The Tanner Lectures on Human Values

THE TANNER LECTURES
ON HUMAN VALUES

35

2016

Allen, Anderson, Atwood, Chakrabarty,
Ginsberg, Pettit, Santner, Singer

Mark Matheson, *Editor*

THE UNIVERSITY OF UTAH PRESS
Salt Lake City

∞ This symbol indicates books printed on paper that meets the minimum requirements of American National Standard for Information Services—Permanence of Paper for Printed Library Materials, ANSI A39.38\-1984.

Printed and bound by Edwards Brothers Malloy, Inc., Ann Arbor, Michigan.

Interior printed on recycled paper with 50% post-consumer content.

THE TANNER LECTURES ON HUMAN VALUES

INTRODUCTION

Obert Clark and Grace Adams Tanner endowed the Tanner Lectures on Human Values in 1978. From the first, the Lectures have served as a leading forum for reflection on scientific knowledge and the advancement of philosophical and humanistic thought. They take place annually at nine major universities in the United States and England and occasionally at other centers of learning around the world. Each of the participating universities is given complete autonomy in selecting its Tanner Lecturer for a given year. The list of scholars, writers, artists, and public figures who have delivered Tanner Lectures is especially distinguished, and this high standard continues through the diligent work of the member universities and the Tanner Lectures Board, which includes the presidents and vice chancellors of these institutions.

Obert Tanner and Grace Adams grew up in the early twentieth century in rural Utah, a society that retained much of its pioneer character. Hard work and dedicated service to others were lived values in their families, and education was a profoundly held ideal. A belief in the dignity and transformative power of learning was nurtured in Obert by his mother, Annie Clark Tanner, who encouraged him to study joyfully, to enter the profession of teaching, and to regard the university as the greatest institutional achievement of humankind. Obert was educated at Utah, Harvard, and Stanford, and he went on to teach religious studies and philosophy at Stanford and Utah for more than thirty years. Somehow during this time he also managed to build the O. C. Tanner Company, the business he began in 1927, into an extraordinary success. Obert's friend Professor Sterling McMurrin, the first director of the Tanner Lectures, once remarked that not since the sixth century BCE, when Thales cornered the wine market in the eastern Mediterranean, had a philosopher been so successful in business. From the early years of this success to his death in 1993, Obert used the wealth produced by his company to endow innumerable educational institutions and civic projects. Over the course of this lifetime of giving, he came to regard the Tanner Lectures as his most important educational and cultural legacy.

The Lectures are thus a product of the values and the vision shared by Obert and Grace. They partake of the spirit of Grace's brightness, wit, and sense of humor as well as Obert's passionate devotion to learning as a means of lifting up the human condition. In the context of an unfolding world culture, the continuing role of the Tanner Lectures will be to contribute in constructive and inspiring ways to our collective intellectual and moral life. Reading through an annual volume of the Tanner Lectures is a remarkable intellectual adventure, and the founders would want the experience to produce both a more abundant life for the individual reader and a more informed and greater dedication to the well-being of the human community.

MARK MATHESON
University of Utah

CONTENTS

The Tanner Lectures on Human Values   v

The Trustees   vii

Preface to Volume 35   xi

Danielle Allen   Education and Equality   1

    Lecture I.   Two Concepts of Education   3

    Lecture II.   Participatory Readiness   27

Elizabeth Anderson   Liberty, Equality, and Private Government   61

    Lecture I.   When the Market Was "Left"   63

    Lecture II.   Private Government   94

Margaret Atwood   Human Values in an Age of Change   123

Dipesh Chakrabarty   The Human Condition in the Anthropocene   137

    Lecture I.   Climate Change as Epochal Consciousness   139

    Lecture II.   Decentering the Human? Or, What Remains of Gaia   165

Justice Ruth Bader Ginsburg   A Conversation with Ruth Bader Ginsburg, Associate Justice of the United States Supreme Court   189

Philip Pettit   The Birth of Ethics   211

    Lecture I.   From Language to Commitment   222

    Lecture II.   From Commitment to Morality   269

Eric L. Santner   The Weight of All Flesh: On the Subject-Matter of Political Economy   321

    Lecture I.   On the Subject-Matter of Political Theology   338

    Lecture II.   Paradoxologies   369

Peter Singer   From Moral Neutrality to Effective Altruism:
                         The Changing Scope and Significance of
                         Moral Philosophy   409

The Tanner Lecturers   431

PREFACE TO VOLUME 35

Volume 35 of the *Tanner Lectures on Human Values* includes lectures delivered during the academic year 2014–2015.

The Tanner Lectures are published in an annual volume.

In addition to permanent lectures at nine universities, the Tanner Lectures on Human Values funds special one-time lectures at selected higher educational institutions in the United States and around the world.

The Tanner Lectures on Human Values

Education and Equality

DANIELLE ALLEN

THE TANNER LECTURES ON HUMAN VALUES

Delivered at

Stanford University
October 8, 2014

DANIELLE ALLEN is director of the Edmond J. Safra Center for Ethics and professor of government at Harvard. When she gave the Tanner Lectures at Stanford, she was UPS Foundation Professor of Social Science at the Institute for Advanced Study in Princeton, New Jersey. She is a political theorist who has published broadly in democratic theory, political sociology, and the history of political thought. Widely known for her work on justice and citizenship in both ancient Athens and modern America, Allen is the author of *The World of Prometheus: The Politics of Punishing in Democratic Athens* (2000), *Talking to Strangers: Anxieties of Citizenship since Brown vs. the Board of Education* (2004), *Why Plato Wrote* (2010), and *Our Declaration: A Reading of the Declaration of Independence in Defense of Equality* (2014). She is the coeditor of the award-winning *Education, Justice, and Democracy* (2013, with Rob Reich) *and From Voice to Influence: Understanding Citizenship in the Digital Age* (2015, with Jennifer Light). She is chair of the Mellon Foundation Board and a member of the American Academy of Arts and Sciences.

LECTURE I.
TWO CONCEPTS OF EDUCATION

THE PROBLEM

We are currently awash in torrents of public conversation about education. As of early September 2014, Randi Weingarten, president of the American Federation of Teachers, had 42,400 tweets to her name. For the period between September 2013 and September 2014, the *New York Times* archive generated 178,000 "articles on education." And education is among Americans' top ten political concerns out of a list of some thirty-five issues.[1] There is so much talk about education that one cannot help but think that perhaps the most sensible thing to do would be to just get on with it: to quit conversing and get back to teaching. In other words, we—and these lectures—are perhaps part of some kind of problem, not a solution.

Aside from their sheer volume, the other notable feature of our countless public conversations about education is how many of them have to do with equality. In 2009, former House Speaker Newt Gingrich and the Reverend Al Sharpton famously joined up for a public tour to advocate educational reform. They identified problems in education as the civil rights issue of our time. Similarly, our many public conversations about income inequality inevitably turn to the topic of education. Thus Thomas Piketty in his recent book, *Capital in the Twenty-First Century*, writes:

> Historical experience suggests that the principal mechanism for convergence [of incomes] at the international as well as the domestic level is the diffusion of knowledge. In other words, the poor catch up with the rich to the extent that they achieve the same level of technological know-how, skill, and education.[2]

He is not the first to make this point. The influential economists Claudia Goldin and Larry Katz also do so, for instance, in their book *The Race between Education and Technology*.[3]

Here too, I must count myself as part of this problem—or, if it not a "problem" then at least the phenomenon of a durable societal obsession with "education" and "equality."[4] For nearly five years now, I have been going around giving lectures under the title "Education and Equality." I have not, however, been plowing a single furrow. My arguments have constantly shifted. My experience has been the pursuit of a highly elusive object of analysis; an adequate framework for thinking about the relationship between education and equality has felt always just beyond reach.

Over the course of my constant worrying on this topic, I have made normative arguments that ideal educational institutions in a democratic society ought to lift the educational level of the entire population as high as possible while also making it possible for those with special gifts to achieve the highest heights of intellectual and creative excellence and simultaneously ensuring that the pathways to those highest heights can be entered into by anyone from any social position. Imagine a western mesa, but one that has jutting out of it peaks like the Rockies with trailheads for the ascent of each peak marked plainly and boldly.[5]

I have also made policy arguments. For instance, I make the case that the achievement of such an ideal requires reforming our approaches to zoning and municipal policy;[6] committing public funding to early childhood education, community colleges, and public universities;[7] distributing admission tickets to elite colleges and universities by means of geographic lotteries over a certain basic threshold of achievement;[8] constructing tuition and aid policies based on transparency about what any given institution actually spends on educating a student;[9] and broadly disseminating the competencies, aptitudes, and skills necessary to convert social relationships that are currently costly—namely, those that bridge boundaries of social difference—into relationships that bring mutual benefit.[10]

Yet, for all the pages and PowerPoint slides, I do not feel that I have been able to come to a resting point in my account of the relationship between education and equality. With these lectures and your help, I am hoping to put this insistent intellectual problem to bed at last.

Why exactly is it so hard to think about education and equality in relation to each other? There is, of course, the fact that equality is simply a difficult concept to talk about. Students often think that to say two things are "equal" is to say that they are "the same." But, of course, "equal" and "same" are not synonyms. To be "the same" is to be "identical." But to be "equal" is to have an equivalent degree of some specific quality or attribute compared to someone else. To talk about equality, one must always begin by asking "equal to whom and in what respect?"

Importantly, the effective use of a concept of equality in a sociopolitical context requires pinpointing whether one means human equality, political equality, social equality, or economic equality. Or, perhaps, in place of the last, one will replace an idea of "economic equality" with an ideal of economic justice, or fairness, or opportunity. Furthermore, there are relations among each of these types of equality. I think clarifying those relationships is among the most important tasks of political philosophy, particularly in our present moment. Yet when we invoke the concept of equality in our conversations about education, for the most part we do not bother to define what we actually mean by it, or to identify which aspect of human experience we wish to pick out for analysis.[11]

Beyond the simple fact that we often leave the idea of equality unspecified in our conversations about educational policy, another issue, too, stirs up my vague unease with how we commonly invoke the concept in these discussions. The quotation from Piketty's *Capital* that I read just a moment ago is revealing. Let me read a bit of it again: "In other words, the poor catch up with the rich to the extent that they achieve the same level of technological know-how, skill, and education."[12]

Note that here the problem that education is used to solve is poverty or, at least, unequal income and/or wealth distributions. This tracks our most common way of discussing equality in relation to education. Discussions of educational reform are very often proxies for conversations about poverty and, insofar as this is the case, it is often unclear how much the conversation actually concerns education itself. Similarly, if one returns to my normative picture and policy prescriptions—the mesa with its peaks; the policies about funding, admission, and municipal planning—you will find that the picture I have painted is entirely about the egalitarian *funding* and *allocation* or *distribution* of some *good* called *education*, but not particularly about whatever the actual good called *education* fundamentally is.

In other words, for all of our talk about education and equality, we do not actually talk very much about how education itself, in itself, relates to equality, regardless of whether the equality we have in mind is human, political, or social, or connected to economic fairness.

And this brings me to the basic problem that motivates these lectures. I think that education itself—a practice of human development—has, intrinsic to the practice, important contributions to make to the defense of human equality, the cultivation of political and social equality, and the emergence of fair economic orders. But I think we have lost sight of just how education, in itself, and putting aside questions of funding and distribution, relates to those egalitarian concerns. If we are to do right by the students we purport to educate, in whatever context and at whatever level, I think we need to recover that vision. Consequently, my goal for these lectures will be to effect a recovery of our understanding of just how education and equality are intrinsically connected to each other.

Here is the plan for what follows. I begin with some conceptual cleanup work. Drawing on the philosophers John Rawls and Hannah Arendt, I hope to secure some basic conceptual architecture for thinking about education. This work will establish what I will call a *humanistic baseline* for understanding what education is. This cleaned-up understanding of education should help clarify our conversations about our goals for both schooling and higher education. This will be the main work of this first lecture, and I will wrap it up by examining just how a "humanistic baseline" for understanding the meaning of education might help us to reframe key policy questions.

In my second lecture, I will turn to the specific policy domain that appears most freshly lit by my account. This is the domain that many people refer to as "civic education." I argue that we should reorient ourselves to a concept of "participatory readiness," and I will lay out a proposed framework for thinking about the desirable content of a new approach to cultivating such participatory readiness. This "participatory readiness" is actually of critical relevance to other egalitarian concerns, including economic ones, and I will suggest that the cultivation of "participatory readiness" in all probability depends fundamentally on the humanistic aspects of the curriculum. In other words, the identification of the "humanistic baseline" for establishing a justification for education will turn out to have in fact provided a foundation for a defense of the humanities, as well as the beginnings of an explanation for how education in itself has egalitarian potential. This means, of course, that the fates of the humanities and the fate of so-called civic education are likely to rise and fall together.

In sum, the task of these lectures is to clarify our understanding of education, its intrinsic connection to equality, and the relevance of the study of the humanities to education's intrinsic egalitarian potentialities.

TWO CONCEPTS OF EDUCATION—THE VOCATIONAL VS. THE LIBERAL?

For all the talk about education in contemporary culture, do we actually have an adequate framework for saying what it is? As an object of anthropological and sociological analysis, education is a relative newcomer. Although Emile Durkheim and W. E. B. DuBois launched the sociology of education in the late nineteenth century, sustained interest did not emerge until after World War II when the field of the anthropology of education came into its own. The late inclusion of education among the practices that an anthropologist or sociologist might study reflects the fact that many of the earliest templates for these disciplines—I am thinking of the work of Friedrich Engels, Karl Marx, Fustel de Coulanges, Henry Maine, and Max Weber—began from analyses of Western antiquity when education was generally not an autonomous social practice but dependent on other social forms. For instance, in ancient Greece, religious ritual, legal practices, military training, and so on largely provided the context for training the young. Some ancients could conceive of education as an autonomous field of social practice—most notably Plato and Aristotle—but their anticipation of "systems of education" was largely unmatched in practice (although Sparta stands as an exception). In contrast, China's extensive network of formal educational institutions began its development in the third millennium BCE. Only when a social practice becomes autonomous—conducted through rituals or institutions built for the sake of that practice and no other—can it be said to have a logic, and also a structure of action-guiding principles and rules emergent from that logic.

In addition to focusing on autonomous social practices, anthropologists and sociologists have sought to understand their conversion into sociopolitical practices. By this conversion I mean the moment when legitimate public officials acquire authority for a practice that has previously been managed mostly by private individuals, as for instance when a society stops allowing individuals to effect retribution for wrongdoing through methods of self-help and instead designates public authorities to manage responses to wrongdoing. This is the moment when *social* practices of *revenge* instead become a *sociopolitical* practice of *punishment*. In other words, at various points in history, phenomena like revenge, mating, raiding, and possession of land and other goods were co-opted by newly developing political realms and turned into punishment, marriage, war, property, and markets. In the history of Western sociopolitical development, we can say that "revenge" had become "punishment" by at least 800 BCE (although this transition was effected more than once, not only in antiquity but again in the medieval period). Education did not undergo an equivalent conversion until well after antiquity had faded away.

The first versions of Western educational institutions were scribal training centers in ancient Egypt and the ancient Near East, and philosophical, rhetorical, and medical schools as well as early schools for children in Greece and Rome.[13] Over the course of late antiquity and the

Middle Ages, educational institutions took shape through the development of centers of religious training in the different monotheistic traditions, and included the emergence of universities in Bologna, Paris, and Oxford in the eleventh century.[14] The emergence of these institutions was followed by others: to pick out just two examples, the establishment in England of schools for poor boys (for instance, Winchester, Eton) as feeders to the new universities, and during the Renaissance the training of artists in the schools of particular painters. But the processes by which political authorities established universal or compulsory education began in Europe only in the seventeenth century, and in the United States were completed only in 1918, when the last of the states then in the Union made education compulsory, at least through age sixteen.[15] As a consequence of the relatively late arrival in Western history of education as a fully autonomous sociopolitical practice on a par with punishment, economics, and war, scholars are still in the early stages of coming to understand its logic.

Despite the relative youthfulness of education as a state practice, it might seem, however, that our current public conversations about education do not in fact evidence any confusion or uncertainty about the nature of education. This is one of the few areas of public policy where politicians from either major party tend to say roughly the same thing. Both Democrats and Republicans clearly articulate what could reasonably be called a neoliberal educational agenda with a focus on educating the national population to succeed in global market competition. Here is Barack Obama from the 2012 Democratic National Convention:

> I promise you, we can out-educate and out-compete any nation on Earth. Help me recruit 100,000 math and science teachers within ten years, and improve early childhood education.
>
> Help give two million workers the chance to learn skills at their community college that will lead directly to a job. Help us work with colleges and universities to cut in half the growth of tuition costs over the next ten years. We can meet that goal together.
>
> You can choose that future for America.[16]

And here is Mitt Romney at the 2012 Republican National Convention:

> I am running for president to help create a better future. A future where everyone who wants a job can find one. Where no senior fears

for the security of their retirement. An America where every parent knows that their child will get an education that leads them to a good job and a bright horizon.

Second, we will give our fellow citizens the skills they need for the jobs of today and the careers of tomorrow. When it comes to the school your child will attend, every parent should have a choice, and every child should have a chance.[17]

The rhetorical affinities extend beyond the presidential campaign trail. Both candidates echoed the language of the preamble to the bipartisan Common Core "college and career readiness" state standards, which were created and promoted by the National Governors Association. Here is a portion of the preamble:

The Common Core State Standards define the rigorous skills and knowledge in English Language Arts and Mathematics that need to be effectively taught and learned for students to be ready to succeed academically in credit-bearing, college-entry courses and in workforce training programs. These standards have been developed to be:

Fewer, clearer, and higher, to best drive effective policy and practice;

Aligned with college and work expectations, so that all students are prepared for success upon graduating from high school;

Inclusive of rigorous content and applications of knowledge through higher-order skills, so that all students are prepared for the 21st century;

Internationally benchmarked, so that all students are prepared for succeeding in our global economy and society; and

Research and evidence-based.

The standards intend to set forward thinking goals for student performance based in evidence about what is required for success. The standards developed will set the stage for US education not just beyond next year, but for the next decade, and they must ensure *all* American students are prepared for the global economic workplace.[18]

In short, in this country, we seem to know just what we should be pursuing in education: college and career readiness as preparation for the global economy. Given that this goal is backed by state power generated by the richest and most powerful government the world has ever known, we have to take seriously the idea that it is of considerable consequence for the future of our own culture at least.

What exactly is the cultural consequence of constructing an educational system around this goal of college and career readiness as preparation for the global economy? As our public conversations have unfolded, the reigning political ideology in education has generated the common critique that the orientation is overly "vocational." The story of how such a vocationally oriented frame of global competiveness came to dominate our public conversations about education is familiar. The Soviet launch of the first satellite in 1957 provoked a sense that this country was falling behind in a Cold War science contest. The response was the National Defense of Education Act, signed into law in 1958. A 1983 Reagan-era report, "A Nation at Risk," further spurred the view that the United States was falling behind. Although its data were later debunked, it included provocative summary sentences such as: "If an unfriendly foreign power had attempted to impose on America the mediocre educational performance that exists today, we might well have viewed it as an act of war."[19] This report is generally understood to have kicked off the era of school reform that still shapes educational discussion and policy. And in 2007, the National Academy of Sciences put out a report called "Rising above the Gathering Storm," which emphasized the need for significant improvements in science and technology education and investment. The report's authors wrote: "An educated, innovative, motivated workforce—human capital—is the most precious resource of any country in this new, flat world. Yet there is widespread concern about our K–12 science and mathematics education system, the foundation of that human capital in today's global economy."[20] This influential report has influenced educational policy conversations, driving an increase of focus on STEM (science, technology, engineering, and mathematics) fields. We can see the influence in Obama's 2013 State of the Union address, when he announced a competition to "redesign America's high schools." Rewards would go, he said at the time, to schools that develop more classes "that focus on science, technology, engineering and math—the skills today's employers are looking for to fill jobs right now and in the future."

Those who critique this educational vision typically invoke the "liberal arts" by way of contrast. Of course, a straightforward dichotomy between vocational and liberal learning is relevant mostly in the context of elite colleges and universities. As Louis Menand has argued, such campuses often suffer from "an allergy to the term 'vocational.'"[21] Nonetheless, the antithesis between "vocational" and "liberal" that has developed on college campuses structures our broader debates about the purposes of education, and these can come to feel stuck in a simple and endless tug of war between those two poles. Is the point of education the life of the mind or the ability to secure a job?

Of course, it is both, and it is, in fact, possible to get past this blockage in public conversation.[22] We can do so by recognizing that our conversations about education have the shape that they do because we are operating with two different concepts of education. In the next section, I would like to clarify those two concepts, in order to lead us to a resolution of the seeming opposition between the vocational and the liberal arts conceptions of education.

TWO CONCEPTS OF EDUCATION: A HUMANISTIC BASELINE

Those of you who are philosophers will already know that in referring to "two concepts of education," I am riffing on Rawls, who in 1955 published an important essay called "Two Concepts of Rules."[23] In this early paper, Rawls pointed out that the perpetual debates among penal theorists over whether the proper justification for punishment was deterrent (and therefore utilitarian) or retributive (and thus based on a commonplace morality) stem from a failure to understand the logic of practices, of which punishment was one of his two examples (promise-keeping was the other). He argued (following David Hume, Ludwig Wittgenstein, and John Austin) that for any given practice, there is a distinction between justifying a practice and justifying a particular action falling under it. For example, there is a distinction between justifying punishment and justifying punishing. The first kind of justification requires answering the question, "Why does the state (generally) punish people?" The second kind of justification requires answering the question, "Why did the state punish that man?"

According to Rawls, the answer to the latter question requires a retributive statement, for instance: "That particular man was punished as a response to the wrong he had done and in proportion to that wrong." The answer to the question of why states generally punish may, however, again according to Rawls, be utilitarian. An example would be: "In order to keep wrong-doing to a minimum by deterring would-be wrong-doers through the example of the punishments of others."[24] But Rawls's neat distinction obscures a few other important distinctions. When we ask, "Why does the state (generally) punish people?" we are in fact asking two questions: first, "why has punishment come to exist as an institution that distinguishes human social organization from hives and galaxies?"[25]; and second, "why is the state justified in operating institutions of punishment?" The first question seeks a causal explanation; the second question seeks a justification for state action.[26]

Take the game of baseball as an example. The emergence of the game as a social practice is *explained* by the end or goal of leisure. But the actions of individuals participating in the game—swinging at balls, running around bases, catching and throwing balls—are *justified* by the goal not of leisure but of scoring more runs than an opponent. And the actions of corporate actors who have co-opted the game of baseball to develop, for instance, a professional version of the sport are justified by the goal of profit. The ends that explain the emergence of a practice, the ends that justify the effort to regulate the practice, and the ends that justify actions undertaken within it are all logically separate; if they turn out to be the same, that coincidence is merely accidental. Thus, it can be a matter of social utility that practices should arise and be co-opted by the state, for which the ends of the actions falling under them are not utilitarian but either moral or eudaimonistic.[27] What do I mean by "eudaimonistic"? The term comes from the Greek word for "happiness" (*eudaimonia*) and designates an ethical outlook organized around the effort of individuals to achieve their full human flourishing by means of the development of their internal capacities.

The case of education resembles that of punishment. Analysts of education move in a perpetual circle when they argue over its proper justification: *economic* competitiveness, the development of *citizens*, or enablement of a eudaimonistic *human flourishing*? We need to recognize that, as with punishment, the logic of education makes two different kinds of justification relevant to the practice: the justification for the state's maintenance of a system of education and the justification for particular instances of teaching carried out within that system.

In order to draw out the point, let us consider the very different schools that emerged in different historical periods prior to the nationalization of education. In chronological order, these are: scribal training centers; philosophical, medical, and rhetorical schools; theological programs; universities; schools of artists. These educational institutions were founded for different reasons—scribal training centers, for instance, to help rulers control their property and the flow of goods; religious training centers, to prepare priests and theologians and thereby to supply religious organizations with manpower. These different schools were thus directed toward diverse ends. But in terms of the activity that occurred within them, which allows classification of all these institutions as fundamentally about the same thing, namely, education, all shared the aspiration to direct the development of human capacities. Whereas the institutions of formal education arise on the basis of diverse justifications, within these different institutions the activity of educating and also the techniques developed to pursue it are identified by a single end: cultivating human development. This is true even when a student chooses a vocational training course for the sake of making money. For that training to succeed, it must still effect the development of the student qua human being, for that is what it means for any of us to cultivate capacities and abilities.

In our current context, then, it is entirely reasonable that the justification for the co-optation of education by the state, for the conversion of education into a sociopolitical practice, might be utilitarian—a state asserts authority over education as a matter of securing social reproduction. Achieving this requires economic and/or military competitiveness for the state and preservation of its state form; in the context of a democracy, the system-level justification for education therefore entails a twinned utilitarian concern for generating economic and/or military competitiveness and for producing citizens prepared to maintain democratic life.[28] But the justification for the actions falling under the practice, particular instances of educating, the micro-level of justification, cannot be utilitarian.

What do I mean by that strong statement? Clearly, people do often provide utilitarian or more broadly consequentialist justifications for education. The point is that when they do so, they may indeed justify the state's involvement in institutions of education but they actually fail to justify the activity of educating as such. Economists, for instance, distinguish between the consumption and investment benefits of education, or between the intrinsic and extrinsic benefits. As Helen Ladd and Susanna Loeb put it:

> Intrinsic benefits arise when education is valued for its own sake such as the pleasure of being able to solve a complex problem or appreciate artistic expression, and extrinsic benefits arise when education serves as an instrument for the attainment of other valued outcomes such the higher income for working parents that is facilitated by having children in school, or the potential for the recipients of education to seek higher paying jobs and fulfilling careers than would otherwise be possible.[29]

But when we scrutinize the extrinsic benefits that are most often identified as flowing from education—higher paying jobs, for instance—we notice that education is only one means of achieving those ends. A person might, for instance, also obtain a higher paying job through cronyism. These extrinsic ends might justify activities other than education; in no way do they necessarily justify education. The ends that define education *as* education, in contrast, and that thereby provide its proper justification, must be ends that can be achieved only through education: these are ends of human development, pursued as such.

Our considered moral judgment, to crib from Rawls, is that the state of affairs where a person has been educated is better than if she has not been; and it is better for her own sake regardless of any consequence of educating her. We recognize educating *as* educating, across different instances of it, because in all cases one party has undertaken to spur the positive human development of another. Across the different examples of education, what counts as success is the activation in the student of positive capacities that had previously been latent. Moreover, we care about the activation of those capacities regardless of the consequences. We do not, for instance, cease educating the child who has cancer because she has cancer. This is not to say that the consequences that flow from activating latent human capacities are unimportant, just that those consequences do not themselves justify the activation.

The important point here is that even when a student pursues education as a means to moneymaking, she is choosing as her means an activity whose form is built around a different set of ends. Of course, as Aristotle long ago pointed out, the ends of moneymaking and of human flourishing are not separate from one another. In order to achieve a broad eudaimonistic human flourishing, we also need the means to live. Close attention to the logic of education reveals any strong distinction between utilitarian and eudaimonistic goals to be overdrawn. Similarly, even if one thinks that one needs to teach a child his tribe's rituals in order to preserve that tribe (a collective utilitarian concern), one also thinks that life in that tribe is in the child's best interest (a eudaimonistic perspective), so one's view about inculcating social norms is tethered to a view about the child's good. An educational system is constituted by a multitude of particular actions that involve the relation between teachers and students, where each student must always be an end in himself. When we try to cultivate good teachers, we seek to instill this instinct. This effort flows from the moral intuition that the appropriate justification for the actual activity of educating is a broad eudaimonism, and not social utility.

Rawls's neat distinction between the justification for rules that structure practices and the justification for rules that structure the activities conducted in the context of that practice thus helps us to see that thinking about education requires us to think on two levels. And we have to understand when each level of justification is relevant. It is reasonable to think about social utility and about how a whole educational system might achieve social utility. It may even be necessary to do that.[30] But the justification for particular instances of educating must instead be eudaimonistic. What we are thinking about as education will not count as such unless we also think about it from the perspective of the individual being educated. In order to count as education, the practice sponsored by those institutions has to affect the development of an individual qua human being, namely, a creature whose flourishing entails the development of a range of valuable cognitive, affective, and intersubjective capacities. I refer to this as the humanistic baseline for the concept of education.

FROM THE HUMANISTIC BASELINE
TO FOUR BASIC NEEDS

The next sort of question we have to ask is this: If any given system of education—regardless of the social ends toward which it is directed—must meet a humanistic baseline in order to count as a system of, specifically, *education*, how do we determine what is involved in meeting that humanistic baseline? What sort of education activates latent potential for general human flourishing? This is also to ask which account of human flourishing we should use to give content to the humanistic baseline for education. As we pursue an answer to this question, we will also have to ask whether it is possible to have an approach to education that integrates the two perspectives provided by its system and the micro-level justifications. A coherent account of the purposes of education surely requires such an integration or alignment.

As we initiate our hunt for an acceptable eudaimonistic account of the nature of education, we can define the stakes of the search by reaching back again, if briefly, to the first theorist of education in the Western tradition. Plato argued that the differences among people are such that each should be educated to perform excellently the one kind of work at which she will excel. This would make us all virtuous and therefore happy, he argued, as would assuming our places in a highly stratified society in which adults perform the single role assigned to them (for instance, political leadership, military service, craftsmanship, trading, or agriculture). But this is not a democratic answer to the question, forced upon us by the logic of practices, of how to justify not merely the institutions of education but also the actions undertaken while educating. And just as Plato's answer is antidemocratic, so too is it illiberal, even if only avant la lettre. Liberalism depends on the idea that the ends of the state and of the individual are separable to a meaningful degree. Plato, of course, argued the opposite view that city and soul cannot, ultimately, adopt divergent aims.[31] He therefore integrated the system-level justification for education and the action-specific justification by proposing a form of education whose purpose was to fit each individual to his assigned social role.

Against Plato, a democratic answer to the question of the kind of education that would achieve full human flourishing starts from a different view of human nature, namely, that despite the differences among us we are all capable of doing multiple jobs, at the very least those of performing our own particular excellence and of acting politically as citizens.[32] To flesh out a democratic account of full human flourishing, we would profit, I think, from turning now to the work of another mid-twentieth-century philosopher, not often considered in concert with Rawls. The person I have in mind is Hannah Arendt. Her 1958 book *The Human Condition* is driven by a consideration of the issue of well-being from the perspective of the individual instead of the social whole.[33] Given the historical proximity of Rawls's 1955 article and Arendt's 1958 book, it is perhaps not surprising that there should be resonances between them. It is more surprising that the lines of thought in contemporary political philosophy that flow from each rush on so separately from one another. Interestingly, Arendt's account in *The Human Condition* provides a valuably democratic account of human flourishing that can serve as a foundation for integrating our two concepts of education: our macro-level social utilitarian concept and our micro-level eudaimonistic concept.

In *The Human Condition*, Arendt famously expounds on the content and import of three core human activities: labor, work, and action. Labor is what we undertake out of biological necessity—what we do, in other words, to feed ourselves. It also encompasses sexual reproduction and the energies devoted to child-rearing. Work is what we do out of creative effort, to build the things—whether physical or cultural—that shape our world and establish our social connections with others. Labor and work overlap with each other insofar as our romantic relationships are products of our social art and, of course, create the context within which we may also pursue biological reproduction. Finally, action identifies the effort we make together as political creatures, struggling in conditions of pluralistic diversity, to come to collective decisions about our polity's course of action.[34]

Arendt's arguments about labor, work, and action have garnered significant scholarly attention, yet one important detail has been overlooked. By describing work, labor, and action as typifying every human existence, Arendt sought to reverse centuries, even millennia, of philosophical effort to differentiate social roles with reference to these activities.[35] Earlier philosophers had assigned to a different social class each of the three domains of activity that for Arendt defined the human condition of each individual. In the idealized Greek city of Aristotle, for instance, securing a stable economic base for life was assigned to a slave class, contributing to the realm of creativity was assigned to tradesmen, and participating in politics, to citizens. Or think again of Plato, who assigned these tasks to farmers, traders, craftsmen, soldiers, and political leaders, and expected very little mobility among these groups.

With her incandescent and liberatory philosophical imagination, Arendt dedifferentiated these three roles and recombined them into an account of the experience of every individual, as themselves the marks of the human condition for each one of us. In an Arendtian account, the potential of the modern union of economics and politics is that we can build polities that are nonstratified such that each individual is responsible for securing his own subsistence (rather than exploiting others[36]); has a life scope that makes it possible to create meaningful social worlds—both intimate and communal; and has a platform for participating in politics. Individual human flourishing, then, depends on the activation of a potential that inheres in all human beings—as a feature of the human condition—to succeed at labor, work, and political action simultaneously.

On the basis of Arendt's arguments in *The Human Condition*, then, we can identify four basic human potentialities that should be activated by education. Through education, we need:

1. To prepare ourselves for breadwinning work;
2. To prepare ourselves for civic and political engagement;
3. To prepare ourselves for creative self-expression and world-making;
4. And to prepare ourselves for rewarding relationships in spaces of intimacy and leisure.

We recognize that the capacities relevant to all these domains are flourishing when we see young people become adults who can support themselves economically without exploiting others, take their place among a world of adult creators, including as creators of rewarding intimate relationships, and participate effectively in their polity's political life. When the humanistic baseline for the micro-level concept of education is given content from such democratic eudaimonism, it orients us toward a pedagogic practice that is in itself egalitarian in that it seeks to meet the same range of needs for all students. Yet there is also another way in which this conceptualization of education makes a contribution to egalitarianism.

When one takes a look at this list of basic educational needs generated from Arendt's democratic eudaimonism, one quickly notices that the utilitarian social justifications for a system of education—that a polity as a whole secures economic competitiveness and, in the case of a democracy, an engaged and effective citizenry—align with two of the four needs any individual requires of education. Each person's individual need to prepare for breadwinning work and for civic and political engagement is simply the other side of the coin of the social need for broad economic competitiveness and an engaged citizenry. In other words, public goods and private goods come together here, and analyzing education in terms of an opposition between them is not necessarily helpful. Similarly, the state's "utilitarian" goods turn out to be features of an individual's "eudaimonistic" good, if merely considered from a different perspective. Although a state seeks an economically successful population, each individual too flourishes only when her potential for successful labor is appropriately activated. And although a democracy needs an engaged and effective citizenry, each individual flourishes only when his potential for action is appropriately tapped.

When we see how the social and the individual come together, bringing the two concepts of education into alignment with each other, we also learn something important about our own contemporary conversations about education. Our current conversations emphasize only one of the social justifications for education—namely, the economic—leaving the state's need to cultivate effective citizens largely to the side. I will return to that topic in my next lecture, for that is where the truly egalitarian work of this humanistic concept of education is done.

Yet for all the surprising proximity between the system-level goals of education and the individual-level goals that emerge from the eudaimonistic account, we should also be grateful that the alignment between social goals and our individual goals is only partial. It should be a cause of relief that two of the basic needs defining the humanistic baseline for the practice of education—for creative self-expression and world-making; and for rewarding relationships in spaces of intimacy and leisure—do not align with the system-level justifications for education. We do not want the state to colonize our social lives as creatures who build our worlds with others through creative self-expression and who pursue rewarding relationships in spaces of intimacy and leisure.

Yet, although we do not wish the state to colonize those spaces, we do need to ensure that the state leaves space for them. That is, if in failing to see those spaces, the state begins to override them, then that is simply another form of colonization. And this brings us to the topic of just how the humanistic baseline for education might point us toward a reorientation of our education policy discussions generally.

Rawls helped us see that we must consider the goals of educational systems, on the one hand, and of teachers with specific students, on the other. Arendt offers us a eudaimonism that permits bringing social and individual goods into alignment with one another on a democratic footing. Thinking clearly about education requires shifting effectively back and forth between these two registers: the social and the individual, categories that track neither a public good/private good distinction, nor a simplistic utilitarian/nonutilitarian distinction. If the state is to support a system of education that remains a system of *education* as distinct from some other practice, it needs to leave institutions the room to educate such that their pedagogic practices meet the requirements of the humanistic baseline.

THE HUMANISTIC BASELINE AND EDUCATION POLICY

This idea of two concepts of education should affect reflection on educational policy by requiring us to consider any given policy proposal through each of two lenses. We can assess a policy for its success in meeting the social goods we have in view—perhaps global economic competitiveness. But we must also assess the policy by asking whether the actions it requires and institutions it establishes also satisfy the humanistic baseline that justifies actual educating.

Let me illustrate this point, very briefly, with a few schematic remarks about the policy topic of accountability. Once one sees that there are in fact two kinds of justification relevant to thinking about education, one realizes that there must also be two kinds of accountability relevant to the practice. The system of education, as a whole, has to be held to account in relation to the utilitarian justification, which justifies drawing the social practice of education within the political realm in the first place; but individual and particular instances of teaching must be held to account in relation to the eudaimonistic justification that should properly structure the relationship between teacher and student.

Does our present approach to accountability employ this distinction? It does not. We wish to hold the system as a whole accountable for the production of economically competitive citizens, but to do so we test individual children, and not for each child's own sake but in order to track change over time in the performance of student cohorts.[37] Individual students are, in other words, made the instruments for judging something other than themselves and their own flourishing. System-level practices of accountability should instead be constructed out of measures that can capture systemwide effects without interfering with the individual teacher–student relationship. We need measurement that touches the system as such, not the particular moves or actions made within it.

Such measures are available. Imaginative educational reformers have already identified some. Thus, Larry Rosenstock, now of High-Tech High in San Diego, a few years ago proposed that we track:

1. Of the entering ninth graders in that education entity (school, district, or state, etc.), what percent graduated from a four year college?
2. Of those students who qualify for free and reduced lunch of those ninth grade entrants, what percent graduated from a four year college?
3. Of those ninth graders not in poverty, what percent graduated from a four year college?
4. Finally, what relative mixtures/concentrations of #2 and #3 were most efficacious for getting the #2's through college?[38]

Similarly, researchers at the Chicago Consortium for School Research have developed an extensive set of indicators to assess the quality of work done by schools and teachers in fostering academic achievement. These indicators are developed on the basis of measures that perform better than standardized tests in predicting student achievement. They also make use of readily available data already independently generated by the practice of educating, so using these data does not interfere with educating. One such indicator is the on-track status of ninth-graders in a given school (with respect to attendance, grades, and course pass-rates); on-track status is a better predictor of high school graduation than eighth-grade test scores or socioeconomic status. Moreover, identification of this first indicator allows for the development of others. Since "schools that cultivate strong student-teacher relationships, make high school relevant for students, and engage their students average fewer failures, better grades, and better attendance," the consortium has developed indicators to help schools judge how well they are doing these foundational things.[39] These reformers are confident that that they can judge which schools are succeeding and which are not, with rubrics and metrics for accountability that track systemic effects but without interfering with the activity of teaching to do so.

What, then, about holding teachers accountable for their success at the activity of teaching itself? Teachers should indeed be held to account, but for the flourishing (or failure to flourish) of individual children along all the dimensions identified in the democratic eudaimonistic justification for education—progress toward economic self-sufficiency, progress toward a capacity for social and cultural creation, and progress toward a capacity to participate in political life. Here it matters that the measures of system-level performance of the kind developed described above can be analytically connected to specific things that teachers do or fail to do, as in the case of the ninth-grade on-track indicator, where students are more likely to be on-track when teachers develop strong student–teacher relationships, make high school relevant (i.e., future-oriented) for their students, and engage them. Measures of system-level performance are most valuable when they are, as in this case, organically linked, as test scores are not, to specific features of the activity of teaching. Such indicators give parents and students tools that are much more powerful than test scores for holding schools accountable because they give parents and students actionable policies and improvements to propose instead of the generic demand that schools "raise scores."[40]

Policy alternatives thus rest on answers to deeper questions posed by the logic of education as a practice. They carry with them implicit answers to the question of how we justify both a system of education and the practice of actually teaching. By forcing to the surface our thinking about the two concepts of education—the state-level and the micro-level concepts—I hope to have provided a framework to support more rigorous analysis of our policy options. By arguing for the importance of a humanistic baseline in thinking about what education is, I also hope to have restored some balance to our policy conversations, which tend to turn around the state-level concept of education. Most important, when we shift our gaze from the social to the individual justification of education, and orient ourselves to the humanistic baseline, democratically defined, we are restoring the egalitarian potential of education in itself. The humanistic baseline requires that we think about the education of all students in the context of a broad notion of flourishing. Thus, the humanistic baseline reinforces an egalitarian orientation toward human dignity that can disappear if we focus exclusively on the state-level justifications of education, which instrumentalize the student.

In my next lecture, I will turn to the topic of civic education or, to use more Arendtian language, preparation for participatory readiness. This is the policy domain in which the egalitarian potentiality of education as such most fully shows itself.

NOTES

1. http://www.gallup.com/poll/1675/most-important-problem.aspx. Education was last on the list of Americans' most important issues in the 1960s and 1970s, but the topic began moving up the charts in 1980 and hit the first position in 2000 (Roper Center at University of Connecticut, Public Opinion Online; from P. McGuinn presentation at the Institute for Advanced Study in the 2009–10 academic year). Its salience has declined since then (as per Policy Agendas Project Web site, http://www.policyagendas.org/page/trend-analysis#), but it still makes Gallup's top ten list.

2. Thomas Piketty, *Capital in the Twenty-First Century*, Kindle ed. (Cambridge, MA: Harvard University Press, 2014), 71.

3. Claudia Goldin and Lawrence F. Katz, *The Race between Education and Technology* (Cambridge: Belknap Press, 2010).

4. The politics of education have generated three different egalitarian ideals: equality of opportunity, equality of outcome, and adequacy. Susana Loeb, Helen Ladd, Rob Reich, and Anna Marie Smith discuss the strengths and weaknesses of these in their chapters in Danielle Allen and Robert Reich, eds., *Education, Justice, and Democracy* (Chicago: University of Chicago Press, 2013).

5. Danielle Allen, "Education and Equality," lecture given at the Institute for Advanced Study, November 2011, https://www.youtube.com/watch?v=zrW6HNi9-QU.

6. Danielle Allen, *Our Declaration: A Reading of the Declaration of Independence in Defense of Equality* (New York: Norton/Liveright, 2014); cf. Clarissa Hayward, *How Americans Make Race: Stories, Institutions, Spaces* (New York: Cambridge University Press, 2013); Richard Rothstein, "Racial Segregation and Black Student Achievement," in Allen and Reich, *Education, Justice, and Democracy*, 173–98; Elizabeth Anderson, *The Imperative of Integration* (Princeton, NJ: Princeton University Press, 2010).

7. Allen, "Education and Equality."

8. Danielle Allen, "Talent Is Everywhere," in *The Future of Affirmative Action: New Paths to Higher Education Diversity after Fisher v. University of*

Texas, edited by R. Kahlenberg (New York: The Century Foundation Press, 2013).

9. Danielle Allen, "What 'Tuition' and 'Fees' Leaves Out on College Costs," *Washington Post*, December 19, 2010, http://www.washingtonpost.com/wp-dyn/content/article/2010/12/17/AR2010121705587.html.

10. Danielle Allen, "Art of Association," Annual Equality Lecture for British Sociological Association, April 2012, https://www.youtube.com/watch?v=hZJA6u OS-jk; Danielle Allen, "What We Should Be Doing with Diversity on Our College Campuses," *Institute Letter*, Summer 2013, http://www.ias.edu/files/pdfs/publications/letter-2013-summer.pdf.

11. There is the related problem to which Aristotle first called attention in Book 5 of the *Nicomachean Ethics*: one must also distinguish between whether one has arithmetic or geometric equality in mind.

12. Piketty, *Capital in the Twenty-First Century*, 71.

13. On scribal schools, see Christopher Woods, "Bilingualism, Scribal Learning, and the Death of Sumerian," in *Margins of Writing, Origins of Cultures: Unofficial Writing in the Ancient Near East and Beyond*, edited by S. Sanders, 91–120 (Chicago: University of Chicago, 2006). We hear about one ancient Greek school for children in Thucydides's *History of the Peloponnesian War*.

14. Ian Wei, *Intellectual Culture in Medieval Paris* (Cambridge: Cambridge University Press, 2012).

15. Michael Katz, *A History of Compulsory Education Laws*, Fastback Series, no. 75. Bicentennial Series (Bloomington, IN: Phi Delta Kappa, 1976).

16. Transcript: President Obama's Convention Speech, National Public Radio, http://www.npr.org/2012/09/06/160713941/transcript-president-obamas-convention-speech.

17. Transcript: Mitt Romney's Acceptance Speech, National Public Radio, http://www.npr.org/2012/08/30/160357612/transcript-mitt-romneys-acceptance-speech.

18. National Governors Association, "Common Core State Standards Initiative Standards-Setting Criteria," http://www.corestandards.org/assets/Criteria.pdf, and on file with the author.

19. A Nation at Risk, US Department of Education Archived Information, http://www2.ed.gov/pubs/NatAtRisk/risk.html.

20. Institute of Medicine, National Academy of Sciences, and National Academy of Engineering. *Rising Above the Gathering Storm: Energizing and Employing America for a Brighter Economic Future* (Washington, DC: The National Academies Press, 2007), 30.

21. Louis Menand, *The Marketplace of Ideas: Reform and Resistance in the American University* (New York: Norton, 2010), 53. See also Amy Gutmann, "What Makes a University Education Worthwhile?" in *The Aims of Higher Education: Problems of Morality and Justice*, edited by Michael McPherson and Harry Brighouse, 7–25 (Chicago: University of Chicago Press, 2015).

22. Indeed, several scholars and leaders in higher education have lately been seeking to achieve that. See Gutmann, "What Makes a University Education

Worthwhile?"; Mike Rose, "Heal the Academic-Vocational Schism," *Chronicle of Higher Education*, September 10, 2012.

23. John Rawls, "Two Concepts of Rules," *Philosophical Review* 64, no. 1 (January 1955): 3–32.

24. I am paraphrasing rather than quoting Rawls's argument. I should also note that Rawls excavates the common utilitarian justification for the basic structure of society, in order, eventually, to replace a utilitarian justification at this level with his justification from "justice as fairness." I adopt his diagnosis of social facts on this ground—namely, that utilitarian arguments are commonly those being used at the macro-level of justification—but without moving from that view to an adoption of the theory of justice. I seek to develop my argument about political obligation instead from the content of moves inside the game, the micro-level.

25. In responding to Rawls's argument about practices, the philosopher Stanley Cavell distinguishes two ways in which the label "practice" might be applied: "We may be conceiving of [a practice] either on a par with institutions like kinship systems, law and religion, institutions which distinguish societies from hives or galaxies, general dimensions in terms of which any community of human beings will be described; or we may be thinking of it as a *specific* institution, on a par with monogamy or monotheism or suttee or death by stoning, institutions in terms of which one society is distinguished from another society, or from the same society at an earlier stage" (Cavell, *The Claim of Reason: Wittgenstein, Skepticism, Morality, and Tragedy* [Oxford: Oxford University Press, (1979) 1999], 299–300). Cavell rightly saw Rawls as concerned with the first category of "practice." I am also concerned with the first category.

26. Here, readers who know Rawls's argument, will notice that I am limiting my use of it to *sociopolitical* practices, which have been co-opted by the state; I am not applying it to practices generally. I am arguing that when Rawls distinguishes between the justification for a practice as such and justification for actions undertaken within the practice, his distinction succeeds, really, only for *sociopolitical* practices, where the state has co-opted some domain of human social activity. In such cases, two actors are relevant to understanding the practice: the state and particular individuals who carry out actions within the domain of the relevant practice. That Rawls's distinction between the two kinds of justification should map onto a distinction between two kinds of actor should come as no surprise. He draws readers' attention to the fact that utilitarianism, understood in its original formulation, concerned social institutions and was used primarily as a criterion for judging social institutions, not for guiding the actions of individuals ("Two Concepts," 18–19 and 19–21). Insofar as he makes space for utilitarianism at the level of justifying practices as such, he is recovering a bounded approach to utilitarianism as relevant mainly to the societal level. When Stanley Cavell criticizes Rawls's argument in "Two Concepts," he focuses on the case of promise-keeping and acknowledges that Rawls's argument works better for punishment, where formal institutions have been set up (Cavell, *Claim of Reason*, 299, 308). In other words, Cavell is

implicitly noting that, if Rawls's argument works, it works for sociopolitical practices.

27. Utility captures the satisfaction that agents take in particular outcomes. Here is one basic formulation: "What does it mean to say that agents are self-interested? It does not necessarily mean that they want to cause harm to each other, or even that they care only about themselves. Instead, it means that each agent has his own description of which states of the world he likes—which can include good things happening to other agents—and that he acts in an attempt to bring about these states of the world. The dominant approach to modeling an agent's interests is *utility theory*. This theoretical approach quantifies an agent's degree of preference across a set of available alternatives, and describes how these preferences change when an agent faces uncertainty about which alternative he will receive. Specifically, a *utility function* is a mapping from states of the world to real numbers. These numbers are interpreted as measures of an agent's level of happiness in the given states" (Kevin Leyton-Brown and Yoav Shoham, *Essentials of Game Theory: A Concise, Multidisciplinary Introduction* [San Rafael: Morgan and Claypool, 2008], 1).

28. If the social justification for democracy is preservation of the state form, then educational systems should look different around the world accordingly as the world continues to hold differences in regime type. On this line of argument, a single international standard for assessing education (such as the PISA [Programme for International Student Assessment] test) will be dangerous to any state whose state-form is not adequately captured by that assessment instrument.

29. Helen Ladd and Susana Loeb, "The Challenges of Measuring School Quality: Implications for Educational Equity," in Allen and Reich, *Education, Justice, and Democracy*, 19–42, 20.

30. This thought runs in the opposite direction from the line of argument that Rawls pulled out of his separation of the two levels of justification. His purpose in pulling apart justification for the rules of the game from justification for particular moves in the game was to establish a framework for a concerted challenge to the use of utilitarianism to justify the former.

31. For a particularly compelling account of how to understand Plato's arguments on this subject, see J. Lear, "Inside and Outside the *Republic*." *Phronesis* 37, no. 2 (1992): 184–215.

32. I call this a "democratic view of human nature" because it is implicit in the construction of democratic institutions that draw everyone into political life while also expecting them to be active in other domains.

33. Hannah Arendt, *The Human Condition* (Chicago: University of Chicago Press, 1958).

34. Democratic politics is fundamentally a project of negotiating difference (and this was always true, even in homogeneous communities; increased demographic diversity simply makes the centrality of plurality more obvious). Josiah Ober, *Democracy and Knowledge: Innovation and Learning in Classical Athens* (Princeton, NJ: Princeton University Press, 2008), and "What Is Democracy?

What Is It Good For?" paper presented at the James Moffett Lecture, Princeton University, September 30, 2010. I owe my reading of Hannah Arendt, and particularly my understanding of the economic significance of the arguments in *The Human Condition*, largely to Patchen Markell in *Politics Against Rule: Hannah Arendt and* The Human Condition (forthcoming).

35. The philosophical practice of establishing, in essence, caste systems where particular social tasks are assigned to particular social classes appears in non-Western traditions as well. See, for instance, Jennifer London, "Circle of Justice," *History of Political Thought* 32, no. 3 (2011): 425–47.

36. On stringent efforts to determine what is necessary given a nonexploitation criterion, see Gerald A. Cohen, *Rescuing Justice and Equality* (Cambridge, MA: Harvard University Press, 2009).

37. Here it is worth noting that, as of 2010, the current U.S. presidential administration advocated replacing the cohort model with a growth model designed to track individual student progress. As of 2010, multiple states were also switching to a growth model for accountability. See Rolf Blank, "State Growth Models for School Accountability," Council of Chief State School Officers, June 2010: "States have increased interest in the use of growth models for school accountability. Growth models are based on tracking change in individual student achievement scores over multiple years. A total of 12 states are utilizing growth models that provide estimates of whether student achievement will meet Adequate Yearly Progress (AYP) state proficiency targets within three years. These models were designed to meet the requirements of the No Child Left Behind (NCLB) Act. In addition, 13 states have developed and implemented growth models as required by state policy; these models use different formulas to measure growth for students and schools. This paper is an overview and description of current state activities with growth models. For more, see http://www.ccsso.org/Resources/Publications/State_Growth_Models _for_School_Accountability_Progress_on_Developing_and_Reporting _Measures_of_Student_Growth.html#sthash.ZOpCt9p1.dpuf. There does not appear to have been much recent change in this area.

38. Larry Rosenstock, e-mail correspondence with author, August 13, 2010.

39. Chicago Consortium for School Research (CCSR), "Graduation and School Culture: What Matters in the Freshman Year," CCSR Report, https://ccsr.uchicago .edu/ssr/school/1777/high/2009/report/report-freshman/section-freshman-intro .html. See also the reports, Elaine Allensworth and John Q. Easton, "The On-Track Indicator as a Predictor of High School Graduation," CCSR (2005), http:// ccsr.uchicago.edu/publications/p78.pdf; Elaine Allensworth and John Q. Easton, "What Matters for Staying On-Track and Graduating in Chicago Public Schools," CCSR (2007), http://ccsr.uchicago.edu/publications/what-matters-staying-track -and-graduating-chicago-public-schools.

40. To this end, the Chicago Consortium on School Research disseminates its reports in "briefs" for parents, teachers, and students on how to make use of the CCSR indicators to support student achievement. For an example of a parent brief, see Allensworth and Easton, "On-Track Indicator as a Predictor."

LECTURE II.
PARTICIPATORY READINESS

λόγος δυνάστης μέγας ἐστίν, ὃς σμικροτάτωι σώματι καὶ
ἀφανεστάτωι θειότατα ἔργα ἀποτελεῖ

Speech is a great power, which achieves the most divine works
by means of the smallest and least visible form.
— Gorgias, "Encomium to Helen"

INTRODUCING PARTICIPATORY READINESS

In my first lecture, I argued that our conversations about education are
often muddled because we fail to distinguish between two concepts of
education: one that justifies the practice at a societal level; and another
that justifies actual instances of particular teachers teaching particular
students. Once we focus on these two concepts of education, we see that
the latter establishes a humanistic baseline for the former. A social system
designated as "education," which may be justified and sustained for utilitarian reasons such as a society's global economic competitiveness, can
retain that label only if the actual instances of teaching conducted
within its ambit are responsive to the eudaimonistic pursuit of human
flourishing that underlies all actual instances of teaching, properly
understood.

Rawls's conceptual tools allow us to switch back and forth between
consideration of the social and the individual. This—the social vs. the
individual—is a better distinction, I think, than one between public and
private goods or between the extrinsic and intrinsic goods of education.
This is because the same phenomenon—for instance, the development of
civic agents—can be considered either for its public good aspect (including its susceptibility to free riding) or for its private benefit. And there
are, of course, not only intrinsic but also extrinsic benefits that flow to an
individual from civic participation.

Once we are prepared to consider education with regard both to a
macro societal-level and a micro-level conception, we meet the question
of whether it is possible to provide content for the humanistic baseline
for education that harmonizes the two concepts. I made the case that,
by drawing on Hannah Arendt's account of basic human needs in *The
Human Condition*, we can do that successfully. On the basis of her text, I
argued that education needs to prepare all students in four ways:

1. For breadwinning work;
2. For civic and political engagement;
3. For creative self-expression and world-making;
4. For rewarding relationships in spaces of intimacy and leisure.

A striking feature of this list of education's aims is that two of them identify goals that—considered from an alternative perspective—are also part of common utilitarian social justifications for education. To say that each person needs preparation for nonexploitative breadwinning work is to consider the issue of societal economic well-being from the perspective of the individual rather than the social whole. Similarly, to say that everyone needs preparation for civic and political engagement is to consider the issue of civic engagement from the perspective of each student rather than the social system.

When we put the Rawlsian and the Arendtian perspectives together, we see that our public discourse about education, our articulations of our collective goals, routinely leave out the civic. This is true despite the fact that civic experience is important to both concepts of education—the social and the individual. We have seen that, for instance, according to the Common Core State standards, again, education "must ensure *all* American students are prepared for the global economic workplace."[1] In general, the rhetoric of educational policy relies almost exclusively on advocating the goals of college and career readiness. The civic has, in short, gone AWOL. My aim, in pursuing the topic of "participatory readiness," is to rectify this.

What exactly is "participatory readiness"? First, the idea of being prepared to participate captures prospects of participation at several social levels: not only the level of the political community but also that of intimate and communitarian relationships. Think again of the four needs I derived from Arendt. Our flourishing as creators entails our engagement in cultural communities of meaning, and even our success in the realm of labor requires participation in social relationships. "Participatory readiness" defines our preparation for civic and political life, but it also undergirds our preparation in all the areas in which we hope to prosper. When young people leave school or college, we hope that they are prepared to participate effectively at work, in communities, and in love. One might well want to pause on the question of what "participatory readiness" entails at the intimate or social level—particularly given the contemporary crisis around sexual assault on college campuses. But the question of what it means to participate well in civic and political life also merits our ful-some attention. The reason to prioritize this topic—despite the urgencies of the social pathologies of our campuses—is its centrality to our political pathology, the problem of inequalities of many kinds.

Before I turn to the components of "participatory readiness," and what we know about the kinds of education that can achieve them, I would like to take a moment to expand on just how civic and political agency, and their cultivation, are relevant to our understanding of equality, and any effort to address issues of inequality, however those are specified.

PARTICIPATORY READINESS AND EQUALITY

The first link between a broad education for "participatory readiness" and equality is obvious. The idea that all students should be educated for political participation—and not merely a select few prepared for political leadership, as in Plato—is already an egalitarian feature of the humanis-tic baseline education, as I have fleshed that out. In seeking to give con-tent to the humanistic baseline for education, I described my employment of a democratic eudaimonism developed from Arendt. My embrace of democracy imported an ideal of political equality to the core idea of human flourishing that education supports. In other words, I follow Hannah Arendt (and others) in seeing a basic human need to participate in the realm of action as the explanation for why, among possible regime types, democracy is not only desirable but also the most just.[2] Given that, by this argument, political participation is necessary for a flourishing life, and given that education is preparation for a flourishing life, our curricula and pedagogies must prepare people for an Arendtian life of action. The goal is to maximize participation and thereby to come closer to realizing an ideal of political equality as well as providing the specific sense of fulfillment that accrues to each individual through the experience of em-powerment. The aspiration in the micro-level concept of education to prepare students to participate in their communities and polities flows from, and in turn, reinforces a commitment to political equality.

The egalitarian significance of this preparation of the young for civic and political life extends, however, beyond politics. It stretches to every domain in which it matters who makes the decisions that define our collective lives. The importance of "participatory readiness" therefore touches even the realm of economics. Here we can return to the many scholars who propose education as the main remedy for income and wealth inequality. They do so accurately, but for the wrong reason.

Most arguments that education is the solution to economic inequality stress education's potential to achieve broad dissemination of skills. Such broad dissemination is expected to drive down the wage premium on expertise and to help compress the income distribution. I am thinking again of Thomas Piketty's arguments but also of the work of Claudia Goldin and Larry Katz. On this line of thought, education is presumed to bring with it positional advantage. That is, those who have more education—more skills—can be presumed to reap more market rewards than those with lesser educational attainment. Narrowing gaps in educational attainment across the population or equalizing the distribution of educational goods should thus also reduce the positional advantage that accrues to education and reduce, for instance, income inequality. Rob Reich, coeditor with me of the volume *Education, Justice, and Equality*,[3] has drawn my attention to the work of the economist Fred Hirsch on the idea of positionality. Hirsch quips, "If everyone stands on tiptoe, no one sees any better."[4] We might also say, "If everyone stands on tiptoe, then no one is too seriously overshadowed."

But there are limits to how much the positional advantage of education can be moderated through the dissemination of technological skills. As the economist Daron Acemoglu and political scientist Jim Robinson have pointed out, arguments such as this presume a stable framework of technology and political institutions. They put this point particularly effectively when critiquing Piketty's account of income and wealth inequality. His argument fails, they propose, because it ignores politics. Thus they write:

> The quest for general laws of capitalism, or any economic system, is misguided because it is a-institutional. It ignores that it is the institutions and the political equilibrium of a society that determine how technology evolves, how markets function, and how the gains from various different economic arrangements are distributed.[5]

Acemoglu and Robinson remind us that, for instance, Marx's predictions that capitalism would generate wage stagnation or a decline in the share of national income accruing to labor failed at least in the case of the United Kingdom, because important British political reforms influenced wages and labor in the opposite direction. I quote again:

> For example, the Industrial Revolution went hand-in-hand with major political changes, including the development of the state and the

Reform Acts, which changed British political institutions and the distribution of political power. The economic consequences of these political changes were no less profound. In 1833 a professional factory inspectorate was set up, which brought the real implementation of legislation on the regulation of factory employment. The Factory Act of 1847 was much more radical than previous measures and it came at a time of intense social mobilization in the form of the Chartist movement. The political fallout of the 1832 democratization also led to the repeal of the Corn Laws in 1846, lowering the price of bread, raising real wages and simultaneously undermining land rents.

In other words, a society's political life intersects with its economic fate. In the case of the United States, Acemoglu and Robinson highlight late nineteenth- and early twentieth-century Populist and then Progressive mobilizations that led to reductions of corporate power, a turn of events that also refuted one of Marx's general laws, they argue.

The preparation of citizens for civic and political engagement supports the pursuit of political equality, but political equality, in turn, may well engender more egalitarian approaches to the economy. In other words, education can affect income inequality not merely by spreading technical skills and compressing the income distribution; it can even affect income inequality by influencing "how technology evolves, how markets function, and how the gains from various different economic arrangements are distributed."[6]

The idea of "participatory readiness" and the concept of equality, in short, have several linkages. An education that prepares students for civic and political engagement brings not only a concept of political equality into play but also the prospect of political contestation around issues of economic fairness. Insofar as technology frameworks and political institutions are malleable, the status of education as a positional good may itself be susceptible to change, and the degree of its positionality will in all likelihood vary with the political context. If an education for participatory readiness can affect a society's level of political competitiveness, it may also drive changes not only in the distribution of education but even in its positionality.[7] Consequently, the most effective way for us to direct our educational system toward egalitarian ends could well be to focus on participatory readiness.

When we think about equality in the context of education, we tend to think above all about distributional questions. We imagine that we will have an egalitarian system when we have managed to fund a system that will genuinely offer the possibility of an equal level of attainment (as distinguished from achievement) to all (or nearly all) students.[8] But we may need to move the conversation one step back and to remind ourselves that fair economic outcomes may themselves depend on genuine political equality. If this is right, then an education for participatory readiness, and not merely for technical skill, is the appropriate way of understanding the linkage between pedagogy and equality.

But if "participatory readiness" is so important, just what should students get ready for? In what do we expect them to participate?

PARTICIPATORY READINESS: READY FOR WHAT?

A basic challenge in answering the question of what students should get ready for is already reflected in a certain instability in our common vocabulary. Would we like to say that we should prepare them for civic engagement? Or for political participation? On this question, we are confused.[9] Thus far in my lectures, I have repeatedly used the pleonastic phrase "civic and political life," and this reflects what I take to be a broadly shared confusion. After all, do those two words not mean fundamentally the same thing? Their etymological roots are similar. "Political" and "civic" come, respectively, from the Greek and Latin terms for "city." Why, then, use both at once? Yet these terms have come to have two distinct rhetorical valences for us. "Civic" is a safe word. It suggests public action undertaken through approved venues and within the confines of long-standing public agendas. "Political" is a more highly charged term. It invokes approved actions such as voting and holding office, but it also suggests protest action, activism, and advocacy, all of which make us nervous when we come to discussions of things like curriculum and pedagogy. We do not, for instance, commonly think that a K–12 education or college education should be organized around teaching people Saul Alinsky's *Rules for Radicals*.[10] Yet Alinsky's text does instill participatory readiness of at least *some kind or another*. And whatever kind it is, we are most likely to call an education in Alinsky "political," rather than "civic."

Our strange uncertainty around the term "political" came home to me with a special force when I had the occasion to watch the video of a recent panel that gathered together three young leaders of digital associations. These young people were engaged in activities such as supporting marriage equality, disseminating Hayekian economic ideas, and claiming space in the public sphere for American Muslims. When asked whether

they thought of themselves as political, each said no.[11] This fact under-
scores the challenge of trying to define the content of an education for
"participatory readiness." We cannot quite bring ourselves to agree on
whether our object is "the civic" or "the political," and this is partly because
we no longer esteem "the political." The lack of equilibrium in our
vocabulary—do we want to talk about the "civic" or do we want to talk
about the "political"—reflects the current absence of any single, unified
conception of what it means to participate in public life.

A historical view can bring perspective to the situation in which we
find ourselves with regard to our conceptions of citizenship. The sociologist and communications scholar, Michael Schudson, has made the important point that models of civic education in any given time and place tend
to track that time's reigning ideology about citizenship.[12] In the case of
the United States, he identifies four separate models of civic agency that
have emerged since the founding—with each model stemming from the
period's reigning ideals and generating a distinctive approach to socializ-
ing the young for political participation.

In the young republic, politics was dominated, Schudson argues, by
a model of the citizen as the "trusted, solid" individual, a (white, male)
property owner, whose central activity was to vote for esteemed leaders
whose wise hands would set the community's course. A religious education directed toward matters of character predominated. With the rise
of populist politics and mass political parties, the citizen evolved into
the "party loyalist," an individual who turned out for party parades and
events, voted for the slate, and reaped economic benefits, such as employment opportunities, through party membership. The intellectual demands were minimal; to vote a party ticket, not even literacy was necessary.
With the rise of the progressive era and the professionalization of political
administration and journalism, the country saw the emergence of "the informed voter" as the model for citizenship. Voting was still the citizen's
main activity, but that citizen was supposed to enter the now private ballot
box having consumed high-quality information provided by journalists.
With the Civil Rights era came the "rights-conscious" citizen; individuals
needed to be both more self-aware about their own rights and more attentive to those of others. The citizen's toolkit now included the courtroom
and tactics such as public litigation.

I think it is currently impossible to find a single, unifying model of
citizenship dominating our culture—and our uncertainty about the terms
"civic" and "political" is just one symptom of this difficulty.[13] Nonetheless,

we can identify a handful of models currently bumping and jostling each other in our collective imagination. To spot them, though, we will need to establish as a backdrop a broad, philosophical conceptualization of the range of action-types that can characterize public life, so that we can consider which features of that range currently have the greatest salience. Just as Hannah Arendt's philosophical views were helpful in identifying the humanistic baseline, her work can advance our thinking here too. We can draw on her account of *action* to limn the backdrop against which to assess just how, in practice, we seem to conceive of the political life these days.

In Arendt's account of action, citizenship is the activity of cocreating a way of life; it is the activity of world-building. The concept, fully understood, extends beyond legal categories of membership in political units. The activity of citizenship—of cocreation and world-building—can occur at many different social levels: in a neighborhood or school, in a networked community or association, in a city, state, or nation, at a global level. As I further specify this idea of civic agency in my own work, it is multifaceted and involves three core tasks.[14] First, there is disinterested deliberation around a public problem.[15] Here the model is the Athenian citizens gathered in the assembly, or the town halls of colonial New Hampshire, or public representatives behaving reasonably in the halls of a legislature. Second, there is prophetic work to shift a society's codes of values; in the public opinion and communications literature, this is now called *frame shifting*.[16] Think here of the rhetorical power of Harriet Beecher Stowe and Martin Luther King Jr. Finally, there is transparently and passionately interested "fair fighting," where a given public actor adopts a cause and pursues it passionately, never pretending to disinterestedness.[17] One might think of the nineteenth-century activists for women's rights, Elizabeth Cady Stanton, Susan B. Anthony, and Matilda Joslyn Gage.

The ideal civic agent combines capacities to carry out all three of these tasks ethically and justly. Let us take the nineteenth-century women's rights activist, Elizabeth Stanton Cady as an example. At the Seneca Falls Convention she had to function in a deliberative mode for the debate about the text of the Declaration of Sentiments. When she drafted that text, however, before the convention's deliberations, she functioned in the prophetic mode, just as she did in her innumerable speeches. Finally, in campaigning for legal change, as in the adoption of the Married Women's Property Act in New York and similar laws in other states, she functioned as an activist.

Yet if deliberation, prophesy, and contestation are the rudimentary components of civic agency, they do not in themselves determine the content of any given historical moment's conception of citizenship. There is no need for each of these functions to be combined in a single role or citizenly persona, nor is there any guarantee that all three will operate in each historical context. Diverse regime types—from the authoritarian to the liberal to the tribal—have been known to try to shut down heterodox prophets. One or another of these roles may be foregrounded, and it is altogether possible for these tasks to become separated from one another, generating distinguishable kinds of civic roles. I think this latter situation obtains today.

Distinct, alternative roles and personae have developed that emphasize one or another of these three core tasks of civic agency or some combination of them. I designate these roles as the "civically engaged individual," the "activist" or "political entrepreneur," and the "professional politician." Following Schudson's example, we can distinguish these roles by how they define the tasks of civic agency; how they connect to the levers of power; and how they place intellectual and psychological demands on their practitioners.[18]

The "civically engaged individual" focuses on the task of disinterested deliberation and actions that can be said to flow from it. Such citizens focus on pursuing "universal" values, "disinterestedness," "critical thinking," and "bi-partisan" projects.[19] Hence our use of the safe word "civic" for this category of civic agency. Next come the activist and the politician. They are "political" actors, and the unsafe and sometimes unsavory nature of the activity conducted through these second two roles explains our use of the word *political* for them. The activist seeks to change hearts and minds and to fight, in the ideal fairly, for particular outcomes, often making considerable sacrifices to do so. Finally, the professional politician, as currently conceived, focuses mainly on "fighting," and not necessarily on "fighting fair." This role, in contrast to the other two, currently represents a degraded form of civic agency in contemporary discourse; one has only to look at Congress's all-time low approval ratings to recognize this.[20]

Each of these citizenly personae has some affinity with one of the models that Schudson analyzes as grounded in a particular historical era. The "civically engaged individual," has a close affinity with the Progessive era's idealization of the "informed voter"; the activist or political entrepreneur with the Civil Rights era's rights-conscious citizen; and the "politician" with the late nineteenth-century model of the party loyalist. Yet at this moment all three of these models of civic agency—or updated versions of them—are elbowing and shoving one another in our public spheres. Given this fact, how do we educate for "participatory readiness"? Do we choose one of these models to emphasize? Or is there a way to integrate our understanding?

All three of these citizenly roles include "voting" in their responsibilities. But beyond that institutional responsibility, these roles develop very different conceptions of how to interact with both formal political institutions and the other levers that can be pulled to effect change.[21] They also develop very different conceptions of the types of speech and ethical orientations that should govern civic and political participation.[22] Each of these citizenly roles also presupposes a different approach to the development of intellectual and psychological capacities.

The civically engaged citizen who embraces the ideal of disinterested deliberation and pursues projects of "universal" value must, in some fashion, be clear about and counteract self-interest, must develop ways of testing whether things count as universal, and requires high-quality information on a wide array of issues.[23] The activist must be clear about interest and goals, must be good at strategic and tactical thinking, must understand "the levers of change," must be good at the techniques of storytelling that facilitate "frame shifting," and must have ethical parameters for thinking about the relationship between ends and means.[24] The professional politician, in the ideal, as opposed to in contemporary reality, would have both sets of the above competencies, as well as having expertise in how political institutions themselves function.

Notably, we have lost sight of the "ideal citizen" who combines success in all three citizenly tasks. That is, we have lost sight of the "statesman," who *is* a professional politician but who nonetheless has developed all of the capacities described above as belonging to the other two roles and is thus capable of disinterested deliberation, of just "frame shifting," and of fighting fair, as opposed to being capable merely of fighting.[25] But, even more important, we have also lost sight of the "ordinary citizen," who is not a professional politician, but who has nonetheless developed all of the competencies described above and who is proud to be involved in "politics."

If we are to embrace an education for "participatory readiness," we must aim our pedagogic and curricular work not at any single one of these three models, but at what lies behind all of them: a more fundamental understanding of what politics is. I embrace an Arendtian account of political life as something positive that consists of the activity of cocreating a way of life.[26] Ultimately, I think that this view of politics generates an account of "participatory readiness" that supports all three models of citizenship: the civically engaged individual, the activist, and the politician. It supports all three roles because each carries out only a subset of the work that constitutes public action. An education that prepares a student for Arendtian action should nourish future civic leaders, activists, *and* politicians. But such an education ought also to permit a reintegration of these role types. As we consider what sorts of pedagogy and curriculum can achieve participatory readiness, we thus have available two possible courses of action. We might direct an education for "participatory readiness" toward the three citizenly personae simultaneously, albeit as distinct and separable, or we might direct that education toward a reintegrated concept of civic agency. Either way, pursuing "participatory readiness" is an ambitious project and requires a much more expansive approach to "civic education" than I have yet seen an example of.

THE CONTENT OF PARTICIPATORY READINESS

What should be the content of an education for "participatory readiness?" An aspiration to answer this question is visible in the June 2013 report, called *The Heart of the Matter*, released by the Commission on the Humanities and Social Sciences established by Congress and organized by the American Academy of Arts and Sciences. This report declared its first goal to be to: "Educate Americans in the knowledge, skills, and understanding they will need to thrive in a twenty-first-century democracy."[27] With this formulation, the report sought to rectify the gap in our public justification for the system of education by restoring a civic component. What is education for? It is for thriving in "democracy," not merely a global economy. So the report argues.

Then the commission detailed the activities for which it thought students should ready themselves. Drawing, among other sources, on the good work of Michael Rebell and the Campaign for Fiscal Equity, the commission followed its goal statement with a recommendation:

> The Commission therefore recommends a new dedication to "participatory readiness" as an educational goal. We urge a nationwide commitment to preparing k-12 students for full participation in a democratic society. The Commission commends the Common Core State Standards Initiative for its inclusion of history and civics in the

basic literacy curriculum. It promotes the competencies necessary for full civic participation in American society: voting, serving on juries, interpreting current events, developing respect for and understanding of differences, along with an ability to articulate one's sense of the common good.[28]

The commission adopted the language of "participatory readiness" but, in its account of the education that achieves this, sketched the contours of civic education largely as we have traditionally known it. This traditional conception focuses on instruction in history and civics, primarily understood as classroom learning about the mechanics of government. Conventionally described as the "how a bill becomes a law" version of civic education, this approach prepares students for "informed" or "dutiful" citizenship, as the media scholar Lance Bennett calls it.[29] This "informed citizen" model is what comes through most strongly in the report.

Yet in the passage quoted above, the commission—on which I need to confess that I served—did extend the basic civic education framework modestly, and in two directions in particular. The report drew attention to the pressing need to prepare students to interact in conditions of diversity and also to the importance of developing in them linguistic competence adequate to offering up compelling visions of the public good. These are extensions on which I believe we can and should build.

There are two problems with the traditional "how a bill becomes a law" approach to civic education, at which the commission's report only hints.

First, to focus on the mechanics of government as the heart of civic education is to focus on only a part of what is needed for the development of participatory readiness. Civic agents do need to understand the strategies and tactics available for bringing about political change, and the structure of political institutions is a part of this. But tactical knowledge is only one of the developmental pillars necessary for civic agency. In addition to tactical and strategic understanding, just as the commission suggests, students also need *verbal empowerment* and *democratic knowledge*. These are the two other developmental pillars supporting civic agency. I will return to both of those concepts in a moment. The second problem with a focus on the institutional mechanics of government as the heart of civic education is that, even as an account of the tactics and strategies of civic agency, it is a limited picture, particularly in this era of new media and a transformed communications landscape. In sum, "participatory readiness" rests on three developmental pillars: verbal empowerment, democratic knowledge, and a rich understanding of the strategies and tactics that undergird efficacy. I will turn to each of these pillars of "participatory readiness" individually.

First, I address verbal empowerment, which consists of interpretive (or exegetical) and expressive skills. Civic and political action must begin from a diagnosis of our current situation and move from that diagnosis to a prescription for a response. Such interpretive work, or in the language of the Declaration of Independence, the work of reading "the course of human events," can be done only in and through language. Data is only one subset of the linguistic resources available to this work of diagnosis and prescription. Conversational work is necessary to clarify the meaning of data—regardless of how big those data are. The analytical skills that constitute acts of interpretation only ever manifest themselves in language: descriptions of the situation that obtains or of what is to be done.

Moreover, success at the movement from diagnosis to prescription requires not merely the verbal skills embodied in acts of interpretation but also expressive skills. For these social diagnoses to become effective, one must convince others of them. The verbal work involved in civic agency extends well beyond our usual focus on deliberation to include also adversarial and prophetic speech. This component of "participatory readiness" used to be taught, from antiquity through the nineteenth century, under the heading of rhetoric.[30]

Second, "participatory readiness" requires what I, building on the work of classicist and political scientist, Josiah Ober, call *democratic knowledge*.[31] Democracy is an egalitarian political form and one of the great paradoxes of egalitarianism is that it functions not through a reduction or diminishment of the need for leadership but through its increase. Democracies spawn vast numbers of collective decision-making bodies. The Athenians famously had a long list of boards of administrators and civic officers, many populated by lottery. As to our own case, during the period of the Revolutionary War, scarcely a day went by when the Continental Congress did not set up yet more committees to carry out congressional business.[32] Tocqueville, of course, noticed how prolific nineteenth-century Americans were at forming associations and, for all of Robert Putnam's tales in *Bowling Alone* of decline in the twentieth century, we in fact continue to be very busy in this regard.[33] Our forms of association have changed, certainly, and for very good reasons, among them that the law of association was fundamentally restructured between

1970 and 1990, but it is by no means clear that associations are any less common now than at earlier points. (In other words, I think Putnam's story is fundamentally wrong, an issue I address elsewhere.[34])

All this associating generates its own science and demands its own art form.[35] Call these simply the science and art of association. I call this science and art, taken together, "democratic knowledge" because they pinpoint bodies of knowledge that grow up in democratic contexts, specifically. Although there are many components to this science and art of association, I consider its relational elements to be among the most important. On this front, democratic knowledge consists of what I call cosmopolitan bonding skills, on the one hand, and bridging skills on the other. The latter is easier to understand. These bridging skills consist of the capacities by which a translator, a mediator, an individual who can surmount social difference can convert a costly social relationship into one that is mutually beneficial to both parties. Cosmopolitan bonding skills, in contrast, relate to the precise nature of the bonds that we form with the people to whom we feel the most affinity, whether that is because of shared kinship, geographical collocation, ethnicity, religion, or similarity of preferences. For the sake of healthy psychological development, all people need bonding relationships.[36] But not all bonding relationships are the same. We need to bond in ways that help to preserve the democracy of which we are a part.[37] Indeed, the question of how we bond is deeply entangled with the question of whether we are able to bridge.[38] Thus, the critical question for a democratic society is how we can bond with those who are like us so as to help us bridge even with those who differ from us. In order for any method of bonding—for instance, that which begins from social homogeneity or that which begins from interest affinity—to support our capacity to bridge, the very experience of bonding must cultivate receptivity toward the potential of participation in our bonding group by social dissimilars. The question of just what sorts of styles and methods of social bonding can be cosmopolitan in this way is a difficult one, which I will not address in this lecture. Suffice it for our purposes simply to mark out the terrain by identifying this, too, as a core component of "participatory readiness." Cosmopolitan bonding skills and bridging skills are both necessary for civic actors to function effectively across political institutions and other spaces for political action. They are also necessary for the formation of solidarity that supports civic and political action outside of institutions.

Finally, verbal empowerment and the acquisition of democratic knowledge require supplementation by tactical and strategic understanding or knowledge of the mechanics of political action. As I have said, this last area is where civic and political education has traditionally focused. The error in focusing here is, of course, the failure to take the domains of verbal empowerment and democratic knowledge fully into account. But there is also another problem with the traditional focus on the mechanics of government, this one stemming from the transformation of public spheres in our new media age. Traditionally, we have thought about this "tactical" part of civic education as requiring lessons in how a bill becomes a law, but a feature of our new media age is that levers of change outside of political institutions are now easier to pull.[39] Consequently, tactical and strategic understanding now also requires learning about how civic agents can interact with corporations and nongovernmental organizations, or as part of social movements. It requires understanding how cultural norms can be changed and how changes in cultural norms bring about broader political changes.[40] It also requires understanding a new architecture of communication. Where once we needed to know how to write letters to the editor and to Congress, now we need to master the architecture and rhetoric of the Internet and social media.[41] We still have a curricular and pedagogic need for the traditional focus of civic education on the Constitution and structure of government but this domain of strategies and tactics now requires expansion.

The core elements of "participatory readiness" are thus: verbal empowerment; strategic and tactical understanding of the levers of political change, broadly conceived; and democratic, associational know-how. This is a nonexhaustive account of the elements of "participatory readiness," but these components are, I think, the most significant human capacities that require cultivation if each of us is to be well-prepared to function as a civic and political actor.

CULTIVATING PARTICIPATORY READINESS

How can we cultivate capacities of these kinds? For the rest of my lecture, I will focus on the relationship between "participatory readiness," and verbal empowerment. We will soon find that the unlikely hero of my story is the humanities, or a liberal arts education. We will also finally see the significance of using the humanistic baseline to define education as it pertains to the actual teaching of actual students.

In the vast universe of educational data one can catch fleeting glimpses here and there of an answer to the question of how teachers can cultivate "participatory readiness." For instance, it is clear that college provides something useful there that our K–12 system generally does not.

As Meira Levinson and others have pointed out, educational attainment is an even better predictor of the likelihood of voting than income.[42] In other words, although we do not talk terribly often or in very consistent ways about how college provides a civic and political education, something is happening on our campuses that engenders "participatory readiness." Importantly, that something is not simply the preparation of students for economic success. It is the importance of the fact that there is an even closer correlation between level of educational attainment and likelihood of voting than between socioeconomic status and likelihood of voting.

There is also an important corollary to the observation that college makes a meaningful difference for "participatory readiness." If, as is shown in Table 1, those who have advanced degrees vote more than those with college degrees, and those with college degrees, more than those with high school degrees, we have what Meira Levinson has called a civic achievement gap. If the goal of an educational system is to achieve participatory readiness for all students, this is an element of our education that we should hope to bring to a satisfactory level by age eighteen, the age of political majority. The civic achievement gap means we are not doing well enough in the K–12 system in cultivating "participatory readiness."

TABLE 1. Percentage of U.S. citizens over 18 who voted in the 2004 and 2008 presidential elections by educational attainment.

	2004 Election (percent)	2008 Election (percent)
Educational Attainment		
Less than high school diploma	30	39
High school graduate	56	55
Some college or associate degree	69	68
Bachelor's degree	78	77
Advanced degree	84	83

Data from Meira Levinson, No Citizen Left Behind, Harvard, 2012, p. 35. Figures calculated using data from U.S. Census Bureau (2010b), tables 4a, 5, 8, 13; US Census Bureau (2010c), tables 4b, 5, 8, 13.

TABLE 2. College Graduates' Civic Engagement.

	Humanities	STEM
Ever voted as one year out (class of 2008)	92.8%	83.5%
Wrote to public officials by ten years out (class of 1993)	44.1%	30.1%

Data from the American Academy of Arts and Sciences. Figures calculated using U.S. Department of Education, National Center for Education Statistics, B&B: 09 Baccalaureate and Beyond Longitudinal Study; B&B: 93/03 Baccalaureate and Beyond Longitudinal Study.

What exactly is happening on college campuses, then, and not in the K–12 system that makes this kind of difference? Not all college is the same, of course, and this fact holds an important key. Students have varying experiences depending, among other things, on their choice of major. Interestingly, there is a statistically significant difference (shown in Table 2) between the rates of political participation that we see from those who have graduated with humanities majors and those who graduate with STEM (science, technology, engineering, and mathematics) majors.

Similarly, participation in social science college curricula is a strong predictor of later political participation, according to Duke University political scientist Sunshine Hillygus.[43] Hillygus conducted the study to control for the possibility of self-selection of those with civic and political interests into social sciences courses, and even with this control in place, she found an effect on later political participation from enrollment in social science courses. Her paper provides strong evidence for a correlation between work in the humanities and social sciences and participatory readiness.

The difference between different educational strands in higher education is mirrored in K–12 education. Just as, those who major in the humanities or take social science courses in college are more likely to participate politically after graduation, so too are those whose verbal skills are higher by the end of high school, as measured by SATs, more likely to become active political participants than those with high math scores. Moreover, the SAT effect endures even when college-level curricular choices are controlled for (see Figure 1).

To identify a correlation is not, of course, to identify causation, but those with more sophisticated verbal skills are clearly more ready to be civic and political participators. This may be because another source of motivation engaged them in politics, and once they were engaged, these

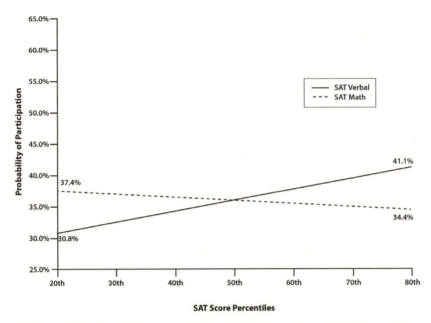

Figure 1. Predicted probability of political participation by SAT percentiles. *Source:* D. Sunshine Hillygus, "The Missing Link: Exploring the Relationship between Higher Education and Political Engagement." *Political Behavior* 27, no. 1 (2005): 39. Reprinted with permission from Springer Science+Business Media Inc.

students sought the verbal skills that they needed to thrive in the domain of political participation. Or the verbal ability may make it easier to engage. We do not have a study that considers levels of engagement before and after significant increases in verbal ability. Nonetheless, what we do have in data such as these is a tantalizing suggestion that the work of the humanities on verbal empowerment is intrinsically related to the development of "participatory readiness." Explaining just how this is so is an important and largely unaddressed research question.[44]

In addition to the data points that one can find scattered here and there as provocative clues to a profound story about the humanities, language, and participatory readiness, one also finds occasional anecdotes that help elucidate the connection between language and civic agency. In a volume called *Citizenship across the Curriculum*, Rebecca Nowacek, an English professor, relates the following story about the discovery by one humanities student of how her major had distinctively prepared her to participate in public life. Nowacek writes:

Early in the collaborative process [of working with two classmates on the knotty local problem of school choice within Milwaukee public schools], an English major told me she felt that the value of her disciplinary knowledge was questioned, even slighted. One of her groupmates was a political science major, well versed in questions of public policy. The other was a speech pathologist, with experience working in the local schools. What could someone who sits reading novels bring to their collaborative inquiry? Whether their skepticism was real or only imagined, the English major felt the need to articulate for her groupmates—and for herself—what her studies of literature had prepared her to contribute to the understanding of this knotty local problem. . . . Ultimately she determined that what she could contribute to her group was her capacity to identify and tease out the significance of patterns in discourse. She conducted a careful reading of local newspaper coverage of school choice, identifying a number of disturbing trends.[45]

This English major's heightened linguistic sensitivity was her special skill. My contention here is that it is also the foundational civic competency. It is the English major who was in a position to diagnose what was actually happening in the community, and the meanings of how particular choices were being framed. We see her interpretive skills at work. We also see her expressive skills. She "felt the need to articulate . . . what her studies of literature had prepared her to contribute" and in response to this need she was able to develop and express a memorable answer. The anecdote is too partial for us to know just what political meaning the English major found in the newspaper or to know precisely how she contributed to the world-making in which she was engaged alongside the political science and speech pathology majors. Yet we do see in this anecdote a deployment of the first political skill: diagnosis. Notably, reading novels—interpreting them—was what had prepared this student for her own life of action, in the Arendtian sense.

This investigation of the relationship between the humanities, verbal empowerment, and participatory readiness is nothing more than a suggestive gesture toward precisely how we might cultivate participatory readiness. If indeed verbal empowerment is at the base of political empowerment, and if indeed the humanities have a special influence there, then we have a case for the humanities in their potential to contribute to "participatory readiness." In other words, in my pursuit of the links between education and equality, in these lectures I have wandered into a defense of the humanities. This is because of the potential of education to advance political equality, a potentiality that depends, I suggest, first and foremost on the humanistic components of the curriculum.

To conclude these lectures, though, I would like to complete these thoughts about the relationship between education and equality. The link that I have suggested among the humanities, language, and participatory readiness brings us to what I think is at the heart of education's egalitarian force. Education's most fundamental egalitarian value is in its development of us as language-using creatures. Our linguistic capacities are what, fundamentally, education taps, and it is their great unfolding that empowers students. This verbal empowerment prepares us for participation in civic and political life. As we cultivate verbal empowerment in our students, we build the foundation for a politically competitive social and political system. We have good reason to expect that a genuinely competitive political system would put matters of economic fairness into play for contestation. This returns us to the idea that, by supporting political equality, educational institutions themselves can affect "how technology evolves, how markets function, and how the gains from various different economic arrangements are distributed." The idea is that there ought to be a developmental "threshold," identified in my account as the cultivation of participatory readiness, that enables human beings to compete politically even with others who have achieved a higher level of educational attainment. The fundamental relationship between education and equality, then, is that the very definition of education rests on a conception of shared human capacities, which, when fully activated, have the potential, by supporting political equality, to move us toward a world that reduces or eliminates the positional aspect of the good of education itself. Consequently, the most valuable way for us to direct our educational system toward egalitarian ends may be by focusing on participatory readiness. Finally, I would suggest that it is perhaps because we have lost sight of the contributions made by the humanities to our educational system that we have also lost sight of the fundamental link between education and equality that I have tried to clarify in these lectures.

EDUCATION FOR POLITICAL EQUALITY

Let me offer a brief conclusion. The great beauty of language's power as a catalyst of human capacity is that we all have access to it, so any of us can choose anywhere, anytime to plumb its depths and climb with it to the heights of human achievement. An adequately egalitarian educational system would maximally activate the latent capacities in the powerful, invisible body of language, which dwells inside each of us. Even when an educational system fails us, we still have access to self-development. We can educate ourselves, and many have. Before the arrival of compulsory education, there were Benjamin Franklin, Abraham Lincoln, Frederick Douglass, and Susan B. Anthony. After its arrival, there were the participants in the Freedom Schools in the South in the summer of 1964. Today we have the Clemente Courses founded by Earl Shorris and Sarah Hirschman's work on People and Stories.[46] When we strip our idea of education of the state apparatus—that is, of the system-level concept— we see again that what remains is what I have been calling the *humanistic baseline*, the idea that education begins as an effort to unfold the powers that mark us as human, the first of which is language, an effort that any of us can undertake in any social circumstance in which we find ourselves. In this fact, we come back to a fundamental human equality and also to the political equality that language opens up as a possibility for us. We come back to the human capacity, latent in our linguistic power, for world-making—through political contestation and prophesy, through art and deliberation. And we come back to the possibility that the cultivation of participatory readiness leads to political institutions that will themselves pull toward social equality and economic fairness.

NOTES

1. National Governors Association, "Common Core State Standards Initiative Standards-Setting Criteria," http://www.corestandards.org/assets/Criteria .pdf, and on file with the author.
2. Hannah Arendt, *The Human Condition* (Chicago: University of Chicago Press, 1958); Amartya Sen, *Development as Freedom* (New York: Knopf, 1999); Josiah Ober, "Natural Capacities and Democracy as a Good-in-Itself," *Philosophical Studies* 132 (2007): 59–73; Danielle Allen 2014a.
3. Danielle Allen and Robert Reich, eds., *Education, Justice, and Democracy* (Chicago: University of Chicago Press, 2013).
4. Fred Hirsch, *Social Limits to Growth* (London: Routledge & Kegan and Paul, 1977), 5.
5. Daron Acemoglu and James A. Robinson, "The Rise and Fall of General Laws of Capitalism," MIT Open Access, August 2014, http://economics.mit.edu /files 9834.
6. *Ibid.*
7. If it is indeed possible for an adequacy framework to reduce the positional aspects of the good of education, then "adequacy" rather than "equality" may actually be the right allocative solution to the distributive justice problem.

8. "Attainment" refers to the number of years of schooling; "achievement" refers to the level of growth achieved during those years of schooling as exhibited by test scores. It is theoretically possible to equalize attainment, but it is not theoretically possible to equalize achievement because of individual variation.

9. Evidence for this claim comes from five years of experience in the MacArthur Foundation research network on youth and participatory politics. The question of which word, "civic" or "political," to use in discussions of how to educate students for public life returns with a strange insistence, and without much prospect of resolution.

10. Saul Alinsky, *Rules for Radicals* (New York: Vintage, 1971).

11. This was a conference panel titled "From Participatory Culture to Political Participation," at the Futures of Entertainment 6 conference, MIT, November 9–10, 2012; for the video of the panel, see http://techtv.mit.edu/collections /convergenceculture/videos/21729-foe6-from-participatory-culture-to-political -participation.

12. Michael Schudson, "Click Here for Democracy: A History and Critique of an Information-Based Model of Citizenship," in *Democracy and New Media*, edited by Henry Jenkins, 49–60 (Cambridge, MA: MIT Press, 2003).

13. Schudson, in contrast, does identify a single model, which he calls the "monitorial" citizen. The "monitorial" citizen fulfills a watchdog function with regard to officeholders.

14. I have pursued an effort to anatomize political speech across numerous publications, including Danielle Allen, *Talking to Strangers: Anxieties of Citizenship Since Brown v. Board of Education* (Chicago: University of Chicago Press, 2004); Allen, *Why Plato Wrote* (London: Wiley-Blackwell, 2010); Allen, *Our Declaration: A Reading of the Declaration of Independence in Defense of Equality* (New York: Norton/Liveright, 2014); Danielle Allen and Jennifer Light, *From Voice to Influence: Understanding Citizenship in a Digital Age* (Chicago: University of Chicago Press, 2015); Allen, "Discourse Ethics for Divided Publics," keynote address at the Conference on Moderation at the University of Warwick, June 2014; and "Art of Association" (unpublished manuscript on file with author, presented at University of California at Berkeley, Yale University Law School, and Columbia Law School).

15. The literature on deliberative democracy is relevant here. See, for instance, the work of Jurgen Habermas, Seyla Benhabib, and Amy Gutmann and Dennis Thompson.

16. For a treatment of King in this direction, see George Shulman, *American Prophecy: Race and Redemption in American Culture* (Minneapolis: University of Minnesota Press, 2008). On frame shifting, see Deva Woodly, *The Politics of Common Sense: How Social Movements Use Public Discourse to Change Politics and Win Acceptance* (Oxford: Oxford University Press, 2015).

17. Here there is a literature from the study of sport on the ethics of fair fighting, which is relevant, as well as the professional ethics of fields like law and journalism.

18. Schudson, "Click Here for Democracy," 49–60.

19. Terms used at the conference panel, "From Participatory Culture to Political Participation."

20. See Gallup's polls on low approval ratings for Congress, http://www.gallup.com/poll/1600/congress-public.aspx.

21. On the levers of change, see Danielle Allen, "Reconceiving Public Spheres," in Allen and Light, *From Voice to Influence*, 178–208.

22. Allen, "Discourse Ethics for Divided Publics."

23. Howard Gardner, "In Defense of Disinterestedness, in Allen and Light, *From Voice to Influence*, 232–53.

24. On the last point, see Karuna Mantena, "Another Realism: The Politics of Gandhian Nonviolence," *American Political Science Review* 106, no. 2 (2012): 455–70.

25. For a particularly powerful treatment of the figure of the statesman, see Melissa Lane, *Method and Politics in Plato's Statesman* (Cambridge: Cambridge University Press, 1998).

26. Cf. D. Allen 2014a.

27. American Academy of Arts and Sciences, *The Heart of the Matter* (Cambridge, MA, 2009), 19.

28. Ibid., 24.

29. See Lance Bennett, Chris Wells, and Deen Freelon, "Communicating Citizenship Online: Models of Civic Learning in the Youth Web Sphere," *Civic Learning Online Project* (2009), www.engagedyouth.org.

30. Here I effectively reproduce Aristotle's division of rhetoric into deliberative, forensic, and epideictic. The forensic (or judicial) aligns with my category of adversarial speech, and the epideictic, which involves pointing out what is noble and shameful, aligns with my category of the prophetic.

31. Josiah Ober, *Democracy and Knowledge: Innovation and Learning in Classical Athens* (Princeton, NJ: Princeton University Press, 2008).

32. For an account of all the committee work involved in the production of the Declaration of Independence, see Allen, *Our Declaration*.

33. Robert Putnam, *Bowling Alone* (New York: Simon and Schuster, 2000). For a portrait of the alternative kinds of association being pursued, one needs to add synthesized data from Robert Wuthnow, *Sharing the Journey: Support Groups and the Quest for a New Community* (New York: Free Press, 1996), and Wuthnow, *Loose Connections: Joining together in America's Fragmented Communities* (Cambridge, MA: Harvard University Press, 2002); Theda Skocpol, *Diminished Democracy: From Membership to Management in American Civic Life,* Rothbaum Series (Norman: University of Oklahoma Press, 2003); Mario Small, *Unanticipated Gains: Origins of Network Inequality in Everyday Life* (Oxford: Oxford University Press, 2009); and Everett Ladd, *The Ladd Report* (New York: Free Press, 1999).

34. See Allen, "Art of Association."

35. Let me provide an example of the relationship between the science and art of associations. Colleagues and I from the MacArthur Foundation Youth and Participatory Politics research network have developed design principles to

guide the use and construction of digital tools whose purpose is to engage youth in equitable and efficacious civic or political action. These design principles are available at http://ypp.dmlcentral.net/projects/digital-platforms-project. This project synthesized three years' worth of research on youth participatory experience, "the science of associations," in order to generate these principles as guidance for the "art of association."

36. Philip Bromberg, *The Shadow of the Tsunami and the Growth of the Relational Mind* (New York: Routledge, 2011).

37. Elizabeth Anderson, *The Imperative of Integration* (Princeton, NJ: Princeton University Press, 2010).

38. Bromberg, *Shadow of the Tsunami*; David Eng and Shinhee Han, "A Dialogue on Racial Melancholia," *Psychoanalytic Dialogues: The International Journal of Relational Perspectives* 10, no. 4 (2000): 667–700; and Eng and Han, "Desegregating Love: Transnational Adoption, Racial Reparation, and Racial Transitional Objects," *Studies in Gender and Sexuality* 7, no. 2 (2006): 141–72.

39. Allen, "Reconceiving Public Spheres."

40. See Woodly, *Politics of Common Sense*; Allen, *Why Plato Wrote*; and Allen, "Discourse Ethics for Divided Publics." See also how Adbusters, which founded Occupy Wall Street, describes its project of "culture-jamming": "We are a global network of culture jammers and creatives working to change the way information flows, the way corporations wield power, and the way meaning is produced in our society," http://www.adbusters.org. "According to Mark Dery (1990), cultural jamming is defined as 'artistic terrorism' directed against the information society in which we live'" (Leah Lievrouw, *Alternative and Activist New Media* [Cambridge: Polity Press, 2011], 72). "The term [culture-jamming] was originally coined by a band by the name of Negativland in 1984. They define it as 'media about media about media' which describes 'billboard alteration and other underground art that seeks to shed light on the dark side of the computer age'" (ibid.).

41. Peter Levine of Tufts University made the case that civic education now requires teaching students to master the "architecture of the internet" at an August 2014 APSA panel on civic education.

42. Miera Levinson, *No Citizen Left Behind* (Cambridge, MA: Harvard University Press, 2012); Sidney Verba and Kay Lehman Schlozman, *Voice and Equality: Civic Voluntarism in American Politics* (Cambridge, MA: Harvard University Press, 1995); Raymond Wolfinger and Steven Rosenstone, *Who Votes?* (New Haven, CT: Yale University Press, 1980).

43. D. Sunshine Hillygus, "The Missing Link: Exploring the Relationship between Higher Education and Political Engagement," *Political Behavior* 27, no. 1 (2005): 25–47. Since I am giving these lectures at Stanford, I feel obliged to point out that Hillygus earned her PhD at this university. Additional tantalizing evidence is available in the work of David Kidd and Emanuele Castano, on the relationship between reading literary fiction and the "theory of mind" function. See David Kidd and Emanuele Castano, "Reading Literary Fiction Improves Theory of Mind," *Science 18* (October) 342 (6156): 377–80, DOI: 10.1126/science.1239918.

44. At the end of *Citizenship across the Curriculum*, David Scobey laments "the one real lacuna in the book's disciplinary range: attention to the role of the arts and humanities in civic life and civic education" (Michael Smith, Rebecca S. Nowacek, and Jeffrey L. Bernstein, *Citizenship across the Curriculum* (Bloomington: Indiana University Press, 2010), Kindle location, 2852–53).

45. Rebecca S. Nowacek, "Understanding Citizenship as Vocation in a Multidisciplinary Senior Capstone," in Smith, Nowacek, and Bernstein, *Citizenship across the Curriculum*, Kindle location 1384–652.

46. Earl Shorris, *Riches for the Poor: The Clemente Course in the Humanities* (New York: Norton, 2000), and Shorris, *The Art of Freedom: Teaching Humanities to the Poor* (New York: Norton, 2013); Sarah Hirschman, *People and Stories: Who Owns Literature? Communities Find Their Voice through Short Stories* (Bloomington, IN: iUniverse, 2009).

REFERENCES

Acemoglu, Daron, and James A. Robinson. "The Rise and Fall of General Laws of Capitalism. August 2014, MIT Open Access. http://economics.mit.edu/files/9834/.

Allen, Danielle. "Democracy and Education: Three Principles?" Unpublished essay, 2013.

———. "Discourse Ethics for Divided Publics." Unpublished essay, 2014b.

———. 2011. "Education and Equality." Lecture given at the Institute for Advanced Study, Princeton, New Jersey, November 16, 2011. http://video.ias.edu/stream&ref=784.2004a.

———. "Helping Students Find Their Place in the World." *Washington Post*, September 23, 2012. http://www.washingtonpost.com/opinions/helping-students-find-their-place-in-the-world/2012/09/23/64552334-029a-11e2-8102-ebee9c66e190_story.html.

———. "A Multilingual America?" *Soundings* 87 (2004): 259–80.

———. *Our Declaration: A Reading of the Declaration of Independence in Defense of Equality.* New York: Norton/Liveright, 2014a.

———. 2015. "Re-conceptualizing Public Spheres." In Allen and Light, *From Voice to Influence*, 178–210.

———. "Talent Is Everywhere," in Kahlenberg, *Future of Affirmative Action*.

———. *Talking to Strangers: Anxieties of Citizenship since Brown v. Board of Education.* Chicago: University of Chicago Press, 2004.

Allen, Danielle, and Jennifer Light, eds. *From Voice to Influence*. Chicago: University of Chicago Press, 2015.

Allen, Danielle, and Robert Reich, eds. *Education, Justice, and Democracy*. Chicago: University of Chicago Press, 2013.

American Academy of Arts and Sciences. *Introducing the Humanities Indicators: An Online Prototype of National Data Collection in the Humanities*. Cambridge, MA, 2009.

———. *The Heart of the Matter*. Cambridge, MA, 2013.

American Council of Learned Societies. *A Report to the Congress of the United States on the State of the Humanities and the Reauthorization of the National Endowment for the Humanities.* New York, 1985.

Anderson, Elizabeth. "Fair Opportunity in Education: A Democratic Equality Perspective." *Ethics* 117, no. 4 (2007): 595–622.

———. *The Imperative of Integration.* Princeton, NJ: Princeton University Press, 2010.

Arendt, Hannah. *The Human Condition.* Chicago: University of Chicago Press, 1958.

———. *Men in Dark Times.* New York: Harcourt Brace, 1968.

———. "Reflections on Little Rock." *Dissent* 6, no. 1 (1959): 45–56.

Arum, Richard, and Josipa Roska. *Academically Adrift.* Chicago: University of Chicago Press, 2011.

Association of American Colleges and Universities (AACU). *AACU Civic Engagement Rubrics.* http://www.aacu.org/value/rubrics/index.cfm?CFID=1084774 &CFTOKEN=68824593/.

Bachen, Christine, Chad Raphael, Kathleen-M. Lynn, Kristen McKee, and Jessica Philippi. "Civic Engagement, Pedagogy, and Information Technology on Web Sites for Youth." *Political Communication* 25, no. 3 (2008): 290–310.

Banaji, Shakuntala. "Framing Young Citizens: Explicit Invitation and Implicit Exclusion on Youth Civic Websites." *Language and Intercultural Communication* 11, 2 (2011): 126–41.

Bennett, Lance, Chris Wells, and Deen Freelon. "Communicating Citizenship Online: Models of Civic Learning in the Youth Web Sphere." *Civic Learning Online Project,* 2009. www.engagedyouth.org.

Bennett, Lance, and Michael Xenos. "Young Voters and the Web of Politics 2004: The Youth Political Web Sphere Comes of Age." CIRCLE Working Paper 42, 2005. http://www.civicyouth.org/PopUps/WorkingPapers/WP42BennettXenos.pdf.

Berman, S. "Civil Society and the Collapse of the Weimar Republic." *World Politics* 49, no. 3 (1997): 401–29.

Billington, Josie. "'Reading for Life': Prison Reading Groups in Practice and Theory." *Critical Survey* 23 (2011): 67–85.

Blank, Rolf K. "State Growth Models for School Accountability." Council of Chief State School Officers, June 2010.

Bowles, Samuel, Glenn Loury, and Rajiv Sethi. "Group Inequality." Working paper, 2009. http://www.columbia.edu/~rs328/GroupInequality.pdf.

Boyer, John, ed. *The Aims of Education: The College of the University of Chicago.* Chicago: University of Chicago, 1997; rev. ed. 2009.

Brighouse, Harry, and Michael McPherson, eds. *The Aims of Higher Education: Problems of Morality and Justice.* Chicago: University of Chicago Press, 2015.

Brodhead, Richard. "Advocating for the Humanities." *Duke Today,* March 19, 2012.

———. "In Praise of the Humanities and the 'Fire that Never Goes Out.'" *Duke Today,* October 23, 2011.

Bromberg, Philip. *The Shadow of the Tsunami and the Growth of the Relational Mind.* New York: Routledge, 2011.

Broughton, Janet. "Commencement for Programs in Celtic, Comparative Literature, Dutch, French, German, Italian, Portuguese, Scandinavian, Slavic, Spanish." Commencement Address, University of California, Berkeley, 2010.

Campaign for Fiscal Equity v. State of New York I, 1995. 86 N.Y.2d 307.

Cavell, Stanley. *The Claim of Reason: Wittgenstein, Skepticism, Morality, and Tragedy*. Oxford: Oxford University Press, 1999 [1979].

CIRCLE Staff. "The Youth Vote in 2012." CIRCLE Fact Sheet, 2013. http://www.civicyouth.org/wp-content/uploads/2013/05/CIRCLE_2013FS_outhVoting2012FINAL.pdf.

Cohen, G. E. *Rescuing Justice and Equality*. Cambridge, MA: Harvard University Press, 2009.

Commission on the Humanities. *The Humanities in American Life: Report of the Commission on the Humanities*. Berkeley: University of California Press, ca.1980. http://ark.cdlib.org/ark:/13030/ft8j49p1jc/.

Dawood, Yasmin. "The Anti-domination Model and the Judicial Oversight of Democracy." *Georgetown Law Journal* 96 (2008): 1411–85.

de Tocqueville, Alexis. *Democracy in America*. Edited by P. Bradley. New York: Vintage Classics, 1990 [1835–40].

Delbanco, Andrew. *College: What It Was, Is, and Should Be*. Princeton, NJ: Princeton University Press, 2012.

Douglas, William O. "The Right of Association." *Columbia Law Review* 63, no. 8 (1963): 1361–83.

Doumas, Leonidas, and John Hummel. 2005. "Approaches to Modeling Human Mental Representations: What Works, What Doesn't, and Why." In Holyoak and Morrison, *Cambridge Handbook of Thinking*, 73–94.

DuBois, W. E. B. *Souls of Black Folk*. In *W.E.B. DuBois: Writings*. New York: Library of America, 1987 [1903].

Emerson, Thomas I. "Freedom of Association and Freedom of Expression." *Yale Law Journal* 74 (1964): 1–35.

Eng, David, and Shinhee Han. "Desegregating Love: Transnational Adoption, Racial Reparation, and Racial Transitional Objects." *Studies in Gender and Sexuality* 7, no. 2 (2006): 141–72.

———. "A Dialogue on Racial Melancholia." *Psychoanalytic Dialogues: The International Journal of Relational Perspectives* 10, no. 4 (2000): 667–700.

Galison, Peter. *Image and Logic: A Material Culture of Microphysics*. Chicago: University of Chicago Press, 1997.

Gardner, Howard. *Frames of Mind: the Theory of Multiple Intelligences*. New York: Basic Books, 2011.

———. *Good Work: When Excellence and Ethics Meet*. New York: Basic Books, 1983.

———. 2015. "In Defense of Disinterestedness." In Allen and Light, *From Voice to Influence*, 232–253.

Gerodimos, Roman. "Mobilising Young Citizens in the UK: A Content Analysis of Youth and Issue Websites." *Information, Communication and Society* 11, no. 7 (2008): 964–88.

————. "New Media, New Citizens: The Terms and Conditions of Online Youth Civic Engagement." PhD dissertation, Bournemouth University, 2010.

Goldstone, Robert, and Ji Son. "Similarity." In Holyoak and Morrison, *Cambridge Handbook of Thinking*, 13–36.

Gutmann, Amy. *Democratic Education*. Princeton, NJ: Princeton University Press, 1999.

————, ed. *Freedom of Association*. Princeton, NJ: Princeton University Press, 1998.

————. "What Makes a University Education Worthwhile." In Brighouse and McPherson, *Aims of Higher Education*, 7–25.

Hayward, Clarissa. *How Americans Make Race: Stories, Institutions, Spaces*. New York: Cambridge University Press, 2013.

Heiland, Donna, and Laura Rosenthal. *Literary Study, Measurement, and the Sublime: Disciplinary Assessment*. New York: Teagle Foundation, 2011.

Hess, Diana. *Controversy in the Classroom: The Democratic Power of Discussion*. New York: Routledge, 2009.

Hess, Diana, and P. McAvoy. *The Political Classroom: Ethics and Evidence in Democratic Education*. New York: Routledge, 2012.

Hillygus, D. Sunshine. "The Missing Link: Exploring the Relationship between Higher Education and Political Engagement." *Political Behavior* 27, no. 1 (2005): 25–47.

Hirschman, Sarah. *People and Stories: Who Owns Literature? Communities Find Their Voice through Short Stories*. iUniverse, 2009.

Holyoak, Keith, and Robert Morrison, eds. *The Cambridge Handbook of Thinking and Reasoning*. New York: Cambridge University Press, 2005.

————. "Thinking and Reasoning: A Reader's Guide." In Holyoak and Morrison, *Cambridge Handbook of Thinking*, 1–12.

Honneth, Axel. "Integrity and Disrespect: Principles of a Conception of Morality Based on a Theory of Recognition." *Political Theory* 20, no. 2 (1992): 187–201.

Inclan, Jaime. Appendix C. "Evaluation of Clemente Course." In *New American Blues*. Edited by Earl Shorris, 402–9. New York: Norton, 1997.

Jackson, Philip. *Life in Classrooms*. New York: Holt, Rinehart and Winston, 1968.

Jay, Paul, and Gerald Graff. "Fear of Being Useful." *Inside Higher Education*, January 5, 2012. http://www.insidehighered.com/views/2012/01/05/essay-new-approach-defend-value-humanities#.ToTw_WhErgk.facebook.

Kahlenberg, Richard D., ed. *The Future of Affirmative Action: New Paths to Higher Education Diversity after Fisher v. University of Texas*. New York: Century Foundation, 2013.

Katz, Michael. *A History of Compulsory Education Laws*. Fastback Series, no. 75. Bicentennial Series. Phi Delta Kappa, Bloomington, IN, 1976.

Kaufman, James, and Robert Sternberg, eds. *The Cambridge Handbook of Creativity*. Cambridge: Cambridge University Press, 2010.

Keohane, Nannerl. "The Liberal Arts as Signposts in the 21st Century." *Chronicle of Higher Education*, January 29, 2012. http://chronicle.com/article/The-Liberal-Arts-as-Guideposts/130475/.

Kidd, David, and Emanuele Castano. "Reading Literary Fiction Improves Theory of Mind." *Science 18* (October 2013) 342 (6156): 377–80. DOI: 10.1126/science. 1239918.

Kiley, Kevin. "Making the Case," *Inside Higher Education*. November 19, 2012. http://www.insidehighered.com/news/2012/11/19/liberal-arts-colleges-re think-their-messaging-face-criticism.

Kohlberg, Lawrence. "The Moral Atmosphere of the School." In *The Unstudied Curriculum: Its Impact on Children*. Edited by Norman Overly, 104–39. Washington, DC: Association for Supervision and Curriculum Development, NEA, 1970.

Koppelman, A. "Should Noncommercial Associations Have an Absolute Right to Discriminate?" *Law and Contemporary Problems* 67, no. 4 (2004): 27–57.

Ladd, Everett. *The Ladd Report*. New York: Free Press, 1999.

Ladd, Helen, and Susanna Loeb. "The Challenges of Measuring School Quality: Implications for Educational Equity." In Allen and Reich, *Education, Justice, and Democracy*, 19–42.

Laden, Anthony. "Learning to Be Equal." In Allen and Reich, *Education, Justice and Democracy*, 62–79.

Lane, Melissa. *Method and Politics in Plato's Statesman*. Cambridge: Cambridge University Press, 1998.

Lareau, Annette. *Unequal Childhoods: Class, Race, and Family Life*. 2nd ed. Berkeley: University of California Press, 2011.

LeBoeuf, Robyn, and Eldar Shafir. "Decision Making." In Holyoak and Morrison, *Cambridge Handbook of Thinking*, 243–66.

Levine, Peter, Cynthia Gibson, et al. *Special Report: The Civic Mission of Schools*. New York: CIRCLE and the Carnegie Corporation of New York, 2003.

Levinson, Miera. *No Citizen Left Behind*. Cambridge, MA: Harvard University Press, 2012.

Leyton-Brown, K., and Y. Shoham. *Essentials of Game Theory: A Concise, Multidisciplinary Introduction*. San Rafael, CA: Morgan and Claypool, 2008.

Lievrouw, Leah. *Alternative and Activist New Media*. Cambridge, UK: Polity, 2011.

Linder, Douglas O. "Freedom of Association after Roberts v. United States Jaycees." *Michigan Law Review* 82, no. 8 (1984): 1878–903.

Linkon, Sherry. *Literary Learning: Teaching in the English Major*. Bloomington: Indiana University Press, 2011.

Livingstone, Sonia. "The Challenge of Engaging Youth Online: Contrasting Producers' and Teenagers' Interpretations of Websites." *European Journal of Communication* 22, no. 2 (2007): 165–84.

London, J. "Circle of Justice." *History of Political Thought* 32, no. 3 (2011): 425–47.

Lundberg, Carol A. and Lauire A. Schreiner. "Quality and Frequency of Faculty–Student Interaction as Predictors of Learning: An Analysis by Student Race/Ethnicity." *Journal of College Student Development* 45 (2004): 549–65.

Macedo, Stephen et al. 2005. *Democracy at Risk: How Political Choices Undermine Citizen Participation, and What We Can Do About It*. Washington, DC: Brookings Institution Press, 2005.

Mantena, Karuna. "Another Realism: The Politics of Gandhian Nonviolence." *American Political Science Review* 106 (2012): 415–70.

Marx, Michael. "Disciplining the Minds of Students: The Study of English." *Change: The Magazine of Higher Learning.* March/April 2005, 40–42.

Mathae, Katherine, and Catherine Birzer, eds. *Reinvigorating the Humanities: Enhancing Research and Education on Campus and Beyond.* Washington, DC: Association of American Universities, 2004. McFarland, Daniel, and Reuben Thomas. "Bowling Young: How Youth Voluntary Associations Influence Adult Political Participation." *American Sociological Review* 71 (2010): 401–25.

Menand, Louis. *The Marketplace of Ideas: Reform and Resistance in the American University.* New York: Norton, 2010.

Milner, Henry. *The Internet Generation: Engaged Citizens or Political Dropouts.* Medford, MA: Tufts University Press, 2010.

Moglen, Seth. "Sharing Knowledge, Practicing Democracy: A Vision for the Twenty-First-Century University." In Allen and Reich, *Education, Justice and Democracy,* 267–84.

Morrill, Richard. "What Is the Value of Liberal Education." *Huffington Post,* November 6, 2012. http://www.huffingtonpost.com/richard-morrill/liberal-education_b_2083994.html.

Nagda, Biren A., Sandra R. Gregerman, John Jonides, William von Hippel, and Jennifer S. Lerner. "Undergraduate Student–Faculty Research Partnerships Affect Student Retention." *Review of Higher Education* 22 (1998): 55–72.

Note. "Civil Rights. Public Accommodation Statutes. New Jersey Supreme Court Holds That Boy Scouts May Not Deny Membership to Homosexuals. Dale v. Boy Scouts of America." *Harvard Law Review* 113, no. 2 (1999): 621–26.

Note. "Discrimination in Private Social Clubs: Freedom of Association and Right to Privacy." *Duke Law Journal* 6 (1970): 1181–222.

Note. "State Power and Discrimination by Private Clubs: First Amendment Protection for Nonexpressive Associations." *Harvard Law Review* 104, no. 8 (1991): 1835–56.

Nowacek, Rebecca S. "Understanding Citizenship as Vocation in a Multidisciplinary Senior Capstone." In Smith et al. 2010: Kindle location 1384–652.

Nussbaum, Martha. *Not for Profit: Why Democracy Needs the Humanities.* Princeton, NJ: Princeton University Press, 2012.

———. *Poetic Justice: The Literary Imagination and Public Life.* Boston: Beacon Press, 1996.

Ober, Josiah. *Democracy and Knowledge: Innovation and Learning in Classical Athens.* Princeton, NJ: Princeton University Press, 2008.

———. "Natural Capacities and Democracy as a Good-in-Itself." *Philosophical Studies* 132 (2007): 59–73.

———. "What Is Democracy? What Is It Good For?" Presented at James Moffett Lecture, Princeton University, September 30, 2010.

Pettit, Philip. *Republicanism: A Theory of Freedom and Government.* Oxford: Oxford University Press, 1997.

Piketty, Thomas. *Capital in the Twenty-First Century*. Kindle edition. Cambridge, MA: Harvard University Press, 2014.

Pitkin, Hanna. *Attack of the Blob: Hannah Arendt's Conception of the Social*. Chicago: University of Chicago Press, 2000.

Putnam, Robert. "Bowling Alone: America's Declining Social Capital." *Journal of Democracy* 6, no. 1 (1995): 65–78.

———. *Bowling Alone: The Collapse and Revival of American Community*. New York: Simon and Schuster, 2000.

———. "*E Pluribus Unum*: Diversity and Community in the Twenty-First Century." *Scandinavian Political Studies* 30, no. 2 (2007): 137–74.

Rawls, John. "Two Concepts of Rules." *Philosophical Review* 64, no. 1 (January 1955): 3–32.

Rips, Lance, and Douglas Medin. 2005. "Concepts and Categories: Memory, Meaning, and Metaphysics." In Holyoak and Morrison, *Cambridge Handbook of Thinking*, 37–72.

Robins, Philip, and Murat Aydede, eds. *The Cambridge Handbook of Situated Cognition*. New York: Cambridge University Press, 2009.

Rose, Mike. "Heal the Academic-Vocational Schism." *Chronicle of Higher Education*. September 10, 2012.

Rothstein, Richard. "Racial Segregation and Black Student Achievement." In Allen and Reich *Education, Justice and Democracy*, 173–98.

Salovey, Peter, and David Sluyter, eds. *Emotional Development and Emotional Intelligence: Implications for Educators*. New York: Basic Books, 1997.

Sanders, Seth L., ed. *Margins of Writing, Origins of Cultures: Unofficial Writing in the Ancient Near East and Beyond*. Chicago: University of Chicago, 2006.

Schudson, Michael. 2003. "Click Here for Democracy: A History and Critique of an Information-Based Model of Citizenship." In *Democracy and New Media*. Edited by H. Jenkins, 49–59. Cambridge, MA: MIT Press, 2003.

Sen, Amartya. *Development as Freedom*. New York: Knopf, 1999.

Sennett, Richard. *The Craftsman*. New Haven, CT: Yale University Press, 2008.

Shorris, Earl. *The Art of Freedom: Teaching Humanities to the Poor*. New York: Norton, 2013.

———. *Riches for the Poor: The Clemente Course in the Humanities*. New York: Norton, 2000.

Shulman, George. *American Prophecy: Race and Redemption in American Political Culture*. Minneapolis: University of Minnesota Press, 2008.

Skocpol, Theda. *Diminished Democracy: From Membership to Management in American Civic Life*. Rothbaum Series. Norman: University of Oklahoma Press, 2003.

Small, Mario. *Unanticipated Gains: Origins of Network Inequality in Everyday Life*. Oxford: Oxford University Press, 2009.

Smith, Michael, Rebecca S. Nowacek, and Jeffrey L. Bernstein. *Citizenship across the Curriculum*. Bloomington: Indiana University Press, ca. 2010.

Soifer, Aviam. *Law and the Company We Keep*. Cambridge, MA: Harvard University Press, 1998.

Sternberg, Robert, and Scott Kaufman, eds. *The Cambridge Handbook of Intelligence.* New York: Cambridge University Press, 2011.

Sternberg, Robert, Todd Lubart, James Kaufman, and Jean Pretz. "Creativity." In Holyoak and Morrison, *Cambridge Handbook of Thinking and Reasoning*, 315–70.

Stout, Jeffrey. *Democracy and Tradition.* Princeton, NJ: Princeton University Press, 2004.

Suárez-Orozco, Carola, and Marcelo Suárez-Orozco. "Conferring Disadvantage: Immigration, Schools, and the Family." In Allen and Reich, *Education, Justice and Democracy*, 133–54.

Sunquist, Eric. "The Humanities and the National Interest." *American Literary History* 24, no. 3 (2012): 590–607.

Szreter, Simon, and Michael Woolcock. "Health by Association? Social Capital, Social Theory, and the Political Economy of Public Health." *International Journal of Epidemiology* 33, no. 4 (2004): 650–67.

Tarrow, Sidney. "Making Social Science Work across Space and Time: A Critical Reflection on Robert Putnam's Making Democracy Work." *American Political Science Review* 90 (1996): 389–97.

Tinto, Vincent. *Leaving College: Rethinking the Causes and Curses of Student Attrition.* 2nd ed. Chicago: University of Chicago Press, 1993.

Tversky, Barbara. "Visuospatial Reasoning." In Holyoak and Morrison *Cambridge Handbook of Thinking*, 209–42.

U.S. Department of Education, National Center for Educational Statistics (NCES). "Baccalaureate and Beyond Longitudinal Study." By Jennifer Wine, Melissa Cominole, Sara Wheeless, Kristin Dudley, and Jeff Franklin. NCES 2006–166. Washington, DC: Government Printing Office, 2006.

———. "Baccalaureate and Beyond Longitudinal Study." By Emily Cataldi, Caitlin Green, Robin Henke, Terry Lew, Jennie Woo, Bryan Shepherd, and Peter Siegel. NCES 2011–236. Washington, DC: Government Printing Office, 2011.

U.S. House. *Proceedings of the 45th National Encampment of the Veterans of Foreign Wars of the United States.* August 22–24, 1944. H. Doc. 182, 1945. Text from *Congressional Documents.* Available from ProQuest Congressional.

———. *Proceedings of the 79th National Convention of the Veterans of Foreign Wars of the U.S.* H. Doc. 96–100/ Text from *Congressional Documents.* Available from ProQuest Congressional.

U.S. Supreme Court. *Board of Directors, Rotary International v. Rotary Club of Duarte.* 1987. 481 U.S. 537.

———. *International Association of Machinists et al., Appellants, v. S. B. Street et al.* 1961. 367 U.S. 740.

———. *NAACP v. Alabama ex rel Patterson.* 1958. 357 U.S. 449.

———. *NAACP v. Button.* 1963. 371 U.S. 415.

———. *Roberts v Jaycees.* 1984. 468 U.S. 609.

———. *Runyon et Ux., DBA Bobbe's School v. McCrary et al.* 1976. 427 U.S. 160.

———. *Tillman v. Wheaton-Haven Recreation Assn, Inc.* 1973. 410 U.S. 431. Van Oorschot, Wim, Wil Arts, and John Gelissen. 2006. "Social Capital in

Europe: Measurement and Social and Regional Distribution of a Multifaceted Phenomenon." *Acta Sociologica* 49, no. 2 (2006): 159–67.

Verba, Sidney, and Kay Lehman Schlozman. *Voice and Equality: Civic Voluntarism in American Politics*. Cambridge, MA: Harvard University Press, 1995.

Volkwein, J. Fredericks, and David Carbone. "The Impact of Departmental Research and Teaching Climates on Undergraduate Growth and Satisfaction." *Journal of Higher Education* 65 (1994): 146–67.

Walton, Gregory. "The Myth of Intelligence: Smartness Isn't Like Height." In Allen and Reich, *Education, Justice and Democracy*, 155–72.

Warren, Mark E. *Democracy and Association*. Princeton, NJ: Princeton University Press, 2000.

Wei, Ian. *Intellectual Culture in Medieval Paris*. Cambridge: Cambridge University Press, 2012.

Wineburg, Samuel. *Historical Thinking and Other Unnatural Acts: Charting the Future of Teaching the Past*. Philadelphia: Temple University Press, 1999.

Wolfinger, Raymond, and Steven Rosenstone. *Who Votes?* New Haven, CT: Yale University Press, 1980.

Woodly, Deva. *The Politics of Common Sense: How Social Movements Use Public Discourse to Change Politics and Win Acceptance*. Oxford: Oxford University Press, 2015.

Woods, Christopher. "Bilingualism, Scribal Learning, and the Death of Sumerian." In Sanders, *Margins of Writing*, 91–120. Wuthnow, Robert. *Loose Connections: Joining Together in America's Fragmented Communities*. Cambridge, MA: Harvard University Press, 2002.

———. *Sharing the Journey: Support Groups and the Quest for a New Community*. New York: Free Press, 1996.

Xenos, Michael, and Lance Bennett. "The Disconnection in Online Politics: The Youth Political Web Sphere and US Election Sites, 2002–2004." *Information, Communication, and Society* 10, no. 4 (2007): 443–64.

Young, I. "Communication and the Other: Beyond Deliberative Democracy." In *Democracy and Difference: Contesting the Boundaries of the Political*. Edited by S. Benhabib, 120–138. Princeton, NJ: Princeton University Press, 1996.

———. *Justice and the Politics of Difference*. Princeton, NJ: Princeton University Press, 1990.

Liberty, Equality, and Private Government

ELIZABETH ANDERSON

THE TANNER LECTURES IN HUMAN VALUES

Delivered at

Princeton University
March 4–5, 2015

ELIZABETH ANDERSON is Arthur F. Thurnau Professor and John Dewey Distinguished University Professor of Philosophy and Women's Studies at the University of Michigan, Ann Arbor. The author of *Value in Ethics and Economics* (1993) and *The Imperative of Integration* (2010), she has written extensively on democratic theory, egalitarianism, affirmative action and racial integration, antidiscrimination law, the ethical limitations of the market, feminist theory, pragmatism, social epistemology, and the interaction of facts and values in the social sciences. She is currently working on a history of egalitarianism from the Levellers to the present, with a special focus on abolitionist movements. She is a fellow of the American Academy of Arts and Sciences, former president of the Central Division of the American Philosophical Association, and winner of fellowships from the Guggenheim Foundation and the American Council of Learned Societies. She is also the principal designer and inaugural director of the Philosophy, Politics, and Economics Program at University of Michigan.

LECTURE I.
WHEN THE MARKET WAS "LEFT"

TWO IMAGES OF MARKET SOCIETY

The ideal of a free market society used to be a cause of the left. By "the left" I refer to egalitarian thinkers and participants in egalitarian social movements, starting with the Levellers in the mid-seventeenth century, continuing through the Enlightenment, the American and French Revolutions, and pre-Marxist radicals of the late eighteenth and early nineteenth centuries. In the United States, the association of market society with egalitarianism lasted through the Civil War.[1] We need to recover an understanding of why this was so, to better grasp the importance of evaluating ideals in their social context, and the problems with current ways of thinking about ideals of equality and freedom.

Consider two of the most famous passages ever written about market society. The first, by Adam Smith, sketches an image of market society as a free society of equals:

> When an animal wants to obtain something either of a man or of another animal, it has no other means of persuasion but to gain the favour of those whose service it requires. A . . . spaniel endeavours by a thousand attractions to engage the attention of its master who is at dinner, when it wants to be fed by him. Man sometimes uses the same arts with his brethren, and . . . endeavours by every servile and fawning attention to obtain their good will . . . . But man has almost constant occasion for the help of his brethren, and it is in vain for him to expect it from their benevolence only. He will be more likely to prevail if he can interest their self–love in his favour, and shew them that it is for their own advantage to do for him what he requires of them. Whoever offers to another a bargain of any kind, proposes to do this. Give me that which I want, and you shall have this which you want, is the meaning of every such offer. . . . It is not from the benevolence of the butcher, the brewer, or the baker, that we expect our dinner, but from their regard to their own interest. We address ourselves, not to their humanity but to their self–love. . . . Nobody but a beggar chuses to depend chiefly upon the benevolence of his fellow-citizens.[2]

The second passage is by Karl Marx. He recasts Smith's image of the market as a mere portal into relations of domination and subordination:

[The] sphere . . . within whose boundaries the sale and purchase of labour-power goes on, is in fact a very Eden of the innate rights of man. There alone rule Freedom, Equality, Property and Bentham. Freedom, because both buyer and seller of a commodity, say of labour-power, are constrained only by their own free will. They contract as free agents, and the agreement they come to, is but the form in which they give legal expression to their common will. Equality, because each enters into relation with the other, as with a simple owner of commodities, and they exchange equivalent for equivalent. Property, because each disposes only of what is his own. And Bentham, because each looks only to himself. . . .

On leaving this sphere of simple circulation or of exchange of commodities, which furnishes the "Free-trader Vulgaris" with his views and ideas, and with the standard by which he judges a society based on capital and wages, we think we can perceive a change in the physiognomy of our dramatis personae. He, who before was the money-owner, now strides in front as capitalist; the possessor of labour-power follows as his labourer. The one with an air of importance, smirking, intent on business; the other, timid and holding back, like one who is bringing his own hide to market and has nothing to expect but—a hiding.[3]

These two passages encapsulate a dramatic change in the egalitarian assessment of market society that took place between the eighteenth and nineteenth centuries. By "egalitarian" I refer to an ideal of social relations. To be an egalitarian is to commend and promote a society in which its members interact as equals. This vague idea gets its shape by contrast with social hierarchy, the object of egalitarian critique. Consider three types or dimensions of social hierarchy: of authority, esteem, and standing. In a hierarchy of authority, occupants of higher rank get to order subordinates around. They exercise arbitrary and unaccountable power over their inferiors. In a hierarchy of esteem, occupants of higher rank despise those of inferior rank and extract tokens of deferential honor from them, such as bowing, scraping, and other rituals of self-abasement that inferiors display in recognition of the other's superiority. In a hierarchy of standing, the interests of those of higher rank *count* in the eyes of others, whereas the interests of inferiors do not: others are free to neglect them, and, in extreme cases, to trample upon them with impunity. Usually, these three hierarchies are joined.

Smith depicts market relations as egalitarian: the parties to exchange interact on terms of equal authority, esteem, and standing. He implies such egalitarian content by contrasting market exchange with begging, a kind of gift exchange in which the subordinate party offers tokens of asymmetrical esteem—"servile and fawning attention"—in return for something he wants. The resort to servile fawning supposes that one's interests have negligible standing in the eyes of the other. The prospective benefactor may turn away a beggar just as a master may shoo away his spaniel from the dinner table. The transaction is humiliating to the beggar, and may involve his submission to the other's authority: servility is how servants behave toward their masters. Behind every gift exchange, ostensibly an altruistic affair, lurks dependency, contempt, and subordination.[4] By contrast, in market exchanges with the butcher, the brewer, and the baker, each party's interests have standing in the eyes of the other. Each party expresses this recognition by appealing to the other's interests as a reason for him to accept the exchange. The buyer is not an inferior, begging for a favor. Equally importantly, the buyer is not a superior who is entitled to simply order the butcher, the brewer, or the baker to hand over the fruits of his labor. Buyers must address themselves to the *other's* interests. *The parties each undertake the exchange with their dignity, their standing, and their personal independence affirmed by the other.* This is a model of social relations between free and equal persons.

Marx depicts this sunny egalitarian story of market exchange as utterly superficial. The market is a "noisy sphere, where everything takes place on the surface."[5] If this is Eden, it is just before the Fall. The action of real importance takes place once the contract is signed and the time comes to execute it. The worker is now dragged out of Eden into the sphere of production. His employer, like God, curses him to toil by the sweat of his brow. Now it is clear where the parties stand in the order of esteem: the capitalist enjoys an "air of importance," his employee is timid and cringing before him. They stand unequally in the order of authority: the capitalist strides in front, with the employee obligated to follow wherever his employer takes him. And they stand unequally in the order of standing: where the capitalist beams, in expectation of profit from the relationship, his worker "has nothing to expect but—a hiding." The performance of the contract embodies a profound asymmetry in whose interests *count*: henceforth, the worker will be required to toil under conditions that pay no regard to his interests, and every regard for the capitalist's profit.

What happened between Smith and Marx to reverse the egalitarian assessment of market society? It is not, as some have supposed, a revaluation of self-interest as a motive for relating to others. Smith *denies* Marx's claim that in market transactions "each looks only to himself." On his account, a successful bargain requires each to consider how they could bring some advantage *to the other*. Without a sympathetic appreciation for what might interest the other in transacting with oneself, and without acknowledging the independent standing of the other as someone whose property rights must be respected, no bargain will be struck.[6] Smith, no less than Marx, reviled selfishness as a basis for relating to others.[7]

What happened, I shall argue, was the Industrial Revolution. Smith wrote at the mere threshold of the Industrial Revolution, well before its implications for relations of production could be fully grasped. Marx wrote in its midst, at a point when workers were bearing its most frightful costs, and enjoying precious few of its benefits. The Industrial Revolution was a cataclysmic event for egalitarians, a fundamental turning point in egalitarian social thought.[8] It shattered their model of how a free society of equals might be built through market society. The history of egalitarianism in the nineteenth century is a history of extraordinary innovation and experimentation with alternative models, some of which rejected market society wholesale, others of which sought various revisions and supplements to it. Most of these experiments—utopian socialism, anarchism, syndicalism, Georgism, communism, democratic state socialism, workplace democracy, to name a few—either failed, were denied a real trial, or never managed to scale up. The most visible successes—notably, social democracy and labor unions—while still with us, are in decline or under stress in our postindustrial, globalized economy.

Intellectually, public discourse is underequipped to cope with these challenges. The Cold War induced a kind of amnesia over what the nineteenth-century struggles were about, presenting a radically reductionist picture of alternatives, especially in the United States. Images of free market society that made sense prior to the Industrial Revolution continue to circulate today as ideals, blind to the gross mismatch between the background social assumptions reigning in the seventeenth and eighteenth centuries, and today's institutional realities. We are told that our choice is between free markets and state control, when most adults live their working lives under a third thing entirely: *private government*.

My aim is to get a clearer view of what this third thing is, what challenges it poses to the ideal of a free society of equals, and how it might be reformed to enable that ideal to be realized under contemporary conditions. To gain clarity, we need to recover the intellectual context of egalitarian thought before the Industrial Revolution, when the market was "left."

EGALITARIANISM BEFORE THE INDUSTRIAL REVOLUTION: MASTERLESS MEN, LEVELLERS, AND LOCKE

The Levellers undertook one of the first egalitarian social movements of the modern world. Arising in the English Civil War and strongly represented in Cromwell's New Model Army, they are best remembered for their calls for constitutional reform, including a nearly universal male franchise, parliamentary representation of districts in proportion to population, abolition of the House of Lords and the Lords' privileges, and religious toleration.[9] Notwithstanding their name, given to them by Cromwell, who feared that democratization threatened a mass redistribution of property, the Levellers were also firm defenders of rights of private property and free trade. Captain John Clarke, in the Putney debates, affirmed that the law of nature establishes a right to property.[10] The Third Agreement of the People, promulgated by John Lilburne, William Walwyn, Thomas Prince, and Richard Overton, denied the state the power to "level mens Estates, destroy Propriety, or make all things Common," to hinder freedom of foreign trade, to exempt anyone from paying their debts, or to enact permanent customs or excise taxes on goods, as these were "extreme burthensome and oppressive to Trade."[11] Lilburne attacked the state-granted monopolies of printing, preaching, and foreign trade as infringing on "the Common right of all the free-men of England" just as much as the recently barred monopolies of soap, salt, leather, and other goods.[12] He included, with full endorsement, the petition of William Sykes and Thomas Johnson against the licensed monopolies of the Eastland merchants, Merchant Adventurers, and other cartels in *Londons Liberty in Chains Discovered*.[13] Walwyn submitted a systematic argument for free trade to Whitehall.[14]

Given the tendencies of market society to generate inequality in income and wealth, what stake did this egalitarian movement see in promoting private property and free trade? To understand this, we must get beyond a narrow interpretation of egalitarianism in terms of current ideas about distributive justice.[15] Egalitarianism, more fundamentally, is about dismantling or taming social hierarchy. The Levellers' support for free trade formed an essential part of a larger program of liberating individuals from interlocking hierarchies of domination and subordination. They saw in free markets some essential institutional components of a free society of equals, based on their proliferation of opportunities for individuals to lead lives characterized by personal independence from the domination of others.

To see this, we must consider the social order against which the Levellers were rebelling. Early modern England was characterized by pervasive hierarchies of domination and subordination. Nearly all people but the King had superiors, who claimed nearly unaccountable discretionary authority to rule their lives. Lords governed their tenants and retainers, masters governed their servants, bishops their priests, priests their parishioners, captains their sailors, guilds their members, male heads of households their wives, children, and servants.

Government was everywhere, not just in the hands of the organizations we identify today with the modern state. The Anglican Church ran its own system of courts, censorship, and taxation. Church courts regularly excommunicated and fined parishioners for infractions of church regulations, even when that conduct was lawful. The church censored publications it regarded as heretical or blasphemous. It exacted tithes from parishioners, regardless of their religious beliefs.[16] Excommunication had consequences beyond expulsion from the church: by the Test Act, only those receiving Anglican Communion were eligible for public office. Guilds, too, operated their own court system, under which they routinely tried, fined, and jailed members who violated (or who merely refused to offer an oath that they had obeyed) the guild's minute regulations regarding matters such as the prices and quantities of goods for sale, and the location and days on which trading was permitted.[17] Under the common law of coverture, a wife's legal personhood was subsumed under her husband's: she could not own property, make contracts, sue or be sued in her own name. Her husband was legally entitled to all of her wages, to control her movements, and to inflict corporal punishment for disobedience. Divorce was very difficult to obtain.[18] Wives often acquired more leeway than the law recognized: mainly through contestation of their husbands' authority and appeal to custom, and rarely through prenuptial agreements and use of scattered laws and jurisdictions that limited coverture. Nevertheless, to speak of husbands' governing their wives was no mere metaphor.[19] In an era where production was not yet separated from the household, servants—that is, any employees under contract— lived under the government of their employers as subordinate members of an extended patriarchal family.[20] Apprentices were bound to service without pay. Under the common law of master and servant, regular employees had to work an entire year from sunup to sundown before acquiring entitlement to wages. Masters (employers) were free to withhold any amount of pay, without prorating, if their servants missed even a single day of work, or if they judged any part of their employees' work substandard. They were entitled to all of their servants' wages from moonlighting. Antienticement laws forbade competing employers to offer contracts to servants under contract to a different master.[21] Again, although custom and market conditions often gave servants more leeway than the law prescribed, they could not be considered free by today's standards.

Various ideologies rationalized these hierarchies.[22] One was the great chain of being. All creatures were linked in a great authoritarian chain of being reaching up to God, it was said, with everyone fixed to their particular link or social rank by birth. Everyone had some creature above and some below their place; even the king and pope were accountable to God; even the lowliest humans had dominion over animals. Breaking ranks would break the chain and unleash catastrophic disorder upon the world, detaching everyone from their connection to God.[23] Another was patriarchalism. The king, as father to his country, stood to his subjects as the father to all the members of his extended family—his wife, children, servants, and slaves. Just as the father enjoyed absolute dominion over the subordinate members of his household, and owned all its property, so the king enjoyed absolute authority over all his subjects, and owned all the land of the realm.[24] A third was the doctrine of original sin. Humanity's inherent proclivities toward sin justified comprehensive external constraint. Every sinner—every person—needed someone with authority over them to keep them in line.[25] Original sin rationalized absolute authority over others, and was the traditional justification for slavery.[26]

In sixteenth-century England, economic and religious changes began to set various individuals loose from traditional lines of authority, creating groups of "masterless men"—people who had no particular individual to whom they owed obedience.[27] The least advantaged were those displaced by agricultural developments, including enclosures and draining of the fens. Some went to London, seeking employment as casual laborers. Some became itinerant entertainers, traders, and cobblers. Some hung on in rural areas as cottagers and squatters in heaths, wastes, and forests, keeping a few animals, taking in knitting, and performing day labor. Some became vagabonds and beggars. Many of these individuals lived outside parishes or were otherwise unchurched. The more advantaged among masterless men were those who attained self-employment in a fixed establishment—yeoman farmers and long-term leaseholders, shopkeepers, artisans, and printers.

The rise of masterless men undermined the argument for authority based on the great chain of being.[28] That argument could explain why people fixed in a subordinate position should obey whoever was already bossing them around. But it could not identify any particular people to boss those unlinked from the chain of authority. Nor were many masterless men much interested in finding masters. They were making their livings on their own.

When Civil War broke out in the mid-seventeenth century, masterless men formed the core of Cromwell's New Model Army, which selected officers by ability rather than birth, and practiced open discussion among the ranks. Many men and officers were Levellers. Although the Levellers are mostly remembered for their constitutional demands to limit the authority of king, lords, and parliament, and to make the state accountable to the people, their egalitarianism challenged other social hierarchies as well: the authority of the Church of England, and priests more generally, over parishioners; of men over women; of guilds and mercantile monopolies over artisans.

The Levellers arose in a time of religious ferment, the seeds of which had been laid in the Reformation. Martin Luther's doctrine of the priesthood of all believers was taken more literally by various Protestant sects than he intended. With the rise of printing and literacy among the people, laypersons began to read and think for themselves in theological matters. If believers enjoyed direct connection to God, unmediated by intervening links in the chain of being, then why grant authority to bishops or even to priests? The central religious conflict of the English Civil War was over church governance: the Puritans wanted to overthrow the Anglican bishops and universalize the Presbyterian system of governance by elders. Far more radically democratic sects arose during this period, such as Baptists, Quakers, Ranters, and Fifth Monarchists, featuring lay preachers. Leading Levellers came from dissenting sects. They demanded religious toleration, the abolition of tithes, church courts, and church censorship. Millennialism—the doctrine of Christ's imminent return to rule earth directly—was common among the sects. Christ's return implied his redemption of human beings from sin, and hence the demise of the doctrine of original sin and its support for authoritarianism. Individuals were thereby restored to their natural (prelapsarian) state of freedom and equality.[29]

Some dissenting sects drew feminist conclusions from their theologies. "The soul knows no difference of sex."[30] Women participated in church governance. Some became popular preachers. Divorce was liberalized, with men and women having equal rights to divorce their spouses. Quaker marriage vows omitted mention of a wife's duty to obey her husband. Margaret Fell, the wife of Quaker founder George Fox, had a prenuptial agreement denying Fox authority over her estate.[31] Leveller John Lilburne insisted that Adam and Eve, and hence all of their progeny "were, by nature all equal and alike in power, dignity, authority, and majesty, none of them having by nature any authority, dominion, or magisterial power one over or above another." Turning the authoritarian doctrine of original sin on its head, he claimed that Adam's sin and that of all other men acting likewise consisted in the arrogant attempt to rule over anyone else without their consent.[32] Since, in the beginning, Adam had no one to rule over but Eve, the feminist implication of Lilburne's view is evident. Women such as Elizabeth Lilburne and Katherine Chidley were active in the Leveller movement. The *Petition of Women*, believed to be written by Chidley, insisted on the equal right of women to petition Parliament, and claimed for women "an interest in Christ equal unto men, as also of a proportionable share in the freedoms of this commonwealth."[33] Fifth Monarchists even advocated women's suffrage.[34]

In the context of patriarchalist justifications of state power, such feminist ideas served also to undermine monarchy. If husbands had no absolute dominion over their wives, then the king's claim to rule his subjects as the male head of household rules over everyone else in the family could not justify absolutism, or indeed much of any authority. If wives could hold title to property independently of their husbands, then the king's patriarchal claim to own all the property in the realm also came to naught.

In this era, support for private property and free trade went hand in hand with challenges to the monopoly of the Anglican Church over religious matters, as well as the king's patriarchalist claims to authority. The Root and Branch Petition of 1640, which called for the abolition of the episcopacy, complained of monopolies, patents, and tariffs, as well as the church's impositions of fines and excommunication for working and opening shop on holy days. Its persecution of dissenters drove clothiers to Holland, to the ruin of England's wool trade and of the poor workers who depended on that trade. The petition also railed against the church's control of the press, which was used to suppress dissenting religious tracts and to publish works claiming "that the subjects have no property in their estates, but that the king may take from them what he pleaseth."[35]

The Levellers' support for private property and free trade should be read in this context. The personal independence of masterless men and women in matters of thought and religion depended on their independence in matters of property and trade. If the king held title to all property, then subjects with land were reduced to mere copyholders, whose customary property rights could be extinguished by laws made without their participation, such as those calling for enclosures and expulsions of residents from fens.[36] If the church could fine dissenters in its own courts for violations of church decrees in restraint of trade, it would destroy their freedom of religion as well as their ways of making a living.

Monopolies were another form of state-licensed private government that threatened the personal independence of small traders and artisans. Whereas free trade promised economic growth, its principal advantage, from the Levellers' point of view, was its promotion of opportunities for economic independence. Abolition of guild monopolies would end the arbitrary and oppressive government of guilds over small merchants and artisans who did not care to obey the rules laid down by the larger ones.[37] (William Sykes, whose cause was championed by Lilburne, had been imprisoned in Rotterdam by England's Merchant Adventurers cartel, for refusing to swear an oath that he had obeyed all of their regulations concerning the cloth trade in Holland.[38]) This was not only a violation of rights to liberty. It was a violation of equality: "Patent societies swelling with a luciferian spirit, in desiring to advance into a higher room than their fellows, did by seruptitious Patents incorporate themselves," despite the fact that "every subject hath equall freedom with them" by the Magna Carta and other laws of England. Monopolies put the people "in a condition of vassalage," and reduce their hearts to "servility."[39]

Abolish the monopolies, and free trade would not merely liberate already existing small artisans from arbitrary private government. It would expand opportunities for many others to create their own businesses—to become self-employed, independent, masterless men. Charters of monopoly limited trade to particular towns. Abolish them, and trade, with its attendant opportunities for attaining independence, would spread across the entire country. Eliminate artificial barriers to trade, and "even servants" could risk investing in it, with the chance of gaining enough profit to become independent taxpayers.[40]

The Levellers did not neglect the benefits free trade would bring to those who would never attain self-employment. Abolition of monopolies would also strengthen the bargaining power of sailors, due to the multiplication of ships needed to bear a higher-volume foreign trade, and to increase the purchasing power of "workmen of all sorts," by reducing prices.[41] The higher volume of trade would also employ many who were, under monopoly, unable to find work and thereby reduced to beggary.[42] As we have seen from Smith's observations, in the order of esteem and standing, earning one's living is better than begging. So free trade advances equality for many, even for those who do not enjoy full independence from the will of a master.

Thus, the Levellers rejected the principal arguments for social hierarchy of all kinds—the great chain of being, patriarchalism, original sin. Their critique of arbitrary and unaccountable state power was part and parcel of their critique of other forms of domination—of the church over all English subjects, of men over women, of lords over tenants, of guilds over artisans. The state underwrote these other forms of government by grants of monopoly (the established Church of England being just another kind of monopoly), restraints on free trade, and invasions of the birthrights of English subjects, which they saw as a form of property.[43] The Levellers supported property rights and free trade for the ways they secured and promoted the personal independence of individuals from the domination of others. These institutions promoted the ability of men and women to become masterless, and increased the dignity and bargaining power of those who remained servants, by raising their wages and real incomes and by lifting beggars from destitution to employment.

Locke, too, was an egalitarian who supported extensive rights to private property and contract. Did he link egalitarianism to rights to property and contract in the same ways as the Levellers? Lacking space for a more extensive commentary, I shall merely note some profound affinities between the Levellers and Locke, writing some decades after them. Locke's constitutional principles—popular sovereignty, a nearly universal male franchise, equality under the law, equal representation of districts, supremacy of the House of Commons—are all Leveller principles.[44] Like them, his egalitarian critique of arbitrary and unaccountable state power is deeply tied to his critique of other forms of government. In particular, his feminism (his insistence that wives are entitled to independent rights to property, freedom of contract, divorce, and personal autonomy from their husbands) is indispensable to his critique of patriarchalist defenses of absolute monarchy.[45] He also insists that property owners are not entitled to take advantage of the poor by conditioning an offer of subsistence on their submission to arbitrary power.[46] As with the Levellers, once we focus on the egalitarian interest in avoiding relations of domination and subjection, it is much easier to see how, in the context of seventeenth-century institutions, market society could be an egalitarian cause.

EGALITARIANISM BEFORE THE
INDUSTRIAL REVOLUTION: SMITH

We have seen that in the seventeenth century, egalitarians supported private property and free trade because they anticipated that the growth of market society would help dismantle social hierarchies of domination and subordination. State-licensed monopolies were instruments by which the higher ranks oppressively governed the middling and lower ranks. Opposition to economic monopolies was part of a broader agenda of dismantling monopolies across all domains of social life: not just the guilds, but monopolies of church and press, monopolization of the vote by the rich, and monopolization of family power by men. Eliminate monopoly, and far more people would be able to attain personal independence and become masterless men and women. Even those who remained servants would gain esteem and standing through enhanced income and bargaining power with respect to their masters.

Did that vision continue through the eighteenth century? We need only consult the leading eighteenth-century advocate of market society, Adam Smith, to know the answer. Today, Smith is read as advocating market society because it would lead to economic growth and an efficient allocation of resources. These are unquestionably significant themes in his writings. However, he did not think that economic growth and efficiency were the leading virtues of market society. Rather, the transition from feudalism to market society, driven by the rise of commerce and manufactures, led to "order and good government, and with them the liberty and security of individuals . . . who had before lived almost in a continual state of war with their neighbours, and of servile dependency upon their superiors. This . . . is *by far the most important of all their effects.*[47]

The critical mediating factor leading to these favorable effects was the transition from gift to market exchange as the principal basis by which individuals satisfied their needs. Feudalism was based on "hospitality": because markets were undeveloped, the landlord could spend his surplus in no other way than by maintaining a hundred or a thousand men. He is at all times, therefore, surrounded with a multitude of retainers and dependants, who, having no equivalent to give in return for their maintenance, but being fed entirely by his bounty, must obey him. . . . The occupiers of land were in every respect as dependent upon the great proprietor as his retainers. Even such of them as were not in a state of villanage, were tenants at will. . . . A tenant at will . . . is as dependent upon the proprietor as any servant or retainer whatever, and must obey him with as little reserve. . . . The subsistence of both is derived from his bounty, and its continuance depends upon his good pleasure. Upon the authority which the great proprietors necessarily had . . . over their tenants and retainers, was founded the power of the ancient barons. They necessarily became the judges in peace, and the leaders in war, of all who dwelt upon their estates. . . . Not only the highest jurisdictions, both civil and criminal, but the power of levying troops, of coining money, and even that of making bye-laws for the government of their own people, were all rights possessed allodially by the great proprietors of land.[48]

To depend on the good will of another for one's subsistence puts one at the mercy of the other, and under his subjection. Gifts are not free: "hospitality" is given in return for obedience. The result is *private government*: the gift-giver's unaccountable dominion over the recipients of his good will. But private government was *bad* government. Not only did it reduce most people to a state of "servile dependency," but the feudal lords were always at war with one another, leaving the country "a scene of violence, rapine, and disorder."[49]

The rise of commerce and manufacturing had ironically beneficial results:

All for ourselves, and nothing for other people, seems, in every age of the world, to have been the vile maxim of the masters of mankind. As soon, therefore, as they could find a method of consuming the whole value of their rents themselves, they had no disposition to share them with any other persons. For a pair of diamond buckles, perhaps, or for something as frivolous and useless, they exchanged the maintenance, or, what is the same thing, the price of the maintenance of 1000 men for a year, and with it the whole weight and authority which it could give them . . . thus, for the gratification of the most childish, the meanest, and the most sordid of all vanities they gradually bartered their whole power and authority.[50]

On Smith's account, the rise of commerce and manufacturing led people to leave the lords' estates to become artisans and tradesmen. Although the latter still depended on the great proprietors' expenditures for a living, now any given lord contributed only a small proportion of the subsistence of any of them. Hence no lord was in a position to command any of them: he got only buckles, not authority, from his payment. The substitution of market exchange for gift exchange thereby liberated artisans and tradesmen from "servile dependency." A similar process liberated the farmers. As the lords dismissed their retainers, they did not need to take so much of the harvest for the maintenance of hundreds or thousands. So the lords also dismissed many tenants at will, while raising rents on the remainder. The latter were willing to pay higher rents only in return for long-term leases. By this means, the farmers were also liberated from servility to the lords. Tenants at will, fearful of eviction if they do not obey every whim of their landlord, must bow and scrape before them. Farmers protected by long-term leases need only pay the rent. The market nexus replaces a relation of domination and subjection with an arm's-length exchange on the basis of mutual interest and personal independence. By undermining the authority of the landlords, market society also increased the power of the national government, which brought peace, order, and the rule of law.[51]

So far, Smith's account of the rise of market society is historical. It does not take into account the *expected* effects of setting markets *free*—of removing all monopolizing constraints on trade. Chief among these constraints were primogeniture and entails, which kept nearly all land locked up and undivided in the possession of the firstborn sons of a few great families. Smith condemned these constraints as "founded upon the most absurd of all suppositions, . . . that every successive generation of men have not an equal right to the earth," but that land ownership be restrained by "the fancy of those who died perhaps five hundred years ago."[52] This arrangement was inefficient, because great landowners are more interested in conspicuous consumption than improving the land, which requires laborious attention "to small savings and small gains."[53] The most efficient agricultural producers are the yeoman farmers, small proprietors who work their own land. Neither sharecroppers nor tenants at will nor even leaseholders had a great incentive to invest in land improvements, because their landlord would appropriate part or all of the gains. Nor was slavery efficient, because slaves have no incentive to work hard.[54] If primogeniture and entail were abolished, great estates would be divided upon the death of the owner, and sold. Land prices would fall because a greater supply of land would reach the market. This would put farms within reach of the most productive—the yeoman farmers. Smith looked to North America as a model of what would happen: even individuals of very modest means could buy their own farms, and yeoman farmers dominated the agricultural sector.[55]

Smith believed that in a fully free market, the commercial and manufacturing sectors would similarly be dominated by small-scale enterprises, run by independent artisans and merchants, with at most a few employees. Large-scale enterprises were a product of state-licensed monopolies, tariffs, and other mercantilist protections. It was only necessary to raise the large concentrations of capital used by joint-stock corporations for four types of "routine" business that required no innovation or entrepreneurial vision: banking, insurance, canals, and water utilities. With or without special state protections, they would tend to fail.[56] In a free market, with barriers to entry eliminated, firms managed by their owners would out-compete the directors of joint-stock corporations because the former, risking their own money, would invest more energy, attention, and skill in their businesses. With many entrants into the open market, rates of profit would fall. When profits are low, few great fortunes can be accumulated, so nearly all capital owners will have to work for a living.[57]

No wonder Smith's pin factory, his model of an enterprise with an efficient division of labor, employed only ten workers.[58] *The Wealth of Nations* was published in 1776. Smith was writing only at the threshold of the Industrial Revolution. The spinning jenny had been invented in 1764, kept secret until it was patented in 1770, and only beginning to be used in a few factories by 1776. No one could have anticipated the rise of Blake's "dark, satanic mills" on the basis of such slender evidence. Smith reasonably believed that economies of scale were negligible for the production of most goods.

Thus we see that Smith's economic vision of a free market society aligns with the Levellers' vision more than a century earlier. Abolish guilds, monopolies, tariffs, restrictions on land sales, and other state-enforced restrictions on "natural liberty," and concentrations of great wealth would be dissipated, while labor would enjoy a "liberal reward."[59] Any remaining inequalities of wealth would hardly matter. In Smith's day, there were only two things great wealth could buy that were beyond the reach of those of modest means: dominion over others, and vanities.[60] For the rich, the rise of market society replaced the pursuit of dominion with the pursuit of trifling vanities. This was a huge win from an egalitarian point of view. Eliminate barriers to free markets, and the fortunes of the rich would be quickly dissipated, while opportunities for self-employment would proliferate.[61] This would be another huge advance for equality. It is a deeply humane vision.

EGALITARIANISM BEFORE THE INDUSTRIAL REVOLUTION: FROM PAINE TO LINCOLN

Imagine a free market economy in which nearly everyone is either self-employed as a yeoman farmer, artisan, or small merchant, or else as a worker in a small firm with high and rising wages, sufficient to enable enough saving so that one could purchase one's own farm or workshop after a few years. Markets would be perfectly competitive, so no one would enjoy market power over others. Profits would be low and everyone would have to work for a living, so labor would not be despised. Material inequality would be limited to individual differences in personal labor effort and skill, not to inequalities in birth, state-granted privileges, capital ownership, or command over others' labor. Everyone would meet on an equal footing with everyone else. All would enjoy personal independence. No one would be subject to another's domination. Would this not be close to an egalitarian utopia, a truly free society of equals?

Egalitarians thought they saw such a utopia emerging in America. This is hard to imagine today, given that the United States is by far the most unequal among the rich countries of the world. Yet from Smith's day to Lincoln's, America was the leading hope of egalitarians on both sides of the Atlantic.

To be sure, slavery was a monstrous blot on that hope.[62] But in the heady years of the American Revolution and the early American republic, optimism reigned. The Northwest Ordinance of 1787 had prohibited the spread of slavery to the northwestern territories. By 1804, all the Northern states had passed laws to abolish slavery. Many thought that slavery was headed for a natural death as an inefficient form of production, as Smith had argued.

In the age of revolutions, America offered opportunities to free workers, unlike any other country in the world. The great majority of the free population was self-employed, either as a yeoman farmer or an independent artisan or merchant. Journeymen had a good chance of owning their own enterprise after a few years. In the North, not only slavery, but other forms of unfree labor, such as apprenticeship and indentured service, were in steep decline.[63] The future appeared to promise real personal independence for all.

Thomas Paine was the great advocate of this vision in the revolutionary era, in three countries. Raised as a Quaker and apprenticed as a staymaker, Paine despised social hierarchy and dedicated his life to political agitation for equality. He was a hero of the American Revolution for writing *Common Sense*, the most popular and influential political pamphlet up to that time. *Common Sense* rallied the colonists not simply around independence, but around the idea that America, as a republic, would show the world how a free society of equals would look. During the French Revolution, he was elected to the National Convention. He was also lionized by American and English labor radicals, who read his writings well into the nineteenth century. The Chartists, active from 1838 to 1848, put him on their reading list.

Paine's economic views were broadly libertarian. Individuals can solve nearly all of their problems on their own, without the state meddling in their affairs.[64] All improvements in productive technology are due to enterprising individuals, who hope that government will just leave them alone.[65] A good government does nothing more than secure individuals in "peace and safety" in the free pursuit of their occupations, enjoying the fruits of their labors, with the lowest possible tax burden.[66] Paine was a lifelong advocate of commerce, free trade, and free markets.[67] He argued against state regulation of wages, claiming that workers should bargain over wages on the free market.[68] Against populist suspicion of finance, Paine was a leading advocate of chartering the Bank of North America, in part to supply credit for artisans, in part as a defense against the state's issuing too much paper money.[69]

Most problems, he argued, are the result of government. Excess printing of paper money (not hoarding, as popular crowds supposed) was the cause of inflation. So he criticized demands for price controls during the Revolutionary War inflation, and argued against price controls at the French National Convention.[70] He called for hard money and fiscal responsibility.[71] In most states—England was his chief example—government is the principal burden on society, waging war, inflating the debt, and imposing burdensome taxes. Government spending is mostly wasteful. Taxation is theft; government is a "system of war and extortion."[72] People living off government pay are social parasites, oppressing the industrious.[73] Government is also the chief cause of poverty, due to "the greedy hand of government thrusting itself into every corner and crevice of industry, and grasping the spoil of the multitude."[74] He proposed a plan to eliminate poverty in England by rebating the oppressive taxes the poor were forced to pay. Cut taxes drastically, and the poor will do fine, while the better off will no longer have to pay poor rates to support the welfare system.[75]

Paine's views on political economy sound as if they could have been ripped out of today's Republican Party playbook.[76] How, given these positions, could he have been the hero of labor radicals in the United States and England for decades after his death in 1809? He shows enormous faith in free markets and does not display a trace of the anticapitalist class conflict that characterized nineteenth-century politics. The answer is that labor radicals saw access to self-employment as central to avoiding poverty and attaining standing as equals in society. In the late eighteenth and early nineteenth centuries, the most radical workers were not the emerging industrial proletariat, but artisans who operated their own enterprises.[77] As such, they were simultaneously capitalists and workers: they owned their own capital, but also had to work for a living. As operators of small businesses, they favored commerce and open access to markets and credit. America, with nearly universal self-employment either actually realized or a seemingly realistic prospect for free workers, offered proof of concept. Paine was the greatest popularizer of the American experiment.

In an economic context in which the self-employed find their status and opportunities threatened by powerful institutions, it does not make sense to pit workers against capitalists. Popular politics instead pits the common working people against elites—that is, whoever controls the more powerful institutions. It may also pit the common working people against idlers—those who, like aristocrats, do not have to work for a living, but live off the labor of others. The Levellers saw the state as underwriting all kinds of oppressive private governments—of landlords, the established church, guilds, patriarchy. In Paine, however, the pre-industrial egalitarian vision narrowed to focus on the state. Nearly all states, other than the United States, were corrupt. Corruption exists whenever the state favors elites at the expense of ordinary working people—when it acts "by partialities of favor and oppression."[78] Paine enumerated several forms of unjust favoritism that oppressed ordinary working people. Idle landlords received special representation in the House of Lords, and a separate set of laws applicable only to them.[79] The state gave charters (monopolies) to elites, at the expense of the right of all people to engage in trade, and at the cost of economic growth.[80] It taxed working people to lavishly fund the king and his court of idlers.[81] It handed out sinecures to buy the votes of members of Parliament, and provide places for the worthless younger sons of aristocrats who, under primogeniture, would receive no inheritance.[82] The worst corruption by far was the state's waging of bloody and colossally expensive wars to support plunder and imperialism, at the cost of exploding tax burdens and public debt. Because the aristocracy controlled the system of taxation, they exempted themselves from most taxes and placed the burdens of funding these wars on working people, through oppressive sales taxes.[83]

Paine's low-tax, free-trade libertarian agenda made considerable sense for an export-led agricultural economy facing high grain prices, as was true for late eighteenth-century America. "The commerce by which [America] hath enriched herself are the necessaries of life, and will always have a market while eating is the custom of Europe."[84] Free market wages were high in a country suffering from chronic labor shortages, and in which self-employment was a ready option for nearly all.[85] When the bulk of the population is self-employed, pleading for relief from state meddling is quite a different proposition than it would be today. There is not much call for employment regulations if there are few employees, and virtually all have a ready exit into self-employment. When no enterprises are large enough to have market power, there is no need for antitrust regulation. When land is abundant and practically free, land use and pollution regulations are hardly needed because people are spread out and environmental effects (as far as people understood at the time) minimal. When people can appraise the quality of virtually all goods for sale on inspection, and nearly everyone grows what they eat, there is little need for laws regulating the safety of consumer goods. Arcane financial instruments could not bring an economy to its knees in an era in which banking was primitive and much of the economy was not monetized. So there was little need for complex financial regulation. In the absence of any notion of central banking or modern monetary policy, the gold standard was a better policy than one allowing states to issue paper money at will—a practice that led to destructive inflation in Paine's day. Paine's America probably came as close as anywhere in the world to avoiding market failures, as contemporary economists define them.

One issue, however, continued to bother Paine near the end of his life: widespread poverty. In *The Rights of Man*, he argued that poverty in

England could be solved by rebating the taxes the poor paid to support England's king, court, sinecures, military, and colonial system. Roll back this wasteful spending, end the poor rates, and there would still be a surplus that could be rebated to the poor or spent on educating their children, which would prevent their falling into poverty as adults.

Implicit in his thinking was a more systematic appreciation of the causes of poverty. It could not be simply due to a corrupt state oppressing the poor with excessive taxes to fund wasteful spending, or to monopolizing and other forms of state favoritism. People needed access to education to avoid poverty. In "Agrarian Justice," Paine went much further in questioning the adequacy even of the system of nearly universal self-employment that he saw in America. The great defect of such a system is that it makes families depend on labor to avoid poverty. What happens when, due to old age, disability, illness, or death, there is no one in the family able to work? The rich had a stock of capital on which they could live without working. To prevent poverty, everyone would need something comparable. Paine proposed a system of universal social insurance, including old-age pensions, survivor benefits, and disability payments for families whose members could not work. In addition, he proposed a system of universal stakeholder grants for young adults starting out in life, which they could use to obtain further education or tools, so their labor would earn enough to avoid poverty. This was the first realistic comprehensive social insurance proposal in the world, and the first realistic proposal to end poverty.

Paine insisted that this did not represent an abandonment of his principles of private property and free markets. Individualist to the last, Paine justified his social insurance system on strict Lockean property principles. Revenues for social insurance would come from an inheritance tax, which in his day amounted to a land tax. This was just, because landowners, in enclosing a part of the earth that was originally held in common by all, had failed to compensate everyone else for their taking. Even if they had mixed their labor with the land in the original appropriation, this entitled them only to the value their labor added to the land. They could not claim to deserve the value of the raw natural resources, or the value of surrounding uses that enhanced the market price of land. Each member of society was entitled to their per capita share of these values. So, landowners still owed a rent to everyone else. By this reasoning, Paine justified social insurance as a universal right, not a charity.[86]

This emergence of a systematic economic account of poverty, not tied to corrupt special favors dealt out by the state, was to remain underdeveloped in Painite radical labor ideology. English radicals such as William Cobbett and the Chartists continued to focus on political corruption as the source of the independent worker's oppression. The idea of social insurance as a systematic solution to a problem inherent in a system that let free markets be the sole mechanism for allocating income had to await the rise of socialism before it was taken up again—and then, ironically, by socialism's enemies. Bismarck, the notorious antisocialist who banned the activities of the German Social Democratic Party, implemented the first social insurance program in the world.

Even as the Industrial Revolution was bringing the presocialist era of egalitarian labor radicalism to an end in Europe—Chartism breathed its last gasp in 1848—the dream of a free society of equals built on independent small producers continued in the United States through the Civil War. This was the ideal on which the antebellum Republican Party was founded. Its central principle, antislavery, was based not so much on the moral wrong slavery inflicted on the slaves (although this was acknowledged), as it was on the threat slavery posed to the self-employed worker. The central platform of the antebellum Republican Party was to prohibit the extension of slavery in the territories. The creation of gigantic slave plantations in the territories would absorb land that would otherwise be available for free men to make it on their own as yeoman farmers, and consign them to wage labor for the rest of their lives.[87] President Lincoln articulated the view of his party. He rejected the theory that all workers must either be wage workers or slaves—either hired or bought by capital— and, if hired, "fixed in that condition for life." This he condemned as the "mud-sill" theory of society—the idea, advanced by proslavery Senator James Hammond of South Carolina, that every society needed an inferior class of people consigned to drudgery, on which to base civilization, just as every soundly built house needs to rest on a mudsill.[88] Lincoln advanced a rival view

> that there is not, of necessity, any such thing as the free hired laborer being fixed to that condition for life. . . . Many independent men in this assembly doubtless a few years ago were hired laborers. And their case is almost, if not quite, the general rule. The prudent, penniless beginner in the world labors for wages awhile, saves a surplus with which to buy tools or land for himself, then labors on his own account another while, and at length hires another new beginner to help him. This, say its advocates, is free labor—the just, and generous,

and prosperous system, which opens the way for all, gives hope to all, and energy, and progress, and improvement of condition to all.[89]

This progress of free labor to full self-employment is what the "society of equals" was all about.[90]

Was the Republican promise truly "for all"? The Homestead Act of 1862 was an attempt to fulfill that promise. However, to masses of wage laborers in the big Northern cities, this was already an unrealistic dream that did not speak to their needs as workers. It was even more unrealistic for free blacks, Chinese indentured servants, Mexican-American peons, and American Indians, who occupied "halfway houses of semifree labor."[91] The Thirteenth Amendment, which abolished slavery, attempted to advance that promise for nonwhites. Under it, peonage and other forms of involuntary servitude were prohibited—although litigation against various forms of peonage continued well into the 1940s, long after the dream of universal self-employment was dashed forever. More revealing for our purposes is the fact that the Thirteenth Amendment was the basis for the Civil Rights Act of 1866, which banned racial discrimination in the sale and rental of property. That a law banning slavery supported a right to buy land made sense only given a background ideology that identified free labor with self-employment, which required that the worker could buy or rent his capital. Yet that promise was left unfulfilled by the failure of the radical Republican's vision of Reconstruction, which would have divided the former slave plantations among the freed people.

Even had the radical Republican program of Reconstruction been enacted, its ideal of free labor was doomed. What began as a hopeful, inspiring egalitarian ideal in the United States self-destructed in three ways.

First, the ideal of universal self-employment never managed to incorporate the unpaid domestic labor essential to family life, which was performed overwhelmingly by women. Congressional debate over the Thirteenth Amendment made it clear that women were excluded from the promise of fully free labor. Notwithstanding the amendment, husbands retained property in their wives' labor.[92] This was a contradiction inherent in the free labor ideal, as the independence of men depended on their command over their wives' labor.[93] Hidden in the ostensible universalism and hyperindividualism of the ideal was a presumption of male governance over their wives'—and children's—labor. The feminist movement, which arose from the abolitionist movement, was to highlight this contradiction, as women came to demand independent and equal standing in the workplace and at home.

Second, the Civil War, which ended slavery in the name of independent labor, ironically propelled the very forces that put the universalization of that ideal farther out of reach, even for the class of white men. It was a powerful driver of industrialization, and hence of the triumph of large enterprises using the wage labor system over the small proprietor.

Third, the ideal contained an implicit esteem hierarchy that was ultimately to turn its egalitarian aspirations upside down. If the only fully respectable labor is independent, self-employed labor, if the way to attain recognition as an equal is to operate one's own enterprise, then what is one to make of those who remain wage laborers for their whole lives? Lincoln was clear: "If any continue through life in the condition of the hired laborer, it is not the fault of the system, but because of either a dependent nature which prefers it, or improvidence, folly, or singular misfortune."[94] Even in 1861, with the frontier still open, the burgeoning pace of immigration and urban industrialization was outrunning the flow of men out West. Lincoln's disparaging judgment of wage laborers is akin to blaming those left standing in a game of musical chairs, while denying that the structure of the game has anything to do with the outcome. Thus, what began as an egalitarian ideal ended as another basis for esteem hierarchy: to raise the businessman on a higher plane than the wage worker.[95]

THE CATACLYSM OF THE INDUSTRIAL REVOLUTION

The Industrial Revolution shattered the egalitarian ideal of universal self-government in the realm of production. Economies of scale overwhelmed the economy of small proprietors, replacing them with large enterprises that employed many workers. Opportunities for self-employment shrank dramatically in the course of the nineteenth century, and have continued to shrink to the present day. The Industrial Revolution also altered the nature of work and the relations between owners and workers in manufacturing, widening the gulf between the two.

There was a hierarchy of masters over journeymen and apprentices in the small-scale preindustrial workshop. Apprentices, in particular, without the right to a wage (like many American interns today), were unfree. Yet several factors constrained this hierarchy. Masters worked side by side with journeymen, performing the same labor while teaching apprentices the same skills. The fact that they performed work of the same kind as their subordinates, in the same workshop, softened the conditions of work. Masters could not make their subordinates labor in a shop whose conditions were so uncomfortable or unsafe that they would be unwilling to work there themselves. Nor could they impose a pace of work more relentless than they would be personally willing to endure. The pace of the typical artisanal workshop was relaxed, and included many breaks. Masters fraternized with their journeymen. Alcohol passed freely between masters and journeymen even during working hours. Finally, in the United States through the early years of the nineteenth century, skilled journeymen enjoyed a reasonable expectation of being able to set up shop for themselves after a few years of wage labor, in the manner Lincoln thought was the norm. With such a short, easy bridge from one rank to the next, it was relatively easy for workers to reconcile the hierarchy that did exist with egalitarian republican values.[96]

The Industrial Revolution dramatically widened the gulf between employers and employees in manufacturing. Employers no longer did the same kind of work as employees, if they worked at all. Mental labor was separated from manual labor, which was radically deskilled. Ranks within the firm multiplied. Leading executives might not even work in the same building. This facilitated a severe degradation of working conditions. Workers were subject to the relentless, grueling discipline of the clock and the machine. Employers, instead of drinking with their workers, preached temperance, industry, punctuality, and discipline. Conditions were harsh, hours long, wages low, and prospects for advancement, regardless of how hard one worked, minimal.

The nineteenth century saw the spread of total institutions across society: the prison, the asylum, the hospital, the orphanage, the poorhouse, the factory. Jeremy Bentham's notorious prison plan, the Panopticon, was his model for these other institutions.[97] Other liberals, such as Joseph Priestley, allied with factory owners and social reformers to promote these new types of hyperdisciplinary institution. Here lay the central contradiction of the new liberal order: "Though these radicals preached independence, freedom, and autonomy in polity and market, they preached order, routine, and subordination in factory, school, poorhouse, and prison."[98]

Preindustrial labor radicals, viewing the vast degradation of autonomy, esteem, and standing entailed by the new productive order in comparison with artisan status, called it *wage slavery*. Liberals called it *free labor*. The difference in perspective lay at the very point Marx highlighted. If one looks only at the conditions of entry into the labor contract and exit out of it, workers appear to meet their employers on terms of freedom and equality. That was what the liberal view stressed. But if one looks at the actual conditions experienced in the worker's fulfilling the contract, the workers stand in a relation of profound subordination to their employer. That was what the labor radicals stressed.

In this light, let us now return to the contrast between Smith and Marx with which this lecture opened. It is often supposed that their differing assessments of market society were based on fundamentally opposed values. Yet both marveled at the ways market society drove innovation, productive efficiency, and economic growth. And both deplored the deskilling and stupefying effects of an increasingly fine-grained division of labor on workers.[99] They differed rather on what they expected market society to offer to workers. Smith's greatest hope—the hope shared by labor radicals from the Levellers to the Chartists, from Paine to Lincoln—was that freeing up markets would dramatically expand the ranks of the self-employed, who would exercise talent and judgment in governing their own productive activities, independent of micromanaging bosses. No wonder Smith's optimistic representation of market relations focused on the butcher, the brewer, and the baker—all independent proprietors. Free market society could be championed as "left," as an egalitarian cause, so long as "by far the most important" of its effects was "the liberty . . . of individuals . . . who had before lived almost in a continual state of . . . servile dependency upon their superiors." With the Industrial Revolution, the pervasiveness of markets in *labor* returned manufacturing workers to an even deeper state of subjection to their superiors than before. Smith, who despised selfishness, disparaged the quest to accumulate vast fortunes, and cited "the disposition to admire, and almost to worship, the rich and the powerful . . . [as] the great and most universal cause of the corruption of our moral sentiments" would not have approved.[100]

Preindustrial egalitarians had no answer for the challenges of the Industrial Revolution. Their model of how to bring about a free society of equals through free markets via near-universal self-employment was shattered. Advocates of laissez faire, who blithely applied the earlier arguments for market society to a social context that brought about the very opposite of the effects that were predicted and celebrated by their predecessors, failed to recognize that the older arguments no longer applied. Thus arose a symbiotic relationship between libertarianism and authoritarianism that blights our political discourse to this day. For what we have yet to adequately grasp is the nature of the challenge before us: *private government*.

NOTES

1. Of course, this usage of the term "left" is anachronistic. But it serves to fix ideas. I hasten to add that some egalitarians of the seventeenth and eighteenth centuries—notably, the Diggers, and Rousseau—rejected market society. My focus in this lecture is on those who embraced it.

2. Adam Smith, *An Inquiry into the Nature and Causes of the Wealth of Nations*, vol. 1, Glasgow Edition of the Works and Correspondence of Adam Smith (Indianapolis: Liberty Fund, 1981), I.ii.2.

3. Karl Marx, *Capital: A Critique of Political Economy*, edited by Frederick Engels, translated by Samuel Moore and Edward Aveling (Chicago: Charles H. Kerr, 1912), 195–96.

4. This is not just cynicism on Smith's part. He points to a transcultural social fact, that every gift implies a debt that, until reciprocated in kind, subordinates the recipient to the giver. See Marcel Mauss, *The Gift*, translated by I. Cunnison (New York: Norton, 1967); William Miller, *Humiliation* (Ithaca, NY: Cornell University Press, 1993), ch. 1.

5. Marx, *Capital*, 195.

6. Thus, the so-called Adam Smith problem—the purported tension between Smith's moral theory, founded on sympathy with others, and his economics, supposedly founded on pure egoism, is dissolved.

7. "All for ourselves, and nothing for other people, seems, in every age of the world, to have been the vile maxim of the masters of mankind." Smith, *Wealth of Nations*, vol. 1, III.iv.10.

8. On this point, I fully agree with Pierre Rosanvallon, *The Society of Equals*, trans. Arthur Goldhammer (Cambridge, MA: Harvard University Press, 2013), 11, 29, 51.

9. For the first statement of the army's program, see "Agreement of the People," in *The English Levellers*, edited by Andrew Sharp (New York: Cambridge University Press, 1647), 92–101. "Agitators"—Leveller officers chosen by their men—debated this proposal with Cromwell and Ireton at Putney in 1647. The Putney debates offer some of the most riveting reading in the history of political thought, at a level of intellectual depth and seriousness vastly exceeding contemporary public discourse. See "Putney Debates," *Puritanism and Liberty, Being the Army Debates (1647–9) from the Clarke Manuscripts with Supplementary Documents*, edited by A. S. P. Woodhouse (Chicago: University of Chicago Press, 1951), 1–124.

10. "Putney Debates, 29 October 1647," *Puritanism and Liberty*, 75.

11. John Lilburne, William Walwyn, Thomas Prince, and Richard Overton, "An Agreement of the Free People of England, 1 May 1649," in *The Levellers: Miscellaneous Writings*, edited by James Otteson, vol. 4 of *The Levellers: Overton, Walwyn and Lilburne* (Bristol: Thoemmes Press, 1649) articles XXX, XVIII, XX, XIX.

12. John Lilburne, "Englands Birth-Right Justified," in *Works of John Lilburne* 62–64, edited by Otteson, vol. 3 of *The Levellers*.

13. John Lilburne, "Londons Liberty in Chains Discovered," *Works of John Lilburne*, 175–77.

14. William Walwyn, "For a Free Trade," in *Works of William Walwyn*, vol. 2 of *The Levellers*, edited by Otteson, 399–405.

15. It would be anachronistic to attribute such ideas to any seventeenth-century thinkers because the modern notion of distributive justice was not invented until the end of the eighteenth century. Samuel Fleischacker, *A Short History of Distributive Justice* (Cambridge, MA: Harvard University Press, 2004).

16. See "The Root and Branch Petition (1640)," *Documents Illustrative of English Church History*, edited by Henry Gee and William John Hardy (New York: Macmillan, 1896), 537–45, http://history.hanover.edu/texts/engref/er97.html, a contemporary document calling for an end to the church's powers in these respects.

17. Thomas Leng, "'His Neighbours Land Mark': William Sykes and the Campaign for 'Free Trade' in Civil War England," *Historical Research* 86, no. 232 (2013): 230–52.

18. William Blackstone, *Commentaries on the Laws of England*, 1st ed. (Oxford: Clarendon Press, 1765), ch. 15.

19. For some legal complexities in the early modern era, see Karen Pearlston, "Review of *Women, Property, and the Letters of the Law in Early Modern England*," *Osgoode Hall Law Journal* 44, no. 1 (2006): 219–21; for documentation of women's contestation of husbands' authority, along with contemporary cultural recognition of its limits, see Don Herzog, *Household Politics: Conflict in Early Modern England* (New Haven, CT: Yale University Press, 2013).

20. Recall John Locke, *Second Treatise of Government* (Indianapolis: Hackett, 1690) §77: "The first society was between man and wife, which gave beginning to that between parents and children; to which, in time, that between master and servant came to be added . . . and make up but one family, wherein the master or mistress of it had some sort of rule proper to a family." Locke here includes employees in the family, and represents it as a kind of government, which, in the state of nature, is not patriarchal. I shall return to Locke's feminism later in this lecture.

21. See Blackstone, *Commentaries*, ch. 14; Karen Orren, *Belated Feudalism: Labor, the Law, and Liberal Development in the United States* (Cambridge: Cambridge University Press, 1991) (documenting the early modern English law of master and servant, and how it continued to govern U.S. employment relations well into the nineteenth century).

22. See Don Herzog, *Happy Slaves* (Chicago: University of Chicago Press, 1989), ch. 1.

23. Arthur O. Lovejoy, *The Great Chain of Being: A Study of the History of an Idea* (Cambridge, MA: Harvard University Press, 1936).

24. Robert Filmer, *Patriarcha: Or the Natural Power of Kings* (London: W. Davis, 1680).

25. Christopher Hill, *The World Turned Upside Down: Radical Ideas during the English Revolution* (New York: Penguin Books, 1991), 155.

26. See Saint Augustine, *City of God*, translated by Marcus Dods (Edinburgh: T. & T. Clark, 1888), XIX.15.

27. Hill, *World Turned Upside Down*, ch. 3, 4.

28. Herzog, *Happy Slaves*, ch. 1.

29. See Hill, *World Turned Upside Down*, esp. ch. 8; Andrew Bradstock, *Radical Religion in Cromwell's England: A Concise History from the English Civil War*

to the End of the Commonwealth (New York: I.B. Tauris, 2011), esp. ch. 5. Thus arose the endlessly repeated conservative charge that egalitarians believe in the perfectibility of human beings. Absurd as applied to today's believers in an egalitarian distribution of income and wealth, democracy, and other secular egalitarian doctrines, the charge makes sense as applied to historical Christian millennialist egalitarian social movements, which needed to refute the authoritarian doctrine of original sin.

30. Samuel Torshell, *The Womans Glorie: A Treatise, First, Asserting the Due Honour of That Sexe, by Manifesting That Women Are Capable of the Highest Improvements and Instancing Severall Examples of Womens Eminencies . . .*, 2nd ed. (London: Printed for John Bellamy, 1650), 11.

31. Hill, *World Turned Upside Down*, 310–12.

32. John Lilburne, "The Free-Man's Freedom Vindicated," *Works of John Lilburne*, 105–6.

33. Elizabeth Chidley, "Petition of Women, Affecters and Approvers of the Petition of Sept. 11, 1648 (5th May 1649)," *Puritanism and Liberty*, 367.

34. Hill, *World Turned Upside Down*, 312.

35. "Root and Branch Petition," articles 10, 12, 24.

36. Michael Levy, "Freedom, Property and the Levellers: The Case of John Lilburne," *Western Political Quarterly* 36, no. 1 (1983): 116–33, here 120.

37. See Walwyn, "For a Free Trade," 403–4 (complaining that the burdens of guild government lie "more heavily upon the more moderate Traders" who suffer from the guilds' "many unreasonable Orde Oathes, fines, Censures" and that they spend too much time "in Courts & meetings about others affaires").

38. Leng, " 'His Neighbours Land Mark,' " 233, 236.

39. Thomas Johnson, *A Plea for Free-Mens Liberties: Or the Monopoly of the Eastland Merchants* (London, 1646) 2, 3, http://gateway.proquest.com.proxy.lib .umich.edu/openurl?ctx_ver=Z39.88–2003&res_id=xri:eebo&rft_id=xri: eebo:citation:99861268/.

40. Walwyn, "For a Free Trade," 403.

41. Ibid., 402, 401.

42. Johnson, *Plea*, 4.

43. "Reason being the fountain of all honest laws, gives to every man propriety and liberty; propriety of interest, freedom of enjoyment and improoovement to his own advantage . . . those who have bereft us of our liberty, have made bold with our propriety" (ibid.).

44. Jacqueline Stevens, "The Reasonableness of Locke's Majority: Property Rights, Consent, and Resistance in the Second Treatise," *Political Theory* 24, no. 3 (1996): 423–63.

45. As Jeremy Waldron decisively demonstrates, in *God, Locke, and Equality: Christian Foundations of John Locke's Political Thought* (Cambridge: Cambridge University Press, 2002), ch. 2.

46. "As justice gives every man a title to the product of his honest industry . . . so charity gives every man a title to so much out of another's plenty, as will keep him from extreme want, where he has no means to subsist otherwise: and a

man can no more justly make use of another's necessity to force him to become his vassal, by with-holding that relief God requires him to afford to the wants of his brother, than he that has more strength can seize upon a weaker, master him to his obedience, and with a dagger at his throat, offer his death or slavery." John Locke, "First Treatise of Government," *The Works of John Locke in Nine Volumes*, 12th ed. (London: Rivington, 1824), §42.

47. Smith, *Wealth of Nations*, vol. 1, III.4.4 (emphasis added).

48. Ibid., III.4.5–8.

49. Ibid., III.4.9.

50. Ibid., III.4.10.

51. Ibid., III.4.11–15.

52. Ibid., III.2.6.

53. Ibid., III.2.7.

54. Ibid., III.2.8–13.

55. Ibid., III.4.19.

56. Smith, *Wealth of Nations*, vol. 2, V.1.E.32. Joint-stock corporations tend to fail because their governance structure cannot solve the principal–agent problem of holding directors accountable to investors. Surveying the history of joint-stock corporations, Smith finds that directors lack expertise, initiative, and energy because they are risking other people's money, and allow employees to squander the corporation's resources (Ibid., V.1.E.18, 27).

57. Smith, *Wealth of Nations,* vol. 1, I.ix.20. It follows that, while a free market economy would be more unequal than primitive society, it would be far more equal than a feudal or mercantilist economy. For further support of the view that Smith's vision of a free market society has egalitarian tendencies, see Deborah Boucoyannis, "The Equalizing Hand: Why Adam Smith Thought the Market Should Produce Wealth without Steep Inequality," *Perspectives on Politics* 11, no. 4 (2013): 1051–70.

58. Smith, *Wealth of Nations*, I.1.3.

59. Other Enlightenment figures shared this view: "It is easy to prove that fortunes tend naturally toward equality, and that excessive differences of wealth either cannot exist or must promptly cease, if the civil laws do not establish artificial ways of perpetuating and amassing such fortunes, and if freedom of commerce and industry eliminate the advantage that any prohibitive law or fiscal privilege gives to acquired wealth." Antoine-Nicholas Condorcet, *Outlines of an Historical View of the Progress of the Human Mind* (G. Langer, 2009), 10th epoch.

60. Medicine was so unreliable that one might be better off not being able to afford a doctor's services. No one could travel in comfort or speed at any expense. The penny press made news available to all. Theaters offered cheap seats. No wonder Smith disparaged the quest for great wealth as not worth the trouble. See *The Theory of Moral Sentiments*, edited by D. D. Raphael and A. L. Macfie, Glasgow Edition of the Works and Correspondence of Adam Smith (Oxford: Oxford University Press, 1976), I.3.2.1, III.3.31, IV.1.6.8.

61. Smith, *Wealth of Nations*, vol. 1, III.4.16.

62. So was the fact that the hope was predicated on mass, violent expropriation of land from its former possessors. In contrast to slavery, which received substantial attention from many Euro-American egalitarians, Native American claims received little attention.

63. Joyce Appleby, *Capitalism and a New Social Order: The Republican Vision of the 1790s*, Anson G. Phelps Lectureship on Early American History (New York: New York University Press, 1984), 89; Eric Foner, *Tom Paine and Revolutionary America* (New York: Oxford University Press, 1976), 32, 43–44.

64. Thomas Paine, *Rights of Man. Part the Second: Combining Principle and Practice*, 8th ed. (London: J. S. Jordan, 1792), 7–8.

65. Ibid., 59n*.

66. Ibid., 60.

67. See for example, Paine, *Rights of Man, Part 2*, 82; Thomas Paine, *The Crisis: In Thirteen Numbers. Written during the Late War. By the Author of Common Sense* (Albany, NY: Charles and George Webster, 1792), no. 3, 40.

68. Paine, *Rights of Man, Part 2*, 150.

69. Foner, *Paine and Revolutionary America*, 183–200.

70. See ibid., ch. 5, for an extended discussion of Paine's thought and activities regarding price controls.

71. Ibid., 190.

72. Paine, *Rights of Man, Part 2*, 16.

73. Ibid., 69.

74. Ibid., 3–4.

75. Ibid., 113–31.

76. The Republican Party, however, has not followed Paine in other respects: his critique of Christianity (Thomas Paine, *The Age of Reason* [Boston: Thomas Hall, 1794]); his feminism (see Eileen Hunt Botting, "Thomas Paine Admidst the Early Feminists," in *Selected Writings of Thomas Paine*, edited by Ian Shapiro and Jane Calvert [New Haven, CT: Yale University Press, 2014], 630–54); his opposition to the death penalty; his opposition to military spending, war, and imperialism. Most of all, Paine, who experienced poverty for much of his life, had profound sympathy for the poor and never disparaged them as lazy, lacking enterprise, or corrupted by "welfare." As we shall see, he argued that everyone had a right to sufficient income to avoid poverty.

77. Craig Calhoun, *The Roots of Radicalism: Tradition, the Public Sphere, and Early Nineteenth-Century Social Movements* (Chicago: University of Chicago Press, 2012).

78. Paine, *Rights of Man, Part 2*, 11.

79. Ibid., 63, 100.

80. Ibid., 92–98.

81. Ibid., 67–69.

82. Ibid., 105–6. When Paine complained that people on government pay were parasites, he was not speaking of magistrates, parish officials, or other government workers who perform actual public services for modest pay. He was complaining of the court, and of sinecures. Genuine civil servants, by contrast, are entitled to reasonable pay (ibid., 54, 72, 119).

83. Ibid., 4, 77–80, 87, 100–102, 155. In contrast to the U.S. Republican Party today, Paine opposed regressive consumption taxes and supported taxes on inheritances and bonds.

84. Thomas Paine, *Common Sense* (Edinburgh: Eighteenth Century Collections Online. Gale, 1776), 33.

85. Paine expressed his objection to wage controls, and preference for market wages, in an era when regulations set *maximum* wages.

86. Thomas Paine, "Agrarian Justice," *The Writings of Thomas Paine, Vol. III (1791–1804)*, edited by Moncure Daniel Conway (New York: Putnam's Sons, 1894), 322–44.

87. Eric Foner, *Free Soil, Free Labor, Free Men: The Ideology of the Republican Party before the Civil War*, with a new introduction (New York: Oxford University Press, 1995) is the indispensable work on this subject.

88. James Henry Hammond, "Speech in the Senate, 35th Congress, Session 1," *Congressional Globe*, March 4, 1858: 71.

89. Abraham Lincoln, "Annual Address before the Wisconsin State Agricultural Society, at Milwaukee, September 30, 1859," *Abraham Lincoln, Complete Works*, edited by John Nicolay and John Hay, vol. 1 (New York: Century Co., 1859), 581.

90. "There is no permanent class of hired laborers amongst us. . . . The hired laborer of yesterday, labors on his own account to-day; and will hire others to labor for him to-morrow. Advancement—improvement in condition—is the order of things in a society of equals." Abraham Lincoln, "Fragment on Free Labor," *Collected Works of Abraham Lincoln,* vol. 3, edited by Roy Basler (New Brunswick, NJ: Rutgers University Press, 1859), 463.

91. Foner, *Free Soil*, Kindle loc. 332–37.

92. Ibid., 434.

93. Ibid., 377–80.

94. Lincoln, "Address before the Wisconsin State Agricultural Society," 581–82.

95. Lincoln may have baked it into the ideological infrastructure of his party. A century and a half after his pronouncement, Eric Cantor, then Republican House majority leader, tweeted on Labor Day 2012: "Today, we celebrate those who have taken a risk, worked hard, built a business and earned their own success," https://twitter.com/ericcantor/status/242654833218293760. Cantor appears to be viscerally incapable of recognizing how a day could be dedicated to honoring wage laborers.

96. Sean Wilentz, *Chants Democratic: New York City and the Rise of the American Working Class, 1788–1850* (New York: Oxford University Press, 2004), 508–16.

97. Gertrude Himmelfarb, *The Idea of Poverty: England in the Early Industrial Age* (New York: Knopf, 1984), 78. See, for example, Jeremy Bentham, *Pauper Management Improved: Particularly by Means of an Application of the Panopticon Principle of Construction* (London: R. Baldwin, 1812).

98. Isaac Kramnick, *Republicanism and Bourgeois Radicalism: Political Ideology in Late Eighteenth-Century England and America* (Ithaca, NY: Cornell University Press, 1990), 97.

99. Smith, *Wealth of Nations*, vol. 2, V.1.F.50.

100. Smith, *Theory of Moral Sentiments*, I.3.3.1.

LECTURE II.
PRIVATE GOVERNMENT

COMMUNIST DICTATORSHIPS IN OUR MIDST

Imagine a government that assigns almost everyone a superior whom they must obey. Although superiors give most inferiors a routine to follow, there is no rule of law. Orders may be arbitrary and can change at any time, without prior notice or opportunity to appeal. Superiors are unaccountable to those they order around. They are neither elected nor removable by their inferiors. Inferiors have no right to complain in court about how they are being treated, except in a few narrowly defined cases. They also have no right to be consulted about the orders they are given.

There are multiple ranks in the society ruled by this government. The content of the orders people receive varies, depending on their rank. Higher-ranked individuals may be granted considerable freedom in deciding how to carry out their orders, and may issue some orders to some inferiors. The most highly ranked individual takes no orders but issues many. The lowest-ranked may have their bodily movements and speech minutely regulated for most of the day.

This government does not recognize a personal or private sphere of autonomy free from sanction. It may prescribe a dress code and forbid certain hairstyles. Everyone lives under surveillance, to ensure that they are complying with orders. Superiors may snoop into inferiors' e-mail and record their phone conversations. Suspicionless searches of their bodies and personal effects may be routine. They can be ordered to submit to medical testing. The government may dictate the language spoken and forbid communication in any other language. It may forbid certain topics of discussion. People can be sanctioned for their consensual sexual activity or for their choice of spouse or life partner. They can be sanctioned for their political activity and required to engage in political activity they do not agree with.

The economic system of the society run by this government is communist. The government owns all the nonlabor means of production in the society it governs. It organizes production by means of central planning. The form of the government is a dictatorship. In some cases, the dictator is appointed by an oligarchy. In other cases, the dictator is self-appointed.

Although the control that this government exercises over its members is pervasive, its sanctioning powers are limited. It cannot execute or imprison anyone for violating orders. It can demote people to lower ranks. The most common sanction is exile. Individuals are also free to emigrate, although if they do, there is usually no going back. Exile or emigration can have severe collateral consequences. The vast majority have no realistic option but to try to immigrate to another communist dictatorship, although there are many to choose from. A few manage to escape into anarchic hinterlands, or set up their own dictatorships.

This government mostly secures compliance with carrots. Because it controls all the income in the society, it pays more to people who follow orders particularly well and promotes them to higher rank. Because it controls communication, it also has a propaganda apparatus that often persuades many to support the regime. This need not amount to brainwashing. In many cases, people willingly support the regime and comply with its orders because they identify with and profit from it. Others support the regime because, although they are subordinate to some superior, they get to exercise dominion over inferiors. It should not be surprising that support for the regime for these reasons tends to increase, the more highly ranked a person is.

Would people subject to such a government be free? I expect that most people in the United States would think not. Yet most work under just such a government: it is the modern workplace, as it exists for most establishments in the United States. The dictator is the chief executive officer (CEO), superiors are managers, subordinates are workers. The oligarchy that appoints the CEO exists for publicly owned corporations: it is the board of directors. The punishment of exile is being fired. The economic system of the modern workplace is communist, because the government—that is, the establishment—owns all the assets,[1] and the top of the establishment hierarchy designs the production plan, which subordinates execute. There are no internal markets in the modern workplace. Indeed, the boundary of the firm is *defined* as the point at which markets end and authoritarian centralized planning and direction begin.[2]

Most workers in the United States are governed by communist dictatorships in their work lives. Usually, those dictatorships have the legal authority to regulate workers' off-hour lives as well—their political activities, speech, choice of sexual partner, use of recreational drugs, alcohol, smoking, and exercise. Because most employers exercise this off-hours authority irregularly, arbitrarily, and without warning, most workers are unaware of how sweeping it is. Most believe, for example, that their boss

cannot fire them for their off-hours Facebook postings, or for supporting
a political candidate their boss opposes. Yet only about half of U.S. workers enjoy even partial protection of their off-duty speech from employer
meddling.[3] Far fewer enjoy legal protection of their speech on the job,
except in narrowly defined circumstances. Even where they are entitled to
legal protection, as in speech promoting union activity, their legal rights
are often a virtual dead letter due to lax enforcement: employers determined to keep out unions immediately fire any workers who dare mention
them, and the costs of litigation make it impossible for workers to hold
them accountable for this.

I expect that this description of communist dictatorships in our
midst, pervasively governing our lives, often to a far greater degree of control than the state, would be deeply surprising to most people. Certainly
many U.S. CEOs, who think of themselves as libertarian individualists,
would be surprised to see themselves depicted as dictators of little communist governments. Why do we not recognize such a pervasive part of
our social landscape for what it is? Should we not subject these forms of
government to at least as much critical scrutiny as we pay to the democratic state? My project in this lecture is to explain why public discourse
and political philosophy largely neglect the pervasiveness of authoritarian governance in our work and off-hours lives and why we should return
our attention to it, and to sketch some thoughts as to what we should do
about it—for neglect of these issues is relatively recent. They were hot
topics of public discourse, academic and legal theorizing, and political
agitation from the Industrial Revolution through the New Deal. Now
they are the province of members of marginalized academic subfields—
labor historians, labor law scholars, and some labor economists—along
with a few labor lawyers and labor activists.

Our currently dominant tools for discerning our work lives were
manufactured before the Industrial Revolution and originally designed
as viewfinders to the future. They were rejected as useless by organized
labor movements that arose in recognition of the fundamental irre-
versible changes in workers' prospects brought about by the Industrial
Revolution. They have been redeployed since the grave decline of organized labor movements, but now as blinders on our actual institutional
landscape of work. We need different instruments to discern the normatively relevant features of our current institutions of workplace
governance. In particular, we need to revive the concept of *private
government.*

PRIVATE GOVERNMENT: THE VERY IDEA

Most modern workplaces are private governments. By this, I do not mean
merely that they are in the so-called private sector, and have some internal structure of authority—as specified, for instance, in the rules for corporate governance. I refer rather to a particular sort of constitution of
government, under which its subjects are unfree.

The notion of "private government" may seem a contradiction in
terms. In the impoverished vocabulary of contemporary public discourse,
and to a considerable extent in contemporary political philosophy, "government" is often treated as synonymous with the state, which, by supposed definition, is part of the "public sphere." The supposed counterpart
"private sphere" is the place where, it is imagined, "government" ends,
and hence where individual liberty begins. Here is a characteristic expression of this view in U.S. public discourse:

> Giving up our very freedom for a system that allow[s] the government
> to further meddle in our private lives . . . [is] not the answer. . . . Every
> single thing government does to increase its own power increases the
> size of *its slice* of the liberty pie . . . Since there are only two slices,
> every time the government's slice of the liberty pie grows, the citizens'
> slice is *reduced*.[4]

That is according to Ken Cuccinelli, the former attorney general of
Virginia. But nothing hangs on him. He is merely expressing a view widely
accepted in public discourse, certainly among libertarians, but not only
among them. Let us unpack the confusions.

First, government exists wherever some have the authority to issue
orders to others, backed by sanctions, in one or more domains of life.[5] The
modern *state* is merely one form of government among others, defined
by Max Weber as "a compulsory organization" that asserts a monopoly on
determining the legitimate use of force over a territory.[6] Popular usage before the nineteenth century is much clearer about the government/state
distinction than we are today. Here is John Adams, replying to Abigail's
famous letter asking him to "remember the ladies":

> We have been told that our struggle has loosened the bonds of gov-
> ernment every where; that children and apprentices were disobedient;
> that schools and colleges were grown turbulent; that Indians slighted
> their guardians, and negroes grew insolent to their masters. But your

letter was the first intimation that another tribe, more numerous and powerful than all the rest, were grown discontented. . . . Depend upon it, we know better than to repeal our masculine systems.[7]

Here Adams frankly acknowledges that government is "every where"— parents (and *govern*esses) exercise government over children, masters over apprentices, teachers over students, guardians over Indians, masters over slaves, husbands over wives. We have seen from my previous lecture that this understanding of the scope of government was equally familiar to actors in seventeenth-century England.

Now consider the public/private distinction. If something is legitimately kept private *from* you, that means it is none of your business. This entails at least one of the following: you are not entitled to know about it, your interests have no standing in decisions regarding it, you aren't entitled to make decisions regarding it or to hold those who do accountable for the effect their decisions have on you. If it is private *to* you, that means it *is* your business, *and* you may exclude others from making it any of theirs. This entails at least one of the following: you are entitled to keep others from knowing about it; you need not consider others' interests in making decisions regarding it; you are not accountable to others for your decisions regarding it; you are entitled to exclude others from making decisions regarding it.

If something is "public," that means it is the business of a more or less well-defined group of people (members of "the public"), such that no one is entitled to exclude any member of the group from making it their business. Publicity in the informational sense typically extends much further than publicity with respect to standing, decision making, and accountability. The latter three categories refer to the governance of the thing in question. Its public status, with respect to governance, involves means by which the public asserts standing to make claims regarding its governance, and organizes itself to make collective decisions regarding it, and/ or hold accountable the individuals elected or appointed to make such decisions.

Privacy is relative to persons. A thing that is private with respect to some persons may be public with respect to others. A private club is private from nonmembers, but generally a public thing to its members: the club will typically have meetings to which its members are invited, in which they learn about the club's activities and finances, insist that their interests be taken into account in its operations, make decisions about it, and hold officers of the club accountable. It follows that there is no single public sphere or a single private sphere in society. There are many spheres, and which are public or private depends on who you are.[8]

Today we associate the state with "the" public sphere, and things that are not the state's business, but individuals' own business, with "the" private sphere. Insofar as these associations are thought to be inherent, the idea of "private government" would appear to be contradictory. Isn't everything in the "private sphere" part of individual liberty, and everything subject to "public" (government, confusedly limited to state) control, a constraint on individual liberty? That is Cuccinelli's idea, which reflects associations entrenched in contemporary public discourse.

But of course the association of the state with the public sphere is not inherent. It is a contingent social achievement of immense importance. The centuries-long struggles for popular sovereignty and a republican form of government are attempts to make the state a public thing: something that is the people's business, transparent to them, servant to their interests, in which they have a voice and the power to hold rulers accountable. Authoritarian governments insist on the opposite—that the affairs of state are the private business of the rulers.

This point generalizes to *all* governments, not just governments run by the state. You are subject to *private government* wherever (a) you are subordinate to authorities who can order you around and sanction you for not complying over some domain of your life, and (b) the authorities treat it as none of your business, across a wide range of cases, what orders it issues or why it sanctions you. A government is private with respect to a subject if it can issue orders, backed by sanctions, to that subject in some domain of that subject's life, and that subject has no say in how that government operates and no standing to demand that their interests be taken into account, other than perhaps in narrowly defined circumstances, in the decisions that government makes. Private government is government that has arbitrary, unaccountable power over those it governs. This of course is a matter of degree. Its powers may be checked in certain ways by other governments, by social norms, and by other pressures.

Note that *the privacy of a government is defined relative to the governed, not relative to the state.* The notion of governments that are kept private from the state is much more familiar: we speak of corporate governance, church governance, and so forth, in referring to legal entities that are private in relation to the state. That notion of private government abstracts from the people who are governed and their relation to these governments. They focus only on the fact that the state is kept out of decision making in these governments. My definition of private government focuses on the fact that, in many of these governments, the governed are kept out of decision making as well.

Now consider the connections of government to freedom. Cuccinelli depicts a zero-sum tradeoff between the liberties of the state and those of its citizens. But there are at least three concepts of freedom: negative, positive, and republican. If you have negative freedom, no one is interfering with your actions. If you have positive freedom, you have a rich menu of options effectively accessible to you, given your resources.[9] If you have republican freedom, no one is dominating you—you are subject to no one's arbitrary, unaccountable will.[10] These three kinds of freedom are distinct. A lone person on a desert island has perfect negative and republican freedom, but virtually no positive freedom, because there is nothing to do but eat coconuts. An absolute monarch's favorites may enjoy great negative and positive freedom if he has granted them generous privileges and well-paid sinecures. But they still lack republican freedom, since he can take their perks away and toss them into a dungeon on a whim. Citizens of prosperous social democracies have considerable positive and republican freedom, but are subject to numerous negative liberty constraints, in the form of complex state regulations that constrain their choices in numerous aspects of their lives.

All three kinds of freedom are valuable. There are sound reasons to make tradeoffs among them. If we focus purely on negative liberty, and purely concerning rival goods, it *might* seem that Cuccinelli is correct that the size of the liberty pie is fixed: one agent's liberty over rival good G would seem to preclude another's liberty over it. But this is to confuse negative *liberties* with *exclusive rights*. There is nothing incoherent about a Hobbesian state of nature, in which everyone has the negative liberty to take, or compete for possession of, every rival good. That would be a social state of perfect negative liberty: it is a state of anarchist communism, in which the world is an unregulated commons. Such a condition would also be catastrophic. Production would collapse if anyone were free to take whatever anyone else had worked to produce. Even the natural resources of the earth would rapidly be depleted in an unregulated commons. Without property rights—rights to exclude others—people would therefore be very poor and insecure. Opportunities—*positive* liberties— are vastly greater with the establishment of a system of property rights.

This is a standard argument for a regime of private property rights. It is impeccable. Yet its logical entailments are often overlooked. Every establishment of a private property *right* entails a correlative duty, coercively enforceable by individuals or the state, that others refrain from meddling with another's property without the owner's permission. Private property rights thus entail massive net losses in negative liberty, relative to the state of maximum negative liberty. If Lalitha has private property in a parcel of land, her liberty over that parcel is secured by an *exclusive right* at the cost of the identical negative liberty of seven billion others over that parcel. If we are good libertarians and insist that the justification of any constraint on liberty must appeal to some other more important liberty, then the libertarian case for private property depends on accepting that positive liberty very often rightly overrides negative liberty. It follows that even massive state constraints on negative liberty (in the form of enforcements of private property rights) can increase total liberty (in an accounting that weights positive liberty more highly than negative, as any accounting that can justify private property in terms of freedom must).

State-enforced constraints on negative liberty can also increase total liberty through their enhancement of republican freedom. This is a venerable argument from the republican tradition: without robust protection of private property rights (which, as we have seen, entail massive net losses of negative liberty), a republican form of government is insecure, because the state is liable to degenerate into despotism, exercising arbitrary power over its subjects. This argument has been carried over in modern libertarian writing.[11]

This form of argument is equally applicable to substate private governments. If one finds oneself subject to private government—a state of republican unfreedom—one can enhance one's freedom by placing negative liberty constraints on the power of one's private governors to order one around or impose sanctions on one's refusal to comply. This may involve state regulation of private governments. For example, a state's imposition of a requirement on employers that they refrain from discriminating against employees on the basis of their sexual orientation or identity enhances the republican and negative freedom of workers to express their sexual identities and choose their sexual and life partners. It also enhances their positive liberties, by enabling more people to move out of the closet, and thereby increasing opportunities for LGBT people to engage with others of like sexual orientation. The state's imposition of negative liberty constraints on some people can thereby enhance all three liberties of many more.

Private government is, thus, a perfectly coherent concept. To grasp it, we need to reject the false narrowing of the scope of government to the state, recognize that one's liberty can be constrained by private governors in domains of activity kept private from the state, and that increased state constraints on people's negative liberties can generate massive net gains in individual positive and republican freedoms. It can even generate net gains in their negative liberties, to the extent that the people being constrained by the state are private governors over others.

WORKPLACE GOVERNMENT AND THE
THEORY OF THE FIRM AS IDEOLOGICAL BLINDER

Employees are pervasively subject to private government, as I have defined it. Why is this so? As far as the legal authority of the employer to govern employees was concerned, the Industrial Revolution did not mark a significant break. Legally speaking, employers have always been authoritarian rulers, as an extension of their patriarchal rights to govern their households.

The Industrial Revolution moved the primary site of paid work from the household to the factory. In principle, this could have been a liberating moment, insofar as it opened the possibility of separating the governance of the workplace from the governance of the home. Yet industrial employers retained their legal entitlement to govern their employees' domestic lives. In the early twentieth century, the Ford Motor Company established a Sociological Department, dedicated to inspecting employees' homes unannounced, to ensure that they were leading orderly lives. Workers were eligible for Ford's famous $5 daily wage only if they kept their homes clean, ate diets deemed healthy, abstained from drinking, used the bathtub appropriately, did not take in boarders, avoided spending too much on foreign relatives, and were assimilated to American cultural norms.[12]

Workers today might breathe a sigh of relief, except that most are still subject to employer governance of their private lives. In some cases this is explicit, as in employer-provided health insurance plans. Under the Affordable Care Act, employers may impose a 30 percent premium penalty on covered workers if they do not comply with employer-imposed wellness programs, which may prescribe exercise programs, diets, and abstinence from alcohol and other substances. In accordance with this provision, Penn State University recently threatened to impose a $100 per month surcharge on workers who did not answer a health survey that included questions about their marital situation, sexual conduct, pregnancy plans, and personal finances.[13] In other cases, employer authority over workers' off-duty lives is implicit, a byproduct of the employment-at-will rule: since employers may fire workers for any or no reason, they may fire them for their sexual activities, partner choice, or any other choice workers think of as private from their employer, unless the state has enacted a law specifically forbidding employer discrimination on these grounds. Workplace authoritarianism is still with us.

The pro-market egalitarian aspiration toward nearly universal self-employment aimed to liberate workers from such governance by opening opportunities for nearly everyone to become their own boss. Why did it fail? Why are workers subject to dictatorship? Within economics, the theory of the firm is supposed to answer this question. It purports to offer politically neutral, technical, economic reasons why most production is undertaken by hierarchical organizations, with workers subordinate to bosses, rather than by autonomous individual workers. The theory of the firm contains important insights into the organization of production in advanced economies. However, it fails to explain the sweeping scope of authority that employers have over workers. What is worse, its practitioners sometimes even *deny* that workers lie under the authority of their bosses, in terms that reflect and reinforce an illusion of workers' freedom that also characterizes much of public discourse. Both the theory of the firm, and public discourse, are missing an important reality: that workers are subject to their employers' *private government*.

The pro-market egalitarian dream failed in part due to economies of scale. The technological changes that drove the Industrial Revolution involved huge concentrations of capital. A steam-powered cotton mill, steel foundry, cement or chemical factory, or railway must be worked by many hands. The case is no different for modern workplaces such as airports, hospitals, pharmaceutical labs, and computer assembly factories, as well as lower-tech workplaces such as amusement parks, slaughterhouses, conference hotels, and big-box retail stores. The greater efficiency of production using large, indivisible capital inputs explains why few individual workers can afford to supply their own capital. It explains why, contrary to the pro-market egalitarian hope, the enterprises responsible for most production are not sole proprietorships.

But economies of scale do not explain why production is not managed by independent contractors acting without external supervision, who rent their capital. One could imagine a manufacturing enterprise renting its floor space and machinery and supplying materials to a set of self-employed independent contractors. Each contractor would produce a part or stage of the product for sale to contractors at the next stage of production. The final contractor would sell the finished product to wholesalers, or perhaps back to the capital supplier. Some New England factories operated on a system like this from the Civil War to World War I. They were superseded by hierarchically organized firms. According to the theory of the firm, this is due to the excessive costs of contracting between suppliers of factors of production.[14] In the failed New England system, independent contractors faced each other in a series of bilateral monopolies, which led to opportunistic negotiations. The demand to periodically renegotiate rates led contractors to hoard information and delay innovation for strategic reasons. Independent contractors wore out the machinery too quickly, failed to tightly coordinate their production with workers at other stages of production (leading to excess inventory of intermediate products), and lacked incentives to innovate, both with respect to saving materials and with respect to new products.[15]

The modern firm solves these problems by replacing contractual relations among workers, and between workers and owners of other factors of production with centralized authority. A manager, or hierarchy of managers, issues orders to workers in pursuit of centralized objectives. This enables close coordination of different workers and internalizes the benefits of all types of innovation within the firm as a whole. Managers can monitor workers to ensure that they work hard, cooperate with fellow workers, and do not waste capital. Because they exercise open-ended authority over workers, they can redeploy workers' efforts as needed to implement innovations, replace absentees, and deal with unforeseen difficulties. Authority relations eliminate the costs associated with constant negotiation and contracting among the participants in the firm's production. To put the point another way, the key to the superior efficiency of hierarchy is the open-ended authority of managers. It is impossible to specify in advance all of the contingencies that may require an alteration in an initial understanding of what a worker must do. Efficient employment contracts are therefore necessarily incomplete: they do not specify precisely everything a worker might be asked to do.

While this theory explains why firms exist and why they are constituted by hierarchies of authority, it does not explain the sweeping scope of employers' authority over workers in the United States. It does not explain, for example, why employers continue to have authority over workers' off-duty lives, given that their choice of sexual partner, political candidate, or Facebook posting has nothing to do with productive efficiency. Even worse, theorists of the firm appear not to even recognize how authoritarian firm governance is. Major theorists soft-pedal or even deny the very authority they are supposed to be trying to explain.

Consider Ronald Coase, the originator of the theory of the firm. He acknowledges that firms are "islands of conscious power."[16] The employment contract is one in which the worker "agrees to obey the directions of an entrepreneur." But, he insists, "the essence of the contract is that it should only state the limits to the powers of the entrepreneur."[17] This suggests that the limits of the employer's powers are an object of negotiation or at least communication between the parties. In the vast majority of cases, outside the contexts of collective bargaining or for higher-level employees, this is not true. Most workers are hired without any negotiation over the content of the employer's authority, and without a written or oral contract specifying any limits to it. If they receive an employee handbook indicating such limits, the inclusion of a simple disclaimer (which is standard practice) is sufficient to nullify any implied contract exception to at-will employment in most states.[18] No wonder they are shocked and outraged when their boss fires them for being too attractive,[19] for failing to show up at a political rally in support of the boss's favored political candidate,[20] even because their daughter was raped by a friend of the boss.[21]

What, then, determines the scope and limits of the employer's authority, if it is not a meeting of minds of the parties? The state does so, through a complex system of laws—not only labor law, but laws regulating corporate governance, workplace safety, fringe benefits, discrimination, and other matters. In the United States, the default employment contract is employment at will. There are a few exceptions in federal law to this doctrine, notably concerning discrimination, family and medical leave, and labor union activity. For the most part, however, at-will employment, which entitles employers to fire workers for any or no reason, grants the employer sweeping legal authority not only over workers' lives at work but also over their off-duty conduct. Under the employment-at-will baseline, workers, in effect, cede *all* of their rights to their employers, except those specifically guaranteed to them by law, for the duration of the employment relationship. Employers' authority over workers, outside of collective bargaining and a few other contexts, such as university professors' tenure, is sweeping, arbitrary, and unaccountable—not subject to notice, process, or appeal. The *state* has established the constitution of the government of the workplace: it is a form of private government.

Resistance to recognizing this reality appears to be widespread among theorists of the firm. Here, for example, is what Armen Alchian and Harold Demsetz say in their classic paper on the subject:

> It is common to see the firm characterized by the power to settle issues by fiat, by authority, or by disciplinary action . . . . This is delusion. The firm . . . has no power of fiat, no authority, no disciplinary action any different in the slightest degree from ordinary market contracting between any two people. I can "punish" you only by withdrawing future business or by seeking redress in the courts for any failure to honor our exchange agreement. That is exactly all that any employer can do. He can fire or sue, just as I can fire my grocer by stopping purchases from him or sue him for delivering faulty products. What then is the content of the presumed power to manage and assign workers to various tasks? Exactly the same as one little consumer's power to manage and assign his grocer to various tasks. . . . To speak of managing, directing, or assigning workers to various tasks is a deceptive way of noting that the employer continually is involved in renegotiation of contracts on terms that must be acceptable to both parties. Telling an employee to type this letter rather than to file that document is like telling a grocer to sell me this brand of tuna rather than that brand of bread. I have no contract to continue to purchase from the grocer and neither the employer nor the employee is bound by any contractual obligations to continue their relationship.[22]

Alchian and Demsetz appear to be claiming that wherever individuals are free to exit a relationship, authority cannot exist within it. This is like saying that Mussolini was not a dictator, because Italians could emigrate. While emigration rights may give governors an interest in voluntarily restraining their power, such rights hardly dissolve it.[23]

Alternatively, their claim might be that where the only sanctions for disobedience are exile, or a civil suit, authority does not exist. That would come as a surprise to those subject to the innumerable state regulations that are backed only by civil sanctions. Nor would a state regulation lack authority if the only sanction for violating it were to force one out of one's job. Finally, managers have numerous other sanctions at their disposal besides firing and suing: they can and often do demote employees, cut their pay, assign them inconvenient hours or too many or too few hours, assign them more dangerous, dirty, menial, or grueling tasks, increase their pace of work, set them up to fail, and, within very broad limits, humiliate and harass them.

Perhaps the thought is that where consent mediates the relationship between the parties, the relationship cannot be one of subordination to authority. That would be a surprise to the entire social contract tradition, which is precisely about how the people can consent to government. Or is the idea that authority exists only where subordinates obey orders blindly and automatically? But then it exists hardly anywhere. Even the most repressive regimes mostly rely on means besides sheer terror and brainwashing to elicit compliance with their orders, focusing more on persuasion and rewards.

Alchian and Demsetz may be hoodwinked by the superficial symmetry of the employment contract: under employment-at-will, workers, too, may quit for any or no reason. This leads them to represent quitting as equivalent to firing one's boss. But workers have no power to remove the boss from his position within the firm. And quitting often imposes even greater costs on workers than being fired does, for it makes them ineligible for unemployment insurance. It is an odd kind of countervailing power that workers supposedly have to check their bosses' power, when they typically suffer more from imposing it than they would suffer from the worst sanction bosses can impose on them. Threats, to be effective, need to be credible.

The irony is that Alchian and Demsetz are offering a theory of the firm. The question the theory is supposed to answer is why production is not handled entirely by market transactions among independent, self-employed people, but rather by authority relations. That is, it is supposed to explain why the hope of pro-market pre–Industrial Revolution egalitarians did not pan out. Alchian and Demsetz cannot bear the full authoritarian implications of recognizing the boundary between the market and the firm, even in a paper devoted to explaining it. So they attempt to extend the metaphor of the market to the internal relations of the firm and pretend that every interaction at work is mediated by negotiation between managers and workers. Yet the whole point of the firm, according to the theory, is to eliminate the costs of markets—of setting internal prices via negotiation over every transaction among workers and between workers and managers.

Alchian and Demsetz are hardly alone. Michael Jensen and William Meckling agree with them that authority has nothing to do with the firm; it is merely a nexus of contracts among independent individuals.[24] John Tomasi, writing today, continues to promote the image of employees as akin to independent contractors, freely negotiating the terms of their contract with their employers, to obtain work conditions tailor-made to their idiosyncratic specifications.[25] While workers at the top of the corporate hierarchy enjoy such freedom, as well as a handful of elite athletes, entertainers, and star academics, Tomasi ignores the fact that the vast majority of workers not represented by unions do not negotiate terms of the employer's authority at all. Why would employers bother, when, by state fiat, workers automatically cede all liberties not reserved to them by the state, upon accepting an offer of work?

Not just theorists of the firm, but public discourse too, tend to represent employees as if they were independent contractors.[26] This makes it seem as if the workplace is a continuation of arms-length market transactions, as if the labor contract were no different from a purchase from Smith's butcher, baker, or brewer. Alchian and Demsetz are explicit about this, in drawing the analogy of the employment relation with the customer–grocer relation. But the butcher, baker, and brewer remain independent from their customers after selling their goods. In the employment contract, by contrast, the workers cannot separate themselves from the labor they have sold; in purchasing command over labor, employers purchase command over people.

What accounts for this error? The answer is, in part, that a representation of what egalitarians hoped market society would deliver for workers before the Industrial Revolution has been blindly carried over to the post–Industrial Revolution world. People continue to deploy the same justification of market society—that it would secure the personal independence of workers from arbitrary authority—long after it failed to deliver on its original aspiration. The result is a kind of political hemiagnosia: like those patients who cannot perceive one half of their bodies, a large class of libertarian-leaning thinkers and politicians, with considerable public following, cannot perceive half of the economy: they cannot perceive the half that takes place *beyond* the market, *after* the employment contract is accepted.

This tendency was reinforced by a narrowing of egalitarian vision in the transition to the Industrial Revolution. While the Levellers and other radicals of the mid-seventeenth century agitated against all kinds of arbitrary government, Thomas Paine mainly narrowed his critique to state abuses. Similarly, the Republican Party kept speaking mainly on behalf of the interests of businesspeople and those who hoped to be in business for themselves, even after it was clear that the overwhelming majority of workers had no realistic prospect of attaining this status, and that the most influential businesspeople were not, as Lincoln hoped, sole proprietors (with at most a few employees, the majority of whom were destined to rise to self-employed status after a few years), but managers in large organizations, governing workers destined to be wage laborers for their entire working lives. Thus, a political agenda that once promised equalizing as well as liberating outcomes turned into one that reinforced private, arbitrary, unaccountable government over the vast majority.

Finally, nineteenth-century laissez-faire liberals, with their bizarre combination of hostility toward state power and enthusiasm for hyperdisciplinary total institutions, attempted to reconcile these contradictory tendencies by limiting their focus to the entry and exit conditions of the labor contract, while blackboxing what actually went on in the factories. In fact, they did drive a dramatic improvement in workers' freedom of entry and exit.[27] Under the traditional common law of master and servant, employees were bound to their employers by contracts of one year (apprentices and indentured servants for longer), could quit before then only on pain of losing all their accrued wages, and were not entitled to keep wages from moonlighting. Other employers were forbidden to bid for their labor while they were still under contract.[28] Workers were liberated from these constraints over the course of the nineteenth century.[29]

This liberation, as is well-known, was a double-edged sword. Employers, too, were liberated from any obligation to employ workers. As already noted, the worst the workers could do to the boss often involved suffering at least as much as the worst the boss could do to them. For the bulk of workers, who lived at the bottom of the hierarchy, this was not much of a threat advantage, unless it was exercised collectively in a strike. They had no realistic hope under these conditions for liberation from workplace authoritarianism.

No wonder a central struggle of British workers in the mid-nineteenth century was for limits on the length of the working day—even more than for higher wages. This was true, even though workers at this period of the Industrial Revolution were suffering through "Engels's pause"—the first fifty to sixty years of the Industrial Revolution during which wages failed to grow.[30] My focus, like theirs, is not on issues of wages or distributive justice. It is on workers' freedom. If the Industrial Revolution meant they could not be their own bosses at work, at least they could try to limit the length of the working day so that they would have some hours during which they could choose for themselves, rather than follow someone else's orders.[31]

That was an immediate aim of European workers' movements in the mid-nineteenth century. As the century unfolded, workers largely abandoned their pro-market, individualistic egalitarian dream and turned to socialist, collectivist alternatives—that is, to restructuring the internal governance of the workplace. The problem was that the options open to workers consisted almost exclusively of private governments. Laissez-faire liberals, touting the freedom of the free market, told workers: choose your Leviathan. That is like telling the citizens of the Communist bloc of Eastern Europe that their freedom could be secured by a right to emigrate to any country—as long as they stayed behind the Iron Curtain. Population movements would likely have put some pressure on Communist rulers to soften their rule. But why should Leviathan set the baseline against which competition took place? No liberal or libertarian would be satisfied with a competitive equilibrium set against this baseline, where the choice of state governments is concerned. Workers' movements rejected it for nonstate governments as well.

To their objection, libertarians and laissez-faire liberals had no credible answer. Let us not fool ourselves into supposing that the competitive equilibrium of labor relations was ever established by politically neutral market forces mediated by pure freedom of contract, with nothing but the free play of individuals' idiosyncratic preferences determining the outcome. This is a delusion as great as the one that imagines that the workplace is not authoritarian. Every competitive equilibrium is established against a background assignment of property rights and other rights established by the state. The state supplies the indispensable legal infrastructure of developed economies as a kind of public good, and is needed to do so to facilitate cooperation on the vast scales that characterize today's rich and sophisticated economies.[32] Thus, it is the state that establishes the default constitution of workplace governance. It is a form of authoritarian, private government, in which, under employment-at-will, workers cede *all* their rights to their employers, except those specifically reserved for them by law.

Freedom of entry and exit from any employment relation is not sufficient to justify the outcome. To see this, consider an analogous case for the law of coverture, which the state had long established as the default marriage contract.[33] Under coverture, a woman, upon marrying her husband, lost all rights to own property and make contracts in her own name. Her husband had the right to confine her movements, confiscate any wages she might earn, beat her, and rape her. Divorce was very difficult to obtain. The marriage contract was valid only if voluntarily accepted by both parties. It was a contract into subjection, entailing the wife's submission to the private government of her husband. Imagine a modification of this patriarchal governance regime, allowing either spouse to divorce at will and allowing any clause of the default contract to be altered by a prenuptial agreement. This is like the modification that laissez-faire liberals added to the private government of the workplace. Women would certainly have sufficient reason to object that their liberties would still not be respected under this modification, in that it preserves a patriarchal baseline, in which men still hold virtually all the cards. It would allow a lucky few to escape subjection to their husbands, but that is not enough to justify the patriarchal authority the vast majority of men would retain over their wives.[34] Consent to an option within a set cannot justify the option set itself.

BACK TO THE FUTURE

My historical investigation explains why a certain libertarian way of thinking about market society and its promise made considerable sense in its original context prior to the Industrial Revolution, and why it was reasonable for egalitarians to support it at that time. But the Industrial Revolution destroyed the context in which that vision made sense. The new context perverted what was once a liberating, egalitarian vision into support for pervasive workplace authoritarianism—arbitrary, hierarchical, private government. The evolving rhetoric of laissez-faire liberalism that arose in the nineteenth century papered over the real issues and represented, in Orwellian fashion, subjection as freedom.

Workers' movements from the mid-nineteenth century through World War II were not fooled by this.[35] That is not to say that they all had sound ideas for how to solve the problem. I have no space to recount the follies of democratic state socialism.[36] Nor do I have space to recount the catastrophes of state communism, which were dominated by the same totalitarian vision of the original designers of total institutions—only dramatically scaled up, more violent, and unmixed with any skepticism about state power. Like the original designers, state communists looked to ideals of neither liberty nor equality, but rather to utilitarian progress and the perfectibility of human beings under the force of private government.

My point is rather that, with the drastic decline of organized labor, and especially with the triumph of ostensibly free markets since the end of the Cold War, public and academic discourse has largely lost sight of the problem that organized workers in the nineteenth century saw clearly: the pervasiveness of private government at work. Here most of us are, toiling under the authority of communist dictators, and we do not see the reality for what it is.

No doubt many of us, especially most of those who are reading these lectures, do not find the situation so bad. My readers, most likely, are tenured or tenure-track professors, who, almost uniquely among unorganized workers in the United States, enjoy due process rights and a level of autonomy at work that is unmatched almost anywhere else among employees.[37] Or, if they are college students or graduates, they are or likely will be the dictators or higher-ranked officials of private governments. Or they will escape the system and belong to the thin ranks of the self-employed who have no employees of their own. The people I am worried about are the 25 percent of employees who understand that they are subject to dictatorship at work,[38] and the other 55 percent or so who are neither securely self-employed nor upper-level managers, nor the tiny elite tier of nonmanagerial stars (athletes, entertainers, superstar academics) who have the power to dictate employment contracts to their specification, nor even the ever-shrinking class of workers under ever-retrenching collective bargaining agreements. That 55 percent is only one arbitrary and oppressive managerial decision away from realizing what the 25 percent already know. But this 80 percent receives almost no recognition in contemporary public and academic discourse.

I do not claim that private governments at work are as powerful as states. Their sanctioning powers are lower, and the costs of emigration from oppressive private governments are generally lower than the costs of emigration from states. Yet private governments impose a far more minute, exacting, and sweeping regulation of employees than democratic states do in any domain outside of prisons and the military. Private governments impose controls on workers that are unconstitutional for democratic states to impose on citizens who are not convicts or in the military.

The negative liberties most workers enjoy de facto are considerably greater than the ones they are legally entitled to under their employers.

Market pressures, social norms, lack of interest, and simple decency keep most employers from exercising the full scope of their authority. We should care nevertheless about the insecurity of employees' liberty. They work in a state of republican unfreedom, their liberties vulnerable to cancellation without justification, notice, process, or appeal. That they enjoy substantially greater negative liberty than they are legally entitled to no more justifies their lack of republican liberty than the fact that most wives enjoyed greater freedoms than they were legally entitled to justified coverture—or even coverture modified by free divorce.

Suppose people find themselves under private government. This is a state of republican unfreedom, of subjection to the arbitrary will of another. It is also usually a state of substantial constraints on negative liberty. By what means could people attain their freedom? One way would be to end subjection to government altogether. When the government is a state, this is the anarchist answer. We have seen that when the government is an employer, the answer of many egalitarians before the Industrial Revolution was to advance a property regime that promotes self-employment, perhaps even to make self-employment a nearly universally accessible opportunity, at least for men. This amounts to promoting anarchy as the primary form of workplace order.

The theory of the firm explains why this approach cannot preserve the productive advantages of large-scale production. Some kind of incompletely specified authority over groups of workers is needed to replace market relations within the firm. However, the theory of the firm, although it explains the necessity of hierarchy, neither explains nor justifies private government in the workplace. That the constitution of workplace government is both arbitrary and dictatorial is not dictated by efficiency or freedom of contract, but rather by the state. Freedom of contract no more explains the equilibrium workplace constitution than freedom to marry explained women's subjection to patriarchy under coverture.

In other words, in the great contest between individualism and collectivism regarding the mode of production, collectivism won, decisively. Now nearly all production is undertaken by teams of workers using large, indivisible forms of capital equipment held in common. The activities of these teams are governed by managers according to a centralized production plan. This was an outcome of the Industrial Revolution, and equally much embraced by capitalists and socialists. That advocates of capitalism continue to speak as if their preferred system of production upholds "individualism" is simply a symptom of institutional hemiagnosia, the misdeployment of a hopeful preindustrial vision of what market society would deliver as if it described our current reality, which replaces market relations with governance relations across wide domains of production.

Workers in the nineteenth century turned from individualistic to collectivist solutions to workplace governance because they saw that interpersonal authority—governments over groups of workers—was inescapable in the new industrial order. If government is inescapable or necessary for solving certain important problems, the only way to make people free under that government is to make that government a public thing, accountable to the governed. The task is to replace private government with public government.

When the government is a state, we have some fairly good ideas of how to proceed: the entire history of democracy under the rule of law is a series of experiments in how to make the government of the state a public thing, and the people free under the state. These experiments continue to this day.

But what if the government is an employer? Here matters are more uncertain. There are four general strategies for advancing and protecting the liberties and interests of the governed under any type of government: (1) exit, (2) the rule of law, (3) substantive constitutional rights, and (4) voice. Let us consider each in turn.

Exit is usually touted as a prime libertarian strategy for protecting individual rights. By forcing governments to compete for subjects, exit rights put pressure on governments to offer their subjects better deals. "The defense against oppressive hours, pay, working conditions, or treatment is the right to change employers."[39] Given this fact, it is surprising how comfortable some libertarians are with the validity of contracts into slavery, from which exit is disallowed.[40] In their view, freedom of contract trumps the freedom of individuals under government, or even the freedom to leave that government. While contracts into slavery and peonage are no longer valid, other contractual barriers to exit are common and growing. Noncompete clauses, which bar employees from working for other employers in the same industry for a period of years, have spread from technical professions (where nearly half of employees are subject to them) to jobs such as sandwich maker, pesticide sprayer, summer camp counselor, and hairstylist.[41] While employers can no longer hold workers in bondage, they can imprison workers' human capital. California is one of the few states that prohibit noncompete clauses. As the dynamism of its economy proves, such contractual barriers to exit are not needed for economic growth, and probably undermine it.[42] There should be a strong legal presumption against such barriers to exit, to protect workers' freedom to exit their employers' government.

The rule of law is a complex ideal encompassing several protections of subjects' liberties. (a) Authority may be exercised only through laws duly passed and publicized in advance, rather than arbitrary orders issued without any process. (b) Subjects are at liberty to do anything not specifically prohibited by law. (c) Laws are generally applicable to everyone in similar circumstances. (d) Subjects have rights of due process before suffering any sanctions for noncompliance. Not all of these protections, which were devised with state authority in mind, can be readily transferred to the employment context. Most of the solutions to problems the state must address involve regulations that leave open to individuals a vast array of options for selecting both ends and means. By contrast, efficient production nearly always requires close coordination of activities according to centralized objectives, directed by managers exercising discretionary authority. This frequently entails that the authority of managers over workers be both intensive (limiting workers to highly particular movements and words, not allowing them to pursue their own personal objectives at work or even to select their own means to a prescribed end) and incompletely specified. The state imposes traffic laws that leave people free to choose their own destinations, routes, and purposes. Walmart tells its drivers what they have to pick up, when and where they have to deliver it, and what route they have to take. In addition, managers need incompletely specified authority to rapidly reassign different tasks to different workers to address new circumstances. Finally, excessively costly procedural protections against firing also discourage hiring. All these obstacles to applying rule-of-law protections in the workplace empower employers to abuse their authority, subject workers to humiliating treatment, and impose excessive constraints on their freedom.

At the same time, it is easy to exaggerate the obstacles to imposing rule-of-law protections at work. Larger organizations generally have employee handbooks and standard practice guides that streamline authority along legalistic lines. Equal protection and due process rights already exist for workers in larger organizations with respect to limited issues. A worker who has been sexually harassed by her boss normally has recourse to intrafirm procedures for resolving her complaint. Such protections reflect a worldwide "blurring of boundaries" among business, nonprofit, and state organizations, which appears to be driven not simply by legal changes, but by cultural imperatives of scientific management and ideas of individual rights and organizational responsibilities.[43] Some but not all of these managerial developments are salutary. They are proper subjects of investigation for political theory, once we get beyond the subject's narrow focus on the state.

A just workplace constitution should incorporate basic constitutional rights, akin to a bill of rights against employers. To some extent, the Fair Labor Standards Act, antidiscrimination laws, and other workplace regulations already serve this function. A workers' bill of rights could be strengthened by the addition of more robust protections of workers' freedom to engage in off-duty activities, such as exercising their political rights, free speech,[44] and sexual choices. Similar protections for employee privacy could be extended in the workplace during work breaks. The Occupational Safety and Healthy Administration (OSHA) prohibitions of particularly degrading, dangerous, and onerous working conditions can be viewed as part of a workers' bill of rights. Nabisco once threatened its female production line workers with three day suspensions for using the bathroom, and ordered them to urinate in their clothes instead.[45] It was only in 1998 that OSHA issued a regulation requiring employers to recognize workers' right to use a bathroom, after cases such as Nabisco's aroused public outrage. Workers in Europe are protected from harassment of all kinds by anti-mobbing laws.[46] This gives them far more robust workplace constitutional rights than workers in the United States, who may be legally harassed as long as their harassers do not discriminate by race, gender, or other protected identities in choosing their victims.

There are limits, however, to how far a bill of rights can go in protecting workers from abuse. Because they prescribe uniformity across workplaces, they can at best offer a minimal floor. In practice, they are also grossly underenforced for the least advantaged workers.[47] Furthermore, such laws do not provide for worker participation in governance at the firm level. They merely impose limits on employer dictatorship.

For these reasons, there is no adequate substitute for recognizing workers' voice in their government. Voice can more readily adapt workplace rules to local conditions than state regulations can, while incorporating respect for workers' freedom, interests, and dignity. Just because workplace governance requires a hierarchy of offices does not mean that higher officeholders must be unaccountable to the governed, or that the governed should not play any role in managerial decision making. In the United States, two models for workers' voice have received the most attention: workplace democracy and labor unions. Workplace democracy, in the form of worker-owned and -managed firms, has long stood as an ideal for many egalitarians.[48] While much could be done to devise laws more accommodating of this structure, some of its costs may be difficult to surmount. In particular, the costs of negotiation among workers with asymmetrical interests (for example, due to possession of different skills) appear to be high.[49]

In the United States, collective bargaining has been the primary way workers have secured voice within the government of the workplace. However, even at its peak in 1954, only 28.3 percent of workers were represented by a labor union.[50] Today, only 11.1 percent of all workers and 6.6 percent of private sector workers, are represented.[51] Although laws could be revised to make it easier for workers to organize into a union, this does not address difficulties inherent to the U.S. labor union model. The U.S. model organizes workers at the firm level rather than the industry level. Firms vigorously resist unionization to avoid a competitive disadvantage with nonunionized firms.[52] Labor unions also impose inefficiencies due to their monopoly power.[53] They also take an adversarial stance toward management—one that makes not only managers but many workers uncomfortable. At the same time, they often provide the only effective voice employees have in workplace governance.

It is possible to design a workplace constitution in which workers have a nonadversarial voice in workplace governance, without raising concerns about monopolization. The overwhelming majority of workers in the United States would like to have such a voice: 85 percent would like firm governance to be "run jointly" by management and workers.[54] In the United States, such a constitution is illegal under the National Labor Relations Act, which prohibits company unions. Yet this structure is commonplace in Europe. Germany's system of codetermination, begun in the Weimar era and elaborately developed since World War II, offers one highly successful model.[55]

It is not my intention in this lecture to defend any particular model of worker participation in firm governance. My point is rather to expose a deep failure in current ways of thinking about how government fits into Americans' lives. We do not live in the market society imagined by Paine and Lincoln, which offered an appealing vision of what a free society of equals would look like, combining individualistic libertarian and egalitarian ideals. Government is everywhere, not just in the form of the state, but even more pervasively in the workplace. Yet public discourse and much of political theory pretends that this is not so. It pretends that the constitution of workplace government is somehow the object of voluntary negotiation between workers and employers. This is true only for a tiny proportion of privileged workers. The vast majority are subject to private, authoritarian government, not through their own choice, but through laws that have handed nearly all authority to their employers.

It is high time that public discourse acknowledged this reality and the costs to workers' freedom and dignity that private government imposes on them. It is high time that political theorists turned their attention to the private governments of the workplace. Since the Levellers, egalitarian social movements have insisted that if government is necessary, it must be made a public thing to all the governed—accountable to them, responsive to their interests, and open to their participation. They were shrewd enough to recognize the pervasiveness of private government in their lives. It is time to go back to the future in recovering such recognition and experimenting with ways to remedy it.

NOTES

1. This is true of the corporate form. Legally, the corporation, *not* the shareholders, owns the firm's assets. In a partnership, an oligarchy governs and owns all the assets.

2. R. H. Coase, "The Nature of the Firm," *Economica* 4, no. 16 (1937): 386–405.

3. Eugene Volokh, "Private Employees' Speech and Political Activity: Statutory Protection against Employer Retaliation" (2012), http://ssrn.com/abstract=2174776/.

4. Ken Cuccinelli, *The Last Line of Defense: The New Fight for American Liberty* (New York: Crown Forum, 2013), 52, 231.

5. This may sound like a positivist account of *law*. But government need not rule by law—that is, general rules of conduct. It can rule by orders or decrees, issued ad hoc to particular persons for particular occasions. I take no stand here regarding a positivist account of law.

6. Max Weber, *Economy and Society*, edited by Guenther Roth and Claus Wittich (Berkeley: University of California Press, 1968), 56.

7. John Adams, "Letter to Abigail, April 14, 1776," *Letters of John Adams Addressed to His Wife*, edited by Charles Adams, vol. 1 (Boston: C. C. Little and J. Brown, 1841), 96–97.

8. I draw on Herzog, *Household Politics*, 89–94, who spends more time distinguishing the entailments of privacy than I do here.

9. Here I focus on "external" conceptions of positive freedom in terms of opportunity sets within individuals' budget constraints, legal permissions, and other external conditions. I set aside psychological notions of positive freedom, such as freedom from addictions, compulsions, or other motives with which the agent does not identify.

10. Philip Pettit, *Republicanism: A Theory of Freedom and Government* (New York: Oxford University Press, 1997), 5.

11. See, for example, Milton Friedman, *Capitalism and Freedom* (Chicago: University of Chicago Press, 1962), linking private property to political and not just economic freedom.

12. Joyce Shaw Peterson, *American Automobile Workers, 1900–1933* (Albany: State University of New York Press, 1987), 57, 72.

13. Natasha Singer, "Health Plan Penalty Ends at Penn State," *New York Times*, September 19, 2013, http://www.nytimes.com/2013/09/19/business/after-uproar-penn-state-suspends-penalty-fee-in-wellness-plan.html.

14. Coase, "Nature of the Firm."

15. Oliver Williamson, "Markets and Hierarchies: Some Elementary Considerations," *American Economic Review* 63, no. 2 (1973): 316–25, here 322.

16. Coase, "Nature of the Firm," 388.

17. Ibid., 391.

18. Only fifteen states do not allow a disclaimer to count as a per se defense against a charge of wrongful discharge under an implied-contract exception to employment-at-will; twenty-two states allow disclaimers and limit implied-contract exceptions to written documents; thirteen states do not recognize any implied-contract exception to employment-at-will. Charles Muhl, "The Employment-at-Will Doctrine: Three Major Exceptions," *Monthly Labor Review*, January 2001: 5.

19. *Nelson v. Knight*, Iowa Supreme Court, No. 11-1857, July 12, 2013.

20. Neela Banerjee, "Ohio Miners Say They Were Forced to Attend Romney Rally," *Los Angeles Times*, August 29, 2012, http://articles.latimes.com/2012/aug/29/news/la-pn-miners-romney-rally-20120829/.

21. Dugan Arnett, "Nightmare in Maryville: Teens' Sexual Encounter Ignites a Firestorm against Family," *Kansas City Star*, October 12, 2013, http://www.kansascity.com/2013/10/12/4549775/nightmare-in-maryville-teens-sexual.html.

22. Armen Alchian and Harold Demsetz, "Production, Information Costs, and Economic Organization," *American Economic Review* 62, no. 5 (1972): 777–95, here 777.

23. Even the addition of immigration rights to new governments—something workers do not enjoy at work—does not dissolve their authority. Within the European Union (EU), citizens are guaranteed the right not only to exit, but to enter other member states. Yet this has not eliminated the authority of EU member states.

24. Michael Jensen and William Meckling, "Theory of the Firm: Managerial Behavior, Agency Costs and Ownership Structure," *Journal of Financial Economics* 3 (1976): 305–60, here 310.

25. John Tomasi, *Free Market Fairness* (Princeton, NJ: Princeton University Press, 2012), 23, 77, 81.

26. This tendency facilitates a common abuse of labor law, in which employers pretend that their employees are independent contractors, to avoid minimum wage, maximum hours, benefits and safety regulations, to shift the burden of

employment taxes on their workers, and to force them to pay for equipment and uniforms. The court test in such cases is always whether the employer exercises control over the worker. See, for example, *Alexander v. FedEx Ground Package System*, 2014 U.S. App. LEXIS 16585 (9th Cir. Aug. 27, 2014), which ruled that FedEx misclassified thousands of its California truck drivers as independent contractors.

27. Josiah Wedgwood, a pioneer of the Industrial Revolution in promoting worker discipline in his pottery factory, was also a major abolitionist.

28. Blackstone, *Commentaries*, ch. 14.

29. Karen Orren tells the story for the United States in *Belated Feudalism*. Similar developments took place in other common law countries and the rest of Western Europe during the nineteenth century. An important lesson of her work is that some nineteenth-century labor law legal doctrines in the United States and England that are thought to be novelties of laissez-faire free contract ideology—for example, that an employer could confiscate a worker's entire accrued wage for the slightest insubordination—were in fact merely continuations of English labor laws established in the feudal era. In other words, laissez faire at the level of market relations left feudal authoritarianism intact at the level of intrafirm relations.

30. Robert Allen, "Engel's Pause: A Pessimist's Guide to the British Industrial Revolution," *Explorations in Economic History* 46, no. 4 (2009): 418–35.

31. Under employment-at-will, the legal reach of employers' authority extended to the entire day, as it still does today except when expressly limited by law, or, in fifteen states, by contract. However, for practical purposes, the separation of the workplace from the home substantially raised the costs and reduced the benefits to many employers of reaching that far, and thereby opened up room for workers to enjoy freedom from their bosses when off duty.

32. As I argue in Elizabeth Anderson, "Equality and Freedom in the Workplace: Recovering Republican Insights," *Social Philosophy and Policy* 31, no. 2 (2015): 48–69. One consequence of this point is that the traditional libertarian argument that the state should simply stop "interfering" with the economy is misguided: it is like saying that the commissioner of baseball should stop interfering with the game by promulgating its rules. It turns out that, to facilitate efficient cooperation at the vast scales of modern developed economies, the rules have to be remarkably complex. This opens up room both for democratic control in the public interest and regulatory capture.

33. For the classic exposition, see Blackstone, *Commentaries*, ch. 15.

34. As I argue in Anderson, "Equality and Freedom in the Workplace."

35. See, for example, Sidney Pollard, "Factory Discipline in the Industrial Revolution," *Economic History Review* 16, no. 2 (1963): 254–71. He notes the "deliberate or accidental modelling of many [factory] works on workhouses and prisons, a fact well known to the working population" (p. 254). I stress that it did not take Marxists or socialists to see the problem in the terms in which I have presented them. American labor republicans also understood it. See Alex Gourevitch, *From Slavery to the Cooperative Commonwealth: Labor and*

Republican Liberty in the Nineteenth Century (New York: Cambridge University Press, 2015).

36. Most famously, the inability of comprehensive centralized planning to use the information needed to allocate resources efficiently. See Friedrich A. Hayek, "The Use of Knowledge in Society," *American Economic Review* 35 (1945): 519–30.

37. Those of you who are adjunct or contingent faculty, on the other hand, understand firsthand what I am talking about.

38. Workplace Democracy Association, "Zogby Poll: As Independence Day Nears, Workplace Democracy Association Survey Finds One in Four Working Americans Describe Their Employer as a 'Dictatorship,'" June 23, 2008, https://workplacedemocracy.wordpress.com/2008/06/23/workplace-democracy-survey/.

39. *Pollock v. Williams*, 322 U.S. 4, at 18 (1944). In this opinion, Justice Jackson, writing for the Supreme Court, struck down a Florida statute criminalizing failure to specifically perform a labor contract on which an advance was made, as contrary to the Thirteenth Amendment prohibition on involuntary servitude. Note the late date of the decision. Risa Goluboff, "The Thirteenth Amendment and a New Deal for Civil Rights," in *The Promises of Liberty: The History and Contemporary Relevance of the Thirteenth Amendment*, edited by Alexander Tsesis (New York: Columbia University Press, 2010), 119–37, explains how Jackson's reasoning reflected New Deal (positive liberty) rather than *Lochner*-era freedom of contract (negative liberty) principles.

40. See Robert Nozick, *Anarchy, State, and Utopia* (New York: Basic Books, 1974), 331; Walter Block, "Toward a Libertarian Theory of Inalienability: A Critique of Rothbard, Barnett, Smith, Kinsella, Gordon, and Epstein," *Journal of Libertarian Studies* 17, no. 2 (2003): 39–85; Stephen Kershnar, "A Liberal Argument for Slavery," *Journal of Social Philosophy* 34, no. 4 (2003): 510–36. For libertarians opposed to the validity of slave contracts, see Murray Rothbard, *The Ethics of Liberty*, rev. ed. (New York: New York University Press, 1998), 40–41; Randy Barnett, "Contract Remedies and Inalienable Rights," *Social Philosophy and Policy* 4, no. 1 (1986): 179–202.

41. Matt Marx, "The Firm Strikes Back: Non-Compete Agreements and the Mobility of Technical Professionals," *American Sociological Review* 76, no. 5 (2011): 695–712; Steven Greenhouse, "Noncompete Clauses Increasingly Pop Up in Array of Jobs," *New York Times*, June 8, 2014, http://www.nytimes.com/2014/06/09/business/noncompete-clauses-increasingly-pop-up-in-array-of-jobs.html; Clare O'Connor, "Does Jimmy John's Non-Compete Clause For Sandwich Makers Have Legal Legs?" *Forbes*, October 15, 2014, http://www.forbes.com/sites/clareoconnor/2014/10/15/does-jimmy-johns-non-compete-clause-for-sandwich-makers-have-legal-legs/.

42. Orly Lobel, *Talent Wants to Be Free: Why We Should Learn to Love Leaks, Raids, and Free Riding* (New Haven, CT: Yale University Press, 2013).

43. Patricia Bromley and John Meyer, "'They Are All Organizations': The Cultural Roots of Blurring Between the Nonprofit, Business, and Government Sectors," *Administration & Society* (2014), DOI: 10.1177/0095399714548268.

44. There may be legitimate limits to this for higher-ranked managers and press agents who are regarded as official spokespersons for their firms. It is one thing to fire an ordinary Pepsi worker for drinking Coke on the job (Suzanne Presto, "Coke Employee Fired for Drinking Pepsi on the Job," *CNN Money*, June 16 2003, http://money.cnn.com/2003/06/13/news/funny/coke_pepsi/index.htm), and quite another for the CEO of Pepsi to publicly disparage Pepsi in comparison to Coke.

45. Mark Linder and Ingrid Nygaard, *Void Where Prohibited: Rest Breaks and the Right to Urinate on Company Time* (Ithaca, NY: ILR Press, 1998), 46.

46. James Whitman and Gabrielle Friedman, "The European Transformation of Harassment Law," *Columbia Journal of European Law* 9 (2002–2003): 241–74.

47. Cynthia Estlund, "Why Workers Still Need a Collective Voice in the Era of Norms and Mandates," *Research Handbook on the Economics of Labor and Employment Law*, edited by Cynthia Estlund and Michael Wachter, 463–90 (Northampton, MA: Edward Elgar, 2013), 470–71.

48. See John Stuart Mill, *Principles of Political Economy*, edited by J. M. Robson (Toronto: University of Toronto Press, 1965), vol. 3 of *Collected Works of John Stuart Mill*, ch. 7, for a classic defense in the liberal tradition. For a contemporary economic view, see Samuel Bowles, Herbert Gintis, and Bo Gustafsson, eds., *Markets and Democracy: Participation, Accountability, and Efficiency* (Cambridge: Cambridge University Press, 1993).

49. See Henry Hansmann, "Employee Ownership of Firms," in *The New Palgrave Dictionary of Economics and Law*, edited by Peter Newman, vol. 2 (London: MacMillan, 1998), 43–47, 45–46. I thank Steve Nayak-Young for this reference.

50. Gerald Mayer, *Union Membership Trends in the U.S.* (Washington, DC: Congressional Research Service, 2004), iv, http://digitalcommons.ilr.cornell.edu/cgi/viewcontent.cgi?article=1176&context=key_workplace.

51. Bureau of Labor Statistics, *Union Members—2014*, USDL-15-0072 (2015), 1, http://www.bls.gov/news.release/pdf/union2.pdf.

52. By contrast, in Europe, unions often deliver benefits to workers across entire industries, and often to workers as a whole, even when their membership is only a small proportion of all workers. For international comparisons, see Jelle Visser, *ICTWSS: Database on Institutional Characteristics of Trade Unions, Wage Setting, State Intervention and Social Pacts in 34 Countries Between 1960 and 2012* (Amsterdam: Amsterdam Institute for Advanced Labour Studies (AIAS), 2013), http://www.uva-aias.net/208/.

53. It does not follow that nonunionized firms are free from monopoly. Monopsonistic conditions are pervasive in labor markets. Alan Manning, *Monopsony in Motion: Imperfect Competition in Labor Markets* (Princeton, NJ: Princeton University Press, 2003).

54. Richard B. Freeman and Joel Rogers, *What Workers Want* (Ithaca, NY: ILR Press; New York: Russell Sage Foundation, 2006), 84.

55. For a brief introduction to Germany's system of works councils, see Rebecca Page, *Co-Determination in Germany: A Beginners' Guide* (Düsseldorf: Hans-Böckler-Stiftung, 2009).

Human Values in an Age of Change

MARGARET ATWOOD

The Tanner Lectures in Human Values

Delivered at

University of Utah
March 25, 2015

A winner of many international literary awards, including the prestigious Booker Prize, MARGARET ATWOOD is the author of more than forty volumes of poetry, children's literature, fiction, and nonfiction. She is perhaps best known for her novels, which include *The Edible Woman*, *The Handmaid's Tale*, *The Robber Bride*, *Alias Grace*, *The Blind Assassin*, *Oryx and Crake*, and *The Year of the Flood*. Her nonfiction book *Payback: Debt and the Shadow Side of Wealth*, part of the Massey Lecture series, was made into a documentary. Her recent novel, *Madaddam* (the third novel in the Oryx and Crake trilogy), has received rave reviews: "An extraordinary achievement" (the *Independent*); "A fitting and joyous conclusion" (the *New York Times*). The trilogy is being adapted into an HBO TV series by celebrated filmmaker Darren Aronofsky. Atwood's most recent collection of short stories is *Stone Mattress*. Her new novel, *The Heart Goes Last*, was published in September 2015 by Random House.

Atwood's work has been published in more than forty languages, including Farsi, Japanese, Turkish, Finnish, Korean, Icelandic, and Estonian. In 2004, she coinvented the LongPen, a remote signing device that allows someone to write in ink anywhere in the world via tablet PC and the Internet. She is also a popular personality on Twitter, with over 750,000 followers.

Atwood was born in 1939 in Ottawa and grew up in northern Ontario, Quebec, and Toronto. She received her undergraduate degree from Victoria College at the University of Toronto and her master's degree from Radcliffe College.

I am very honored to be here with you today. It is gratifying that you think I could have something to say that might be, marginally, at least, worth hearing. The topic I was asked to speak about is, however, somewhat daunting—"Human Values in an Age of Change." Yikes, as those of my generation used to say. Given the choice between "My Summer Vacation" and "Human Values in an Age of Change" as a high school essay topic, I would have beelined for the summer vacation, snore-making as it would have been, since I certainly would not have written about what I really did on my summer vacation, such as writing stories in the mode of Edgar Allan Poe. But "Human Values in an Age of Change" would have been way too ambitious for me.

I knew what an age of change was—we had just invented the hula hoop, plus Fire and Ice lipstick and oat cereal with holes in it—but human values? What were those? And were they the same as humane values, such as "Don't kick your dog?" I suspected not. For every human value has its evil twin. Such is our fate.

I was already well into the reading of science fiction, and the possibility of beings that shared some human functions but were not human was something that troubled my waking dreams. H. G. Wells's tentacled Martians that relished the drinking of human blood through straws, sort of like a soda, were definitely not human; but what about Ray Bradbury's Martians, or John Wyndham's Chrysalids? Or the thinking, feeling robots of Karl Capek's *R.U.R*? What about Donovan's Brain, that lived in a glass aquarium full of brain food and had brain superpowers, and was intent on manipulating the stock market? What—in other words—are the essential human characteristics, without which we cease to be us? Now that we have opened Pandora's Box, which is the ability to change the human genome and thus alter our own descendants, it seems even more pertinent to ask that question.

I have been recently reprimanded, by the way, for having said that science fiction (as opposed to speculative fiction, which takes place on this planet, with scenarios that are possible now, involving our own species, Homo sapiens)—proper involves things that are not possible and that take place in a galaxy far, far away and in another time, such as talking squids in outer space. It was thought that I was sneering upon these loquacious squids. But such—I protest!—was not at all my intention. What, I ask you, is *wrong* with talking squids in outer space? I for one will be very cross if it is ever proved definitely that outer space contains no talking squids. There are many water planets, and if they harbor life, such life would therefore have to be aquatic; and squids are not unintelligent.

Maybe I should have said "talking octopi," as octopi are very clever indeed. They can take the lids off jars, which is a darn sight more than I can sometimes do these days. A talking squid (or octopus) in outer space is as good a point of departure as any for a consideration of essential human characteristics. This ultra-squid (or octopus) would not talk in the same way that we do, lacking the necessary vocal apparatus, but the possibilities for semaphoric communication are quite good. One tentacle *Yes,* two tentacles *No,* three tentacles *Make that a fish latte,* four tentacles, *Would you like some octopoid sex*? Eight tentacles, *My octopus army with its powerful suckers is now going to rip your puny spaceship to shreds.* The essentials of what needs to be said, as you will immediately recognize. Consensus, nourishment, procreation, and defense. Somebody tell Congress. Better still, elect an octopus. But I digress.

That would be one way of approaching "Human Values in an Age of Change"—via the talking cephalopods. But there are many other ways; because the title is a bit one-size-fits-all generic. In fact it sounds a little like an ad for life insurance, for example: Shot of a granddad playing with the grandkids, with some old-timey music in the background. "Granddad, did you have a photo album when you were young?" "Yes, honey, but it was made of paper." "Paper? What's that? MY photo album is in the Cloud!" "What's the Cloud, honey?" "The Cloud is on my iPad! And you'll always be in my photo album in the Cloud, Granddad!" Indicating that lifestyles we are comfortable recognizing at present will be passed down to the next generations, despite rapid increases in confusing technology, even if granddad croaks. But especially if Granddad, before croaking, has taken out a hefty policy to insure that his descendants can pay their monthly Wi-Fi bills.

Granddad, being no fool despite the fact that he may not immediately know what LMAO means, has conspired with a bunch of other granddads and grandmoms, or maybe just a bunch of dads and moms, or maybe just a bunch of people over the age of thirty, to invite me here to speak to you today. These wise folks suspect I have a foot in both camps—the human values camp, problematic though the notion of an essentialist quality called *human* is rapidly becoming, as increasingly sophisticated androids and biotech baby-designing possibilities hit the radar; and the age of change camp, with its dizzying discoveries and inventions and society-changing technologies and fears of planetary catastrophe.

I can indeed speak to both camps, being one of the few white-haired people on the planet who knows what ROTFL means, thanks to the young people on my Twitter, who obligingly answer questions such as "Is *bad-ass* a good thing or a bad thing?" when I ask them. So thanks, kids. I have learned a lot from you. And thanks, more elderly inviters, whoever you may be. And let's hope I can get through "Human Values in an Age of Change" without having a heart attack and toppling off the podium.

That perked you up! OMG, you may have thought: could she really? An action moment! How awful! How thrilling!

I have just demonstrated one of the first principles of narrative art, which is: introduce uncertainty. Otherwise known as "suspense." Alfred Hitchcock, when asked how long he could have his actors hold a kiss on-screen, said "Two minutes." "Isn't that awfully long?" they asked. "Yes," he replied, "but first I put a bomb under the bed." You have to admit that at my mention of a possible disaster happening to myself, right before your very eyes, you popped awake. Or at least a little more awake than you were before.

Narrative art belongs to one of the essential human-value clusters, by the way. All societies that we know anything about tell stories, and have a group of core stories that they prize above others. Anthropologists have gone about collecting areas of interest and accomplishment that appear to be shared by all human societies we know anything about; these include complex languages, probably our oldest and most powerful technology; symbolic thinking and representation, also very old; singing and music; the visual arts, including body and clothing decoration; food and cooking; the ability to count (but not trigonometry; that's new); dwelling places; children and procreation, gender, and sex; heating and light, or energy sources; toolmaking; beliefs and practices concerning animals; origin stories and religious observances; exchanges, including trading and justice (good for good, bad for bad); and an interest in what happens to people after they die.

Those are some shared human interests. Then there are the values attached to segments of them. The values themselves come in two parts: what we think we ought to do, and what we actually do—by no means always the same. We in this culture hold up monogamy as a virtue. I leave you to imagine how often that value, though respected on the surface, is not practiced in fact.

The details of the values can change from culture to culture (a tassel here, a piece of jade there, a taboo against eating turtles over there, a head covering on the other side, some blue tattoos to the north), but the areas of interest are shared.

How could it be otherwise? What interests us relates to what kind of creature we are. Our interests and our values are inextricably tied to that, and all our stories and all our arts and technologies are utterings (or out-erings) of those interests and values. We never make art or invent new tech that is not an expression of a human wish and our desire to fulfill it, or a human fear and the desire to protect ourselves from it.

Put another way: If we were super-intelligent spiders with the ability to invent and manufacture technologies, including biotechnologies, we would be focused on the development of large, juicy, domesticated flies, and of bottled fly juice, and of super-filament web-enhancers. For male spiders, we would be inventing little suits that would render the male spider invisible and intangible so he could creep up on the female and im-pregnate her without getting eaten.

If, on the other hand, we were super-intelligent ravens, we would be inventing little Swiss army knives that would allow us to open dead car-casses so we would not have to depend on wolves, polar bears, or people to do it for us.

But instead we are a eusocial species of hominids, "eusocial" meaning a species that raises its young over generations, in a nest or fixed location that is therefore defended by more than just a parent or parents caring for offspring, thus forming a society with differentiated roles. We share this quality with ants and bees, and with naked mole rats. Though some would say we are not altruistic enough to be truly eusocial. The jury is out. Still, it would explain some of the things we do on a regular and sometimes de-plorable basis.

Take war.

If you were one of those children who poked anthills with a stick, you will know that there is a set of ant values or imperatives. "Defend the nest" is foremost among these. In ants, that means: (1) when poked with a stick, hide the kids, otherwise known as eggs and larvae; and (2) swarm all over the intruding foot and up the pant leg if available, and bite for all you're worth. In people, who are symbolic thinkers—with the good things and the bad things that come with being a symbolic thinker—the "nest" can be your own home and family. Or it can be your car, thus ac-counting for road rage. Or it can be your town, your state, your country, your ethnic group, your religion, your favorite band, or your football team. We have all felt the anger that happens when our nest is attacked, in any of its manifestations. In its most problematic incarnation it leads to wars, among people as among ants. Some wars are wars of acquisition (make the nest bigger by invading another's territory and taking their stuff); and some are wars of resistance (keep the others from invading your territory and taking your stuff.) But all wars are group efforts having to do with territory, and with a division of labor.

"Defend the nest," among people as among ants, also manifests itself as that old slogan of the Three Musketeers, "All for one and one for all." At its best, this can appear as acts of pure altruism—soldiers who throw themselves on grenades to save their comrades, people who jump into freezing water to rescue strangers, or those who take a public moral stand in the face of repressive laws or governments and get themselves jailed or shot for doing it. Odd though it may seem in a society that does not value the arts as highly as it values, say, making a lot of money, artists are usually in the front lines when it comes to being shot, because dictators and authoritarian governments know the power of art. That is one way of celebrating the humanities, though not a way we would like to see put into practice here.

At its worst, "defend the nest" can appear as mob rule, witch burning, riots, and the like.

That is one example of a human interest with positive and negative values stemming from it. But let's turn to something closer to my heart, which is that body of story-telling practices (on whatever diverse platforms) that we might call the narrative arts.

•   •   •

Why do people everywhere, in all cultures, tell stories?

Our ancestors spent a very long time in the Paleolithic Period before written languages appeared, so "history" as we know it is just a thin skin of icing on an otherwise very large and somewhat impenetrable cake. What our predecessors were doing during all those years, as the ice ages came and went—in addition to meeting the basic needs for food and shelter—must have included a great deal of what we would now call *the arts* and *religion* and *the humanities*, though it was not until very recent times that we began to call them by those separating names, and to specialize in them. Those ancient ones were also working out various forms of what we would now call *science*, or at least *applied science*—this mushroom will kill you; here is how you make a chert arrowhead, and so forth.

Thus the deep roots of what we now call *the humanities* are very, very old. There is a bone flute dated to forty thousand years ago on which you can play Mozart. There is a shell with a homo-erectus-made design on it that carbon-dates to four hundred thousand years. These kinds of art-making behaviors must have contributed enough to the enterprise at hand—the survival and flourishing of the group—that they were selected for, though we can only guess at the uses made of the various forms of art. We do know that extremely young children soak up languages like little sponges, that they show an interest in music and dance—melody and rhythm—very early, that they are inclined to use visual tools, such as crayons on the wallpaper, well before they have enough small-motor control to make recognizable pictures, and that they can understand a narrative sequence—a story—this happens, then this, then this—before they can talk.

We cannot truly know, but it is tempting to think that both musical systems and articulated languages—containing, for instance, a past tense and a future tense, and the ability to create similes and metaphors—are our oldest human technologies. Music fosters bonding, and helps members of communities to feel and act together. (Hint: that's what hymns are for, not to mention march music and national anthems.) Narrative skills would have been invaluable in many ways: for origin stories—*here's where we came from*—but especially for helping the young survive and prosper by way of story, a far more effective way of communicating than, for instance, graphs and charts, say those who study such things.

This is the story about how Uncle Drood got eaten by a crocodile because he went swimming *right there*. Do not do the same! On the other hand, here is how we hunted the gazelles last year; if you listen to the story about it, you will be better equipped to hunt gazelles yourself, when the time comes.

It has recently been proposed by the brain people that the processes involved in memory did not evolve to help us remember the past, but instead to help us anticipate the future—thus a function with an obvious survival application. Another positive result of the narrative arts—novels included—is increased empathy, or *feeling with*. Empathy enlarges our ability to understand other people, we are told; a valuable life skill if you are a member of a small interdependent group, as most people were until very recently. And useful even today, unless you want to interact with nothing but the Siri voice on your phone. "Siri," we asked her recently. "Does cat urine cause dementia?" "I am trying to understand your request," she replied.

But you did not need higher math to survive or flourish in a small Paleolithic group. The number of objects we can count by looking at them assembled on a tabletop, without using fingers or an abacus, is seven, we are told. Although we can learn arithmetic and algebra if we apply ourselves, we are not soaking them up at the age of two. And they were very late to appear in human history. It isn't that we couldn't count. We just needed some tech help doing it. Most of the Mesopotamian clay tablets written in cuneiform are temple inventories. Only a few are poems, such as *Gilgamesh* and the Sumerian Inanna hymn cycle. Why? People could easily memorize the poems, but not the numbering inventories.

So we come into this world equipped with nascent capabilities for "the arts." Inside every one of us is an artist of some sort. (Maybe not a very good artist. But an artist nonetheless.) You can take the humanities out of the curriculum, but you can't take the humanities out of the humans. They are built in.

●　◆　●

People are in the habit of making a distinction between the sciences on the one hand, and the humanities on the other—though both are part and parcel of who we are. But each understands basic questions differently. For instance: *Who are we?*

Science can only speak authoritatively about what can be measured, and about hypotheses that can be proven by repeatable experiments. So from the scientists you will get a lot of fascinating stuff—we are a DNA pattern closely related to, but differing crucially from, those of the other primates; we are a carbon-based air-breathing life form reducible to a few pounds of minerals and a lot of H_2O; we are composed, in part, of many nonhuman but symbiotic intestinal and cellular nanobioforms, without which we would die. Science can tell us *what* we are, but who we are may well be a different sort of question. Not everything about us is the sum of our material parts, or so I fondly believe. But those who think they can ignore those material parts altogether are sadly deluded.

And, if you ask the anthropologists and archaeologists the same question—*who are we*—they will say we all exist in a culture, like other social animals, and in our case that ever-fluctuating cultural matrix is composed of a huge number of waxing and waning memes that carry various emotional charges, including modern meme clusters like "Elvis Presley" and ancient ones like "Easter egg," and almost forgotten but once potent ones like "bubble gum," and very modern ones like "Twitter."

If you ask the theologians, you will get yet another set of answers, which I trust will contain the phrase "a living soul," or something like it. This will start a furious argument with the natural scientists, who will insist that the soul be produced so it can be weighed and measured, and the theologians will say that this is impossible, since a spirit is not material, and the scientists will say that in that case there is no pointing talking about it, since it is nonexistent, and so on.

Whereas the anthropologists might say that whether a soul can be shown to exist is beside the point: insofar as people believe in souls and act as if they believe in them, they are a formative part of culture and of human life, at that time, there. And so forth.

But, from the students of literature, you would get instead some pertinent quotes, such as Hamlet's rumination: "What a piece of work is a man! How noble in reason, how infinite in faculty! In form and moving how express and admirable! In action how like an angel, in apprehension how like a god! The beauty of the world. The paragon of animals. And yet, to me, what is this quintessence of dust?"

The modern smarty-pants might cry, "He's depressed! Quick! Take a Zoloft!" Which would be impertinent, because Hamlet is, on many counts, right: "The beauty of the world, the paragon of animals," check. At least in our own eyes. The quintessence of dust, also check. And also in our own eyes. We exist on a continuum, from very high to very low. The humanities might be said to be the study of that continuum.

◆   ◆   ◆

Are our human values changing? Our human interests are not—they remain constant—but the way we are approaching those interests and attaching values to manifestations of them may in fact be in flux. As it usually is.

For instance, the whole human being is coming back into fashion. After a century of more and more specialization, there is a movement to link together areas of study previously considered separate. We are seeing this in all areas; in medicine, for instance, there is a new interest in treating the whole patient, not just his left tonsil. People are getting tired of being viewed as mere collections of body parts; and doctors are getting tired of being viewed as just a means to a profit margin. Some of them actually want to help people. People. Not only their toes.

There is a new book called *Art and Energy*, by Barry Lord, that connects the kind of energy used in each historical period—wood, slaves, coal, oil, electricity, renewables—with the kind of art made and valued at those times. It seems obvious once said—why wouldn't there be a connection?—but it is fascinating to note that someone is now actually making it. According to Lord, we are transitioning from an age of carbon energy and consumerism to an age of renewables and stewardship. *Use it and toss it* will go out of fashion; *conserve it and save it* will come in. And thus the nature of new artworks is changing.

Parallel work is being done by Ian Morris at Stanford, correlating the kinds of food sources and energy used in a given period to the social values of that period. Among hunter-gatherers, there was more gender equality than among agriculturalists, for example. Among the agriculturalists, hierarchies, with kings at the upper end and peasants or slaves at the lower end, were the norm; men plowed, women wove, and so forth. And now, in the age of keyboards—not requiring a lot of upper-body strength—genders are becoming more equal once again. I think we will see quite a lot more of this kind of crossover study in the years to come.

That may be what is happening at the academic level, but what about the mega-level—the human race itself? Where are we headed? And is it a good place?

Here is my big pronouncement: It is the best of times, it is the worst of times. (Hint: Charles Dickens. *Tale of Two Cities*.) In the "best of times" corner, the pace of the increase in knowledge and discovery in all areas of science is breathtaking. Inventions and procedures that were merely theoretical even ten years ago are with us now, and new wonders appear, it seems, every week, spurred on by mind-bending advances in computing and data processing. Among the most riveting projects are those involving genetics: through genetic studies, we can open a window into the deep past, trace the connections among organisms, and seek answers to questions such as, what part of the prehuman brain changed to allow for advanced language and symbolic thinking? In genetic engineering, we may soon be able to cure inherited disease. And that is just one part of the amazing human multiexperiment now taking place. Artificial intelligence, the Internet of things, the ability to make ourselves smarter, healthier, older for longer, and, yes, cuter and hunkier—it's all on the table.

In the worst of times corner, there are a lot of contenders.

As the planet warms—we won't argue about the causes just now, but the facts themselves are inescapable—as the planet warms, (1) the sea expands, (2) more evaporation takes place, so there is (3) more precipitation in some places; and (4), more hot air rises, causing stronger winds and more extreme weather events, leading to (5) lower food production, which will lead to more political instability, as people in stricken areas fight for resources. This is not me making it up, it's the Pentagon, so if you want to accuse them all of being lunatics, be my guest. (Hint: they've got some weapons.) Moreover, warming in temperate zones will lead to an influx of invasive species, and the spread of tropical diseases. Having fun so far?

More important: Did your blood pressure go up? Probably not, because you have heard it before; also I communicated it in a general way, and did not include an individual protagonist with whose struggles you could identify. We gnaw our nails over Tiny Tim, but not over statistics.

Which is of course where the artists come in, because that's what art—narrative art, visual art, movies, TV, dance, history—all the things the humanities are, and also study—that's what art does. Art makes it personal. To understand war, you can read about strategy and tactics. And you can also read *The Iliad*. Which is more real? The former. Which touches us more deeply? The latter. It's real in a different way.

I was lucky enough to be in Greece this past summer, and to stand in the amphitheater where the great plays of Sophocles were first performed. Sophocles was a war veteran. Some of his plays are about war and the damage it can do to individuals. Right now, in the United States, there is a theater group that performs to war vets. The effect is therapeutic—much more so than therapies of other kinds. Because art can take you inside a mind, it can show you what trauma *feels* like. To be understood on such a deep level is transformative; no mere clinical description comes anywhere close.

In a mirror project, vets who had suffered brain damage from explosions but could not describe what that felt like were asked to make masks of themselves *showing* what it felt like. The resulting created objects—which you can see in the National Geographic—are extraordinary. And they are extraordinary, not only as expressions of personal emotion, but also as art. They are what T. S. Eliot would have called the objective correlative of damage. Have a look.

We make art because that is who we are. We are art-making beings. And we understand art at a deep level for the same reason. Any educational system that ignores this fact is ignoring our essential human being. If all you want is a trade school—something that will help people get jobs—that's fine, and there's nothing wrong with it. But if you are interested in human wholeness, the humanities must be engaged.

That's not just my personal opinion. It's our opinion. It's us.

At weddings, funerals, and other threshold moments of life, we do not recite our income tax reports. If we recite, it is likely to be poetry. We speak; we sing; we engage in rituals that are meaningful to us, because they connect us, not only with ourselves, but with our communities and with the human race.

Or, as John Donne once put it, back in the seventeenth century:

No man is an island entire of itself; every man
is a piece of the continent, a part of the main;
if a clod be washed away by the sea, Europe
is the less, as well as if a promontory were, as
well as any manner of thy friends or of thine
own were; any man's death diminishes me,
because I am involved in mankind.
And therefore never send to know for whom
the bell tolls; it tolls for thee.

The Human Condition in the Anthropocene

DIPESH CHAKRABARTY

The Tanner Lectures in Human Values

Delivered at

Yale University
February 18–19, 2015

DIPESH CHAKRABARTY is the Lawrence A. Kimpton Distinguished Service Professor of History, South Asian Languages and Civilizations, and Law at the University of Chicago. He is the author of many articles and books including "The Climate of History: Four Theses," *Critical Inquiry* (2009), *The Calling of History: Sir Jadunath Sarkar and His Empire of Truth* (2015), *Provincializing Europe: Postcolonial Thought and Historical Difference (2008; 2000), Habitations of Modernity: Essays in the Wake of Subaltern Studies* (2002), *Rethinking Working-Class History: Bengal 1890–1940* (2000; 1989). He is a founding member of the editorial collective of *Subaltern Studies*, a founding editor of *Postcolonial Studies*, and is a consulting editor of *Critical Inquiry*. Chakrabarty is currently working on a book on climate change and on a collection of essays on history's relationship to the present. He was elected fellow of the American Academy of Arts and Sciences in 2004 and honorary fellow of the Australian Academy of the Humanities in 2006. He was recently named the recipient of the 2014 Toynbee Foundation Prize for his contributions to global history.

LECTURE I.
CLIMATE CHANGE AS EPOCHAL CONSCIOUSNESS

For some time now, I have been interested in thinking about the question of how the intersecting themes of globalization—a story about the growing connectivity of the world—and global warming make up for us our sense of the times we are living through. Individually considered, these themes appear to be of different origins. The idea of a global age grew in the hands of humanistic scholars. Planetary climate change, on the other hand, was a phenomenon defined and discovered by scientists. The science of climate change has its immediate roots in the Cold War period and had in particular to do with the realities of the nuclear bomb and competitive research on atmosphere and space. Climate change—or global warming—became a public concern in the late 1980s when scientists advised governments that this was the biggest threat human civilization had ever faced and that the threat came from our civilization's dependence on the cheap and plentiful energy that fossil fuels provided. Climate change, they said, was anthropogenic in nature and what was worse, it was going to affect the poor of the world more than the rich, who were much more responsible for the emission of excessive greenhouse gases.

Much of the debate on global warming or climate change has since turned around the question of responsibility. Both the Rio Earth Summit of 1992 and the Kyoto Protocol of 1997 emphasized the formula that countries and peoples bore "common but differentiated responsibilities" for actions dealing with climate change.[1] Today I want to discuss this expression: "common but differentiated responsibilities." Why responsibility should be differentiated is easy to understand. Climate change is a back-loaded problem. We do not suffer immediately from the effects of our emissions today. Carbon dioxide and other greenhouse gases stay around in the atmosphere for quite a while (some dissipate sooner than others), and the consequences we suffer at any one point in time are the result of past emissions. Because the developed world has been responsible for most of the past emissions, it was agreed—on the "polluter pays" principle—that the richer countries ought to pay more for controlling, mitigating, or preventing the damages caused by climate change.

The expression "differentiated responsibilities" is what brings the story that scientists tell—about the relationship between climate and earth processes—into a relationship with the familiar stories of globalization: the uneven and iniquitous history of world capitalism, the emergence of global media and connectivity, and so on. It situates climate change as a climactic point in the history of globalization. So much for the expression "differentiated responsibility." But how will we understand the word *common* that is also a part of the formula: "common but differentiated"? Was "common" simply an empty and rhetorical bargaining device, used to placate the richer countries that insisted on the responsibility of emerging powers like China and India? Was it a word meant simply to defer the responsibility of the emerging powers—the idea that they would become responsible, too, but only *after* they had industrialized and had emitted enough greenhouse gases to qualify? But then there was also the recognition—and it has only grown with every report that the Intergovernmental Panel on Climate Change (1988) has published since 1990— that the problem of global warming produces its own timeline for urgent and global action, irrespective of the question of responsibility, if we are to avert the truly "dangerous" effects of climate change that unfortunately and unfairly would affect the poor more than the rich.

Scholars agree that planetary climate change cannot be addressed as a planetary problem—as distinct from the many actions we can take regionally or locally—unless there is a "global political will" that will help humans deal with their shared planetary crises. As the historian John L. Brooke writes at the very end of his magisterial *Climate Change and the Course of Global History*:

> What is needed is a new legal framework to shape the transition to a new system of energy and the market. If an earth system crisis is averted, it will be because the politics of economic transformation was able to unfold quickly enough to make a difference.... What is necessary, what all of the pragmatists are working for, and what the pessimists despair of, and what the deniers reject in antihistorical, antiscientific ideological animus, entrenched interest, and a good bit of wishful thinking, is a global solution. We hold it in our collective capacity to address the earth system crisis that is now upon us. That capacity must be mobilized by an informed political will."[2]

For a host of reasons, the global response has been much slower than needed. In countries such as India where corruption and environmental pollution are supreme concerns, global warming does not even merit the same level of public discussion as it does in Europe and North America.

Global warming is, one may be led to think, simply not as global an issue as globalization.

Bruno Latour recently remarked with his characteristically wry sense of humor that we still behave as though we were all "climate skeptics," even those who do not deny the science.[3] I do not make it my aim here to explain why global response to climate change has not been as forthcoming as many would like it to be. Some persuasive explanations have been proffered including the argument that climate change is a classic instance of a "wicked problem," a problem you can diagnose rationally but not practically solve as it impinges on too many other problems that cannot all be solved together.[4] These lectures, however, have a much more modest aim. I want to share some thoughts with you on the word *common* in the expression "common but differentiated responsibilities." I submit to you that the word is much less obvious than the idea of "differentiated responsibility." Its meaning is not given. Both the word *common* and what it may stand for have to be *composed*, in the Latourian sense of that word. These lectures are meant as a small contribution toward that task of composing the common.

The story of globalization and the idea of "differentiated responsibility" are an important but insufficient part of this project. It is true that we can never *compose* our planetary collectivity by ignoring the intensely politicized and necessarily fragmented domain of the global that understandably converts scientists' statements about humans as the cause of climate change into a charged discussion about moral responsibility and culpability. But we cannot think the common by immersing ourselves in the international politics of climate justice either, for such politics will always reduce climate change to globalization and its discontents—that is, to the familiar themes of human power and inequalities. What Clive Hamilton said recently in response to an essay by Ulrich Beck is pertinent: "one cannot come to grips with climate change if it is cast *only* as a problem of power relations and differences between humans."[5] We need to start somewhere else.

EPOCHAL CONSCIOUSNESS

My starting point in these lectures is the observation that, for all their overlaps, the narratives of globalization and the stories that climate scientists tell concerning global warming have a very particular difference separating them. Humans are central to all stories of globalization, celebratory or critical. Stories of globalization are homocentric in nature. The science of global warming, on the other hand, invites us to see humans on an expanded canvas of history, spanning the geological history of the planet and the story of life on it. By "life," I mean natural reproductive life, *zoe*, not *bios*, to follow Georgio Agamben's and Hannah Arendt's reworking of Aristotle and to bracket for the moment the disagreements that Aristotle scholars have expressed regarding Agamben's Arendt-inspired reading of this opposition.[6] Life, not humans, emerges as one of the main concerns of the literature on climate science. I will describe these points of view, respectively, as homocentric and zoecentric views of the world. I will spend the time at my disposal today in setting up a framework for situating and handling this distinction. Tomorrow, I will elaborate further on the implications of the distinction for thinking about the word *common* in relationship to the expression "differentiated responsibility."

From where and how does a humanist historian begin to think in order to contribute to the work of composing "the common" without in the process denying all that divides us in the space of politics? While others may propose different starting points here, let me begin by retrieving an idea that was mooted in the period when the fear of a nuclear winter was a widely shared feeling. The particular idea I have in mind is the German philosopher Karl Jaspers's conception of what he called an *epochal consciousness*.

Jaspers is not an arbitrary choice. Two aspects of his category "epochal consciousness" have some relevance to what I am trying to do here: (a) Jaspers's thinking on "epochal consciousness" comes out of a particular tradition—mainly German—of taking the whole of humanity as the object of philosophy of history; and (b) the fact that Jaspers invented this category to find a form of thinking that did not foreclose the space of actual politics—in his case, the Cold War—and yet created a space of thinking, a perspectival and ethical space, that he imagined as "prepolitical." Prepolitical in a particular sense: a form of consciousness that does not deny, decry, or denounce the divisions of political life while seeking to position itself as something that comes *before* politics or thinking politically, as a pre-position as it were to the political. In other words, the question behind my thought experiment is: is it possible to develop a shared perspectival position that can inform—but not determine—competitive and conflicted actions by humans when faced with the unequal and uneven perils of dangerous climate change?

In his book, *Man in the Modern Age*, published in German in 1931 and in English in 1933, Jaspers spelled out the idea of "epochal consciousness" as a problem that had haunted European intellectuals "for more than a century." Furthermore, he argued that it was a problem that had become urgent "since the [Great] war" from which time "the gravity of the peril [to humanity] ha[d] become manifest to everyone." Jaspers explained the context for "epochal consciousness" as follows: "Man not only exists but knows that he exists. In full awareness he studies his world and changes it to suit his purposes. He has learned how to interfere with 'natural causation.' . . . He is not merely cognisable as extant, but himself freely decides what shall exist." Epochal consciousness was thus a "modern" phenomenon, a phenomenon possible only after Man had learned to "interfere with 'natural causation.'" But one has to keep in mind that as a form of consciousness, it is an ideational entity, a product of thought, or as Jaspers put it, "Man is mind, and the situation of man as man is a mental situation."[7] Epochal consciousness is not a position to which everybody naturally gravitates; one occupies it by following a certain path of thinking.

Let us follow Jaspers a little further. Although there had been "transcendental" and universal conceptions of history before—Christian, Judaic, or Islamic—passed on "from one generation to another," the continuity of this chain, argued Jaspers, was "severed" in the sixteenth century with "the deliberate secularization of human life." This was the beginning of the process of European domination of the globe: "It was an age of discovery. The world became known in all its seas and lands; the new astronomy was born; modern science began; the great era of technique was dawning; the State administration was being nationalized." The French Revolution was perhaps the first event that found expression in forms of "epochal consciousness" in the work of philosophers. It was "the first revolution whose motive force was a determination to reconstruct life upon rational principles after all that reason perceived to be the weeds of human society had been ruthlessly picked up and cast into the flames." Even though the "resolve to set men free developed into the Terror which destroyed liberty," the fact of the Revolution, wrote Jaspers, left men "uneasy about the foundations of an existence for which they thenceforward held themselves responsible, since [existence] could be purposively modified, and remoulded nearer to the heart's desire." Jaspers mentions Kant, Hegel, Kierkegaard, Goethe, Tocqueville, Stendhal,

Niebuhr, Talleyrand, Marx, and, among others, Nietzsche as bearers of different forms of epochal consciousness, ending his series with Walther Rathenau's *Zur Kritik der Zeit* (1912) and Oswald Spengler's *Untergang des Abendlandes* (The Decline of the West) (1918) as two books displaying forms of epochal consciousness that preceded his own, *Man in the Modern Age*.[8] And we can, of course, add to this list other names of the twentieth century including those of Martin Heidegger and Hannah Arendt. Epochal consciousness, in each case, was thus tied to the question of humans' perceived capacity to project themselves into the world as collective, sovereign agents.

Epochal consciousness is both a form of thought and a genre of writing, for the form could find its fully formed expression only in writings that sought to grapple with this consciousness. Jaspers's own book, *The Atom Bomb and the Future of Man* (1958), is a case in point. It was in this book that Jaspers sought to capture an age through a critical discussion of certain historical statements that summed up for him the dominant motifs of the time. His opening sentences are ones we could use to dramatize the fundamental choices of our times: "An altogether novel situation has been created by the atom bomb. Either all mankind will physically perish or there will be a change in the moral-political condition of man. This book is an attempt to clarify what strikes us as a choice between two fantasies."[9] You could replace "the atom bomb" with "global warming" while remembering Jasper's point that both outcomes are fantasies. But he makes it clear that he needed these fantasies to work toward a new "moral-political condition of man." I will register some differences with Jaspers in the course of these lectures, but let us stay with him a little longer before going our different ways.

Jaspers explains why dealing with epochal consciousness called for a new mode of thinking that stood at a distance from academically specialized routine disciplinary thought—that is, from modes of thinking that Jaspers called *departmental*. Because epochal consciousness seeks to ingest a slab of historical time in its entirety, it cannot be comprehended from what Jaspers calls a *departmental position*. He writes:

> The purpose of this book is not to take a "departmental position," as, for example, from the viewpoint of philosophy as an academic discipline. I mean to address that part of man which is above departments. We have special fields in science, organized departments in administration, a diversity of specialists in politics; we defer to the authority

of expert knowledge, of professional standing, of official position, of membership in groups, nations, states. But all divisions *presuppose* the unity of the whole. Departments have a limited meaning. The whole which unites them also limits their realm of validity; it is their source and their guidepost. The whole, on the other hand, is common to all and belongs to no one or everyone.[10]

Moving forward, Jaspers explains that this nondepartmental (i.e., non-specialized) thinking is best understood from the point of view of a general "listener or reader" who listens to experts and specialists explaining their view of a global problem—"physicist, biologist, military man, politician, theologian"—who each individually "declare[s] himself incompetent outside his special field," while the "listener or reader . . . is supposed to understand them all, to check their statements understandingly as best as he can, to gain an over-all insight and to judge them, in his turn, on an over-all basis." But "where is this complete man?" asks Jaspers, and answers: "He is every individual including the lecturing specialist."[11] Yet, clearly, this general reader or the complete man is not the empirical "every individual," for Jaspers himself admitted that even as he was writing his book, not every individual wanted to discuss the bomb, just as, today, however portentous the crisis of planetary climate may be, not everybody feels the urgency to discuss it. Reflecting further on this problem concerning the crisis precipitated by the bomb, Jaspers wrote: "We let it stand as if it did not concern us, since at this moment, here and now, it is not yet acute. As the sick man forgets his cancer, the healthy man his mortality, the bankrupt his plight—is this how we react to the atom bomb, covering up the horizon of our existence and muddling through, unthinkingly, a while longer?" A somewhat angry and impatient question no doubt, but one that was forced to acknowledge that the "everyman" epochal consciousness addressed was not every empirical individual; and yet Jaspers struggled to produce a form of thought that issued from and addressed the position of an imagined general listener or reader, joining Jaspers in thinking at the "limit of departmental thinking," and on "the existence of issues that concern the whole and are up to everyone."[12]

The other important characteristic of epochal thought, as Jaspers conceived of it, was a negative one: it was not oriented to finding solutions. Such thought was "granted to man," wrote Jaspers, "without giving him the rest of a conclusion." Therefore, it "takes stamina" and "calls for endurance in the tensions of insolubility," for what it brings to bear on philosophy "is not merely a matter of academic [i.e., departmental or specialized discipline-based] training but a reality in man as a truly human, as a rational being."[13] Again, I will disagree later with Jaspers's characterization of rationality as "truly human," but let us follow his thought to its logical end. An epochal consciousness cannot be charged with the function of producing solutions for an epochal crisis because all possible concrete solutions of an epochal problem—and Jaspers welcomes them all—will be partial or departmental, one important department being that of politics, the specialization of politicians. "Purely political thinking"—thinking that calculates and calibrates conflicting interests and strategizes accordingly—is "at a loss in extremities," where it needs "the resolve of the human being in whom a change is wrought by extremity [such as the possibility of a nuclear winter]." This resolve can only come from "something above politics," something that Jaspers would describe as ethical, non-goal-oriented, something suprapolitical, and rational for no other reason than that it is of man's essence, as Jaspers thinks of it. Not having faith in it was to lose "faith in man."[14] Epochal consciousness is ultimately ethical. It is about how we comport ourselves with regard to the world under contemplation in a moment of global crisis; it is what sustains our horizon of action.

Jaspers was well aware that while we can, in the gesture of a deity, "construct for ourselves an image of the whole ['This is what God sees!' as an astronaut once said, looking at Earth]," the "opinion that we can know what the whole, historically or at this actual moment, really is, is fallacious." However one chooses to "regard the epoch," it remains one of a number of obtainable perspectives of orientation." One is never actually outside of the whole one imagines, which is why, Jaspers writes, "my original impulse to comprehend the whole was foredoomed to shipwreck through the inevitable tendency of the whole to be shattered into fragments—into particular glimpses and constellations out of which, building in reverse order, I attempt to reconstruct the whole." But he warned at the same time that "to conceive these antitheses in too absolute a fashion would be a mistake." For the whole remains a heuristic device. We use it to get beyond our submersion in particulars and especially in departmental thinking. It is a methodological part of "the endeavor to get to the bottom of things."[15] But if one's image of the whole always shatters into fragments because it ultimately runs the risk of collapsing back into politics—in other words, my image of the whole can be vulnerable to the charge that it is itself political—then the point only goes to show

how precariously perched the idea of "epochal consciousness" must be. It remains a thought experiment in the face of an emergency that requires us to move toward composing the common. But it is a conceptual struggle that risks being consumed by the political and thus rendered partisan. This is a risk that someone moving toward epochal consciousness has to take.

FROM THE WORLD TO THE GLOBE OR THE PLANET

I will return to the idea of epochal consciousness in the next lecture where I will have more to say about how the crisis of climate change—or the period of the Anthropocene—marks a fundamental shift in the human condition. In order to do so, however, I need to develop two more distinctions: between what I will call *homocentric* and *zoecentric* views of the world, and a pragmatic and artificial one—for I take the words to have the same meaning in English—between the Latin *homo* and the Greek *anthropos*. I find this pragmatic distinction useful for the argument at hand.

Some of the epochal themes that have marked the writings of many European theorists of the world during the period beginning from the Cold War to the fall of the Berlin Wall in 1989 may be listed as follows: (a) the end of the Europeanization of Earth; (b) the question of constructing a multicivilizational post-European world that could counter the risk of technology promoting a culture of uniformity (the idea that technology uproots man); and (c) the emergence of the planet or the globe or the "whole earth" as a space for human dwelling as such. Some of these themes have carried over into and structured contemporary discussions of globalization. But they have done so with a difference. We have to remember also that much of the literature on globalization and postcolonial theory was directed against a particular fear that accompanied this world-historical consciousness of European, especially German, intellectuals. Thinkers such as Heidegger, Jaspers, Gadamer, and Schmitt were all concerned about the possibility that once Europe lost control of the world it had brought together under its imperial aegis, only technology would hold the world together, producing a dull uniformity in world cultures that would leave humans feeling homeless. This was one reason that they were all interested in dating the period from when Europe became only a province of the world. Hans-Georg Gadamer, from whose prose I once borrowed the expression "provincializing Europe," wrote in 1977 that Europe got "provincialized" as early as 1914. Only in the realm of the "natural sciences" could Europe prevail as something of an entity.[16] Jaspers expressed similar sentiments in 1931: "After thousands of years during which civilisations progressed along detached and even divergent roads, the last four and a half centuries have witnessed the European conquest of the world, which the last hundred years have completed.... Today, however, we feel that for us this century of expansion is over and done with."[17] In his *The* Nomos *of the Earth*, Schmitt dated the decline of geopolitical Eurocentrism from even earlier than 1914. For him, the death of a Eurocentric construction of the world that began in the sixteenth century—the *jus publicum Europaeum*—happened in the nineteenth century, sometime between the conclusion of the Napoleonic Wars in 1815, the introduction of the Monroe Doctrine (retrospectively so-called) in 1823, and the rise of Japan as a Great Power by the turn of the twentieth century: "The transition to a new, no longer Eurocentric world order began with the inclusion of an East Asian Great Power."[18]

The uniform figure of the "mass-man" haunted many German thinkers, from Heidegger to Adorno, as a nightmare of modernity. To quote Jaspers, again, in 1931:

> With the unification of our planet there has begun a process of leveling-down which people contemplate with horror. That which has already become general to our species is always the most superficial, the most trivial, and the most indifferent of human possibilities. Yet men strive to effect this leveling-down as if, in that way, the unification of mankind could be brought about.... [Films show that p]eople dress alike. The conventionalities of daily intercourse are cosmopolitan; the same dances, the same types of thought, and the same catchwords (a compost derived from the Enlightenment, from Anglo-Saxon positivism, and from theological tradition) are making their way all over the world.[19]

"Technicisation," Jaspers admitted, was "a path along which we have no choice but to advance."[20] Yet the fear of technology uprooting people from their own cultures remained: "The historical civilisations and cultures have become detached from their roots, and are merged in the technico-economic world and in a vacant intellectualism."[21]

Jaspers took these concerns into the book on the bomb he wrote some twenty-five years later: "We human beings meet each other less and less on the ground of our respective faiths, more and more in the common uprooting vortex of our existence. Technology with its consequences is initially ruinous for all age-old traditional ways of life."[22] Heidegger made the same point in his famous or infamous interview in *Der Spiegel* in 1966: "[T]echnology tears men loose from the earth and uproots them."[23] And Gadamer, writing on "The Future of the European Humanities," in 1983 (before anybody could imagine the fall of the Berlin Wall), wondered if the spread of the capitalist market and technology would lead eventually to a world unity or its opposite: "will the continuation of the industrial revolution lead to the leveling of the cultural articulation of Europe and the spreading of a standardized world civilization, ... or ... will history remain history with all of its catastrophes, tensions, and its manifold differentiations, as has been the essential characteristic of humanity since the building of the Tower of Babel?"[24] "The homelessness with which the modern industrial world threatens humans," added Gadamer, would only drive the latter "to search for home," something that in turn could lead to the unattractive path of "catastrophes and tensions." The "authentic task" of a globalized world would "lie in the area of human coexistence" but for that to happen each culture needed the security of its authentic identity, for "only where strength is, is there tolerance."[25]

These themes constitute an intellectual prehistory of the contemporary literature on postcolonial criticism and globalization. They feature also in Schmitt's *The* Nomos *of the* Earth, written at the same time as Jasper's book on the bomb. But Schmitt tells a changing story of *nomos* that was once land-bound. A certain historical dis-orienting of *nomos* begins in Schmitt's narrative with the expansion of Europe, a process that eventually produced the vision of this planet as the globe. Once Europeans took to exploring and "conquering" the deep seas with the maritime expansion of Europe—the history of large-scale deep-sea whale hunting could be one index of this—*nomos* gradually ceased to be something land-based, thus producing, at the intellectual level of jurisprudential thought, a separation between the ought and the is, between *nomos* and *physis*. "The first *nomos* of the world was destroyed about 500 years ago when the great oceans were opened up."[26] The coming of air travel and eventually the space age could only expand this separation between *nomos* and *physis* and leave humans—it is interesting that both Gadamer and Schmitt appear to agree on this—with two options in the future: either feeling "homeless" (as the globe is the home for nobody) or living in a technologically united world in which all humans come to call the planet their home. Schmitt thought that the destruction of the separation of land and sea whereby the sea became as divisible as land, made "the whole world, our planet, . . . a landing field or an airport, a storehouse of raw materials, and a mother ship for travel in outer space." But that only posed the question of "a new *nomos* of the earth" more powerfully than ever. Writing in a period of a bipolar world caught in the "cold war" of capitalism and so-called socialism, Schmitt saw one possible future in "an ultimate, complete unity of the world" carried out by the victor or victors in this struggle.[27]

In a 2008 essay published in the *American Historical Review*, the historian Benjamin Lazier described this historical thinking—and, of course, historiography—as marked by a veritable lexical spill: from "world histories" to "global histories," and then from the latter to histories of planetary concerns, to go, for instance, by Alison Bashford's and Joyce Chaplin's recent publications.[28] Of course, words like *world*, *globe*, or *planet* are not stable entities. World history once looked like global history until the 1990s, when the very phenomenon of globalization prompted historians to ask whether "world history" needed to attune itself to a distinctly "global age"—as Michael Geyer and Charles Bright put the question in 1995—and whether, indeed, the word *global* could ever be fully subsumed in the word *world*, as Bruce Mazlish asked in a seminal article in 1991.[29]

A similar instability, I would argue, has attended the fate of the word *planetary* as it has traveled from the literature on globalization where analysts used the words *globe* and *planet* as one and the same, to the literature on climate change. Consider, for example, the use of the words *globe* and *planet* or *global* and *planetary* in the following sentences culled from Schmitt's classic text, *The* Nomos. Schmitt would write:

> The first attempts in international law to divide the earth as a whole according to the new global concept of geography began immediately after 1492. These were also the first adaptations to the new, planetary image of the world.
>
> The compound term "global linear thinking" is . . . better than "planetary" or similar designations, which refer to the whole earth, but fail to capture its characteristic type of division.
>
> The English island [at the time of the Treaty of Utrecht in 1713] remained a part of the European planetary order. . . .

I speak of a new *nomos* of the earth. That means that I consider the earth, the planet on which we live, as a whole, as a globe, and seek to understand its global division and order.[30]

It can be seen from each of the above quotations that for the theoretical approach Schmitt was attempting to develop to understand the production of the global in human history, *planetary* was simply another word for *global*. They referred to the planet we live on, the earth taken "as a whole." This is exactly how many of the later scholars of globalization would use the word *planetary*—to refer to the earth as a whole. This was, of course, a fulfillment of what many, from Heidegger to Sloterdijk, had seen as the "age of the world-picture" or "the global age."[31] From this point of view, the famous 1968 NASA picture of the earth taken from space portraying the planet as a sphere that rises over the horizon of the moon—the one titled "Earthrise"—may be seen as the culmination of this use of the picture of the earth as a globe, the planet on which we humans happen to live (see Figures 1 and 2). It is humans looking in and picturing the whole earth to be their home. This planet is what the globe is; other planets are not in our field of view.

These pictures symbolized for observers the theme of human dwelling, its fulfillment as well as its breakdown. Heidegger expressed this crisis well in his 1966 interview in *Der Spiegel*: "I do not know if you were frightened, but I at any rate was frightened when I saw pictures coming from the moon to the earth. We don't need any atom bomb. The uprooting of man has already taken place. The only thing we have left is purely technological relationships. This is no longer the earth on which man lives."[32] "Should the emancipation and the secularization of the modern age," asked Hannah Arendt in beginning her book *The Human Condition*, "end with . . . [a] fateful repudiation of an Earth who was the mother of all living creatures under the sky?"[33]

Thus the epochal consciousness that the history and narrative of globalization produced—through the years of the Cold War and beyond—turned around the question of dwelling, human dwelling on earth, in a process whereby the globe, an outcome of the history of European expansion and the growth of capitalism as a world-system, encountered the planet Earth simply because the Earth was there to be so encountered. The globe and the planet in the end merge into one another insofar as the globalization theorists are concerned. This was the "lexical spill," as Lazier puts it, "from the word 'earth' to the words 'Earth,' 'planet,' and

Figure 1. *Earthrise.* As seen from *Apollo* 8 in orbit around the moon, 1968.
Source: NASA.

'globe.'" The parallel turn in the environmental movement, "from 'environment' to 'globe' as in 'global environment,'" he points out, goes in tandem with this "globalization of the world picture."[34]

There are three things to be noted about this consciousness of globalization: (a) it turns, as I said, on the question of humans dwelling together in a global world when technology weaves the planet into a huge network of connections; (b) the history it recalls is the history of the last five hundred or so years, the history of European expansion, of globalizing capital with all its inequities, and of modern technology; and (c) although the environmental concerns of the past four decades did call attention to man's relationship to his environment including other species, this epochal consciousness remained profoundly homocentric. Humans were at the center of this narrative, however it was told.

Figure 2. *Blue Marble.* As seen from *Apollo* 17, 1972.
Source: NASA.

THE PLANET/GLOBE DIVERGENCE
AND THE PLACE OF *ZOE*

The story of planetary climate change carries on with the narrative of globalization but also departs from it in a radical manner. The science of climate change has roots going back to nineteenth- and twentieth-century investigations by European and American scientists, both amateur and professional. But, more immediately, it is a product of the Cold War, the detonation of nuclear bombs that made for new oceanographic and atmospheric studies by the United States.[35] Spencer R. Weart and Joshua P. Howe have recently told this story in fascinating detail.[36] The science, one could say, was mainly American. Its immediate context lay in the competition between the United States and the Soviet Union for mastery of space. The story of planetary climate change is not even a culminating point in the history of the "ecological crisis" for humans that Gadamer, Schmitt, and many others had acknowledged and discussed as a coming danger.[37] The "climate crisis" could not have been foreseen from within the logic of the available narratives of "environmental pollution" attributable to humans or with the help of the methodological tools that allow us to reconstruct something like a history of capital. Diagnosing global warming entailed the involvement of other kinds of sciences. Understanding the phenomenon of climate change required the development of a form of planetary thinking that was interdisciplinary. It involved knowledge of earth systems functioning (itself a development of the 1980s, with the beginnings harking back to the 1960s), of geology, and the history of life on the planet in addition to what globalization theorists take an interest in, which is the history of the world market for production and consumption (or to use a nontheoretical word: *capitalism*).[38] By introducing new questions of scale—astronomical scales for space, geological scales for time, and scales of evolutionary time for the history of life—all in search of understanding the relationship between the history of the planet's atmosphere and its life-carrying capacity, and thus promoting what may be called a life, or zoecentric, view of the history of the planet, the literature on global warming works at a tangent to the completely homocentric narrative of globalization. This tension is best seen in the work of someone we will consider in the next lecture, James Lovelock of the Gaia fame.

Both globalization narratives and scientists' concern over "dangerous" climate change share an interest in human well-being. But whereas globalization theorists argue about the capacity of existing economic and political institutions to deliver well-being for all humans, the science of planetary climate change ends up making the conditions for the flourishing of life in general on the planet into a condition of what Charles Taylor calls "ordinary human flourishing."[39] The two sets of literature also thus develop a tension between their two master categories: humanity and the human species. Elaborating on this tension and its implications is the task I will set myself in my second lecture.

The beginnings of the divergence between homocentric perceptions of the planet and what I have called the *zoecentric* view of it, may be seen in some of the key responses to that 1968 Christmas Eve American astronauts' view of "earthrise" over the moon, a topic on which Robert Poole has written an engrossing book.[40] Immediate responses to the sight of the

Earth seen from space evoked thoughts about human dwelling, with astronauts spontaneously expressing the hope that Fred Hoyle, the astronomer, Arthur C. Clarke, the science fiction writer (who in turn had been influenced by Arnold Toynbee's ideas about "the unification of the world"), and others had articulated in the 1950s: that humanity might now see the whole earth as their home, bringing an end to all nationalist and other ideological strife.[41] Alongside these reactions that focused on man, there were others that focused on life as such. The microbiologist René Dubos remarked: "How drab and grey, unappealing and insignificant, this planet would be without the radiance of life;" and the ecologist David Worster spoke of the "thin film of life" that covered this planet.[42]

The difference between "homocentric" and "zoecentric" views of the world is perhaps best illustrated through some remarks that James Lovelock made in passing in his book, *The Ages of Gaia*, while recalling the time when he teamed up with his friend, Michael Allaby, to write a fictional book called *The Greening of Mars*, trying to imagine how humans might begin to inhabit the red planet.[43] Apparently, Allaby wanted a world in which "to act out a new colonial expansion; a place with new environmental challenges and free of the tribal problems of the Earth"—a vision of "*terraforming* . . . a word often used when considering this act [of making a place habitable] for planets."[44] Terraforming, to Lovelock's ears, had "the homocentric flavor of a planetary-scale technological fix, redolent of bulldozers and agribusiness." He preferred the ecopoetic expression "the making of a home," a process whose imagination does not begin with humans but with life. "To make Mars a fit home for life," writes Lovelock, even as he believed that Mars was too arid to host life, "we shall first have to make the planet comfortable for bacterial life."[45] It is this latter view that places humans firmly within a larger view of life and planetary dynamics that I am calling *zoecentric* for my purposes here.

Both these views were copresent, for instance, in what the American modernist poet and the Librarian of Congress, Archibald MacLeish, famously wrote on December 25, 1968, in immediate response to the picture of "earthrise." His prose poem called "Riders on Earth Together, Brothers in Eternal Cold" was pregnant with the tension between homocentric and zoecentric views of the place of humans:

1. Homocentric: "To see the earth as it truly is, small and blue and beautiful in that eternal silence where it floats, is to see ourselves as riders on the earth

together, brothers on that bright loveliness in the eternal cold—brothers who know now they are truly brothers."

2. Zoecentric: "For the first time in all of time men have seen . . . whole and round and beautiful and small as even Dante . . . had never dreamed of seeing it; as the Twentieth Century philosophers of absurdity and despair were incapable of guessing that it might be seen. And seeing it so, one question came to the minds of those who looked at it. 'Is it inhabited?' they said to each other and laughed—and then they did not laugh. What came to their minds a hundred thousand miles and more into space—'half way to the moon,' they put it—what came to their minds was life on that little, lonely, floating planet; that tiny raft in the enormous, empty night. 'Is it inhabited?' "[46]

Indeed, the habitability of the planet is a problem we will come back to in the next lecture.

INTRODUCING A PRAGMATIC DISTINCTION: ANTHROPOS AND HOMO

It must be of interest to scholars in the humanities that the word *human* has turned out to be one of the most contested and disputed categories of the social and political literature on climate change. The use of the word *anthropos*, for instance, in the expressions "anthropogenic climate change" or "the Anthropocene"—or for that matter the use of the word *human* in calling something "human-induced climate change"—has invited the not-unreasonable retort: why blame all humans or humans in general when the addiction to fossil fuel is shared by only a minority of humans, the global rich, the consuming classes of the world, and, of course, by interested groups such as the producers and marketers of fossil fuels and their advocates? Scholars from China, India, and other countries have often complained that the word *anthropos*, when used thus, ends up falsely and unfairly implicating the poor and their "survival emissions" of greenhouse gases in the crime of those whose "luxury emissions" are actually responsible for the current crisis of global warming.[47]

The word *anthropos* in the expression "anthropogenic climate change" has a very particular orientation. Earth has seen dramatic and planetary climate changes before. When we call this particular episode of climate change anthropogenic, we do so in order to distinguish this present episode of climate change from previous ones that were caused by nonanthropic geophysical/geological forces such as shifts in tectonic plates, volcanic eruptions, impact of asteroids, and so on. Thus we put this current episode of warming of the planet in a series of similar episodes, and the qualifier "anthropogenic" has the same function as have the different sound values of different letters in a Saussurean chain of signs: to differentiate itself from what precedes and follows it. The word does not designate or connote an inward-oriented sense of uniqueness of humans. "Anthropos" here has no moral value, for it does not signify culpability. It is there simply to suggest that the kind of geophysical force usually needed to change the climate of the planet as a whole was supplied this time—unlike at any other time in the history of the planet—mainly by actions of humans. It is a causal term that does not signify any moral culpability.

A similar point may be made about the use of "anthropos" in attempts by geologists to define and justify a naming of a new geological epoch called the Anthropocene that is meant to signify a shift from the Holocene period that is usually regarded as having begun some 11,700 years ago.[48] Some scholars, mainly from the Left, have expressed deep discomfiture with the label "Anthropocene" and attacked it for its presumed ideological nature. Why not call it "capitalocene," they have asked, when it is the capitalist mode of production that made our greenhouse gas emissions and technologies have an impact on the climate of the planet.[49] Yet it is arguable that names of geological periods are not usually required to say something about the causes that brought particular periods about. The name Holocene, meaning "recent times," suggests nothing about why an interglacial warm period began in the geological time it designates. Similarly, the debate about the name "Anthropocene" is more about whether or not geologists now could scientifically argue that future geologists, millions of years from today, will detect consistent and planet-wide synchronous signals in particular strata of the Earth suggesting that the planet was significantly modified by the work of a species called "Homo sapiens."[50] The name does not assign moral responsibility.

But the moment we define climate change not just as a physical phenomenon but as dangerous—thus the expression "dangerous climate change"—we are in the realm of values and hence of disagreement and politics. Consider, again, two very different rhetorical moves from two recent books by two climate scientists—Raymond T. Pierrehumbert and David Archer, both at the University of Chicago—each dealing with questions of scale that are involved in thinking about the crisis of anthropogenic global warming. Pierrehumbert, writing a text book for college seniors and graduate students, thus writes of how the problem may seem to future humans or some other intelligent species—his tone is calm, dispassionate, self-possessed, and does not at all sound like a call to action, for scale here is a spur to disciplinary imagination:

> As seen by paleoclimatologists 10 million years in the future, whatever species they may be, the present era of catastrophic release of fossil fuel carbon will appear as an enigmatic event which will have a name of its own, much as paleoclimatologists today refer to the PETM [55 Ma] or the K-T [$_{66}$ Ma] boundary event. The fossil carbon release event will show up in ^{13}C proxies of the carbon cycle, . . . through mass extinctions arising from rapid warming, and through the moraine record left by retreating mountain glaciers and land-based ice sheets. As an event, it is unlikely to permanently destroy the habitability of our planet.[51]

Compare this with the move with which David Archer opens his book, *The Long Thaw*, aimed at communicating to a general reading public the urgency of action needed on climate change. Confronting the question as why we "mere mortals" *should* "worry about altering climate 100,000 years from now," Archer asks his reader: "How would it feel if the ancient Greeks . . . had taken advantage of some lucrative business opportunities for a few centuries, aware of potential costs, such as, say a stormier world, or the loss of 10% of agricultural production to rising sea levels—that could persist to this day?"[52]

Archer clearly goes further than Pierrehumbert in speaking of agency and responsibility. His moral and rhetorical question points up an important problem in the politics of climate change. It is this: that motivating human action on global warming necessarily entails the difficult task of making available to human experience a cascade of events that unfold on different scales, at once human and *in*human. The problem of intergenerational ethics both straddles and illustrates this divide: if our greenhouse gas emissions are changing the climate of the planet for the next hundred thousand years, as Archer shows, how many generations beyond us should we—or even can we—really care for?[53] Our capacity to thus care, a capacity that has evolved over a long period of time, may not be unlimited. And Archer, in any case, is speaking here not of the "anthropos" of "anthropogenic climate change" but of a very specific cultural and ethnic branch of humanity, those to whom ancient Greeks represent an acme of civilizational achievement.

The human problem of climate change cannot be defined without some discussion of human values, ethics, suffering, and attachments—topics on which the physical sciences have limited purchase. The idea of a "dangerous climate change" is not in itself a scientific idea. Understanding and defining "planetary climate change" depend on scientific knowledge. But "dangerous" is not a scientific word. As Julia Adeney Thomas has recently said, "historians coming to grips with the Anthropocene cannot rely on our scientific colleagues to define 'the endangered human' for us." "'Endangerment,'" she points out, is never a "simple scientific fact" but "is a question of both scale and value."[54] It is thus when we think of the climate crisis through the idea of moral—and not causal—responsibility that climate change becomes a question of justice and hence a political question as well. Who should own the moral responsibility for the emission of greenhouse gases? Who should bear the cost of mitigation and adaptation? Should the "polluter pays" principle apply? Global warming then poses problems of intrahuman justice. The figure of humanity differentiates itself from the "anthropos" (of the Anthropocene, say) at this point. We think of the political figure of humanity as having two, somewhat contradictory, characteristics. First, it is an entity that is capable of projecting itself into the future as a purposeful agency even though the purpose may not always be one that wins universal approval. But we also think of this humanity as always already divided by issues that in turn give rise to issues of justice. It is never an operative, singular agency. Its unity as a political actor is always "to come."

One could argue that this category "humanity" is a product of the very process of the gradual mondialization of the world, the superimposition of the world with the globe or the planet. It reflects a modern formation, something brought into being by the technoeconomic networks that made this planet the home we saw from space. Let us call this figure of one-but-divided humanity by the Latin word *homo* simply to distinguish it from the Greek *anthropos* that has already been claimed by scientists. When we read the word *homo* used in this sense into the word *anthropos* (as discussed above) in the context of anthropogenic global warming, we see climate change as a continuation of the story of capitalist globalization accentuating all the human inequities that are central to that story, however told.[55] But planetary climate change and the Anthropocene are also events driven by nonhuman, nonliving vectors that work on multiple scales, some of which work on geological scales while some

have an influence within the time horizon of one or two human generations. What works over hundreds of thousands, if not millions, of years
cannot be brought within the realm of policy and politics. But the moment we say "we" should do something to prevent dangerous climate
change, we raise questions about damages, costs, and responsibility, and
we read what I have called *homo* back into the word *anthropos* as used in
the expressions "anthropogenic" or "the Anthropocene." In the politics
of climate justice, one may therefore say that homo comes to be where
anthropos was.[56]

NOTES

I am grateful to the Tanner Lectures Committee, Yale University, for the invitation
to deliver these lectures. Thanks are also due to Michael Warner, Daniel Lord
Smail, Wai Chee Dimock, and Gary Tomlinson—as well as to the members of my
audience—for their formal and informal comments. I have also benefited from discussions with Fredrik Jonsson, Ewa Domanska, Rochona Majumdar, and Gerard
Siarny.

1. J. Timmons Roberts and Bradley C. Parks, *A Climate of Injustice: Global Inequality, North-South Politics, and Climate Policy* (Cambridge, MA: MIT Press,
   2007), 3.
2. John L. Brooke, *Climate Change and the Course of Global History* (New York:
   Cambridge University Press, 2014), 558, 578–79.
3. Bruno Latour, "Facing Gaia: Six Lectures on the Political Theology of Nature,"
   The Gifford Lectures on Natural Religion, Edinburgh, 18–28 February 2013, 109.
4. Mike Hulme, *Why We Disagree about Climate Change: Understanding Controversy, Inaction and Opportunity* (Cambridge: Cambridge University Press,
   2009), 333–35. For examples of the general idea of "wicked problem" applied to
   many different areas, see Valerie A. Brown, John A. Harris, and Jacqueline Y.
   Russell, eds., *Tackling Wicked Problems: Through the Transdisciplinary Imagination* (London: Earthscan, 2010).
5. Clive Hamilton, "Utopias in the Anthropocene," paper presented at a plenary
   session of the American Sociological Association, Denver, August 17, 2012,
   p. 6. My thanks to Professor Hamilton for sharing this paper.
6. See, for instance, James Gordon Finlayson's (somewhat ill-tempered) critique
   of Agamben in the former's " 'Bare Life' and Politics in Agamben's Reading of
   Aristotle," *Review of Politics* 72 (2010): 97–126, and especially the remark that
   "Aristotle's distinction between mere life and the good life is not . . . captured
   by the semantic differences between the words *zoe* and *bios*" (111). See also the
   Aristotle scholar Adriel M. Trott's disagreement with Agamben on a similar
   point in his *Aristotle on the Nature of Community* (Cambridge: Cambridge
   University Press, 2014), 6–7. There is actually a progressive restriction of the
   meaning of *zoe* that takes place in Agamben's text. His citation (7–8) of a passage from Aristotle's *Politics* shows the latter excluding forms of life incapable

of expressing the pain/pleasure distinction from the idea of "bare life," *zoe*, and later in Agamben's own discussion (8) it becomes clear that *zoe* in his text stands for the bare life of humans alone. Agamben's expansion of Foucault's idea of biopolitics still leaves out a lot of what I mean to include here in the word *zoe*. Giorgio Agamben, *Homo Sacer: Sovereign Power and Bare Life* (Stanford, CA: Stanford University Press, 1998; first published in Italian in 1995), 1–11. But see also Agamben's comment that "the principle of sacredness of life has become so familiar to us that seem to forget that classical Greece, to whom we owe most of our ethico-political concepts, not only ignored this principle but did not even possess a term to express the complex semantic sphere we indicate with the single term 'life'" (6). Rosi Braidotti, *The Posthuman* (Cambridge: Polity, 2013), refers to *bios* as "the portion of life traditionally reserved for *anthropos*" and *zoe* as "the wider scope of animal and non-human life," "the dynamic self-organizing structure of life itself," as "generative vitality" (60).

7. Karl Jaspers, *Man in the Modern Age*, translated by Eden Paul and Cedar Paul (New York: Henry Holt and Company, 1933; first published in German, 1931), 1, 4.

8. Ibid., 5–6, 7–8, 8–16.

9. Karl Jaspers, *The Atom Bomb and the Future of Man*, translated by E. B. Ashton (Chicago: University of Chicago Press, 1963), vii. An earlier 1961 edition was published under the title, *The Future of Mankind*. The original German edition was published in 1958.

10. Ibid., 9 (emphasis added).

11. Ibid., 16.

12. Ibid., 6, 16.

13. Ibid., 10, 12–13.

14. Ibid., 23, 25, 26, 316.

15. Further, "Contrasted with the real situation of the individual, every generally comprehended situation is an abstraction. . . . But images of situations are spurs whereby the individual is stimulated to find his way to the root of what takes place" (Jaspers, *Man in the Modern Age*, 28–31).

16. Hans-Georg Gadamer, "Martin Heidegger," in *Philosophical Apprenticeships*, translated by Robert R. Sullivan, 45–54 (Cambridge, MA: MIT Press, 1985; first published in German, 1977), 45.

17. Jaspers, *Man in the Modern Age*, 18.

18. Carl Schmitt, *The Nomos of the Earth in the International Law of the Jus Publicum Europaeum*, translated and annotated by G. L. Ulmen (New York: Telos Press, 2006), 191 and Part 3 generally.

19. Jaspers, *Man in the Modern Age*, 87.

20. Ibid., 213.

21. Ibid., 88.

22. Jaspers, *Atom Bomb*, 74.

23. Heidegger cited in Benjamin Lazier, "Earthrise; or, The Globalization of the World Picture," *American Historical Review* (June 2011): 602–30, here 609.

24. Hans-Georg Gadamer, "The Future of the European Humanities," in *Hans-Georg Gadamer: On Education, Poetry, and History: Applied Hermeneutics*, translated by Lawrence Schmidt and Monica Reuss, edited by Dieter Misgeld and Graeme Nicholsonm, 193–208 (Albany: State University of New York Press, 1992), 200.

25. Gadamer, "Future of the European Humanities," 206–7.

26. Schmitt, *The* Nomos, 352.

27. Ibid., 354–55.

28. Lazier, "Earthrise"; Alison Bashford, *Global Population: History, Geopolitics, and Life on Earth* (New York: Columbia University Press, 2014); Joyce Chaplin, *Round about the Earth: Circumnavigation from Magellan to Orbit* (New York: Simon and Schuster, 2012).

29. Michael Geyer and Charles Bright, "World History in a Global Age," *American Historical Review* 100 (October 1995): 1034–60; Bruce Mazlish, "Comparing Global History to World History," *Journal of Interdisciplinary History* 28, no. 3 (Winter 1998): 385–95.

30. Schmitt, *The* Nomos, 87, 88, 173, 351.

31. Heidegger, "The Age of the World-Picture," in Martin Heidegger, *The Question Concerning Technology and Other Essays*, translated by William Lovitt, (New York: Garland Publishing, 1977), 115–54 ; Peter Sloterdijk, "Globe Time, World Picture Time," in *In the World Interior of Capital*, translated by Wieland Hoban, 27–32 (London: Polity, 2013; first published in German in 2005).

32. Cited in Lazier, "Earthrise," 609. See also his discussion of Husserl's statement that "the planet as such could not be the proper scene for the human being" (611).

33. Hannah Arendt, *The Human Condition*, 2nd ed., introduction by Margaret Canovan (1958; Chicago: University of Chicago Press, 1998 [1958]), 1–2.

34. Lazier, "Earthrise," 614. See also Bashford, *Global Population* and Chaplin, *Round about the Earth.*

35. Sverker Sörlin, "The Global Warming That Did Not Happen: Historicizing Glaciology and Climate Change," in *Nature's End: History and the Environment*, edited by Sverker Sörlin and Paul Warde, 93–114 (New York: Palgrave, 2009).

36. Spencer R. Weart, *The Discovery of Global Warming*, rev. and exp. ed. (Cambridge, MA.: Harvard University Press, 2008 [2003]); Joshua P. Howe, *Behind the Curve: Science and the Politics of Global Warming* (Seattle: University of Washington Press, 2014). See also Joe Masco, "Bad Weather: On Planetary Crisis," *Social Studies of Science* 40, no. 1 (February 2010): 7–40; and Masco, "Mutant Ecologies: Radioactive Life in Post-Cold War New Mexico," *Cultural Anthropology* 19, no. 4 (2004): 517–50.

37. Gadamer saw weapons and the "desolation of the natural basis of our home, the earth" as the twin dangers threatening "the human conditions for life in general." Gadamer, "The Diversity of Europe" in *On Education*, p. 223. Schmitt writes: "Given the effectiveness of modern technology, the complete unity of the world appears to be a foregone conclusion. But no matter how effective modern technology may be, they can destroy completely neither the nature of

man nor the power of land and sea without destroying themselves." *The No-mos,* 354–55.

38. For a quick history of Earth systems science, see Weart, *Discovery of Global Warming,* 144–47.

39. Charles Taylor, *A Secular Age* (Cambridge, MA: Harvard University Press, 2008).

40. Robert Poole, *Earthrise: How Man First Saw the Earth* (New Haven, CT: Yale University Press, 2008).

41. Ibid., 37–41, 103, 133–34.

42. Ibid., 8–9.

43. James Lovelock and Michael Allaby, *The Greening of Mars: An Adventurous Prospectus Based on the Real Science and Technology We Now Possess—How Mars Can Be Made Habitable by Man* (New York: St. Martin's Press, 1984).

44. James Lovelock, *The Ages of Gaia: A Biography of Our Living Planet* (New York: Norton, 1995 [1988]), 173, 174.

45. Ibid., 174, 175, 180–81; see also: "Our first objective would be to introduce a microbial ecosystem that could convert the regolith into topsoil, and at the same time to introduce surface-dwelling photosynthetic bacteria" (187).

46. Archibald MacLeish, "Riders on Earth Together, Brothers in Eternal Cold," *New York Times,* December 25, 1968, available at http://cecelia.physics.indiana .edu/life/moon/Apollo8/122568sci-nasa-macleish.html.

47. For details, see Dipesh Chakrabarty, "Postcolonial Studies and the Challenge of Climate Change," *New Literary History* 43 (2012): 25–42.

48. Jan Zalasiewicz et al., "When Did the Anthropocene Begin? A Mid-Twentieth Century Boundary Level Is Stratigraphically Optimal," *Quaternary International* 30 (2014): 1–8, http://dx.doi.org/10.1016/j.quaint.2014.11.045. Thanks to Dr. Zalasiewicz for letting me see a copy of this article before publication.

49. See, for example, the essay by Andreas Malm and Alf Hornborg's, "The Geology of Mankind? A Critique of the Anthropocene Narrative," *Anthropocene Review*, March 18, 2014 (published online January 7, 2014).

50. Jan Zalasiewicz, Mark Williams, and Colin N. Waters, "Can an Anthropocene Series Be Defined and Recognized?" in *A Stratigraphical Basis for the Anthropocene*, edited by C. N. Waters et al., *Geological Society, London, Special Publications* 395 (2014): 39–53, http://dx.doi.org/10.1144/SP395.16.

51. Raymond T. Pierrehumbert, *Principles of Planetary Climate* (Cambridge: Cambridge University Press, 2010), 66.

52. David Archer, *The Long Thaw: How Humans Are Changing the Next 100,000 Years of the Earth's Climate* (Princeton, NJ: Princeton University Press, 2009), 9–10.

53. For a very significant book on the problem of intergenerational ethics in the context of climate change, see Stephen M. Gardiner, *A Perfect Moral Storm: The Ethical Tragedy of Climate Change* (Oxford: Oxford University Press, 2011).

54. Julia Adeney Thomas, "History and Biology in the Anthropocene: Problems of Scale, Problems of Value," *American Historical Review* (December 2014): 1587–88.

55. Intergovernmental Panel on Climate Change (IPCC), *Climate Change 2001: A Synthesis Report. A Contribution of the Working Groups I, II, and III to the Third Assessment Report of the IPCC*, edited by R. T. Watson and the Core Writing Team (New York: Cambridge University Press, 2001), 12, cited in Steve Vanderheiden, *Atmospheric Justice: A Political Theory of Climate Change* (New York: Oxford University Press, 2008), 9.

56. This formulation was prompted by a fascinating lecture on "the philology of the Anthropocene" that I heard given by Robert Stockhammer of the LMU University of Munich at a 2014 conference on "Meteorologies of Modernity."

LECTURE II.
DECENTERING THE HUMAN? OR,
WHAT REMAINS OF GAIA

I want to share with you some further thoughts about the fault line that runs through the nonidentity I proposed in the previous lecture: homo and anthropos, a pragmatic and artificial distinction through which I want to capture the two figures of the human that discussions on climate change help us to imagine.

CLIMATE JUSTICE AND HOMOCENTRISM

When we think of climate change as representing a climactic point in the history of capital or of globalization, global warming appears to be entirely a matter amenable to issues of intrahuman justice, even as we acknowledge that anthropogenic climate change affects life beyond human life and impacts on the inanimate world as well. A zoecentric view is passed over in favor of a homocentric one. Consider, for instance, the following passage that occurs early in an otherwise engaging discussion on a possible "political theory of climate change" in Steve Vanderheiden's book on atmospheric justice. It begins with what you will recognize, following yesterday's discussion, to be a zoecentric position on the climate crisis:

> Carbon is one of the basic building blocks of life on the planet earth, with CO_2 the dominant means by which carbon is transmitted between natural carbon sinks, including living things. In an exchange known as the *carbon cycle*, humans and other animals take in oxygen through respiration and exhale CO_2, while plants absorb and store CO_2, emitting oxygen and *keeping terrestrial life in balance*.[1] [emphasis added]

Vanderheiden acknowledges that without the greenhouse gases (GHG) and "the *natural greenhouse effect*," the planet would be inhospitably cold for life in general, and for human life in particular. "While some life," he writes, "might be possible to sustain within a small range of temperature variability beyond that seen since the last Ice Age, the climatic equilibrium produced by 10,000 years of GHG stability is responsible for the development of *all terrestrial life* [emphasis added], and even tiny changes from that equilibrium could throw those ecosystems dramatically out of balance."[2]

Yet, in spite of fully acknowledging that the climate crisis concerns "the balance" of "all terrestrial life" on the planet—whatever such "balance" might mean—and therefore needs to be thought of in terms of at least thousands of years, Vanderheiden's questions of justice and inequity circle around problems of human life and human life alone, and problems that are actionable only on much smaller, human measures of time. As he himself says: "While anthropogenic climate change is expected to visit significant and in some cases catastrophic harm on the planet's *nonhuman species* [emphasis added]," his pursuit of issues of climate justice would follow the Intergovernmental Panel on Climate Change (IPCC) in focusing exclusively on "the planet's human habitats and populations." Vanderheiden gives a good, practical reason for this approach: we do not yet know how to compose a global climate regime that would include representation for "animals and future generations"—not to speak of nonanimal life forms or even the inanimate world. He refers to the work of the political theorist Terrence Ball to argue that even if we represented these groups "by proxies in democratic institutions, giving at least some voice to their interests, . . . they would necessarily remain a legislative minority."[3] Thus it is acknowledged, on the one hand, that "the global atmosphere is a finite good" and is so not just for humans, for it is "vital for the continuation of life on this planet" while being "instrumental for human flourishing" as well. This is the lesson of the sciences. And yet, on the other hand, when it comes to justiciable issues of inequality with regard to climate change, the absorptive capacities of this "one atmosphere"—which, it is acknowledged, "must be shared between *all* the planet's inhabitants"—are divided up *only* among humans ("the world's nations or citizens") with no discussion of what might be the legitimate share of nonhuman forms of life![4] From here it takes only one step to forget nonhuman life altogether and declare global warming to be synonymous with issues of human justice and even to see it as a problem that cannot be remedied *until* issues of human justice are satisfactorily addressed. See how the quotation below moves from a moral recommendation—"concern for equity and responsibility *should not be* dismissed . . ."—to a conditional statement—"anthropogenic climate change . . . *cannot be genuinely addressed unless* . . ."—and finally to a statement that posits a relation of identity between global justice and climate change:

> Concern for equity and responsibility should not be dismissed as secondary to the primary goal of avoiding catastrophic climate change,

for ... anthropogenic climate change is also a problem of justice and so cannot be genuinely remedied unless the international response aims to promote justice [including the poor nations' "right to develop"]. ... Global justice and climate change [are] ... manifestations of the same set of problems.[5]

LOVELOCK, GAIA, AND ZOE

If I had to illustrate in this context a point of view completely opposed to the homocentric view espoused by Vanderheiden, that is, a zoecentric point of view, I would cite a statement from James Lovelock's book, *The Vanishing Face of Gaia*. In a chapter titled "The Climate Forecast," Lovelock argues for the need to "consider the health of the Earth [as a living planet] without the constraint that the welfare of humankind comes first." "This way," he explains, "I see the health of the Earth as primary, for we are utterly dependent upon a healthy planet for survival."[6] We know what Lovelock means by a "healthy" planet: it is one where Gaia remains in charge, that is, life acts as a self-regulatory system and plays a role in maintaining planetary conditions conducive to the continuation of life. In the language of his "Gaia hypothesis": "the Earth's atmospheric composition is kept at a dynamically steady state by the presence of life; moreover if organisms could affect atmospheric composition then maybe they could regulate the climate of the Earth to keep it favorable for life."[7] Now, Lovelock's Gaia theory has faced many criticisms including some very well-known ones from Richard Dawkins.[8] That "life"—thought of "as a planetary scale phenomenon"—is almost an indefinable, metaphysical category is acknowledged by many, including Lovelock himself.[9] Toby Tyrell, a professor of earth systems science at the University of Southampton has recently published a book aiming to be a serious refutation of the Gaia theory while acknowledging that many of Lovelock's insights—though not maybe his whole theory—are accepted today as part of normal science.[10]

It is not necessary for our purposes either to rehearse here the details of the scientific debate around Gaia or to take sides in this debate.[11] Suffice it to note that Lovelock's comparative work on the issue of the presence of life on Mars and Earth gave rise to a fascinating question: Why has this planet been so consistently and continuously hospitable to life for billions of years and to multicellular life for hundreds of millions of years? How has oxygen been maintained at a constant level (21 percent) of the atmosphere for a very, very long time? Any more oxygen, and life would go up in flames; any less, a lot of life would die of suffocation.[12]

This is what led the geologists Jan Zalasiewicz and Mark Williams to call earth "the Goldilocks planet." Mars has weather, "including spectacular planet-wide dust-storms." "It might even harbour a few simple microbes. But it will never be a green and pleasant land." Venus, starting its life with "probably about as much water as the Earth possesses," suffered runaway planetary warming.

> The Earth is the Goldilocks planet. . . . The Earth has been, so far and all in all, *just* right for life, not just right at any one time, but continuously so for three billion years. There have, of course, been some close calls, times of mass extinction. But, life has always clung on to bloom once more. That makes the Earth's history more remarkable than any children's story.[13]

Not everyone has been convinced that it is a good question to ask why the Earth has been so continuously friendly to life over such a long period of time. The question, some scientists point out, seems natural to us humans because, as complex creatures with big brains, we can come only at the end of a long line of continuous evolution of life. But life—the passage from the very first instance of life to us—may have been just a matter of enormous luck. "We are here, so it happened, but, given the number of solar systems overall—'someone throws the dice 10^{22} times'—what else would you expect?"[14] The geophysicist Raymond Pierrehumbert does not think that the success of life on this planet is a gigantic fluke but admits that "the book is far from closed" on the "habitability problem."[15] Some others, with reason, say that we need to study more earthlike planets with similar shares of oxygen in their atmospheres before we can tell what makes a planet so welcoming of life as to evolve complex, intelligent species that can formulate and contemplate this problem—but nothing can be said on the basis of a sample of one![16] Toby Tyrrell, who is critical of the idea that Gaia behaves like a homeostatic superorganism protecting life under all circumstances, settles for a position he shares with Andrew Watson (once Lovelock's collaborator in creating the famous Daisy worlds model): the fact that the planet has never snuffed out life completely since the life began is ascribed to a combination of "both luck and environment stabilizing mechanisms, albeit mechanisms that do not work all that well."[17]

The climate crisis thus raises very significant questions about the conditions for life on the planet and invites us to see humans in the context of those questions. These questions stem from what I have called the zoe-centric view of the world. We cannot get to this point of view through the homocentric per capita emissions figures of the climate justice litera-ture. The relevant figures here are not those for per capita emissions but the story of the expansion of the human species on the planet up to a point where we became indisputably the most dominant species putting pressures on many other life-forms. The Dutch scholar Rob Hengeveld's work explains the problem here nicely. For most of their existence, humans fitted into a pattern of life where one life-form's wastes were re-sources for another life-form, and life subsisted on this natural process of recycling of wastes. Now, thanks to our numbers and the sale of our production and consumption, we produce a lot of waste that cannot be decomposed or recycled. Plastics that are involved in many, many depart-ments of our lives are one such example. And the so-called excess CO_2 is another one. At the same time, our dependence on plentiful and cheap energy—presently supplied by fossil fuels—has become unavoidable, as managing a population of the size of ten to twelve billion (predicted for the end of this century) or even the present seven billion people calls for the creation of complex organizations that produce an ever-increasing demand for energy.[18]

The relatively recent growth of the human population is connected to the story of fossil fuel, whether we look back on human history or antici-pate our futures. After all, it was fossil fuel energy, "and only fossil fuel energy, [that] made it possible to break with the old agrarian pattern and construct the industrial world," writes the "peak oil theorist" John Mi-chael Greer.[19] The benefits (for humans) of plentiful and cheap energy derived from fossil fuel have been innumerable: food improved, both in quality and quantity, improvement in housing and clothing, more hy-gienic and healthier conditions in many places, public safety (better polic-ing), and better illumination.[20] The exponential growth of both human population and our average life span in the twentieth century—and here, of course, the poor are included in both figures—have generally had much to do with fossil fuels through the use of artificial fertilizers, pesticides, pumps for irrigation, and the use of petrochemicals in the manufacture of common pharmaceutical products such as antibiotic medicines.[21]

Emerging powers like India and China justify their continued use of coal (the most offending fossil fuel) and increasing emissions by referring to the need to raise billions of Chinese and Indians out of poverty. China is already the biggest emitter in the world and surpasses European Union figures for emission in per capita terms.[22] This is not simply a story about carbon emissions. It is also about the pressure humans as a species exert on the lives of other species, and thus ultimately on our own conditions of life. The issue is not unconnected to the climate crisis for, as many scholars have pointed out, the warming of the atmosphere and the seas not only raises sea levels threatening coastal settlements, cities, and islands, it also changes marine biodiversity by making the seas more acidic.[23] That increasing numbers of humans threaten the biodiversity of the world is now a commonplace of ecological writings.[24] And, as Vaclav Smil has pointed out, humans and the animals they eat and keep now consume around 95 percent of what the biosphere produces, leaving only 5 percent for genuinely wild animals.[25] The poor are a part of this species life of humans, even while it is true that they do not bear much responsibility for the emission of greenhouse gases.

The more people we have on this planet, even if the majority of them are poor, the more complex our societies become (for the administrative apparatus needed to manage populations enlarges and ramifies), and the greater the amount of "free" energy needed to maintain these societies.[26] If by the end of this century we have ten to twelve billion humans as predicted, we will need even more than we have today of cheap and plentiful energy to sustain such a population, not less. The Duke University geologist, Peter K. Haff, recently argued that maintaining a human population so large entails technology becoming enmeshed with biology. He has put forward a suggestive concept of "the technosphere" in "defining the world [humans] now inhabit." Modern civilization and its "present 7×10^9 human constituents," he argues, could not survive without "the proliferation of technology across the globe . . . the set of large-scale networked technologies that underlie and make possible rapid extraction from the Earth of large quantities of free energy and subsequent power generation, long-distance communication . . . including regional, continental and global distribution of food and other goods." This networked technology supplying the condition of possibility for the existence of so many human lives is what he calls "the technosphere"—humans, he argues, are merely the sentient aspect of this complex whole. The human population "at anything like its current size," writes Haff, "is deeply dependent on the existence of the technosphere." "Without the support structure and the services provided by technology," there would be a major collapse of the human population.[27] Technology, he argues, thus represents "the opening phase of a new paradigm of Earth history." Having become the precondition for the existence of a very large human population and for the animals humans consume, technology may thus be considered "the next biology."[28] It is as if the legacy of Gaia thinking, as Latour puts it with his characteristic witticism, is "to have forced every one of us to render explicit the [growingly technical] breathing conditions we require: out of the suffocating archaic past, running toward an otherwise suffocating future!"[29] Haff's thesis about the technosphere as he defines it also complicates the question of agency and the distribution of causal and moral responsibility in the process of emission of greenhouse gases. If animals whose lives humans have industrialized produce a significant share of methane in the atmosphere, if industrialized lives of humans add another significant amount of the same family of greenhouse gases, and if such lives are sustainable only on the basis of access to cheap and plentiful energy, then even the talk that blames the human species for causing the climate problem gets the question of agency wrong. Clearly, "anthropogenic" climate change results from the industrialization of both human and (certain) animal lives to a point where together they form a causal complex—an ensemble of technology and human and nonhuman lives—while only humans can be assigned some "moral" responsibility (for causal responsibility remains distributed).

It is at this point that some familiar themes regarding the finitude of the Earth suggest themselves. For if human population rose to ten or twelve billion by the end of this century and people exercised, fairly, their right to more energy and development, where would the additional, cheap, and plentiful energy come from? If it all came from renewables, it would mean humans hogging much of the finite amount of energy the Earth receives from the Sun every day; would humans then be depriving other Earth processes and life-forms of the latter's share of the energy this planet receives? Haff imagines humans one day using geoengineering to capture "the energy of photons in space that would have missed the Earth and then transmit the energy down to the Earth's surface (in the form of microwaves)."[30] Latour cites some relevant figures supplied by geologists: human civilization is "already powered by around 12 terawatts (10^{12} watts)." If the world were to be developed to the point of U.S. levels of consumption, the energy count would grow to 100 terawatts, a figure Latour rightly describes as "stunning...if one considers that plate tectonic forces are said to develop no more than 40 terawatts of energy."[31] Besides, adds Latour, we would need five more earth-size planets (to find the necessary global hectares)![32] Setting his sights somewhat lower, Vaclav Smil, the renowned environmental scientist, writes in the very last sentence of his remarkable book, *Harvesting the Biosphere: What We Have Taken from Nature*: "If the billions of poor people in low-income countries were to claim even half the current per capita harvest prevailing in affluent economies, too little of the Earth's primary production would be left in its more or less natural state, and very little would remain for the mammalian species other than ours."[33]

There is a case for climate justice between the rich and the poor of the world, no doubt. Yet justice arguments are not very good at thinking limits. Arguments for climate justice base themselves on per capita emissions on the democratic, humane but homocentric assumption that every human being has equal rights to the world's carbon sinks that the developed nations have hogged for themselves so far. The popularity of this position with governments like India's was reflected, for instance, in what the Indian environment minister, Prakash Javdekar, said in an interview with the *New York Times* in September 2014, placing the "responsibility for what scientists call a coming climate crisis on the United States, the world's largest historic greenhouse gas polluter," and dismissing "the idea that India would make any cuts to carbon emissions":

> "What cuts? . . . That's for more developed countries. The moral principle of historical responsibility cannot be washed away." . . . It would be at least 30 years, he said, before India would likely see a downturn. "India's first task is eradication of poverty," Mr. Javadekar said . . . "Twenty percent of our population doesn't have access to electricity, and that's our top priority. We will grow faster, and our emissions will rise."

"In the coming decades, as India works to provide access to electricity to more than 300 million people," adds the *Times* reporter, "its emissions are projected to double, surpassing those of the United States and China."[34]

Zoecentric views, on the other hand, do not place the emphasis so much on per capita emissions as on humanity as a species, a dominant one that has industrialized its own life-forms and those of many other species with an eye to its own flourishing alone. The size of the human population therefore matters. There are climate-justice thinkers who try to reconcile the two and create a "contraction and convergence scenario," whereby humans attain a state where all nations are equally developed, the richer nations of today having learned to reduce their levels of consumption, and where all humans try to control for their overall numbers and resource consumption.[35] But here, again, some global calendars emerge that are severely mismatched. The calendar for attaining distributive justice between humans with regard to atmospheric space is, basically, an indefinite and open calendar. We do not know when and how, using the inevitable hybrid mixture of normative and politically pragmatic and realist arguments that make up the stuff of everyday politics, the world will become more just. But the IPCC presents us with a very definite and finite calendar for global action if "dangerous climate change," that is, an average rise of more than two degrees Celsius, were to be averted. As Toby Tyrrell puts it:

> We are currently driving the Earth outside the envelope of its recent history. During the last 800,000 years . . . atmospheric CO_2 has never made up more than 0.03% (300 parts per million) of the atmosphere. In contrast, . . . we have already caused it to rise to nearly 400 parts per million, and the rate of increase is still accelerating. The speed at which we are adding carbon dioxide to the atmosphere is probably unprecedented during the last 50 million years or more.[36]

The chances of limiting the temperature rise to 1.5 degrees and 2 degrees Celsius at the present rate of emissions decline to 66 percent in 6 and 21 years, and to 50 percent in 10 and 28.4 years, respectively.[37] Even this calendar may be too optimistic. "The planet has warmed by 0.8°C above the pre-industrial average already," remarks Clive Hamilton, cautioning that the "inertia in the system means that 2.4°C is already locked in, with heating reaching 4°C perhaps in [the] 2070s." A rise of four degrees, in Hamilton's words, is "uncharted territory."[38] The justice calendar and the calendar for global action spelled out by the IPCC probably will not harmonize. Our search for climate justice and its attendant politics may very well mean that we have to travel the via dolorosa of dangerous climate change; perhaps our struggles for climate justice will have to be conducted in a world that is even more climate-stressed and far more unjust than the one we have at present.

CLIMATE CHANGE AND EPOCHAL CONSCIOUSNESS

Climate change as epochal consciousness, then, is constituted around a split between the homo, humanity as a divided political subject, and the anthropos, collective and unintended forms of existence of the human, as a geological force, as a species, as a part of the history of life on this planet. The idea of anthropos decenters the human by subordinating human history to the geological and evolutionary histories of the planet. Epochal consciousness, Jaspers said, "[is] granted to man without giving him the rest of a conclusion." To inhabit such consciousness "takes stamina," he wrote, for "it calls for endurance in the tensions of insolubility."[39] To say this, as I have remarked before, is not to foreclose on the space for short-term politics and conflicts over issues of justice between humans. Nor, for this reason, do we have to rush to Malthusian solutions by calculating the carrying capacity of the planet, or indulge in genocidal-sounding conjectures of exactly how many people the planet can actually support at our current standard of living. But an epochal consciousness acknowledges the moods that drive such thinking and recognizes them as belonging to a spectrum of moods the climate crisis engenders.

Jaspers did not think of epochal consciousness instrumentally, as a pragmatic solution to planetary problems. "This kind of thinking," he wrote, "is not a means to the self-preservation of mankind. It would be futile to incorporate it in a plan, which would always spoil it." But he felt optimistic about the use-value of such consciousness or thinking. "Its existence," he added, "may result in a life that would, by virtue of freedom and against the menace of the atom bomb, save mankind's existence as well." What gave Jaspers this confidence was his idea of reason. His idea of reason was not naive. He did not forget "human ferocity, rapaciousness, love of adventure, the lust of feeling superior to life in flinging it away, etc." He was not unaware of the "blind selfishness" that drives a lot of economic calculations and that "alienates man from himself." Nor was reason a matter of technological innovation "which produces instruments of production and of destruction simultaneously, to the point where both unlimited production and total destruction are possible."[40]

Jaspers addressed his thoughts to fellow humans whom he saw as capable of standing on the common ground of reason, something he defined as the "true essence" of man. In all of human history, he wrote, "only one thing is immobile and adamant: the premise of a will to reason, to boundless communication, and to the love that potentially links all men." Further on, he writes: "If we distrust reason, if we doubt the human susceptibility to reason, we have no faith in man." But he also saw epochal consciousness as inevitably imbricated in efforts at creating "the common": "To refuse to give up this chance [of communication between fellow human beings] shows [a lack of] faith in man as man," and cited Nietzsche: "Truth begins when there are two." Jaspers makes it very clear that he is addressing his fellow human as a thinker, and not the departmental figure of the professional philosopher: "Reason belongs to man as such. It can grow in anyone who thinks honestly, patiently, and unselfishly." And reason has the potential to create a human brotherhood that could stand above and beyond the narrow feelings of group solidarity that divide humans. Science only links humans "purely intellectually" while "reason also belongs to all men, but it belongs to their whole being and is not merely a special field of comprehension. It links men who may differ completely in other respects, in their ways of life, their feelings, their desires; it links them more strongly than they are divided by all their diversities."[41]

In the tradition of thinking to which we are all heirs, Jaspers has not been alone in finding in reason and in humans' capacity for taking a planetary/global perspective a real potential for humanity consciously taking on the role of an intelligent species with a capacity to manage the planet for the benefit of all, including nonhumans. In the twentieth century, anti-imperial thinkers as diverse as Rabindranath Tagore and Frantz Fanon had similar thoughts. The tradition, however, is older. In a recent essay, Deborah Coen has drawn our attention to the thinking of Eduard Suess, the nineteenth-century Viennese liberal politician who was also a pioneering scholar of geology and who coined the term *biosphere*; he was optimistic that geology was a subject that could help combat narrow tribal affiliations of humans. As Coen remarks, Suess saw a "planetary perspective" leading to "a politics that would not privilege mankind over other living things."[42] He wrote:

> Prejudices and egoism, above all the pettiness of the things with which we are accustomed to dealing . . . have placed barriers around each of us which constrict our view. If they are removed, if we resolve to leave behind the narrow conceptions of space and time which bourgeois life offers us, and no longer to view the world from the base, self-centered perspective, which sees advantages here, disadvantages there for us or our species, but rather to admit the facts in their naked truth, then the cosmos reveals to us an image of unspeakable grandeur.[43]

Within my own field, history, this assumption that thinking on large scales leads to a sense of human solidarity or "global citizenship" has found a resurgent expression in a branch of historical scholarship that calls itself Big (or sometime Deep) History. In the hands of a pioneer of this movement, David Christian—as in the writings of other Big Historians—the history of the human species merges seamlessly with the history of "humanity." Christian writes:

> In this expanded form, history will . . . allow individuals and communities throughout the world to see themselves as part of the evolving story of an entire universe, just as they once mapped themselves on to the cosmologies of different religious traditions. . . . Understanding of this shared history will help educators generate a sense of global citizenship, just as nationalist historiography once created a sense of solidarity within different nation-states.[44]

In support of his proposition, Christian directly cites the world-history pioneer William McNeill's 1986 presidential address to the American Historical Association as a source of his inspiration. McNeil had written:

> Instead of enhancing conflicts, as parochial historiography inevitably does, an intelligible world history might be expected to diminish the lethality of group encounters by cultivating a sense of individual identification with the triumphs and tribulations of humanity as a whole. This, indeed, strikes me as the moral duty of the historical profession in our time. We need to develop an ecumenical history, with plenty of room for human diversity in all its complexity.[45]

Cynthia Stokes Brown's version of human history ends up "trusting to the demonstrated capacity for innovation that humans have shown in their history" the hope "that . . . sustainable techniques will emerge."[46] J. L. Brooke, at the end of his masterful survey of the role of climate in human evolution and history, acknowledges that "the emergence of the modern economy has made humanity an agent in abrupt climate change and, more broadly, in abrupt planetary change." He writes:

> In a flash of either geological or human evolutionary time, human populations have doubled and redoubled to more than 7 billion, twenty-four times the number inhabiting the earth 1,000 years ago; six times the number two centuries ago. In just the past sixty years, human populations have more than doubled, . . . and our role in building greenhouse gases has tripled, and we have begun to disrupt the natural systems and services that have sustained us for millions of years.

His hope, however, is vested in "our collective capacity," our "wits," and in our ability to develop a political will that he hopes "will suffice to ensure the sustainability of future generations." His final words: "We hold it in our collective capacity to address the earth system crisis that is now upon us. That capacity must be mobilized by an informed political will."[47]

The idea that humanity, a subject that can project itself into the world, is capable of exercising sovereignty over what humans do as a dominant species or as a geophysical force, also turns up in many other areas of the literature on the climate crisis. There are those who acknowledge the anthropogenic nature of global warming and yet find the ultimate solution in some understanding of the specialness of humans, in their ability to be not just "humanity" but a rational "species" as well. Mark Lynas, the climate change journalist, literally exhorts humans to become the "god species" in his book by that name, by cheerfully adopting geoengineering as a way to solve or manage the problem of climate change. "Can humanity manage the planet—and itself—towards [the] transition to sustainability?" he asks. His answer: "grounds for optimism are at least as strong as the grounds for pessimism, and only optimism can give us motivation and passion we will need to succeed. . . . The truth is that global environmental problems are soluble. Let us go forward and solve them."[48] Erle Ellis, a geographer at the University of Maryland, wrote in the *New York Times* of September 13, 2013, that the idea that "humans must live within the natural environmental limits of our planet denies the reality of our entire history, and most likely the future. . . . The only limits to creating a planet that future generations will be proud of are our imaginations and our social systems. In moving towards a better Anthropocene, the environment will be what we make it." In fact, he calls *this* "the science of the Anthropocene."[49]

These ideas find an echo in Toby Tyrrell's book on Gaia, but an echo that reverberates twice, as it were, and thus interferes with itself. "Because our own activities are already having a great impact on the natural world and show no signs of slowing," Tyrrell thinks that humans will be left with no option but to "embark on some degree of active . . . management" of the Earth. He goes further and adds the reassuring remark that "safely managing a planet is in some ways analogous to safely managing an airplane." But then he points out the most critical distinction: we designed and built the airplane, while the planet "is a system we do not fully understand."[50] To apply to his own argument the criticism he makes of

Lovelock: the fact that the Earth has a history does not mean that it was designed (while the airplane was!). As he additionally points out, we often discover disasters after the fact. The ozone hole crisis was "accidental and unintentional" and "it is only thanks to a minor quirk of fate that this wasn't very much worse."[51] Managing the planet may not at all be similar to managing an airplane! Who would want to get on an airplane whose design we did not fully understand?

It indeed seems fallacious to think that homo (in our scheme) could take the place of anthropos—or humanity that of the human species—though many see this as possible. Consider a recent statement of Amartya Sen on the climate crisis and on human responsibility to other species. Sen argues for the need for a normative framework in the debate on climate change, one that he thinks—and I agree—should recognize the growing need for energy consumption by humans if the masses of Africa, Asia, and Latin America are going to enjoy the fruits of human civilization and to acquire the capabilities needed for making truly democratic choices. Sen also recognizes that human flourishing can come at the cost of other species and therefore advocates a form of human responsibility toward nonhumans. Here is how his argument goes:

> Consider our responsibilities toward the species that are threatened with destruction. We may attach importance to the preservation of these species not merely because the presence of these species in the world may sometimes enhance our own living standards.... This is where Gautama Buddha's argument, presented in *Sutta Nipata*, becomes directly and immediately relevant. He argued that the mother has responsibility toward her child not merely because she had generated her, but also because she can do many things for the child that the child cannot itself do.... In the environmental context it can be argued that since we are enormously more powerful than other species, ... [this can be a ground for our] taking fiduciary responsibility for other creatures on whose lives we can have a powerful influence.[52]

Think of the problems that follow from this purely homocentric placing of humans in loco parentis with regard to "creatures on whose lives we can have a powerful influence." We never know of all the species on which our actions have a powerful influence; often we find out only with hindsight. Peter Sale, the Canadian ecologist, writes about "all those species that may be able to provide goods [for humans] but have yet to be discovered and exploited, and those that provide services of which we simply are unaware."[53] Moreover, human flourishing directly puts us at war with many bacteria and viruses, not to speak of the animals we have already—or almost—squeezed out of existence. Could we ever be in a position to value the existence of viruses and bacteria hostile to us, except insofar as they influence, negatively, our lives? How could the work of humans either anticipate or replace the work we do also as a species, where our history happens, as in the case of all species, through natural selection processes that are random and blind?

FALLING INTO DEEP HISTORY

We can now turn to the problem that distinguishes our situation from the threat of a nuclear winter that Jaspers faced in conceiving his idea of epochal consciousness. A novel and singular phenomenon shapes our age, *planetary* climate change, something that humans never had to face in recorded or remembered history. They faced regional climate changes and other environmental problems to be sure, but something is profoundly different about our times. The time of human history—the pace at which we tell stories of individuals and institutions—has now collided with the timescales of two other histories, both deep time, the time of evolution of life on the planet, and geological time. The latter are histories whose paces we used to take for granted in telling the human story, in particular the story of human motives, aspirations, and the psychosocial dramas and institutions that make up our social lives. These narratives were all built on the assumption that geological and evolutionary developments were like a backdrop on the stage on which our very human dramas unfolded for our own enjoyment. These earth-scale phenomena—earthquakes, for instance—sometimes erupted into our narratives, no doubt, but they provided, for the most part, a background to our actions. In our own lifetime, however, we have become aware that the background is no longer just a background. We are part of it, both in contributing to the loss of biodiversity that may become the Sixth Great Extinction Event, and at the same time as a geophysical force, changing the climate and the geology for the planet for millennia to come. It appears that we are ringing out the Holocene and ushering in a new geological epoch whose proposed name is the Anthropocene, for it signifies the extent and the duration for which our species has modified the physical nature of the Earth.[54]

This temporary (in terms of earth history) collapsing of the human and geological chronologies has not gone unnoticed by scientists. A recent publication by the geologist Jan Zalasiewicz and his collaborators, who have been working to substantiate and formalize the name of the epoch of the Anthropocene, cite a series of worldwide and synchronic stratigraphic signals enabling them to suggest with confidence that "the Anthropocene . . . be defined to begin historically at the moment of the detonation of the Trinity A-bomb at Alamogordo, New Mexico, . . . [on] July 16, 1945." They write: "With the onset of the Industrial Revolution, humankind became a . . . pronounced geological factor, but . . . it was from the mid-20th century that worldwide impact of the accelerating Industrial Revolution became both global and near-synchronous." The date thus combines both an important event in human history—the test explosion—and "the source of a chemostratigraphic [global] signal."[55] If the Anthropocene is ever formalized by the International Union of Geologists, it will mean that long after fossil fuel-based civilizations are gone, the Earth will still bear in its rocks the signs of "our" having been here.[56]

But who is that "we?" We are simultaneously a divided homocentric humanity, and a dominant species and thus a part of the history of life on this planet; and we are also the sentient-moral aspect of Peter Haff's "technosphere," and a geological agent, to boot. With this collapsing of multiple chronologies—of species history and geological times into our very own lifetimes, within living memory—the human condition has changed. This changed condition does not mean that the related but different stories of humans as a divided humanity, as a species, and as a geological agent have all fused into one big story, and a single story of the planet and of the history of life on it can now serve in the place of humanist history. As humans we have no way of experiencing—as distinct from cognitively knowing or deducing (from the effects of our human desires and actions)—these other modes of being that are also open to us today. Humans, humans as a species, and humans as the makers of the Anthropocene are three distinct categories; we construct their archives differently, and employ different kinds of training, research skills, tools, and analytical strategies to construct them as historical agents, and they are agents of very different kinds.[57] It is obvious that humans cannot live denying their evolved characteristics—the designing of all human artifacts, for instance, will always be based on the assumption that humans have binocular vision and opposable thumbs—but having big and complex brains may very well mean, contrary to the argument that proponents of Big and Deep History have put forward, that our big and deep histories can exist alongside our small and shallow pasts, that our internal sense of time—that phenomenologists study, for instance—will not always align itself with evolutionary or geological chronologies.[58]

But the relatively recent collapsing of these differently scaled chronologies now stares us in the face creating an affect that I liken to the affect of falling: we have fallen into "deep" history, into deep, geological time. This falling into "deep" history carries a certain shock of recognition—recognition of the otherness of the planet and its very large-scale spatial and temporal processes of which we have, unintentionally, become a part.[59] What do I mean by falling into deep history? It is somewhat like pasts flashing up at a moment of emergency, as Walter Benjamin once famously put it. Being from the Indian subcontinent where diabetes has acquired epidemic proportions, I sometimes explain this experience by drawing an analogy with how an Indian person's sense of his or her own pasts suddenly undergoes a rapid expansion when he or she is diagnosed as diabetic. You go to the doctor with (potentially) a historian's view of your own pasts: a biography that you could place in certain social and historical contexts. The diagnosis, however, opens up completely new, impersonal, and long-term pasts that could not be anybody's own in the possessive-individualist sense of which the political theorist C. B. Macpherson once wrote brilliantly. Subcontinental people will most likely be told that they have a genetic propensity toward diabetes because they have been rice eaters (for at least a few thousand years); if they were academic and from a Brahmin or upper caste family in addition, then they had practiced a sedentary lifestyle for at least a few hundred years; and it would perhaps also be explained to them that human muscles' capacity for retaining and releasing sugar was still related to the fact of humans having been hunters and gatherers for the overwhelming majority of their history—suddenly, evolution![60] You do not have experiential access to any of these longer histories but you fall into a sudden awareness of them!

Such falling into deep or big history is what the tension in epochal consciousness between the homocentric and the zoecentric views of the world is all about. One can inhabit the tension but not resolve it (for, as categories constructed here, anthropos is not homo). I accepted Jaspers's category of epochal consciousness as something that, with revisions, may be of use to us as we struggle to compose the "common" of the Kyoto formula of "common but differentiated responsibilities." I also found it helpful to work with Jaspers's idea that such consciousness denoted a thought space that came before and above/beyond politics, without however foreshortening the space for political disputation and differences.

But Jaspers grounded this consciousness in "reason" that he saw as the essence of the human being. I argued that, given our falling into the times of evolutionary and geological histories, reason could not be a satisfactory resolution of the tension between the homocentric and zoecentric views of the place of human.

How do we think of this tension then? A certain slippage in Jaspers's prose suggests a way forward. Jaspers writes: "Reason is more than the sum of acts of clear thinking. These acts, rather, spring from a life-carrying basic mood, and it is this mood we call reason."[61] The word for "basic mood" in the original German text is *Grundstimmung*, a profoundly Heideggerian word pointing to the problem of attunement.[62] Moods, an ontological and not psychological category, disclose the world, claimed Heidegger, in more primordial ways than does cognition: "the possibilities of disclosure which belong to cognition reach far too short a way compared with the primordial disclosure belonging to moods, in which Dasein is brought before its Being as 'there.'"[63] And then again: "From the existential-ontological point of view, there is not the slightest justification for minimizing what is 'evident' in states-of-mind, by measuring it against the apodictic certainty of a theoretical cognition of something which is purely present-at-hand."[64]

Heidegger thus points out two aspects of "mood" that are relevant to our discussion here. Moods disclose the world more primordially or in a more profoundly phenomenological sense than does cognition. Cognition is present-at-hand, general conceptions mediated by abstract categories. It is also placeless. Climate change, as defined by climate scientists, is such a present-at-hand description of the world. It is placeless in being, literally, planetary. Moods, on the other hand, are about place: they are what brings Dasein before its Being "as there." What is translated in John Macquarrie and Edward Robinson's edition of *Being and Time* as "state-of-mind" is actually the German word *Befindlichkeit* ("the state in which one may be found") that, as the translators point out, has no etymological connection with the English word "mind," "which fails to bring out the important connotation of finding oneself."[65]

So the question that arises is: If we take into account the basic moods that underlie human responses to scientists' present-at-hand propositions about planetary climate change, moods that range from fear, denial, skepticism, pragmatism, to optimism (even of the undue kind), what is the nature of the world, not the abstract concept of the Earth, but the lived world, the place that is disclosed, where epochal consciousness finds itself? Here I would suggest, as I have already suggested elsewhere, our falling into deep or big history is also about a Heideggerian "thrownness," the shock of the recognition that the world-earth is not there simply as *our* place of dwelling, as the astronauts thought looking at the floating sphere from space. This thrownness is about the recognition of the otherness of the planet itself: an awakening to the awareness that we are not always in practical and/or aesthetic relationship with this place where we find ourselves. Its very long-term and dynamic pasts that we could, in the history of "civilization," mostly take for granted in going about our daily business, are now something that our smaller histories of conflicting attachments, desires, and aspirations have run up against, suddenly leaving us not only with an identifiable range of moods but also with our own sense of having been decentered from the narratives that we ourselves tell of this place. The expression "anthropogenic climate change" sounds as if it is all about humans—only until we realize that what we call "global warming" is merely a very particular case of the more generic category "planetary warming" that, in its most general theory, has nothing to do with humans at all, for it has happened on this planet long before there were humans, just as it happens even on planets that have no life. The fact that this planet has life and processes that support life—the story of *zoe*—only forces on us the recognition that however we strategize, the planet remains a coactor in the processes that will delay or hasten climatic shifts.

Given this phenomenological aspect to epochal consciousness, our affective responses to climate change—from denial to moods of heroism—all seem understandable and will no doubt continue to influence the politics of global warming. Motivating globally coordinated human action on global warming necessarily entails the difficult, if not impossible, task of making available to human experience a cascade of events that unfold on multiple scales, many of them inhuman. This act of persuading humans to act brings us up against the politics of climate change. Politics means having to deal with divisions among humans. It is precisely because we humans are not politically one that histories of intrahuman (in)justice and welfare will remain relevant and necessary to the efforts we make to cope with climate change. But at the same time the crisis of climate change, by throwing us into the inhuman timelines of life and geology, also takes us away from the homocentrism that divides us. As I said before, epochal consciousness is not about thinking politically. It is about thinking around politics while taking care that the space for politics is not foreclosed by that move. Our political histories will continue to divide us as we muddle our way through this crisis. But we may have to think of these divisive political histories not simply in the context of the history of capitalism but on the much larger canvas of geological and evolutionary histories.

We can follow Lovelock and ask: Will humans, even in and through all their conflicts and differences, recognize "the needs of the Earth even if [their] response time is slow?"[66] That remains the critical question for the future. How we answer it will also shape our understanding of the word *common* in the expression "common but differentiated responsibilities."

NOTES

1. Steve Vanderheiden, *Atmospheric Justice: A Political Theory of Climate Change* (Oxford: Oxford University Press, 2008), 6. See also the discussion on p. 79.

2. Ibid., 7.

3. Ibid., 264n8.

4. Ibid., 79, 104.

5. Ibid., 251–52.

6. James Lovelock, *The Vanishing Face of Gaia: A Final Warning* (New York: Basic Books, 2009), 35–36.

7. Ibid., 163.

8. Lovelock deals with some of these criticisms in his *The Ages of Gaia: A Biography of Our Living Earth* (New York: Norton, 1995 [1988]), 30–31.

9. "We all know intuitively what life is. It is edible, lovable, or lethal. Life as an object of scientific inquiry requiring precise definition is much more difficult. . . . All branches of formal biological science seem to avoid the question." Ibid., 16–17; see also 39, 60, 200–201.

10. Toby Tyrrell, *On Gaia: A Critical Investigation of the Relationship between Life and Earth* (Princeton, NJ: Princeton University Press, 2013). For an (a)stringent critique of Tyrrell, see Bruno Latour, "How to Make Sure Gaia Is Not a God of Totality? With Special Attention to Toby Tyrrell's Book on Gaia" (unpublished ms., presented at the colloquium "The Thousand Names of Gaia," Rio de Janeiro, September 2014). Michael Ruse, in his book *The Gaia Hypothesis: Science on a Pagan Planet* (Chicago: University of Chicago Press, 2013), helpfully points out how much of the scientific debate on Gaia still turns around the divide of reductionist/holistic approaches. Latour also comments on this point.

11. For some recent views of scientists, see Timothy Lenton, "Testing Gaia: The Effect of Life on Earth's Habitability and Regulation," *Climatic Change* 52 (2002): 409–22; James E. Lovelock, "Gaia and Emergence: A Response to Kirchner and Volk," *Climatic Change* 57 (2003): 1–3; Tyler Volk, "Seeing Deeper into Gaia Theory: A Reply to Lovelock's Response," ibid., 5–7; James W. Kirchner, "The Gaia Hypothesis: Conjectures and Refutations," *Climatic Change* 58 (2003): 21–45; Tyler Volk, "Natural Selection, Gaia, and Inadvertent

By-Products," ibid., 13–19; and Ruse, *Gaia Hypothesis*. For a history of these debates—apart from Lovelock's own books—see Ruse, *Gaia Hypothesis*, and John Gribbin and Mary Gribbin, *James Lovelock: In Search of Gaia* (Princeton, NJ: Princeton University Press, 2009), chs. 7–10.

12. Lovelock, *Ages of Gaia*, 28–29; see also the chapter, "The Contemporary Atmosphere," in James Lovelock, *Gaia: A New Look at Life on Earth* (Oxford: Oxford University Press, 1995; first published in 1979), ch. 5.

13. Jan Zalasiewicz and Mark Williams, *The Goldilocks Planet: The Four Billion Year Story of Earth's Climate* (Oxford: Oxford University Press, 2012), 1–2.

14. Ruse, *Gaia Hypothesis*, 219. The number 10^{22} was an estimate of the number of solar systems based on the then-prevailing assumption that all of the universe was visible.

15. Raymond T. Pierrehumbert, *Principles of Planetary Climate* (Cambridge: Cambridge University Press, 2010), 14.

16. Tyrrell, *On Gaia*, p. 176.

17. Ibid., 188–89.

18. See figures for global population and energy use, 1750–2010, given in Will Steffen et al., "The Trajectory of the Anthropocene," *Anthropocene Review* (2015): 1–18. See also Rob Hengeveld, *Wasted World: How Our Consumption Challenges the Planet* (Chicago: University of Chicago Press, 2012), part 2, ch. 1, section D.

19. John Michael Greer, "Progress vs. Apocalypse," in *The Energy Reader*, edited by Tom Butler, Daniel Lerch, and George Wuerthner, 96–99 (Sausalito, CA: Foundation for Deep Ecology, 2012), 97. Early modern historians might justifiably debate the relationship between the transition from traditional to modern agriculture and onset of the Industrial Revolution. In broad terms, however, the deep dependency of both industrialization and modern agriculture on fossil fuels is clear. I have benefited from discussion with Gerard Siarny on this topic.

20. Hengeveld, *Wasted World*, 53, 98.

21. See Vaclav Smil, *Harvesting the Biosphere: What We Have Taken from Nature* (Cambridge, MA: MIT Press, 2013), 221; Butler, Lerch, and Wuerthner, *Energy Reader*, 11–12. See also Hengeveld, *Wasted World*, 31: "almost throughout human history, life expectancy was short—normally up to only some thirty-odd years." See also 50–51.

22. Steffen et al., "Trajectory of the Anthropocene."

23. Lisa Ann-Gershwin, *Stung! On Jellyfish Blooms and the Future of the Ocean* (Chicago: University of Chicago Press, 2013), ch.10; Naomi Oreskes, "Scaling Up Our Vision," *Isis* 105, no. 2 (June 2014): 379–91, especially 388; James Hansen, *Storms for My Grandchildren: The Truth about the Coming Climate Catastrophe and Our Last Chance to Save Humanity* (New York: Bloomsbury, 2009), 165–66.

24. Hengeveld, *Wasted World*, 164–65.

25. See Smil, cited in Dipesh Chakrabarty, "Climate and Capital: On Conjoined Histories," *Critical Inquiry* (Fall 2014): 1–23.

26. Hengeveld, *Wasted World*, 66–70, 129.

27. P. K. Haff, "Technology as a Geological Phenomenon: Implications for Human Well-Being," in *A Stratigraphical Basis for the Anthropocene*, edited by C. N. Waters et al., *Geological Society, London, Special Publications* 395 (2014):, 301–9, here 301–2, http://dx.doi.org/10.1144/SP395.4.

28. Ibid., 302.

29. Bruno Latour, "Facing Gaia: Six Lectures on the Political Theology of Nature," Being the Gifford Lectures on Natural Religion, Edinburgh, February 18–28, 2013, Lecture 5, 107.

30. Haff, "Technology," 308.

31. Latour, "Facing Gaia," Lecture 4, 76.

32. Ibid., Lecture 5, 126.

33. Smil, *Harvesting the Biosphere*, 252.

34. "Emissions from India Will Increase, Official Says," report by Coral Davenport, *New York Times*, September 23, 2014. I am grateful to Sheldon Pollock for drawing my attention to this report.

35. See Thomas Athanasiou and Paul Baer, *Dead Heat: Global Justice and Global Warming* (New York: Seven Stories Press, 2002), 75, cited in Vanderheiden, *Atmospheric Justice*, 74.

36. Tyrrell, *On Gaia*, 212–13. The ppm concentration of atmospheric carbon dioxide was 394.28 in December 2012, 396.81 in December 2013, 398.78 in December 2014, and 400.18 during the week of February 1, 2015. These figures are averages prepared by the Mauna Loa Observatory in Hawaii, and obtained from http://co2now.org/.

37. Carbon Brief, http://www.carbonbrief.org/blog/2014/11/six-years-worth-of -current-emissions-would-blow-the-carbon-budget-for-1-point-5-degrees/.

38. Clive Hamilton, "Utopias in the Anthropocene," paper presented at the plenary session of the American Sociological Association, Denver, August 17, 2012, p. 3. My thanks to Professor Hamilton for sharing this paper. See also Robert J. Nicholls et al., "Sea-level Rise and Its Possible Impact Given a 'Beyond 4°C World' in the Twenty-First Century," *Philosophical Transactions of the Royal Society A* 369 (2011): 161–81; and Richard A. Betts et al., "When Could Global Warming Reach 4°C?" ibid., 67–84. Betts et al. report that their "best estimate is that a temperature rise of 4°C would be reached in the 2070s, and if the carbon-cycle feedbacks are strong, then 4°C could be reached in the early 2060s" (83), while the calculations of Nicholls et al. suggest that the number of people displaced from the coastal regions of south, southeast, and east Asia, if adaptations measures failed, would range, under different scenarios, from 72 to 187 million people (172).

39. Karl Jaspers, *The Atom Bomb and the Future of Man*, translated by E. B. Ashton (Chicago: University of Chicago Press, 1963), 10, 12–13.

40. Ibid., 217–18, 213–14.

41. Ibid., 222, 223, 307, 229.

42. Deborah R. Coen, "What's the Big Idea? The History of Ideas Confronts Climate Change," unpublished ms. (2014), 19. I am grateful to Dr. Coen for sharing a copy of this essay with me.

43. This quotation from Suess is taken from Brigitte Hamman, "Eduard Suess als liberaler Politiker," in *Eduard Suess zum Gedenken*, edited by Günther Hamman, 70–98 (Vienna: Akademie der Wissenschaften, 1983), 93, cited in Coen, "What's the Big Idea?" 18–19.

44. David Christian, "The Return of Universal History," *History and Theory* 49 (December 2010): 6–27, here 7–8.

45. McNeill cited in ibid., 26.

46. Cynthia Stokes Brown, *Big History: From the Big Bang to the Present* (New York: New Press, 2012 [2007]), xvii.

47. John L. Brooke, *Climate Change and the Course of Global History* (New York: Cambridge University Press, 2014), 558, 578–79.

48. Mark Lynas, *The God Species: How the Planet Can Survive the Age of Humans* (London: Fourth Estate, 2011), 243–44.

49. Erle C. Ellis, "Overpopulation Is Not the Problem," *New York Times*, September 13, 2013. Clive Hamilton's book, *Earthmasters: The Dawn of the Age of Climate Engineering* (New Haven, CT: Yale University Press, 2013) powerfully argues that geoengineering could indeed endanger human flourishing. See also Mike Hulme, *Can Science Fix Climate Change?* (London: Polity, 2014).

50. Tyrrell, *On Gaia*, 210–11.

51. Ibid., 213.

52. Amartya Sen, "Energy, Environment, and Freedom: Why We Must Think about More Than Climate Change," *New Republic*, August 25, 2014, 39.

53. Peter F. Sale, *Our Dying Planet: An Ecologist's View of the Crisis We Face* (Berkeley: University of California Press, 2011), 223.

54. Oreskes, "Scaling Up Our Vision," 388. On the question of extinctions and why they pose a problem for human existence, see the discussion in Sale, *Our Dying Planet*, 102, 148–49, 203–21, 233. Also Elizabeth Kolbert, *The Sixth Extinction: An Unnatural History* (New York: Henry Holt, 2014).

55. Jan Zalasiewicz et al., "When Did the Anthropocene Begin? A Mid-Twentieth Century Boundary Level Is Stratigraphically Optimal," *Quaternary International* 30 (2014): 1–8, http://dx.doi.org/10.1016/j.quaint.2014.11.045. Thanks to Dr. Zalasiewicz for letting me see a copy of this article before publication.

56. We should acknowledge here the deeply contested nature of this yet-to-be-formalized term, *Anthropocene*, debated not only by social scientists but by geologists themselves. See S. C. Finney, "The 'Anthropocene' as a Ratified Unit in the ICS International Chronostratigraphic Chart: Fundamental Issues That Must Be Addressed by the Task Group" and P. L. Gibbard and M. J. C. Walker, "The Term 'Anthropocene' in the Context of Geological Classification," in *A Stratigraphical Basis for the Anthropocene*, pp. 23–28, 29–37. See also the exchanges between Zalasiewicz et al. and Whitney J. Autin and John M. Holbrook in "Is the Anthropocene an Issue of Stratigraphy or Pop Culture?" *GSA Today*, October 2012.

57. See Dipesh Chakrabarty, "Postcolonial Studies and the Challenge of Climate Change," *New Literary History* 43 (2012): 25–42.

58. Here I register—with respect and admiration—a small but significant conceptual disagreement with some of the propositions that Daniel Lord Smail has put forward in his thought-provoking book, *On Deep History and the Brain* (Berkeley: University of California Press, 2008). The book opens with the statement: "If humanity is the proper subject of history, as Linnaeus might have well have counseled, then it stands to reason that the Paleolithic era, that long stretch of the Stone Age before the turn to agriculture, is part of our history" (2). I agree, and I do not: it depends on how one understands the words *humanity* and *our*. They are open to multiple meanings. Smail similarly remarks (201), with regard to the genes ("of considerable antiquity") that are "responsible for building the autonomic nervous system," that "this history is also world history since the equipment is shared by all humans though it is built, manipulated, and tweaked in different ways by different cultures." But the physical feature of the autonomic nervous system is something humans share with many other animals, so this could not quite be a world history of humans alone. I elaborate on these differences in a forthcoming paper provisionally titled, "From World-History to Big History: Some Friendly Amendments."

59. See Dipesh Chakrabarty, "Climate and Capital: On Conjoined Histories," *Critical Inquiry* (Fall 2014): 1–23.

60. The archaeologist Kathleen D. Morrison states that the "codification of several elite cuisines based on irrigated produce, especially rice" can be documented from "the first millennium C.E. in South India." See her "The Human Face of the Land: Why the Past Matters for India's Environmental Future," NMML Occasional Paper, History and Society, New Series no. 27 (New Delhi: Nehru Memorial Museum and Library, 2013), 1–31, here 16.

61. Jaspers, *Atom Bomb*, 218.

62. Karl Jaspers, *Die Atombombe und die Zukunft des Menschen* (Munich: R. Piper & Co Verlag, 1958), 300.

63. Martin Heidegger, *Being and Time*, translated by John Macquarrie and Edward Robinson (Oxford: Basil Blackwell, 1985; first published in 1962), 173.

64. Ibid., 175.

65. Ibid., 172n2.

66. Lovelock, *Ages of Gaia*, 171.

A Conversation with Ruth Bader Ginsburg, Associate Justice of the United States Supreme Court

JUSTICE RUTH BADER GINSBURG

THE TANNER LECTURES IN HUMAN VALUES

Delivered at

The University of Michigan
February 6, 2015

RUTH BADER GINSBURG was nominated by President Clinton as associate justice of the United States Supreme Court in June 1993 and took the oath of office on August 10, 1993. Prior to her appointment to the Supreme Court, she served from 1980 to 1993 on the bench of the United States Court of Appeals for the District of Columbia Circuit. From 1972 to 1980, Justice Ginsburg was a professor at Columbia University School of Law; from 1963 to 1972, she served on the law faculty of Rutgers, the State University of New Jersey. She has served on the faculties of the Salzburg Seminar in American Studies and the Aspen Institute for Humanistic Studies, and as a visiting professor at many universities in the United States and abroad. In 1978, she was a fellow at the Center for Advanced Study in the Behavioral Sciences in Stanford, California.

Justice Ginsburg has a bachelor of arts degree from Cornell University, attended Harvard Law School, and received her LL.B. (J.D.) from Columbia Law School. She holds honorary degrees from many universities, including Michigan, Yale, Princeton, and Harvard.

In 1972, then-Professor Ginsburg was instrumental in launching the Women's Rights Project of the American Civil Liberties Union. Throughout the 1970s she litigated a series of cases solidifying a constitutional principle against gender-based discrimination. Justice Ginsburg is a member of the Council on Foreign Relations, the American Academy of Arts and Sciences, and the American Philosophical Society. She has written widely in the areas of civil procedure, conflict of laws, constitutional law, and comparative law.

Editor's Note: Justice Ginsburg chose to present her Tanner Lecture in the form of a conversation about her personal history, her work as an attorney, and her judicial opinions. She was joined in this discussion by professors Kate Andrias and Scott Hershovitz of the University of Michigan Law School. Andrias and Hershovitz both served as law clerks for Justice Ginsburg, and their questions reflect their knowledge of her life experience and her history on the Supreme Court. The conversation took place before a lively audience of 3,500 at the University of Michigan's Hill Auditorium.

Justice Ginsburg (JG): Thank you! Please be seated so we can get started.

Kate Andrias (KA): Justice, thank you so much for joining us this morning. We have combined questions that were submitted online with some of our own. And to start, we want to talk about how you become a lawyer. As President Schlissel mentioned, when you enrolled at Harvard Law School in 1956 you were one of nine women in a class of about five hundred. What made you decide to go to law school when so few women did?

JG: I will answer the question in two parts. First part, I was an undergraduate at Cornell University in the early 1950s. It was not the best of times for our country. Senator Joseph McCarthy from Wisconsin held sway. He was a man who saw a communist in every corner. People were hauled before the House Un-American Activities Committee and the Senate Internal Security Committee. They were asked questions about their affiliations with socialist organizations in the thirties. The professor for whom I worked as a research assistant, Professor Robert Cushman, taught Constitutional Law. He wanted me to understand that our country was straying from its most basic values. But there were lawyers standing up for people in the entertainment industry who were blacklisted, and for writers and academics. Those lawyers were reminding our Congress that we have a First Amendment that secures our right to think for ourselves and not as "Big Brother" thinks we should. And we have a Fifth Amendment that protects us against self-incrimination. The idea was that law is a profession, but it also arms you with the skill to help make things a little better for other people. So that was one tug.

The other part was played by my dear spouse. Both of you knew Marty. We decided that whatever we would do in our post-college years, we would do it together.

Fortunately for me, medicine was eliminated because golf practice (Marty was on Cornell's varsity team) interfered with afternoon science labs. Our choice then became business school or law school. In those ancient days, the Harvard Business School did not admit women. The Law School first admitted women in '50–'51. So business school was scratched, and that left law school.

Now, I should add that my family had some reservations about my career choice because most law firms in the 1950s and 1960s wanted no "lady lawyers." Marty and I married a week after I graduated from Cornell. My family's reservations vanished. Their view became, "If she wants to be a lawyer, let her try. If she doesn't succeed, she'll have a man to support her."

Scott Hershovitz (SH): Justice, let's talk a little bit about your early career as a lawyer. Everyone knows that you are an advocate for gender equality, but before that, you were a professor of procedure. What got you interested in procedure?

JG: Procedure was the first class I attended at the Harvard Law School, I had a great teacher, Benjamin Kaplan. He was skilled in the Socratic Method, but he never used it to embarrass or humiliate students. He would sometimes take a less than coherent answer a student gave and rephrase it so it sounded brilliant. There was a young man in that class, his name was Tony Lewis. He was a well-known journalist enrolled at Harvard as a Nieman Fellow. For many years, he was the Supreme Court reporter for the *New York Times*. The first day in class, he answered the professor's questions just right. I aimed to speak in class as often as Tony Lewis. I attribute my fondness for procedure to my teacher, Benjamin Kaplan, and fellow student, Tony Lewis.

In 1963, I started teaching at Rutgers Law School in Newark. Rutgers had lost its principal procedure person, Clyde Ferguson. Clyde left to become dean of the Howard Law School. Rutgers searched for an African American male to replace him. Failing in that quest, the next best thing was a woman. For me, it proved to be more than a little bit of luck.

KA: How did you transition to work on gender equality issues?

JG: From civil procedure? There were two magnets. One, my students. In 1970, the students wanted Rutgers to offer a course on women and the law. Such a course had been started at NYU and at Georgetown. I repaired to the library. In the space of a month, I read every federal decision published up to that time about women's status under the law. Now, that was no mean feat. Precious little appeared in print on that topic, less than would be generated today in a couple of months. I put together some materials and taught a course on women and the law. The other magnet: new complainants were coming to the ACLU. I had signed up as a volunteer lawyer for the ACLU's New Jersey affiliate. Among the new complainants were pregnant schoolteachers made to take what was euphemistically called "maternity leave" rather early in their pregnancy. It was a euphemism because the leave was unpaid and there was no guaranteed right to return. If the school district wanted the teacher back, the superintendent would call.

One of the explanations for that practice: "We don't want the children to think their teacher has swallowed a watermelon." From the women's perspective: "We are ready, willing, and able to work. There's no reason why we should not be allowed to continue."

Another category of complainants, blue-collar women who sought health insurance for their families through their place of employment. A common practice, employers offered family coverage only to male workers. Women were considered secondary wage earners, "pin money earners." The man was the worker who counted. As head of the family, he alone qualified for family coverage.

On the Rutgers campus itself, the undergraduate college was all male. There was a smaller, very fine women's college, but the state was providing education to many more boys than girls.

Those are typical of the new complaints coming into the ACLU around 1970, and the legal director in Newark asked if I could handle them. I wasn't the initiator. My students and the new complainants tugged my occupations in a new direction. Until then, most women simply accepted the way things were. In the 1970s, the Women's Movement experienced a revival all over the world. In its wake, women in the USA, in increasing numbers, decided they shouldn't simply submit to the way things were, they should be part of making things the way they should be.

SH: I am wondering if you could tell us more about your work with ACLU Women's Rights Project—what your legal strategy was. Sometimes people compare you to Thurgood Marshall; they say that you were the Thurgood Marshall of the Women's Rights Movement. I am wondering what you make of the comparison and whether the legal strategies were similar or different.

JG: Thurgood Marshall inspired partisans of social change. People know about *Brown v. Board of Education*, but many do not know about all the building blocks Marshall had in place before he took on legally enforced separation of the races in public schools. Before *Brown*, there was a law school case, a couple of university cases. By the time *Brown* v. *Board* reached the Supreme Court, it seemed inevitable that the court would move in the direction it did. Marshall didn't ask the court to take a giant stride. A step-by-step approach was his successful strategy. I copied that strategy, but I am uneasy when people compare me to Thurgood Marshall. His life was on the line when he went to a small town in the South to represent someone charged with a capital crime he probably didn't commit. My life was never in danger.

KA: Can you tell us more about some of the cases you brought and whether there is one case in particular that you think of as your most important victory?

JG: Perhaps I should first describe the turning-point case, *Reed v. Reed*. As a preface, I should explain that until 1971, the Supreme Court never saw a gender classification it didn't like, or at least, that it regarded as unconstitutional. Consider a case decided in 1948, *Goesaert v. Cleary*. The plaintiff was a woman who owned a tavern. Her daughter was her bartender. But the State of Michigan had recently passed a law prohibiting women from working as bartenders unless the woman was the wife or the daughter of the bar owner.

Mother Goesaert was put out of business by that law. The Supreme Court observed that bars can be dangerous places, and held that

Michigan's law was legitimate because it protected women against the sometimes foul atmosphere in taverns. No law precluded women from being barmaids, bringing drinks to tables. Those women were not sheltered by a bar from dangerous men. Without recognizing that irony, the Supreme Court declared it constitutional to exclude women from bartending.

Fast forward from Goesaert's case in 1948 to Sally Reed's case in 1971. Sally was a woman from Boise, Idaho. She and her husband had a son. The couple divorced. When the child was of "tender years," Sally was given custody. When the boy reached his teens and needed to be prepared for a man's world, the father applied for custody and Sally opposed his application. She thought the father would not be a good influence on the son. Sadly, she turned out to be right. This boy became severely depressed and one day used one of his father's many guns to kill himself.

Sally wanted to be appointed administrator of his estate, not for any monetary reason. There was very little in the estate; a small bank account, a guitar, a record collection, that was about it. Her former husband applied some weeks later. Sally assumed she would get the appointment because she applied first. The probate court judge told her, "I'm very sorry about this, but the law settles the matter for me." It reads, "As between persons equally entitled to administer a decedent's estate, males must be preferred to females."

It was the perfect turning-point case. Sally Reed was excluded arbitrarily, simply because she was a woman. Her case was in no sense made-up. Sally Reed was an everyday woman.

In the seventies, we never had to look for plaintiffs, they were all out there. After *Goesaert* v. *Cleary*, the Michigan bartender's case in 1948, the next gender discrimination case was heard in 1961, during the tenure of the "Liberal Warren Court." A woman, Gwendolyn Hoyt, was charged with murdering her philandering, abusive husband. It was a freak accident. He had humiliated her to the breaking point. She saw her young son's baseball bat in the corner of the room, took it, and with all her might, hit her husband over the head. He fell to the ground. End of their altercation, beginning of the murder prosecution.

Gwendolyn Hoyt had the idea that if women were on her jury, they might better understand her state of mind. Not that they would acquit her, but they might find her guilty of the lesser offense of manslaughter rather than murder.

But Hillsborough County, Florida, where Gwendolyn Hoyt lived, did not put women on the jury rolls. Florida had a system some regarded as pure favor to women. Women were not on the jury roster to begin with, but any woman who wanted to serve could go down to the clerk's office and sign up.

You can imagine how many people, male or female, would sign up voluntarily if they were not compelled to serve.

Anyway, Gwendolyn Hoyt was convicted of murder by an all-male jury. The Warren Court found that Florida's exclusion of women from the jury rolls made sense, for after all, women are "the center of home and family life," and should not be distracted from their homecare responsibilities.

Ten years later, the court displayed a different understanding. Warren Burger was then the chief justice. He did not have the liberal reputation that Earl Warren did, and yet the court ruled unanimously in Sally Reed's favor. We knew from that unanimous decision that the court was ready to catch up with the change that had already occurred in society. By 1971, women were not content to be pigeonholed or placed on a single track. They wanted to have opportunities to do whatever their God-given talents enabled them to do.

In the course of the seventies, laws, both state laws, like the Michigan Bartender Law, and federal laws drawn on gender lines, were removed from the statute books. The first effort of the ACLU's Women's Rights Project was to make sure that public opinion was on our side. Next, we urged legislative change, and if that failed, constitutional challenges could be mounted in court.

I have described Sally Reed's case. Let me tell you about Stephen Wiesenfeld's. It is probably the best illustration of what is wrong with sex-role stereotyping. Stephen Wiesenfeld's wife was a public school teacher. She had a healthy pregnancy, teaching into the ninth month. When Steven and Paula went to the hospital for the birth of their child, the doctor came out and told Steven, "You have a healthy baby boy, but your wife died of an embolism."

Steven vowed that he would not work full-time until his child was in school full-time. He could just about make it with the Social Security benefits provided for a child left with a sole-surviving parent, plus the earnings limit—the amount he could make on top of the Social Security benefits.

He went to the Social Security office, asked for an application for child-in-care benefits, and was told, "the benefits are for mothers, they're not available to fathers." A sole-surviving parent who was female would get the benefits enabling her to care for a child, but the sole-surviving male parent did not qualify.

Wiesenfeld's case was argued, first of all, as discrimination against the woman as worker. Paula Wiesenfeld paid the same Social Security taxes as her male coworker, but when she died, her family did not get the same protection. Stephen Wiesenfeld was disadvantaged as a parent because he would not have the opportunity to work only part-time. He would have to work full-time and could not be his child's personal caretaker.

The court's majority recognized that the discrimination started with the woman as worker. Others thought the law discriminated against the male as parent. And one, who later became my chief—he was then Justice Rehnquist—said that the scheme was totally arbitrary from the point of view of the baby.

Why should the baby have the care of a parent, a sole-surviving parent, only if the parent is female? I think it was the lone case in which the chief voted to hold a gender-based law unconstitutional. We did not ask to "strike down" the law. We certainly did not want to take away mothers' benefits. Instead, we urged, this law is imperfect. Congress wanted mothers to get the benefits. The last thing in the world Congress would want is to remove the benefits from women.

So to perfect the law, to make it constitutional, the court had to "equalize up," to convert "surviving mother" to "sole-surviving parent, male or female." Many law teachers told me, "You can't do that." The court can strike down the law and then leave it to the legislature to reenact the measure shorn of gender bias. The court eventually accepted the position that if there is an unconstitutional omission in a statute, then the court should ask, "Suppose the legislature knew that what it had passed was not permissible, what would it prefer? Would it rather have the law stricken or would it prefer to extend the law to cover the class unconstitutionally left out?"

After Stephen Wiesenfeld's cases, a series of other Social Security cases were brought on behalf of husbands and widowers, cases I called "Wiesenfeld without the baby."

The final case in that series involved unemployment compensation, in particular, a social welfare benefit available when the parent was unemployed. When Congress learned that some women were signing up as the unemployed parent, it changed the law to cover only unemployed fathers. In a 1979 decision, the court considered the constitutionality of the law.

"Congress had changed unemployed parent to unemployed fathers," the court noted, but Congress got it right the first time. So the court restored "unemployed parent." In that case, the majority acknowledged what I just explained. If the law is imperfect, sometimes the appropriate cure is not to strike it down but to extend it to the left-out people.

SH: Let's talk a little bit about your time at the court. The opinion that you may be best-known for is *United States v. Virginia*. Can you tell us a little about the Virginia Military Institute (VMI) case and how it relates to the cases that you have just been telling us about?

JG: The Virginia Military Institute is a state school. It offers an advantageous educational opportunity. VMI graduates do not necessarily become soldiers; only about 15 percent of VMI graduates go into the military. But the institute fostered an old boy's network. Graduates who had positions in business and commerce would help younger graduates along their way. Virginia did not offer anything comparable for women. One interesting facet of the VMI case is that the plaintiff was the United States of America. Not too many years before, there had been litigation against the United States for excluding women from West Point, from Annapolis, from the Air Force Academy. Those cases were litigated on behalf of women who wanted to go to those schools.

In the course of the litigation, the government decided it would rather switch than fight, and it opened up the military academies to women. By the time we got to VMI, the United States was arguing on behalf of women ready, willing, and able to go to VMI.

Sometimes people ask me, "Why would a woman want to go to VMI and undergo that kind of rigorous military training?" I reply, "I wouldn't want to. Perhaps you wouldn't want to. Perhaps the gentlemen over there wouldn't want to, but there are some women who want to and have everything it takes, all the qualifications necessary to succeed. Why shouldn't they have that opportunity?" The VMI case yielded a seven to one judgment. Justice Scalia was the lone dissenter.

My husband commented, "Ruth, it took you twenty years to win the Vorchheimer's case." What was the Vorchheimer's case? Philadelphia had two public high schools for gifted children; their names told the story.

One was called Central—it was all boys. The other was called Girls' High. A girl, Susan Vorchheimer, wanted to go to Central because it had better math and science facilities, and incomparably better athletic facilities. She won in the District Court, the federal trial court. She lost in the Court of Appeals 2–1. So the federal judges stood 2–2 at that point. In the Supreme Court, one justice was recused, the rest divided evenly 4–4. When that happens, the court is unable to make a decision. Instead, it automatically affirms the decision of the Court of Appeals.

That meant that the Third Circuit judgment—that Central High could remain all male—stood. Years later, a Pennsylvania court, under Pennsylvania's Equal Rights Amendment, held that Central could not remain all male.

KA: In recent years, you have gotten more attention for your dissents than for your majority opinions. Which of your dissents do you think is the most important?

JG: The most important . . . I can't pick just one. But Shelby County is high on my list. Some of you have seen the film *Selma*, and you know the background of the Voting Rights Act of 1965, a very important law that Congress renewed periodically. States and certain localities in the bad old days had barred African Americans from voting, and the federal law said to those prior offenders, "If you want to change any of your voting laws, you have to preclear the change either with the Justice Department or with a three-judge federal court in the District of Columbia. The formula was challenged as outdated. Congress, by an overwhelming majority, both sides of the aisle, had renewed the Voting Rights Act with the same formula. The court agreed with the challengers that the formula was outdated. Everyone knew it was impossible for the Congress then sitting to change it. So a major civil rights protection was effectively rendered unconstitutional.

I viewed Shelby County as a "who decides" case. The legislature had overwhelmingly voted to extend the Voting Rights Act. Should nine unelected judges trump that decision of the legislative branch? My answer was "no." The members of the political branches probably know more about voting and elections than the unelected Supreme Court justices do. So I would have preserved the Voting Rights Act. The problem with changing the formula was simply this: What senator, what representative was going to stand up and say, "My state is still discriminating. It should still be on the list."

Sometimes, a dissent can have an immediate impact. My favorite example is the Lilly Ledbetter case. Lilly worked for a Goodyear Tire plant. She was an area manager. She was hired in the 1970s, the first woman to hold such a job. Many years later, she found a slip of paper in her mailbox at the plant. It had a series of numbers. They showed the pay received by other area managers. Lilly's name, although she worked there for well over a decade, was at the very bottom. The most junior person, someone she had helped train, earned more than she did. So she decided she had a good Title VII lawsuit. Title VII is the principal antidiscrimination in employment federal statute. It says employers cannot discriminate because of race, religion, national origin, or sex.

Lilly won in the trial court. She got a substantial verdict, but the Supreme Court said she sued too late. Title VII says, "You have to complain within 180 days of the discriminatory incident." Lilly complained about discrimination that began at the end of the seventies, so she was way out of time, the court held. What I tried to explain in my dissent was that women who take a job that, up to then, had been done mostly by men, do not want to be seen as complainers. They don't want to rock the boat. Besides, suppose she had complained early on—well, first, she would have to know, because salary figures were not given out. Second, the employer would almost certainly defend by saying, "It has nothing to do with Lilly being a woman. She just doesn't do the job as well as the guys." But now she has been working there over a decade, and she has gotten good performance ratings through the years. So the defense that she does not do the job as well is no longer available. Now, she has a winnable case.

Her view was that the discrimination she encountered is repeated every month. Every paycheck reflects that differential so she should—if you interpret Title VII properly—have 180 days from each paycheck to complain. Congress with amazing rapidity amended Title VII to adopt that paycheck theory—that the clock started to run anew with every paycheck that reflected the discriminatory differential.

The Lilly Ledbetter dissent had an immediate impact. Most of my dissents, I hope, will be the law someday.

SH: Justice, two of your colleagues have given Tanner Lectures before. Justice Scalia took the opportunity to defend originalism, and Justice Breyer defended his view of active liberty and said that the Constitution should be interpreted to promote democratic engagement. What is your approach to the Constitution? Do you think of yourself as having an -ism?

JG: My approach to the Constitution is influenced by the first three words, "We the people." If we go back to 1787, who were "we the people"? A very select group. They were white, property-owning men. I think the genius of our Constitution is that, over the span of more than two centuries, the notion of who counts among "we the people" has grown. At the start, Native Americans were left out, people held in human bondage, women, until 1920, were not part of the political community, and newcomers to our shores. We the people, today, is a much more embracing concept than it was in 1787. The founders probably expected that that's the way it would be and should be—that these grand ideas they planted, like due process of law, would be adjusted to govern the society that exists at a particular time. To take a simple example: the Eighth Amendment, cruel and unusual punishment. Many people visit Historic Williamsburg, Virginia. They visit the jail and see various devices designed to punish people, like putting them in a stock. We do not allow that kind of public humiliation today. We don't allow twenty lashes. So cruel and unusual punishments means something different today than it meant originally.

The difference between my approach and Justice Scalia's is illustrated in a comic opera that will have its world premiere on July 11 in Castleton, Virginia. The opera is called Scalia/Ginsburg. It opens with Scalia's rage aria. It is, for those who know music, a Handelian aria. Handel is long, long dead so there are no copyright problems. The composer and librettist is a young man, Derrick Wang, and he has created a marvelously inventive piece. Scalia's rage aria goes like this.

"The Justices are blind. How can they possibly spout this? The Constitution says absolutely nothing about this." I answer that he is "searching for bright line solutions to problems that don't have easy answers, but the great thing about our Constitution is, like our society, it can evolve." And then the singer launches into a spirited refrain, "Let it grow. Let it grow."

There is a scene I like better than my colleague does. Justice Scalia is locked up in a dark room. He is being punished for excessive dissenting. I enter to rescue him. I make my entrance through a glass ceiling.

KA: Justice, the court obviously plays an important role in interpreting the Constitution. You have said that the Supreme Court went too far and too fast in *Roe v. Wade*. What do you mean by that?

JG: *Roe v. Wade* is a 1973 decision. At the time of Roe, abortion law was in a state of flux all over the country. Some states, including my home state, New York, also California, Alaska, and Hawaii, allowed a woman access to an abortion in the first trimester, if that was her choice. A number of states had moved to a middle ground, recognizing grounds for abortion: rape, incest, danger to the woman's health. Texas had the most extreme law in the nation, no abortion unless it was necessary to save the woman's life; impairment of her health was not good enough, only her life counted. I thought the Supreme Court would strike down that most extreme law, and then there would be a continuing dialogue in the country. State legislatures would react to the court's decision. Instead, the court wrote an opinion that made every law in the nation, even the most liberal, unconstitutional in one fell swoop. I spoke earlier about *Brown v. Board* and Thurgood Marshall putting the building blocks in place. The Women's Rights Project started with cases like Sally Reed's and it built up from there.

Roe was a stunning opinion, although it was not really controversial at the time it was released. *Roe v. Wade* is a 7–2 decision. There were only two dissenters, Justice Rehnquist and Justice White. My thought was that if the court had been more modest, then the change would continue to move in the direction in which it was already moving. Instead, there was a single target for those who opposed a woman's free choice, and that one target was *Roe v. Wade*, a decision by unelected justices. It was much easier to target that decision than to be fighting in the trenches, state legislature by state legislature.

Unquestionably the right judgment was reached in *Roe*. I criticized not the judgment, but the opinion, on two grounds. One, a criticism best expressed by a great constitutional law scholar, Paul Freund. He said, "The problem with *Roe v. Wade* is like that of the little boy who gets trotted out at his parents' dinner party and to impress the guests, he's asked to spell 'banana.'" He replies, "Well, I know how to start spelling banana. I just don't know where to stop." That's what I saw as the problem with the decision in *Roe v. Wade*.

SH: Justice, after Justice Stevens left the bench, he published a book in which he proposed six amendments to our Constitution. Do you have amendments you would like to see added?

JG: I have one, beyond all others and that is the Equal Rights Amendment. I am sometimes asked, "Well, isn't the Equal Protection Clause good enough?" My answer is "no." Think of this historically. There was a woman, Virginia Minor. After the Fourteenth Amendment was adopted, she wanted to vote. The amendment says, she urged, "nor shall any state deny to any person the equal protection of the laws." "I am a person and I am a citizen," so I must have the right to vote. The Supreme Court answered her plea by saying, "Of course you're a person and you are a citizen, but so too are children. And who would suggest that children should have the right to vote?" That was back in the 1870s.

The post–Civil War amendments had one purpose: to end the legacy of slavery. At the time the Fourteenth Amendment was adopted, many states placed restrictions on married women. The woman who married lost her right to contract, to sue and be sued in her own name, to hold property in her own right. The Congress that put out the Thirteenth, Fourteenth, and Fifteenth Amendments for ratification had no intention of changing any of that.

As I said a while ago, the idea of equality is much broader than the initial impact of it. So perhaps today, under the Equal Protection Clause, the rights that the Equal Rights Amendment would have secured—most of them—the same result might be achieved under the Equal Protection Clause. But every constitution in the world written after World War II has a statement to the effect that women and men are persons of equal citizenship stature.

I would like to take my pocket Constitution out, show it to my three granddaughters, and say, "This is a prime value of our society, just like free speech and freedom of religion. The equality of men and women, their equal citizenship stature, is a basic tenet of our society." And for that reason, I would like to see that statement in our Constitution, just as it is in every post–World War II constitution.

KA: Could you tell us what the Supreme Court decision is that you would most like to see overruled?

JG: I mentioned the Voting Rights Act decision, but I would have to say, first, if I had any decision I could change, it would be *Citizens United*. I am very glad, very proud to be a citizen of the USA, but when I go abroad and people ask, "How can it be that you allow unlimited campaign contributions? Certainly, the office holder is going to be beholden to the big money person who finances his or her campaign." Other democratic nations have very severe limits on private financing of candidates for public office. And people abroad say of the current situation in the United States, "You have all the democracy money can buy."

I think there will come a time, maybe not too far down the road, when the people are disgusted with this, and then the pendulum will swing the other way.

SH: Supreme Court justices are the only senior officials in our government who decide for themselves when to retire, and some people think that instead of having that system, we should have a system of fixed terms. Which system do you think is better?

JG: The most important thing is that you preserve the independence of the judges. Some systems, like Germany, have a long—I think the term for their Constitutional Court is either twelve or fourteen years, nonrenewable. Nonrenewable, so the judge won't worry about a reappointment, how a vote on a particular issue would affect reappointment. That's the way they guarantee the independence of the judges. In our system, Article III of the Constitution says that judges, all federal judges, not just Supreme Court justices, shall hold their office during good behavior. I might speculate about other systems, but the truth is, our Constitution is powerfully hard to amend. I know that as a citizen of the District of Columbia. District dwellers would like to end taxation without representation. The failed effort to ratify the Equal Rights Amendment is another example.

So we have a Constitution that is very difficult to amend, and I do not think life tenure for federal judges is going to be something that really exercises the public. Of course, I am terribly biased and prejudiced on this subject. But think of Justice Stevens, who stepped down when he was ninety. Scott has already mentioned that since his retirement, he has written a couple of books. In his last year on the court, the year he turned ninety, he was no slower than he was when I was a new justice. He was still the fastest justice responding to an opinion another justice circulated.

So it is a decision an individual has to make. I have said that as long I can do the job full steam, I will stay in it. But when I begin to slip, as inevitably I will, when that happens, that will be the time for me to go.

KA: As we have talked about, you focused a lot of your career on the rights of women. Your dissent in *Hobby Lobby* points out one way in which women are still disfavored by the law. Could you talk a little bit about that dissent and other areas of the law where women are still at disadvantage?

JG: Hobby Lobby was decided under a law called the Religious Freedom Restoration Act, and from the majority's point of view, they were championing the right of the owners of the Hobby Lobby to practice their religion. And I had no doubt about the genuineness of their religious belief and their right to practice their own religion. But what they did not have the right to do, in my judgment, was to force their religious belief on a workforce that did not share that view. I used in my dissenting opinion an expression by a great law teacher, Zechariah Chafee. Speaking of freedom of expression, he said, "I have a right to swing my arm, until it touches the other fellow's nose, and that's when I have to stop."

KA: As we have talked about, there has been lots of positive change for women, for people of color, for gays and lesbians over the course of your career, and we hope perhaps more change is coming. But lower-income women still face a host of challenges, and the situation for lower-income Americans, in general, is getting worse. We were wondering if you think there's a role for a law and judges in addressing economic inequality, or are those issues better handled through politics?

JG: A court does not have the power of the purse. So if you want a spending program, that cannot be created by a court. The major problems, I think, must be solved legislatively, to raise the money through taxes for social programs, and to create those programs. We were, until very recently, the only democratic industrialized nation that did not have universal health care. That is not a program the court can adopt. A court can say yes or no, or it can extend the law in the way I described. But it cannot create the kind of programs that would be needed if we are seriously to have a handle on the economic inequality that exists in the country. There are modern constitutions that guarantee economic and social rights, as well as political rights, but rights of that nature are aspirational. And ever since *Marbury v. Madison*, we have treated our Constitution not as an aspirational document, but as law on the ground, the highest law we have, a law that trumps other laws.

So we do not have economic and social rights in our Constitution. If we did, there is no way a court could provide a decent shelter for every person, enough to eat. Those programs have to be adopted by the legislature.

KA: We wanted to switch to talk a little bit about family life. You have two new female colleagues, Justice Kagan and Justice Sotomayor, and many people are struck by the fact that neither one is married or has had children. Do you think that having a family makes it harder for women to reach the highest levels of government, or the legal profession? And what could we do about that?

JG: Whenever the comment is made—that the woman has to give up her family life if she is going to rise to the top of the tree in her profession—I think about Justice O'Connor, who raised three sons, or my colleague on the D.C. Circuit, Pat Wald, who has five children. I attribute my success largely to my partner in life, my husband, but also to my children. I succeeded as a law student because law school was not the only thing in my life. That is, I worked hard, I attended all of my classes and studied in the library in the afternoon. But four o'clock was children's hour.

My days were concentrated on studies, but then I had this respite, this time with my daughter until she went to sleep, and then I went back to the books. Each part of my life was a respite from the other, and I was not so overwhelmed about law, law school, or study as the only thing in life that mattered.

I remember how nervous I was about taking practice exams my first year. Harvard had a cruel system. There were no exams until the very end of the year, but there were practice exams in January or February.

In one of those unforgettable moments in life, I was at the kitchen table studying, when my daughter crawled in. She had a mouth full of moth balls she came upon in a drawer containing my sweaters. We rushed her to the Cambridge City Hospital. I listened to her scream when her stomach was pumped. Thank goodness she hadn't actually ingested anything, but at that moment, I realized, "These practice exams really aren't all that important." After that I had a more relaxed attitude about them.

SH: Justice, one of your law clerks recently wrote an article in the *Atlantic* about the advice you gave him about being a stay-at-home dad. I think a lot of people find it natural to look to you for advice because you and Marty had such a wonderful relationship. You both had extraordinary careers and you raised two successful children. So we are wondering: what advice do you have for the rest of us?

JG: More than a little bit of luck is involved in raising a child who has a happy, satisfying adulthood, as my children do. My children are ten years apart. With my daughter, I overcompensated, dreadfully. On weekends, I took her to museums and children's shows. I took her to the Amato Opera when she was four years old. That was pushing things a bit. She stood up as the soprano was singing, and shouted at the top of her lungs, because that's how the soprano sounded to her. I quickly ushered her out. We waited four more years, and then went to the Met, choosing the opera carefully. It was *Così fan tutte* in an English translation. Jane loved it. By the time my son James came along, my husband and I were both busy with our careers, so he didn't have the same intense education every weekend. Jane never had a meal without beautiful long-playing records loaded on the Victrola. My son, who has a passion for music, just came by it naturally.

SH: In the years since Kate and I worked for you, I think it's safe to say you've achieved a new level of notoriety. Can you tell us a little bit about what it's like to be the Notorious R. B. G.?

JG: When all this started, my law clerks had to tell me about Notorious B. I. G. He's no longer alive, but we do have something in common.

We both grew up in Brooklyn. Notorious R. B. G. was started by a student at NYU Law School. I think it's wonderfully amusing. Early on, there were T-shirts, and the latest is a tattoo, fake, I hope. The creators of Notorious R. B. G. came to court and they sat in at a session. They have posted some serious stuff. As the Clinton Library released papers, they picked up items leading to my nomination by the president. Some of the items were revelations. Notorious R. B. G. is going to be a book. These are very speedy people. Recently, they interviewed my personal trainer, and they anticipate a fall release.

They asked my trainer, "What does she do?" He responded, "Well, I'll tell you and then you try it." They were intimidated.

SH: Justice, we are just about out of time, but there are a lot of young people on the audience and we would be interested to give you an opportunity to give them advice—advice for young women, advice for young men, advice for everybody.

JG: I've loved the law. I've loved everything I've done in it. But one thing I know is that if I had regarded the law as just a business . . . Oh, let me, first, tell you about beginnings that Justice O'Connor and I shared. She was at the top of her class in Stanford, but as in my case, there were no job offers. She volunteered to work free for a county attorney for four months, and said, "If you think I'm worth it after four months, you can put me on the payroll." That's how she got her first job. I was tremendously fortunate to have been alive and a lawyer when the Women's Movement came alive, and I had a talent that could help move that social change along. I have gotten tremendous satisfaction from things I have done that I wasn't paid to do. And if you think of yourself as a professional, you are not going to be content working just to turn over a buck. If you do only that, then you will have an occupation, much like a plumber, your skill will enable you to earn a living. But if you think of yourself as a true professional armed with a skill that can help others less fortunate—whatever it is that's your passion, whether it's the environment, helping newcomers to our shores, whatever it is—if you can work to help repair tears in your communities, to make things a little better for people in need, you will gain satisfaction no paycheck could give you.

Lawyers have an obligation to serve the public in that way. After all, lawyers have a monopoly on certain services, and at least in exchange for that privilege, they ought to conceive of themselves as servants of the people. That would be my advice to you. Pursue whatever is your passion, in addition to the job for which you get paid.

SH: Justice, thanks so much for coming today. It was such a special privilege for all of us, and we are glad you trekked out to Michigan in the dead of winter to share your wisdom with us this morning. Thank you.

JG: Thank you for being such sympathique interviewers. Thank you to all in the audience for listening so patiently.

NOTE

The original transcript of this lecture has been edited here for clarity and to aid reader comprehension.

The Birth of Ethics

PHILIP PETTIT

THE TANNER LECTURES IN HUMAN VALUES

Delivered at

University of California, Berkeley
April 7–9, 2015

PHILIP PETTIT is L. S. Rockefeller University Professor of Politics and Human Values at Princeton University, where he has taught political theory and philosophy since 2002. Since 2012–13 has held a joint position as Distinguished University Professor of Philosophy at the Australian National University, Canberra. Born and raised in Ireland, he was a lecturer in University College, Dublin, a research fellow at Trinity Hall, Cambridge, and professor of philosophy at the University of Bradford, before moving in 1983 to the Research School of Social Sciences, Australian National University. There he held a professional position jointly in Social and Political Theory and Philosophy until 2002. Prof. Pettit was elected fellow of the American Academy of Arts and Sciences in 2009, honorary member of the Royal Irish Academy in 2010, and corresponding fellow of the British Academy in 2013. He has also been awarded numerous honorary professorships and degrees.

Prof. Pettit works in moral and political theory and on background issues in the philosophy of mind and metaphysics. His single-authored books include *The Common Mind* (Oxford University Press, 1996), *Republicanism* (Oxford University Press, 1997), *A Theory of Freedom* (Oxford University Press, 2001), *Rules, Reasons and Norms* (Oxford University Press, 2002), *Penser en Société* (Presses Universitaires de France, 2004), *Examen a Zapatero* (Temas de Hoy, 2008), *Made with Words: Hobbes on Mind, Society and Politics* (Princeton University Press, 2008), *On the People's Terms: A Republican Theory and Model of Democracy* (Cambridge University Press, 2012), *Just Freedom: A Moral Compass for a Complex World* (Norton, 2014), and *The Robust Demands of the Good: Ethics with Attachment, Virtue and Respect* (Oxford University Press, 2015).

INTRODUCTION

FROM REDUCTION TO GENEALOGY

According to the ethical point of view, as commonly understood, there are two striking aspects to the natural and social world we human beings inhabit. First, the options we confront in decision making vary in their overall desirability, however desirability is conceptualized. And second, we are often fit to be held responsible in making a choice for choosing or failing to choose the most desirable option. Specifically, we are fit to be held responsible for the option we choose in the presence of a capacity—an unimpaired, unimpeded capacity—to register and act on considerations of desirability. Depending on what we do, we are appropriate targets for the praise and blame of others and can appropriately feel pride or guilt in how we perform.

The concepts of the desirable and the responsible are essentially prescriptive or normative. To hold that one option in a given choice is more desirable than alternatives is to prescribe its performance, on the assumption that other things are equal. To hold that an agent is fit to be held responsible for the choice is to maintain that other things are equal and that it is appropriate, therefore, to prescribe the most desirable option in advance or, depending on what was actually chosen, to deem the choice praiseworthy or blameworthy in retrospect: to commend or condemn the action or, if you are the agent, to feel pride or guilt about how you behaved.

Because of being inherently prescriptive, ethics raises a problem for those of us who think that the world we live in is an austere place that conforms to the image projected in natural science and mathematics. For prescriptive properties like desirability and responsibility—that is, fitness to be held responsible—do not look to be of a kind with mathematical properties.[1] And neither do they seem to be at home in the naturalistic world of science. They are unlikely to pull weight in any of the laws that science seeks to identify, and they do not plausibly materialize in virtue of effects that those laws explain.

Naturalistic philosophers have sometimes responded to the problem raised by debunking the idea that, by naturalistic lights, desirability and responsibility are bona fide properties. They have opted for representing ethical talk as fundamentally emotive or expressive, for example, rather than taking it to be descriptive of any features of items in the world.[2] Or they have held that in speaking ethically we treat desirability and responsibility as if they were real properties when actually they are not: consciously or otherwise, so this story goes, we operate with a fiction.[3]

The idea in these lectures is to resist downgrading ethical discourse in any such manner and, without forsaking naturalism, to try to vindicate the assumption that there really are properties like desirability and responsibility in the world and that they have an impact on our actions. These properties are not on a par with natural properties like mass and charge and spin, of course, which characterize the fundamental building blocks of our universe. The assumption is that just as the pixels on a television screen support patterns or properties at a higher level—the patterns we register in following any TV program—so the patterns we discern in distinguishing desirable actions and responsible agents are supported at a lower level by the fundamental elements—ultimately, perhaps, wavicles or strings—out of which the world is built.

The standard way to vindicate this sort of realism about higher-level, ethical properties, at least within a scientifically based view of the universe, is to try to provide a naturalistic reduction of ethical talk. Such a reduction would argue, first, that there is nothing more to the realization of an ethical property than the realization of a suitably supportive natural configuration—there may be an endless variety of these—as there is nothing more to the realization of a pattern on a TV screen than the realization of a suitably supportive configuration of pixels. And it would try to show, second, that whatever facts we register about the ethical property, or indeed the property presented on the TV screen, we might in principle have registered by noting how things stand at the lower, supportive level. It would maintain, roughly, that there is a sense—there are many candidates for what this sense is—in which the higher-level language can be reduced to lower-level terms.[4]

These lectures explore a distinct way of vindicating a naturalistic realism about ethical properties like desirability and responsibility. The idea is not to argue for a particular way of reducing ethical talk to naturalistic talk but to provide a naturalistic genealogy of how ethical talk could have arisen, in particular a genealogy under which ethical judgments play a role in registering bona fide aspects of the world and in shaping our responses to that world. The aim is to vindicate ethics, taken literally or realistically, in naturalistic terms. And the plan is to achieve that aim by explaining how we, the products of a natural and cultural evolution, could have come to develop notions of desirability to refer to aspects of the options we face, to shape our choices between those options, and to determine our fitness to be held responsible for what we do.[5]

To vindicate a naturalistic realism about ethics, establishing that there are bona fide properties like desirability and responsibility in the world, is not to deny that those properties may be inherently anthropocentric. The exercise pursued here takes those properties to consist in patterns that become visible, and only become visible, from within a perspective that presupposes access to distinctively human practices. The anthropocentric character of the properties identified does not argue against construing them, however, in a naturalistic, realist fashion. The colors that we perceive on the surfaces of objects are detectable, and perhaps only detectable, from within the sort of visual processing systems we and our biological ilk bring to the world. But their anthropocentric character does not, or should not, lead us to reject a naturalistic realism about such colors.

A CONJECTURAL HISTORY OF ETHICS

For purposes of these lectures, vindicating ethics can be taken henceforth to mean vindicating a naturalistic realism, however anthropocentric, about desirability and responsibility. A genealogical vindication would start with a possible, naturalistically intelligible form of human society where people do not have access to ethical concepts, and then show how naturalistically intelligible adjustments would lead them to develop and deploy such concepts in charting their world. It would amount to a conjectural history of ethics, as it might have been described in the eighteenth century. This does not aim at a conjectural narrative about how ethics really emerged—the goal is not a just-so story—but at an explanation of how ethics would really have emerged under certain conjectural conditions.[6] The aim is to establish the naturalistic emergability of ethics.[7]

I start in this exercise with a naturalistically plausible, if historically unlikely social state where members lack an ethics or morality; they do not have access to the network of practices and concepts associated with desirability and responsibility. And I then try to show that people in that state would plausibly have had motives and opportunities sufficient to push them onto a trajectory of development culminating in the ethical. They would have been led, as by an invisible, nudging hand—and not, for example, as a result of foresight and planning—to invoke standards of desirability, and to hold one another responsible for living up to those standards.

In the social state imagined at the origin of this development, natural language has already emerged, presumably on the basis of a naturalistically intelligible process of natural and social evolution. People use that language, however, only for purposes of giving one another reports on how things are in their environment, according to their own beliefs: whether the blackberries have ripened on the hill, what the weather is like farther north, how the prospects are looking for a big-game hunt. In particular, they make no ethical pronouncements bearing on issues of what it is desirable to do or on who is fit to be held responsible for something done.

Anticipating later discussion, the claim is that once people can use words to communicate their representations of the world in this manner, they are more or less bound to develop further speech acts of avowal and pledging, co-avowal and co-pledging, and to put themselves thereby in a world where ethical practices and concepts can gain traction. Or at least they are bound to do this, on the assumption that they display a variety of characteristically human features. However culturally malleable, for example, they are disposed by nature to exercise joint attention, consciously focusing on data they take to be available to all, albeit from different perspectives[8] However altruistic in other ways, they are deeply invested in promoting their own welfare and that of their kin. And however individually resourceful, they need to establish and maintain relationships and networks of mutual reliance in order to promote that welfare: they need to be able to rely on others and to get others to rely on them.[9]

It is unlikely that there ever was a time or place in the trajectory of human development when our ancestors used language solely for making reports on their shared world. And it is even more unlikely that a society at any place or time would have existed in isolation from other societies, as simplicity requires us to assume here. For this reason, I use the name of Erewhon to refer to our starting society. This name, borrowed from a nineteenth-century novel, is an anagram of "nowhere" and may serve to remind us of the unhistorical nature of the community with which the narrative begins. We may think of Erewhon as a possible scenario rather than as an earlier stage in human history and treat the narrative as an exploration of how ethics would be liable to emerge in that possible world.

Our narrative about Erewhon is also unfaithful to history in assuming an equality of power that discounts rigid hierarchies of gender or class; it projects a picture of communicative exchanges in which power and domination play no role. Our species has been on Earth for at least a hundred thousand years and we know that since the agricultural revolution that occurred about seven or eight thousand years ago, inequality of power has been the rule, not the exception. In supposing a relatively egalitarian Erewhon, then, the narrative does not reflect recent human history.

This particular inaccuracy need not be very troubling, however. There is some ground for thinking that preagricultural societies were much more egalitarian than agricultural, so that it is not clear how far we are departing from history on this front.[10] And in any case a departure from history on that front would not be a problem for the enterprise undertaken here. It would scarcely be a strike against the naturalistic intelligibility of ethics that suitable practices and concepts could only have arisen naturalistically in an egalitarian community; that might teach a lesson about the nature of ethics but it would hardly put its naturalistic credentials in doubt.

But not only is the starting point in our narrative unhistorical; more importantly, the process invoked in the account of how ethics could emerge in Erewhon is also unrealistic. The protagonists in that story are individualistic adults in strategic search of opportunities to satisfy primarily self-regarding desires.[11] This model is an unrealistic representation of a species in which a prime concern must always have been the protection and nurture of children; a primary characteristic must have been an attachment to family, clan, and tribe; and the crucial factor in sustaining development must have been socially transmitted customs and skills.[12]

THE EXPLANATORY PURPOSE

The point of our unhistorical, unrealistic narrative is to show that despite not having access to prescriptive concepts or practices to begin with, the inhabitants of Erewhon would be more or less inevitably pushed toward the formation of ethical concepts and the development of ethical practices. The idea is not that they would have motives to enter a social contract with one another to establish shared moral standards; even to conceive of such a contract, they would already have to be possessed of ethical concepts. The proposal rather is that, starting as mere reporters, they would be moved in all likelihood to adopt the profile of avowers and pledgers and that, with avowal and pledging established as shared activities, they would be moved in turn to develop properly ethical practices and concepts. The narrative documents an unplanned process of more or less inevitable emergence, not a history of contractual agreement. It is developed in the spirit of David Hume, who stressed the benefits of an emergence story over any story of a would-be contract.[13]

Even though our narrative focuses on Erewhon, then, it can teach an important lesson about Earth. If it is sound, it demystifies ethics, showing that it can emerge on the basis of the wholly naturalistic elements invoked in the story. Thus it demonstrates that the concepts of desirability and responsibility, and the practices with which they are associated, are not naturalistically mysterious. They are capable of materializing among agents of a kind with human beings and of assuming an important part in the regulation of their lives together. And they are capable of doing this as a result of naturalistically intelligible adjustments to naturalistically plausible opportunities.

Why work with an unhistorical, unrealistic model in seeking to demonstrate the emergability and intelligibility of ethics? One reason is that the model is theoretically tractable. Positing rational agents with defined purposes, determinate abilities, and relatively equal power, it allows us to provide plausible accounts of how they would be likely to respond to certain opportunities, how their aggregate responses would be likely to generate new opportunities, and how they would be likely to respond to these in turn. It enables us to posit and track a more or less inescapable trajectory of development among the inhabitants of Erewhon.

But another reason for working with this model is that the very austerity of its assumptions can help to give us confidence that ethics is inescapable for creatures like us. The individualistic, opportunistic model that it introduces is a worst-case scenario from the point of view of explaining our human fixation on issues of desirability and responsibility. If ethics is inescapable in such a scenario, as the genealogy suggests, then it is even more likely to be inescapable in better-case scenarios. If people would have naturally evolved a sense of ethics in the dry wood of the model, we may hope that they would certainly have done so in the green wood of our actual history.

How does the story presented relate to an historical, evolutionary account of ethics? Histories that purport to tell us about the emergence of ethics often offer only accounts of the emergence of ethical, in particular altruistic, patterns of behavior.[14] What an actual history of ethics ought to provide is a story about the joint, mutually reinforcing emergence of ethical patterns of behavior, on the one side, and of ethical concepts on the other, in particular concepts in the families of desirability and responsibility. It is hard to say how far the conjectural history outlined here has much to tell us about actual history. But it has at least this positive lesson to teach: that if it is possible to explain how ethics could have emerged under plausible but unhistorical pressures, it ought to be possible to explain how it emerged under the pressures operative in actual history.

THE CONJECTURAL HISTORY OF MONEY

The most familiar analogue to the project undertaken here is the conjectural history of money that is standardly offered in an attempt to demystify financial arrangements: to make sense of money in individualistic, economic terms. The starting state in that story is a barter society—as in our case, a society of relatively equal power—where people are interested in exchanging various commodities or services but, lacking money, cannot easily find suitable partners. You want the dog that I can provide but I do not need the service that you would give me in recompense. I want something that a third person can furnish but that individual does not want my dog or anything else I can currently offer. People in such a society might improve things by writing IOUs in a suitable domain—for example, in the provision of puppies—but this would have similar, if looser limitations. So what might relieve them of the problem they face?

The standard story is that at a certain point it is very likely that some commodity like gold or cattle or tobacco would assume a special status, being recognized as a commodity that everyone wants, or that everyone believes everyone wants, or that everyone believes everyone believes everyone wants, or whatever.[15] And at that point, it would be in the interest of each to gain access to that special good or to IOUs issued by individuals or groups who could provide it. People can be sure of finding providers for the things they want if and only if they have enough of that good, or at least of reliable IOUs in that good, to offer providers an attractive trade.

With these developments, that good and the corresponding IOUs would constitute a medium of exchange, a metric for putting prices on things, and a means of building up purchasing power. In other words, it would become deserving of our name of money. And it would come to resemble our contemporary form of money even more closely if certain other conditions were fulfilled: if the government accepted it in payment of taxes, for example; if the issuers of IOUs became reliable enough to count as banks; if the supply of IOUs was controlled by a central bank that guarded against oversupply and undersupply; and, to mark a recent development in world finance, if those IOUs came to be backed solely by their trading value, not by the guarantee of being able to cash them in.

This narrative demystifies the appearance of money, and our access to the concept of money. It shows that however puzzling it may seem, money is not essentially mysterious: it could have emerged as a by-product of the accumulating, unplanned effects of people's interest in conducting and facilitating trade. The narrative contrasts with a social contract story, for example, because it does not presuppose that people had the concept of money prior to establishing the institution. The idea is that institution and concept would have become simultaneously available in a cascade of individually intelligible developments.

A PHILOSOPHICAL PROJECT

But while the project taken up here is usefully analogized to the economic story about money, it still has a recognizably philosophical character. Think of Wilfred Sellars's myth of Jones, according to which we could have developed concepts of mental experience and attitude, and begun to practice folk psychology, by seeking a theoretical explanation for our dispositions to make certain utterances and to take corresponding actions. Think of David Lewis's demonstration that as self-interested rational agents we could have coordinated with one another in familiar predicaments, and given rise to regularities of the kind exemplified by conventions of language and the like. Think of Donald Davidson's argument that as masters of a finite Tarskian truth theory, we could have become positioned to understand any of a potentially infinite number of sentences. Think of Edward Craig's claim that we could have developed the concept of knowledge, and the practice of justifying claims to knowledge, out of an interest in determining who should count as good informants by criteria available to everyone in the community. Or think of Bernard Williams's explanation of how a community of mutual informants could have evolved norms of truth and truthfulness without relying on any prior sense of a truth-telling obligation.[16]

All of these projects are designed to serve three functions akin to the functions served by the narrative about money. They are meant to identify the putative role and utility of certain practices: the explanatory role of folk psychology; the coordinating role of conventions; the role of recursion in enabling us to understand indefinitely many sentences; the role of knowledge ascriptions in identifying reliable informants; and the role of truth-related norms in organizing a speech community. They are designed to make sense of how people could have come to develop terms and concepts equivalent to our concepts of mental states, social conventions, sentence meanings, knowledge claims, and truth-related norms. And they do this for each case in a usefully demystifying manner. There is said to be nothing mysteriously first-personal about the psychological understanding to which we lay claim; nothing individualistically unintelligible about our dependence on conventions; nothing impossible for finite minds about understanding indefinitely many sentences; nothing about states of knowledge that makes them more puzzling than other mental states; and nothing about our attachment to truth and truthfulness that requires an independent sense of the obligatory.

What those stories seek to achieve in their respective domains, the story sketched here aims at achieving in the domain of ethics or morality. It seeks, first, to show how practices akin to our ethical practices would be likely to emerge in a purely reportive society like Erewhon; second, to explain why that development would provide referents for the use of ethical concepts like our concepts of desirability and responsibility; and third, to do this in a demystifying way that does not make any naturalistically implausible assumptions.

The approach adopted also resembles the method of creature-construction championed by Paul Grice, foreshadowed by Jonathan Bennett, and used, for various purposes, by philosophers like Michael Bratman and Peter Railton.[17] On that methodology we are invited to imagine how we might design a simple naturalistic creature and build on that design, in successive naturalistic steps, until we come to a creature that can apparently think in familiar psychological and ethical terms. The approach taken here might be recast as an attempt to do something similar at the level of community. The goal is to build on a naturalistic design, in successive naturalistic steps, until we come to a community like the community you and I inhabit where people think in terms of desirability and hold one another responsible for living up to desirable standards.

LECTURE I.
FROM LANGUAGE TO COMMITMENT

BACKGROUND CONCEPTS

This first lecture looks at how the members of the reportive community of Erewhon are very likely to resort to avowals and pledges, and indeed co-avowals and co-pledges, where these do not yet involve them in ethics. The second lecture explores the reasons why the capacity for making such avowals and pledges is going to put them within reach of ethical practices and concepts, leading them to make judgments of desirability and to hold one another responsible to those judgments.

As understood here, reporting, avowing, and pledging are all forms of communication in the sorts of conventional, compositionally constructed signs that are characteristic of natural language. In the normal case of communication, I use those signs with two intentions. The primary intention is to convey some information to an audience and the secondary to achieve that result, at least in part, by making the primary intention manifest to them.[18] Making that intention manifest, by some accounts, involves making it into a matter of common awareness: each of us is in a position to be aware of the intention, in a position to be aware that each is aware of it, and so on.[19] We need not dwell on these complexities here but it is important to recognize that they are in place; they are what distinguish communication in natural language, or so at least it seems, from the transmission of information by the signaling systems used among other species.[20]

Reporting, avowing, and pledging are all varieties of communication in this sense, although they are tailor-made to different domains. I may report any fact about the world or any fact about myself, such as that I have a certain belief or desire or intention. But while I can avow a belief or desire or intention, I cannot avow a fact about the world. And, as we shall see later, while I can pledge an intention, I cannot pledge any other sort of attitude, or of course any fact about the world.

There is a basis for distinguishing between reporting, avowing, and pledging, however, that is independent of the domain in which they may be put to communicative use. And this is the distinction that will be of concern here. It derives from a difference in the extent to which the different speech acts allow me to explain a miscommunication in a face-saving way: that is, in such a way that, if you accept my explanation—if you think it is credible or adequate—then you will not take me to have been careless or untruthful in the message I conveyed; or at least not as careless or untruthful as I may have seemed. You will not take me to have proved myself an unreliable interlocutor.

The explanation of a failure that deflects the charge of unreliability counts in ordinary parlance as an excuse: it saves my claim to be a cooperative, reliable communicator. Excuses may partially rather than fully explain a failure but for simplicity they will be taken throughout these lectures to constitute full explanations of failure. Reports leave room for two salient sorts of excuses; avowals leave room for just one; and pledges leave room for neither.[21]

Suppose I report to you that something is the case: say, to take a first-person state of affairs, that I weigh less than 170 pounds. And now imagine that you discover that I weigh much more: inviting me to step on an undoubtedly reliable set of scales, it is clear that I am at least 180 pounds. There are two salient sorts of excuses that I may offer in the attempt to show that I was careful about determining the facts and truthful or sincere in communicating them. First, I may offer a misleading-world excuse to the effect that the home set of scales on which I was relying for evidence turns out to be inaccurate. Or second, I may offer a changed-world excuse to the effect that I did weigh less than 170 pounds at the time I made my report, although (sadly) I no longer weigh that now. The misleading-world excuse draws attention to a failure of my words to match the world, the changed-world excuse to a failure of the world to remain matched to my words.

Among the reports I make about the world there are likely to be reports I make about my own attitudes or mind. Thus I may report that I have such and such a belief or other attitude, taking the evidence of introspection or reflection on behavior to show that I believe or desire or intend such and such. And in the case of any misreport on my mind, as with any misreport whatsoever, I may try to excuse it in either of two ways. I may invoke a misleading-mind excuse, arguing that the reason I did not prove to have the attitude I ascribed to myself is that the evidence about what I thought or felt was misleading; I got myself wrong in the way in which I might have gotten a third person wrong. Or I may invoke a changed-mind excuse, claiming that the reason I did not prove to have the attitude—the reason I did not display it later in action—is that my attitude changed before the time for action: on discovering new facts, for example, I ceased to hold the belief I had earlier reported.

The contrast between reports, avowals, and pledges shows up in this domain, where I communicate about my mind. Where I may offer either of two face-saving excuses with an attitudinal report—explanations that aim to save my claim to be a reliable communicator—I may offer only one in the case of an avowal, and neither in the case of a pledge. I take steps in the case of an avowal of attitude that enable me to put aside the misleading-mind excuse and I take steps in the case of a pledge of attitude that enable me to put aside the changed-mind excuse as well. I act in each case so as to deprive myself of the relevant excuse.

Consider the case of avowal first. Here the misleading-mind excuse is unavailable and only the changed-mind excuse can be invoked. Suppose, for example, that I choose to communicate to you that I believe that p, not by reporting on my belief as I might report on the belief of a third party, but just by reporting or asserting that p, thereby expressing my belief state. And now imagine that you discover that I do not actually believe that p: you find that I do not act as if it were the case that p, for example, or you overhear me testifying credibly to a third party that it is not the case that p. How may I excuse my failure to communicate the truth about my belief?

I may certainly claim, with whatever degree of plausibility, that my belief changed since speaking with you, thereby invoking a changed-mind excuse. But I cannot plausibly say that I must have gotten my belief that p wrong when I spoke to you. I showed that I had that belief, after all, by asserting or reporting that p, presumptively in response to the data at my disposal. And knowing that that is so—knowing that this shows that I believed that p—I did not have to consult any introspective or other evidence to determine that I was in that belief state. Thus I foreclosed the possibility of explaining why I misled you by saying later that I was myself misled by such evidence.[22]

Where an avowal rules out one of the excuses that a report tolerates, as in the example given, a pledge rules out both. Suppose I say that I intend to go to your art exhibition this evening and fail to turn up. What I said will count as an avowal of intention insofar as I cannot excuse myself by saying I must have gotten my intention wrong. It will count as a pledge of the intention, however, if it is a matter of common awareness—say, because of the conventions in place—that given how I chose to express myself, I cannot excuse a failure to act on the intention in either of the two salient ways: I cannot claim that I was misled about my mind, in particular my intention, and I cannot say that I changed my mind since speaking with you. To communicate an intention in this manner, fore-closing both sorts of excuses, is to pledge that attitude as distinct from reporting it or even avowing it.

Avowals and pledges, as conceptualized here, are voluntary acts of communicating an attitude in which I take active steps to put aside one or both of the relevant excuses for failing to display it. The avowed attitude is one that I might have reported, the pledged attitude is one that I might have avowed or reported. In each case it is an attitude about which I might possibly have been misled, as I see things, or which I might possibly change; there is nothing that makes it immune to misreading or alteration. In avowing such an attitude, I set aside a misleading-mind excuse that, by assumption, I might have kept in place. And in pledging an attitude I set aside both a misleading-mind excuse and a changed-mind excuse that, by assumption, I might have kept open.

In describing the developments in Erewhon, charting its transition to ethics, the narrative that follows relies heavily on this excuse-based way of distinguishing between reports, avowals, and pledges. But before beginning to chart those developments it is worth noting two important points. The first is that the excuses introduced in making these distinctions are all epistemic in character and contrast with what we may describe as practical excuses. The second is that the notion of an excuse employed is not itself an ethical notion; it may be understood and employed among Erewhonians, long before they come to ethics.

The excuses invoked in distinguishing between reports, avowals, and pledges all direct us to breakdowns of an epistemic kind. They cite problems that allegedly blocked me from tracking the facts properly, in particular the facts about my mind. In the one case this is a failure on my side to match my words to a misleading mind; in the other it is a failure on the side of the mind to remain unchanged and matched to my words. But there are problems that may be cited in excusing a miscommunication that have a very different, practical character.

Practical excuses, by contrast with epistemic, cite behavioral problems that purport to explain why my assertions or actions did not correspond to what I believed—the assumption is that my beliefs were in order—and why for that very different reason I miscommunicated the facts. They might invoke a problem that inhibits me from telling you what I actually accepted—"I was coerced or induced not to tell the truth"—or a problem that prevents me from acting as I had told you I would act: "I broke a leg before I could do so." Epistemic excuses focus on something that goes wrong in my processing of information; practical excuses focus on something that breaks the linkage between the information I process and the things I say or do. Both may assume the form of partial excuses rather than excuses of a complete sort, but the assumption throughout these lectures, as noted earlier, is that they come only in the form of complete excuses. This assumption makes the presentation easier, without leaving partial excuses as a mystery; the amendments required by admitting them should be fairly clear in the different cases discussed.[23]

Apart from epistemic or practical excuses, it is useful to recognize a third category of explanation that may be offered on a person's behalf for a failure to live up to their words, whether words uttered in report, avowal, or pledge. This is the explanation that suggests roughly that at the earlier time of utterance or the later time of action the agent was not fully adult or able-minded. The idea is that the agent is exempt, as it is often put, from being held to his or her words, not just excused for failing to live up to them.[24]

It is important to register that the excuses introduced to explain the difference between reporting, avowing, and pledging are of an epistemic character, since otherwise the basis for that taxonomy may seem dubious. But it is even more important to register that, like practical excuses and exemptions, they do not presuppose access to ethical concepts. Otherwise they could not be invoked without circularity in a naturalistic genealogy.

An excuse in an ethical sense would explain an action—say, a miscommunication—in a way that deflects the charge that the agent should be held responsible for acting badly. But excuses as they are invoked here are designed strategically to secure a result that is describable without resort to the notion of responsibility, or any other ethical concepts. They are invoked to show that, despite appearances to the contrary—despite my having uttered misleading words—still I am someone on whom it makes self-interested sense for you and others to rely. Even without access to concepts of desirability and responsibility, there is every reason in Erewhon why I should want to establish such reliability in my own case. And equally there is every reason why I should be able to recognize when others have established it in theirs.

Once we recognize that excuses should be given only a strategic sense in the genealogy provided for ethics, it should be clear that something similar applies to the notions of avowing and pledging. Such acts naturally count, by ordinary criteria, as acts of commitment in which I put my good name on the line. But they need only be commitments in the strategic, game-theory sense of precommitments, not in any distinctively ethical sense. In making a precommitment, say to performing a certain action, I place a side-bet on doing what I say I will do, where I stand to lose my stake should I fail to do it. By analogy, in making an avowal or pledge, I bet on myself to display the attitude avowed or pledged, where the stake is the cost that I will have to bear if, having failed to display the attitude, I cannot invoke the excuse or excuses foreclosed by the avowal or pledge. That cost will consist in being identified as an unreliable interlocutor.

This lecture is described as moving from language to commitment. But, as these observations underline, the sort of commitment it introduces is strategic rather than ethical in character. The second lecture will move from commitment in that sense to morality proper. It will seek to show how the strategic commitments embedded in the avowals and pledges of Erewhonians will push them towards the adoption of a moral viewpoint, organizing their lives around concepts of desirability and responsibility.

The Reportive Community

Where the genealogy of money begins with a purely barter society, the genealogy of ethics begins with a purely reportive community. This is a community of people, the Erewhonians, who have evolved to the point of being able to use a natural language in communicating with one another but who use it intentionally for the sole purpose of giving reports to one another on how things are in their shared world. I and others in Erewhon make use of conventionally established signs to communicate voluntarily and overtly that things are thus and so: the berries on the hill are ripening, the weather up north is getting better, the prospects for the big-game hunt are looking good. And that is all that we intentionally use such signs to do.

We will each benefit in Erewhon from being able to rely on others to be careful about determining how things stand and to be truthful in making reports; this will expand the range of beliefs on the basis of which we can act with confidence. And we will each benefit by being able to get others to rely on us, going along with the picture we offer of the world and with the plans we make on the basis of that picture. But none of us can expect others to prove suitably reliable or reliant unless we resist the temptation to mislead them and make sure to prove reliable ourselves.

You will have little or no incentive to tell me the truth about what you know, or to rely on me in future, if I have shown myself unwilling to tell you the truth about what I know. On the contrary, you may retaliate against me by refusing some information or collaboration I seek, or by being less than careful in determining the facts I ask about or less than truthful in reporting them to me. You may even retaliate out of an explicit desire to teach me the lesson that if you are to prove reliable and reliant, then I must establish that I too am a reliable person; you may practice a variation of tit for tat in our interaction.[25] In addition, it may also be clear that if I prove to be unreliable you are likely to report this to others—that would help establish your own reliability with them—and so cause me quite a heavy reputational loss.[26]

Under conditions like these it is almost inevitable that we Erewhonians will be generally careful about determining what is the case—this will be supported anyhow by self-regarding motives—and will be truthful in communicating to others what we take to be the case ourselves. We will each generally try to tell the truth, recognizing that this is the only way of establishing a reputation for being reliable and that establishing such a reputation is essential for being able to rely on others or get others to rely on us. The regularity will constitute a social norm or pattern in a more or less familiar sense of the term.

Let a regularity of behavior count as a social norm insofar as conditions such as the following are fulfilled.

- Almost everyone in the community conforms to the regularity.
- Almost everyone expects conformity to attract a good opinion among others and nonconformity—except perhaps in retaliation—a bad opinion.
- Almost everyone is motivated to conform to the regularity, at least in part, by that expectation.[27]

A regularity that fits these conditions is a pattern maintained in a society as a result of the attitudes of the inhabitants toward conformity. That it is actually maintained, as the first condition stipulates, distinguishes it from a standard honored more in the breach than in the observance, such as the ideal of bipartisanship in politics. That it reflects the mutually expected attitudes of inhabitants toward conformity, as the second condition holds, means that it is distinct from a regularity to which others are manifestly indifferent, such as the regularity whereby most people sleep at night, not during the day. And that it is maintained by that expectation, at least in part, means that it is distinct from a regularity such as taking steps to guard against penury in old age; it is unlikely that people are motivated in any degree by the good opinion they may expect this to win among others.

But while a social norm is distinctive on these three fronts, it may or may not represent a requirement of an ethical or moral kind: that is, a properly "normative" or prescriptive requirement that tells us what to do. A pattern that constitutes a social norm of behavior—say, a pattern of retaliation for injury or discrimination against women—may not be morally permissible, let alone morally required. And a pattern may be morally required, even required by everyone's lights—say, a pattern of moderation in retaliating against injury—without being established as a social norm.

Telling the truth is bound to become a social norm in Erewhon, although in the absence of ethical concepts it will not be marked out by any of us in the society as ethically required or desirable. Each of us will have a strategic interest in winning an opinion and reputation for reportive reliability among others. This will motivate us to be careful about forming true beliefs and, in particular, to be truthful in making reports based on those beliefs. So the upshot ought to be that almost everyone in our society will speak the truth in communicating with others; almost everyone will expect conformity with this regularity to establish a good reputation for them in the minds of others and failures to tell the truth, a bad reputation; and almost everyone will conform on the basis, at least in part, that their reputation depends on it.

For parallel reasons, we may expect our community to establish norms, not just against deception, but also against killing, violence, unfairness, and the like, at least in dealing with other members of the same community. In each of these cases too everyone has a motive, derived from their interest in establishing themselves as reliable partners in interaction, to conform to a suitable regularity, giving rise thereby to a corresponding norm. This observation, as appears in the next lecture, may help to explain why members of the community are likely to converge in developing recognized standards of desirability to which they can hold one another.

Even in the presence of a truth-telling norm, there will be epistemic grounds on which I or someone who takes my side may argue that although I spoke falsely, you should not give up on me as a reliable reporter. I may persuade you that I failed to tell the truth despite taking all the care

I could about determining the facts and despite being truthful in reporting what I took to be the facts. I may be able to show that the world as it
presented itself to me was misleading: the berries on which I reported
really did look ripe, although perhaps only because of the setting sun. Or
I may be able to show that the world changed between the time of my report and your action: a third party came and picked the berries before
you got to them. My failing to tell the truth in the presence of a plausible
epistemic excuse, whether of the misleading-world or changed-world variety, is not a failure that should induce you to give up on me as a reporter.
It explains why I failed to tell the truth in a way that saves my reputation
as a truth-teller.

Given that there is a norm of truth-telling in place among us—or indeed a norm of any kind—we Erewhonians can be described as regulating or policing one another into conformity with it. But it is important
to distinguish this form of mutual regulation in truth-telling from the
practice, which is described in the next lecture, of holding one another
responsible—holding one another to account—for telling the truth. The
regulation envisaged here falls short of the responsibility practice in two
striking ways. First, we may pursue it without being aware of the norm
that we regulate one another into sustaining, and so without sustaining
it intentionally; and second, we may practice it without any sense of the
moral or ethical appeal of the norm.

Within Erewhon, to take up the first feature, we may regulate one
another into truth-telling without being aware or conscious of the abstract
regularity that we consequently uphold. We may each act in response,
now to this individual, now to that, without having any idea of the general pattern we collectively elicit as a result of those responses. Let a rule
as distinct from a pattern be expressed by a verbal formula like "tell the
truth," which dictates behavior of that patterned kind. While sustaining
a regularity or norm of truth-telling, we may not be able to spell out the
regularity as a rule; we may not recognize that the upshot of our shared
responses on the truth-telling front is to establish conformity with such a
rule; and we may not intentionally conform to the rule or intentionally
seek to get others to conform.[28]

Our regulation for truth-telling is not only liable to be unconscious
and unintentional, however. Whether or not it becomes conscious, to
take up a second feature, we are also likely to pursue it without any sense
of its moral or ethical appeal. On the story told, we each support the truth-
telling regularity or norm out of a desire, now in this case, now in that, to

prove reliable to others. But that is not because proving reliable promises to have impersonal merits of a moral kind. It is only because any failure to prove reliable will make us uncongenial to others and cost us severely; it will involve a strategic loss, diminishing our ability to rely on them in future exchanges or get them to rely on us.

THE AVOWAL OF BELIEF

The Attraction and Accessibility of Avowing Belief

By the story told so far, we Erewhonians are invested in the benefits of mutual reliance and are generally willing therefore to take on the associated costs of proving reliable ourselves; we are willing to be careful and truthful in the reports we make about the world. The investment in mutual reliance means that we must have a particular interest, not just in proving reliable, but in communicating that we desire or intend to be reliable, and that we hold the beliefs that answer to our reports about the world. Thus we must also invest in conveying our attitudes to one another, communicating that we hold this or that belief, are moved by this or that desire, and are bound to this or that intention or plan: presumably, beliefs, desires, and plans that are consistent with peaceful, mutually reliant community. Communicating an account of our attitudes toward one another—in particular, a credible account that ascribes congenial attitudes—we can boost the prospect of establishing relations of mutual confidence and reliance.

What means are we likely to adopt, then, in communicating those attitudes? Should we rely on reporting our attitudes to one another in just the way that we report other aspects of the world? Or should we resort to avowing or pledging? The question arises for our beliefs in the first place, and in the second for other attitudes like desire and intention. The first topic to be discussed, then, is the mode in which we may be expected to communicate our beliefs to one another; the second is the mode in which we may be expected to communicate our other, noncredal attitudes.

The earlier discussion of avowal points up an observation that shows that I will be able to communicate my beliefs to others in Erewhon, not just by making reports on those beliefs, but also by avowing them. Suppose that instead of reporting that I seem to believe that a man I know, Jones, is reliable, I simply say: Jones is reliable. It appears in that case that I cannot excuse my later acting as if Jones were a liar by saying that I must have been misled about the belief I held when I said that he is reliable.

And that being so, the communication I made cannot count as a report. It would allow me to excuse my failing to display the belief expressed by saying that I changed my mind about Jones since the time when I spoke to you. But it would not allow me to invoke a misleading-mind excuse in the same way. It would count by the earlier definition as an avowal of that belief rather than a report.

Why would my saying to you that Jones is reliable communicate, not just that he is reliable, but also that I believe that he is reliable? And why would it communicate this belief in the mode of an avowal that forecloses a misleading-mind excuse?

The key to answering the first question is to recognize the tight link between the idea of making a report and the idea of purporting to have a belief in the content of the report. When I report that Jones is reliable, this linkage means that it ought to be a matter of common belief between us that I purport to believe that he is reliable. The evidence of that linkage is salient for each of us, the evidence that that evidence is salient is itself salient to each of us, and so on.[29] When I make the report that Jones is reliable, then, it ought to be the case that we each believe that I purport to believe that he is reliable, that we each believe that we each believe that I speak with this purport, and so on. Queried about what we believe at any level in that hierarchy we are each going to be disposed, assuming we understand the query, to give the appropriate response.

Thus when I make the report that Jones is reliable I inevitably communicate that I have the corresponding belief. Insofar as the report is intentional, it is intentional on my part that I also convey that information about my belief and that I do so, at least in part, by means of making it manifest that I intentionally convey the information.[30] The semantic message of what I say may be that Jones is reliable but the pragmatic message—the message conveyed by what I do in making the report—is that I *believe* that he is reliable. The semantic message bears on the belief content that I report, the pragmatic message bears on the belief state that I express in giving that report.

Turning now to the second question, why would the pragmatic or expressive message that I convey about my belief in Jones's reliability foreclose my excusing a miscommunication by claiming that the evidence about my mind was misleading? Once again, the key to the answer is the conceptual connection between making a report and purporting to have a belief in its content. This linkage means that I showed that I believe that

Jones is reliable by asserting or reporting, in response to the data at my disposal, that he is reliable. And knowing that this shows that I believed that he is reliable, I can know that I have that belief without consulting any independent evidence about myself, say of an introspective or behavioral kind. Thus I foreclosed the possibility of explaining why I misled you by saying later that I was myself misled by such introspective or behavioral evidence. Not relying on being led by such evidence—and this, as a matter of common awareness—I can hardly claim in excusing a miscommunication to have been misled by it.[31]

Sooner or later we Erewhonians are bound to recognize that communicating a belief by expressing it allows of only one of the excuses that reporting the belief would have permitted. Might we be tempted to resort in that case to play safe and choose to report our ground-level beliefs about any matter rather than communicating them expressively? Rather than expressing the ground-level belief that Jones is reliable, might it push me toward reporting that belief in words such as "My belief seems to be that Jones is reliable," thereby expressing the higher-order belief that I hold the belief that Jones is reliable?

It may at first seem that it would. The cost of my miscommunicating a higher-order belief without being able to invoke a misleading-mind excuse—the cost of miscommunicating a belief about whether I believe that Jones is reliable—would not be very high; you and others are unlikely to rely very much on the truth of a message about my beliefs about my beliefs. But the cost of miscommunicating a ground-level belief about the world without being able to invoke a misleading-mind excuse—the cost of miscommunicating a belief that Jones is reliable—is likely to be quite high; you and others are liable to rely quite heavily on the truth of any such message about my beliefs about the world.

But the resort to higher-order reports about our worldly beliefs would not be likely to attract us, all things considered. For the very fact that the pragmatic or expressive mode of communication allows of only one excuse for error provides a motive for why any one of us should positively cherish it. By communicating a belief in this manner I manifestly take on a greater risk than if I had reported it: I expose myself to the cost of not being able to explain a miscommunication about that belief by recourse to the allegedly misleading character of my mind. And by manifestly taking on such a risk, I make my words more expensive and give you and others firmer ground for expecting them to be true. Why, you may think, would I take on that risk unless I was pretty sure that I would not have to pay the cost of being unable to excuse a possible miscommunication by appeal to a misleading mind?[32]

Suppose you want to know about my belief about Jones's reliability. And assume that I am anxious to be able to get you to accept whatever communication I make; I am anxious to be treated as someone whose words are credible, both in this instance and more generally. If I hedge and say that it seems to me that I believe that he is reliable, then it will be clear to you that even if I prove not to have that belief, I will be able to get off the hook—I will be able to provide a plausible excuse for having mis-reported my belief—by saying that I must have gotten my belief wrong. But in that case it will be clear that my words are pretty cheap and are not very credible. If I refuse to hedge in that reportive manner, however, and say simply that Jones is reliable, then it will equally be clear that I have foreclosed access to that easy excuse, that I am taking a considerable risk in communicating my belief in that expressive mode, and that my words therefore are highly credible.

It is bound to be appealing for each of us in Erewhon to give the words we utter as much credibility as we can, assuming we are pretty confident about what we say. And that means that communicating our belief-states pragmatically rather than semantically, at least when they matter in our relationships to others, is bound to be very attractive. Taking on that risk may help to ensure that others actually believe what we say, which is likely to appeal on a number of counts. For one thing, it is likely to get others to rely on us in the instance in question, which may be important for our other purposes. And for another, it will enable us to prove reliable in living up to those words, thereby improving our general reputational standing.

To choose the pragmatic or expressive communication of a belief, foreclosing the misleading-mind excuse but not the changed-mind ex-cuse, is generally to avow that belief, by the terminology adopted here. It is to opt voluntarily for that mode of communication over the salient al-ternative of just reporting it. And presumptively, it is to opt for that form of conveying the belief, at least in part, because it represents a more ex-pensive and so more credible form of communication; absent that effect, there would be little reason for me or others to opt for avowal. It provides me with a potentially more effective means of getting you to believe what I say.[33]

An avowal will not only be more credible for being more expensive; it will also be more credible for being manifestly adopted on the grounds of being more expensive. In avowing a belief in conscious awareness of reducing excuses for error, I will manifestly back myself not to have to suffer the cost of being unable, as a result of the avowal, to excuse a failure to act on that belief. I will bet on myself, as a matter of common awareness, not to have to incur that cost. In effect, I will put my money where my mouth is, giving you the firmest grounds for taking me at my word.

While foreclosing resort to the misleading-mind excuse raises the cost and the credibility of an avowal, however, it does not make it prohibitively costly. It leaves the changed-mind excuse in play, for starters, since I will not have foreclosed this. And of course it also leaves room for the various practical, un-foreclosed excuses that I might offer in seeking to establish that despite having miscommunicated a belief, you may take me to be a cooperative and reliable interlocutor. Thus I might excuse myself in the wake of such a miscommunication by explaining that someone had a gun to my head and that I could not speak truthfully without risking my life. And I might achieve the same result by explaining that I was totally disabled from speaking the truth, say as a result of a psychological malaise like paranoia; in that case I am exempted from penalty, in the sense explained earlier. These observations apply to every form of avowal and pledging to be considered in the evolving narrative, although they will not be registered explicitly in every case.

The Feasibility of Avowing Beliefs

These observations suggest that given the ready availability of avowing as distinct from just reporting our beliefs, we in Erewhon are likely to cherish the possibility of avowal; we are likely to rely on avowal to give as much credibility to our communications about our beliefs—certainly to communications that matter in relationships with others—as our confidence allows. But how can we ever be confident enough to put aside the possibility of invoking a misleading-mind excuse for a failure to display a belief avowed? It is one thing for us to have a motive for avowing our beliefs rather than just reporting them. It is quite another for us to be in a position where we have sufficient confidence about what we believe to be able sensibly to take this line.

What might make it possible for me, then, to have the required level of confidence that I know what I believe? What might enable me to have sufficient confidence that I believe that Jones is reliable, for example, or that the berries on the hill are ripening, that the weather up north is improving, or that the prospects for the big-game hunt are bright? I will recognize any such belief as one that I could be wrong to ascribe to my-self, as avowal presupposes; thus it is not like a belief that, as I see it, is true by definition or true on the basis of some unquestioned revelation. So what might make it possible for me to know that I hold it and to be prepared to put aside the misleading-mind excuse?

To answer this question, it is necessary to turn briefly to more general matters. In order to serve a reporting function in a community, natural language must provide the means for speakers like you and me to com-municate how things are, according to our beliefs. And this means that when we take care to determine whether or not it is the case that p, to pick an arbitrary sentence from their language, and when we then report truthfully or sincerely that p, we must tend in general to hold the belief that p. If this were not generally the case—if their conscientious reports were correlated only contingently with their beliefs—then their words would be uninterpretable; they would lack the reliable connections with prompting conditions and prompted actions that would enable others to make sense of them.[34]

What is it going to mean, whether in Erewhon or elsewhere, for me to take care about determining that it is or is not the case that p? It cannot mean introspecting my beliefs to see if I actually hold the belief that p. In that case I could never be brought to assent to a proposition that I previ-ously disbelieved or in which I had no belief either way. And taking care over whether or not it is the case that p can often lead me to form a belief in a proposition—that p or that not-p—that I did not previously believe. So the exercise must involve something of a different character.

In the absence of further alternatives, taking care over determining that it is or is not the case that p can only mean attending to the data on whether or not p, where these are mediated by perception or memory or existing beliefs. Attending to those data will lead me to assent to or dis-sent from the proposition before me, or to withhold judgment. And if I take care to exercise such attention conscientiously, not neglecting any aspect of the data, then I may expect the belief-state to materialize in a suitably robust form. I may expect it to stay in place just so long as the data remain unchanged, and regardless of collateral differences: say, dif-ferences in how attractive or unattractive it may be in other respects to hold by that belief.

If I find myself deferring to the data and assenting to the proposition that p after such an exercise, then I can generally assume that I have thereby come to form the belief that p, whether for the first time or in reaffirmation of a belief already held. In either case I now believe that p in the sense, roughly, that I am disposed robustly to act and adjust as if it were the case that p.[35] If I did not come to form a corresponding belief as a result of such careful assent, then I would not be the sort of being whose language would be interpretable by others.

The upshot of these general considerations appears to be that I can know that I believe something—that is, believe it on a presumptively robust basis—when I find that I assent to it after paying careful attention to relevant data. That conclusion is independently plausible, being borne out by the fact that we often answer the question as to whether we believe that p by thinking about the data and saying sincerely "p"; we often treat it as a question about whether the data elicit in us a belief that p.[36]

But still, the conclusion needs to be qualified, for there is one important complexity to be added to the account of how I can know what I believe. Suppose that I form a belief that p on the basis of data supporting the assertion that p but that there are factors on the horizon of which the two following things are true. First, if they materialized at a certain time, then I would be likely to cease to display the belief formed. And second, I would not be willing to excuse a failure to display that belief by appealing to a change of mind; on the contrary I would be inclined to avow the belief again as soon as those factors went away.

To illustrate the possibility, suppose I am brought by consideration of the data to assent to the proposition that the gambler's fallacy is a fallacy; we may assume that gambling has a place in Erewhon. It may be, first, that the belief is liable to disappear in the excitement of the casino—when there is a run of blacks, I feel sure that red is likely to come up next. And it may be, second, that I would not be disposed in such a case to invoke the excuse that I changed my mind about the matter during my visit to the casino; on the contrary, I would continue to maintain outside the casino that the fallacy is indeed a fallacy.[37]

We may describe any factor that fits these two conditions as a disrupter of the belief I form. It is a disrupter in terms internal to my own practice, not in a sense that invokes external normative standards. What it means for something to count as a disrupter is simply that while it may cause me to drop a belief it affects, it does not induce a change of mind that I would happily cite as an epistemic excuse for no longer displaying the belief. The excitement of the casino would be likely to cause me to drop the belief that the gambler's fallacy is a fallacy. But even if it did I would not treat the excitement of the casino as an epistemic excuse of the changed-mind variety.

With the notion of a disrupter in place, it is possible to offer a more nuanced account of self-knowledge. As someone competent in the natural language of my Erewhonian community, I can know that I believe something "p"—this is the content of an assertion in that language—when I satisfy two conditions. First, I am evidentially careful in registering relevant data before assenting to it. And second, I am executively careful, if needed, in guarding against potential disrupters of the belief and remaining sensitive to the data.

How can I muster sufficient confidence, then, to be able to avow a belief that p as distinct from merely reporting it? Assuming that I take care to register all relevant data and to avoid potential disrupters—assuming that I take evidential and executive care—the answer is: by deferring to a body of data that robustly elicits it; alternatively, by assenting to "p" or making up my mind that p on the basis of robustly effective data. I know that I believe that p by virtue of knowing what it is that I do in taking that action, whether it be described as deferring to the data, or assenting to the proposition, or making up my mind about it. In a seventeenth-century phrase, I have a maker's knowledge of believing that p, not the knowledge of an observer, even an introspective observer.[38] I can speak for what I believe with an authority of a special, practical sort.[39]

The norm governing truth-telling in Erewhon does not register anything about avowals as distinct from reports. But if the considerations just rehearsed are sound, then it is plausible to expect that in Erewhon we will adjust that norm, consciously or otherwise, to cover avowals. The same is true, not just for norms governing the avowals of belief but also for norms governing the other avowals and the pledges that figure in the discussion that follows. Given the purposes of the narrative, however, it need not register that development explicitly in each case, and need not try to spell out the adjusted shape that the norm would take.

THE AVOWAL OF OTHER ATTITUDES

The Attraction and Accessibility of Avowing Other Attitudes

As it is going to be manifestly attractive for me and others in Erewhon to avow our beliefs rather than just report them, so the same is true for the other attitudes we may wish to communicate to others. Or at least that will be so with attitudes that are important in our relationships with others and that we must want others to recognize in us. Thus suppose that I am confident in holding about myself that I wish to prove reliable to others, that I prefer talking about a difference to squabbling over it, that I intend to go on a hunt tomorrow, or that I have affection for you as a friend. If I want to convey such an attitude to you with a suitable degree of credibility, then it will be useful to be able to avow the attitude rather than just report it. Avowing it will mean communicating that I have it in such a manner that I cannot excuse a failure to live up to it by claiming that I must have been misled about my attitude. And such a mode of communication will give you much firmer ground for taking me at my word, relying on my possession of the attitude, than if I reported on its presence in a way that kept that excuse open.

But there is a problem in explaining how I can avow a desire or any other noncredal attitude; the means are not so straightforwardly accessible as in the case of belief. I can avow a belief that p, as we know, by asserting that p. But I cannot avow a desire that q by asserting that q; such an assertion would express a belief that q rather than a desire that q. While I may be strongly motivated to avow a desire, then, it seems that I may lack the means of doing so. Certainly I cannot avow a desire in a way that corresponds to the straightforwardly expressive means of avowing a belief.[40]

The expressive means of avowing a belief is of fundamental importance because it is going to be saliently available as well as saliently attractive in Erewhon, even at the stage where we are exclusively interested in making worldly reports to one another. But suppose that the expressive avowal of belief has become standard practice in Erewhon, as the preceding argument suggests that it would. Suppose that it has become a matter of common awareness, in other words, that in Erewhon we will generally want to avow the beliefs we hold rather than just reporting them and that a standard way of doing this is just to express those beliefs: to say "p" in communicating that we believe that p. Under those circumstances, it is plausible that we will begin to recognize other, nonexpressive means of avowing our beliefs. And it turns out that those other means of avowing beliefs offer us models for the avowal of attitudes like desires as well.

The attraction for me and for others in Erewhon of avowing as distinct from reporting beliefs that are important in our relationships with others is going to be obvious to all. And so it is likely to be a matter of common awareness that avowing such beliefs has a much greater appeal for us than reporting them: we will each have access to evidence of that appeal, of evidence that we each have access to that evidence, and so on.[41] But if this is a matter of common awareness, then the default assumption we will each make with others is that in communicating relevant beliefs to us they are meaning to avow them. They are meaning to speak for what they believe while putting aside the possibility that they may have gotten those beliefs wrong: the possibility that they may have been misled about their own minds.

Suppose then that in the presence of that default assumption, I do not say "p" in expressive mode but resort to the ascriptive mode, as in saying "I believe that p." Should I be taken to be merely reporting on my belief rather than avowing it? It should be clear that in many contexts—specifically, contexts where I act as if I am willing to avow the belief—you will naturally take me to be using the ascriptive remark with the same force that an expressive remark would have had: that is, with the force of an avowal. In such a case you would expect me to go out of my way to indicate that I am merely reporting on the belief, if indeed that was what I was doing. You would expect me to resort to oblique phrasing, as in saying that it seems to me that I believe that p, or that I think that what I want to say is that p, or that I am inclined to believe that p, or whatever.

Absent such phrasing, you will naturally take an ascriptive assertion like "I believe that p"—an assertion in which I ascribe the belief to myself—to have the same avowal force as the expressive assertion "p." And equally you are likely to assign the force of an avowal to other remarks too: say, to an explanatory remark such as "The data explain why I believe that p." In either sort of case, ascriptive or explanatory, you will expect me to be ready to stand by the belief, and not to hedge in the manner of a self-reporter. Hedging in that manner would be unusual enough for you to expect that I would do more to indicate that I was hedging, if indeed that is what I was wanting to do. That this is what would happen in Erewhon is borne out by the fact that this is what happens in actual languages. You would hardly expect to be taken as a mere self-reporter if you said that you believed that Jones was reliable. In order to mark out your utterance as merely the report of a belief you would have to say that your own impression was that he was reliable, or that you were inclined to make the judgment, or something of that markedly tentative kind.

Assuming that this line of argument is sound, consider now the point at which we in Erewhon have established a practice that allows us to avow our beliefs in ascriptive and explanatory assertions as well as in expressive. At that point, so it turns out, we will have provided ourselves with a salient means of avowing noncredal attitudes as well credal.

Saying in ascriptive mode "I desire prospect R"—say, I desire to prove myself reliable—is not necessarily going to be taken as a mere report that I have that desire but will be heard in appropriate contexts as an avowal. And the same will be true of saying in similar mode that I prefer talking to squabbling, that I intend to go on a hunt tomorrow, or that I like you.[42] Again, saying that there are factors that explain why I desire R or prefer talking to squabbling is not necessarily going to count as a detached explanation but will be taken in suitable contexts as an avowal of the attitude explained. Or at least this will be so with communications in which the attitudes I convey are important in my relationships with others.[43] Thus I will be expected to go out of my way to indicate that I am hedging my bets if that is what I am doing in communicating such an attitude. I will be expected to resort to quaint phrasings, as in saying, "My sense is that I have a desire for R," or "It's possible that I like you," or something of that kind.[44]

The Feasibility of Avowing Other Attitudes

But it is one thing to show that like others I will have a motive and a means of avowing desires and other noncredal attitudes in Erewhon. It is quite another to show that I can be confident enough of having any such attitude to be willing to avow it: to be willing to discount the possibility that I may be misled about my own inclinations. In the case of belief, I can find a sufficient basis for confidence in the fact that the data to which I defer with suitable care robustly elicit assent to the proposition. In order to avow any attitude like desire I need similar grounds to be confident about holding it. But where might I find an effective basis for confidence in this case? The question is particularly challenging because the attitude is one, as avowal presupposes, that I could be wrong to ascribe to myself.

The most plausible answer, which fits with a long tradition of thinking, is that I can find such a basis in the properties that robustly lead me to adopt the attitude, eliciting desire or affection, preference or intention: for short, in the desiderata or attractors present. Thus I can be sure of desiring R insofar as R has properties that attract me to it here and now and that promise to attract me robustly across possibilities where those properties remain in place. Or at least I can be sure of desiring R insofar as I guard, as needed, against potential disrupters of the desire: that is, factors like wayward whims or impulses that are liable to remove the desire without disposing me to claim an excusing change of mind.

The desiderata that serve to elicit desire come in many different forms. They include neutral properties that can make a scenario attractive for anyone in any situation: that it would be fun, that it would secure peace, that it would reduce suffering. They include agent-relative properties that can make a prospect attractive for anyone in a certain relationship or position: that it would create an advantage for my child or further the prosperity of my tribal group. And they include properties that can make a scenario attractive for anyone with a certain need or taste: that it would satisfy my hunger, relieve my boredom, or preserve my sense of who I am.

By analogy with the case of desire, I can be sure of liking you insofar as your attractive features give you a robust hold on my affections. Or at least that is so to the extent that I also guard against potential disrupters, as I will see them: for example, against the effects of prolonged absence or shifts of mood. Again I can be sure of preferring talking to squabbling insofar as it features desiderata like creating a sense of calm or offering an opportunity for mutual understanding that appeal to me here and now and that promise to remain appealing across a variety of circumstances. Or at least that is so to the extent that I also guard against vicissitudes of taste or inclination that I see as potential disrupters of that preference.

To hold that attitudes of these kinds are grounded robustly in desiderata, as beliefs are grounded in data, is to go along with the idea, long accepted in philosophical tradition, that there are motivating reasons that generally lead human beings to form any such disposition. Those attitudes do not appear out of the blue, so this orthodoxy holds, but are elicited by features that people ascribe to their targets; or at least that is so when they are not subject to disruption and failure.[45]

Although this picture is not endorsed on all sides, it is deeply intuitive. Decision theorists reject it insofar as they treat preferences as primitive rankings, ignoring the possibility that reliable attractors or desiderata lie at their origin. But their view can be seen as a convenient simplification, not a position defended on independent grounds.[46]

Opponents of the picture also include particularists, as they are often known.[47] While they agree that the properties of objects of desire play a characteristic role in eliciting that attitude—or at least in eliciting the corresponding moral judgment—they deny that those properties always weigh in the same direction; the pleasure of an innocent activity may weigh in its favor, the pleasure of doing something noxious like torturing another may weigh against.[48] But this runs counter to the familiar idea that in deliberating about what we want, we weigh the pros and cons attaching to each option and form our desire on the basis of the resultant effect. And while examples like the pleasure case may seem to put that idea in question, they can be taken equally to show that it is not pleasure as such that counts as a desideratum with us but rather innocent pleasure.[49]

If desiderata play a role of the kind ascribed in this picture, we may expect that we members of Erewhon will have terms for the relevant attractors and will be able to employ those terms to explain our attitudes and by the same stroke avow them. Thus I will explain and avow corresponding desires by describing various scenarios as being a lot of fun or providing a chance to learn something or promising relief from boredom. I will explain and avow a preference for talking over squabbling by pointing to the advantages it offers in generating calm and comprehension. And I will explain and avow an affection by citing your attractive features as a friend. The predication in each case will play the role of an avowal of the relevant attitude insofar as it forecloses a misleading-mind excuse for not acting on that attitude. And it will play the role of an explanation for that avowal insofar as it identifies the property of the object in virtue of which I am robustly drawn to it.

We Erewhonians are disposed to avow rather than report the beliefs we hold, at least when they are important in our relationships with one another: at least when it matters to us that others should rely on our having those beliefs. And by analogy we are disposed to avow rather than just report our desires and other noncredal attitudes, when they matter in our relationships and we want others to rely on our having them. What now appears is that as we can rely on the robust role of data in eliciting beliefs to enable us to avow those states, so we can rely on the robust role of desiderata in eliciting noncredal status in order to be able to practice avowal in this case as well.

On the picture supported, I will form a desire or affection, a preference or intention, insofar as I defer to corresponding desiderata in the way in which I defer to the data supporting a proposition in assenting to it. And I will be in a position to know that I desire or feel, prefer or intend, something—whether for the first time or not—by virtue of knowing that I defer to the relevant desiderata in that way. I make up my mind in response to those attractors and I know the attitudes I form on the basis of knowing what I am doing. It is not by virtue of introspective observation that I know that I have the attitudes I avow but rather, as in the belief case, by virtue of a sort of maker's knowledge.

THE PLEDGING OF ATTITUDES

By the definitions given earlier, to make a pledge as distinct from an avowal in communicating an attitude is to go one stage further in making the communication credible. It is to raise the cost of the communication by foreclosing not just the possibility of excusing a failure to live up to it by reference to a misleading mind but also the possibility of doing so by reference to a changed mind. If I avow the intention of going with you on a hunt, then I can scarcely excuse my failure to turn up by saying that I was misled about my intention but I can certainly excuse it by saying that I changed my mind since speaking to you. But if I pledge the intention to join you on the hunt, in the sense introduced, then I cannot avail myself of this excuse either. The intention is not immune to being misread, and not immune to change, but the pledge rules out the possibility of my invoking either possibility to excuse my failure to turn up. It will take something like a practical excuse, such as that I broke a leg, to persuade you that I was nonetheless disposed to act in a cooperative manner.

It should be clear that in Erewhon, I and others are going to have a motive for pledging attitudes, if pledging is indeed possible. In particular, we are going to have a motive for pledging the congenial or collaborative intentions that matter in building or maintaining relationships with one another. Pledging an attitude is even more expensive than avowing it, since it exposes me to a greater risk of not having any excuse for failing to act on the attitude. It will be highly credible because of the risk that I choose to take in opting for it. And it will be all the more credible because of the fact that in opting for it I convey the message that I fully recognize the cost of failure but back myself not to incur it.

But however attractive it may be, pledging is only going to emerge in the community if it also proves to be an accessible and feasible option. In order to be an accessible option we will have to be able to identify a linguistic means of communicating a pledge akin to the expressive, ascriptive, and explanatory means of communicating an avowal. But presumably we will be able to find some way of conveying a pledge, if the option of pledging is feasible. And it will be feasible just in case there is some basis, saliently available to each of us, for giving ourselves enough confidence about maintaining an attitude to be able to pledge it: that is, to be able to rule out not just the possibility that we may have been misled about our attitude but also the possibility that we may yet change that attitude.

The question, then, is whether I could ever have enough confidence in maintaining an attitude to be able to set aside the two standard, epistemic ways of excusing a failure to display it. The question is particularly challenging because the assumption, as we saw, is that the attitude in question is not immune to being misread or immune to change. It arises only with attitudes that, from my perspective, it may actually be wrong to ascribe to myself and it may be wrong to expect to remain unchanged.[50]

Might I be able, then, to pledge a belief? In particular, might I be able to pledge a regular, empirically vulnerable belief of the kind that I recognize I might not maintain; more in a moment on religious beliefs and the like? We live in a changing, incompletely grasped world and although I may think that the data are sufficient to elicit belief in an empirical proposition "p", enabling me to avow that belief in it, I could never be sure that the data would not later be overturned or outweighed. Indeed for me to consider pledging such a belief would betray a misconception about the very attitude of belief. It would show that I did not treat it as responsive to potentially changing data.[51]

Might I be able to pledge any other attitudes besides belief? In order to do so, I would have to be able to identify desiderata or attractors related to those attitudes. And in deferring to those desiderata, I would have to be confident enough about their remaining effective—and about my ability to guard against disruption of their effect—to be able to foreclose the changed-mind excuse as well as the misleading-mind excuse. Is there any reason to think that I might be able to muster such confidence? Surprisingly, there is.

Were I to pledge such an attitude, then the very fact of making the pledge would bring a desideratum or attractor into existence that might serve in the required role. It would make it the case that sticking with the attitude had at least this appealing feature: that it would show that I can be relied upon to keep my word. So the question, then, is whether I could rely on that feature to enable me to pledge a desire for R, a preference for talking over squabbling, or an intention to join you on a hunt. The answer is that I could rely on that feature to be able to pledge an intention but not to be able to pledge any of the other attitudes.

Suppose that I pledge a certain preference—say, for hunting over gathering; that many of the desiderata that attracted me to hunting cease to be appealing; but that I continue to choose hunting because of wanting to show that my word is my bond. Would the preference for hunting remain in place as a result of the pledge? No, it would not. I can hardly count as preferring hunting in the relevant sense—that is, liking it more than gathering—when I only continue to choose it because of having given my word. Preference in the sense at issue here requires me to be attached to hunting on the basis of desiderata other than the attractor that a pledge would put in place. This same sort of problem arises with anything that we are likely to regard as a desire for a prospect R and, of course, with any attitude like affection. I would not count as maintaining the desire or the affection just because I acted as if it were in place but only for the sake of presenting myself as faithful to my word.[52]

This problem does not arise, however, with an intention or plan or anything of that kind. Suppose that in speaking with you I pledge an intention or plan to join you on the hunt, wanting the thrill of chasing prey over open sunny spaces. And imagine that it rains heavily on the appointed day, but that I turn up nevertheless because of having given you my word. Do I count as still holding and acting on the intention pledged? Yes, I do. With an intention as distinct from a desire or affection or preference, the attitude does not have to be sourced in certain sorts of desiderata in order to count as remaining in place. And so the attractor that pledging an attitude creates in favor of maintaining the attitude can serve in this sort of case—although only, it appears, in this sort of case—to give me the confidence required for being able to make a pledge.

We saw earlier that I put myself in a position to avow an attitude on the basis of consciously deferring to a suitable body of data or set of desiderata, where I am careful to register the data or desiderata available and to guard against the possibility of disruption. I know that I think or feel something with sufficient confidence to be able to avow that attitude, by virtue of knowing that I defer to those data or desiderata: by virtue, in that sense, of a sort of maker's knowledge. The same sort of maker's knowledge will enable me to tell that I intend something with sufficient confidence to be able to pledge the intention. In consciously recognizing and deferring to the desideratum that the very act of pledging brings into play—the desideratum that consists in proving that I live up to my word—I can achieve the degree of confidence required. Or at least I can do this to the extent that I can guard against the disruption of my response to that attractor.

Someone may balk at restricting the speech act of pledging to intentions or plans, on the grounds that many people claim to pledge religious beliefs, political beliefs, and perhaps even beliefs in matters that they take to be a priori: for example, beliefs in classical logic. But the best gloss on such a pledge is to treat it as pledging an intention: say, the intention to treat certain texts or authorities or frameworks as definitive, letting them shape the construal to be given to any other sources of evidence. It is certainly possible to organize life around such voluntarily adopted fixtures. And as this is possible in the actual world, so it would be possible also for those of us who live in Erewhon. The possibility is not relevant to the narrative, however, and will not figure significantly in the evolving story.

The notion of pledging an attitude, in particular an intention, reflects the more regular idea of promising to act in a corresponding way. But the notion of promising in ordinary usage has a strong moral or ethical flavor. It is represented as an act such that if I make a promise to do something, then I have an ethical obligation, however defeasible, to do it. Pledging, as introduced at this point, has no such ethical connotations. When I make a pledge in Erewhon, as when I make an avowal, I back myself to act as thereby advertised, manifestly exposing myself to serious retaliatory and reputational costs in the event of failure. What I do is more akin to making a side-bet that I will hold and act on the intention pledged—a side-bet strategically designed to entice you and others to rely on me—than it is to giving you a promise in the ordinary, moralized sense of that term.

Pledging, by the account offered here, is considerably more costly, and hence more credible, than avowing. If I pledge to act on a certain intention, as in pledging to join you on the hunt, then my stake in living up to those words is higher than my stake would have been, had I merely avowed an intention to join you. And hence you can rely with greater assurance on my joining you than if I had just avowed the intention. But as in the case of avowal, of course, the cost of pledging need not make the act prohibitively expensive. If I fail to join you on the hunt but can invoke the practical, un-foreclosed excuse of a broken leg in explanation of the failure, then I do not lose my stake. And the same is going to be true when I can plead an exempting disability like a temporary bout of insanity to explain the failure. Any such factor can persuade you that, despite the failure, you need not despair of me as a cooperative and reliable interlocutor.

THE CO-AVOWAL AND CO-PLEDGING OF ATTITUDES

The Authorization Presupposed in Co-avowal

When I avow or pledge an attitude I play the role of spokesperson rather than reporter in relation to myself. I speak for myself, as we might say, rather than speaking about myself. I do not convey the attitude in the way in which I might try to communicate the attitude of another, reporting on it in a manner that keeps both epistemic excuses alive. In an avowal I assume the authority to voice an attitude while closing down the possibility that I may have been misled by my own mind. In a pledge I assume the authority to voice an attitude while closing down the possibility both that I was misled about my mind and that I might yet change my mind.

In speaking about your attitudes as a random other, there is a distance between me in the interpreting role and you in the role of the interpreted. In speaking for myself in avowals and pledges—in assuming the role of spokesperson for myself—I reduce or remove that distance. I present myself as the person spoken for and speak, therefore, without fear of an interpretive failure: without fear of a failure to read my mind aright, in the case of an avowal; without fear of misreading or changing my mind in the case of a pledge. Uttered with the authority of a spokesperson, my words are not supported by my skill as the person speaking to track the independently formed attitudes of the person spoken for. They are supported rather by a dual, strategically prudent commitment: as the person spoken for, to conform to what the person speaking says; and as the person speaking, to ascribe only such attitudes as the person spoken for is likely to be willing to display.

As it is possible for me to speak for myself in this way so it is possible in certain contexts for me or someone else to speak for a number of people, being authorized by each of them to make avowals—better, co-avowals—in their collective name, or indeed to make pledges or co-pledges in the collective name. The case of particular relevance to the evolving narrative is co-avowal. Suitably authorized, I will be able to avow a shared attitude in a way that forecloses the possibility of anyone's invoking a misleading-mind excuse—anyone's claiming that I got them wrong—in order to excuse their not displaying the attitude avowed. I will be able to co-avow the attitude in the name of the group.

Co-avowal can mean avowing attitudes in the name of an incorporated agent, as when someone acts as spokesperson for a body like a company or church or state. But when someone co-avows the attitudes of such an incorporated group they also co-avow the attitudes of its members, qua members. And in that respect the co-avowal is a special case of a more general possibility. The general possibility, which will be the main focus of interest, materializes in any case where I or you or another avows an attitude in the name of the members of a group, whether or not that group constitutes an organized agency. One co-avows the attitude and the rest of us co-accept it: we each treat it as an attitude such that we cannot invoke the misleading-mind excuse for failing to live up to the co-avowal; we cannot claim that in our particular case the spokesperson got the attitude wrong.

It might seem that co-avowal in this sense requires the prior authorization of the spokesperson by other members of the group. That is what Thomas Hobbes assumes when he suggests that the paradigm of authorization is my being appointed by you and others to speak for all of us, as "a representer, or representative, a lieutenant, a vicar, an attorney, a deputy, a procurator, an actor."[53] Hobbes is particularly concerned with the case where I speak for all of us as an organized group agent—say, a corporation or commonwealth—and not just as individuals. But his assumption about the need for prior authorization might be taken to apply to any case of co-avowal, not just to the case where the individuals involved constitute an organized agency.[54]

Advance authorization of the kind at issue may obviously be appropriate in special circumstances where I speak for all of us in a more or less formal capacity. But the authorization on the basis of which I can co-avow certain attitudes in common with you and others need not have its origin in any such ex ante arrangement, however tacit. I may presume on being authorized and claim authorization in the absence of ex post protest at my avowal of a purportedly shared attitude.

On this picture I will signal that I am speaking for what each of us in a certain group thinks or feels, whatever form that signal takes, and I will presume on having the authority of a spokesperson insofar as no one objects to what I say in that role. I do not speak in this case with your advance license, your ex ante authorization. Rather I speak on the presumption that no one will reject my authority and that if no one rejects it, then the absence of rejection will have the same effect as ex ante authorization. You and others do not say "Yea" in advance to my playing the role of spokesperson but neither do you say "Nay" in the wake of my assuming such a role. And that amounts to the same thing. It means that you authorize me in a virtual rather than an actual manner: you authorize me, not by what you said, but by what you might saliently have said and chose not to say.

It is this general form of presumptive authorization that is of most interest here. It raises two questions, parallel to questions that arose with individual avowal. First, would co-avowal be accessible and attractive for us in Erewhon? And second, would it be feasible? Would any of us have a basis of confidence sufficient to make it into a plausible pursuit: that is, sufficient to give us reason to expect that when we speak for others, they will go along?

The Accessibility and Attraction of Co-avowal

In considering the motives that each of us has for avowing or pledging attitudes, the assumption has been that in communicating with one another in Erewhon we trade independent utterances in a series of exchanges; we each pay the cost of reliably communicating information to another for the reward of being generally able both to rely on others and to induce their reliance on us. On this picture, I make a report or avowal or pledge on my side, you make a report or avowal or pledge on yours. And the main concern on my side, exactly analogous to the main concern on yours, is to prove sufficiently reliable in conveying those messages to be able, as occasion demands, to rely on you and to get you to rely on me.

This assumption about communication is fine for the purposes pursued in the discussion so far. But the accessibility and attraction of co-avowal is going to be obvious only in light of a further observation. This is that in reaping the benefits of mutual reliance, we in Erewhon are bound to pursue exchanges of information that have a more complex, conversational structure. This observation is crucial, because it turns out that conversationally structured exchanges inevitably involve the presumptive form of co-avowal.

Suppose that you and I and others exchange information with a view to resolving a problem we face, whether as individuals or as a community: perhaps a problem about how to resolve a conflict, what to believe about something, or what to do in pursuit of some end. If I am to contribute usefully to a conversation like this, I must speak on the basis of presuppositions about what we each believe and want and intend; if I am wrong about the shared presuppositions then what I say will not engage the concerns of others properly. But in speaking on the basis of such presuppositions I effectively co-avow them in the name of each of us in the conversation. On the presumption that I will not be opposed, it will be manifest to all that I take the beliefs or desire or intentions as attitudes that we, the members of the relevant group, are each prepared to accept as properly avowed in our joint names.[55]

When the presuppositions are unopposed, the contribution I make to the conversation in expressing a belief or desire or whatever will be to propose, again on the presumption that I am not going to be opposed, that that attitude is also one that we each accept or can be expected to accept as members of the group. If you and others go along with the presuppositions I make and the proposal I put forward, this will establish between us a shared presuppositional base and create a new opportunity for you or someone else to co-avow yet another attitude and, on the presumption that your proposal is accepted, to add further to that base. And if things proceed smoothly along this path, then we may hope to reach a point where our shared set of presuppositions is extensive enough to be able to solve the problem with which we started. It may be enough to eliminate or corral potentially dangerous conflicts, for example, to establish a common belief about some contentious issue, or to make possible the various forms of coordination or incorporation that involve co-pledging.

The presuppositional base built up in such a smoothly progressing conversation is well-described as common ground that we manage to establish between us.[56] It consists in a set of attitudes such that it is a matter of common awareness among those of us engaged in the conversation that we are each prepared to treat those attitudes as properly co-avowed in our name: in that sense, we each co-accept the attitudes. When we go along with a conversation, accepting the different elements in the common ground, we each foreclose the possibility of excusing our failure to live up to the co-avowed attitude by claiming that the co-avower got our attitude wrong.

The attitudes that are built into the common ground between us may include desires as well as beliefs but it is worth noting at this point that there is a great difference between the extent to which the two sorts of attitudes lend themselves to co-avowal. With anything I have solid ground for believing there will be others who share that ground and the belief will be co-avowable in relation to them. But that is not so with all the things I have solid ground for desiring. With some of those things, there may be many people who share that ground but with other things, there may be few or no people who do so. Desires that prove resistant to co-avowal will typically be grounded in agent-relative desiderata to do with what will facilitate my success in some area, help my children, satisfy my curiosity, or whatever.

The difference between belief and desire in these respects will be at the center of concern in the next lecture.

Not all conversations will progress smoothly, of course. Even if my presuppositions are accepted, someone may reject the addition to the common ground that I propose in my initial contribution to the conversation, or indeed in any later contribution. And what goes for me in this regard goes for each of us; none of us can be assured that our contribution at any point will be accepted. But when rejection occurs, this will presumably trigger a round of rejoinders and revisions—it would be in no one's interest just to walk away from every divergence of attitudes—and this can eventually put things back on a progressive path. Conversations in Erewhon may sometimes fail, as they may fail in any society. But, plausibly, they will often succeed.

This image of conversational exchange is easily illustrated. I tell you that there are deer gathering on the southern side of the woods, presupposing for example that we each want to join in a hunt and that we each know where the woods are. You go along with that presupposition, accept my assertion and add, on the basis of the now richer common ground—and perhaps on the basis of the further presupposition that three makes a better hunting party—that a certain friend is available to join us. As the conversation progresses, perhaps now including the friend as well, we each end up co-avowing a desire to hunt. "The hunt is on," one of us may say, or "OK, we're all for hunting." And, explicitly or implicitly, we co-avow a belief that the best time to hunt is now, and we each manifestly avow or indeed pledge a desire and intention to take part, making this too a part of the common ground.

In Erewhon, as in any plausible society, we will each have a motive for taking part in conversations of this kind; after all, they are essential for mutual reliance, enabling us to form, maintain, and develop peaceful, helpful, and collaborative relationships. What the analysis shows is that there is no useful conversation without a pattern of co-avowal and co-acceptance. Contributors each avow attitudes in the name of all those involved, putting them forward as attitudes that everyone avows or can be expected to avow from the standpoint they share. And, whether or not they make any active contribution, participants each accept that any co-avowed attitude that no one opposes is one that they are individually prepared to avow as a member of the group.

This analysis of conversation connects closely with the work of Robert Stalnaker on assertion and related topics.[57] He emphasizes that "the essential effect of an assertion is to change the presuppositions of the participants in the conversation by adding the content of what is asserted to what is presupposed."[58] And he also recognizes that in presenting certain presuppositions and assertions as expressive of the attitudes of each, every participant presumes on the authorization of others for doing this and is ready to retreat if ex post authorization is denied. Thus he says that the effect of assertion in changing presuppositions, reshaping the common ground between parties, "is avoided only if the assertion is rejected."

What holds about the content of an assertion holds equally, as Stalnaker recognizes,[59] with any presuppositions that an assertion puts in place less obtrusively; an utterance can change common ground, not by just asserting something, but also by intruding a would-be presupposition of all parties. Suppose I say in a conversational context, "The present king of Erewhon is bald." I thereby identify as a would-be presupposition the proposition that Erewhon currently has a king as well as proposing the new presupposition that the king is bald. But you or others can play the same role in rejecting my would-be presupposition as you can in rejecting the content of my assertion. If you each let it pass, then the utterance will count as co-avowing the belief that there is a king of Erewhon, as it will count as co-avowing the belief that the king is bald. You must reject my presumed authority if you are to stop me from changing the common ground in this way.

No man is an island and, as these observations show, no speaker holds just by insulated attitudes. Conversation is essential for gaining the benefits of mutual reliance that we have been emphasizing throughout but it imposes costs on those of us who submit themselves to its discipline. It means that as members of this or that group any one of us may have to avow beliefs and desires in the name of many as well as in our own name alone. And it means that as members of this or that group each of us has to accept that we cannot excuse a failure to live up to any successfully co-avowed attitude by appealing to a misleading mind: that is, by claiming that the spokesperson involved got our mind wrong.[60]

The Feasibility of Co-avowal

So much for the means and motives that I, like everyone else, will have in Erewhon for making co-avowals in the name of others as well as myself. But now, as in earlier cases, we must turn to the question of feasibility. What could give me confidence enough to be ready to speak for a plurality of individuals, avowing a belief or desire as an attitude that you and others also hold as members of the same group? Where could I find grounds to avow attitudes on the default assumption that they are your attitudes as well as mine?

We saw that in order to avow a belief in my own name I have to think that the data supporting the proposition believed are sufficient to elicit that belief robustly and that my sensitivity to those data is secure: for example, secure against the sort of disruption illustrated by the casino case. And we saw too that in order to avow a desire or other such attitude in my own name, I have to rely on the desiderata at the origin of the desire being sufficient and my sensitivity to those attractors being secure. What might enable me, then, to avow a belief or a desire in the name of you and others as well as myself? Presumably, the fact, as I must take it to be, that you are responsive in the same way to the same data and desiderata, and that you are secure in your responsiveness to them. I must take this to be the case when I venture to speak for us, not just for me, and to avow an attitude in our common name.

Would it be reasonable on my part, or on the part of anyone else in Erewhon, to rely on our being exposed to the same data and desiderata and to be responsive to them in the same manner? It appears to be part of human nature that we exercise joint attention, being consciously directed to matters that we each assume to be available to all, albeit from different perspectives.[61] That being so, I will often be in the position of recognizing that you and others are exposed in common with me to a certain body of data or a certain set of desiderata. Many of us will have access to data not available to others but we may still confront a patently common, intersecting body of data, as when the data in your case suggest that p&q, the data in mine that p&r. Again many of us will recognize special desiderata that are not available to others, and perhaps not available by a sort of necessity: the welfare of your child may matter to you in a way it cannot matter to me, and vice versa. But that is consistent with there being common desiderata or attractors that are effective for both of us: say, that there should be peace and prosperity in the land.

It is one thing, however, to assume that you and I and others may often face a manifestly common body of data or common set of desiderata. It is quite another to suppose that we are each disposed to respond to that common base in a common manner: to suppose that as the data or desiderata are likely to lead me, so in general they are likely to lead you. So the question is whether this further assumption is also a reasonable one to make, in Erewhon or elsewhere.

Suppose that the data you rely on in forming a belief are not good or complete by my lights. Or suppose that the desiderata you are moved by in forming a desire are not attractors that I can see as relevant, even allowing for differences of taste and background, or are only a proper subset of the desiderata I take to be relevant. This will be no problem so long as I can point out my worries about the idiosyncratic or incomplete basis on which you form your attitudes and you respond appropriately. You may change the attitude in response to my complaint or you may show me, perhaps with the help of an anthropologist or psychotherapist, that the basis is not as quirky or patchy as it seemed.

But suppose that you are not disposed or able to do this and continue to display a form of sensitivity to data or desiderata that is completely alien to me. Suppose that without giving me reason to assign different meanings to your words—if it is possible to avoid such differences—you present to me as someone for whom the effect of data is not the same as it is with me; or as someone for whom the role of desiderata is played by different properties from those that make any sense to me. Whether on a wider or narrower front, you and I do not work with the same logic of attitude-formation.

If you were as alien as this, then I could not relate to you as in practice we human beings generally relate to one another. I could only see you as someone to whom I had to adjust, as I might adjust to a force of nature, not as someone conversable: someone I could reach in the space of words.[62] I would be likely to be bewildered and at a loss in such a case. In the end, indeed, I might even be forced to assume that you are a subject for treatment, not conversational interaction.[63]

Elizabeth Anscombe suggests that I would be bewildered and at a loss even if you failed to make sense on quite a narrow front.[64] She argues the point by asking how we would think of a person who seeks something as unlikely as a saucer of mud but cannot do anything to make sense of that desire: cannot present it to us under an aspect with recognizable attractor potential. In order to find the person conversable we would have to see some aspect under which the saucer of mud appeals: say, as an ornament or as a reminder of our mortality. We would not have to be moved by the prospect of having such an ornament or a reminder, as our interlocutor is presumably moved, but we would at least have to recognize why such ornaments or reminders might have an appeal.

Assuming that it is essential for interpersonal interaction that human beings can treat one another as generally conversable, there is no problem about assuming that in Erewhon we each have a more or less similar sensitivity to data and desiderata, as we do when we co-avow and co-accept certain attitudes. Such a common sensitivity probably comes in good part from our nature. But even if it was not wholly supplied by nature we each would have to simulate or internalize it in order to establish ourselves as someone on whom others could rely and with whom they could converse and do business.

The assumption of mutual conversability is not only needed to explain how we in Erewhon can presume on enjoying a similar sensitivity to data and desiderata, thereby providing a basis for co-avowal. Although not registered earlier, it is also needed to explain why any one of us might be prepared to accept even the individual avowals or pledges of another. You may be content to avow a belief in light of robustly supportive data, and to avow a desire or pledge an intention in light of robustly supportive desiderata. But I would hardly be content to rely on your avowal and pledge if the data or desiderata on which you relied struck me as alien and unmoving. I would be likely to find your avowals and pledges compelling only to the extent that I found that at some level we shared a similar sensitivity to data and desiderata.

As we in Erewhon have a motive to practice co-avowal, then, so we are bound to have the capacity to do so in a range of cases. We can assume a common logic of attitude formation and, identifying the data and desiderata at our common disposal, we can presume on speaking for others as well as ourselves in avowing corresponding beliefs or desires. Or at least we can presume on doing this to the extent that we can assume that all of us who accept a co-avowal made in our name will recognize the possibility of disruption, as we must do in the case of avowals and pledges that we make in our individual names, and will guard against it.

Disruption can be introduced by any factors that might lead us not to live up to a co-avowed or co-accepted attitude without providing us with what we might treat as a changed-mind excuse. The disrupters in the case of co-avowed or co-accepted attitudes will include the sorts of intertemporal factors mentioned in the individual case—the momentary illusion or impulse—as well as disrupters of a particularly interpersonal character such as the tendency to favor a partial perspective or a selfish preference, letting it weaken the force of the data and desiderata shared in common with others. Individuals can expect to be able to make avowals in their own name only if they guard against disruption. And equally they can expect to be able to co-avow or co-accept attitudes in a common name only if those spoken for guard against the disrupters relevant in this case too.

We saw earlier that it is a sort of maker's knowledge that gives me enough confidence to be able to avow or pledge an attitude in my own name. The line developed here shows that it is something of the same sort that can give me enough confidence to co-avow an attitude in the name of a group. Suppose I recognize that a body of data or desiderata that is available to me in common with you and others is sufficient to elicit a certain belief or desire and that you are disposed to respond to it in the same way as me. In consciously deferring to that base, making up my mind on the attitude to form, I am positioned to know that I hold that attitude. And in consciously recognizing that you and others are responsive in the same way to the same data and desiderata, I am positioned to know that you and others hold that attitude too. Or at least I am positioned to know that you are likely to form that attitude under the stimulus of my co-avowal. I have a comaker's knowledge, as we might say, of our each holding the attitude.

The co-avowals we make may be expressive, ascriptive, or explanatory in form. Thus in the case of the deer-hunt I may say either that the hunt is on or that we're all for hunting or indeed that hunting would be fun or something of that kind. More generally, I may co-avow a belief that p by uttering "p" in a context where this manifestly implicates you and others; or by saying, "We believe that p" or "I take it we all believe that p"; or by claiming that the data show that p or something of that kind. And I may co-avow a desire for R, if not by an expression like "Oh for R," at least by an ascription of the form, "We desire R," or by an explanation such as "R would give us all some pleasure."

This discussion of co-avowal completes a review of the elements needed for the purposes of the second lecture, but it may be useful to add a word on co-pledging as well as co-avowal. Co-pledging an attitude must mean co-pledging an intention, for reasons already rehearsed. It is bound to be attractive for us in Erewhon to be able to pursue common goals with a number of others on the basis of sharing in a co-pledged intention. I will co-pledge an intention on behalf of a group when I speak for what we will do in a manner that closes down the possibility both that I am misled about their intention and that they might yet change their mind. But how could I or anyone else have sufficient confidence that the others in a group are tied in this way to an intention I co-pledge?

One possibility, of course, is that I am authorized in advance to speak in pledging mode for what the group intends to do; or that I am authorized to speak in that way on one aspect of the group performance, others on other aspects; or indeed that a voice constructed out of different inputs from within our membership is authorized as our common voice, whether on all or on only some of the relevant aspects. This, arguably, is what happens when we form a corporate agent, and acquiesce in pursuing the intentions—and the other attitudes—that the authorized spokesperson announces.[65] In this case we act together like a single agent, robustly pursuing a coherent set of goals in robust accord with a coherent set of judgments, where those goals and judgments are determined by the authorized voice.

The other possibility for co-pledging an intention arises when, short of forming a group agent, we the members of a group acquiesce in enacting a particular, episodic goal with sufficient salience for any one of us to be able to presume on the authorization of others in pledging an intention in the name of all the parties involved to realize that goal. This will occur in Erewhon, for example, as it may occur anywhere, when it is salient to all of us in the group—indeed perhaps a matter of common awareness among us— that there is a plan whereby we can achieve something together that we cannot achieve apart; that this is something we each wish to achieve in view of the manifestly present, manifestly effective desiderata; and that if one or more of us takes up their part in implementing the plan, then the others will quickly join in. Under such conditions we members will each go along with the plan and act on a joint intention in pursuing this or that particular end: say, in saving a drowning child or in undertaking a mountain adventure.[66] And in any such case it will be possible for one of us to presume on the authority of others in pledging the intention in the name of all.[67]

CONCLUSION

The main steps covered in the narrative so far should now be fairly clear.

- Erewhon is a society in which by hypothesis we members are competent in natural language but use it only to communicate in reports about our shared world.
- In Erewhon we will want to be able to rely on others and to get others to rely on us and this will give us a motive to prove reliable in giving our reports: to be careful and truthful in what we say.

- That motive will also prompt us to want to communicate our general attitudes to one another, in particular those beliefs, desires, and intentions that help to establish that we are congenial and reliable parties in interaction.

- In communicating our beliefs, one salient option will be to do this by expressing and thereby avowing our beliefs rather than reporting them; to express a belief that p is to assert simply that p.

- Avowal will make our words more costly, since we cannot explain a failure to live up to them, as we might explain words used in a report, by the misleading-mind excuse; and by doing this it will make them more credible and more useful in communication.

- The default attraction of avowal will mean that, unless we go out of our way to indicate otherwise, we will be taken to avow beliefs even when we speak nonexpressively: even when we self-ascribe a belief or explain its hold on us.

- As we will be attracted to avowing beliefs, so we will be attracted to avowing desires and other noncredal attitudes too; we can avow them by means of ascriptive or explanatory modes of self-attribution, if not by expressive ones.

- The attraction of avowal extends also to pledging, which involves closing down not just the misleading-mind excuse but also the changed-mind excuse; pledging an attitude will be more costly, and more credible, than avowing it.

- Pledging may not be possible with beliefs and desires, but it is certainly possible with intentions and plans; pledging an intention will mean setting aside the possibility not just of having misread it, but also of changing it.

- As I may avow beliefs and desires in my own name, so I may co-avow them: that is, avow them in the name of all of us in a certain fixed or fluid group.

- I may do this with the prior authorization of others but also, and more commonly, on the basis of their presumptive authorization; in this case I will count as authorized to the extent that others do not reject what I claim to say in our common name.

- Conversational exchange inevitably involves such presumptive authorization for co-avowal, since it evolves smoothly only when we participants manifestly co-accept the presuppositions and the proposals made by a speaker.

- We are bound to practice co-avowal in Erewhon, since the mutual reliance that we seek is going to materialize fully only to the extent that we can converse with one another and converge on common standpoints.

- This is also true of co-pledging, where that may materialize on the basis either of episodic cooperation between some individuals—acting on a joint intention—or on the basis of incorporating as a group agent.

The social practices that are likely to emerge in Erewhon will have an impact on how we see the world, in particular the social world, we share. They will make various patterns salient to us that would otherwise have been unavailable, so that the view from within those practices will contrast with the view from the bare perspective of natural science. The practices will not direct us to particulars or properties that are naturalistically mysterious, since any patterns that become visible will achieve salience in the process of naturalistically intelligible interactions with one another and with our common environment. But the emerging patterns may still serve to provide us with referents for demonstrably ethical concepts and novel ways of organizing our lives together around those concepts.

This is the guiding promise behind these lectures, holding out the prospect of a genealogy of ethics that serves to vindicate it. The second lecture tries to make good on that promise. It attempts to show how the view from within practices of avowal and co-avowal, pledging and co-pledging, allows notions of desirability and responsibility to gain application and to play an organizing role in the lives of Erewhonians. If successful, the argument demonstrates the near inescapability of ethics for any creatures like us— any creatures endowed with our natural capacities and motives—that have access to natural language. Even if we take ethics at face value as revealing facts about desirability and responsibility, we can insist that it is an unmysterious part of a naturalistic world and that it plays an important role in our lives.

NOTES

1. According to a currently popular version of non-naturalism, pure normative truths are treated like the truths of mathematics and hold with a necessity akin to mathematical necessity. For an excellent presentation, see T. M. Scanlon, *Being Realistic about Reasons* (Oxford: Oxford University Press, 2014). I do not address that position in this text but seek to provide an alternative in light of which I hope it may lose its appeal.

2. Charles L. Stevenson, *Ethics and Language* (New Haven, CT: Yale University Press, 1944); Alfred J. Ayer, *Truth and Logic* (London: Gollanz, 1982); Simon Blackburn, *Spreading the Word* (Oxford: Oxford University Press, 1984); Allan Gibbard, *Wise Choices, Apt Feelings* (Oxford: Oxford University Press, 1990).

3. J. L. Mackie, *Ethics* (Harmondsworth: Penguin, 1977); Richard Joyce, *The Evolution of Morality* (Cambridge, MA: MIT Press, 2006).

4. There are as many forms of non-reductive naturalism, so called, as there are accounts of reduction. I prefer to think that the varieties of naturalism are all reductive and vary only in how constraining they take reduction to be. For a good account of the shape that a reductive naturalism has to take, see Frank

Jackson, *From Metaphysics to Ethics: A Defence of Conceptual Analysis* (Oxford: Oxford University Press, 1998); and David Chalmers and Frank Jackson, "Conceptual Analysis and Reductive Explanation," *Philosophical Review* 110 (2001): 315–60). And for how it might apply in the ethical case, see also Frank Jackson and Philip Pettit, "Moral Functionalism and Moral Motivation," *Philosophical Quarterly* 45 (1995): 20–40; reprinted in Frank Jackson, Philip Pettit, and Michael Smith, *Mind, Morality and Explanation,* 189–210 (Oxford: Oxford University Press, 2004).

5. Thus the genealogy of ethics, as I pursue it here, is philosophical rather than historical in character, seeking only to tell us how ethics could have emerged, not how it did. And, as noted, it is also vindicatory, not debunking. In both respects, it clashes with the sense of genealogy employed by Friedrich Nietzsche, *On the Genealogy of Morals* (Cambridge: Cambridge University Press, 1997); see Bernard Williams, *Truth and Truthfulness* (Princeton, NJ: Princeton University Press, 2002); and Alexander Prescott-Couch, "Williams and Nietzsche on the Significance of History for Moral Philosophy," *Journal of Nietzsche Studies* 45 (2014): 147–68.

6. Rousseau seems to have thought in this way about his project in the Second Discourse: "The Inquiries that may be pursued regarding this Subject ought not be taken for historical truths, but only for hypothetical and conditional reasonings; better suited to elucidate the Nature of things than to show their genuine origin" (Jean-Jacques Rousseau, *The Discourses and Other Early Political Writings,* edited by Victor Gourevitch [Cambridge: Cambridge University Press, 1997], 132). I am grateful to Alison McQueen for drawing my attention to this. For the various strands in Rousseau's genealogy, see Frederick Neuhouser, *Rousseau's Critique of Inequality: Reconconstructing the Second Discourse* (Cambridge: Cambridge University Press, 2015).

7. I see no essential conflict between the genealogical approach I take and the attempt to seek a naturalistic reduction. Here I differ from Joshua Gert, *Normative Bedrock: Response-Dependence, Rationality, and Reasons* (Oxford: Oxford University Press, 2012), 32–33.

8. Michael Tomasello, *A Natural History of Human Thinking* (Cambridge, MA: Harvard University Press, 2014).

9. The current text takes the notion of reliance that it employs as fairly intuitive. For a useful analysis, see F. M. Alonso, "What Is Reliance?" *Canadian Journal of Philosophy* 44 (2014): 163–83.

10. Christopher Boehm, *Hierarchy in the Forest: The Evolution of Egalitarian Behavior* (Cambridge, MA: Harvard University Press, 1999); and Carles Boix and Frances Rosenbluth, "Bones of Contention: The Political Economy of Height Inequality," *Americal Political Science Review* 108 (2014): 1–22.

11. In assuming that Erewhonians are opportunistic agents of this kind, the genealogy may seem to be of a type with those attempts to show that if we were able to prescribe on the basis of long-term prudence for what we ought to do, then this would support prescriptions of a distinctively altruistic or ethical sort: those prescriptions would present themselves as good prudential policies.

But the genealogy developed here is quite different from any enterprise of that kind, since, for all it requires, Erewhonians at the beginning of the story may not be capable of any prescriptions of the sort that might be based on judgments of desirability—even personal, long-term desirability—or responsibility. The opportunistic rationality displayed in Erewhon need not be mediated, so the assumption goes, by any such prescriptive or normative reasoning. On the relationship between rationality and reasoning, see Philip Pettit, *The Common Mind: An Essay on Psychology, Society and Politics* (New York: Oxford University Press, 1993); and John Broome, *Rationality through Reasoning* (Oxford: Wiley Blackwell, 2013).

12. Kim Sterelny, *The Evolved Apprentice: How Evolution Made Humans Unique* (Cambridge, MA: MIT Press, 2012).

13. David Hume, *Political Essays* (Cambridge: Cambridge University Press, 1994).

14. This charge is laid against a range of studies in Peter DeScioli and Robert Kurzban, "A Solution to the Mysteries of Morality," *Psychological Bulletin* 139 (2013): 477–96, here 478. For an exception, see Philip Kitcher, who describes ethics as "an evolving practice, founded on limited altruistic dispositions that were effectively expanded by activities of rule giving and governance," in *The Ethical Project* (Cambridge, MA: Harvard University Press, 2011), 412.

15. Carl Menger, "On the Origin of Money," *Economic Journal* 2 (1892): 239–55.

16. Wilfred Sellars, *Empiricism and the Philosophy of Mind* (Cambridge, MA: Harvard University Press, 1997); David Lewis, *Convention* (Cambridge, MA: Harvard University Press, 1969); Donald Davidson, *Inquiries into Truth and Interpretation* (Oxford: Oxford University Press, 1984); Edward Craig, *Knowledge and the State of Nature* (Oxford: Oxford University Press, 1990); and Williams, *Truth and Truthfulness.*

17. Paul Grice, "Method in Philosophical Psychology," *Proceedings and Addresses of the American Philosophical Association* 68 (1975): 23–53; Jonathan Bennett, *Rationality* (London: Routledge and Kegan Paul, 1964); Michael Bratman, *Shared Agency: A Planning Theory of Acting Together* (Oxford: Oxford University Press, 2014); and Peter Railton, "Reliance, Trust, and Belief," *Inquiry* 57 (2014): 122–50.

18. Dan Sperber and Deirdre Wilson, *Relevance: Communication and Cognition* (Oxford: Blackwell, 1986); and Paul Grice, *Studies in the Ways of Words* (Cambridge, MA: Harvard University Press, 1989).

19. Lewis, *Convention.*

20. Thom Scott-Phillips, *Speaking Our Minds: Why Human Communication Is Different, and How Language Evolved to Make It Special* (London: Palgrave Macmillan, 2015).

21. There is a further excuse that is normally foreclosed even by reporting, or at least by reporting in a shared language: namely, that what I meant by the words used in my report are not what you took them to mean.

22. For an extended, broadly congenial, account of avowals in more or less this sense, see Dorit Bar-on, *Speaking My Mind: Expression and Self-knowledge* (Oxford: Oxford University Press, 2004).

23. Any excuse I offer for a failure to tell the truth, be it epistemic or practical in character, will tend to show that my action was not uncooperative; it was not the product of a lack of carefulness or truthfulness in communication. But as with an excuse for any sort of failure, it may exonerate my action, as it were, without exonerating me as a person. This possibility will materialize in a case where the factor that explains my failure at a certain time—say, ignorance of some fact or an alcoholic hangover—is due to a failure at some earlier time for which I did not have an excuse; in our examples, this will be my not having bothered to learn some important fact or my having drunk to excess. The distinction between excuses that exonerate an enduring agent and excuses that do not have this particular effect is important in other contexts but we may ignore it for our purposes here.

24. On exemptions, see R. J. Wallace, *Responsibility and the Moral Sentiments* (Cambridge, MA: Harvard University Press, 1996) and John Gardner, *Offences and Defences: Selected Essays in the Philosophy of Criminal Law*, (Oxford, Oxford University Press, 2007).

25. Robert Axelrod, *The Evolution of Cooperation* (New York: Basic Books, 1984).

26. Geoffrey Brennan and Philip Pettit, *The Economy of Esteem: An Essay on Civil and Political Society* (Oxford: Oxford University Press, 2004).

27. For an earlier version of this conception of a norm, see Philip Pettit, "*Virtus Normativa*: Rational Choice Perspectives," *Ethics* 100 (1990): 725–55; reprinted in Philip Pettit, *Rules, Reasons, and Norms*, 309–43 (Oxford: Oxford University Press, 2002); and Brennan and Pettit, *Economy of Esteem*. The current version appears in Philip Pettit, "Value-mistaken and Virtue-mistaken Norms," in *Political Legitimization without Morality?* edited by Jörg Kühnelt, 139–56 (New York: Springer, 2008); and Philip Pettit, *The Robust Demands of the Good: Ethics with Attachment, Virtue and Respect* (Oxford: Oxford University Press, 2015). It is modeled on David Lewis's account of convention (Lewis, *Convention*). This notion of a social norm picks up points made in a variety of approaches. See, for example, H. L. A. Hart, *The Concept of Law* (Oxford: Oxford Unviersity Press, 1961); Peter Winch, *The Idea of a Social Science and Its Relation to Philosophy* (London: Routledge, 1963); James Coleman, *Foundations of Social Theory* (Cambridge, MA: Harvard University Press, 1990); Elliott Sober and David Sloan Wilson, *Unto Others: The Evolution and Psychology of Unselfish Behavior* (Cambridge, MA: Harvard University Press, 1998); Jon Elster, *Alchemies of the Mind: Rationality and the Emotions* (Cambridge: Cambridge University Press, 1999); and Scott J. Shapiro, *Legality* (Cambridge, MA: Harvard University Press, 2011). For a recent, insightful development of the idea of esteem-based norms, see Kwame Anthony Appiah, *The Honor Code: How Moral Revolutions Happen* (New York: Norton, 2010). And for an overarching theory that is reconcilable with that adopted here, although it uses terminology somewhat differently, see Geoffrey Brennan, Lina Eriksson, Robert E. Goodin, and Nicholas Southwood, *Explaining Norms* (Oxford: Oxford University Press, 2013).

28. Regulation for truth-telling would become conscious in the event, often assumed in discussion of norms, that the three clauses in our definition of a norm were fulfilled as a matter of common awareness among members of the community. In that case we would each see evidence for the pattern of behavior and expectation involved, see that this evidence is available to all, see that the evidence that it is available to all is itself available to all, and so on. In effect, we would each recognize that there is a rule to which everyone conforms on the basis of expectations about how others are likely to respond. While this may be quite a plausible development, it is still worth noting that regulation does not presuppose that it has occurred and may operate without being consciously targeted on upholding a rule.

29. This point is supported at length in Lewis, *Convention*.

30. Standard accounts of communication, as we have seen, require a primary intention to convey certain information and a secondary intention to achieve that result by making the primary intention manifest. But this is unnecessarily strong. It is surely enough, as may hold in the present case, that I intentionally convey the information and intentionally do so by relying on the very manifestness of my intentionally conveying it. To intend a result, in ordinary usage, presupposes that you desire it as such. To bring about a result intentionally requires only that you desire a package that includes the result, not that you desire the result as such. I will communicate my belief that Jones is reliable in saying that he is reliable, even if I do not desire or intend as such to inform you about my belief. It is enough for communicating the belief that I intentionally inform you about it, recognizing that the manifestness of my intentionally doing so will help to bring about that result.

31. There is also a regress argument for this conclusion. The misleading-mind excuse would be in place only if it were the case that I relied upon certain evidence, perhaps of an introspective kind, to determine that I held the belief that Jones is reliable; only in that case could I excuse a miscommunication by saying that the evidence was misleading. But if I had evidence that I hold the belief that Jones is reliable, then that would not only constitute evidence that I do indeed hold the belief; it would also provide evidence sufficient to elicit the higher-order belief that I hold the belief. And presumably I might then express this higher-order belief in words such as: I believe that I believe that Jones is reliable. But if I needed evidence that I believe that Jones is reliable in order to express the belief that he is reliable, then by the same principle I would need evidence that I believe that I believe that Jones is reliable in order to express the higher-order belief. And that would open up an endless regress.

32. On the linkage between expense and credibility in animal signaling, see John Maynard Smith and David Harper, *Animal Signals* (Oxford: Oxford University Press, 2004).

33. Suppose that I report that I believe that p because of wanting to hedge my bets. In that case I will express the higher-order belief that I believe that p. But such an expression may not count as an avowal in the sense defended here: that is, in the sense of an attempt to make my claim more credible. It may be just the

difficulty of going to any higher level, and not the attraction of communicating that belief with maximum credibility, that leads me to express it rather than report it.

34. Davidson, *Inquiries into Truth*.

35. The assumed concept of belief is broadly functional in character, building on the notion of credence in decision theory; see Robert C. Stalnaker, *Inquiry* (Cambridge, MA: MIT Press, 1984) and Philip Pettit, "Practical Belief and Philosophical Theory," *Australasian Journal of Philosophy* 76 (1998): 15–33. There is a serious issue as to how credences relate to acts of assent—and to the states of mind that those acts express—but in this context I generally ignore the problem. See Philip Pettit, "Making up Your Mind," *European Journal of Philosophy* 23 (2015).

36. Gareth Evans, *The Varieties of Reference* (Oxford: Oxford University Press, 1982).

37. Victoria McGeer and Philip Pettit, "The Self-regulating Mind," *Language and Communication* 22 (2002): 281–99.

38. I associate the notion of maker's knowledge with Hobbes and Vico (Philip Pettit, *Made with Words: Hobbes on Language, Mind and Politics* [Princeton, NJ: Princeton University Press, 2008], ch. 1), but Rae Langton cites an employment of the idea in Maimonides (Rae Langton, *Sexual Solipsism: Philosophical Essays in Pornography and Objectification* [Oxford: Oxford University Press, 2009], ch. 13).

39. Victoria McGeer, "Is 'Self-knowledge' an Empirical Problem? Renegotiating the Space of Philosophical Explanation," *Journal of Philosophy* 93 (1996): 483–515; Richard Moran, "Self-Knowledge: Discovery, Resolution, and Undoing," *European Journal of Philosophy* 5 (1997): 141–61; and Victoria McGeer, "The Moral Development of First-Person Authority," *European Journal of Philosophy* 16 (2008): 81–108. See also Alex Byrne, "Transparency, Belief, Intention," *Supplementary Proceedings of the Aristotelian Society* 85 (2011): 201–21.

40. I put aside a possibility like "Oh to q!"

41. Lewis, *Convention*.

42. In the ascriptive avowal of a belief or other attitude, it is worth noting that I do not just communicate that I have the belief—say, the belief that p—or the attitude—say, the desire for R; I also communicate that I have the belief that I hold that belief or harbor that desire. While I give expression to that higher-order belief, however, I do not strictly avow it. This is because it is not for the sake of communicating the belief more credibly, only because I have no option in the matter, that I put aside the misleading-mind excuse in this case.

43. Thus I may not be taken to make an avowal if I communicate an attitude that is manifestly of little or no possible significance for others such as "When I'm alone, I like to read novels."

44. Our observations on the avowal of noncredal attitudes bear indirectly on a familiar debate in metaethics as to what is the relationship between a moral attitude of approval or disapproval and an utterance that communicates the presence of that attitude: say, "I approve of X," or "You ought to do X," or "X

is right." In their simplest forms, one of the standard approaches suggests that this sort of utterance expresses the attitude in the way that an assertion that p expresses a belief, another that it reports the attitude in the way in which an assertion that it seems to me that I believe that p might report a belief. But these standard alternatives—expressivism and subjectivism, as they are sometimes called—are certainly inadequate (Frank Jackson and Philip Pettit, "A Problem for Expressivism," *Analysis* 58 [1998]: 239–51); reprinted in *Mind, Morality and Explanation*, edited by Frank Jackson, Philip Pettit, and Michael Smith, 252–66 (Oxford: Oxford University Press, 2004). In ignoring the role of the belief, simple expressivism would fail to explain why ethical utterances are voluntary acts of communication. In ignoring the difference between reporting and avowing, simple subjectivism would fail to explain why the utterance forecloses the misleading-mind excuse and helps put the speaker on the hook for any failure to live up to the attitude.

45. Philip Pettit and Michael Smith, "Practical Unreason," *Mind* 102 (1993): 53–80; reprinted in *Mind, Morality and Explanation*, edited by Frank Jackson, Philip Pettit, and Michael Smith, 322–53 (Oxford: Oxford University Press, 2004).

46. Philip Pettit, "Decision Theory and Folk Psychology," in *Essays in the Foundations of Decision Theory*, edited by M. Bacharach and S. Hurley, 147–75 (Oxford: Blackwell, 1991); reprinted in Philip Pettit, *Rules, Reasons, and Norms* (Oxford: Oxford University Press, 2002), 192–221; and Franz Dietrich and Christian List, "A Reason-Based Theory of Rational Choice," *Nous* 47 (2013): 104–34.

47. Jonathan Dancy, *Ethics without Principles* (Oxford: Oxford University Press, 2004).

48. Ibid.

49. For a critique of particularism on these general lines—and for a critique of the closely related doctrine I call "interpretivism"—see Pettit, *Robust Demands of the Good*. For a deeper-running complaint about particularism, see Frank Jackson, Philip Pettit, and Michael Smith "Ethical Particularism and Patterns," in *Particularism*, edited by B. Hooker and M. Little, 79–99 (Oxford: Oxford University Press, 1999); reprinted in *Mind, Morality and Explanation*, edited by Frank Jackson, Philip Pettit, and Michael Smith, 211–32 (Oxford: Oxford University Press, 2004).

50. Suppose I have an attitude that I see no possibility, for independent reasons, of ever changing: it might be an idée fixe or an obsessive urge that I cannot seem to drop. With such an attitude I might be able to predict that I will maintain it, and have sufficient confidence to avow that predictive belief. And I might pretend to pledge it, treating it as an attitude that I might have been restricted to reporting or avowing. But I cannot really pledge it in the sense operative here: I cannot take a voluntary step to ensure that I will maintain it. I am indebted to an exchange with Pamela Hieronymi and Jay Wallace on this point.

51. It is possible to be moved to hold a belief by practical considerations, such as the comfort derived from holding it, but it is hardly possible to maintain that

you would stick by the belief for such reasons in face of counterevidence: that it would support your holding by the belief in a suitably robust way.

52. Of course I may pledge to work at maintaining an affection, or perhaps even a desire or preference, committing myself to take steps aimed at preserving the hold of suitable attractors on my sensibility.

53. Thomas Hobbes, *Leviathan*, edited by E. Curley (Indianapolis: Hackett, 1994), ch. 16, 174.

54. Hobbes (ibid., ch. 16) argues that a multitude can become a group agent, being "made one person," by means of advance authorization. He thinks that that is the way that a private body may form—say, a company of merchants, in an example he uses elsewhere—with members authorizing some one officer to make avowals, and indeed pledges, in their collective name under a limited "commission" from them. And he thinks that that is the way in which a commonwealth or state may come into existence, with members authorizing a sovereign spokesperson "without stint." The commission in this case is unlimited, he holds, since he defends an absolutist view of the power that a sovereign has to enjoy if the polity is to be stable and successful. He acknowledges that the entity whose voice a group authorizes may be also a committee that operates by majority voting but denies that it can be a set of mutually constraining individuals or committees such as the competing branches and offices of government that a mixed constitution would allow. He is mistaken on both those counts but this is not the place to explore such issues (Pettit, *Made with Words*; and Christian List and Philip Pettit, *Group Agency: The Possibility, Design and Status of Corporate Agents* [Oxford: Oxford University Press, 2011]).

55. The things I presuppose—or more generally "implicate"—are plausibly going to be identifiable on the assumption that I satisfy constraints like the maxims of conversation—quality, quantity, relation, and manner—analyzed by Paul Grice, "Logic and Conversation," in *Syntax and Semantics*, vol 3., edited by P. Cole and J. L. Morgan, 41–58 (New York: Academic Press, 1975). For a more general perspective, in which relevance is the crucial factor, see Sperber and Wilson, *Relevance*.

56. Robert C. Stalnaker, "Assertion," in Stalnaker, *Context and Content* (Oxford, Oxford University Press, 1999) 78–95; Sperber and Wilson, *Relevance*; and Michael Tomasello, *Origins of Human Communication* (Cambridge, MA: MIT Press, 2008).

57. See also David Lewis, *Philosophical Papers*, vol. 1 (Oxford: Oxford University Press, 1983), ch. 13. For some imaginative applications and developments of the approach shared between Lewis and Stalnaker, see Langton, *Sexual Solipsism*, including the chapter jointly written with Caroline West.

58. Stalnaker, "Assertion," 86.

59. Ibid., 87.

60. Needless to say, the argument here assumes it is acceptable to set aside the effect of power and domination in driving a conversation; this is an aspect of the power equality built into the model, as mentioned in the Introduction.

61. Tomasello, *A Natural History of Human Thinking*.

62. Philip Pettit and Michael Smith, "Freedom in Belief and Desire." *Journal of Philosophy* 93 (1996): 429–49; reprinted in *Mind, Morality and Explanation*, edited by Frank Jackson, Philip Pettit, and Michael Smith, 375–96 (Oxford: Oxford University Press, 2004).

63. P. Strawson, *Freedom and Resentment and Other Essays* (London: Methuen, 1962).

64. G. E. M. Anscombe, *Intention* (Oxford: Blackwell, 1957).

65. List and Pettit, *Group Agency*; and Philip Pettit, "Group Agents Are Not Expressive, Pragmatic or Theoretical Fictions," *Erkenntnis* 79 (2014): 1641–62.

66. There is a large literature on joint intention of this kind. For a congenial perspective, see Bratman, *Shared Agency*, and for other important views, see Raimo Tuomela, *The Importance of Us* (Stanford, CA: Stanford University Press, 1995); Margaret Gilbert, *Joint Commitment: How We Make the Social World* (Oxford, Oxford University Press, 2015); and John Searle, *Making the Social World: The Structure of Human Civilization* (Oxford: Oxford University Press, 2015).

67. The formation of a group agent discussed in the first sort of case is almost certain to involve the members in supporting a joint intention—perhaps voluntarily, perhaps under pressure—to establish an authorized voice behind which they can rally, thereby achieving the coherence of goals and judgments required for corporate agency. See Philip Pettit and David Schweikard, "Joint Action and Group Agency," *Philosophy of the Social Sciences* 36 (2006): 18–39.

LECTURE II.
FROM COMMITMENT TO MORALITY

According to the argument in the first lecture, a simple, reportive community like Erewhon would not be a steady or stationary society. It would contain within itself the seeds of its own transformation, providing its members with motives sufficient to take them beyond giving reports. On pain of having few excuses for failure, those individuals would back themselves to live up to certain self-ascribed attitudes; they would commit themselves in a strategic sense of the term to those attitudes. Their commitments would include avowals and pledges in regard to individual attitudes, and co-avowals and co-pledges in regard to attitudes that they share or expect to share in certain groups.

Nothing in the developments reviewed so far would take the players in our drama into the realm of ethics. They do not make judgments of desirability, and they do not hold one another responsible for living by any judgments of that kind. The challenge in this lecture is to carry forward the project begun in the last and show why the commitments that the protagonists make in avowals and pledges are liable and indeed likely to bring them into ethical space.

The lecture takes up that challenge in two stages: first, by arguing that the players are in a position where it is natural for them to begin to think in terms of desirability; and second, by arguing that having come to think in that mode, they are going to be in a position to hold one another properly responsible to such judgments.

THE NOTION OF DESIRABILITY

Before embarking on the first stage of this argument, it is necessary to articulate what it is to think in terms of desirability. That something is desirable may mean in some contexts that you are permitted to desire it, but it means more generally that you ought to desire it—desiring it is obligatory or mandatory—and this is how it will be taken here. The fact that something is desirable in that sense presupposes that it is one option in a set of alternatives, and requires that you should rank it above the others; it counts not just as desirable in a generic way but, specifically, more desirable than the other options. The alternatives in any such context may be basic alternatives like X, Y and Z or, allowing for ties, disjunctive alternatives like X or Y. In the case of actions these will represent possibilities such that it is up to you whether or not to realize them. Thus you can opt between doing X or Y or Z or indeed doing X or Y: in this case you choose the disjunction, letting some contingency or chance determine which disjunct is realized.

While the ascription of desirability in the intended sense always introduces a ranking of alternatives, however, it may do so *pro tanto* or *secundum quid*. On the first reading, to say that X is desirable is to hold that it ought to be desired insofar as it displays a certain property or set of properties, F; it ought to be desired qua F, as it is sometimes said. On the second, it means that X ought to be desired *simpliciter;* it ought to be desired outright or unreservedly, not just insofar as it has a certain profile or aspect.[1]

The first task in this narrative is to explain how Erwhonians might develop ranking concepts of desirability, in particular a concept of unreserved or outright desirability. The concept of the unreservedly desirable plays a central role in ethics or morality, so it is assumed here, because of its connection with the more frequently invoked notion of rightness.

As desirability is taken here in a ranking sense—that is, to mean ought to be desired among a presumptive set of alternatives—rightness is taken in a similar way. The question of rightness arises only when there is a set of options in play for an agent or set of agents, and the right option, basic or disjunctive, is that which the agent ought to choose. Is the right option in any such choice set necessarily the unreservedly desirable option? On one pattern of usage, it is: the right option is simply the most desirable option. But on another pattern, the right option is the most desirable option that it would be wrong or blameworthy for the agent not to take. On this second usage, the most desirable option overall will not be the right option if it counts as supererogatory: that is, if it is so demanding that regardless of its desirability, it would not be appropriate to blame the agent for failing to take it.

Should the right option be equated with the most desirable of all the options or with the most desirable option among "erogatory" alternatives? Either equation would work from purposes of the genealogy pursued here, but in what follows rightness will be understood on the second pattern; this has the advantage of registering more clearly the distinction between the obligatory and the supererogatory. On this way of construing the notion of rightness, it is impossible to give an account of how Erewhonians might get to make use of a concept like that of rightness, prior to having an explanation of how they might get to hold one another responsible for how they perform. The concept of rightness can only appear at the end of the lecture, then, when the issue of responsibility has already been addressed. In the meantime, the focus will be on the concept of desirability, in particular unreserved desirability, and how it might make an appearance in Erewhon.

What is it to think in terms of the desirable? There are three generic and three specific constraints that such thinking must satisfy. The generic constraints apply to thinking in terms of any form of desirability, reserved or unreserved, and indeed to thinking in any prescriptive terms whatsoever: say, as we shall see, to thinking in terms of what is credible or ought to be believed. The specific constraints apply to thinking in terms of unreserved desirability, although perhaps not to thinking in terms of desirability more generally. The generic constraints reflect the role that any judgments of desirability must play in relation to desire, the specific constraints reflect assumptions about the sort of evidence to which such judgments—or at least judgments of unreserved desirability—are responsive.

The first generic constraint is that the desirability of any possible scenario relative to alternatives—say, any option among the options that define a choice—is grounded in the independent features of the alternatives on offer. That scenario cannot cease to be more desirable than competitors without a change in the distribution of independent properties across alternatives; fix those properties and the relative desirability of the alternatives will be fixed too. Why believe in the supervenience of desirability on other properties, as this constraint is often described? The answer is, because it is encoded in the ordinary use of language. When I hold one alternative to be more desirable than another, it is always appropriate to ask about what makes it more desirable: what distinguishes it in independent terms from the other alternatives.

The second generic constraint on desirability judgments is that it is always possible for me or any agent to judge that one alternative in a choice set is desirable, yet not actually desire it; the judgment of desirability can come apart from the appearance of a corresponding desire. This scarcely needs defending, since dissonance and conflict of that sort is a datum of common experience.

The third constraint is that in any such case of divergence, it is going to count as a failure on my part, other things being equal, if I act on my desire and against my judgment of what is desirable. Other things will not be equal, for example, if I make conflicting judgments of reserved desirability, taking one alternative to be desirable under one aspect, a second to be desirable under another, and so on. And other things will not be equal if my judgment of what is desirable is faulty. But absent those possibilities, the idea is that I will not function properly if I fail to let the judgment of desirability govern what I do. The idea is plausible, since it will be perfectly reasonable to ask me to explain myself in any situation where I fail in that way.

These constraints may be named after what they impose or allow: grounding in the first case; divergence in the second; governance in the third. As they apply to any form of desirability, so they apply to unreserved or outright desirability in particular. The first, grounding constraint, shows up in the fact that if I am told that one option is unreservedly desirable, another not, it always makes sense to ask about what is the difference—the independent difference—between them. The second, divergence constraint, is reflected in our pervasive sense that we may often desire what we think is not unreservedly desirable or fail to desire what we think is. And the third, governance constraint, reflects the fact that we treat judgments of unreserved desirability as having the role of guiding us, and if necessary, correcting us, in the formation of desire and intention.[2]

Apart from these generic constraints, there are three more specific constraints that judgments of unreserved desirability should satisfy; they may also be satisfied by some judgments of reserved desirability but, given the interest in rightness, our focus will be on the unreserved case. These constraints reflect assumptions about the sort of evidence to which judgments of desirability are responsive and may be more controversial than the generic constraints. There are two grounds for endorsing them. First, they fit with plausible, widely supported intuitions. And second, they make the exercise on hand more rather than less difficult to complete: they raise the bar to be crossed in providing a plausible explanation of how residents of Erewhon could come to master and apply the concept of the unreservedly desirable.

The first of the three specific constraints is that when I judge or believe that one among a set of alternatives is unreservedly desirable— when I assent to the proposition ascribing unreserved desirability to it—the property that I ascribe is not the property of being unreservedly desirable$_{me}$, where this is distinct from the property, unreservedly desirable$_{you}$, that you would ascribe if you were the one assenting to the proposition. The constraint is that "unreservedly desirable" is not indexical in the manner of "mine" or indeed "now"; it does not assume a different referent, depending on the identity of the utterer or of the context of utterance.

Thus when I say that it is unreservedly desirable for a person to do something and you deny that it is unreservedly desirable, we are not talking past one another, addressing different properties and responsive to different bodies of evidence. This will be so in either of two salient cases. It will hold if I mean that it is unreservedly desirable for you, independently of position or relationship, to perform the act in question, as in saying that it is desirable in that sense that you relieve pain or promote peace. And equally it will be so if I mean that it is unreservedly desirable for you, given a certain position or relationship, to perform that action, as when I say that it is desirable in that sense for you to favor your child, or if you have made a promise, to keep it.[3]

Where the first constraint holds that judgments of unreserved desirability do not vary in content as between speakers, the second holds that neither do they vary in truth-value. The first constraint is that you and I address the same proposition when, given the same context, I say that something is unreservedly desirable and you deny this. The second is that in such a case at most one of us is correct about that proposition. It cannot be that from my standpoint as an assessor—from the standpoint that my evidence gives me—the alternative at issue truly is unreservedly desirable, and from yours it truly is not; if it is unreservedly desirable from one standpoint, it is unreservedly desirable from all. There may be nothing incoherent about the claim that truth-value may be assessor-sensitive, so that a given proposition should be deemed true from within one standpoint of assessment and false from within another.[4] But, so the second constraint holds, this is not the case with propositions about unreserved desirability.

The third specific constraint on unreserved desirability is that whether an action has this property or not cannot turn on the particular identity of a person, time, or place involved in the action: it cannot be responsive to evidence about such particularities. If it is desirable in that way for someone to do something in this situation, there must be something nonparticular that characterizes that person, and something nonparticular that characterizes that situation, that would make it unreservedly desirable for any relevantly similar agent to perform the action in any relevantly similar situation. This constraint is one of universalizability, as it is often called.[5] It requires that for every particular judgment of unreserved desirability, say that it is desirable for A to do X in situation S, there must be a nonparticular or universal truth to the effect that it is unreservedly desirable for anyone like A—anyone with A's ability, motives, and so on—to perform an action of an X-kind in an S-like situation.

The fact that the concept of the unreservedly desirable satisfies these three more specific constraints implies that the concept of rightness—the concept of the most desirable alternative among 'erogatory' options—satisfies them too. And that implied claim is independently plausible. If the right or the obligatory is to serve its characteristic community-wide role in assessing options and actions, and in determining the responsibility of different agents, then it must be non-indexical and non-relative; it must allow different people to address the same content on the basis of the same criteria of assessment. And equally it must support universalizability by not privileging the particularities of any agent or situation of choice.

Given this understanding of what it is to judge that something is unreservedly desirable, it is possible to explore how far the members of our Erewhonian community, equipped with strategically commissive practices of avowal and pledging, are likely to come to form such judgments. The argument to be offered is that making avowals and co-avowals—in particular, avowals and co-avowals of desire—is going to provide me and others in the community with a perspective from within which it is natural to begin to think in terms of the desirable and the undesirable. Pledges do not figure much in this account but they play a later role in explaining why it is also going to be natural for us to hold one another responsible to standards of unreserved desirability.

THE VIEW FROM WITHIN AVOWAL

When I speak for myself in Erewhon, avowing a belief or a desire—these two attitudes will be the focus of discussion from now on—I rely on a basis for holding the belief or desire that I take to be relatively robust, not just a basis that happens to influence me as a matter of present contingency. The basis for belief is provided by the data at my disposal such that attending to those data, so I take it, elicits the belief. And the basis for desire is provided by the desiderata at my disposal such that attending to them, so I take it, elicits the desire. The data elicit the belief robustly, the desiderata the desire, insofar as the eliciting effect is not a function of some contingent, collateral factor: say, a wish to be someone with such an attitude; absent distorters, it is an effect that data and desiderata may be expected to generate robustly over other variations in my situation.

Given that basis for confidence about the belief or desire, I step out of the contingencies of the here and now when I avow the attitude. Taking the basis in data or desiderata as sufficient to elicit the attitude robustly, I treat the belief or desire as something I can stand by with relative assurance. I treat it as firmly enough entrenched for me to be able to self-ascribe it in a way that puts misleading-mind excuses beyond my reach.

Or at least I do this to the extent that I take myself to be adequately protected against the disrupting impact of distorters. No matter how effective the protection, I have to recognize that I may occasionally fail to display the attitude ascribed as a result of a distorting influence.

Thus, persuaded by the data to avow that the gambler's fallacy is a fallacy, I still have to recognize that I may lose sight of this truth in the excitement of the casino and that if I do, I will be unwilling to excuse myself by saying that I changed my mind. I will be unwilling to help myself to that excuse, so I foresee, because the change of mind will only have been temporary. Again, persuaded by the desiderata at hand to avow the desire to tell my friends the truth about some embarrassing episode, I may still have to recognize that the shame of doing so face to face may inhibit me from owning up to the episode with some particularly judgmental friends and that if it does, I will be unwilling to say that I changed my mind about wanting to relate the episode to them. I will be unwilling to help myself to that excuse, so I foresee, because the change of mind will have been local to those friends; the desiderata relevant with others will have been present equally in their case.

Think now about how I am likely to view such disrupters, when in the wake of a failure I have to admit that they caused me not to live up to my avowed attitude. I may or may not cite them as practical excuses for the failure, of course, or at least as factors that diminished my practical ability. But whatever I do in that regard, I will certainly disown the actions that they led me to take, whether that be placing a heavy bet on red after a run of blacks, or beating a hasty retreat from meeting with a judgmental friend. I will hold that those actions do not reflect who I am; I will present them as the product of contingent influences or motives that I do not identify with, not as reflections of my robust dispositions.

If I am disposed to take this view in retrospect, however, that has implications for the view I must take in advance of any failure. It means that as I avow the attitude in question, backing myself to live up to it, I must not only hold the attitude avowed and be aware of holding it. I must also assume that I hold the attitude as a result of the impact of relevant data or desiderata, not as a result of a disrupting influence. If I thought that my holding it was the effect of such an influence, then I would not have the confidence required for avowal.

Thus when I hold an avowed belief that things are thus and so—when I find that scenario avowedly persuasive—I do more than hold by the simple belief that they are thus and so. I hold also by the sophisticated belief that the data support the proposition that things are thus and so, robustly eliciting my belief; or, equivalently, that it is not because of the presence of a contingent distorter that I am led to believe that they are that way. In other words I hold by the simple belief under the assumption—in general, no doubt, a default rather than a confirmed assumption—that there is nothing suspect at its origin. If I thought that there was a suspect distorter at work in eliciting the belief, after all, then that would give me pause about avowing it: I could no longer have the confidence to bet on myself to stick with it.

The same line of thought applies with other attitudes that I avow. When I hold an avowed desire that things be thus and so—when I find that scenario avowedly attractive—I do more than enjoy an attraction to their being that way. I enjoy that attraction but hold at the same time by the belief that relevant desiderata robustly ground the attraction: that the attraction is not due to the contingent influence of any distorter. I stand by the attraction, perhaps letting it shape my actions, under the default or perhaps confirmed assumption that there is nothing suspect at its origin.[6] If I thought that there was a distorting factor at work in generating the attraction then, as in the case of belief, that would give me pause about avowing the desire: I could no longer have the confidence to bet on myself to stick with that desire.

The upshot of this line of argument is that from within the perspective of avowal it is inevitable for me, as it will be inevitable for my fellow Erewhonians, that I should find a use for two presumptively prescriptive concepts: on the one side, that of what I ought to believe, given my avowals of belief; and on the other, that of what I ought to desire, given my avowals of desire. What I ought to believe qua someone who avows beliefs is anything for which, in the presumptive absence of contingent distorters, I find data enough to elicit belief robustly. What I ought to desire qua someone who avows desires is anything in which I find desiderata enough to elicit desire robustly, again in the presumptive absence of distorters. The robustly persuasive, seen from within the practice of avowal, presents as what I ought to believe; the robustly attractive presents from within that practice as what I ought to desire.

Both of these observations are going to be available to me and others in Erewhon and available as a matter of common awareness; the evidence supporting them is salient for all, the evidence that that evidence is salient is itself salient for all, and so on.[7] But that means that not only will each of us in Erewhon be in a position to make use of the concept of what we individually ought to believe and desire—that is, what we ought to believe or desire in light of our avowals; it will also be a concept that we can each use, with manifestly the same referent, in regard to any individual. For each person who avows attitudes we will be able to identify in the one case what we take to be individually credible for that person—this, in the sense of what they ought to believe, not what they may believe—and in the other what is individually desirable for the person.[8]

The concepts of the individually credible and desirable are prescriptive concepts insofar as they satisfy the grounding, divergence, and governance constraints outlined earlier. First, whether something is credible or desirable relative to me is grounded in its relations to data or desiderata; these will explain why a proposition is credible, a prospect desirable. Second, what I find credible may diverge from my actual beliefs, what I find desirable from my actual desires, since distorters may play a role in generating my actual attitudes. And third, assuming that the judgment is not faulty, what I find credible governs or determines what I ought to believe, what I find desirable governs what I ought to desire: this, at any rate, insofar as I go in for the personal avowal of such attitudes. The practice of personally avowing attitudes requires that I ought to believe what I find credible and ought to desire what I find desirable; I could dismiss those requirements as irrelevant only on pain of renouncing the practice.[9] And so it must count as a failure on my part—an inconsistency with what I assume in following that practice—that I do not hold the robustly supported beliefs, or the robustly supported desires, that I avow.

The connection between these prescriptive concepts and the practice of avowal means, in terms introduced above, that the individually desirable is desirable in an aspectual or reserved sense and that something parallel holds of the individually credible. The individually credible or desirable is something I ought to believe or desire insofar as I personally avow the corresponding belief or desire; it is credible or desirable under the aspect it presents from within that practice. And that something is credible or desirable under that aspect does not yet entail that it is unreservedly credible or desirable. The point will be important in later discussion.

With access to the concepts of the individually credible and individually desirable, I and others in Erewhon can form beliefs to the effect that something is credible or desirable in that way. And of course we can even avow such beliefs. Avowal is a potentially recursive operation such that we may avow a belief in a content—that something is credible or desirable in some way—whose very availability to us as a content to be believed itself presupposes the prior use of avowal. While the practice of avowal enables us to gain access to the concepts of the individually credible and desirable, applying these to what we find robustly persuasive and attractive, it enables us at the same time to form and to avow beliefs in propositions that ascribe those very properties of credibility and desirability. This observation applies to all the properties of credibility and desirability to be discussed in this lecture.

How in Erewhon might I avow a belief in the individual credibility of a proposition "p" or in the individual desirability of a prospect R? The usual linguistic devices will be at my disposal. I may express such a belief by saying simply that it is credible that p, or that R is desirable. I may self-ascribe such a belief, and still retain the force of an avowal, by saying that I believe that it is credible that p or that R is desirable. Or I may resort to remarks that serve in context to explain, not why I believe that p or desire R—I may not actually do so—but why it is credible that p or why R is desirable: I may say, for example, "The data stack up in support of 'p'" or "R would be a lot of fun."

These observations show that like others in Erewhon I would naturally be led, just in virtue of making personal avowals, to develop a prescriptive viewpoint on myself. I cannot practice avowal without privileging a robust personal standpoint: the standpoint in which I am responsive to robustly effective data in the case of belief, and to robustly effective desiderata in the case of desire. This standpoint is ideal in the sense that it neutralizes the contingent distorters—the obstacles or limitations—that may affect me as I actually form my attitudes. And so, assuming that standpoint, I can prescribe for how my actual self ought to perform.[10] I can prescribe that actually I ought to stick with a belief that the gambler's fallacy is a fallacy when I go to the casino, or that actually I ought to speak truthfully in face-to-face meetings with my friends. And the wish to live up to my avowals may even lead me to prescribe that should it prove impossible to guard effectively against relevant obstacles or limitations, then I ought to avoid temptation: I ought not to go to the casino or I ought to avoid difficult face-to-face encounters.

THE VIEW FROM WITHIN CO-AVOWAL

My individual perspective in avowal lets me identify the robustly and hence avowedly persuasive and attractive, and leads me to give it prescriptive status, treating it as representative of the individually credible, on the one side, the individually desirable on the other. But my perspective in co-avowal, and indeed co-acceptance, allows me to do something parallel at the social level and complicates the prescriptive concepts to which I and others in Erewhon will enjoy access. Before developing this argument, however, it is important to register that co-avowal may be bounded or unbounded and that bounded co-avowal may take as many different forms as there are different bounds.

Co-avowal, Bounded and Unbounded

With any conversation, there is always a projected group of parties to the conversation and there is always a presupposed ground that is accepted in common by those parties. Conversational co-avowal will be bounded if either of these is taken as fixed and allowed to determine the other; it will be unbounded if they are each allowed to change.

There are two sorts of bounded exchange. In a first variety, I and other speakers may seek accommodation with all the members in a given group, being prepared to make compromises—even compromises that disregard what one or another of us sees as relevant data or desiderata—in order to establish common ground. In a second variety, I and other speakers may treat some common ground as so unquestionable—this, perhaps, because each of us takes it to be revealed doctrine—that we are not prepared to give it up for the sake of keeping dissenting members on our side; we are prepared to stand on that ground and hope to find members with whom we can share it. In the one case we keep the members fixed and let the ground move; in the other we keep the ground fixed, at least in part, and let the membership move.

Conversational co-avowal is unbounded when it is not constrained on either front. As a contributor to the conversation I will start from presumptively solid common ground and speak to others who presumptively share that ground; these may constitute a present or just a prospective audience. But in doing this I will remain open to change in two ways: first, by not fixing the membership of the group in advance; and second, by not fixing in advance the ground to be found in common with that membership. I will be happy to let the ground that is co-avowed with others shift from its initial or any later shape insofar as others change my perception of relevant data or desiderata. Equally I will be happy to let the membership include any others who accept the common ground or are persuasive in arguing for a change, and to exclude any others who reject the common ground but do not provide persuasive arguments in their defense. And as that is true of me, so it is also true of every other participant.

On the unbounded model of conversation, as on the bounded models, I put forward the claims I make on ground that I assume others will share. The others I address in the unbounded case, whether in speech or writing, direct or recorded, are any others who will give me a hearing. I put forward my claims as presuppositions and proposals that I co-avow in the name of such others as well as myself. I essay attitudes on ground that I expect those others—at the limit, perhaps, all presumptively conversable others—to find sufficient. But I am open to the possibility that I may be led by any other to change the ground that I hold fixed and the attitudes I co-avow in our names or co-accept on the basis of another's avowal.

Much of what we say in avowing our standing beliefs and desires, whether in responding to queries, in posting on blogs, in publishing our views, or of course in giving lectures, we say in the spirit of co-avowal. We put forward our attitudes, not in a confessional or autobiographical mode—not on the assumption that our audience is primarily interested in us—but rather in a dialectical mode that invites our interlocutors, real or imagined, to accept what we say or to challenge us where they disagree. As we speak in this mode, we aspire to find a viewpoint that others can share and to contribute to an ongoing conversation. In the unbounded case, we may even think of that conversation continuing into the future or continuing from the past. It was in this spirit that after a day on his farm, the superannuated Machiavelli would enter the courts of ancient men, as he famously records, and feed on the food of their conversation.

Given this distinction between bounded and unbounded conversations and groups, how are things likely to present themselves from within the standpoint of co-avowal? While this issue arises with both bounded and unbounded groups, it assumes a particular importance in the case of the unbounded group and this will be the main focus of attention. Like personal avowal, co-avowal in the name of an unbounded group is inescapable, whereas co-avowal in the name of a bounded group is contingent on happening to belong to such a group. Unbounded co-avowal is inescapable because it is implicit in any exercise of talking things through—and by extension thinking them through—from a standpoint that is presumptively available to anyone. It reflects interests that none of us can put aside, not just contingent personal interests, or interests contingently shared with a number of others.[11]

From within the Co-avowal of Belief

Suppose that I co-avow a belief that p, opening up a potential, unbounded conversation with anyone at any time or place, however remote. And suppose that some others go along, acquiescing in the co-avowal, offering further co-avowals themselves, and, in an exercise involving various episodes of rejection, rejoinder, and revision, coming to reach a set of beliefs that any one of us is in a position—indeed is manifestly in a position—to avow in all our names and, by aspiration, in the names of any others who join us. In the domain explored this exercise will reveal certain propositions as co-avowedly persuasive: elicited robustly, as a matter of common awareness, by evidence available from within the common standpoint that we share.

It will be manifest to each of us in such a case that due to one or another disrupting factor, we may occasionally fail to believe what is robustly or co-avowedly persuasive within this group: for example, fail to live up to commonly recognized data, as might be illustrated once again in the casino case. But, recognizing what the interpersonally tested data elicit, we must each be disposed to disown any such belief we might form: that is, to treat the factor as disrupting the performance required of us within the standpoint presumptively shared with an open number of others.

This means that what is robustly and co-avowedly persuasive from the common standpoint of this group is a prescriptive category on a par with what is robustly and avowedly persuasive from an individual standpoint. What is robustly and co-avowedly persuasive in this way constitutes the commonly credible, as we in Erewhon might come to articulate it. And the prescriptive status of the commonly credible shows up in its satisfying the grounding, divergence, and governance constraints listed earlier.

What I find commonly credible is grounded in the evidence I identify in common, as I think of it, with an open group of others. It may diverge from what I actually believe under the influence of what I am disposed to see as distorters of that common evidence. And, assuming that my judgment of credibility is not faulty, in such a case it would be a failure on my part not to let it govern my beliefs: it would amount to a breach of the practice in which I rely only on robustly effective data to determine what to believe in common with an unbounded set of others.

How does the commonly credible in this sense relate to the individually credible? The individually credible is that which is robustly elicited, absent distortion, by data I can access on my own. The commonly credible is that which is robustly elicited, absent distortion, by data I can access in common with an open number of others. What counts as data in the one standpoint counts as data in the other; to anticipate later discussion, data are different in that respect from desiderata. But the data available in the common standpoint are likely to be wider than the data available in the individual, so that the common standpoint is bound to have an advantage.

Any data I can access on my own I must treat as accessible in common with others, at least in principle; thus I must be open to co-avowing the belief it elicits, in the name of an unbounded group. But for all I know at any point there may be data accessible in common with others that I have not yet identified; they may only come to light in the future, perhaps only in a future after my death. And so what is commonly credible is going to count as more commanding than what is individually credible. No matter what I previously believed, and no matter what I found individually credible, the discovery that something is commonly credible ought to lead me to believe it henceforth.[12]

The standpoint from within which I believe—and avow the belief—that something is individually credible is idealized, as appeared earlier; it represents a standpoint from within which I can prescribe for my actual self. We now see that the standpoint from within which I believe—and no doubt avow or co-avow the belief—that something is commonly credible transcends and absorbs that standpoint. It represents the ultimate point of idealization from which I can prescribe matters of belief for my actual self. There is no tussle between the individually and the commonly credible, then, and no problem about which to follow in determining what I should hold. This marks a deep contrast, to anticipate later discussion, with the case of desirability.

But as the commonly credible will become defined for the members of an unbounded group, so a counterpart ideal—the jointly credible, as it may be put—is likely to be defined for the members of any bounded group: say, a group devoted to some cause or some creed, whether or not organized as a group agent. How does the commonly credible relate to that which we are liable to find robustly and co-avowedly persuasive from within such a bounded group? How does the commonly credible relate to what is jointly credible, now from within this group, now from within that?

It should be clear that the commonly credible must also transcend the standpoint represented by any such grouping. The beliefs we form in bounded groups are inevitably shaped by a constraint that is independent of data. This may be the desire to find a compromise among a fixed set of members, including perhaps some who are not suitably attentive to the data. Or it may be the desire to stick with a certain core of doctrine, regardless of how far it outruns the data, even perhaps conflicts with the data. Or, to take the case of an incorporated agent, it may be the need to find a set of beliefs that are coherent enough for a group agent to act on, even if this makes it less than fully responsive to the beliefs of members.[13]

The fact that the commonly credible transcends the categories of the individually and jointly credible means that what is commonly credible—what is credible in light of data available in a common viewpoint, open to the future—is going to count as what is unreservedly credible.[14] The commonly credible will be a master category in relation to what is jointly credible in any such grouping, as it will be a master category in relation to what is individually credible for any one of us. This, as will appear, marks a deep contrast between the categories of the credible and the desirable.

From within the Co-avowal of Desire

We now turn from the co-avowal of belief to the co-avowal of desire. Suppose that I co-avow a desire for R, aspiring to speak to an open audience in an unbounded conversation on the topic. And suppose that those who pay attention at any time or place acquiesce in that avowal, offering further co-avowals themselves, and coming in an exercise involving rejection, rejoinder and revision to reach a set of desires that any one of us is in a position—indeed is manifestly in a position—to avow in all our names and, by aspiration, in the names of others whom we allow to join us. Within the domain explored, this exercise will reveal certain scenarios as robustly and co-avowedly attractive for all of us: they will appeal to us in light of desiderata that we are each disposed to acknowledge from within the common standpoint we assume.

What sorts of scenarios are likely to prove robustly and co-avowedly attractive from within this standpoint? The issue is more complex than with the co-avowedly persuasive. What count as data for one are presumably going to count as data for all. But what attracts one person—even what attracts one person robustly, on the basis of recognized desiderata—may fail, even fail with a certain inevitability, to be attractive from a standpoint shared equally with others. I may desire my daughter's welfare on the basis, precisely, that she is my daughter, where others will only desire her welfare as they might that of a random person. With such an agent-relative desideratum in play, what is robustly attractive from within my individual standpoint may clash with what is robustly attractive from within a standpoint that I purport to share with others. From within my individual standpoint I may avow a desire that my daughter do especially well; from within a common standpoint I may avow a desire that all children thrive equally.

Returning to the question, then, what scenarios are likely to show up as robustly and co-avowedly attractive from within the standpoint of an open group? One set of candidates are those scenarios that are attractive in virtue of promising to realize agent-neutral desiderata we each care about in the same, relatively unconditional way. Plausible unconditional attractors may make it robustly attractive for all of us that norms like truth-telling or non-violence or fair-dealing should obtain; that the species should survive into an indefinite future; that the planet should be able to sustain a high degree of biodiversity; that there should be no unnecessary suffering; and so on.

Another set of candidates for being robustly and co-avowedly attractive for all of us may overlap with this first set. They are scenarios that are attractive to all of us, given that they offer the best prospect of satisfying a certain agent-relative desideratum on the part of each. Suppose we belong to different religions and that it is an agent-relative desideratum for each of us that we should be able to practice our own religion in peace. Even if none of us treats a world with freedom of religion as robustly attractive on an agent-neutral ground about which we converge—even if we do not ascribe a desideratum in common to that scenario—we are likely to treat it as robustly attractive on different, albeit concordant grounds: I, on the ground that in a world of confessional competition it gives me the best prospect of practicing my own religion; you, on the ground that it gives you the best prospect of practicing yours; and so on.

Whether or not they are also robustly attractive on convergent, agent-neutral grounds, there are many scenarios that are likely to be robustly attractive because of enjoying the concordant support of distinct agent-relative desiderata. These will probably include scenarios in which we each look after the welfare of our own children; we each keep our promises to one another; we are each secure against assault by others; and so on. We may or may not find such scenarios suitably attractive on convergent grounds but we will almost certainly find them suitably attractive on concordant grounds.

We each have to recognize that we may fail to live up to what we find robustly and co-avowedly attractive from a common standpoint due to the influence of potential disrupters. These will include the self-centered preferences that may detach us from the common point of view as well as the wayward impulses that may affect any one of us individually. But when we take something to be commonly attractive, we must assume that we are each going to guard against such disrupters, disowning any desires that they might introduce and seeking to stay faithful to the shared standpoint.

This means that like the co-avowedly persuasive, the co-avowedly attractive is a prescriptive category, directing us to what is desirable from within a standpoint that we share with an open number of others; this is the category of the commonly desirable, as we in Erewhon may think of it. The commonly desirable satisfies the grounding, divergence, and governance constraints associated with all normative or prescriptive categories. It is grounded in the attractor properties, convergent or concordant, that make something attractive to me and others qua members of an open group. It may come apart from what I actually desire—say, as a result of disruption—even when I purport to occupy a common standpoint with others and to think as a member of an open-ended group. And assuming that it is not faulty, I should allow my judgment of the commonly desirable to guide or dictate what I actually desire, at least so far as I operate as one member in an open group of others. Since the commonly desirable is responsive to the robust attractors that our practice in co-avowal and co-acceptance takes as determinants, it would be a failure on my part, so far as I genuinely share in that practice, to endorse some conflicting desire of my own.

As avowal is recursive, so too is co-avowal. Once the category of the commonly desirable becomes available in Erewhon, we members are likely to form, avow, and co-avow beliefs in propositions to the effect that this or that scenario is commonly desirable. And this, despite the fact that the property of being commonly desirable will only have become available to us in virtue of our having practiced co-avowal in respect of what we desire.

As I may avow a belief in the individual desirability of a scenario by expressive, ascriptive, and explanatory devices, so I may resort to such devices in co-avowing a belief in its common desirability. Depending on context, I can co-avow the common desirability of a prospect, R, by saying that it is desirable or commonly desirable, by saying that we desire it or believe that it is desirable or commonly desirable, or by explaining its desirability appropriately: for example, by reference to how much fun it would be or to how it would give us each fair returns.

I am naturally led, just by virtue of making individual avowals of desire, to develop a prescriptive point of view: a robust personal standpoint from which I can judge my actual performance, letting what I desire be assessed in terms of whether it is individually desirable. In the same way I am naturally led, just in virtue of the co-avowal and co-acceptance of desire that I practice in unbounded conversation, to develop a second prescriptive standpoint on desire: a robust common standpoint from which I can judge what I desire, letting it be assessed in terms of whether it is commonly desirable.

How does the individually desirable relate to the commonly desirable? In many cases they may coincide, as when it is both individually and commonly desirable that I should tell the truth to others; it is something I would prescribe for my actual self both from the robust personal standpoint and the robust common standpoint. But it should be clear that in many cases these standpoints are quite likely to come apart. The role of agent-relative desiderata in determining what is individually desirable means that what I would prescribe from an ideal, individualized standpoint may diverge from what I would prescribe from the ideal, socialized counterpart.

This means that neither the individually desirable nor the commonly desirable can play the role of the unreservedly desirable. The categories target what is robustly productive of desire, in the one case under the identification of robustness that goes with my practice of individual avowal, and in the other under the identification that goes with our practice of common co-avowal. Those practices may come apart in a way in which the corresponding practices in the case of belief do not. And so neither has a position in relation to the other that might give it a claim to direct us toward a master category: that of the unreservedly desirable.

We have been looking at what is likely to count as co-avowedly attractive from the point of view of an unbounded group and at what is commonly desirable in the sense of being robustly attractive from within the standpoint of the group. But the argument developed in the case of that group suggests that we can derive parallel conclusions for this or that bounded group. As the perspective of the unbounded group will direct us to the category of the commonly desirable, so the perspective of any bounded group will point us toward the category of what is jointly desirable for members of that group in their part as members; this will be identified by what proves to be robustly attractive to them in that role.

We the members of Erewhon, like the members of any society, are likely to find ourselves in any of a number of bounded groups; indeed our own community, as distinct from neighboring societies, will constitute one example. And within such a partial grouping, as within the unbounded community imagined, we will each conduct conversational exchanges with others in which we co-avow and co-accept a range of desires that reflects the properties that matter from our shared standpoint, identifying scenarios that we will see as jointly attractive.

These properties will include group-relative properties that matter to us as members—the welfare of our club, the prosperity of our community—but that may not matter to us in other roles. And so for each such grouping there is likely to be a notion of the jointly desirable that operates prescriptively but is in potential conflict with rival forms of desirability. It is liable to conflict with what counts as jointly desirable from the standpoint of other bounded groups. And of course it is liable to conflict with what counts as individually or commonly desirable.

The upshot of these observations is that each of us in Erewhon is going to be led by the inexorable pull of avowal and co-avowal into countenancing a range of prescriptive, idealized standpoints. As I avow a desire in my own name, I have to privilege what is robustly I-attractive, treating the possibility of disruption as a failure against which the avowal requires me to guard. And as I avow a desire in the name of a group, I have to privilege the robustly we-attractive in a parallel way, where that may mean what robustly attracts us in an unbounded group or what robustly attracts us in one or another bounded grouping.

The category of the robustly attractive that I identify in each case corresponds to a distinct prescriptive ideal of desirability, satisfying the constraints outlined earlier. What I see as desirable in the individual, common, or joint sense must be grounded in the properties that serve as robust attractors from within the corresponding practice. What I see as desirable in any such sense may diverge from what I actually desire. And, on pain of breaching the requirements of the relevant practice of avowal or co-avowal, I must let the perception of what is desirable in any of these senses govern the desires I actually form in the relevant area. In each case, fidelity to the practice will require me to let the desire that is avowed or co-avowed under it have a governing role in determining what I actually desire.

TOWARD THE UNRESERVEDLY DESIRABLE

A Breakthrough and a Setback

If the argument so far is sound, then in the wake of the developments charted, I and you and others in Erewhon will enjoy a conceptual breakthrough but suffer at the same time a conceptual setback. The conceptual breakthrough occurs in the areas of both belief and desire, the setback is confined to the area of desire alone.

The breakthrough is that we will become able to think in prescriptive terms, enjoying a position from within which we can distinguish between things as we actually believe or desire them to be and things as we ought to believe or desire them to be. How we ought to believe and desire things to be, in this way of conceiving of them, is how we would hold or want them to be, if we conformed to the constraints associated with a standpoint we privilege. Depending on context, this is the standpoint of the avowed self, or the self projected in one or another form of co-avowal. And by parallel it may be the standpoint of the pledged self, or the self projected in some form of co-pledging. It is the standpoint of the self as spokesperson for itself, now in one context, now in another.

It is a real gain for us in Erewhon to be enabled on this basis to think and talk in prescriptive terms, avowing beliefs as to what is credible and we ought to believe, what is desirable and we ought to desire. In the purely reportive life we enjoyed previously, we might have responded to incentives now in this manner, now in that; we might have generated in aggregate social patterns like those of general truth-telling; and we might even have been in a position to recognize and welcome that result. But there would have been no standpoint from which we could have seen ourselves as measuring or not measuring up to one or another ideal. And there would have been no basis for personal aspiration and criticism, or aspiration and criticism interpersonally shared.

All of that changes with the development of acts of avowal and pledging, and the appearance of the concepts of credibility and desirability that they bring onstream. Those shifts enable us to recognize that how we are may or may not be how we are committed by relevant practices to being, and that when we do not conform to the requirements of those practices then we display a sort of failure. We fall short in ourselves of the self we spoke for; we believe what is not credible, or desire what is not desirable, by the lights of that bespoken self. And when we recognize the actuality of failure, we simultaneously grasp the possibility and attainability of success. We see it as within our grasp: what we can become, if only we let the bespoken self shape the self we actually are.

The perspective of the bespoken self is also, it should be noted, the perspective of the beholden self. For the self we speak for in avowing or pledging, co-avowing or co-pledging, is a self that we have given others the right, under the rules of relevant practices, to expect us to display. It is a self such that if we do not display it, then the rules of avowal or pledging give them the right to ignore certain excuses, to treat us as uncooperative, and to impose associated retaliatory and reputational costs.

This conceptual breakthrough ought to be welcome in itself, opening up a wholly new way of thinking, and holding out the possibility of aspiration and criticism. But it ought also to be welcome insofar as it is bound to serve our interest in being able to rely on others and to get others to rely on us. For with the extra resources available in any given context, we will each have an enhanced capacity to assure others of our reliability. I will be able not just to avow or co-avow a belief that p or a desire for R, but to avow or co-avow a belief that p is credible or that R is desirable. And in reaching for such an extra means of communicating my belief or desire, inviting you to rely on me, I will signal that I must pay an even heavier reputational cost, should I fail in the absence of excuse to live up to what I say.

But while the breakthrough into prescriptive space is a huge benefit for us Erewhonians, it comes in the area of desire at a serious cost. Although it may serve us well in this or that insulated context—say, in a context where just individual desirability, common desirability, or one or another form of joint desirability is relevant—it will not do so when there is a prescriptive clash between those modes of desirability. Those modes of desirability are all aspectual in character, as we have seen, and different options may be desirable in different modes; one of my alternatives may be individually desirable, another commonly desirable, and yet another desirable from the joint standpoint of some contingent grouping. It might be, for example, that in a time of need it is individually desirable that I devote my efforts to my children, jointly desirable from the standpoint of my neighborhood that I devote them to the welfare of those who live nearby, and commonly desirable that I put them at the service of people as a whole: say, the general population of Erewhon.

I must be able to resolve this problem in any particular case, deciding which option I should take in light of the rival claims, since otherwise I will be irredeemably ambivalent, unable to decide between the conflicting standpoints. And I must be able to resolve this problem in a way that is manifest to my fellows, since otherwise I will be unable to present myself as a non-ambivalent agent that they understand and on whom they can rely. I will be multiply and inconsistently bespoken, on the one side; multiply and inconsistently beholden, on the other.

BEYOND THE SETBACK

I might resolve this problem brutely by declaring in each particular case, or in cases generally, that such and such a mode of desirability is the winner, without providing any explanation of why it scores better than the rivals. That would not be an appealing way to go, however. It would be tantamount to letting a lottery decide the issue and would project the image of being a more or less random self, not a self for which I can speak and expect to command a hearing: not a self that I can expect to be taken seriously by others, or indeed by myself. It might enable me to escape ambivalence but would do so only at the cost of embracing arbitrariness.

But there is a more appealing way for me or any other to resolve the problem raised. This would be to treat the grounding attractors that determine the individual or common or joint desirability of options as features that may be weighed against each other across categories, determining in aggregate which option in any given choice is to be selected. The local balance of features in one practice determines what is individually desirable from my perspective, in another what is commonly desirable, in yet another what is jointly desirable from the standpoint of this or that grouping. The idea in this resolution would be to let the global balance of features across those different categories determine what is desirable according to me in a practice-neutral sense: in a sense that treats no particular practice as special.

It may be that we in Erewhon depend on practices of avowal and co-avowal to access concepts of the individually, commonly, and jointly desirable. And it may be that none of those concepts has the status of a master category, as the concept of the commonly credible has that status in the case of belief. But with any choice we face that still leaves us with the salient possibility of allowing the desiderata that support competing, practice-relative judgments of desirability to enter into competition with one another and to determine which alternative in the choice answers best to the desiderata as a whole. It leaves us with the option of recruiting the desiderata mobilized within each practice in a further role, letting them interact with one another to fix what counts as desirable in a sense that is no longer tied to any particular practice.

Given the notions of what is desirable in one or another practice-relative manner, the concept of what is desirable in a manner that is not bound to any particular practice ought to be readily available to us. And it ought to be clear that the introduction of such a concept would serve an important function in our psychologies. It would enable me—or you or any other—to escape the specter of ambivalence. And it would do this without exposing me to the charge of arbitrariness in how I make up my mind.

The concept of the practice-neutrally desirable ought to be attractive in Erewhon, not just because of enabling each of us to resolve intrapersonal conflicts, but also because it holds out the prospect of making certain interpersonal conflicts resoluble as well. I and you and others will identify the practice-neutrally desirable on the basis of the aggregate desiderata—recognized as a matter of common awareness between us—that stack up in support of different options in any choice. And that means that there is at least the possibility that we may be able to agree about the option the agent should choose—perhaps even co-avowing or co-accepting a belief in its desirability, whether across a bounded or un-bounded community—and that we should conceive of the issue as one that we may sensibly debate; we should conceive of it as an issue shared across people, not as a different issue for each person.

We will certainly be able to achieve agreement in any case where one option in the choice satisfies all the desiderata satisfied by others, and satisfies them in a higher measure or, satisfying them in at least equal measure, satisfies other desiderata as well. And equally we will be able to achieve agreement in other cases to the extent to which the weightings we attach to different desiderata are in more or less the same range. The desiderata that we recognize may be weighted differently to the point where there is no agreed resolution available in certain cases as to what it is desirable for the agent to choose, in which case it will be indeterminate whether this or that option is practice-neutrally desirable. But the concept of practice-neutral desirability will at least allow us to think that we may achieve resolution and not have to give up in advance on the prospect; we may put ourselves in a position to co-avow a belief in the desirability of this or that alternative in a choice.

The role that the concept of the practice-neutrally desirable can play in helping to resolve interpersonal as well as intrapersonal conflicts should lead us in Erewhon to cast it as a concept capable in principle of resolving both. Construed in that way, the concept would hold out the prospect of a result that we ought to embrace, given our interest in establishing relationships of mutual reliance. Those relationships will be the more readily available, the more we can converge with one another in our judgments of practice-neutral desirability.

These observations argue that as we in Erewhon would each come to access a range of practice-relative concepts of desirability, so in all likelihood we would evolve a corresponding concept of practice-neutral desirability. This argument marks a crucial development in the narrative, for the concept of the practice-neutrally desirable is vanishingly close to the concept of the unreservedly desirable, as was outlined earlier. The concept of the practice-neutrally desirable would not single out the options to which it applies under certain aspects only; it would go beyond what is desirable only pro tanto—only under the aspect it presents from within a certain practice—to what is desirable simpliciter. And, so it turns out, it would satisfy both the generic constraints and the specific constraints that the concept of the unreservedly desirable may be expected to satisfy.

The notion of the practice-neutrally desirable straightforwardly satisfies the generic constraints of grounding, divergence, and governance, If one option in a choice counts as practice-neutrally desirable and others not, then there must be a difference in the desiderata that ground their relative desirability. If an option is desirable in that sense by my judgment, it may still be that what I desire diverges from that judgment; the desiderata supporting the judgment may fail as a result of disruption to elicit the desire. And, assuming that the judgment is not faulty, it ought to dictate or govern what I actually desire. It would be a manifest failure on my part not to let the judgment play that role, for it would amount to a failure not to let my desire be guided by the desiderata registered in the judgment.

The first of the specific constraints on the concept of the unreservedly desirable requires that you and I should have the same content in mind when we judge that it is desirable for anyone, whether anyone in general or anyone in a certain position, to choose a given option. And the second requires that it should be true or false that the option is desirable—assuming the issue is determinate—ruling out the possibility that it might be true by your criteria as an assessor, false by mine. The concept of the practice-neutrally desirable is bound to meet these constraints insofar as it is designed to facilitate the resolution of interpersonal as well as intrapersonal resolution. If it is to play that role in any range of cases, it must rule out both the relativity of content that the first constraint forbids and the relativity of truth-value that the second constraint outlaws. It must direct us to a range of issues that we may hope to explore and perhaps resolve in common.

Finally, does the notion of the practice-neutrally desirable satisfy universalizability, the third more specific constraint associated with the unreservedly desirable? Is it the case, for example, that when I say it is practice-neutrally desirable for someone independently of position or relationship to relieve suffering, I must hold that it is desirable in the same sense for anyone to relieve suffering? And is it the case that when I say it is desirable in that sense for someone in the position of a parent to give special care to their own child, I must hold that it is desirable in the same sense for anyone in a parental relationship to give such care to their own child?

The plausible answer in each case is, yes. What makes an action practice-neutrally desirable under the story told about Erewhon is the fact that in aggregate the desiderata derived from relevant practices weigh up in favor of the action. But whether they are agent-neutral or agent-relative in character, the desiderata must be general properties, if they are to enable each of us to prove conversable to others. In the agent-neutral case the general property might be that of relieving suffering, in the agent-relative that of being an agent who looks after their own child. And so, if they weigh up in favor of A's doing an action X in situation S, then they must weigh up in favor of the relevantly similar B doing an X-like action in any S-like situation.

These considerations argue that the concept of practice-neutral desirability, which Erewhonians would be likely to evolve under the pressures described, can be identified with the familiar concept of unreserved desirability. With this argument then, it becomes plausible to endorse the claim that the practices of avowal and pledging that are likely to emerge in Erewhon would push inhabitants to come to think, not just in terms of practice-relative forms of desirability, but in terms of an outright form as well: in terms of desirability, period.

The concept of what is right or obligatory figures more prominently in ethics than that of the unreservedly desirable. But, as noted earlier, if Erewhonians come in addition to have the ideas of responsibility and blame, they are also going to be in a position to introduce a concept that plays the role of the right, under the construal adopted here. It will be right for someone to choose a certain option under that construal if it is unreservedly desirable that they should choose it and if they would be blameworthy—if they would be fit to be held responsible—for not doing so. And that means that the concept of the right cannot be introduced into the narrative until it has been extended to encompass responsibility as well as desirability.

Some Observations about Unreserved Desirability

Before moving on to issues of responsibility, however, it is worth making some observations about the Erewhonian concept of practice-neutral desirability. These will help to display the implications of identifying that concept with the concept of the unreservedly desirable.

It is likely, to make a first point, that we in Erewhon will agree about the practice-neutral desirability of many types of choice, or at least about the desirability of most instances of those types. Consider choices of the kind that are generally resolved by strategically supported social norms of the kind considered in the first lecture. Each of us is likely to be sensitive to the desiderata, relevant to individual, joint, or common desirability, that argue for the practice-neutral desirability of conforming to such a norm. Thus it is likely that we will agree in thinking that at least when other things are equal, it is practice-neutrally desirable to tell the truth, abstain from violence, not steal what belongs to others under local conventions, and the like. It is likely that with such examples we would be prepared to co-avow or co-accept a belief in their desirability, whether on a bounded or unbounded basis.

Although we may readily agree on the extension of practice-neutral desirability in such run-of-the-mill cases, however, a second point to note is that we may disagree strongly in other cases. Indeed we may even think that there is no fact of the matter to be resolved in those cases: we may treat the question as to whether a certain choice is practice-neutrally desirable as indeterminate.

That we are likely to disagree about the desirability of various choices derives from the fact that we may differ in the relative weights that we assign to relevant desiderata—nothing in the narrative rules out this possibility—and be led by those desiderata in different directions. While disagreeing about such choices, we may each think that our opponents are wrong and that further reflection on the desiderata—say, on the importance they give those desiderata in other contexts—would lead them in our direction. Or, despairing of even the theoretical possibility of reaching agreement, we may conclude that there is no resoluble fact of the matter at issue between us: the question dividing us is indeterminate.

Moved by the costs to the mother, for example, I may think that abortion is practice-neutrally desirable, at least in certain cases; moved by the prospects for the foetus, you may think that taking the child to term in such cases is practice-neutrally desirable. And confronted with that divide, we may treat the difference as one of a disagreement that is worthy of further discussion. Or we may decide that the issue is indeterminate, reflecting an indeterminacy about the relative importance of the costs to the mother and the prospects for the foetus.

But this observation about possibilities of disagreement and indeterminacy should be balanced against a third point: that in any such case, there is always a prospect of conceptual evolution and eventual convergence. Mutual conversation and exchange may reveal that a desideratum we take to support a judgment of desirability in one context applies in a context where we hadn't invoked it previously and requires in consistency that we make a corresponding judgment of desirability there.

Thus it may be that invoking the notion of equality in arguing against discrimination between males, we may be led to recognize that it also argues against discrimination across gender. We may come to a ground-level agreement on the extension of the property of practice-neutral desirability to such a case. Or, consistently with ground-level disagreement, we may at least agree at a higher level that the extension to that case is determinate. In the case of higher-level agreement we may co-avow or co-accept the desiderata, suitably weighted, that we take to make the question resoluble. In the case of ground-level disagreement, we may also co-avow or co-accept certain particular judgments of desirability.

A fourth and final observation about practice-neutral desirability bears on the issue of amoralism. We are likely to react negatively to anyone's failure to agree with us, at least when the evidence is clear, about something that we regard as determinately desirable: that is desirable in terms of commonly endorsed, commonly weighted desiderata; for short, desirable in terms of accepted standards. But will this be the case, even if the person claims to be an amoralist who does not recognize the category of the practice-neutrally desirable? Yes, it will. Amoralists are likely to have a hard time of it in Erewhon.

Amoralists can scarcely reject the claims of different modes of desirability, since these appear in light of more or less inescapable practices.

And they can scarcely deny the relevance of the desiderata invoked in those practices, since that would put their very conversability in question. How then can they deny the possibility of allowing these desiderata, in the event of conflict—or at least in the event of some conflicts—to determine in aggregate the option that is practice-neutrally desirable? Certainly they cannot deny this without argument. And since they will come out as losers in most arguments, at least by the views of their adversaries, they are likely to be treated like self-serving offenders.[15] Thus they will not be allowed any excuse for refusing to act as it is practice-neutrally desirable for them to act, by the common perceptions of the community.

THE CHALLENGE OF RESPONSIBILITY

The observations made in this discussion give us solid ground for thinking that Erewhonians would evolve a conception of desirability akin to that with which people operate in more familiar worlds. They would inevitably develop practices of avowing and pledging, co-avowing and co-pledging their attitudes, as registered in the first lecture. Those practices make it more or less inevitable that they would introduce practice-relative notions of desirability. And, confronted with conflicts between those notions, it is equally inevitable that they would develop the concept of what is practice-neutrally desirable: in effect, so it was argued, the concept of what is unreservedly desirable.

If it is to give us a potential explanation of the emergence of ethics, however, the narrative must also explain how the inhabitants of Erewhon can come to think in terms of responsibility as well as desirability. It must explain how we who have evolved the concept of the unreservedly desirable would go on to hold one another responsible in various choices for not selecting the unreservedly desirable option. That is the next challenge that the genealogy has to confront.

The Notion of Responsibility

As in the case of desirability, it is essential in pushing forward this project to have a good sense of what fitness to be held responsible connotes in everyday usage and practice; otherwise it will not be clear what is needed for the narrative to achieve success. There are various accounts in the literature of what it means to hold someone responsible for having done something. But rather than going into the debate between these approaches, the line taken here will be to present an account that has two now familiar considerations in its favor. First, it satisfies many of the common connotations of saying that someone is fit to be held responsible for an action. And, second, it offers a rich account of those connotations that makes the task to be discharged by the narrative about Erewhon more rather than less difficult to accomplish; it does not tilt the scales in favor of success.

What responsibility connotes in ordinary usage is best articulated for the scenario where I hold you responsible for something I see as an undesirable choice: an offence or misdeed. This is a case in which the implications of being fit to be held responsible are sharp and the costs high, so that the received understanding of responsibility is likely to be at its clearest. And if it proves possible to articulate the concept of responsibility for this scenario, then the lessons should carry over to the case where I hold you responsible for having done something good rather than something bad.

Suppose, then, that I hold you responsible for a misdeed of some kind. Let this be an action like telling a lie, when there are no special considerations that make it desirable in the context on hand to hide the truth. On the account to be adopted here, there are three aspects to holding you responsible in this way or, alternatively, to treating you as fit to be held responsible. They come out nicely in three distinct messages that I convey if in the case of such a misdeed I say: "you could have done otherwise."[16]

First, those words convey a recognition that despite not having acted like someone with the capacity to respond to salient reasons of desirability—to the desiderata that make telling the truth desirable—you did indeed have that capacity at the time of choice: you possessed it, albeit you did not manifest it. Second, the words convey an exhortation after the event to have done otherwise; they communicate that I maintain an attitude that might have been expressed before the event in a regular exhortation to act as the reasons of desirability require. And third, the words convey censure or blame for not having done otherwise; they constitute a reprimand or penalty in themselves—this may be associated, of course, with independent penalties of custom or law—and they communicate at the same time that that penalty is deserved: you do not have an excuse, so I suggest, that might let you off the hook.

According to the first of these connotations, if I say "You could have done otherwise" in response to a misdeed, then I credit you with a capacity to have done otherwise in the situation where you made your choice. This connotation has two elements to it, one negative, the other positive.

The negative connotation is that you were not hindered in either of two commonly recognized ways. First, you were not subject to an agency-debilitating condition like paranoia or obsession or delusion or something of that kind; this radical form of practical excuse would exempt you from being held responsible.[17] And, second, there was no unforeclosed excuse, epistemic or practical, that got in the way of your action. You were in a position to realize that what you said was a lie and that telling a lie in that situation was undesirable. And you were able to act voluntarily on that perception: no one had a gun to your head, for example, and you were not under any other pressure of that kind.

The absence of exemption means that your capacity to respond to the desirability of truth-telling was unimpaired, as it might be said, the absence of excuse that the capacity was unimpeded: there was nothing recognizable in place to block either your recognition of the relevant reasons of desirability or your acting on those reasons. The lack of impairment means that you had the generic capacity to respond to the desirability of truth-telling—to register and act on it—and the lack of impediment means that nothing stopped you from exercising that capacity: you had the situation-specific capacity to respond appropriately. This covers the negative element in the first connotation of holding you responsible. But what does it mean in positive terms to hold that, despite your failure, you had the situation-specific capacity to register the desirability of telling the truth and act as it required?

If you were sensitive to the relevant considerations or reasons of desirability, and you were not affected by the impairment or impediment that might suspend that sensitivity, then your failure to respond appropriately must count as a surprise.[18] Presumably you would have responded appropriately in most variations on that situation where the sensitivity was still in place and there was no impairment or impediment to its activation: that is, to your registering and acting on the considerations. That is the positive element in the first connotation of holding you responsible. It must have been the case, so the presumption goes, that despite the fact that you did not actually respond appropriately, you would have done so over the bulk of variations on the actual situation where the same considerations or reasons continued to obtain and you remained unaffected by exempting or excusing factors.[19] It must have been the case, in short, that it was something of a fluke that you did not register those considerations or act as they required.[20]

There are cases where this connotation of holding you responsible would seem unlikely to be satisfied. Suppose I recognize that you are a habitual liar and that I am not surprised by a lie you just told me. And imagine that still I hold you responsible for the lie, not countenancing any exempting impairment or excusing impediment. How can I seriously believe, in holding you responsible in that way, that just as you were at the time of action, you would have told the truth across most relevant variations on the circumstances? How could I have believed it prior to action in making it clear to you that I would be holding you responsible for acting as the relevant reasons of desirability require? One of the benefits of the narrative presented below is that it makes it intelligible why in Erewhon I might adopt such a view, interacting with you on the assumption that that you are possessed of the appropriate level of capacity. To anticipate, the narrative suggests that not to do so would be to refuse to deal with you within the participant stance of conversation—a stance natural in a society of mutual reliance—preferring instead to treat you in a detached, objective manner as a subject for manipulative treatment.[21]

The second connotation of holding you responsible for a misdeed like telling a lie is that my saying that you could have done otherwise is exhortatory in character. By making this remark, I do not just communicate, as I might communicate to an observer, that as a matter of fact you would generally have done otherwise over variations on the situation where the same reasons were in place and no exemptions or excuses were introduced. And I do not intend to convey just the message that it was a mere fluke that you did not display the disposition in which the capacity consists.[22] Rather I communicate a form of impatience with your failure, a refusal to accept it as a brute fact.

This effect of saying you could have done otherwise means that the remark constitutes a retrospective exhortation, as it might be phrased, to have done otherwise. Normal exhortation is prospective, bearing on a choice that lies before you. I might have exhorted you prior to your choice by saying, "You can respond to the reasons of desirability and tell the truth; you can register and act on those reasons!", where this is meant to support the injunction: "Just do it!" When I say in holding you responsible that you could have done otherwise, I communicate that it would have been appropriate for anyone aware of your situation to have issued such a prospective exhortation prior to the choice. After all, I will communicate that this earlier exhortation would not have been appropriate, if I concede later that you could not have done otherwise than you did. It is plausible, then, that in saying that you could have done otherwise, I stand by that prior exhortation, whether or not anyone put it to you at the time of choice. In that sense I am naturally taken to exhort you retrospectively to have done otherwise and, by implication, to exhort you to do better in situations of the kind that lie in the future.

The third effect of saying that you could have done otherwise in the case of a misdeed is to censure or reprimand you. Not only do I recognize your capacity to have responded to reasons and told the truth, and not only do I maintain the attitude that I might have expressed earlier by exhorting or enjoining you to tell the truth. I also indict you for the failure to have told the truth. In remarking that you could have done otherwise, I highlight your failure in a presumptively unwelcome manner and thereby reprimand and penalize you for not having told the truth. Moreover I present this reprimand as one that you manifestly deserve; not being able to excuse what you did, it is a reprimand you cannot complain about having to endure.

With these aspects of the responsibility practice spelled out, the question to be explored is whether I and you and other members of Erewhon are likely to hold one another responsible for living up to certain standards of desirability. There is good reason to think that we would evolve this sort of practice. In particular, there is good reason to think that we would come to use the remark, "You could have done otherwise," or some cognate utterance, with the three connotations or effects described.

REGULATING FOR DESIRABILITY

Before developing the argument for this conclusion, however, it is worth noticing that whether or not we evolved the practice of holding one another responsible in Erewhon, we would certainly be likely to regulate one another into responding appropriately to those judgments of unreserved desirability on which we manifestly agreed. We would regulate one another into conformity with such a pattern in the way in which, by the account in the first lecture, we would regulate one another into conformity with a pattern like truth-telling.

In the scenario explored in the first lecture, we have an interest in proving ourselves to be reliable and reputable truth-tellers; unless we do so we cannot expect to be able to rely on others or to get others to rely on us. This interest leads us each to tell the truth in general, seeking to win a reputation for having the disposition to tell the truth reliably. And that means that just by being there as an audience for one another, ready to make a judgment on whether someone is a careful and truthful speaker, we provide an incentive for one another to tell the truth. We regulate or police one another into conformity with the standard of telling the truth and may be expected to elicit a general pattern of truth-telling.

Suppose now, in line with the evolving narrative, that we share certain standards of unreserved desirability, being responsive to similarly weighted desiderata; that we think there are determinate answers to questions of desirability where those desiderata are the determinants of desirability; and that we each think that anyone who is seeing clearly—anyone not subject to exemption or unforeclosed excuse—will agree with us in the judgment we make in those cases. On the story told so far, we must each reliably respond to such considerations or reasons of desirability—we must recognize and act on their requirements—in the absence of exemption or unforeclosed excuse. If we fail to do so then we cannot expect to be able to rely on others or to get them to rely on us. And that implies that we will each have a reputational incentive to respond appropriately to such reasons.

Absent exemption or unforeclosed excuse, then, we in Erewhon must be expected to regulate or police one another into generally registering the requirements of accepted considerations of desirability and into generally acting as they require. This form of mutual regulation will fall well short of holding one another responsible to those considerations, however, since for all it requires the exercise may not be conscious or intentional. We may regulate one another into responding to the requirements of accepted considerations without any awareness of doing so and without any intention to achieve such an effect. The regulation practiced may be just an unforeseen, aggregate consequence of our individually seeking a reputation for being reliable in our responses.

If I hold you responsible for responding in this sense to accepted considerations of desirability, I do something much richer than anything I need do in policing you in this way. Thus if I blame you for not acting as the considerations required, I will normally blame you consciously and intentionally. This will certainly be so if I express the blame in words, as in saying, "You could have done otherwise." But it will also be the case if I assume an attitude of blame and keep it to myself. It barely makes sense—although it may convey something metaphorically—to imagine that I might blame you but only unconsciously or unintentionally.

But while regulating one another for responding to accepted reasons of desirability falls short of holding one another responsible to such reasons, the regulative regime may still play an important role in supporting the responsibility practice. This will appear in the story to be told of how we in Erewhon might come to hold one another responsible. The narrative assumes that we are subject to a reputational discipline in which, as a matter of common awareness, we expect one another to be responsive to the expectations of reliability—in particular, reliability in responding to the requirements of accepted considerations of desirability—that we elicit or license in one another.

It should be no surprise that the practice of holding one another responsible depends on the presence of a basic regulative infrastructure of this kind, for that practice itself has a clear regulative rationale. In recognizing your capacity to have acted on relevant reasons, in exhorting you retrospectively to have done so, and in censuring you for your failure, it should be clear that I am working with the assumption that I can thereby influence and even reform you. I may not blame you with an explicitly reformative intention: my primary intention may be just to draw attention to your failure to respond to what by shared lights are the demands of desirability. But there would scarcely be any point in holding you responsible for such failures, if I thought that there was no possibility of getting you to change.[23]

It is time now to return to the narrative and explain why we in Erewhon might go beyond blind regulation and hold one another responsible for living up to accepted reasons of desirability; in particular, to show how we might begin to use something like the remark, "You could have done otherwise," with the three effects associated with holding you responsible. It will be enough to show that such a remark would naturally have those effects, uttered within the Erewhonian world where the concept of unreserved desirability has gained a hold. For if it can saliently have such effects, and thereby implement a system of mutual regulation, then that will give each of us a motive for making the utterance in response to this or that misdeed.

The effects to be explored are the effect of recognizing the offender's capacity to have done otherwise; the effect of exhorting the offender retrospectively to have done otherwise; and the effect of reprimanding the offender for the failure, communicating the message that the reprimand is deserved: there is nothing they can say to excuse themselves. These may be described respectively as the recognition effect, the exhortation effect, and the censure effect.

THE RECOGNITION EFFECT

There are two possible readings of the remark "You could have done otherwise" that I might utter in Erewhon, responding to an offence against some standards of desirability: presumptively, standards that I take you to agree with me in endorsing. On one reading it would mean, in the sense explicated, that you had the capacity to do otherwise: sticking with our example, that you had the capacity to respond to accepted reasons of desirability and tell the truth. On this reading, strictly taken, it would mean that you were disposed in the situation of choice to respond robustly to those reasons—to respond to them in any situation similar to the actual circumstances in which the reasons were present and there was no exemption or unforeclosed excuse—and that your failure to do so was a fluke. On a rival reading of the remark, however, it would mean just that you would have done otherwise if you were a different sort of person: that you would have told the truth if you had had a better education, for example, or had not lived in bad company for so long.

Why would the remark attract the first reading, and have the default effect of communicating the recognition of a capacity to respond appropriately to relevant reasons? Why would I not be moved by the evidence of your failure to conclude that actually you were not responsive to the requirements of shared standards of desirability: you were not disposed, just as you were, to register the relevance of those considerations and to act as they required?

It would certainly be reasonable to ignore the evidence of a particular failure if you had already demonstrated that capacity over a range of similar cases. But it is a default assumption in the practice of holding one another responsible that, even in the absence of such a record, the person who offends against accepted standards of desirability—assuming there is no exemption and no unforeclosed excuse—is fit to be held responsible for the offence and so must have had a capacity to respond to relevant reasons in the exercise of the choice. Is it possible to explain why we who live in Erewhon might be led to support a default assumption of this kind? Plausibly, it is.

Erewhon is a world where we each expect in our own case that others will rely on our words, when we expose ourselves to their scrutiny and their sanction and are not blocked from living up to those words by any exemption or any unforeclosed excuse. We expect that others will act on the assumption that our subjection to that reputational discipline will help to ensure our reliability. This means that it must be a matter of common assumption in Erewhon that the reputational discipline we invite and impose on one another is sufficient, in the absence of exemption or unforeclosed excuse, to ensure an important result: the presence of capacities to conform to patterns we routinely endorse. The observation holds, as registered earlier, not just with conforming to a pattern like truth-telling, but also with conforming to a pattern like that of responding reliably to accepted reasons of desirability.

Suppose now that I take you to accept the reasons of desirability that require you to tell the truth but that you actually tell a lie and do so in the absence of exemption or unforeclosed excuse. To judge that you did not have the capacity to respond to those reasons in the situation where you acted would be to treat you as someone beyond the reputational discipline within which we relate to one another. It would be to suspend the assumption of capacity that operating under that discipline supports and to give up on you in resignation or despair. Thus, if I take you as a fellow subject of that discipline, I must be disposed to treat you as possessed of that capacity and to think that you committed the offence simply because you failed to exercise the capacity.

This argument is worth spelling out more carefully. Taking you to be subject to the reputational discipline that characterizes our relationships in Erewhon, I am bound to think that your exposure to the expectations of others—in particular, expectations that you elicit or license—is likely to provide you with a powerful motive to live up to them and, in that sense, to establish a capacity to do so. But insofar as you manifestly endorse considerations of desirability that clearly argued for telling the truth in the situation in which you acted—insofar as you co-avow or co-accept those considerations—it is clear that I and others would have expected you to live up to them by telling the truth. And that means that it is equally clear, and certainly clear by my lights, that you had the motive and capacity to do so. Thus I must think that you failed to live up to those considerations and tell the truth in the presence of a capacity to have done so, and not that the failure was due to the absence of such a capacity.

This is to say that in the case considered I have epistemic grounds, albeit grounds of an unusual sort, to ascribe a capacity to have done otherwise to you. The grounds are not that you had the capacity, just as you were in yourself, to respond appropriately to the relevant considerations. Rather they are that you had the capacity, as someone empowered by the reputational culture in which we are commonly immersed, to have responded appropriately and told the truth.

These grounds will be available to me, of course, only insofar as I refuse to treat you as an outside or outlier: someone beyond the reputational community. But it makes good practical sense to assume by default that you are not someone of this kind. In Erewhon, as characterized in the narrative, the very possibility of cooperation and community depends on our each making a default assumption in dealing with one another that our words are our bonds and, more generally, that we can be relied upon to live up to the expectations that we elicit or license in others.[24] To reject that default in dealing with you would be to deny in effect that you were one of us.

I might be driven to withdraw the assumption in your particular case, of course—I might be forced to treat you as a pathological liar, for example—if your failure was repeated time and time again. But the cost of ostracizing you in this way would be enormous, since it would mean giving up on the possibility of our having a reputational influence on you within the community. It would make little sense to adopt such an attitude of hopeless resignation in light of a single offence, or even a limited record of offence. Doing so would be a resort of utter despair.

THE EXHORTATION EFFECT

If these considerations are sound, then when I say that you could have done otherwise in wake of a misdeed, in particular some misdeed where you were not subject to an exempting or an unforeclosed excusing condition, then I should be taken to convey by those words that you had the capacity to do otherwise. You were someone disposed reliably, if not invariably, to respond to reasons of desirability and act as they require. On the account offered earlier, however, those words should convey a second message too, if they are to represent an instance of holding you responsible. They should communicate that I think it would have been appropriate for anyone to exhort and enjoin you, prior to the action, to respond appropriately to those reasons. In that sense they should have the effect of a retrospective exhortation.

Suppose, then, that I say that you could have done otherwise in wake of a misdeed such as telling a lie, where it is granted that the action offends against recognized standards of desirability, and that it was performed in the absence of an exemption or an unforeclosed excuse. Is there any reason to think that in Erewhon these words would naturally have a retrospectively exhortatory significance? For reasons related to the reputational discipline just invoked, it turns out that there is.

In Erewhon, as already argued, we each make good use of the reputational pressures that others bring to bear on us when they form expectations, by our license, about what we will think and do. Those pressures force us to be careful to advertise only attitudes we can live up to and to be careful about living up to the attitudes we advertise. They ensure, in effect, that we have resources enough to establish ourselves as reliable partners and neighbors, giving us each capacities that we might not have had in their absence. In particular, they give us the capacity to respond to accepted reasons of desirability, enabling us in the absence of exemption or unforeclosed excuse to register what they require in any instance—say, to tell the truth—and to act on that requirement.

On this account, the capacity any one of us has to respond to reasons of desirability is liable to depend not just on our own internal powers, but on the social or reputational environment in which we operate; it is likely to have an ecological character.[25] This lesson is evidentially available to all of us, as is that availability itself, the availability of that availability, and so on. And so we are likely to hold it as a matter of common awareness in the community.

But if this is a matter of common awareness, then it must be equally a matter of common awareness that when I speak to you prior to your making a choice and say that there are reasons of desirability to do something such as telling the truth, or just that you can tell the truth, then I assume a role in which I may expect to have an influence on you. I am in a position to speak, not just in the manner of someone recording your capacity to tell the truth—say out of a concern for historical accuracy—but also in the manner of someone consciously hoping to elicit that capacity in the very act of ascribing it.

I do not speak just descriptively in saying or implying that you have the capacity, then, as I might do in saying that you have a ruddy complexion; I do not record a situation that obtains independently of what I say. Nor of course do I speak performatively, as I might do in saying "I resign"; I do not record a situation that is made to be true by the very words I utter.[26] I speak evocatively, so it might be put, using words that serve at once to record a situation—your having the capacity to tell the truth—and to make it more likely to obtain. I speak with the manifest expectation, and presumably the intention, of evoking the very capacity I ascribe.[27]

Suppose, then, that when I say "You can tell the truth," it is generally understood that I am likely to be speaking in this evocative manner, exhorting you to tell the truth and supporting by implication the injunction to tell the truth. What does that imply for how I am likely to be speaking when I say in the wake of your failure that you could have done otherwise: you could have told the truth? Plausibly, it implies that I am almost certainly speaking in the manner of retrospective exhortation.

Let "You can tell the truth" have the force of an exhortation when uttered prior to a choice. That is more or less bound to ensure that "You could have told the truth," uttered in the wake of a choice, is going to communicate the message that despite your failure, it would have been appropriate to exhort and enjoin you to tell the truth prior to the choice. And that will be so whether or not I or anyone else actually issued the prior exhortation. The remark will communicate that I maintain the attitude that might have been expressed earlier by "You can tell the truth." And so, as the second effect requires, it represents a form of retrospective exhortation.

THE CENSURE EFFECT

The observations so far show that having developed along the lines charted, I and you and others in Erewhon would satisfy the first two conditions associated with holding someone responsible. Thus I would be in a position, absent considerations of exemption or unforeclosed excuse, to give default recognition to your capacity to respond to the reasons of desirability that required to tell the truth, even in the wake of failure. And I would be in a position to speak with an exhortatory, injunctive force in saying in the wake of any such failure that you could have done otherwise. The final question is whether I could also be taken to censure you by making such a remark, imposing the penalty of a reprimand and implying at the same time that this penalty—and perhaps an associated form of punishment—is deserved.

By the account developed so far, my saying you could have done otherwise in the wake of a misdeed—say, a lie—presupposes that it was manifestly appropriate for anyone prior to your action to exhort and enjoin you to respond to reasons of desirability and tell the truth; by assumption, the option of telling the truth was unreservedly desirable in the circumstances, by our shared lights. But if it was manifestly appropriate for anyone to have enjoined you to respond to reasons of desirability and to tell the truth, then in the wake of the failure, it is manifestly appropriate for me to register that you acted in violation of such an injunction. And that is something I can be plausibly taken to do in saying that you could have done otherwise. In the context, this amounts to registering that you did not act as it would have been appropriate for anyone to enjoin you to act. In saying that you could have done otherwise, I stand by the appropriateness of the injunction and mark your failure to satisfy it.

This in itself is to impose a recognized penalty on you. For it is to express a bad opinion of your failure to act as you might appropriately have been enjoined to act. In effect, it is to issue a reprimand for the way you behaved. And not only does the remark constitute a reprimand; it also communicates that the reprimand is itself deserved. In saying that you could have done otherwise, conveying the message that you acted against an appropriate injunction, I indicate that you were not subject to an exempting or unforeclosed excusing condition; its presence would have meant that in a relevant sense you could not have done otherwise than you did. And in indicating the absence of such factors, I emphasize that there is nothing, under our practices, that might lead me to withdraw the reprimand. I put you on the hook and, since you do not have any available excuse for what you did, you cannot complain about my doing so.

CENSURE IN A NATURALISTIC WORLD

Anti-naturalists hold that in order for you to deserve a reprimand—in order for you to count as blameworthy—it must be the case, not only that there was no available excusing or exempting factor at the origin of your action, but that there was no regular causal factor whatsoever at its source. The idea is that in order to be blameworthy the action must have issued from an uncaused will. It must be something that you brought about as an agent, not something that was occasioned within you, say by a chance failure of normal functioning. The action must have been up to you, and only up to you, in a sense that rules out naturalistic causation.

On standard naturalistic premises, such as those assumed in these lectures, there are no events that cannot be traced to natural causal or chance antecedents. And so it is particularly important on this approach that the practice of holding responsible should not imply that if some causal or chance factor affected your performance, you are off the hook. Happily, however, the practice that emerges in Erewhon can make perfect sense, even if naturalism is sound. The narrative shows that you can be blameworthy in a significant sense even if the action for which I censure you can be causally traced to some dysfunctional blip or glitch, or just to brute chance.

The exhortatory, injunctive practice that obtains in Erewhon appears and survives, by the narrative adopted, because of a wish on the part of members to increase their perceived reliability by exposing themselves to costs in the case of failure: in particular, a failure to live up to the requirements of accepted standards of desirability. The practice allows that if a special set of causes—those associated with exemptions and unforeclosed excuses—can be adduced to explain a failure, then you do not incur those costs and cannot deserve a reprimand; you are off the hook. But assuming that there are causes of failure apart from these—or assuming that chance can play a role in generating failure—the practice cannot allow such factors to let you off the hook. Otherwise it would lose its regulatory point and frustrate the wish that supports it. No practice of holding people responsible to certain standards could have an impact on their performance if offenders could get off the hook just by arguing that their offence was the effect of a natural cause.

Assume that in Erewhon we treat exempting and unforeclosed excusing factors as having the following feature: that if they are present, then even the costs that we face for failing to live up to our advertised attitudes are not going to be enough to get us to display those attitudes. And assume in addition that we think that the other factors that might occasion such a failure—factors like the neural blip or glitch, of which we may know little—are different in precisely that respect: even if they are present, the costs that we face for not living up to our advertised attitudes are sufficient to trump them, although perhaps only in the light of experience and education. In a phrase, assume that in suitable contexts we treat exempting and unforeclosed, excusing factors as ones we cannot regulate one another into overcoming and that we treat other causal factors as ones we can; we treat the former as resistant to the effects of regulation, the latter as susceptible to those effects.

Under these assumptions, it will make perfect sense in Erewhon for us to treat offences that derive from regulation-resistant factors as not deserving blame and offences that derive from regulation-susceptible factors as deserving blame. And of course it will make sense for us to be open to experience in determining which items should be put in the resistant category, and which in the susceptible. It may be true, as noticed earlier, that the practice of holding one another responsible is distinct from the practice of blind regulation. But in the approach suggested there is a deep and continuing connection between the two. It is ultimately because of its regulative point that the practice of holding one another responsible can make the distinction between misdeeds that are deserving of blame and those that are not.[28]

Why, then, should you pay the costs associated with a misdeed that is due to a regulation-susceptible factor: say, the unknown neural blip or glitch? Why should you be expected to treat a reprimand as deserved? In a word, because the glitch counts as an influence that you are able, by the common sense of Erewhonians, to overcome: you have all the motivation and resolution required to carry you past it, especially given the force that you unleash in exposing yourself to the possibility of reputational loss. Factors that count as regulation-resistant ones that you are unable to overcome in the same way. They are not special because they obstruct the operation of an allegedly uncaused will; any causes would serve to do that. They are special because they stand out among natural causes by virtue of the fact that there is not much that you can do, no matter how motivated you are, to overcome them.[29]

This observation take us to the denouement. Just as the developments charted in the present narrative make sense of why I and you and others in Erewhon should give one another the recognition and exhortation associated with the practice of holding responsible, so they make sense of why we should also impose the censure associated with that practice. Thus, the narrative not only explains why we would develop the concept of desirability, it also makes sense of why we would begin to hold one another responsible for living up to certain standards of unreserved desirability. It shows that we would be led, as by an invisible hand—and not, for example, as the result of planning or contract—to make certain judgments of desirability and to hold one another responsible for acting according to those judgments.

BACK TO RIGHTNESS

Before concluding the discussion, however, there is one loose end to tie up. By most accounts it is the concept of the right or obligatory that is central to ethics, not the concept of the desirable. So how does it fit into our picture?

On the line adopted earlier, it is right or obligatory for an agent to choose one option rather than another if and only if, first, that option is unreservedly desirable and, second, the agent would be blameworthy for not choosing it. Thus if we Erewhonians are disposed in many cases to hold one another responsible for failures to do what is unreservedly desirable, then the concept of the right or obligatory will be within our ready reach. We will be prepared to hold that it would have been right for an agent to select a certain option just in case that option was unreservedly desirable and the agent can be held responsible for a failure to perform it, attracting the sort of recognition, exhortation, and censure just discussed.

This is not to say that the category of the right or obligatory would take over completely from that of the desirable. Certain options might be unreservedly desirable, by standards accepted across the community, without counting as right or obligatory. They might require such a level of sacrifice that we would not be prepared to blame people for failing to perform them: we would balk in the case of an offence at ascribing to them the capacity to have responded to the relevant standards. Hence there would be room for a divergence between the category of the unreservedly desirable and the right or obligatory. Those options that are not obligatory would count, in the received term, as supererogatory.

CONCLUSION

It may be useful in conclusion to remind ourselves of the main steps taken in this second lecture.

- The aim in explaining the emergence of ethics in Erewhon is to account for how we inhabitants could come to think in terms of desirability and responsibility.
- On the desirability front it is essential to explain how we could come to think of one option in a set of alternatives as unreservedly desirable, not just desirable under a certain aspect.
- From within the perspective of avowal, we Erewhonians are bound to distinguish between what we actually believe or desire and what our avowals require us to believe or desire.
- Our avowals require us to form beliefs robustly on the basis of data and to form desires robustly on the basis of desiderata, resisting any pressures that count as potential distorters by practice-related criteria.
- From within the practice of avowal, then, we must treat robustly persuasive propositions as credible or ought-to-be-believed, robustly attractive scenarios as desirable or ought-to-be-desired, counting it as a failure if our actual beliefs and desires diverge.

- The practice of co-avowal may involve co-avowing in the name of an open or a closed group; it gives rise to a concept of the commonly credible or desirable in the first case, the jointly credible or desirable in the second.

- In the case of credibility, the commonly credible naturally figures as a master category: what any one of us ought to believe in light of the practice of open co-avowal, we ought to believe unreservedly.

- In the case of desirability, no category has this master status and it is essential for us to have a basis for resolving issues about what to choose in cases where different options are individually, commonly, and jointly desirable.

- The natural way for us to do this is to allow for the aggregation of desiderata across the practices associated with these forms of desirability and the identification in a problematic choice of an option that is practice-neutrally desirable.

- The concept of the practice-neutrally desirable satisfies the constraints governing the ordinary concept of the unreservedly desirable and ensures the success of the genealogy on this front.

- But would we Erewhonians hold one another responsible for living up to the requirements of accepted standards of unreserved desirability? That is the second challenge for a genealogy of ethics.

- Holding you responsible for a misdeed involves ascribing a capacity not to have done it, exhorting you retrospectively to have done it, and reprimanding and penalizing you for failing.

- In Erewhon we rely on one another to impose a reputational discipline that enables us each to live up to others' expectations and it is a matter of common belief that we enjoy reputationally enhanced capacities on this front.

- Thus it is going to be a default assumption among us that if you offend against accepted standards of desirability in the absence of exemption or unforeclosed excuse, I can reasonably credit you with the capacity to have done otherwise.

- For similar reasons I can hold that you might have been appropriately exhorted before acting to take the unreservedly desirable option and I can reaffirm that exhortation retrospectively by saying "You could have done otherwise."

- Finally, by uttering those words I can mark your failure in an unwelcome way, thereby reprimanding and penalizing you; and I can do this in conditions where it is manifest that you cannot object to my doing so.

- With this account of how we Erewhonians might have come to think in terms of desirability and responsibility, it is also possible to make room for the right or obligatory. An option will be right just in case it is unreservedly desirable and the failure to enact it would be blameworthy.[30]

NOTES

1. This may also be described as what you ought to desire, all things considered or, in John Broome's phrase, *pro toto* (John Broome, *Rationality through Reasoning* [Oxford: Wiley Blackwell, 2013]). This phrasing not only marks the contrast with what you ought to desire *pro tanto* but also points to the explanation for why you ought to desire something *simpliciter*: namely, because of its properties overall.

2. Huck Finn does well overall by not letting his slave-culture sense of what is unreservedly desirable affect his spontaneous desire to help out the enslaved Jim. But he still displays a form of failure in not being guided by the judgment of desirability to which that sense of things leads him. It is just that that failure is a happy fault: it compensates for the worse failure that consists in his sense of unreserved desirability being warped by the slave culture and his judgment of desirability being therefore mistaken. That sense of desirability gives him a poor map and it is just as well that he does not navigate by it: that he relies instead, as we might say, on an intuitive analogue of dead reckoning.

3. In this second case, "unreservedly desirable" works the way "prudent" does. As it is prudent for you to look after your future, for me to look after mine, it may be unreservedly desirable for you to favor your child, unreservedly desirable for me to favor mine. It is important to register that "unreservedly desirable," like "prudent," may vary between contexts in the property it ascribes but that nevertheless it is not indexical in character. The point also applies to "right," used in a corresponding way. I am grateful to John MacFarlane for discussion of this issue.

4. John MacFarlane, *Assessment Sensitivity: Relative Truth and Its Applications* (Oxford: Oxford University Press, 2014).

5. R. M. Hare, *The Language of Morals* (Oxford: Oxford University Press, 1952).

6. Frank Jackson and Philip Pettit, "Moral Functionalism and Moral Motivation," *Philosophical Quarterly* 45 (1995): 20–40; reprinted in Frank Jackson, Philip Pettit, and Michael Smith, *Mind, Morality and Explanation* 189–210 (Oxford: Oxford University Press, 2004).

7. Lewis, *Convention.*

8. Consider the measures that are strategically attractive for any one of us in Erewhon, as tracked in the first lecture: measures like telling the truth and establishing ourselves as reliable reporters. We might have seen these as individually desirable, if we had had access to that concept. But there is no reason to think that we must have access to that concept in order to behave strategically. As noted earlier, the genealogy presented does not assume that we Erewhonians had access to the concept of the individually desirable–or to any desirability concepts–at the purely reportive stage charted in the first lecture.

9. The practice requires these responses in the way in which we say that the law requires us to behave thus and so. On this sense of how a practice can be a source of requirements, see Broome, *Rathionality through Reasoning*, ch. 7.

10. This is to say that the ideal self may advise that the actual self should behave in a manner that takes account of difficulties the ideal self does not itself have to

deal with. On this lesson, which also applies in the idealizations considered later, see Michael Smith, *The Moral Problem* (Oxford: Blackwell, 1994).

11. It is perhaps something like this that Richard Rorty has in mind when he appeals to the conversation of humanity. Richard Rorty, *Philosophy and the Mirror of Nature* (Oxford: Basil Blackwell, 1980).

12. This is not to deny that there are some standpoints, say those associated with a form of oppression to which I am personally not subject, such that it may take enormous efforts of empathy on my part—and a willingness to trust the testimony of those occupying that standpoint—for me to grasp what is revealed therein. Similar points apply, of course, in the case of the commonly desirable. See Karen Jones, "Second-hand Moral Knowledge," *Journal of Philosophy*, 96 (1999): 55–78.; and for a general perspective, see Miranda Fricker, *Epistemic Injustice: Power and the Ethics of Knowing* (Oxford: Oxford University Press, 2007).

13. Christian List and Philip Pettit, *Group Agency: The Possibility, Design and Status of Corporate Agents* (Oxford: Oxford University Press, 2011); and Lara Buchak and Philip Pettit, "Reasons and Rationality: The Case for Group Agents," in *Weighing and Reasoning*, edited by I. Hirose and A. Resner, 207–31 (Oxford: Oxford University Press, 2014).

14. This observation may offer some support for the pragmatist thought that the true is that which is destined to be agreed upon.

15. Their adversaries in such a case will take it to be commonly credible—and so credible, period—that the relevant actions are unreservedly desirable. And so they will take the amoralists to reject the claims of the commonly credible without offering any persuasive rejoinder.

16. To hold you responsible for a misdeed is not necessarily to make any utterance. But it is to assume the attitude that might be expressed by saying that you could have done otherwise or had reason to do otherwise or something of the kind.

17. R. Jay Wallace, *Responsibility and the Moral Sentiments* (Cambridge, MA: Harvard University Press, 1996); and John Gardner, *Offences and Defences: Selected Essays in the Philosophy of Criminal Law* (Oxford: Oxford University Press, 2007).

18. This will be a surprise, of course, only if I am truly holding you responsible, not pretending to hold you responsible. Thus it will not be a surprise if I am going through the motions of holding you responsible, because of endorsing the assumption, not that you have the capacity to do otherwise, but that you are capable of developing that capacity as a result of being treated as if you already had it. This would not be to treat you as responsible, strictly speaking, but to treat you as "responsibilizable": capable of being made fit to be held responsible by being held responsible, when strictly you lack such fitness. On that theme, see Philip Pettit, "Responsibility Incorporated," *Ethics* 117 (2007): 171–201.

19. Michael Smith, "Rational Capacities, or: How to Distinguish Recklessness, Weakness and Compulsion," in *Weakness of Will and Practical Irrationality*, edited by S. Stroud and C. Tappolet, 17–38 (Oxford: Oxford University

Press, 2003); and Victoria McGeer and Philip Pettit, "The Hard Problem of Responsibility," *Oxford Studies in Agency and Responsibility*, vol. 3, edited by D. Shoemaker, 160–88 (Oxford: Oxford University Press, 2015).

20. There are two dimensions to the notion of a degree of capacity, which might be described as dependability and durability. A disposition to respond to reasons of desirability will score higher in dependability the more likely it is to survive temptations, and score higher in durability the more likely it is to survive disrupters. Where temptations have to be registered as considerations that counter reasons of desirability, disrupters need not be: like distractions or mood swings they can operate behind the back of the agent. See Pettit, *The Robust Demands of the Good,* ch. 2, and Victoria McGeer and Philip Pettit, "The Empowering Theory of Trust," in *The Philosophy of Trust,* edited by Paul Faulkner and Thomas Simpson (Oxford: Oxford University Press, 2016). Only dependability is taken into account in the text.

21. See Peter Strawson, *Freedom and Resentment and Other Essays* (London: Methuen, 1962) and Philip Pettit and Michael Smith, "Freedom in Belief and Desire." *Journal of Philosophy* 93 (1996): 429–49; reprinted in *Mind, Morality and Explanation*, edited by Frank Jackson, Philip Pettit, and Michael Smith, 375–96 (Oxford: Oxford University Press, 2004).

22. Pamela Hieronymi, "Rational Capacity as a Condition on Blame," *Philosophical Books* 48 (2007): 109–23.

23. Strawson, *Freedom and Resentment and Other Essays;* Victoria McGeer, "Strawson's Consequentialism," *Oxford Studies in Agency and Responsibility* 2 (2014): 64–92.

24. We may elicit or license suitable expectations by what we positively say but also by what we fail to say: for example, by our failure to reject the manifest assumption on the part of others that we endorse certain judgments of unreserved desirability.

25. Victoria McGeer, "Civilizing Blame," in *Blame: Its Nature and Norms*, edited by J. D. Coates and N. A. Tognazzini, 162–88 (Oxford: Oxford University Press, 2013); and McGeer and Pettit, "Hard Problem of Responsibility." The idea of an ecological capacity is borrowed from Manuel Vargas, *Building Better Beings: A Theory of Moral Responsibility* (Oxford: Oxford University Press, 2013). Using concepts introduced earlier, a capacity might depend on ecology for being dependable or for being durable or both.

26. David Lewis, *Philosophical Papers*, vol. 1 (Oxford: Oxford University Press, 1983), ch. 12.

27. McGeer and Pettit, "Hard Problem of Responsibility."

28. I am particularly indebted to Victoria McGeer for the line in this paragraph, as I am indebted on the topic of responsibility in general to our joint work (ibid.).

29. The idea that you might be willing to accept the penalty for a failure that has a natural cause, provided that cause is not a recognized excuse, is borne out by the way we treat causes of moral failure such as laziness or weakness of will. Neither of these factors counts in ordinary terms as an excuse. And yet each is frequently invoked as a cause of the failure to act appropriately. Why do we

treat laziness and akrasia as causes of failure but not causes of the sort that might excuse it? Plausibly, it is because we think of them as hurdles that people of normal motives and resources are capable of overcoming.

30. I presented lectures based on this text at the Australian National University in March 2015 and then at the Tanner Lectures in Berkeley in early April 2015. I learned enormously from the many comments received at those events and afterward and am in the debt of too many people to list. However, I must mention my Tanner commentators, Pamela Hieronymi, Richard Moran, and Michael Tomasello. Apart from offering enlightening commentaries on the material, to which I hope to respond in a separate publication, they were most generous with their informal advice and criticism.

REFERENCES

Alonso, F. M. "What Is Reliance?" *Canadian Journal of Philosophy* 44 (2014): 163–83.

Anscombe, G. E. M. *Intention*. Oxford: Blackwell, 1957.

Appiah, Kwame Anthony. *The Honor Code: How Moral Revolutions Happen*. New York: Norton, 2010.

Axelrod, Robert. *The Evolution of Cooperation*. New York: Basic Books, 1984.

Ayer, A. J. *Language, Truth and Logic*. London: Gollanz, 1982.

Bar-on, Dorit. *Speaking My Mind: Expression and Self-knowledge*. Oxford: Oxford University Press, 2004.

Bennett, Jonathan. *Rationality*. London: Routledge and Kegan Paul, 1964.

Blackburn, Smon. *Spreading the Word*. Oxford: Oxford University Press, 1984.

Boehm, Christopher. *Hierarchy in the Forest: The Evolution of Egalitarian Behavior*. Cambridge, MA: Harvard University Press, 1999.

Boix, Carles, and Frances Rosenbluth. "Bones of Contention: The Political Economy of Height Inequality." *Americal Political Science Review* 108 (2014): 1–22.

Bratman, Michael. *Shared Agency: A Planning Theory of Acting Together*. Oxford: Oxford University Press, 2014.

Brennan, Geoffrey, Lina Eriksson, Robert E. Goodin, and Nicholas Southwood. *Explaining Norms*. Oxford: Oxford University Press, 2013.

Brennan, Geoffrey, and Philip Pettit. *The Economy of Esteem: An Essay on Civil and Political Society*. Oxford: Oxford University Press, 2004.

Broome, John. *Rationality through Reasoning*. Oxford: Wiley Blackwell, 2013.

Byrne, Alex, "Transparency, Belief, Intention," *Proceedings of the Aristotelian Society* 85 (2011): 201–21.

Buchak, Lara, and Philip Pettit. "Reasons and Rationality: The Case for Group Agents. In *Weighing and Reasoning*. Edited by I. Hirose and A. Resner. Oxford: Oxford University Press, 2014.

Chalmers, David, and Frank Jackson. "Conceptual Analysis and Reductive Explanation." *Philosophical Review* 110 (2001): 315–60.

Coleman, James. *Foundations of Social Theory*. Cambridge, MA: Harvard University Press, 1990.

Craig, Edward. *Knowledge and the State of Nature*. Oxford: Oxford University Press, 1990.

Dancy, Jonathan. *Ethics without Principles*. Oxford: Oxford University Press, 2004.

Davidson, Donald. *Inquiries into Truth and Interpretation*. Oxford: Oxford University Press, 1984.

DeScioli, Peter, and Robert Kurzban. "A Solution to the Mysteries of Morality." *Psychological Bulletin* 139 (2013): 477–96.

Dennett, Daniel. *Brainstorms*. Brighton: Harvester Press, 1979.

Dietrich, Franz, and Christian List. "A Reason-Based Theory of Rational Choice." *Nous* 47 (2013): 104–34.

Elster, Jon. *Alchemies of the Mind: Rationality and the Emotions*. Cambridge: Cambridge University Press, 1999.

Evans, Gareth. *The Varieties of Reference*. Oxford: Oxford University Press, 1982.

Fricker, Miranda. *Epistemic Injustice: Power and the Ethics of Knowing*. Oxford: Oxford University Press, 2007.

Gardner, John. *Offences and Defences: Selected Essays in the Philosophy of Criminal Law*. Oxford: Oxford University Press, 2007.

Gert, Joshua. *Normative Bedrock: Response-dependence, Rationality, and Reasons*. Oxford: Oxford University Press, 2012.

Gibbard, Allan. *Wise Choices, Apt Feelings*. Oxford: Oxford University Press, 1990.

Gilbert, Margaret. *Joint Commitment: How we Make the Social World*. Oxford: Oxford University Press, 2015.

Grice, Paul. "Logic and Conversation." In *Syntax and Semantics*, vol 3. Edited by P. Cole and J. L. Morgan. New York: Academic Press, 1975.

———. "Method in Philosophical Psychology." *Proceedings and Addresses of the American Philosophical Association* 68 (1975): 23–53.

———. *Studies in the Ways of Words*. Cambridge, MA: Harvard University Press, 1989.

Hare, R. M. *The Language of Morals*. Oxford: Oxford University Press, 1952.

Hart, H. L. A. *The Concept of Law*. Oxford: Oxford University Press, 1961.

Hieronymi, Pamela. "Rational Capacity as a Condition on Blame." *Philosophical Books* 48 (2007): 109–23.

Hobbes, Thomas. *Leviathan*. Edited by E. Curley. Indianapolis: Hackett, 1994.

Hume, David. *Political Essays*. Cambridge: Cambridge University Press, 1994.

Jackson, Frank. *From Metaphysics to Ethics: A Defence of Conceptual Analysis*. Oxford: Oxford University Press, 1998.

Jackson, Frank, and Philip Pettit. "Moral Functionalism and Moral Motivation." *Philosophical Quarterly* 45 (1995): 20–40; reprinted in Frank Jackson, Philip Pettit and Michael Smith. *Mind, Morality and Explanation*. Oxford: Oxford University Press, 2004.

———. "A Question for Expressivists." *Analysis* 58 (1998): 239–51.

Jackson, Frank, Philip Pettit, and Michael Smith. "Ethical Particularism and Patterns." In *Particularism*. B. Hooker and M. Little, 1999.

Jones, Karen. "Second-hand Moral Knowledge." *Journal of Philosophy* 96 (1999): 55–78.

Joyce, Richard. *The Evolution of Morality.* Cambridge, MA: MIT Press, 2006.

Kitcher, Philip. *The Ethical Project.* Cambridge, MA: Harvard University Press, 2011.

Langton, Rae. *Sexual Solipsism: Philosophical Essays in Pornography and Objectification.* Oxford: Oxford University Press, 2009.

Lewis, David. *Convention.* Cambridge, MA: Harvard University Press, 1969.

———. *Philosophical Papers*, vol 1. Oxford: Oxford University Press, 1983.

List, Christian, and Philip Pettit. *Group Agency: The Possibility, Design and Status of Corporate Agents.* Oxford: Oxford University Press, 2011.

Lyon, A. *Resisting Doxastic Pluralism: The Bayesian Challenge Redux.* University of Maryland. College Park, 2015

MacFarlane, John. *Assessment Sensitivity: Relative Truth and its Applications.* Oxford: Oxford University Press, 2014.

Mackie, J. L. *Ethics.* Harmondsworth: Penguin, 1977.

Maynard Smith, John, and David Harper. *Animal Signals.* Oxford: Oxford University Press, 2004.

McGeer, Victoria. "Civilizing Blame." In *Blame: Its Nature and Norms.* Edited by J. D. Coates and N. A. Tognazzini, 162–88. Oxford: Oxford University Press, 2013.

———. "Is 'Self-knowledge' an Empirical Problem? Renegotiating the Space of Philosophical Explanation." *Journal of Philosophy* 93 (1996): 483–515.

———. "The Moral Development of First-Person Authority." *European Journal of Philosophy* 16 (2008): 81–108.

——— "Strawson's Consequentialism." *Oxford Studies in Agency and Responsibility* 2 (2014): 264–92.

McGeer, Victoria, and Philip Pettit. "The Empowering Theory of Trust." In *The Philosophy of Trust.* Edited by Paul Faulkner and Thomas Simpson. Oxford: Oxford University Press, 2016.

———. "The Hard Problem of Responsibility." In *Oxford Studies in Agency and Responsibility*, vol. 3. Edited by D. Shoemaker, 160–88. Oxford: Oxford University Press, 2015.

———. "The Self-regulating Mind." *Language and Communication* 22 (2002): 281–99.

Menger, Carl. "On the Origin of Money." *Economic Journal* 2 (1892): 239–55.

Moran, Richard. *Authority and Estrangement: An Essay on Self-knowledge.* Princeton, NJ: Princeton University Press, 2001.

———. "Self-Knowledge: Discovery, Resolution, and Undoing." *European Journal of Philosophy* 5 (1997): 141–61.

Neuhouser, Frederick. *Rousseau's Critique of Inequality: Reconconstructing the Second Discourse.* Cambridge: Cambridge University Press, 2015.

Nietzsche, Friedrich. *On the Genealogy of Morals.* Cambridge: Cambridge University Press, 1997.

Pettit, Philip. *The Common Mind: An Essay on Psychology, Society and Politics.* New York: Oxford University Press, 1993.

———. "Decision Theory and Folk Psychology." In *Essays in the foundations of Decision Theory*. Edited by M. Bacharach and S. Hurley. Oxford: Blackwell, 1991; reprinted in Philip Pettit. *Rules, Reasons, and Norms*. Oxford: Oxford University Press, 2002.

———. "Group Agents are not Expressive, Pragmatic or Theoretical Fictions." *Erkenntnis* 79 (2014).

———. *Made with Words: Hobbes on Language, Mind and Politics*. Princeton, NJ: Princeton University Press, 2008.

———."Making Up Your Mind." *European Journal of Philosophy* 23 (2015).

———. "Practical Belief and Philosophical Theory." *Australasian Journal of Philosophy* 76 (1998): 15–33.

———. "Responsibility Incorporated." *Ethics* 117 (2007): 171–2001.

———. *The Robust Demands of the Good: Ethics with Attachment, Virtue and Respect*. Oxford: Oxford University Press, 2015.

———. Value-mistaken and Virtue-mistaken Norms. *Political Legitimization without Morality?* Edited by Jörg Kühnelt, 139–56. New York: Springer, 2008.

———. "*Virtus Normativa*: Rational Choice Perspectives." *Ethics* 100 (1990): 725–55; reprinted in Philip Pettit, *Rules, Reasons, and Norms*. Oxford: Oxford University Press, 2002.

Pettit, Philip, and David Schweikard. "Joint Action and Group Agency." *Philosophy of the Social Sciences* 36 (2006): 18–39.

Pettit, Philip, and Michael Smith. "Freedom in Belief and Desire." *Journal of Philosophy* 93 (1996): 429–449; reprinted in Frank Jackson, Philip Pettit, and Michael Smith. *Mind, Morality and Explanation*. Oxford: Oxford University Press, 2004.

———. (1993). "Practical Unreason." *Mind* 102 (1993): 53–80 reprinted in Frank Jackson, Philip Pettit, and Michael Smith. *Mind, Morality and Explanation*. Oxford: Oxford University Press, 2004.

Prescott-Couch, Alexander. "Williams and Nietzsche on the Significance of History for Moral Philosophy." *Journal of Nietzsche Studies* 45 (2014): 147–168.

Railton, Peter. "Reliance, Trust, and Belief." *Inquiry* 57 (2014): 122–50.

Rorty, Richard. *Philosophy and the Mirror of Nature*. Oxford: Basil Blackwell, 1980.

Rousseau, Jean-Jacques. *The Discourses and Other Early Political Writings*. Edited by Victor Gourevitch. Cambridge: Cambridge University Press, 1997.

Scanlon, T. M. *Being Realistic about Reasons*. Oxford: Oxford University Press, 2015.

Scott-Phillips, Thom. *Speaking Our Minds: Why Human Communication Is Different, and How Language Evolved to Make It Special*. London: Palgrave Macmillan, 2015.

Searle, John. *Making the Social World: The Structure of Human Civilization*. Oxford: Oxford University Press, 2015.

Sellars, Wilfred. *Empiricism and the Philosophy of Mind*. Cambridge, MA: Harvard University Press, 1997.

Shapiro, Scott J. *Legality*. Cambridge, MA: Harvard University Press, 2011.

Smith, Michael. *The Moral Problem*. Oxford: Blackwell, 1994.

———. "Rational Capacities, or: How to Distinguish Recklessness, Weakness and Compulsion." In *Weakness of Will and Practical Irrationality*. Edited by S. Stroud and C. Tappolet. Oxford: Oxford University Press, 2003.

Sober, Elliott, and David Sloan Wilson. *Unto Others: The Evolution and Psychology of Unselfish Behavior*. Cambridge, MA: Harvard University Press, 1998.

Sperber, Dan, and Deirdre Wilson. *Relevance: Communication and Cognition*. Oxford: Blackwell, 1986.

Stalnaker, Robert C. *Inquiry*. Cambridge, MA: MIT Press, 1984.

———. "Assertion." In Stalnaker, *Context and Content* (Oxford, Oxford University Press, 1999) 78–95.

Sterelny, Kim. *The Evolved Apprentice: How Evolution Made Humans Unique*. Cambridge, MA: MIT Press, 2012.

Stevenson, Charles L. *Ethics and Language*. New Haven, CT: Yale University Press, 1944.

Strawson, P. *Freedom and Resentment and Other Essays*. London: Methuen, 1962.

Tomasello, Michael. *A Natural History of Human Thinking*. Cambridge, MA: Harvard University Press, 2014.

———. *Origins of Human Communication*. Cambridge, MA: MIT Press, 2008.

Tuomela, Raimo. *The Importance of Us*. Stanford, CA, Stanford University Press, 1995.

Vargas, Manuel. *Building Better Beings: A Theory of Moral Responsibility*. Oxford: Oxford University Press, 2013.

Wallace, R. Jay. *Responsibility and the Moral Sentiments*. Cambridge, MA: Harvard University Press, 1996.

Williams, Bernard. *Truth and Truthfulness*. Princeton, NJ: Princeton University Press, 2002.

Winch, Peter. *The Idea of a Social Science and Its Relation to Philosophy*. London: Routledge, 1963.

The Weight of All Flesh:
On the Subject-Matter of Political Economy

ERIC L. SANTNER

THE TANNER LECTURES IN HUMAN VALUES

Delivered at

University of California, Berkeley
April 15–16, 2014

ERIC L. SANTNER is the Philip and Ida Romberg Distinguished Service Professor in Modern Germanic Studies at the University of Chicago. He came to Chicago in 1996 after twelve years of teaching at Princeton University. He has been a visiting fellow at various institutions, including Dartmouth, Washington University, Cornell, and the University of Konstanz. He works at the intersection of literature, philosophy, psychoanalysis, political theory, and religious thought. His books include: *Friedrich Hölderlin: Narrative Vigilance and the Poetic Imagination*; *Stranded Objects: Mourning, Memory, and Film in Postwar Germany*; *My Own Private Germany: Daniel Paul Schreber's Secret History of Modernity*; *On the Psychotheology of Everyday Life: Reflections on Freud and Rosenzweig*; *On Creaturely Life: Rilke, Benjamin, Sebald*; *The Neighbor: Three Inquiries in Political Theology* (with Slavoj Žižek and Kenneth Reinhard); *The Royal Remains: The People's Two Bodies and the Endgames of Sovereignty*. He edited the German Library Series volume of works by Friedrich Hölderlin and coedited with Moishe Postone, *Catastrophe and Meaning: The Holocaust and the Twentieth Century*. His work has been translated into German, Spanish, French, Korean, Hebrew, Polish, Italian, and Portuguese. Eric Santner delivered the Tanner Lectures in Human Values at the University of California, Berkeley, in the spring of 2014; they will appear in 2015 with Oxford University Press under the title, *The Weight of All Flesh: On the Subject-Matter of Political Theology*.

INTRODUCTION

I

In my previous book, I argued that the subject matter that Ernst Kantorowicz elaborated in his famous study of medieval and early modern political theology, *The King's Two Bodies*, never disappeared from the life of the citizen-subjects of modern, constitutional states.[1] My claim was rather that the "stuff" of the king's glorious body—the virtually real supplement to his empirical, mortal body—was in some sense dispersed into new locations as a spectral materiality—I called it a *surplus of immanence*—that called on the scene new forms and practices of knowledge, power, and administration charged—or rather: *sur-charged*—with coming to terms with and, indeed, cultivating these "royal remains" injected into the life of the People. To use Freud's locution for the pressure of the drives, these remains now insisted as an uncanny *Arbeitsanforderung* or demand for work. This was, in other words, work in excess of any apparent teleological order, work that kept one busy beyond reason. Among these new forms I counted first and foremost the new modalities of statecraft analyzed by Michel Foucault under the heading of the disciplines and biopower. My claim, however, was that what these new forms of knowledge and control were at least in part "on to," the subject matter they were tracking without fully being able to conceptualize it, came into view in Freud's theory and practice as, precisely, *subject-matter*: a peculiar and often unnerving materiality, a seemingly formless or *informe* remainder of processes of subject-formation. I argued that psychoanalysis could itself be understood as the science of "royal remains" insisting—beyond reason—as a quasi-discursive and quasi-somatic pressure in the souls of modern citizen-subjects. The usual genealogy of Freud's new science—its neurological lineage—was thus to be supplemented by one addressing its emergence out of a displacement and redistribution of "emergency powers" previously concentrated in, *enjoyed* and *embodied* by, the sovereign person, in a word, by a political theological lineage. My further claim was that a variety of modernist aesthetic projects had found their own ways to elaborate and give provisional form to the *informe* surplus of immanence pushing against the skin of "modern man," to the inflammatory pressure emerging at a newly configured jointure of the somatic and the normative, a new symbolic knotting or suturing of *physis* and *nomos*, of man's being as animal and his being as locus of initiative in the space of reasons, commitments, responsibilities. In the following I would like to continue these investigations by extending them into a realm I had heretofore neglected, that of political economy. In a certain sense I will be repeating my previous argument but now with a view to its relation and relevance to Marx's conception of the critique of political economy. This then is very much a *partial* repetition: one concerned with the "partial object" of political economy with respect to which no one ever remains fully impartial.

II

A crucial point of reference in *The Royal Remains* was provided by Jacques-Louis David's famous painting, *The Death of Marat*, which I took to be an emblem of the troubled transition from the representational regime of the King's Two Bodies to that of the People's Two Bodies. My reading took its lead from T. J. Clark who rather boldly proposed that one view the painting as the inaugural work of European visual modernism. For Clark, *Marat* enjoys this status insofar as its particular—and particularly intense—engagement with politics "tells us something about its [modernism—E.L.S.] coming to terms with the world's disenchantment in general."[2] The public service—we might say: liturgical labor—performed by earlier painters such as Velázquez was, according to Clark, "to transmute the political, to clean it of the dross of contingency, to raise it up to the realm of allegory"; David succeeds—and so becomes modern—precisely by failing to do any such thing, by articulating its impossibility, by allowing his painting to turn—and in some sense to keep turning—"on the impossibility of transcendence" (22). And all of that in the context of a new liturgy meant to consolidate the consistency of the People as uncontested bearer of the principle of sovereignty.[3] We might say that what David's painting puts on display is precisely the insistent *remainder* of such efforts at sublimation/allegorization, that it offers them as the new subject matter—and I would add: quasi-carnal *subject-matter*—of painting.

The simultaneously political and painterly form of the impossibility of transcendence or, as we might put it, the political and painterly form of a new surplus of immanence, appears as an abstract materiality that would seem to issue from Marat's mutilated body and fill the upper half of the painting. As Clark puts it, David's treatment of the body "seems to make Marat much the same substance—*the same abstract material*—as the empty space above him. The wound is as abstract as the flesh" (36; emphasis added). The flesh that can no longer be figured as the virtually real, glorious body of the king becomes the *abstract material* out of which the painting is largely made. The empty upper half of the painting stands in for a missing and, indeed, impossible representation of the People: "It embodies the concept's absence, so to speak. It happens upon representation as technique. It sets its seal on Marat's unsuitability for the work of incarnation" (47). The scumbled surface forming the upper half of the painting thus no longer functions as a simple absence but rather as a positive, even oppressive presence, "something abstract and unmotivated, which occupies a different conceptual space from the bodies below it. This produces," Clark continues, "a kind of representational deadlock, which is the true source of the *Marat*'s continuing hold on us" (48). This is the "endless, meaningless objectivity produced by paint not quite finding its object, symbolic or otherwise, and therefore making do with its own procedures" (48). This is what Clark means when he speaks of painting "turning" on the impossibility of transcendence. That characterization brings to mind—well, to my mind—a short text by Kafka:

Es wurde ihnen die Wahl gestellt Könige oder der Könige Kuriere zu werden. Nach der Art der Kinder wollten alle Kuriere sein. Deshalb gibt es lauter Kuriere, sie jagen durch die Welt und rufen, da es keine Könige gibt, einander selbst die sinnlos gewordenen Meldungen zu. Gerne würden sie ihrem elenden Leben ein Ende machen, aber sie wagen es nicht wegen des Diensteides.

(They were given the choice to become kings or messengers. Just like children they all chose to be messengers. For this reason there are only messengers; they race through the world and, because there are no kings, they call out to one another proclamations that have become meaningless. They would happily put an end to their miserable life but because of their oath of office they don't dare.)[4]

We might say that a new form of *business*—of quasi-official busy-ness and busy-body-ness—comes itself to function as the work of incarnation, as the production site of the flesh of the People. For Clark, such agitated racing about is precisely what is *happening* in the upper half of David's painting, a spectral state of affairs—the messengers have outlived their purpose—that constitutes a kind of *shame* that will forever haunt modernism. (At some level Clark seems to be saying that *artists* would like to put an end to their miserable life but because of their oath of office they do not dare.) We might even say that the abstract material out of which the upper half of the painting is made just is the ectoplasmic substance of this haunting: "In a sense . . . I . . . am saying that the upper half is a display of technique. But display is too neutral a word: for the point I am making, ultimately, is that technique in modernism is a kind of shame: something that asserts itself as the truth of picturing, but always against picturing's best and most desperate efforts" (48). In David, this shame emerges precisely at the point and in the space where "'People' ought to appear" (ibid.). What appears at the missing place of the new sovereign body is rather a kind of dreamwork made painterly flesh in the pure activity of painting; the empty upper half of the image forms not so much a vacancy as the site of an excess of pressure, a signifying stress that opens onto a vision of painting as *Triebschicksal*, as a vicissitude of the drive recalling the seemingly senseless running about—the uncannily busy bodies—of Kafka's messengers:

> And yet the single most extraordinary feature of the picture . . . is its whole upper half being empty. Or rather (here is what is unprecedented), not being empty, exactly, not being a satisfactory representation of nothing or nothing much—of an absence in which whatever the subject is has become present—but something more like a representation of painting, of painting as pure activity. Painting as material, therefore. Aimless. In the end detached from any one representational task. Bodily. Generating (monotonous) orders out of itself, or maybe out of ingrained habit. A kind of automatic writing. (45)

Keeping Kafka's text in mind, we might characterize this writing as *traumamtliches Schreiben*, a neologism that brings together the meanings: dream, trauma, and *Amt* or office. My argument in the following will be that Marx's labor theory of value concerns precisely this dimension of the *traumamtlich* as the site at which a surplus of immanence—the royal remains left to the People—comes to be elaborated and managed as the real subject-matter of political economy. His theory concerns, that is, the flesh as a social substance *materially abstracted* from the busy body of labor, a substance he will famously refer to as *gespenstische Gegenständlichkeit*, the spectral objectivity/materiality of value. As will become clear, what is truly at issue in Marx's labor theory—the nature of this spectral stuff and its modes of production—spans the distinction between industrial and "office" work.

To return to *The Death of Marat*: that this inaugural moment of modernism is one that already pertains to political economy and to the "busy-ness" matters with which it is concerned is signaled in the painting by way of a small, easily overlooked detail. Clark dedicates considerable attention to the bits of paper visible in the painting, the most legible of which is Charlotte Corday's own letter of introduction and appeal to Marat's benevolence. More important for Clark is the barely legible scrap on the orange cart that would appear to be Marat's own last letter. Apropos of the words just out of sight in the letter and presumed to be "de la patrie," Clark asks,

> But is there a final phrase at all? Of course there looks to be something; but it is so scrappy and vestigial, an extra few words where there really is no room left for anything, that the reader continually double-takes, as if reluctant to accept that writing, of all things, can decline to this state of utter visual elusiveness. Surely if I look again—and look hard enough—the truth will out. For spatially, this is the picture's starting point. It is closeness incarnate. (40)

Clark adds that these bits of painted writing "become the figure of the picture's whole imagining of the world and the new shape it is taking. . . . The boundaries between the discursive and the visual are giving way, under *some pressure the painter cannot quite put his finger on, though he gets close*" (42; emphasis added).

But as Clark has so persuasively argued, it is in the swirling, vertiginous void that fills the picture's upper half that this pressure finds its "proper" place—its *nonresting place*—in the visual field. The spectral materiality of the flesh torn from the body of the king finds its inaugural *modern* figuration in that dense, agitated, painterly writing on the wall. Clark is right, then, to see in the painting the opening onto a new aesthetic dimension and one that has a very precise historical index. What makes modernism modernism is that its basic materials are compelled to engage with and, as it were, model the dimension of the flesh inflamed by the representational deadlock situated at the transition from royal to popular sovereignty. What in historical experience can no longer be elevated—sublimated—by way of codified practices of picture-making to the dignity of religious, moral, or political allegory, introduced into a realm of institutionally (and, ultimately, transcendentally) authorized meanings, now achieves its sublimity in a purely immanent fashion. The vicissitudes of this abstract materiality itself become the *subject-matter* of the arts: what art deals with, the formal and thematic subject matter of its aesthetic negotiations; but also where the subject is inscribed, where it is libidinally implicated and *at work* in the image.

Toward the very end of his chapter on the painting, Clark returns to the remaining bit of paper resting on the crate, an assignat for five livres. This piece of revolutionary currency first issued in 1790 as an emergency measure in response to the flight of gold and coin from the country would come to be guaranteed, at least in principle, by the value of confiscated properties of the Church and aristocracy. The currency lost most of its value in a matter of years and by 1797 this experiment in financial engineering was finally declared to be a failure (as Clark notes, the Terror, by intensifying the force and pace of expropriations, initially led to a temporary increase in the value of the currency). This was the same year that the English Parliament passed a law releasing the Bank of England from the obligation to convert paper currency into coin upon demand.[5] For Clark, the presence of the assignat in the painting serves as a placeholder for a fundamental uncertainty that must have haunted the revolution as a whole and Jacobins like David in particular, one that concerned the "arbitrariness of the sign"—and so the possible lack of any ultimate reference—under which the revolution was staged: "To believe in oneself as ushering in Nature's kingdom, and to think there was no time to lose if it was to be secured against its enemies; and yet to know in one's heart of hearts that what was being built was just another form of artifice, was wayward and unpredictable as the rest. Another arbitrariness. Another law for the lion and the ox" (50). Clark suggests, in other words, that the question haunting the revolution and at some level symbolized by the fragile value of its currency concerned the ultimate source of legitimacy for the displacement and redistribution of the exceptional power and authority previously concentrated in the sovereign person.

What I will be exploring in the following is a more specific question signaled, in my view, by the presence of the assignat in this inaugural painting of modernism, namely, that of the role of political economy in this displacement and redistribution. What the assignat indicates, in my reading, is that the *abstract material* that seems to flow from the body of Marat to the upper half of the painting darkly figures—in a nonfigural manner—what would ultimately provide the substance of value circulating through the new bourgeois order: the (surplus) value *materially abstracted* from the body of labor, the very "stuff" that would, in Marx's view, come to form the medium of the social bond in capitalist societies. What David's painting bears witness to is thus not only the passage from royal to popular sovereignty—and the impasses haunting the representation of the People for postmonarchical societies—but also from the political theology of sovereignty to the political economy of the wealth of nations. What is at issue in this peculiar effluence that comes to fill the upper half of David's painting is, I am arguing, a shift in the nature of the medium in which our precious subject-matter circulates and in which our fundamental social bonds are sealed. We will, in other words, be tracking in the domain of political economy what I have characterized as a surplus of immanence released into the social body by the ostensible "excarnation" of sovereignty. Marx, as I have noted, analyzed this surplus under the rather remarkable heading of *gespenstische Gegenständlichkeit*, spectral materiality. It is, I will argue, only against this background that we can fully grasp the logic behind Jacques Derrida's decision to accompany his study of the spectral in Marx's work by a running commentary on *Hamlet*.

The editors of a volume of essays on the "Republican Body" have put the subject-matter at issue quite succinctly: "With democracy the concept of the nation replaced the monarch and sovereignty was dispersed from the king's body to all bodies. *Suddenly every body bore political weight....* With the old sartorial and behavioral codes gone, bodies were less legible, and a person's place in the nation was unclear."[6] My interest here is in the nature of the *matter* that accounts for the new political weight and value of every citizen and in political economy as a site in which this weight begins to be taken into account precisely by efforts to weigh it, reckon with it, subject it, as it were, to double-entry bookkeeping without ever really grasping the real nature of the "double" involved. My claim is that the fantasmatic substance once borne by the bearer of the royal office becomes a *traumamtlich* dimension of social life elaborated above all in economic activities and relations. The King's Two Bodies becomes, as it were, every body's busy-ness.

III

In a recent book-length essay on the unique temporal ubiquity of contemporary global capitalism with the telling title, *24/7*, Jonathan Crary has argued that sleep represents the last fragile remnant of the human lifeworld not yet fully colonized by the mad rhythms of production and consumption, the site where our busy bodies can still, if only for ever more brief intervals and often only with the help of medication, withdraw from their "oath of office."[7] Building on Marx's reflections on the "natural barriers" to capital accumulation, Crary implicitly compares the "triumphal installation of a 24/7 world" (17) with an act of *decreation* whereby the most basic distinctions established by the act of creation—those between night and day and darkness and light—have been revoked. "More concretely," he writes, "it is like a state of emergency, when a bank of floodlights are suddenly switched on in the middle of the night, seemingly as a response to some extreme circumstances, but which never get turned off and become domesticated into a permanent condition. The planet becomes reimagined as a non-stop work site or an always open shopping mall of infinite choices, tasks, selections, and digressions" (17). A prerogative belonging to the sovereign—the decision on the state of emergency/exception—has, in a word, at some level bled into the chronic rhythms of economic life. What Crary is suggesting is that exposure to the exceptional force of law (that can in principle suspend its application) and exposure to the exigencies of an economic machine that now runs 24/7, enter into a zone of indistinction, to use Giorgio Agamben's favored formulation. To be caught in the glare of such floodlights that would seem to decreate night and day is, paradoxically, to be rendered ever more creaturely, ever more purely enjoined to the mere management of life, however infinite and entertaining the choices it might comprise.[8] To use Nietzsche's famous term, the life of "the last man" is, in all its blithe nihilism, an infinitely busy one.

Against this background, one might link the manic state of those creaturely messengers described in Kafka's short fragment to the moment in *The Castle* when the novel's protagonist, K., is shocked out of his cognac-induced somnolence by the sudden lighting of the courtyard where he had been resting under blankets in a sleigh, ostensibly waiting for the mysterious castle official Klamm: "At that—just as K. was engaged in taking a long sip—it became bright, the electric light came on, not only inside, on the stairs, in the passage, and in the corridor, but outside above the entrance. Footsteps could be heard descending the stairs, the bottle fell from K.'s hand, cognac spilled onto a fur, K. jumped from the sleigh."[9] We might say that both the messengers and K. are addressees of an imperious interpellation that no longer issues from this or that identifiable agent or official but from a lifeworld that has itself come to resemble a kind of office that never goes dark. In this sense, "24/7" can be viewed as another formula for what I have characterized as the *traumamtlich* dimension of modern life.

Here one will recall that K.'s fundamental dilemma pertains to the question as to whether he was truly "called" to be a land surveyor by the castle, whether he has a proper vocation there, a proper *Berufsarbeit*, to use the term favored by Max Weber in his account of the spirit of capitalism. In a certain sense, K. is demanding of the castle officials that they issue a proper *Arbeitsanforderung* or demand for work. K.'s business at the castle would, at some level, seem to be to reanimate the old spirit of capitalism that calls one to a proper calling. What he encounters instead is a sort of constant chatter that provides no orientation, but only diffuse "excitations" (from *ex-citare*, to call out or summon).[10]

This is quite literally the case in the episode early in the novel when K. tries to clarify the nature of his *Berufsarbeit* by calling the castle authorities from the telephone at the inn where he has spent the first night of his sojourn in the village at the foot of the castle hill. Overcoming the general suspicion among the patrons at the inn that his efforts would remain fruitless, K. picks up the phone. What he hears on the other end is something like the acoustic equivalent of the battery of floodlights in Crary's image of a state of exception that has become the norm of the unworlded world, the decreated creation, of 24/7:

> From the mouthpiece came a humming [*aus der Hörmuschel kam ein Summen*], the likes of which K. had never heard on the telephone before. It was as though the humming of countless childlike voices—but it wasn't humming either, it was singing, the singing of the most distant, of the most utterly distant, voices—as though a single, high-pitched yet utterly strong voice had emerged out of this humming in some quite impossible way and now drummed against one's ears as if demanding to penetrate more deeply into something other than one's wretched hearing. K. listened [*horchte*] without telephoning, with his left arm propped on the telephone stand and he listened thus [*horchte so*]. (20)

What Crary ultimately wants to underline with that image of floodlights—and the essay as a whole might be viewed as an unpacking of this basic insight—is the belonging together of the logic of the security state, with its demand for constant vigilance and ubiquitous surveillance, and that of neoliberal political economy with its demand for constant production, consumption, communication, interconnectedness, interindebtedness, and profit-oriented self-management. The pressure of 24/7 vigilance informs, that is, not only the security apparatus of the state but its political economy as well. The blurring of the boundaries between corporate and state data mining—our most recent "extractive" industry supported, in turn, by the mining of rare earth metals—would then be only one symptom of this convergence of political and economic tendencies in a ubiquitous pressure for productive wakefulness.[11] Sleep, as Crary argues, would thus indeed seem to represent something like a final frontier where the exigencies of a 24/7 world—a world at some level unworlded or, as I have put it, decreated—run up against the recalcitrance of human embodiment. The paradox of a 24/7 environment would thus seem to be that only in sleep do we inhabit a truly human world, one not fully adapted to, (de)created for, the inhuman rhythms of 24/7 routines of work, consumption, connectivity, and vigilance.

In his novels, Kafka's protagonists are everywhere falling asleep at precisely the wrong moment. In one of the final episodes of *The Castle*, for example, we find K. walking the corridors of the *Herrenhof*, the inn where castle officials stay when they have business in the village. He is still searching for ways to reach Klamm, if only by way of further intermediaries. He finally enters a room where he hopes, if only by chance, to find one of those intermediaries, Erlanger, "one of the first secretaries of Klamm" (239). He finds himself in "a small room, more than half of it occupied by a wide bed" (257). The bed's inhabitant, another secretary named Bürgel, welcomes K. and initiates him into various aspects of his life as a castle official, which, as Bürgel suggests, is the only life one has there since, as he puts it, "we don't acknowledge any distinction between ordinary time and work time. Such distinctions are alien to us" (262). All life is, in a word, official life, *amtliches Leben*—or more accurately: *traumamtliches Leben*, one in which the distinction between living and dreaming has been officially suspended, where the *Arbeitsanforderung* of one's office ramifies into the most intimate parts of one's life. All space thereby becomes a kind of office, and a bed a form of office furniture: "Oh, for anyone who could stretch out and sleep soundly, for any sound sleeper, this bed would be truly delicious. But even for someone like myself, who is always tired but cannot sleep, it does some good, I spend a large part of the day in it, dispatching all my correspondence and questioning the parties" (259). The rest of the chapter is for the most part taken up by Bürgel's vague and convoluted account of rare contingencies that might in principle allow "a party" to achieve his goals with castle authorities, goals normally impossible to achieve even with "a lifetime of grueling effort," as he puts it (261). The reader gets the very strong sense that Bürgel is effectively hypnotizing K., seducing him into somnolence, by way of a description of the possibilities of the sort of decisive and saving action that K. has been seeking all along, possibilities that are, however, effectively available only there, in the "here and now" of Brügel's own speech. K. is put to sleep by a discourse on the need for vigilance; he sleeps through the moment being described to him as his singular possibility of salvation. In Freudian terms, it is as if K. falls asleep at the precise point of a possible analytic breakthrough in the "here and now" of the transference. Kafka, ever the master of proliferating ambiguities, also hints that this "act" of falling asleep might itself be viewed as the true and heroic triumph K. had been pursuing all along. This and other such hints, however, get immediately taken up into the darker story of constantly—and somehow inevitably—missed chances.

In a 24/7 economy it is clear that one is "chronically" at risk of missing an opportunity, of failing to be vigilant, of failing to be in the know. Crary thus emphasizes the *fantasmatic* aspect of life lived under the pressure of its demands:

> Now there are numerous pressures for individuals to reimagine and refigure themselves as being of the same consistency and values as the dematerialized commodities and social connections in which they are immersed so extensively. Reification has proceeded to the point where the individual has to invent a self-understanding that optimizes or facilitates their participation in digital milieus and speeds. Paradoxically, this means impersonating the inert and the inanimate.... Because one cannot literally enter any of the electronic mirages that constitute the interlocking marketplaces of global consumerism, one is obliged to construct *fantasmatic compatibilities* between the human and a realm of choices that is fundamentally unlivable. (99–100; emphasis added)

As Kantorowicz has argued, such fantasmatic compatibilities—at least with respect to wakefulness—were in the late middle ages and early modernity conceived as part and parcel of the office of the king. More precisely, they were seen as part of the charge of the king's virtually real

double. The ideal of the *rex exsomnis*, the king who has no rest, added the
dimension of perpetual vigilance to the other attributes sustained by the
king's "second body," those of his ubiquity, his character of *lex animata*,
and his infallibility.[12] One might thus view the 24/7 regime of neoliberal
capitalism as a sort of popularization/democratization of the ideal of the
rex exsomnis and its diffusion into the broader fabric of social life. Thus
24/7 would be another "name" for the displacement or *Entstellung* of the
political theology of sovereignty by the political economy of the wealth of
nations, of the metamorphosis of the King's Two Bodies into the People's
Two Bodies.[13] We might say that at this point, the psychopathology of
everyday (waking) life and the interpretation of dreams enter into a zone
of indistinction.

Michel Foucault has for his part argued that the attribute of perpetual vigilance entered into our general conception of governmental power
largely by way of the ideal of "pastoral" care developed in biblical and classical antiquity and further elaborated in Christianity. As Foucault put it
in the first of his Tanner Lectures delivered in 1979,

> The Greek leader had naturally to make decisions in the interest of
> all; he would have been a bad leader had he preferred his personal in-
> terest. But his duty was a glorious one: even if in war he had to give up
> his life, such a sacrifice was offset by something extremely precious:
> immortality. He never lost. By way of contrast, shepherdly kindness is
> much closer to "devotedness." That's his constant concern. When they
> sleep, *he* keeps watch.

With respect to the ideal of shepherdly vigilance, Foucault adds, "First,
he acts, he works, he puts himself out, for those he nourishes and who are
asleep. Second, he watches over them."[14]

In the second lecture, in which he takes up the modern elaborations
of at least certain strands of pastoral power, Foucault addresses the institution of the police that was, in the seventeenth and eighteenth centuries,
understood broadly as public policy or civil administration. Among the
areas of concern of police administration we find a return of the dimension of glory—now under the heading of *splendor*—that he had first seen
as standing outside the purview of the pastoral paradigm. Drawing on
one of the first utopian programs for a fully policed state, Turguet de
Mayenne's *Aristo-Democratic Monarchy*—a work that includes the first
mention of the term "political economy"—Foucault divides the duties of

the police into two categories: "First, the police has to do with everything providing the city with adornment, form, and splendor. Splendor denotes not only the beauty of a state ordered to perfection; but also its strength, its vigor." The second category, which Turguet brings under the heading of "communication," includes the charge of fostering "working and trading relations between men, as well as aid and mutual help." Summarizing his findings, Foucault suggests that the task of the police—their fundamental charge—was in effect to cultivate a sort of *sur-charge* or *surplus of life* on behalf of the state: "As a form of rational intervention wielding political power over men, the role of the police is to supply them with *a little extra life*; and by so doing, supply the state with a little extra strength."[15] The following reflections will attempt to gather these motifs into a coherent story about the fate of this surplus life, the vicissitudes of this splendid surcharge of animation that became the *subject-matter* of classical political economy and has become an ever more dominant dimension of contemporary capitalism. As we shall see, the story concerns historical dislocations and displacements in the sites, procedures, and fantasies in and through which social bonds are formed in the flesh of embodied subjects, flesh that at a certain moment in our history comes to be weighed in balances that ever more determine our individual and collective destinies.

During the final, proofreading stage of the preparation of this volume, I was alerted to Gil Anidjar's new work on the historical semantics of blood, an element and medium at times opposed to, at times figured as the very life and soul of, the virtual real dimension I address here under the heading of *flesh*.[16] Reading Anidjar at this late date made me feel a bit like Shylock in the trial scene in *The Merchant of Venice*—a scene I will discuss in detail below—when Portia, in the guise of a young doctor of law, informs him that this bond allows him to cut a pound of flesh from Antonio's body but that he must do so without spilling a drop of the latter's Christian blood. Anidjar's work compellingly insists on the insistence of blood in the story I have tried to tell here, a story about the transformation of social bonds and the fantasies that in large measure sustain them.[17] My own sense is that we are, in the end, both addressing the same dimension—the same *subject-matter*—of social bonds as they have been elaborated in the Christian West but that where I focus on the aspect of *congelation*, Anidjar emphasizes the eternal recurrence, if I might put it that way, of *liquefaction*. We are, that is, addressing different *states* of the subject-matter at issue in the elaboration of social bonds in the early modern and modern State, in the former within a political theology of sovereignty, in the latter within a political economy of wealth. As we shall see, Marx himself addresses these two aspects or states in his analysis of the commodity form (his example here is so and so much fabricated linen):

> Human labor-power in its fluid state, or human labor, creates value, but is not itself value. It becomes value in its coagulated state [*in geronnenem Zustand*], in objective [*gegenständlicher*] form. The value of the linen as a congealed mass of human labor [*als Gallerte menschlicher Arbeit*] can be expressed only as an "objectivity" [*Gegenständlichkeit*], a thing which is materially different from the linen itself and yet common to the linen and all other commodities.[18]

It is this objectivity or materiality that our very doings invoke or conjure that Marx characterizes as spectral, as *gespenstisch*, and it is above all this aspect, one that Marx, two paragraphs later, explicitly links to the *Leibesgestalt*, the fleshly form, of the sovereign, that is my concern in these pages.

I would like to conclude these preliminary remarks by citing a brief passage from Rainer Maria Rilke's 1910 novel, *The Notebooks of Malte Laurids Brigge*, a work I discussed in detail in the final chapter of *The Royal Remains*. As I argued there, Rilke's poetic anthropology of modernity tracks the royal remains into the fabric of everyday life, shows what can happen, that is, once the King's Two Bodies come to belong to every body, become every body's busy-ness. The novel's protagonist, a young and now impoverished Danish aristocrat wandering the streets of Paris and struggling to become a writer, visits, at one point, the psychiatric clinic at Salpêtrière in the hopes of finding relief from agonizing anxieties he is unable to master on his own. While waiting to be seen by these new sorts of masters—in Foucault's terms, these biopolitical experts—the anxieties begin to take shape—to congeal—as the carnal pressure of a sort of second head pushing against the boundaries of the skin. It is a pressure that Malte first experienced in the steadily decaying manor houses—the *Herrenhäuser*—of his childhood, houses at one time linked, as the novel makes clear, to the Danish royal house. At the center of the experience is the registration of a demand—an *Arbeitsanforderung*—to sustain this uncanny carnality, this "extra life," with his own blood:

And then . . . for the first time in many, many years, it was there again. What had filled me with my first, deep horror [*Entsetzen*], when I was a child and lay in bed with fever: the Big Thing [*das Große*]. . . . Now it was there. Now it was growing out of me like a tumor, like a second head, and was a part of me, although it certainly couldn't belong to me, because it was so big. It was there like a large dead animal which, while it was alive, used to be my hand or my arm. And my blood flowed through me and through it, as through one and the same body. And my heart had to beat harder to pump blood into the Big Thing: there was barely enough blood. And the blood entered the Big Thing unwillingly and came back sick and tainted. But the Big Thing swelled and grew over my face like a warm bluish boil, and grew over my mouth, and already my last eye was hidden by its shadow.[19]

As the novel as a whole makes clear, what Malte experiences here as *Entsetzen* or horror is linked to the historical *Ent-setzen* or deposition of the king and more generally of the form of life organized, at a symbolic and imaginary level, by way of the political theology of sovereignty. The subject matter of Malte's *Entsetzen* is the appearance in the real of his *subject-matter*, a surplus of inflamed and agitated flesh with no proper sociosymbolic resting place. It was, as I will be arguing in the following pages, the genius of capitalism to keep this dimension from going to waste or rather to convert this waste product of political theology—these *Königsreste*—into the treasure of political economy, the fundamental substance of which Marx characterized as *gespenstische Gegenständlichkeit*. Under Marx's gaze, what Rilke still elaborated as a psycho-politico-theology of everyday life thereby comes into focus as a psycho-economico-theology of everyday life, a life whose uncanny surplus—whose subject-matter—becomes the subject matter of political economy.

LECTURE I.
ON THE SUBJECT-MATTER OF
POLITICAL THEOLOGY

I

As I have indicated in the introduction, I am attempting to unpack the ambiguity embedded in the phrase, "the subject matter of political economy." My claim is that what is generally studied under the heading of political economy—its subject matter in the conventional sense—demands a special sort of materialism, one attuned to the strange matter or materiality generated by the emergence and sustenance, under ever changing historical circumstances, of human subjectivity. If political economy has a proper subject matter, it has to do with an improper "surplus of matter," a locus of pressure that drives the pursuit of the wealth of nations, that first turns the rational pursuit of ends into a drive. (In the following, when I want to emphasize this second meaning, I will use the hyphenated form: *subject-matter*. The topic or subject matter of this book is, one could say, the modern vicissitudes of *subject-matter*.) No doubt a great deal hangs on the nature of this impropriety, this state of being out of place, unowned, and unclean, a cluster of meanings that brings to mind the famous definition of dirt as "matter in the wrong place." Freud, one will recall, cited that definition in an essay in which he showed "primitive accumulation" in the economic realm to be not so much incremental as excremental in nature, to be linked in a fundamental way to the dirty business of *waste*, the work of *waste management*, and the character traits that may be called for in response to its demands.[20]

Some years ago, Jacques Derrida addressed the "hauntological" dirt of political economy in his sprawling study, *Specters of Marx*.[21] The question that interests me here is one that Derrida repeatedly invokes—or to use his own favored term: *conjures*—without fully developing. It has to do with the guardian spirit of his study, *Hamlet*, and with the historical transformations that link the crisis of sovereignty staged in Shakespeare's play to Marx's elaboration of the spectral objectivity/materiality—Marx calls it *die gespenstische Gegenständlichkeit*—immanent and indeed vital to the commodity form. The nature of this "vitality," this "animation," is, in my view, what is ultimately at issue in the spectral analysis of capitalist modernity and links this project to the larger field of contemporary thinking on the concept of life and of so-called *vibrant matter* more broadly. My hunch is that what is behind the contemporary efflorescence of new materialisms in the humanities is not only a new ethical sensitivity to the liveliness and agency of nonhuman animals, things, "actants," and environments. In my view, they have emerged in large measure under the pressure that Rainer Maria Rilke—in many ways the canonical poet of vibrant matter—characterized as the "vibration of money," the flows, fluxes, and intensities—the vibrancies—of capital in our everyday life.[22] The new materialisms attempt, however, to dispense with "subject-matter," the materiality proper to human subjectivity. The modern and postmodern mutations of that subject-matter that function, as I see it, as a hidden object/cause, as the real *Anstoss*, of the new materialist turn, are my concern here.

To return to the frame of Derrida's study, Hamlet/Marx: What finally links the ghost of a violently deposed king to a central, if fantasmatic, feature of economic life under capitalism, to what we might call its *virtual real*? To relocate the question I first asked in my previous book, *The Royal Remains*, I want to ask here what remains of the royal in that domain of activity in which, to use Adam Smith's famous formulation, we seem merely to actualize our basic human capacity to truck, barter, and exchange one thing for another. What allows for the apparent metamorphosis of at least some part or aspect of the king's deposed body—some *partial object* of political theological legitimacy—into the substance of value of commodities?[23]

At some level the question concerns the shift from one form of fetishism to another, from the fetishism of persons to that of objects of exchange. It is the question of a shift in the locus of the Thing that was with the king, to the (ever more imperious) realm of commodities that thereby come to promise "the real thing." In *Capital*, Marx makes only a few brief references to the earlier, ostensibly premodern mode of fetishism. In his initial presentation of the relative form of value in his analytical reconstruction of the commodity form, Marx writes, for example: "An individual, A, for instance, cannot be 'your majesty' to another individual, B, unless majesty in B's eyes assumes the fleshly form [*Leibesgestalt*] of A, and, moreover, changes facial features, hair and many other things, with every new 'father of his people.'" In a later passage, Marx cites Hegel's notion of a *Reflektionsbestimmung* or reflexive determination as the key to this sort of relational identity: "For instance, one man is king only because other men stand in the relation of subjects to him. They, on the other hand, imagine that they are subjects because he is king."[24]

The point is that the king acquires his royal flesh, comes to enjoy the second, glorious body that forms the subject matter—in both senses of the term—of Ernst Kantorowicz's magisterial study, *King's Two Bodies*, by virtue of his place within a specific set of sociosymbolic relations sustained—or better: *entertained* (in German: *unterhalten*)—by way of the liturgical practices of courtly life beginning with those of anointment, consecration, and ritual acclamation. As Kantorowicz puts it, "the vision of the king as a *persona geminata* is ontological and, as *an effluence of a sacramental and liturgical action* performed at the altar, it is liturgical as well."[25] And as Slavoj Žižek has concisely written apropos of such "effluence," "What is at stake is . . . not simply the split between the empirical person of the king and his symbolic function. The point is rather that this symbolic function *redoubles his very body*, introducing a split between the visible, material, transient body and another, sublime body, a body made of a special, immaterial stuff."[26] What is crucial here is that a symbolic investiture establishes not simply the jointure of body and office—a new suturing, as it were, of the somatic and the normative—but generates in addition, at—or better: *as*—the locus of that suture, the pressure of a surplus carnality, of an additional bit of flesh, that can be—and historically has been—elaborated and figured as a kind of second, virtually real and, indeed, glorious body.[27] It is in this context that Žižek refers to Lacan's remarks apropos of Hamlet's inability to slay Claudius: "What stays Hamlet's arm? It's not fear—he has nothing but contempt for the guy—it's because he knows that *he must strike something other than what's there*."[28] The problem is, in a word, in finding the proper locus of the strike, the locus, that is, of a "special, immaterial stuff" (along with its mode of production). The problem becomes only further exacerbated once the king no longer serves as the principal bearer of sovereignty. New topologies will be needed to orient new kinds of "strikes."

Marx's theory of the fetishism of the commodity and the labor theory of value on which it is based is a contribution to just such a new topology; they allow us, precisely, to approach and analyze this immaterial stuff in its new, thingly location. They concern, I am arguing, a kind of metamorphosis of the king's royal flesh into the spectral materiality of the product of human labor, into the substance of value qua congelation of abstract, homogeneous human labor. What Marx characterizes as the dual character of the labor embodied in commodities is, in a word, a two-body doctrine transferred from the political theology of sovereignty to the realm of political economy. The famous "metaphysical subtleties and theological niceties" [*metaphysische Spitzfindigkeit und theologische Mucken*] that Marx discovered in the realm of commodities once belonged, as Kantorowicz's study makes abundantly clear, to the realm of the king; they are aspects of what I have characterized as *royal remains*.[29] Marx's point is that these remains will remain a locus of unfreedom until we learn to work through them in their simultaneously ontological and liturgical dimensions or, as Derrida characterized the zone at which these two dimensions converge, in their "hauntological" aspect.

   This is, in my view, what generates such difficulties for a Marxist theory and practice of revolution. Marx argues, in effect, that a revolutionary, too, *must strike something other than what's there*. It is this very difficulty that Walter Benjamin tried to adumbrate in his discussion of the *general strike* in his famous essay, "Critique of Violence," and that he would continue to elaborate as the properly messianic dimension of human action. This difficulty is no doubt behind so much of our recent preoccupation with messianism, the messianic, and "messianicity," to use the term Derrida introduces in his Marx book. And as the reference to Lacan also reminds us, this is the very field of action that Freud tried to open as the space of the psychoanalytic clinic. *Striking something other than what's there* would thus seem to be a task located at the intersection of political and libidinal economy, a zone that resonates with tensions vital to the messianic tradition of religious thought and action.

   I will have more to say about Marx's contributions to the mapping of this zone in the next lecture. The crucial signpost in that mapping is his notion of the fetishism of the commodity, our relation, that is, to its special, immaterial stuff. For now I would like to return to the historical question about the mutations and dislocations of that stuff, to what I have characterized as a metamorphosis of the subject-matter of political theology into that of political economy. We might think of it as a shift from the "sovereign form" to the "commodity form" of social mediation, of those processes, that is, through which people come to be bound to one another, to "subjectivize" their social ties within a historical form of life that thereby comes to matter for them.

II

The metamorphosis we are tracking is registered in its own peculiar way in Benjamin Franklin's famous advice to a young tradesman, counsel that became one of Max Weber's central proof-texts for his thesis about the Protestant origins of the "spirit of capitalism." It is worth noting that in his famous study, Weber's argument had already blurred the boundaries between spirit and specter. Weber's central claim was that an irrational kernel of cultic doctrine and practice, one condensed in the notion of the vocational call or *Berufung* (along with the activity of laboring in a call, of *Berufsarbeit*), formed the impetus of the economic rationality of modern capitalism. Weber famously characterized the *manic frugality* of this rationality as a paradoxical mode of enjoyment, one he named "worldly asceticism." As Franklin puts it in a passage cited by Weber: "He that kills a breeding-sow, destroys her offspring to the thousandth generation. He that murders a crown, destroys all that it might have produced, even scores of pounds."[30] The strangeness of Franklin's formulation derives not only from its elevation (in the first metaphor) of a once decried perversity proper to chrematistics—the art of making money—to the highest virtue; it derives as well from the fact that the metaphor of the murdered crown owes its meaning to a prior displacement, murderous or not, of the *sovereign* of the realm by the *coin* of the realm, one prefigured by the imprint of the sovereign's own figure on coins. We can murder a crown in Franklin's sense—perform *economic regicide*—only if the political theology of sovereignty has already been largely absorbed by and translated into the terms of the political economy of the wealth of nations, only when stuff of the king's "surplus body" has been transformed into that of surplus value, the product of a certain mode of human labor the glorious amplification of which Franklin enjoins the young tradesman to enjoy. My argument will be that such enjoyment constitutes the libidinal core of what I see as the *doxology of everyday life* in modern capitalist societies.

Aristotle provides the canonical account of the "fertility" of money as unnatural, as a perversion of nature, in his efforts in Book 1 of the *Politics* to clarify the boundary between the management of the household—economy proper—and the art of gaining wealth. The latter is presented as having no natural limit and thus as inherently *masslos*, without proper measure. Freud will of course make the same claim about human sexuality: it is inherently perverse, inherently in excess of teleological function (the reproduction of the family qua basic economic unit). Like the *clinamen* of the ancient atomists, human sexuality emerges on the basis of a constitutive swerve, in this case from a norm that is established only retroactively. In the terms Derrida uses in his discussion of Marx, Aristotle would seem to want to "exorcize" the perverse dimension of chrematistics from the *oikos*, a dimension that, Aristotle suggests, enters human life by way of coined money, an institution first introduced in Greece only a few centuries earlier. (As with nearly all later standard economic theory, Aristotle assumes that money was introduced to resolve practical and logistical obstacles presented by the practice of barter; as David Graeber and others have suggested, such views might be characterized as "infantile economic theories" concerning the emergence of money and markets, theories on a par with what Freud analyzed under the heading of infantile sexual theories concerning the emergence of babies and the nature of the "exchanges" going on between parents.[31]) That questions of the vitality proper to human flourishing—in contrast to the perversely "vibrant matter" of money—are involved are clear from Aristotle's claim that those bent upon the accumulation of money without limit "are intent upon *living only*, and not upon *living well*," something exemplified in the life of our canonical misers from Plautus's Euclio to Molière's Harpagon to Balzac's Gobseck and Dickens's Scrooge.[32] What these misers all show, however, is that such "bare living" can have its own peculiar intensity and jouissance and indeed one that brings it into uncanny proximity with a life of virtue, though one that would perhaps have been unrecognizable to Aristotle.[33] We might call it: compulsive fidelity to the *clinamen*.

The boundary zone between human life and the perverse vitality of money qua symbolic medium of exchange takes center stage in Shakespeare's *The Merchant of Venice* in the guise of the pound of flesh around which the action of the play largely orbits. I would like to dwell on the role that this famous "piece of the real" comes to play in the play or, perhaps better, on the *work* it performs in the play's narrative and dramatic economy. My hunch is that Derrida's appeal to *Hamlet* to draw out the spectral dimension at issue in Marx's thought can be made if supplemented—if fleshed out—by reflections on the *Merchant*. In order to grasp the stakes of Shakespeare's most famous tragedy—especially for modern readers—we need, I am suggesting, the resources of his most problematic comedy. (As a nonspecialist, discussing Shakespeare always feels terribly presumptuous; hopefully one will view this trespass less as tragic hubris and more as a bit of comedic *chuztpadik*.)

There can be little doubt that this work is deeply informed by the Pauline tradition concerning the notion of the flesh and the larger semantic field in which it figures, one articulated as a series of oppositions. Not only flesh and spirit but also: letter and spirit; literal and figural; particular and universal; law and love; and no doubt many more. As I have suggested, what ultimately drives the formation of this series of oppositions along with the various individual and collective "dramas" associated with them is the ultimately enigmatic jointure of the somatic and the normative that defines human life. What Paul, too, is struggling with in these oppositions is the difficulty of conceptualizing the substance of that jointure, this third element in excess of both the somatic and the normative that both links and leaks into the two domains as the uncanny cause of various inflammatory conditions. Whether such conditions are determined to be "auto-immune" or not will depend, in the end, on how one comes to understand this third element and whether it needs to be cured, managed, quarantined, put to work, put into play. Freud, for his part, staked his own new science on the hypothesis that this element was the very subject-matter of human sexuality—what he called *libido*— and that our "sexuation" comprises the generic site of its turbulent and often traumatic emergence, of our (surplus) life in the flesh.[34] The shift from the political theology of sovereignty to the political economy of the wealth of nations is, I am arguing, a shift from one "epochal" mode of shaping our life in the flesh to another.

To begin, it is worth recalling that the first metaphor invoked by Franklin to illustrate the fecundity of capital is used by Shylock in his initial negotiation with Antonio. As a usurer, Shylock embodies the perversion of chrematistics in its purity, a perversion that is of course less visible in the practices of Antonio, the real merchant of the play's title. The fact that people often think that the title refers to Shylock is echoed in the first question asked by Portia (dressed as Balthazar, a young doctor of law) in the famous trial scene: "Which is the merchant here? And which the Jew?" (4.1.176). According to Aristotle, however, they both belong together as those who pursue a spurious kind of wealth:

> There are two sorts of wealth-getting. . . . One is a part of household management, the other is retail trade: the former necessary and honorable, while that which consists in exchange is justly censured; for it is unnatural, and a mode by which men gain from one another. The most hated sort, and with the greatest reason, is usury, which makes a gain out of money itself, and not from the natural object of it. For money was intended to be used in exchange, but not to increase at interest. And this term interest [*tokos*, lit. "offspring"], which means the birth of money from money, is applied to the *breeding of money* because the offspring resembles the parent. Wherefore of all modes of getting wealth this is the most unnatural.[35]

It was W. H. Auden who first noted that Antonio would seem to be guilty of yet another perversion of nature and natural fecundity, namely, homosexuality. And indeed, the various forms of lack that seem to lay at the bottom of his melancholy have encouraged at least one reader to see him not simply as a sinner or *pécheur*—one given over to the life of the flesh—but also as a new incarnation of the *roi-pêcheur*, the wounded Fisher King who can no longer fulfill his office as head of the Grail Society—who can perhaps reign but no longer govern—and so has become dependent on new forms of nourishment/enrichment that are material and unnatural rather than spiritual and supernatural.[36] As we shall see, for both Foucault and Agamben that the king reigns without governing represents the culmination of the process whereby the political theology of sovereignty is absorbed into the political economy of the nation-state and the modes of management adapted to life in commodity-producing societies. In this context it is worth recalling Hans Jürgen Syberberg's stunning dramaturgical innovation in his film version of Wagner's *Parsifal*. There the status of the *roi-pêcheur* as king who reigns but no longer governs—we might say: who is valid but no longer has any meaning, *der gilt, aber bedeutet nicht*—is externalized as a fleshy remnant of the "second body," as a free-floating bit of *gespenstische Gegenständlichkeit* (perhaps just about a pound's worth), now displayed on a pillow carried by the members of the Grail Society.[37] It is a disturbingly apt rendering of the epochal caesura between the no longer viable political theology of sovereignty and the not yet hegemonic political economy of the wealth of nations, a caesura in which the royal remains remain as yet unclaimed. Syberberg's staging emphasizes the aspect of a stalled sacrament, a Eucharist no longer able to establish the communion and community of a *corpus mysticum*.[38]

The play takes off, of course, from Bassanio's desire to dig out from the mountain of debt in "money and love" he admits to owing Antonio. The pursuit of the beautiful, virtuous, and wildly wealthy Portia is his way of doubling down on those debts, of staking everything on one last gamble. And indeed the entire play is organized around the seemingly inextricable knots tying money and *eros* together, knots tied, in turn, by a series of oaths, contracts, and covenants. Antonio agrees to finance the venture, but lacking liquidity he ends up turning to Shylock, thereby breaking with his custom of generally avoiding the giving or taking of interest on loans.[39]

In their initial encounter in the play, Shylock appears to justify the taking of "usance" by reference to Jacob's innovative pastoral intervention that caused Laban's "ewes" to birth the striped lambs that were by prior agreement to be his. When asked by Antonio whether this scriptural reference were "inserted to make interest good," that is, whether his gold and silver were, in essence, so many ewes and rams, Shylock curtly replies: "I cannot tell; I make it breed as fast." In an aside to Bassanio, Antonio characterizes Shylock's brief "midrash" as an example of *hermeneutic* usury, of squeezing out of Scripture a surplus sense that serves one's own advantage. Antonio repeats the metaphor after hearing Shylock's inventory of insults and curses that he, Antonio, had, over the years, heaped upon the Jew: "If thou wilt lend this money, lend it not / As to thy friends, for when did friendship take / A breed for barren metal of his friend? / But lend it rather to thine enemy, / Who, if he break, thou mayst with better face / Exact the penalty" (1.3.143–47). Here Antonio seems to be engaging in his own bit of Biblical exegesis by alluding to the Deuteronomic stipulation that prohibited Jews from lending to their Jewish brethren (this Old Testament passage is thought to be among the first documented *prohibitions* of usury in antiquity).

After listing the insults he has had to endure, Shylock effectively turns the other cheek and offers to Antonio an interest-free loan. He does, of course, insist "in merry sport" on the famous penalty: "let the forfeit / Be nominated for an equal pound / Of your fair flesh, to be cut off and taken / In what part of your body pleaseth me" (1.3.160–64). That Antonio accepts the offer as a sign that "there is much kindness in the Jew" suggests that Shylock's offer to "take no doit / Of usance" (ibid., 150–52) was read as a sign of quasi-Christian fellowship, as the extension of the narrow, "particularist" sphere of Jewish brotherhood into the universal one of the Church. At this point, a surplus of "usance"—we might say: of *jew-usance*, Jewish enjoyment of usury—is seemingly replaced by a surplus of kindness, one that provisionally serves as a sign of being of the same kind. In the end, of course, all bets are off and this economy of kindness is undone in the most exorbitant ways in large measure, no doubt, because of Shylock's own forced forfeiture of flesh, his daughter Jessica. Keeping with Portia's famous characterization of the quality of mercy, we might say that Shylock is, in the end, mercifully strained to choose Christian "kindness." As Mladen Dolar has argued, the final gift of mercy Shylock is compelled to accept—he is made an offer he cannot refuse, as Don Corleone would have put it—introduces a new level and intensity of indebtedness. We might summarize Dolar's argument by saying that Portia's achievement in this context is to "portially" adjust the logic of the debt economy ostensibly represented by Shylock in the direction of its infinite *amourtization*.[40]

As I have noted, the figure of the "pound of flesh" is profoundly overdetermined in the play. We do not actually know until quite late in the play what part of the body is involved in the penalty added to the contract "in merry sport." It is not unreasonable to assume that Shylock is invoking the rite of circumcision, that the penalty in question involves a demand that, so to speak, Antonio put some *foreskin* in the game. But not unlike the "anal object" in Freud's understanding, the figure of the pound of flesh quickly enters into a series of equivalences—consonant with but also exceeding the Pauline field of terms—that extend from money to child to foreskin to phallus to the literal and spiritual flesh of the heart, while the cutting of the flesh oscillates—"vibrates"—in meaning between butchery, circumcision, castration, homicide, and the cruel rigor of the debtor–creditor relation and of contract law more generally. Indeed, the flesh and its cutting seem to mark the very site and action of the opening of the space of possibility of this series of equivalences and the "primary process" of their associative movement, that is, of the very splitting between and various modes of jointure of the literal and figural, the concrete and the abstract, the material and the spiritual. These primary processes are also palpable in the play through the proliferation of punning beginning with Antonio's offer to Bassanio, upon hearing of his friend's plan to get clear of debt, to share with him "my purse, my person, my extremest means" (1.1.141). The puns in the play function as sites where, as it were, the word becomes flesh and the flesh becomes word, sites where words themselves come to assume the status of "partial objects." The pound of flesh finally offers us the figure of a value that can be extracted—or perhaps better: *materially abstracted*—from a living body and weighed in the balances. What is weighed here is, however, no longer that which makes a king a king—the partial object of political theology—but something in or of the body that has been invested not with royal office but with economic value in a mercantile society.

There would seem to be little room for reflection about sovereignty in the play, little concern with the transformation of the King's Two Bodies into the People's Two Bodies and the management of the latter by way of political economic calculations. I would suggest, however, that just such a shift in the meaning of what is weighed in the balances is underlined by one of the biblical texts alluded to in the trial scene, the Book of Daniel. At different points in the scene, each party—first Shylock and then, for the other side, Gratiano—claims to see in Portia their own Daniel, their own learned and upright judge (Daniel means, in Hebrew, "God is my judge"). Portia, for her part, appears in the guise of a young doctor of laws whose name, Balthazar, evokes the name given to Daniel by his Babylonian masters, Beltheshazzar, as well as that of the king himself, Belshazzar. According to Daniel's interpretation of the writing on the wall of the king's vision, the sovereign has reached the end of his royal road: "This is the interpretation of the matter: MENE, God has numbered the days of your kingship and brought it to an end; TEKEL, you have been weighed in the balances and found wanting; PERES, your kingdom is divided and given to the Medes and Persians" (Daniel 6:26–28).

The biblical intertext inscribes into the trial proceedings a crisis of royal sovereignty and therewith the beginnings of the metamorphosis of the subject-matter of political theology into that of political economy, of a partial object of political theological legitimacy—now found to be wanting—into what Marx would identify as the spectral materiality of the commodity, the value materially abstracted from the body of the worker and transferred, as so and so much special, immaterial stuff, as so much flesh, to the product of labor qua commodity. In the Shakespearean figure of the pound of flesh we glimpse, I am arguing, what will be produced when the "Un-Nature" of chrematistics comes to be directly conjoined with the laboring body, when they form a single, wildly fecund matrix producing, of course, not just a pound of flesh but as Franklin put it, "many scores of pounds." In *The Merchant of Venice*, a play written in the midst of England's transformation into a mercantile society, the way of all flesh long exemplified by the rise and fall of kings begins to be registered as the *weight of all flesh*, the rise and fall of the value of the substance of value.[41] As the play makes clear, such a transformation was imagined to be, at least on some level, linked to—we might say: haunted by—Jews, Judaism, Jewishness.

III

To return to Derrida, one will recall that he introduces the first chapter of his Marx book with a citation from act 1 of *Hamlet* in which the hero takes on the mandate of his father's ghost to set right what has been put out of joint by, precisely, the murder of a crown (1.5.187–89). Derrida for his part justifies the recourse to Shakespeare not only by noting Marx's own tendency to cite the poet but above all by underlining the famous opening line of *The Communist Manifesto*, "Ein Gespenst geht um in

Europa—das Gespenst des Kommunismus": "As in *Hamlet*, the Prince of a rotten state, *everything begins by the apparition of a specter*" (4; emphasis added). Derrida quickly goes on to propose a *grand récit* of such apparitions, one exhibiting the sort of historicity without historicism that will allow him, later in the book, to posit a "messianicity" without messianism:

> Haunting is historical, to be sure, but it is not *dated*, it is never docilely given a date in the chain of presents, day after day, according to the instituted order of a calendar. Untimely, it does not come to, it does not happen to, it does not befall, one day, Europe, as if the latter, at a certain moment of its history, had begun to suffer from a certain evil, to let itself be *inhabited* in its inside, that is, haunted by a foreign guest. Not that that guest is any less a stranger for having always occupied the domesticity of Europe. But there was no inside, there was nothing inside before it. *The ghostly would displace itself like the movement of this history*. Haunting would mark the very existence of Europe. It would open the space and the relation to self of what is called by this name, at least since the Middle Ages. (4; emphasis added)

Paraphrasing somewhat, the claim is that the European *economy*—its domesticity, its *oikos*—has always been troubled by an alien presence—something *unheimlich*—immanent to its very constitution. Against this background, one is tempted to replace the word, *das Unheimliche*, with *das Unökonomische*, "the Un-Economic." Both terms point to some excess, some surplus, in the household that both does and does not belong there, that is produced there but ought not to be there, a surplus that is not just too much stuff, too many commodities, but rather something more akin to a disturbing sort of remainder, to "matter in the wrong place." It is, as Marx was to show, something that generates its share of confusion for the science of political economy. As I have noted, the anxiety pertaining to some excess in the *oikos* was already there in Aristotle's efforts to keep a certain improper and *un-natural* chrematistic stranger outside the household. What does management of the household—*oikonomia*, economics—mean if it is *sur-charged* with managing spirits?

It is worth recalling that in a remarkable essay on *Hamlet* from 1956, Carl Schmitt rehearses parts of his own earlier *grand récit* of the Eurocentric global order, of what he referred to there as the *Nomos der Erde*.[42] He proceeds by focusing on what he explicitly refers to as the *Mehrwert* or surplus value that, in his view, served to elevate Shakespeare's play from

Trauerspiel to genuine tragedy and, indeed, transform it into a "living myth." Schmitt's search for the source of the sublime object of the play leads him along various paths of interpretation that need not detain us here. In the context of the present discussion, his crucial insight is that the surplus value circulating in *Hamlet* pertains not only to the turbulence generated for the figure of the sovereign by the religious strife of the period, turbulence that, in his view, came to be embodied in the person of James I. Equally important is the claim that at the core of this turbulence lay another, even greater challenge to the political theology of the sovereign: the emergence of England as a mercantile economy or what Schmitt characterizes as England's "elemental appropriation of the sea [*dem elementaren Aufbruch zu der grossen Seenahme*]" (59):

> Measured in terms of the progress toward civilization that the ideal of continental statehood . . . signifies, Shakespeare's England still appears to be barbaric, that is, in a pre-state condition. However, measured in terms of the progress toward civilization that the Industrial Revolution . . . signifies, Elizabethan England appears to be involved in a phenomenal departure from a terrestrial to a maritime existence—a departure, which, in its outcome, the Industrial Revolution, caused a much deeper and more fundamental revolution than those on the European continent and which far exceeded the overcoming of the "barbaric Middle Ages" that the continental state achieved. (65)[43]

What endows *Hamlet* with its surplus value is, in other words, the fact that in it are registered historical currents that would culminate in economies organized around the production of surplus value and a world order in which the political theology of sovereignty will be more or less absorbed into the political economy of nation-states (pushing, for their part, against the limits of their internal and external juridical organization). I am suggesting, then, that *The Merchant of Venice* renders explicit what in *Hamlet* is registered only as a sort of underlying dreamwork summoned forth—or as we might say: *excited*—by structural transformations of the social order. It was Schmitt himself who argued apropos of *Hamlet* that, "even the dreams that the dramatist weaves into his play must be able to become the dreams of the spectators, with all the condensations and displacements of recent events" (36). But as Schmitt also argues, these "recent events" include the opening of a *structural interregnum* that would not fully take shape in the lifetime of the London audience of

Shakespeare's play. *Merchant* helps to identify the key historical forces at issue in this opening along with the semantic and symbolic transformations it brings in its wake. As Ben Nelson has argued, these transformations ultimately push beyond the Pauline encoding of social relations still operative in the play; they push, that is, from the universal brotherhood of Christian society toward the "universal Otherhood" that characterizes the social relations of modern commercial societies.[44] These are societies organized around the production, circulation, and accumulation of the special, immaterial stuff once retained by the sublime physiology of the king.

For Derrida as well as for me, what ultimately distinguishes the spectral historicity of Europe from other histories of the "European Spirit"—the Hegelian as well as the Schmittian one—comes down to the dimension that I have been calling the *flesh*:

> As soon as one no longer distinguishes spirit from specter, the former assumes a body, it incarnates itself as spirit, in the specter.... The specter is a paradoxical incorporation, the becoming-body, a certain phenomenal and carnal form of the spirit. It becomes, rather, some "thing" that remains difficult to name: neither soul nor body, and both one and the other. For it is *flesh and phenomenality* that give to the spirit its spectral apparition. (6; emphasis added)[45]

And as Derrida emphasizes, this "thing" that remains so difficult to name appears, in the context of *Hamlet* and in medieval and early modern sovereignty more generally, in—or perhaps better: with—*the body of the king*. It is, as I have been arguing, the very thing that leads to the strange doctrine explored by Kantorowicz in his *King's Two Bodies*. But as we have seen in our discussion of *Merchant,* once the political theology of sovereignty begins to give way to new paradigms of governmentality, to use Foucault's term, the flesh comes to be managed at new sites and in new ways; it comes to count—to be counted and weighed—as the subject-matter of political economy.

IV

At this point I would like to make a few further remarks about what distinguishes the matter or materiality I am attempting to track in the transition from the "sovereign form" to the "commodity form" of social mediation from what seems to be at issue in the new materialisms that have appeared over the past years under a variety of different names. I am thinking here less in terms of right or wrong and more in terms of a difference in subject matter insofar as these new materialisms are intent on dispensing, precisely, with "subject-matter," the spectral materiality proper to human subjectivity, one with its distinctive "flesh and phenomenality."

Jane Bennett, for example, presents the notion of flesh according to the perspective of what she calls "vital materiality" this way:

> Vital materiality better captures an "alien" quality of our own flesh, and in so doing reminds humans of the very *radical* character of the (fractious) kinship between the human and the nonhuman. My "own" body is material, and yet this vital materiality is not fully or exclusively human. My flesh is populated and constituted by different swarms of foreigners. The crook of my elbow, for example, is "a special ecosystem, a bountiful home to no fewer than six tribes of bacteria" [Nicholas Wade]. . . . The *its* outnumber the *mes*. In a world of vibrant matter, it is not enough to say that we are "embodied." We are, rather, *an array of bodies*, many different kinds of them in a nested set of microbiomes.[46]

The moral and political wager of this approach is that an awareness of such diverse tribes and populations of "its" and "mes"—a kind of multiculturalism at the cellular, or even molecular level—will inhibit us from producing and consuming "in the same violent and reckless ways" that have characterized modern industrial and postindustrial societies heretofore. As Bennett puts it, being mindful "that the human is not exclusively human, that we are made up of its," will contribute to the formation of "the newish self that needs to emerge, the self of a new self-interest" (113). A curious encounter: Adam Smith meets Gilles Deleuze.

The vital materiality that interests me here is one that is, as Freud put it, composed not of multiple, single or multicellular "its" but rather something he called "It" precisely because it remains so difficult to name (recall Derrida's remarks on the "thing" with the king that remains so difficult to name: "neither soul nor body, and both one and the other"). To put it simply, the "intensities" that occupied—or better: *preoccupied*—the crook of the elbow, among other body parts, of Freud's hysterics were not caused by tribes of bacteria but rather by a complex disorder of the "tribe" to which these hysterics belonged, a disorder that in one way or another— and psychoanalysis is the effort to understand those ways—congealed as the uncanny cause of their desire, the "un-economic" dimension of their libidinal economy.

Bennett's reading of Kafka's famous story about the creature named "Odradek" (the title of the story is "Die Sorge des Hausvaters"[47]) offers an example of what can get lost in the homogenization of alterity performed in the name of multiplicity and hetereogeneity, something that is stated almost explicitly at the conclusion of her reading of the text: "Odradek exposes this continuity of watery life and rocks; he/it brings to the fore the becoming of things" (8). For Bennett, Odradek is Kafka's name for self-organizing matter, for spontaneous structural generation in the interstices between inorganic and organic vitality: "Wooden yet lively, verbal yet vegetal, alive yet inert, Odradek is ontologically multiple. He/it is a vital materiality and exhibits what Gilles Deleuze has described as the persistent 'hint of the animate in plants, and of the vegetable in animals'" (8). I have already discussed this text in detail in the first "volume" of my study of the afterlife of political theology so I will not go into great detail here.[48] But it is crucial to underline what gets lost if one ignores that afterlife—its specific forms of "vital materiality"—with respect to a text written in the midst of the breakup of the Austro-Hungarian Empire into a "swarm" of independent and at times tribally conceived nation-states (the text was published in 1919).

As many scholars have noted, the word *Odradek*, which Kafka's narrator suggests might have Germanic and/or Slavic roots, seems to signify, on the basis of family resemblances with words from these and other linguistic "households," a figure of radical rootlessness and nonbelonging— *Od-radix, Od-adresa*. The meanings scholars have adduced for this word that, as the narrator indicates, may not have a meaning at all, include: deserter from one's kind; apostate; degenerate; a small creature whose business is to dissuade; a creature that dwells outside of any kind, rank, series, order, class, line, or use; a creature beyond discourse or *Rede;* waste or dirt—*Unrat*—and so, once again, "matter in the wrong place." All this suggests, I think, that Odradek's *ontological* statelessness—this is what Bennett emphasizes—cannot be separated from the sense of *political* statelessness evoked by the linguistic and historical overdetermination of its name (if it even is a proper name). It was precisely through the breakup of the Austro-Hungarian Empire that the state of statelessness came to be, as Hannah Arendt argued, the political symptom par excellence of modern Europe. And it was the particular "tribe" to which Kafka, along with Freud and Shylock, belonged—a tribe associated, of course, with a peculiar hybrid language between Germanic and Slavic—that came to embody a kind of foreignness that had no natural fit within any state. This was a tribe whose members could never be fully "naturalized," absorbed without remainder, and indeed thought by many of its own members to be, at its core, *passionately detached* from any historical nation-state. One might think of it as a tribe whose very form of life in some sense *mattered in the wrong place*.[49] It is, then, not so much a "newish self" forged on the basis of a vital materiality and new sense of self-interest that Kafka's text helps us to envision but rather the uncanny dimension of the "Jewish self" that he himself no doubt experienced as profoundly linked to a series of other dilemmas. Perhaps the most important of these was the dilemma of a writerly existence, an existence lived in passionate detachment from other social bonds and one apparently incompatible with being a *Hausvater*, the head of a household or *oikos*. We might say that Odradek is, among other things, a figure of *Un-economic* man par excellence, a paradoxical "busy-body" serving no apparent use and yet not ever quite going to waste.

In the short fragment already cited in the preface, Kafka linked the "busy-ness" of such bodies, their form of life, to that of manic bureaucrats whose official duties and writings, whose "office work" has been cut loose from its erstwhile source of purpose and legitimation:

> They were given the choice to become kings or messengers. Just like children they all chose to be messengers. For this reason there are only messengers; they race through the world and, because there are no kings, they call out to one another proclamations that have become meaningless. They would happily put an end to their miserable life but because of their oath of office they don't dare.[50]

Against this background and remembering Kafka's own "office writings" as an insurance official busy with issues of workmen's compensation—compensation for the damaged flesh of laboring bodies—Kafka's own literary writings become legible as the very paradigm of what I have referred to as *traumamtliche Schriften*—the traumatic dream protocols of officious busy bodies. It is a genre that is, I am suggesting, especially attuned to the subject-matter of political economy. My hunch is that it is above all by assuming our responsibility for *this* subject-matter and for the ways in which we serve to sustain its current configurations, that we can begin to become truly responsive to the multiple forms of vibrant matter that border on and move through the human.

v

I would like to return once more to Shylock and the nature of the "Jewish labor" to which he is assigned and that takes place with reference to him in the economy of *The Merchant of Venice*. In his magisterial study of "Anti-Judaism"—not so much *in* as *as* the Western Tradition—David Nirenberg argues that the figure of the Jew in the West is essentially the figure—or perhaps better: the occasion—of a certain kind of work. This is the work that societies are in some way or another compelled to engage in to make sense of the world in the face of fundamental impasses and antagonisms generated by the logic of their own social organization. We might call this heavy lifting the *work of the real*, work no doubt correlated to the sense that the Jews, excluded from participation in most occupations and forms of labor, don't do *real work*. For Nirenberg, the Jews are not so much the subject or agent of the work at issue as its *Anstoss*, its uncanny cause and object.

"Why," Nirenberg asks, "did so many diverse cultures—even many cultures with no Jews living among them—think so much about Judaism? *What work* did thinking about Judaism do for them in their efforts to make sense of their world?"[51] Nirenberg uses Marx's disturbing reflections on the "Jewish Question" to point the direction for his own efforts to answer these questions:

> Marx's fundamental insight . . . was that the "Jewish Question" is as much about the basic tools and concepts through which individuals in society relate to the world and to each other, as it is about the presence of "real" Judaism and living Jews in that society. He understood that some of these basic tools—such as money and property— were thought of in Christian culture as "Jewish," and that these tools therefore could potentially produce the "Jewishness" of those who used them, whether those users were Jewish or not. "Judaism," then, is not only the religion of specific people with specific beliefs, but also a category, a set of ideas and attributes with which non-Jews can make sense of and criticize their world. Nor is "anti-Judaism" simply an attitude toward Jews and their religion, but a way of critically engaging the world. (3)

For Marx, then, the critique of political economy was inseparable from an engagement with the "Jewish Question," one that, as Nirenberg underlines, must inevitably fall short if it simply puts fears and habits of thought about Jews, Judaism, and Jewishness "to a *new kind of work*: that of planning a world without private property or wage labor" (4; my emphasis).

Nirenberg's own project proposes to show how, from ancient Egypt to the present day, "different peoples put old ideas about Judaism *to new kinds of work* in thinking about the world; to show how this work engaged the past and transformed it; and to ask how that work reshaped the possibilities for thought in the future" (5; emphasis added). As Nirenberg tells it, Western anti-Judaism is ultimately the story of the transmission of the demands of this peculiar sort of labor, of a fundamental, even foundational, *Arbeitsanforderung*, to use the word Freud favored in his efforts to characterize the nature of the drives. The story comes very close to repeating Derrida's brief sketch of European history as a compulsively repeated series of displacements of a spectral substance that no amount of conjuration, necromancy, and exorcism manages to fully elaborate and master. The specters of Marx have, for Nirenberg, too, a long history but it is one that cannot be separated from the history of anti-Judaism in the West. And as is well-known, at least since the time of Paul's canonical formulations, at the heart of that history is the preoccupation with the matter of the flesh in its divergence—its *clinamen*—from and threat to the spirit. Not surprisingly, then, Nirenberg also turns to Shakespeare, in this case not to *Hamlet* and the spectral dimension of political theology but to *The Merchant of Venice* where, as I have argued, the *haunting grounds* of the King's Two Bodies begins to yield to those of the marketplace.

Once again, what is at issue is the nature of the "Jewish labor" performed within the economy of the play, which for Nirenberg is, ultimately, that of working out a response to the fundamental question made urgent by the rise of a mercantile economy: "How can a society built on 'Jewish' foundations of commerce, contract, property, and law consider itself Christian?" (274). What is at issue is, thus, a kind of meta-work or *pre-occupation*, work done to facilitate a set of responses to a new organization of work, to the emergence of new relations of production. In psychoanalytic terms, this would be work "beyond the pleasure principle," a form of work done in advance of the work governed by the pleasure and reality principles, work that in some sense helps to install and sustain those principles. (As Lacan might say, though this work brings no pleasure it is not without its own form of jouissance.) The play lays out a field of signifiers—a network of facilitations or *Bahnungen*, to use Freud's word—along which a surplus or surcharge of semiotic pressure, a *signifying stress* generated at least in part by these new relations of production, can move and be discharged, a movement that will culminate in a fateful charge against Shylock, which threatens to bring the comedy to the edge of the tragic. Paradoxically, the play pulls back from that edge by way of the cruel irony of placing the Jewish usurer in the position of becoming, finally, a Christian merchant of Venice.

As Nirenberg emphasizes—much as Schmitt did with respect to *Hamlet*—the anxieties and confusions associated with the increasing importance of contractual relations in the emerging mercantile economy of England helped to generate this pressure in the first place and to initiate its "Jewish" dreamwork. But what are we then to make of the fact that Shylock seems, at least with respect to his loan to Antonio, to be singularly uninterested in profit, in the amplification of his wealth? Why does he refuse the offer of receiving, in lieu of his bond, many times the sum of his principle? Why the insistence on the pound of flesh, on having his bond?

To begin, one might say that with respect to Antonio, this bit of business is, for Shylock, both personal and historical. It was never about the money; it concerned, rather vengeance for the injustice—we might say the radical and brutal *unkindness*—that Shylock and his kind have had to suffer—since time immemorial—from the likes of Antonio and his kind, injustice amplified by the loss of his daughter to the fleshpots of the aristocratic, Catholic world (Shylock at times comes across as a puritan reformer, one suspicious of music, masques, and other "Catholic" frivolities). That Shylock proposes a pound of Antonio's *fair flesh* as penalty for nonpayment of the loan suggests that what was at issue all along here was *fairness* and indeed of a kind that exceeds that of economic calculation, that of a "fair deal." Shylock seeks vengeance for the fundamental unfairness of being posited as a being ontologically lacking in all the fair qualities, a lack that allows the Christian world to treat and refer to him—this happens repeatedly in the play—as a dog (historically, the beautiful Jewess is always the possible exception). It is in other words clear that up to now—up to the beginning of the action of the play—Shylock has figured for the community as representative embodiment of *jew-usance*, as what is perceived to be the perverse libidinal economy demanded by an emerging mercantile economy. Shylock is ultimately seen—is *classified*, we might say—not so much as belonging to a different cultural and religious kind but rather as a figure of the *unkind*, one who unsettles the logic of kinds—Kafka's name for such a figure was, as have seen, Odradek—and this in large measure because he is seen as embodying what is fundamentally unsettling in the social transformations the larger society is undergoing. There is certain self-reflexivity at work here. We might say that Shylock's rage pertains to *the way he is represented in the play*, to the role to which he is assigned in it as representative of the social disorder attending to the emergence of a mercantile economy, an economy in which the global merchant Antonio is really the key player, the truly representative figure. One can almost understand Shylock wanting a piece of this guy. The self-reflexivity I have noted suggests that at least to a certain extent, Shakespeare understood this.

But I also want to suggest that Shylock's insistence on the (pound of) flesh—an insistence that clearly exceeds any sense of economic rationality—should also be understood as an insistence *of* the flesh as the dimension in which social bonds are sealed.

At the most basic level, the source of anxiety and confusion that haunts the play concerns the nature of social bonds, what it is that binds friends, couples, communities, confessions, nations, peoples together at a moment of profound social, political, and economic transformation. As Shylock seems to know, social bonds always involve the dimension of the flesh. We might say that they are, ultimately, written in and with the flesh, that "part" of us inflamed by the normative pressure of the bonds at issue. They always imply, that is, *a becoming-flesh of the given word*. Shylock's insistence on having his bond could be understood, then, as an explicit insistence on and of this truth, one otherwise dispersed in the play into a series of slighter transactions, most notably the final comedy of errors pertaining to the rings and the pledges they signify.[52] But the play also shows that when the nature of social bonds and the forms of normativity associated with them change—in this case, we are moving from political theological normativity to a space of meaning governed by the normative pressures of political economy—so do the locations, actors, and scenes of that writing, of the relevant *Aufschreibesystem*, to use Friedrich Kittler's term. This is the system of social inscription—Foucault would call it a *dispositif*, Agamben, perhaps with Kafka's *Penal Colony* in mind, a *machine*—through which a signifier comes to represent the subject for other signifiers, an operation that always leaves a remainder of inflamed flesh that, like Shylock himself, insists, in and through those signifiers, on getting a fair hearing or at the very least—Beckett might say: *unnullable least*—on making its presence felt.[53]

VI

In her own reading of *Merchant*, Julia Lupton highlights, among other things, the tense transitional space between the two key "systems" at work in the play, the political theology of sovereignty and the political economy of an emerging commercial society that already prefigures, in her view, fundamental features of modern liberalism.[54] The tension between the two systems comes to a head in the trial scene in which, by means of a legal ploy, Portia/Balthazar shifts the juridical coordinates by which Shylock's petition is to be adjudicated, a ploy that Nirenberg, among others, has characterized as "outjewing the Jew." One will recall that she initially acknowledges the force of Shylock's claim and does so in words that closely mirror his own earlier appeal to the sanctity of contract on which the commercial life of Venice depends: "There is no power in Venice / Can alter a decree established; / 'Twill be recorded for a precedent / And many an error by the same example / Will rush into the state. It cannot be" (4.1.226–29). It is precisely at this point that Shylock first characterizes Portia/Balthazar as "A Daniel come to judgment!" (4.1.230).[55] Within moments, however, Portia/Balthazar comes up with her surprising and surprisingly literal reading of the contract—this is where she ostensibly outjews the Jew—according to which Shylock must not only extract *exactly* one pound of flesh but must do so without shedding a drop of blood: "The bond doth give thee here no jot of blood. / Take thy bond, take thou thy pound of flesh; / But in the cutting it, if thou dost shed / One drop of Christian blood, thy lands and goods / Are by the laws of Venice confiscate / Unto the state of Venice" (4.1.314–20; it is Gratiano who now claims Portia/Balthazar as an upright judge and second Daniel). As Lupton points out, this novel—and rather questionable—legal argument marks a shift from commercial to criminal law, one that promises to give Shylock, as Portia/Balthazar puts it, something like a surplus of justice: "justice more than thou desir'st" (4.2.330). This surplus marks a return of the political theology of sovereignty at the very point at which political economic reckoning was poised to win the day:

Whereas Venetian civil law had protected the "commodity of strangers"—international commercial transactions—in the minimal public sphere constituted by the economic contract, criminal law in this instance shields the rights of citizens, over against the "aliens" in their midst. The open port of Venice now retreats into its interior islands, reasserting the lines dividing the citizen and the noncitizen. Finally, the power of judgment and mercy, the sacral attribute of kings, is now forcibly taken from the civil litigant-turned-defendant and delivered to the Duke who shifts from being . . . nominal figurehead . . . to empowered monarch. (95–96)

In a word, the duke shifts from being a sovereign who reigns but does not govern to one who reigns in excess of governing.[56] I am thus tempted to say that what would appear to be merely a clever legal tactic on the part of Portia/Balthazar, her claim, that is, that Shylock is allowed to cut a pound of flesh but drop no "jot" of (Christian) blood, alludes to the *virtual reality* of the element at issue, to the flesh as the special, immaterial stuff that now goes into the composition of the king's body, now into the substance of value.

Standing before this resurgent sovereign, Shylock now acquires the attributes of creaturely life; he

suddenly stands before the law as mere life or bare life, the life of the creature over against the civic life incarnated by Antonio . . . . Shylock, reduced to a mere "jot" and bare "Iewe," stands shorn of the multiple covenants, laws, and promises, the material and spiritual bequests, that had bound him *as alien* to the civic life and history of Venice through the city's corporate structure and political theology. (96)

But as Lupton sees it, Shylock's status, if we might still call it that, as "unnullable least" is strictly correlative to his partial reintegration, one that comes by way of the duke's act of mercy, the benevolent aspect of the sovereign exception. Though he remains a "Jewish *iota* . . . that both dots and blots—completes and decompletes—the Christian-civic synthesis embraced by his daughter," Shylock embodies, for Lupton precisely the sort of "discontented contentment" that accompanies the "provisional and procedural inscription in the polity" that would be institutionalized in liberalism. For Lupton such a mode of inscription is opposed to "a mystical or ecstatic union sealed by imaginary forms of national identification" (100). It is, thus, Shylock who thereby "emerges as the strongest forerunner of modern citizenship at the close of act 4" (100). What is staged in Shylock's fate, according to Lupton, is the "death into citizenship" that will eventually be demanded of all members of liberal societies, a mortification that in some sense never ceases. For Lupton, the spectral presence of Shylock at the end of the play exercises its own sort of ethical force, functions as the embodiment of the regulative idea of modern liberalism:

> Shylock's legal and psychological condition at the end of the play demonstrates the extent to which naturalization in a diverse polity not only can but should remain structurally incomplete, maintaining memories of suspended modes of affiliation that never dissolve completely into a new identity. In my reading Shylock undergoes not so much a forced conversion as a nominal or procedural one; his reluctant consent is measured and limited, like the rule of law itself. It is worth asserting that however ambivalent we may feel about Shylock's conversion, there is *nothing tragic* in his destiny. (100–101)

As compelling as I find Lupton's reading, I am not, in the end, persuaded by her claim concerning liberal society's ostensible evacuation of the imaginary forms of identification proper to medieval and early modern corporate societies, forms that depend, as Marx insisted, on the fetishism of persons grounded in the logic of reflexive determinations. Indeed, my argument is that modern liberal societies largely relocate and restage that dimension in a variety of other scenes and according to new sets of dramaturgical—or better: *liturgical practices*. And this is, as I understand it, what Marx ultimately meant by proposing that the key to the critique of political economy lay in grasping the displacement of the fetishism of persons by the fetishism of the commodity. The practices and social relations through which the production, exchange, and consumption of commodities would come to be organized—the ostensible subject matter of classical political economy—become the site in which, precisely, new "mystical and ecstatic" unions are sealed. This is what Marx meant with his infamous remarks about the theological, mystical, necromantic, and animistic aspects of life under modern capitalism.

In the next chapter I will try to say more about these liturgical practices that mediate the transition from the glorification/valorization of sovereigns—the modes of production of the king's sublime body—to the self-valorization of capital, that is, the shift to new forms of the production of glory, splendor, and valor.

In the end, the question will be what to make—or rather, *what liberal, civil society will make*—of the "unnullable least" that remains of Shylock along his path toward citizenship under the protection of what remains of sovereign power and authority. How much, we might ask, does Shylock's own creaturely flesh now weigh in the balances? Can it be evaluated, reckoned with? How will it be put to work? These are, I think, the questions that Marx will take on in his efforts to understand the secret of the commodity form, a form that required, in his view, the prior emancipation of workers from all traditional affiliations and bonds. What remains of Shylock is, I am suggesting, related to what will become for Marx the *gespenstische Gegenständlichkeit* that emerges at the threshold of the transition from the fetishism of persons—above all of sovereigns and their sublime, virtually real bodies—to the fetishism of things, a transition marking the reconstitution and organization of the flesh of the social bond.

NOTES

1. Eric Santner, *The Royal Remains: The People's Two Bodies and the Endgames of Sovereignty* (Chicago: University of Chicago Press, 2011).

2. T. J. Clark, *Farewell to an Idea: Episodes from a History of Modernism* (New Haven, CT: Yale University Press, 1995), 15. Subsequent references are made in the text. See chapter 4 of Santer, *Royal Remains* for a more in-depth discussion of the painting.

3. Clark notes that as one of the Museum section's important Jacobins, David very likely took part in producing the *Ordre de la Marche* for the highly stage-managed activities in the context of which his painting was presented to the public, activities that followed the execution of Marie Antoinette. See Clark, *Farewell to an Idea*, 15ff.

4. Franz Kafka, *Beim Bau der chinesischen Mauer und andere Schriften aus dem Nachlaß* (Frankfurt a. M.: Fischer, 1992), 235–36. Unless otherwise noted, translations are mine.

5. For a discussion of these two events in the context of the "spectral" history of financial instruments in modern capitalism, see Joseph Vogl, *Das Gespenst des Kapitals* (Zurich: Diaphanes, 2010).

6. Sara Melzer and Kathryn Norberg, eds., *From the Royal to the Republican Body: Incorporating the Political in Seventeenth- and Eighteenth-Century France* (Berkeley: University of California Press, 1998), 10–11; emphasis added.

7. Jonathan Crary, *24/7* (London: Verso, 2013). Subsequent references are made in the text. As Crary notes, his essay can be understood as a continuation and updating of Anson Rabinbach's groundbreaking study of the modern preoccupation with fatigue as a threat to both political and economic survival. See Rabinbach, *The Human Motor: Energy, Fatigue, and the Origins of Modernity* (Berkeley: University of California Press, 1992).

8. For a fuller discussion of this paradox, see Eric L. Santner, *On Creaturely Life: Rilke, Benjamin, Sebald* (Chicago: University of Chicago Press, 2006).

9. Franz Kafka, *The Castle*, translated by Mark Harman (New York: Schocken, 1998), 103–4. Kafka's novel is a crucial point of reference for Crary as well.

10. Kafka thereby already provides us with a sense of the libidinal economy of what Luc Boltanski and Eve Chiapello have called the "new spirit of capitalism." See their *The New Spirit of Capitalism*, translated by Gregory Elliot (London: Verso, 2007).

11. One is tempted to say that when, in the wake of the 9/11 disaster, New York City's mayor Rudolf Giuliani appealed to the citizens of the city to go shopping as a sign of a return to normality, he was at some level reminding them of their duty or "oath of office" in a regime of 24/7 business, a duty linked, in turn, to the series of states of exception—suspensions of law in the name of security—invoked in the aftermath of the terrorist attacks.

12. Ernst Kantorowicz, *The King's Two Bodies: An Essay in Medieval Political Theology* (Princeton, NJ: Princeton University Press, 1957), 143n167, 496.

13. Alexei Penzin has made this argument in *Rex Exsomnis: Sleep and Subjectivity in Capitalist Modernity*, in dOCUMENTA (13): 100 Notes—100 Thoughts (Osfildern: Hatje Cantz, 2012). I am grateful to Penzin for sharing material from his work-in-progress on a critical cultural history of sleep.

14. Michel Foucault, *Omnes et Singulatim: Towards a Criticism of "Political Reason,"* Tanner Lectures on Human Values, delivered at Stanford University, October 10 and 16, 1979, http://foucault.info/documents/foucault .omnesetsingulatim.en.html, 229–30.

15. Ibid., 246.

16. See Gil Anidjar, *Blood: A Critique of Christianity* (New York: Columbia University Press, 2014). I am grateful to Marcia Klotz for alerting me to Anidjar's work.

17. As Anidjar phrases the fundamental question of his study, "Does blood 'itself' insist, then? And if so, what is the nature of this insistence?" (ibid., 22)

18. Karl Marx, *Capital: A Critique of Political Economy*, vol. 1, translated by Ben Fowkes (New York: Vintage, 1977), 142. The German text is taken from Karl Marx, *Das Kapital: Kritik der politischen Ökonomie, Erster Band* (Berlin: Karl Dietz Verlag, 2008), 65–66.

19. Rainer Maria Rilke, *The Notebooks of Malte Laurids Brigge*, translated by Stephen Mitchell (New York: Vintage, 1990), 61–62.

20. See Sigmund Freud, "Character and Anal Eroticism," in *The Standard Edition of the Complete Psychological Works of Sigmund Freud*, edited by James Strachey (London: Hogarth, 1981), 9: 169–75.

21. Jacques Derrida, *Specters of Marx: The State of Deb, the Work of Mourning, and the New International,* translated by Peggy Kamuf (New York: Routledge, 1994). Subsequent references are made in the text.

22. Rilke uses the formulation in a letter to Lou Andreas-Salomé of March 1, 1912. See *Rainer Maria Rilke / Lou Andreas-Salomé: Briefwechsel,* edited by Ernst Pfeiffer (Frankfurt a. M.: Insel, 1989), 266.

23. See Santner *Royal Remains.*

24. Marx, *Capital,* 143, 149 (translation modified). The German text is taken from Marx, *Das Kapital.*

25. Kantorowicz, *King's Two Bodies,* 59 (emphasis added).

26. Slavoj Žižek, *For They Know Not What They Do: Enjoyment as a Political Factor* (London: Verso, 1991), 255.

27. As I have suggested in the preface to these lectures, I understand this surplus carnality in relation to the "little extra life" that, as Foucault argued, is administered by the police—that guardian of the state's splendor—in early modern societies. See once more, Foucault, *Omnes et Singulatim,* 229–30.

28. Cited in Žižek, *For They Know Not,* 256 (emphasis added). The citation is from Lacan's seminar, "Death and the Interpretation of Desire in *Hamlet,*" from 1959. Žižek is above all interested in the mutation of the king's two bodies into what he refers to as "Lenin's two bodies," that is, how the people come to be conscripted in the liturgical production of the special stuff of the totalitarian leader and party who—thanks to the logic of reflexive determinations—can offer themselves as the incarnation of objective reason of history. "In so far as the stuff they are made of is ultimately their body, this body again undergoes a kind of transubstantiation; it changes into a bearer of *another* body within the transient material envelopment" (258).

29. See Marx, *Capital,* 163; *Kapital,* 85.

30. Cited in Max Weber, *The Protestant Ethic and the Spirit of Capitalism,* translated by Talcott Parsons (London: Routledge, 2001), 15.

31. See David Graeber, *Debt: The First 5,000 Years* (Brooklyn, NY: Melville House, 2011).

32. Aristotle, *Politics,* 1, 9: 1257–58, translated by Benjamin Jowett, in Richard McKeon, ed., *The Basic Works of Aristotle* (New York: Random House, 1941), 1139.

33. Much of my thinking about avarice developed in the course of a team-taught seminar with Mladen Dolar on the topic at the University of Chicago, autumn 2013. I am deeply grateful to Mladen and to the seminar participants for numerous insights regarding this strangely virtuous sin.

34. The Freudian view is already prefigured in Paul's conception of the flesh as an amplification of human sentience by what he calls, in Romans 7, "another law . . . which dwells in my members": "I do not understand my own actions. For I do not do what I want, but I do the very thing I hate. Now if I do what I do not want, I agree that the law is good. So then it is no longer I that do it, but sin which dwells within me. For I know that nothing good dwells within me, that is, in my flesh. I can will what is right, but I cannot do it. For I do not do

the good I want but the evil I do not want is what I do. Now if I do what I do not want, it is no longer I that do it, but the sin which dwells within me. So I find it to be a law that when I want to do right, evil lies close at hand. For I delight in the law of God, in my inmost self, but I see in my members another law at war with the law of my mind and making me captive to the law of sin which dwells in my members." *The Writings of Saint Paul*, edited by Wayne A. Meeks (New York: Norton, 1972), 79–80.

35. Aristotle, *Politics*, 1, 10: 1255–70; emphasis added.

36. See Marc Shell, *Money, Language, Thought: Literary and Philosophic Economies from the Medieval to the Modern Era* (Baltimore: Johns Hopkins University Press, 1982), 47. I am grateful to Mar Rosàs Tosas for pointing out the minimal diacritical difference between the two words.

37. The thought of validity without meaning, *Geltung ohne Bedeutung*, is elaborated by Gershom Scholem in his epistolary exchange with his friend, Walter Benjamin, on the meaning of revelation in the works and world of Franz Kafka. I will return to this exchange of letters at the conclusion of the next lecture. *The Correspondence of Walter Benjamin and Gershom Scholem: 1932–1940*, edited by Gershom Scholem, translated by Gary Smith and André Lefèvre (Cambridge, MA: Harvard University Press, 1992).

38. The historical and conceptual complexity of this concept, so central to our understanding of the way in which human bodies enter into normative "corporations," is explored in detail in a work to which Kantorowicz noted his own considerable indebtedness, Henri Cardinal de Lubac, *Corpus Mysticum: The Eucharist and the Church in the Middle Ages*, translated by Gemma Simmonds, Richard Price, and Christopher Stephens (Notre Dame, IN: University of Notre Dame Press, 2006).

39. That Antonio initially uses the word "excess" rather than "interest" could perhaps allude to the 1571 definition of usury as interest beyond an acceptable rate, generally pegged at 10 percent. It should also be noted that among the complaints lodged against usury was that it represented, so to speak, a first instance of a 24/7 economy: interest-bearing capital never sleeps.

40. In a recent essay on the play, Mladen Dolar has argued that in the end the Christian offer of mercy effectively outbids the ostensibly Jewish insistence on the letter of the law (in this case, contract law) by infinitizing the debt of the recipient of mercy. As Dolar writes, "the crux of the matter is that mercy, behind the cloak of its generosity . . . hinges on a surplus and extortion. Justice is equivalence, the just punishment and reward . . . according to the letter. Mercy is the surplus over the letter, over law and justice, not as coerced taking, but as voluntary giving. But the gift indebts, all the more since its terms are not specified, and if they were to be specified this would cease to be mercy. Hence it opens an unspecified debt, a debt with no limits, an infinite debt. One is never worthy of mercy and however much one gives in return, as a response, it is never enough, it can never measure up to the free gift which has no equivalent, not in what one possesses. Hence one has to give what one doesn't possess, which is the Lacanian definition of love—mercy demands its equivalent only

in love. Mercy is a usurer which, by not demanding a circumscribed surplus [I am tempted to add: *circumcised* surplus—ELS] opens an absolute debt. It demands not 'an equal pound of flesh', but 'an equal pound of soul'—this is why Shylock is granted mercy only on condition that he gives up his creed and converts to Christianity, the religion of love." Mladen Dolar, "The Quality of Mercy Is Not Strained," unpublished manuscript. I am grateful to Dolar for sharing his text with me.

41. A more fully "fleshed out" reading of *Merchant* would, of course, have to take into account the other storyline in the play concerning life, love, and precious metals, namely, that of the three caskets. Portia, who, in the guise of Balthazar, "legally" forces Shylock to choose Christian love and mercy over the ostensibly Jewish letter of the law of contract, was herself bound by the letter of an "old testament" with respect to her choice of a husband. According to Freud's reading of the motif of the three caskets, Bassanio's victorious choice of the lead casket—a choice that wins him not only love but also considerable amounts of silver and gold—itself masks a deeper truth concerning wishful disavowals of forced choices. See Sigmund Freud, "The Theme of the Three Caskets," in *The Standard Edition*, 12:289–302. What he characterizes as Bassanio's unpersuasive—and seemingly forced, *gezwungen*—"glorification of lead"—represents, for Freud, an acknowledgment of the ineluctability of death. We will return to the subject matter (both with and without hyphen) of glory and glorification in the second lecture.

42. Carl Schmitt, *Hamlet or Hecuba: The Intrusion of the Time into the Play*, translated by David Pan and Jennifer Rust (New York: Telos, 2009). Subsequent references are made in the text. Derrida strangely omits this work from his reflections on the hauntological nexus linking Shakespeare and Marx.

43. Against this background, figures such as the Earl of Essex and Walter Raleigh—two examples of what Schmitt sees as a new elite of *adventure capitalists*—might be seen as typologically related to the figure of Antonio in *Merchant*.

44. See Ben Nelson, *The Idea of Usury: From Tribal Brotherhood to Universal Otherhood* (Chicago: University of Chicago Press, 1969). *Hamlet* and *Merchant* are each in their own way caught up in the turbulence of this "conversion." In this context, see also Dietrich Schwanitz, *Das Shylock-Syndrom: Oder Die Dramaturgie der Barberei* (Frankfurt a. M.: Eichborn, 1997).

45. Here Derrida seems to be endorsing what he elsewhere calls into question, namely, the translation of the German word *Leib* as flesh—*chair*—or at the very least as the uncanny combination of flesh and phenomenality. See, for example, his *On Touching—Jean-Luc Nancy*, translated by Christine Irizarry (Stanford, CA: Stanford University Press, 2005).

46. Jane Bennett, *Vibrant Matter: A Political Ecology of Things* (Durham, NC: Duke University Press, 2010), 112–13. Subsequent references are made in the text.

47. Stanley Corngold translates the title as "The Worry of the Father of the Family," in his edition of *Kafka's Selected Stories* (New York: Norton, 2007), 72–73.

48. See Santner, *Royal Remains*, 83–86.

49. Franz Rosenzweig's account of Jewish singularity in *The Star of Redemption* more or less turns into positive—though uncanny—features the negative attributes that Richard Wagner attributes to Jews in his famous essay, "Judaism and Music." I discuss these matters in my *On the Psychotheology of Everyday Life: Reflections on Freud and Rosenzweig* (Chicago: University of Chicago Press, 2001).

50. Kafka, *Beim Bau der chinesischen*, 235–36.

51. David Nirenberg, *Anti-Judaism: The Western Tradition* (New York: Norton, 2013), 2 (emphasis added). Subsequent references are made in the text.

52. As Portia says to Gratiano, who admits to having given his ring to Balthazar's clerk, "You were to blame, I must be plain with you, / To part so slightly with your wife's first gift, / A thing stuck on with oaths upon your finger, / And so riveted with faith unto your flesh" (5.1.179–82). Gratiano, for his part, had just begrudgingly expressed his regret to Nerissa for breaking his oath by means of further sworn testimony that links the "hoop of gold" to the flesh of the genitals and the heart: "By yonder moon I swear you do me wrong! / In faith, I gave it to the judge's clerk. / Would he were gelt that had it, for my part, / Since you do take it, love, so much to heart" (5.1.155–59).

53. See Samuel Beckett, *Worstward Ho*, in *Three Novels by Samuel Beckett* (New York: Grove Press, 1996), 106. Kittler borrowed the term *Aufschreibesystem* from the memoirs of Daniel Paul Schreber, a text on the basis of which Freud wrote one of his five case studies and to which Jacques Lacan dedicated a yearlong seminar. My own study of the case, *My Own Private Germany: Daniel Paul Schreber's Secret History of Modernity* (Princeton, NJ: Princeton University Press, 1996), lays much of the groundwork for the current project. Its focus is Schreber's experience of investiture crisis, of the failure of the symbolic processes of social inscription that then return in delusions that literalize and concretize those processes as the operations of actual machinery in and on the body, operations that seem to transform Schreber into a creature of intensified flesh marked as both feminine and Jewish.

54. Julia Lupton, *Citizen-Saints: Shakespeare and Political Theology* (Chicago: University of Chicago Press, 2005). Subsequent references are made in the text.

55. In his own earlier appeal to the binding force of contracts, Shylock rubs the duke's nose in the darker side of Venetian commercial society:

> What judgment shall I dread, doing no wrong?
> You have among you many a purchased slave,
> Which, like your asses and your dogs and mules,
> You use in abject and slavish parts
> Because you bought them. Shall I say to you
> "Let them be free! Marry them to your heirs!
> Why sweat they under burdens? Let their beds
> Be made as soft as yours, and let their palates
> Be seasoned with such viands"? You will answer
> "The slaves are ours!" So do I answer you:

The pound of flesh which I demand of him
Is dearly bought: 'tis mine and I will have it.
If you deny me, fie upon your law:
There is no force in the decrees of Venice.
I stand for judgment. (4.1.90–104)

56. Dolar offers a concise formulation of this excess: "Sovereignty is based on exception, the sovereign can suspend the law, and mercy is precisely the exception to the law, it is beyond law, beyond the contract, the reciprocal bond, as a surplus depending on the caprice of the sovereign, who can freely grant it or not beyond any obligation. Mercy is the state of exception at its purest." Dolar, "The Quality of Mercy Is Not Strained."

LECTURE II. PARADOXOLOGIES

The shift from the fetishism of persons—above all that of the singularly representative person, the *Staatsperson* or sovereign—to that of things takes place in the context of a long process of secularization that ostensibly drains the shared institutions of the public sphere of transcendental resources of legitimation; it is a process that, so the story goes, disenchants the world more generally, evacuates from all aspects of life the last vestiges of otherworldly, animating spirits, be they divine or demonic. The critical thrust of Marx's theory of the fetishism of the commodity has been to demonstrate just how wrong this story is. Max Weber, who first introduced the concept of the disenchantment of the world, formulated his own critical skepticism on this matter with the concept of the *spirit*—indeed, we might say *specter*—of capitalism. For Weber, the Reformation contributed to the disenchantment of the world—think of the devaluation of priestly sacraments—at the price of injecting into it a proliferation of harassing voices that never cease to remind the faithful to keep busy, essentially, never to cease to economize, and all *for the greater glory of God*. As we shall see, Weber's argument will be that the Protestant ethic effectively transforms work itself into a sort of obsessive-compulsivie *doxology*, the liturgical praise or glorification of God.

It is, I would suggest, Marx's labor theory of value that first opens the horizon within which Weber's argument unfolds. For Marx, however, it is not that secular society remains secretly bound to transcendence but rather that our ostensibly disenchanted world vibrates with a *surplus of immanence* that profoundly informs our dealings in the world, makes us into "busy-bodies" trying to discharge an excess of demand—an excessive *Arbeitsanforderung*, to use Freud's locution for the pressure of the drives—that keeps us driven even when we are ostensibly "idling," keeps us *negotiating* even in the midst of *otium*. Recalling T. J. Clark's characterization of modernism as "turning on the impossibility of transcendence," we might say that moderns keep obsessively *turning* or *spinning* in one fashion or another and do so ever more according to the rhythm of "24/7." This is what Marx means when he claims that although the commodity "appears at first sight an extremely obvious, trivial thing," if looked at in the right way it shows itself to be "a very strange thing, abounding in metaphysical subtleties and theological niceties (*ein sehr vertracktes Ding... voll metaphysischer Spitzfindigkeit und theologischer Mucken*)."[1] But it is not so much *we* who continue to engage in metaphysics and theology but rather our *busy bodies*. For Marx, it is commodity and so value-producing labor—rather than labor as such or a religiously inflected work ethic—that is fundamentally doxological. Both the Marxist critique of political economy and the Freudian engagement with libidinal economy are, although at rather different levels, ultimately in the business of intervening into precisely this *busy-ness*, this uncanny mode of stress. The Freudo-Marxist concept of stress I am developing here is no doubt continuous with other approaches to ideology and efforts to isolate its "sublime object."[2] I hope, though, that by focusing on the afterlife of political theology in secular modernity—essentially, its mutation into political economy—it will be possible to shed new light on these matters.

As I have already noted, this surplus of immanence "at work" in the commodity is of a radically different nature than the vibrant matter, actants, and assemblages of the new posthumanist materialisms. The "animation" at issue for Marx is something that is ultimately deadening—or rather: *undeadening*—for human beings, something that drives them while holding them in place, a condition Walter Benjamin once referred to as "petrified unrest," *erstarrte Unruhe*.[3] For the new materialists, by contrast, "vibrant matter" is the very promise of a new sense of aliveness for a "newish self." Marx's critical intervention aims at a deanimation of this undeadness while the new materialisms seek to open human life to the "agency" of nonhuman material assemblages. What both approaches share, of course, is the very question as to the nature of human flourishing and the sense of urgency of this question. The fundamental difference may just be that the Marxist project—along with that of psychoanalysis—operates within a Judeo-Christian tradition for which the *creatureliness* of human life—I will have more to say about this term—is inseparable from being subject to normative pressures of various kinds, the generic source of which is our life with language. Life lived under normative pressure is a life suffused by questions of responsibility, answerability, and obligation. Such questions would, in turn, seem to draw us inevitably into the orbit of the semantic field of *debt*, of what we owe to others, to society, and to oneself. The new materialisms, for their part, take up more "animist" traditions and habits of thought that aim to disperse the normativity proper to human orders of meaning into self-perpetuating patterns of organized matter (we are back, perhaps, at the difference between the Jewish and the "newish"). It is no doubt for this reason that the figure that keeps emerging as a key point of contestation in these debates is Spinoza, the great Jewish thinker of self-perpetuating being or *conatus* grasped under the heading of an *Ethics*. But that is a story that takes us beyond the scope of the present inquiry. I would simply note that in his final book, *Moses and Monotheism*, Freud tried to give an account of what he took to be the obsessive-compulsive *conatus* of Judaism itself.[4]

II

Before we can say more about the mutation of fetishism in the transition from political theology to political economy, we need to get clear about the nature of the disavowal—of the "unknown knowns"—at work in the first form, the fetishism of persons. What is it that is both affirmed and denied in the fetishistic activity, above all in the liturgical labor that, so to speak, congeals in the virtual reality of the king's second, sublime body? It is not, I think, simply the knowledge that the sovereign is really, after all, just another mortal being and that his kingship is just a fiction or social construction; it is not, that is, the knowledge of the "trick" of the *Reflexivbestimmung* noted by Marx, that is, that the king is a king because his subjects treat him as a king (and not because he is already king). Bringing together the political theological problematic of the state of exception and the psychoanalytic concept of the partial object, Slavoj Žižek offers a concise formulation of what, I think, is really at stake in the fantasmatic physiology of the royal personage:

> The emergence of this sublime body is . . . linked to the illegal violence that founds the reign of law: once the reign of law is established, it rotates in its vicious circle, "posits its presuppositions," by means of foreclosing its origins; yet for the synchronous order of law to function, *it must be supported by some "little piece of the real" which, within the space of law, holds the place of its founding / foreclosed violence*—the sublime body is precisely this "little piece of the real" which "stops up" and thus conceals the void of the law's vicious circle.[5]

For Žižek, the "little piece of the real"—what Lacan famously called the *objet a*—holds the place of the *anarchic* dimension of the space of juridico-political normativity. To put it in terms I have used in earlier work, what I am calling the "flesh"—the stuff out of which the sovereign's sublime body is composed—emerges out of the entanglement of the somatic and normative pressures that constitute creaturely life. By "creaturely" I do not simply mean nature, living things, sentient beings, or even what the religiously minded would think of as the entirety of the "vibrant matter" of God's creation—*deus sive natura*—but rather a dimension specific to human existence, albeit one that seems to push thinking in the direction of theology. It signifies a mode of *exposure* that distinguishes human being from other kinds of life: not simply to the elements or to the fragility, vulnerability, and precariousness of our mortal, finite lives, but rather to an ultimate *lack of foundation* for the historical forms of life in which human life unfolds. This is what Žižek means when he speaks of the law's rotation in a vicious circle; it is a rotation around a gap that opens at the jointure of the somatic and the normative, life and forms of life. This gap, this crucial *missing piece of the world*, to which we are ultimately and intimately exposed as social beings of language, is one that we thus first *acquire* by way of our initiation—Heidegger would say *thrownness*—into these forms of life, not one already there in the bare fact of our biological being. We could say that the vulnerability of biological life becomes potentiated, amplified, by way of exposure to the radical contingency of the forms of life that constitute the space of meaning within which human life unfolds, and that it is only through such an-archic "potentiation" that we take on the flesh of creaturely life.

Creatureliness is thus a dimension not so much of biological as *ontological vulnerability*, a vulnerability that permeates human being as that being whose essence it is to exist in forms of life that are, in turn, contingent, contested, susceptible to breakdown, in a word, *historical*.[6] The normative pressure that suffuses human life always includes an excess, a "too much" of pressure that indexes the contingency of the norms in question. We are not simply answerable to one another according to the relevant norms of our social being, that is, as recognized bearers of normative statuses; we are also always subject to surplus or supplementary "negotiations" that, to use Žižek's terms, orbit around the void of the law's vicious circle, the lack of any ultimate grounding or authorization of those normative statuses. It is these surplus negotiations that *give flesh* to a form of life, infuse the bindingness of its norms with a dimension of psychosomatic passion. To put it somewhat differently, what "covers" the dimension of risk proper to our ontological vulnerability is the subject-matter elaborated by individual and social fantasy as *formations of the flesh*. Our investiture with normative statuses—this is what Lacan meant by entering the "symbolic"—always involves a dimension of libidinal investment of the subject and by the subject. We never simply just have an entitle-ment or "office"; whether we like it not, we *enjoy it*, and this enjoyment is the stuff that dreams are made of.

It would be more accurate to say that the gap at the jointure of the somatic and the normative is always multiple and layered. It concerns the lack of ultimate foundations of the normative order, its lack of anchorage in, its nondeducibility from, the great chain of being. But it also concerns the jointure itself: the *missing link* between the somatic and the norma-tive, a sort of blind spot at the point at which the latter "emerges," as one now tends to put it, from the former. Finally there is the gap immanent to biological life itself, the point at which, at least in human being, it reaches a limit that requires supplementation by cultural prosthetics. The over-lapping of these multiple gaps provides the site of the fleshly surplus en-joyed by humans as distinct from other living things.[7]

The political theology of sovereignty implies, among other things, that the sovereign incarnates and so represents this vulnerability for his subjects, and thereby allows them in some sense to avoid the void. It is the "business" of the sovereign, that is, to *cover the void* in two fundamental senses: to veil it with his or her glorious body; but also, on the basis of that very glory, to stand surety for it as for a primordial debt. The royal flesh—and this is the essence of the fetishism of persons—marks a kind of wound or tear in the fabric of being by covering it in these two senses, which means that the royal virtues always, at some level, serve to sustain the virtual reality of the sublime, royal flesh. My concern continues to be the ways in which what had been, to a large extent, localizable in early modernity, invested within the sphere and "physiology" of the traditional master or sovereign, disperses into the texture of the social space at large—into the life of the People—and so into the very soul of the mod-ern citizen-subject. Marx's theory of the fetishism of the commodity is, I am suggesting, above all a contribution to an understanding of that pro-cess of dispersion. For Marx it is above all political economy that, as it were, *inherits the royal remains*, the dispersed and now "popularized" flesh of the king's sublime body in its function as glorious guarantor cov-ering the missing link at the "anthropogenetic" knotting of the somatic and the normative. Political economy circumscribes the domain in which the production process not only of the wealth of the nation but also of the People's Two Bodies is managed, kept in business / busy-ness. The theory of the fetishism of the commodity serves as a kind of warning not to lose site of the *gespenstische Gegenständlichkeit* of the People's second, sublime body, the virtually real product of commodity-producing labor. The labor theory of value is, I am suggesting, ultimately a theory of the production of the spectral flesh of the sovereign People, a process that depends, we might say, on the exchange of a (decapitated) head for an invisible hand in ceaseless motion. This motion—the imperative of capital accumulation—is, I am arguing, the political economic version of what Žižek characterized as the law's vicious circle, its rotation around an anarchic kernel, a foreclosed origin. Another way of putting it would be to say that political economy converts the fundamental dynamic of the drive into a *debt drive*, a ceaseless effort to redeem or indemnify a lack at the origin of the normative order to which we are, so to speak, joined at the hip.[8]

III

We can think of the king's sublime body as the congelation of a certain kind of labor, as the substance of the "royal value" produced by that labor. The elaboration of this value takes place above all by way of the liturgical practices—*liturgy* (from *laos*, people, and *ergon*, work) just means "public work"—in and through which the sovereign is acclaimed and sustained as sovereign. Such practices performatively enact the *Reflexivbestimmung* of sovereignty noted by Marx. By, as it were, *fleshing out* the conceptual operation of that reflexive determination, this work produces a virtual real *that can take on a life of its own*. This is why insight into the conceptual operation—the structure of a reflexive determination—fails to produce the critical effects one might expect. This was, at bottom, Freud's insight with respect to the therapeutic effects of insight into the logic of an analysand's symptoms by way of interpretation and analytic construction; for the most part, these effects simply fail to materialize. They fail, that is, as interventions into the relevant materiality, the subject-matter at issue. The "business" of a neurosis—the specific mode of *busy-body-ness* that constitutes it—requires an intervention into the labor process itself along with the quasi-somatic, quasi-normative pressures informing it, something that Freud for good reason called *working through*.

Over the past decades there has been a resurgence of interest in the concept of liturgy; not so long ago, a special issue of the journal *Telos* even proposed the notion of a new "liturgical turn" in political and social theory.[9] A good deal of this new work has concerned itself with ways to reanimate liturgical practices heretofore relegated to the religious sphere, to find in liturgical traditions resources of resistance against the flatness of a secular life artificially pumped up by what are characterized as the pseudo-liturgies of capitalist modernity. Among the more recent contributions to this literature, Giorgio Agamben's *The Kingdom and the Glory: For a Theological Genealogy of Economy and Government*, stands out for a number of reasons. First, he avoids the simple and, I think, too facile opposition between ostensibly genuine and patently fake liturgical practices by focusing on a dimension that both attempt to cultivate, namely, *glory*. He furthermore situates his investigation against the background of what he, like so many other contemporary thinkers, sees as the global, neoliberal absorption of political thought and action by forms of economic rationality and behavior. What Agamben develops under the heading of the "archaeology of glory" turns out to be a rich resource for the analysis of this development. Finally and more generally, the "liturgical turn" allows us to revisit various questions previously explored under the heading of ideology. Ideology is a concept that, I think, still remains too attached to the ideational, to thought and image, to the ways in which people make sense of the world, while the concept of liturgy focuses our attention on the practices in and through which they form and consolidate the value—and so, at some level, the valor, the glory, the splendor—of their social being.

The concern with the fate of politics in modernity is not new. Weber, Schmitt, Arendt, Adorno, even Heidegger argued that forms of the economic-technical administration and management of life were becoming hegemonic in the modern world, that *homo economicus* was coming to fully displace or absorb *homo politicus*. Some of the names of this hegemony—names signaling an ostensibly postpolitical age—are familiar: Hannah Arendt called it "the social"; Theodor Adorno spoke of "the administered world"; Martin Heidegger used a nearly untranslatable word, *das Gestell* (sometimes translated as "enframing"); more recently, Alain Badiou has coined the term "democratic materialism." Agamben, for his part, follows Michel Foucault's lead by framing his investigation as one pertaining to the forms of "governmentality" that ostensibly supplant the juridico-political field of sovereignty in modernity.

Foucault formulated this transformation in a number of different ways, most notably as the displacement of sovereign forms of power by a series of institutions and practices that did not so much reign or rule juridical subjects as manage and administer the lives of individuals and populations. At least for a time, Foucault grouped these practices under two headings: the "anatomo-politics of the human body" and the "bio-politics of the population."[10] Regarding the former, Foucault speaks of a disciplinary physics of power that supplants what had once been thought of as the magical effects of the king's touch:

> The *body of the king*, with *its strange material and physical presence*, with the force that he himself deploys or transmits to some few others, is at the opposite extreme of this new physics of power . . . : a physics of a relational and multiple power, which has its maximum intensity not in the person of the king, but in the bodies that can be individual-ized by these relations.[11]

With respect to the biopolitical administration of populations, the body of the king figures equally as Foucault's key point of departure. In his lectures at the Collège de France in 1975–76, for example, he opens his account of the postrevolutionary "embourgeoisement" of the nation-state (and so the emergence of the defining sphere of modern political economy, civil or bourgeois society) with remarks that could have been taken from Kantorowicz's *King's Two Bodies*. What makes a nation, he writes, is the fact that its members "all have a certain individual relationship—both juridical and physical—with the real, living, and bodily person of the king. It is the body of the king, in his *physical-juridical* relationship with each of his subjects, that creates the body of the nation."[12] It is precisely the dispersal and reorganization of this "physical-juridical relationship"—of this paradigmatic yet still exceptional jointure of the somatic and the normative—that is of interest to Foucault.

What is crucial to keep in mind here—and I think that this is what Foucault often fails to do—is that this hyphenation of the physical and the juridical "secretes" a new element or dimension, that of the flesh.[13] Foucault is, in a word, touching here on what I have characterized as a metamorphosis of the King's Two Bodies into the People's Two Bodies and the emergence of new forms of power adapted to the management of the latter, of what is *more* than the body in the bodies of its citizen-subjects. Foucault's investigations lead us to conclude that the threshold of modernity is marked by the "massification" of the physical-juridical flesh of the king, its dispersion into populations that for that very reason must be placed in the care of biopolitical administration. What this means is that whenever Foucault speaks about the object of biopolitics—man-as-species, populations—he is also, although never explicitly and perhaps never even intentionally, addressing the fate in modernity of the royal remains of political theology, the dimension of the flesh in its new, modern form: *masses of busy bodies*. Biopolitics is always mass politics in the sense of dealing with the massive presence of a sublime object—the virtual reality of a fleshy mass—now circulating in and agitating the life of the People, which means, in turn, that political economy, the domain that Foucault came to see as a central site of biopolitical administration, acquires a certain sacramental dimension, the aspect of a "mass." It is no surprise, then, that Marx would discover "metaphysical subtleties and theological niceties" in the midst of our life with commodities.

In another series of lectures concerned with the shift from classical sovereignty to biopolitical forms of administration—from *reigning* to *governing*—Foucault writes:

> When it became possible not only to introduce population into the field of economic theory, but also into economic practice, when it became possible to introduce into the analysis of wealth this new subject, this new *subject-object*, with its demographic aspects, but also with the aspect of the specific role of producers and consumers, owners and non-owners, those who create profit and those who take it, when the entry of this *subject-object*, of population, became possible within the analysis of wealth, with all its disruptive effects in the field of economic reflection and practice, then I think the result was *that one ceased analyzing wealth and a new domain of knowledge, political economy, was opened up.*[14]

Again, what Foucault is saying here is, I am suggesting, that the subject matter of political economy includes an *un-economic subject-matter* the disruptive force of which derives, precisely, from its uncanny, spectral materiality, its status as *gespenstische Gegenständlichkeit*.

There is another passage in this same series of lectures that helps to clarify a crucial aspect of Foucault's engagement with the subject-matter of political economy or what he refers to as its "subject-object." Addressing the semantic history of the institution "police," Foucault recalls that beginning in the seventeenth century it refers broadly "to the set of means by which the state's forces can be increased while preserving the state in good order" (313), that is, to the array of matters we would today group under the heading of public policy. He goes on to note the use, in various sources, of a "rather strange word for describing the object of the police," namely, *splendor*: "What is splendor? It is both the visible beauty of the order and the brilliant, radiating manifestation of a force. Police therefore is in actual fact the *art of the state's splendor* as visible order and manifest force" (314; emphasis added). One might say that the fundamental charge—or better: *sur-charge*—of police/policy and the science it would become—in German, *Polizeiwissenschaft*—was the protection and administration not so much of the *Herrschaft* of the state as its *Herrlichkeit*, not so much its rule as its glory. Police, public policy, and, finally, political economy, were charged, that is, with securing and managing the substance of the social bond in its newfound glory as—or rather, as an immanent surplus to—the wealth of nations.

IV

Before turning to Agamben, I would like to mention very briefly the important work done by Joseph Vogl in addressing the historical shifts of concern here. In an essay on the modern desire for/of the state, "Staatsbegehren: Zur Epoche der Policey," Vogl for the most part cleaves closely to Foucault's conceptual frame in tracking the shift in German political discourse from the early modern sovereign reign over juridical subjects to the modern governmental project of "policing" the lives of individuals and populations.[15] He borrows from Kantorowicz's work to characterize the split introduced into the populations of modern states as one between two bodies: a juridical one that remains within the discursive orbit of law and rights, and an ostensibly empirical one that becomes increasingly the subject matter of a political anthropology whose forms of knowledge emerge out of the administrative practices of *Policey*.

> Alongside questions of natural right and reason, alongside the representation and limitation of sovereign power and the abstract body of the State-Person [*Staatsperson*], there emerged a materiality and reality of the state that was put together from the directions of diverse forces and an aggregation of self-interested individuals; [this new materiality] could not simply be systematized by way of juridical principles and laws: over against the force of law and the sovereign personage there emerged a physics of the state's forces. (611–12)

This Foucauldian assessment is, I think, all perfectly right up to a point. What is finally missed is, I think, a dimension that escapes the conceptual grasp of both juridical rationality and the new anthropology, of both law and "physics." It is the dimension that Foucault himself points to with the notion of *splendor*, namely, something in the empirical body that is *more* than the body, a surplus that, though it emerges on the basis of a symbolic investiture, of an "official" inscription in a symbolic order, cannot be simply equated with the symbolic fiction of office let alone with the empirical body of its incumbent. What this account misses is the impossible dimension of public policy and risk management, the demand to cover what I have characterized as the ontological vulnerability proper to creaturely life. What ultimately comes to cover that dimension of risk is, as we have seen, a special, immaterial stuff elaborated by individual and social fantasy as formations of the flesh. These formations are to a very large extent sustained by the liturgical dimension—the "public work"—enacted in what otherwise appears as the policing of empirical bodies and forces. The "public work" in the *Policey* aims, that is, at what is in the body that is *more* than the body. This dual aspect of "police work" will, I am arguing, find its crucial modern form in the dual aspect of labor articulated in Marx's labor theory of value.

Vogl however goes a long way to recuperate this loss by emphasizing the role played by aesthetic theory and practice—his main point of reference is Schiller—in, as it were, covering or filling "the gap between sovereign representation and empirical state body" (613), in securing the jointure of norms and living bodies at a moment of profound social reorganization. In Vogl's view, around 1800 *Policey* and aesthetics—along with an emergent political economy—ultimately join hands in trying to come to grips with the "abstract material" that, as we have seen with respect to David's *Death of Marat*, began to come into view as a quasi-autonomous dimension in the visual field of an incipient modernism. If, as Vogl suggests, Schiller's aesthetic theory and practice are born "aus dem Geist der Policey" (618), it is crucial to emphasize that what infuses— what *sur-charges*—the *Geist* or spirit of police work with its particular passion is the spectral aspect of its object and the need to extract from it the splendor of the state. If there is indeed a form of empiricism at work here it is a peculiar one: call it the empiricism of the flesh as the virtual-real dimension—as the fundamental *subject-matter*—of public policy. This still basically Foucauldian account of the emergence of *Policey* corresponds, in the terms of Jacques Lacan's discourses, to a displacement of the "discourse of the Master" by that of the "discourse of the University."[16] In the discourse of the Master, the subject-matter of the social bond serves to sustain/entertain the Master in his sovereign glory, nourish the king's sublime metabolism—his two bodies—while in the discourse of the University it becomes the "subject-object" of an administrative-managerial paradigm charged with optimizing its potential (one might recall, in this context, Malte Laurids Brigge's visit to the Salpêtrière). Over the course of the eighteenth and nineteenth centuries, *Policey* effectively yields to the regime of political economy as the primary locus of the production of splendor.

V

Agamben's research aims at providing what the subtitle of his study refers to as a "theological genealogy of economy and government."[17] Foucault rightly grasped that what characterized the modern period was the supplementation and partial supplanting of sovereignty by forms of what he called "governmentality" central to which was, as we have seen, political economy. What he failed to see, however, was just how deep the theological roots of the semantic field of *oikonomia* go:

> the fact that . . . the Foucauldian genealogy of governmentality can be extended and moved back in time, right up to the point at which are able to identify in God himself, through the elaboration of the Trinitarian paradigm, the origin of the notion of an economical government of men and the world, does not discredit his hypotheses, but rather confirms their historical core to the very extent to which it details and corrects their historico-chronological exposition. (111)

It is not first in the early modern period that the sovereign begins to *reign* as the provider of general, universal, and simple laws rather than *govern* in the pastoral sense of providing for the individual and special needs of the people—tasks assumed by new forms and agents of knowledge-power; this difference between what in the theological tradition is referred to as *general* and *special providence* is, Agamben claims, the very signature of the Christian dispensation from the start and forms the basis for what he refers to as the "bipolar machine" of power in the West. Among the terms of that bipolarity whose constantly changing articulations he sees as constitutive of the history of politics in the West, Agamben lists: Sovereignty / Administration-Management; Law / Order-Police; Constituent Power / Constituted Power; Legitimacy / Legality.

Much of the book is dedicated to reconstructing (in at times over-whelming detail) efforts by the Church Fathers to elaborate the Trinitarian paradigm of this machine, to conceptually guarantee the unity in differ-ence of the Father qua transcendent substance or Being of God, on the one hand, and the Son understood as the *visible hand* of God's redemptive ac-tion in the world, on the other. The details of these efforts, along with those of the Monarchist, Arian, and various Gnostic challenges they were meant to overcome, need not detain us here.[18] They largely serve to prepare the reader for Agamben's most significant insight, namely, that the pole of the machine associated with governing, managing, "economizing," has, as Fou-cault said of the police at the beginning of the seventeenth century, largely been dedicated to the cultivation of splendor, glory, *Herrlichkeit*.

Over the course of his "archaeology of glory," Agamben draws on the work of several twentieth-century scholars all of whom to a greater or lesser extent home in on the intimate relation of liturgical doxologies—the ritual praise and glorification of God that constitutes so much of the cultic activity of the Church—and the acclamations that have histori-cally accompanied the investiture of rulers, whether ancient emperors, Christian kings, or, closer to the historical experience of some of those same scholars, the German *Führer*. (As Agamben reminds us, Nazi Ger-many produced some of the most famous acclamations in the modern period, most notably *Heil Hitler* and *Ein Reich, Ein Volk, Ein Führer*.) Among them: Carl Schmitt, Erik Peterson, Ernst Kantorowicz. What this archaeology turns up is, as Agamben puts it, an archaic sphere in which religious and juridical action and speech become indistinguish-able, a sphere he had explored up to this point with respect to the seman-tic field of the sacred. "If we now," he writes, "call 'glory' the uncertain zone in which acclamations, ceremonies, liturgies, and insignia operate, we will see a field of research open before us that is equally relevant and, at least in part, as yet unexplored" (188). This field is framed by two fun-damental questions: First: Why does power—heavenly or earthly—need glory? And second: What are the historical modes and relations of the production, circulation, and consumption of glory?

Perhaps the most important source in Agamben's efforts to get this new field off the ground is Erik Peterson's 1935 book, *The Book of Angels: Their Place and Meaning in the Liturgy*.[19] Peterson argues that the liturgy—the people's work—that makes up the holy mass is best under-stood as the Church's striving to participate in the hymnic glorification of God—the doxologies—that, for Peterson, constitute the very being of the angels, or at least the ones that truly matter for the mass (all ange-lologies articulate a complex division of labor that need not detain us here):

> Their authentic being is not grounded in their immobility but in their movement, which they manage with the beating of those wings that Isaiah first describes with an unmatched power of perception. To this beating of wings . . . there corresponds a distinctive gushing forth in word, in call, in song, of the Holy, Holy, Holy. In other words, the authentic being of these angels is grounded in this overflow into word and song, in this phenomenon. (137–38)

It is for this reason that knowledge of God—*theology*—culminates in praise of God, that is, in liturgical doxology. "For of what use," he continues, "are all the virtues of the angels, if their praise of God, their most authentic life, that for which alone they exist, *that through which their innermost form of being is set to vibrating* [*das, wodurch ihre innere Seinsform in Schwingungen gerät*], is not attainable by human beings?" (138; emphasis added).[20] What Peterson above all emphasizes is the public and, so, fundamentally political character of the cultic activity—of the doxological labor—aimed at reproducing the frequencies that constitute the "vibrant matter" of angelic being.

Peterson will ultimately want to claim that the peculiar theopolitical dimension of the liturgy elevates the Church above all political theology by, precisely, appropriating the core political dimension of doxologies, their resemblance to acclamations of rulers. By taking part in a heavenly worship—one sustained by angelic doxologies—the earthly Church converts political theological acclamation—Peterson personally witnessed the new efflorescence of such acclamations in Nazi Germany—into theopolitical glorification:

> Characteristic for this worship in heaven is the way in which political and religious symbolic expressions are thoroughly intermingled, which is shown most clearly in the resemblance of the doxologies to acclamations. That the heavenly worship described in Revelation has an original relationship to the political sphere is explained by the fact that the apostles left the earthly Jerusalem, which was both a political and a cultic center, in order to turn toward the heavenly Jerusalem, which is

both a city and royal court, and yet also a temple and cult site. With this is connected the further point: that the Church's anthem transcends national anthems, as the Church's language transcends all other languages.... Finally, it is to be noted that this eschatological transcending has as its ultimate result the fact that the entire cosmos is incorporated into its praise. (116)[21]

Ernst Kantorowicz published his own study of ritual acclamations immediately after the war and some ten years before the publication of *The King's Two Bodies*. The study, *Laudes Regiae: A Study in Liturgical Acclamations and Medieval Ruler Worship*, focuses on the history of a particular acclamation—it begins with the phrase, *Christus vincit, Christus regnat, Christus imperat*—central to Carolingian political theology. As Agamben's discussion of this earlier study strongly suggests, it could be seen as a first attempt to grasp the nature of the labor that would congeal into the sublime flesh of the king's royal physiology. This comes across above all in the treatment of the coronation of Charlemagne in Rome. Regarding this rite of royal investiture, Kantorowicz argues that the *laudes* are essentially constative utterances lacking in performative force *and yet somehow crucial*:

> The laudes acclamation, representing the recognition of the king's legitimacy, was an accessory manifestation, impressive by its festal and solemn character, *but not indispensable*; for legally the liturgical acclaim *added no new element of material power* which the king had not already received earlier by his election and coronation.... By means of this chant, the Church professed and publically espoused the king in a solemn form. However, *the weight of this profession or espousal cannot be measured by legal standards*. (*Laudes*, 83; cited in Agamben, 191; emphasis added)

As I have been suggesting, the *weight* at issue is that of the flesh, this virtual real element that enters into the composition of the king's sublime body. The *laudes*, then, are king-creating powers of a special sort, those that, to paraphrase Marx once more, flesh out the reflexive determination of the being of the king and thereby "cover" it, gloriously secure it or, to use more recent economic terminology, *securitize* it. Kantorowicz seems to suggest that the vibrant matter of this flesh is ultimately composed of,

or at least transferred to the king, by way of the sonorous mass of ac-
claiming voices: "The shouts of the Romans and the laudes, as they then
followed one after the other without a break, seem to have formed one
single tumultuous outburst of voices in which it is idle to seek the particular cry which was 'constitutive' and legally effective" (*Laudes,* 84; cited
in Agamben, 192). We might say, then, that what Kantorowicz later elaborated under the heading of the king's second body is a *sublimate* of just
such a sonorous mass, a *congelation of its vibrant doxological matter.*[22]

VI

Agamben's insight is that there is no political theology of sovereignty
without a theological economy of glory, no constitution of *Herrschaft*
without the doxological production of *Herrlichkeit*—no *Herrschaft* that
is not, at some level, "entertained," *unterhalten,* by *Herrlichkeit.* Agamben argues, in effect, that what might at first appear to be a superstruc-
tural feature of a ruling state apparatus is, essentially, its *libidinal economic
base,* one that produces and shapes the glorious flesh of the social bond. It
involves, as we have seen, a mode of production organized according to
the circular logic of reflexive determinations. To put it in terms of what
we might characterize, by way of an allusion to Freud, as *the economic
problem of Christianism,* we could say: We glorify God because he is glorious; the glory that God's creatures owe to God and produce through
cultic praise is already an essential attribute of God; the earth is full of
the glory that the faithful must return to God by way of doxologies. This
work would thus appear to be a mode of God's own self-glorification, a
peculiar sort of divine auto-affection that makes use of creaturely life as
its instrument or tool. Paraphrasing Karl Barth's efforts to capture the
paradoxical logic of doxological labor, Agamben writes, "The circularity
of glory here attains its ontological formulation: becoming free for the
glorification of God means to understand oneself as constituted, in one's
very being, by the glory with which we celebrate the glory that allows us
to celebrate it" (215). One begins to sense the obsessional pattern and
rhythm here, doxology's resemblance to what Freud characterized as the
self-amplifying dynamic of the superego (the key, for Freud, to the economic problem of masochism). At least in the context of an obsessional
neurosis, the ego is, in some sense, under constant pressure to live for the
greater glory of the superego, to "fatten" its status as *Über*-ich, which might
indeed be better translated as *surplus-ego.* Agamben summarizes the dynamic as an embedded series of paradoxes:

Glory is the exclusive property of God for eternity, and will remain eternally identical in him, such that nothing and no one can increase or diminish it; and yet, glory is glorification, which is to say, something that all creatures always incessantly owe to God and that he demands of them. From this paradox follows another one, which theology pretends to present as the resolution of the former: glory, the hymn of praise that creatures owe to God, in reality derives from the very glory of God; it is nothing but the necessary response, almost the echo that the glory of God awakens in them. That is (and this is the third formulation of the paradox): everything that God accomplishes, the works of creation and the economy of redemption, he accomplishes only for his glory. However, for this, creatures owe him gratitude and glory. (216)

The superegoic dimension of the paradox of glory fully emerges in the motto of the Ignatius Loyola, *Ad majorem Dei gloriam*, which Agamben reads as the driving force of Jesuit labor:

One thing that is clear is that he takes the paradox of glory to its extreme, since the human activity of glorification now consists in an impossible task: the continual increase of the glory of God that can in no way be increased. More precisely . . . the impossibility of increasing the inner glory of God translates into an unlimited expansion of the activity of external glorification by men, particularly by the members of the Society of Jesus. (216)

Readers of Weber will recognize here the core argument of his study of the "spirit/specter of capitalism." As Weber shows, what we have been calling the paradox of glory converges with the logic of predestination in Calvinism according to which not only the dispensation of grace but also its withholding serve as manifestations of divine glory, which, in turn, calls on us to respond with acts of thanksgiving and glorification. As Weber puts it, "All creation, including of course the fact, as it undoubtedly was for Calvin, that only a small proportion of men are chosen for eternal grace, *can have any meaning only as means to the glory and majesty of God*" (59–60; emphasis added). There is nothing that does not testify to the glory of God and for that very reason we must dedicate our lives to the further glorification of God. For the reformers, a Christian life was dedicated to God's glory, to live and work *ad majorem Dei gloriam*. As Weber argues, work itself thereby becomes a form of what we might call *the dox-ology of everyday life*. It must be performed as liturgical practice, as a mode of production of glory. To use Peterson's terms, our work must ceaselessly resonate, as a response to a calling, with the vibrating being of the order of angels.

Against this background, Agamben's own philosophical and political project—and they would seem to be inseparable for him—emerges as a fundamentally *paradoxological* one. It consists of various attempts to strike at—or perhaps better: to induce a "general strike" in—the doxo-logical apparatus, our *glory-producing labor*. Agamben sees that labor as the striving to capture in a separate sphere—religion, economics, politics, culture—a fundamental inoperativity, a sabbatical *otium*, marking the absence of a purpose and destination proper to human life. It is a matter of suspending our incessant *neg-otiations,* of unplugging from what keeps us in the business of being busy-bodies—of vibrating—in the sense I have been elaborating here. What is at stake in the doxologies and ceremonials that seem merely to accompany power is, he suggests, a fetishistic dis-avowal of *what does not work* in human life; they present so many manic attempts to capture, incorporate, inscribe in a separate sphere "the inop-erativity that is central to human life." The "flesh wound" that cannot be countenanced is not, as Freud would have it, at the place of the missing maternal phallus, but rather of a missing task or *telos* proper to human life:

> The *oikonomia* of power places firmly at its heart, in the form of festi-val and glory, what appears to its eyes as the inoperativity of man and God, *which cannot be looked at*. Human life is inoperative and with-out purpose, but precisely this *argia* and this absence of aim make the incomparable operativity [*operosità*] of the human species possible. Man has dedicated himself to production and labor [*lavoro*], because in his essence he is completely devoid of work [*opera*], because he is the Sabbatical animal par excellence. (245–46; emphasis added)[23]

What is here translated as "operativity" might better be rendered as *busy-ness* or even *busy-body-ness*, a neologism that also, I think, captures much of what Heidegger is after in his phenomenology of everyday *Dasein* and its existential mode of "falling," of living within a diffuse and generalized mode of *Geschäftigkeit*.

What I have been calling the flesh covers, for Agamben, what the tradition has thought under the heading of *zoe aionios*, eternal life, which, he suggests, is "the name of this inoperative center of the human, of this political 'substance' of the Occident that the machine of the economy and of glory ceaselessly attempts to capture within itself" (251). Recalling Žižek's formulation concerning the reign of law, glory, we could say, is one of the names of the "substance" that, as he put it, " 'stops up' and thus conceals the law's vicious circle." What Žižek calls the "illegal violence that founds the reign of law" is for Agamben a manifestation of the struggle to capture "the inoperative center of the human." What Agamben is after with the notion of "inoperativity" is, I am suggesting, much the same thing that Žižek—among other Lacanians—often attempts to name with formulations such as "the big Other doesn't exist." For Agamben as well as for Žižek, what is at issue is the transferential dynamic at work in the reflexive determination of the Other underlined by Marx. The subject *works* at sustaining/entertaining the *Instanz* or agency—feeding it with the splendor of surplus value—that, in turn, entitles the subject to enjoy its entitlements, its being in the Other. Against this background, a properly Marxist view of class struggle and revolutionary action would ultimately involve some form of intervention into these transferential relations, transactions, negotiations. This brings us to what we earlier referred to as a certain messianic dimension of the Marxist tradition and the need to strike something other than what is there. It would seem to involve the call for a strike on the liturgical labor in and through which the transferential dynamic is enacted, labor that, as Weber powerfully argued, is itself always already a response to a call. This struggle of call and countercall, doxology and paradoxology, will thus always be at least one aspect of what it means to engage in class struggle.

VII

Among the more confusing parts of Marx's labor theory of value are those where he refers to its core subject matter as abstract, undifferentiated, homogeneous human labor and appears to equate that with the purely physiological expenditure of energy, muscle, nerves, and so on, in the labor process.[24] The confusion runs the risks of losing sight of the relevant *subject-matter* in the so-conceived subject matter. Recall that Marx posits the notion of abstract labor on the basis of what he sees as the *real abstraction* operative in the circulation of commodities. In *The*

Wealth of Nations, Adam Smith had himself already apologized for the "obscurity [that] may still appear to remain upon a subject *in its own nature extremely abstracted*."[25] As soon as commodities are exchanged in denominations of a general equivalent of value—so and so much money— the specific, concrete labor that goes into them—tailoring rather than weaving—becomes in some sense a matter of indifference. Of significance, instead, is only the quantity of *value-producing* labor. Tailoring produces not only shirts but also and more importantly so and so much value, value that appears, in turn, as the exchange value of those shirts. That value may be equal to that of so and so much cotton, wheat, iron, or whatever commodity. Homogeneous labor is the labor that has, as Marx likes to say, *congealed* as value rather than taken phenomenal *shape* as this or that particular commodity. It is the labor that produces the value of, precisely, *whatever commodity*, labor that is thus at some level—the level that counts, that gets counted—commanded with utter indifference as to its specific nature.[26] It is not we who are indifferent when we command the labor of others by purchasing this or that commodity; it is our money that is indifferent and it is the money that does the talking here, issues the commands, speaks in imperatives, takes the other to (his or her) task.

What is produced in response to such commands—*Arbeitsanforderungen* structurally indifferent to the specific form of labor at issue— is precisely what Marx characterized as the spectral materiality of the commodity: "Let us now look at the residue of the products of labor. There is nothing left of them in each case but the same spectral materiality [*gespenstische Gegenständlichkeit*]; they are merely congealed quantities of homogeneous human labor [*Gallerte unterschiedsloser menschlicher Arbeit*], that is, of human labor-power expended without regard to the form of its expenditure."[27] Marx's own language has led readers to conclude that what he means with such formulations is simply a certain amount of physiological effort or output of energy.[28] They have understood what Marx calls the "dual character of the labor embodied in commodities" (131) as referring to the specific shape and nature of a particular, concrete form of labor, on the one hand—tailoring, weaving, baking—and the purely physiological expenditure of tissue and energy—I am tempted to call it an expenditure of "biopower"—on the other. Among the passages often cited to support this view we find the following:

> If we leave aside the determinate quality of productive activity, what remains is its quality of being an expenditure of human labor-power.

Tailoring and weaving, although they are qualitatively different productive activities, are both a productive expenditure of human brains,
muscles, nerves, hands etc., and in this sense both human labor. Of
course, human labor-power must itself have attained a certain level
of development before it can be expended in this or that form. But
the value of a commodity represents human labor pure and simple,
the expenditure of human labor in general. (134)

The remarks that immediately follow this passage suggest, however,
that the very perspective or gaze that makes the double character of labor
appear in this apparently straightforward and natural way must itself be
seen as the object of Marx's critique of political economy. What remains
of productive labor once we abstract from its qualitative dimension is,
precisely, an *abstract materiality* generated by the historical relations of
production *to which this gaze belongs*. What appears to be physiological
expenditure pure and simple—so and so much biopower—is, at a different level, the substance of the social bond at the point at which political
economy assumes its hegemonic place in the (self)governmental machine. As Moishe Postone has put it, "*die Materie* in Marx's 'materialist'
critique is . . . social—the forms of social relations."[29] What is at issue is,
in a word, not a pound of brains, muscles, nerves, hands, and so on, but
rather of *flesh*. In Foucauldian terms, we might say that what appears on
the face of it as "biopower" in the sense of measurable physiological expenditure is part of a larger matrix of biopower or biopolitical operations
that, as Marx puts it, go on behind the backs of those involved: "And just
as, in civil society, a general or a banker plays a great part but man as such
plays a very mean part, so, here too, the same is true of human labor. It is
the expenditure of simple labor-power, i.e. of the labor-power possessed
in his bodily organism by every ordinary man, on the average, without
being developed in any special way" (135). It is in his anticipation of questions concerning this notion of simple labor-power that Marx shows
his hand:

Simple average labor, it is true, varies in character in different countries
and at different cultural epochs, but in a particular society it is given.
More complex labor counts only as *intensified*, or rather *multiplied*
simple labor, so that a smaller quantity of complex labor is considered equal to a larger quantity of simple labor. *Experience shows that
this reduction is constantly being made* [emphasis added]. A commodity

may be the outcome of the most complicated labor, but through its *value* it is *posited* as equal to [the verb is *gleichsetzen*] the product of simple labor, hence it represents only a specific quantity of simple labor. The various proportions in which different kinds of labor are reduced to simple labor as their unit of measurement are *established [festgesetzt] by a social process that goes on behind the backs of the producers* [emphasis added]. (135)

As Postone summarizes these and similar remarks in *Capital*, "the appearance of labor's mediational character in capitalism as physiological labor is the fundamental core of the fetish of capitalism."[30] What disappears from view, what is disavowed in the fetishism of the commodity, is precisely the process of "reduction" that produces the *Gallerte*, the gelatinous mass in and through which our sociality is constituted as a kind of quasi-religious, quasi-secular mass in the liturgical service of the self-valorization of Value.

With the shift from the "sovereign form" to the "commodity form" of social mediation, labor becomes the new locus for the production of the flesh of the social bond. Commodity-producing labor is charged, that is, not only with the production of goods to satisfy the needs and wants of a rapidly expanding *bürgerliche Gesellschaft* or civil society; it is *sur-charged* with a task of social mediation that had earlier belonged to hierarchically arranged symbolic statuses or "estates" revolving, at least since the late middle ages and early modernity, around a central locus of sovereign power and authority.[31] For Marx, *value* is now the locus of this surcharge and the labor theory of value concerns itself with its production and circulation. We could add that however one might choose to cultivate (or deconstruct) one's ethnic, religious, sexual, or cultural identity, political economy continues to lay claim to the *vital subject-matter* around which our lives now revolve and with respect to which we are for the most part measured and governed. This is what is at issue in the shift from the fetishism of persons to the fetishism of things; the political theology of the king's two bodies yields to political economy as the domain surcharged with the management—the *oikonomia*—of the subject-matter, the flesh of the social bond.

It should thus come as no surprise that when he introduces the immanent dynamic of capital as the self-valorization of Value—the quasi-autonomous life of this *surcharge* of our vibrant and vital matter—Marx will resort to the original Trinitarian terms of economic theology:

It [value] differentiates itself as original value from itself as surplus-
value, just as God the Father differentiates himself from himself as
God the Son, although both are of the same age and form, in fact one
single person; for only by the surplus-value of £10 does the £100 originally advanced become capital, and as soon as this has happened, as
soon as the son has been created and, through the son, the father,
their difference vanishes again and both become one, £110. (256)

We might add: *ad majorem Dei gloriam.*

VIII

That value is related to valor, glory, radiance, splendor, and that its substance results from the "change of state" that bodily expenditure undergoes under the pressure of real abstraction or "reduction"—call it the
alchemy of capitalism—has long been in plain sight in the choice of objects historically used to incarnate this substance in the sphere of exchange relations: precious metals and, above all, gold. Gold is where the
flesh of abstract, homogeneous human labor is, so to speak, directly de-
posited; this substance extracted from the earth serves as the glorious
garment in which the spectral materiality extracted/abstracted from
laboring bodies shines forth as the very substance of splendor.[32]

What is "cast" in the role of the general equivalent of value must be
at some level superfluous to human needs, must be something that one
can do without. It must, in a word, embody the ambiguous virtues of
waste in the sense of pure superfluity, of what exceeds the needs of the
maintenance of life but serves, rather, to "entertain" it. It is no doubt for
these reasons that psychoanalysis has so often posited a link between ex-
crement and money. Something emerging from one's own body, something the child in some sense works at producing as its own precious
substance, is cast by his caregivers as, precisely, *matter in the wrong place*,
the sort of superfluity that demands to be quickly evacuated and made
to disappear: our first experience of waste management. For Freud, Ferenczi,
and others, the anal jouissance attached to evacuation—a jouissance that
includes the complex negotiations with those caregivers concerning
the value and meaning of these first gifts—comes to be sublimated as the
positive sense of superfluity attached to what will be extracted from the
bowels of the earth and cast into or, rather *as*, the light—the *lux*—of
luxury.[33] This sublimity manifests itself in the aesthetic dimension of
precious metals.

Citing passages from Marx's *Contribution to the Critique of Political Economy*, Jean-Joseph Goux, whose work on the homologies linking diverse forms of symbolic economies has deeply informed my own thinking on these matters, concisely summarizes the aesthetic features that, as it were, help *to make gold gold*, namely,

> Those qualities "that make them the natural material of luxury, ornamentation, splendor, festive occasions, in short, the positive form of abundance and wealth. They [gold and silver] appear, in a way, as spontaneous light brought out from the underground world"; gold dazzles the eyes with its orange rays, or reflects "only the color of highest intensity, viz. red light." It is in these "values people take out on holidays," in these products representing "pure and simple superabundance," that what Marx elsewhere calls the world of "profane commodities" converges as if toward the universal form that gives them their value. In short, society "acclaims gold, its Holy Grail, as the glittering incarnation of its inmost vital principle."[34]

Among the more famous lines in German literature concerning the status of gold in human life, not surprisingly, are from Goethe's *Faust*, a play preoccupied with the "impossible" jointure of the somatic and the normative, the sensuous and the spiritual, the demonic and the angelic. After finding a casket containing jewelry placed in her closet by Mephistopheles, Gretchen puts them on and admires herself in a mirror:

> Were these fine ear-bobs mine alone!
> They give one quite another air.
> What use are simple looks and youth?
> Oh, they are well and good in truth;
> That's all folk mean, though—pretty, fair.
> The praise you get is half good-natured fuss.
> For gold contend,
> On gold depend
> All things and men. . . . Poor us![35]

The last lines read in the original: "Nach Golde drängt, / Am Golde hängt / Doch alles. Ach wir Armen." The verbs *drängen* and *hängen* convey the sense, missing from the translation, of an impersonal passion or drive that seizes on human life. And "wir Armen" can signify not only

"poor us" but also "we poor folk." I say this because Gretchen's class status is underlined from her very first encounter with Faust when he addresses her on the street as *schönes Fräulein*, as "fair young lady" (2605ff.).
Her response is: "I'm neither fair nor lady" (2607). In later conversations
she emphasizes in considerable detail the harshness and hardships of her
home life, in a word, just how much domestic labor she must do and the
toll it has taken on her. The characterization of her room as a "kleines
reinliches Zimmer" evokes not only a sense of Gretchen's *Reinheit* or
purity—this is what, for example, Kierkegaard emphasizes about her—
but also of the work invested here in home economics, something conveyed in the translation with the pedestrian formulation, "a clean little
room."

Furthermore, what is translated above as "What use are simple looks
and youth," reads, in German, "Was hilft euch Schönheit, junges Blut?"
The phrase *junges Blut* signifies much more than youth; it conveys the
sense of *young flesh*.[36] And indeed, after his first encounter with Gretchen,
Faust threatens to part from Mephistopheles if he fails to procure her for
him. In Walter Arndt's translation: "Let me be plain, and hear me right, /
Unless I have that sweet delight / Nestling in my embrace, tonight, / The
selfsame midnight hour will part us" (2635–38). The original reads: "Und
das sag' ich ihm kurz und gut, / Wenn nicht das süße junge Blut / Heut'
Nacht in meinen Armen ruht; / So sind wir um Mitternacht geschie-
den." Faust is addressing Mephistopheles as a sort of pimp and indeed
puts it almost explicitly so in his initial imperative, "Hör, du mußt mir
die Dirne schaffen!" (2618), a command rendered in English as "Here, get
me that young wench—for certain!" The tragic love story of Faust and
Gretchen begins, thus, not only as a story of seduction but also as one of
prostitution based on the equivalence of young flesh and gold. What is
furthermore clear is that what must happen for this story to proceed is
that Gretchen must be torn from the form of traditional if difficult life in
which she is embedded. She must become "modern" and does so by entering into the system of exchange relations—relations in which flesh is directly exchangeable with gold—on the "ground floor," as it were.

Against this background it makes good sense that Mephistopheles
first presents himself to Faust by way of the famous lines that at some
level capture the paradoxical logic of commercial economies as theorized
by Adam Smith more or less contemporaneously with the composition of
the early drafts of the play. When Mephistopheles introduces himself as
"Part of that force which would / Do ever evil, and does ever good" (*Ein*

Theil von jener Kraft, / Die stets das Böse will und stets das Gute schafft; 1335–36), it is hard not to hear the resonances of Smith's famous characterization of the logic of the market whereby the greater good is produced precisely by way of what at the very least looks like an abandonment of Christian moral teachings:

> But man has almost constant occasion for the help of his brethren, and it is in vain for him to expect it from their benevolence only. He will be more likely to prevail if he can interest their self-love in his favor and shew them that it is for their own advantage to do for him what he requires of them. . . . It is not from the benevolence of the butcher, the brewer, or the baker, that we expect our dinner, but from their regard to their own interest. We address ourselves, not to their humanity but to their self-love."[37]

The logic of the "oldest profession," the exchange of gold for flesh, is, like Faust, rejuvenated—finds new blood—by way of the Mephistophelian dynamic placed at the heart of political economy, a dynamic that, in the second part of the play, is potentiated, taken to a new level, by way of Faust's introduction of paper money into the financially drained empire. Among the precedents for this Faustian feat of financial engineering were, as we have noted, the introduction of paper currency—the assignat—by the revolutionary government in France the brief viability of which was sustained by an infusion of wealth—not so much *junges* as *altes Blut*—seized from Church and aristocracy under the bloody regime of the Terror.

IX

As I have been arguing, the inner movement of capital can be grasped as a form of the dynamic logic of doxology the paradigm of which is, as Agamben has compellingly argued, the Trinitarian *oikonomia*. The labor theory of value is, in other words, a theory of the fundamentally doxological nature of capitalism. The English translation of one of Marx's key concepts is actually helpful in this context. Just before introducing the Trinitarian allegory of the transformation of money into capital, Marx lays out in more explicitly Hegelian terms the logic at work in the elaboration of the subject-matter of political economy, of what in political economy is *not only substance but also subject*. The passage, though well-known, is worth quoting at length:

The independent form, i.e. the monetary form, which the value of commodities assumes in simple circulation, does nothing but mediate the exchange of commodities, and it vanishes in the final result of the movement. [At this point, that is, value does not yet function as a medium of social relations—ELS.] On the other hand, in the circulation M-C-M both the money and the commodity function only as different modes of existence of value itself, the money as its general mode of existence, the commodity as its particular or, so to speak, disguised mode. It is constantly changing from one form into the other, without becoming lost in this movement; it thus becomes transformed into an automatic subject. If we pin down the specific forms of appearance assumed in turn by *self-valorizing value* [*der sich verwertende Wert*] in the course of its life, we reach the following elucidation: capital is money, capital is commodities. In truth, however, value is here the subject of a process which, while constantly assuming the form in turn of money and commodities, it changes its own magnitude, throws off surplus-value from itself considered as original value [*sich als Mehrwert von sich selbst als usprünglichem Wert abstößt*], and thus *valorizes itself* independently. For the movement in the course of which it adds surplus-value is its own movement, *its valorization is therefore self-valorization* [*seine Verwertung also Selbstverwertung*]. By virtue of being value, it has acquired the occult ability to add value to itself. It brings forth living offspring, or at least lays golden eggs.[38]

The word *valor* nicely brings out the semantic field we have been exploring: glory, splendor, hymnic praise, and so forth. The paradoxes of glory elaborated by Agamben are the very ones that Marx lays out here with respect to value. Value-producing labor—this is what he characterizes as abstract homogeneous human labor—figures for Marx as the tool or instrumental cause of value's own self-valorization just as the faithful, liturgically joining in the angelic doxologies, serve the process of God's self-glorification. This is what is ultimately meant by religious *service*, by *Gottesdienst*.[39] Marx's abbreviation for the self-valorization of value— M-C-M—could thus be understood as the basic doxological formula of capitalism, its underlying *Sancta, Sancta, Sancta*, one that, as Peterson argued with respect to angelic being, goes on 24/7. Once the political theology of sovereignty disperses into the political economy of the wealth of nations, the doxological acclamations that once congealed in the king's sublime body metamorphose into the less theatrical but no less liturgical productivity that congeals in the commodity as the substance of its value.

Against this background one can now better see what Hannah Arendt gets wrong about Marx's understanding of labor. In *The Human Condition*, she argues that Marx shares in a modern tendency to posit labor as the hegemonic form of the *vita activa* to the detriment of the work of fabrication or making, on the one hand, and, more important, the kinds of action that constitute the space of politics proper, on the other (action that must, in turn, be nourished by labor and sheltered by fabrication). She sees Marx's standpoint as one that more or less cedes the space of making and acting to that of what she calls "the social," a domain that emerges once the mode of activity proper to the *oikos* expands out and absorbs the activities that once fabricated the stage for and animated the public sphere. From a purely social viewpoint, which, she writes, "is the viewpoint of the whole modern age but which received its most coherent and greatest expression in Marx's work,"

> all laboring is "productive." . . . The social viewpoint is identical . . . with an interpretation that takes nothing into account but the life process of mankind, and within its frame of reference all things become objects of consumption. Within a completely "socialized mankind," whose sole purpose would be *the entertaining of the life process*—and this is the unfortunately quite unutopian ideal that guides Marx's theories . . . all work would have become labor because all things would be understood, not in their worldly, objective quality, but as results of living labor power and the functions of the life process.[40]

For Arendt, what is above all lost in "socialized mankind" is what distinguishes, to use the Aristotelian terms cited earlier and that inform her thinking on these matters, *living well* from *mere living*. For Arendt, the emergence of "socialized mankind"—really another name for what Foucault grasped as the regime of biopolitics—signals the collapse of human life into the *conatus* ostensibly common to all "vibrant matter." The virtues that define what it means to live well are those exhibited above all on the stage of politics and involve, though doubtlessly in a quite different sense than in Christianity, the dimension of splendor, glory, greatness, radiance. Commenting on Pericles's Funeral Oration as reported by Thucydides, Arendt writes that there as in Homer "the innermost meaning of the acted deed and the spoken word is independent of victory and defeat.... Unlike human *behavior ... action* can be judged only by the criterion of *greatness* because it is in its nature to break through the commonly accepted and reach into the extraordinary" (205; emphasis added). Pericles (or Thucydides), "knew full well," she continues, "that he had broken with the normal standards for everyday behavior when he found the *glory* of Athens in having left behind 'everywhere everlasting remembrance of their good and their evil deeds.' The art of politics teaches men how to bring forth *what is great and radiant*" (206; emphasis added).[41] But as I have tried to show, Marx's fundamental point is that capitalism is a social formation organized precisely around splendor and glory; the labor theory of value is fundamentally a theory of the production of glory, of the liturgical dimension of labor performed in the service of the greater valor, glory, splendor, of Value.[42]

The conclusion to be drawn from all of this is that the critique of political economy is always an engagement with the dimension of glory and the liturgical labor that we are all, at some level, called to perform as citizen-subjects of capitalist modernity. The critique of political economy is, in a word, always at some level *paradoxological*: a working through of the doxological dimension of work. The urgency of this critique has only intensified with the most recent developments of capitalist modernity into ever more radical versions of what Guy Debord called the society of the spectacle. There, what Arendt characterizes as the "entertaining of the life process," actually becomes something like *entertainment* in the everyday sense of the word. In the society of the spectacle the management of life is, so to speak, just another day in the entertainment business or what Adorno called the culture industry. This also turns out to be Agamben's position at the end of his own archaeology of glory. Bringing together Debord's analysis and Carl Schmitt's view that what we now refer to as "public opinion" assumes the function of acclamations in modern democratic societies, Agamben writes:

> What is in question is nothing less than a new and unheard of concentration, multiplication, and dissemination of the function of glory as the center of the political system. What was once confined to the spheres of liturgy and ceremonials has become concentrated in the media and, at the same time, through them it spreads and penetrates at each moment into every area of society, both public and private. Contemporary democracy is a democracy that is entirely founded

upon glory, that is, on the efficacy of acclamation, multiplied and disseminated by the media beyond all imagination. (256)[43]

One thinks here perhaps of "news" organizations such as Fox News in which the production of *doxa qua opinion* is understood as the production of a certain mode of ostensibly patriotic *doxa qua glory* (in such contexts it also becomes clear that the delivery of news and information has become another branch of the entertainment industry). The ancient Greek word for common opinion or belief that first takes on religious meaning when used in the Septuagint to translate *kavod*, the Hebrew word for glory, retains its sacral aura in occult, though in some sense intensified, form at the very point at which it seems to return to its purely "secular," everyday social meaning.

It is no doubt in this context that we should also situate contemporary discussions about the pros and cons of social media and the effects of being constantly "wired," "plugged in," "online." We know by now that social media function by monetizing our sociality, by, for example, converting our own everyday "acclamations"—our likes and dislikes—into commodities. Our participation in social media thus tends to blur the boundaries between production and consumption (the phrase, being "online," suggests participation in a virtual assembly or production line). Our consumption of the services provided by social media is so often free because it is part of the production process of data commodities, the raw materials of marketing strategies designed to display the splendor of commodities calling us to further consumption (perhaps even of more social media). In and through our participation in social media our labor as medium of social relations becomes so fully transparent that it in some sense disappears, ceases to be identifiable as labor. At this point, life as a whole becomes business, busy-ness, the life of a busy-body whose flesh vibrates with bits of digital sociality.

x

I would like to conclude by turning—or in my case, returning—to the famous debate between Walter Benjamin and Gershom Scholem concerning the status of "revelation" in Kafka's writings, a debate that we can now see as one concerned with the paradoxes of glory and the status of Kafka's writings as exercises in paradoxological thinking.[44] The central point of contention between the two friends concerns the status of theological trace elements in Kafka's work. Scholem insists that Kafka's work is suffused with the radiance of revelation, but a revelation, as he puts it, "seen from the perspective in which it is returned to its own nothingness" (letter of July 7, 1934). Scholem will later characterize this "nothingness of revelation" as "a state in which revelation appears to be without meaning, in which it still asserts itself, in which it has validity but no significance [*in dem sie gilt, aber nicht bedeutet*]," a revelation "reduced to the zero point of its own content, so to speak" (letter of September 20, 1934).[45] These remarks are meant to counter his friend's claim, made in his now well-known essay on Kafka, concerning the status of *Studium*, of learning and study, in Kafka's writings: "The gate to justice is study. Yet Kafka doesn't dare attach to this study the promises which tradition has attached to the study of the Torah. His assistants are sextons who have lost their house of prayer; his students are pupils who have lost the Holy Writ [*Schrift*]."[46] For Scholem this represents, as he puts it to his friend, "one of the greatest mistakes you could have made." For Scholem it remains absolutely crucial that the pupils of whom his friend speaks "are not so much those who have lost the Scriptures but rather those students who cannot decipher it" (letter of July 7, 1934). In a further attempt to clarify his position, Benjamin writes, "you take the 'nothingness of revelation' as your point of departure, the salvific-historical perspective of the established proceedings of the trial. I take as my starting point the small, nonsensical hope, as well as the creatures for whom this hope is intended and yet who on the other hand are also the creatures in which this absurdity is mirrored" (letter of August 11, 1934). It is in this context, he continues, "that the problem of Scripture [*Schrift*] poses itself":

> Whether the pupils have lost it or whether they are unable to decipher it comes down to the same thing, because, without the key that belongs to it, the Scripture is not Scripture, but life. Life as it is lived in the village at the foot of the hill on which the castle is built. It is in the attempt to metamorphize life [*in dem Versuch der Verwandlung des Lebens*] into Scripture that I perceive the meaning of "reversal" [*Umkehr*], which so many of Kafka's parables endeavor to bring about. . . . Sancho Panza's existence is exemplary because it actually consists in rereading one's own existence—however buffoonish and quixotic.[47]

For Scholem, then, Kafka's works are suffused with a barely visible effluence or radiance—a radiance composed out of the validity-without-meaning, the *Geltung-ohne-Bedeutung,* of tradition. It is a light that continues to transmit, to bear the trace of the sacred—we might say: the bare life of the sacred—while for Benjamin the energy of this light has been fully absorbed, fully converted into the "vibrations" of the busy-bodies—this strange order of angels—barely living at the foot of the Castle hill. This is, I would argue, the sort of "bare life" that Benjamin had, in an early fragment, characterized as life caught in the cult of "capitalism as religion."

In this highly abbreviated text, Benjamin proposes to radicalize Weber's thesis on the spirit of capitalism by arguing that modern capitalism was not only deeply informed in its beginnings by religious fervor, but had itself mutated into a fully fledged and all-absorbing religious form of life which, as he puts it, "serves to allay the same anxieties, torments, and disturbances to which the so-called religions offered answers."[48] Benjamin goes on to identify three basic aspects of what he refers to as "the religious structure of capitalism": "In the first place, capitalism is a purely cultic religion, perhaps the most extreme that ever existed. In capitalism, things have a meaning only in their relationship to the cult; capitalism has no specific body of dogma, no theology. It is from this point of view that utilitarianism acquires its religious overtones" (288). There is considerable room for disagreement here. Indeed one could argue that the classical theories of the self-regulation of the market from Smith's "invisible hand" to contemporary mathematical modeling of market dynamics form precisely this body of dogma.[49] The second feature Benjamin identifies is "the permanence of the cult." This concerns precisely what I have referred to as the *doxology of everyday life*, an organization of time that serves to eliminate the distinction between workday and holiday, workday and Sabbath: "Capitalism is the celebration of a cult *sans trêve et sans merci*. There are no 'weekdays.' There is no day that is not a feast day, in the terrible sense that all its sacred pomp is unfolded before us; each day commands the utter fealty of each worshiper" (288).[50]

Finally, and perhaps closest to the spirit of Kafka's universe, Benjamin locates the third aspect of "capitalism as religion" as its tendency to universalize the condition of indebtedness and consciousness of guilt, to make it absolute and so without the possibility of absolution. "Capitalism," Benjamin writes, "is probably the first instance of a cult that creates guilt, not atonement [*der erste Fall eines nicht entsühnenden sondern verschuldenden Kultus*]. . . . A vast sense of guilt that is unable to find relief seizes on the cult, not to atone for this guilt but to make it universal" (288). What Benjamin anticipates here is the phenomenon of *sovereign debt* by which I mean not simply the debt owed by nation-states but the *sovereignty of debt* over human life and its possibilities more generally.

Against this background, what Benjamin, in his letters to Scholem, refers to as *Umkehr* or reversal can, I think, be seen as pertaining to those modes of engagement with glory that I have called *paradoxological*. It involves an effort to reach into the doxological machine—the machine that sustains the religious structure of capitalism—and pull its plug, if even for a fleeting moment of Sabbatical inoperativity in which, perhaps, something new might be spelled out by, precisely, *spelling out the spell* cast by the doxology of everyday life. The repetition of such moments, their stringing together into a constellation, constitutes something on the order of what Freud called *working through*, a process that involves, as we have seen, an effort to strike something other than what's there. What Benjamin's preoccupation with Kafka in particular and literary language more generally suggests—Benjamin, one will recall, saw himself, above all, as a kind of literary critic—is that the "spelling" at issue here may ultimately fall within the purview of literature. A second field thus opens up next to the "archaeology of glory," the literary practice and theory of paradoxology. My hope is that my reflections here have helped to provide some provisional indications as to what the relevant sort of *fieldwork* might look like.

NOTES

1. Karl Marx, *Capital: A Critique of Political Economy*, vol. 1, translated by Ben Fowkes (New York: Vintage, 1977), 163. German from *Das Kapital: Kritik der politischen Ökonomie. Erster Band* (Berlin: Karl Dietz Verlag, 2008), 85.

2. My thinking on such matters continues to be inspired and informed by Slavoj Žižek's work on the mutations of ideology in modernity, though it has become ever more difficult to keep up with his writings.

3. Benjamin takes the phrase from a poem by Gottfried Keller. See Eric L. Santner, *On Creaturely Life: Rilke, Benjamin, Sebald* (Chicago: University of Chicago Press, 2006), 81, for a discussion of Benjamin's formulation.

4. I have discussed Freud's *Moses* at considerable length in "Freud's *Moses* and the Ethics of Nomotropic Desire," in *Sexuation*, edited by Renata Salecl, 57–105 (Durham, NC: Duke University Press, 2000).

5. Slavoj Žižek, *For They Know Not What They Do: Enjoyment as a Political Factor* (London: Verso, 1991), 260.

6. Jonathan Lear has developed the notion of ontological vulnerability in *Radical Hope: Ethics in the Face of Cultural Devastation* (Cambridge, MA: Harvard University Press, 2006).

7. It makes sense that in his effort to capture the point at which dreams reach into a dark zone of illegibility—one that also marks the ultimate object-cause

of dreams—Freud invokes the figure of the *navel* (of the dream), a bodily site that appears now as a hole, now as an uncanny excess of knotted flesh.

8. Pursuing a line of thought first laid out by Elaine Scarry in *The Body in Pain* (Oxford: Oxford University Press, 1987), David Graeber has compellingly argued that the emergence of markets is always at some level grounded in violence, a violence that gets "covered" by the surplus value embodied by its victims, whether as flesh left on the ground in war or, more important, as the spectral materiality—a term he does not use himself—generated by enslavement, by *tearing* the vanquished from the fabric of their social being. The enslaved embody the ontological vulnerability of human life by converting it into a surplus of glory for the victor. Referencing the work of Orlando Paterson, Graeber describes the way in which the degradation of the vanquished gets converted into what he calls the *surplus dignity*—honor, magnificence, greatness, splendor—of the victor: "this ability to strip others of their dignity becomes, for the master, the foundation of his honor. . . . One might say: honor is surplus dignity. It is that heightened consciousness of power and its dangers, that comes from having stripped away the power and dignity of others; or at the very least, from the knowledge that one is capable of doing so. At its simplest, honor is that *excess dignity* that must be defended with the knife or sword." Graeber underlines the fact that the use-value of the enslaved can be irrelevant in such politico-symbolic operations, that is, that their value lies largely in their role in the production of glory, magnificence, *Herrlichkeit*, rather than in any purposeful project. They are, at some level, deployed as displays not of useful but rather of *wasted life*. See David Graeber, *Debt: The First 5,000 Years* (Brooklyn: Melville House, 2011), 170.

9. *Telos*, no. 113 (Fall 1998), edited by Russell Berman and Paul Piccone.

10. Michel Foucault, *The History of Sexuality. Volume 1: An Introduction*, translated by Robert Hurley (New York: Vintage, 1990), 139.

11. Michel Foucault, *Discipline and Punish: The Birth of the Prison*, translated by Alan Sheridan (New York: Vintage, 1977), 208; emphasis added.

12. Michel Foucault, *Society Must Be Defended: Lectures at the Collège de France, 1975–1976*, translated by David Macey (New York: Picador, 2003), 217; emphasis added.

13. Recall, once more, Žižek's concise formulation cited in the first lecture: "What is at stake is . . . not simply the split between the empirical person of the king and his symbolic function. The point is rather that this symbolic function *redoubles his very body*, introducing a split between the visible, material, transient body and another, sublime body, a body made of a special, immaterial stuff." Žižek, *For They Know Not What They Do*, 255.

14. Michel Foucault, *Security, Territory, Population: Lectures at the Collège de France, 1977–1978*, translated by Graham Burchell (New York: Palgrave, 2007), 76–77; emphasis added. Subsequent references are made in the text.

15. Joseph Vogl, "Staatsbegehren: Zur Epoche der Policey," *Deutsche Vierteljahrsschrift für Literaturwissenschaft und Geistesgeschichte* 74 (2000): 600–626. Subsequent references are made in the text.

16. These are Lacan's attempt to map the minimal structure of social bonds, the logic of the social mediation/circulation of subject-matter across historical change. Lacan presents his theory of discourses in Jacques Lacan, *The Other Side of Psychoanalysis: The Seminar of Jacques Lacan. Seminar XVII,* translated by Russell Grigg (New York: W. W. Norton, 2007).

17. Giorgio Agamben, *The Kingdom and the Glory: For a Theological Genealogy of Economy and Government,* translated by Lorenzo Chiesa (Stanford, CA: Stanford University Press, 2011). Subsequent references are made in the text.

18. Agamben summarizes the task of the Church Fathers this way: "At the end of classical civilization, when the unity of the ancient cosmos is broken, and being and acting, ontology and praxis, seem to part ways irreversibly, we see a complex doctrine developing in Christian theology, one in which Judaic and pagan elements merge. Such a doctrine attempts to interpret—and, at the same time, recompose—this fracture through a managerial and non-epistemic paradigm: the *oikonomia*. According to this paradigm, the divine praxis, from creation to redemption, does not have a foundation in God's being, and differs from it to the extent that it realizes itself in a separate person, the *Logos*, or Son. However, this anarchic and unfounded praxis must be reconciled with the unity of the substance. Through the idea of a free and voluntary action—which associates creation and redemption—this paradigm had to overcome both the Gnostic antithesis between a God foreign to the world and a demiurge who is creator and Lord of the world, and the pagan identity of being and acting, which made the very idea of creation unconvincing. The challenge that Christian theology thus presents to Gnosis is to succeed in reconciling God's transcendence with the creation of the world, as well as his noninvolvement in it with the Stoic and Judaic idea of a God who takes care of the world and governs it providentially. In the face of this aporetic task, the *oikonomia*—given its managerial and administrative root—offered a ductile tool, which presented itself, at the same time, as a *logos*, a rationality removed from any external constraint, and a praxis unanchored to any ontological necessity or preestablished norm" (65–66).

19. The *Book of Angels* appears in Erik Peterson, *Theological Tractates,* translated by Michael Hollerich (Stanford, CA: Stanford University Press, 2011), 106–42. Subsequent references are made in the text. German text cited from the German translation of *The Kingdom and the Glory: Herrschaft und Herrlichkeit: Zur theologischen Genealogie von Ökonomie und Regierung,* translated by Andreas Hiepko (Frankfurt a. M.: Suhrkamp, 2010).

20. Throughout his study, Peterson takes pains to distinguish Christian from Jewish doxology. He notes, for example, "that the Christian liturgy was not satisfied just to repeat the simple expression of the prophet, according to which the seraphim 'cry and say': 'Holy, holy, holy is the Lord of Hosts.' . . . In contrast to Isaiah, the *eternal duration* of the cry of the 'Holy' is . . . emphasized. . . . This stress on the *unceasing praise* of God by the angels is unknown in Judaism" (119; emphasis added). We might say that Peterson, a convert to Catholicism, emphasizes the Protestant work ethic of the angels. Or to recall our discussion

of the "quality of mercy" in *The Merchant of Venice*, Christian doxology, as Peterson understands it, is the liturgical form of what I earlier characterized as a "portially" reformed debt economy, one that introduces into life the demands of its *infinite amourtization*.

21. Samuel Brody's fine dissertation on Martin Buber argues that the Jewish philosopher developed his own profoundly anarchic theopolitical perspective, one that also took aim at the resurgence of political theology in fascist movements. See "This Pathless Hour: Messianism, Anarchism, Zionism, and Martin Buber's Theopolitics Reconsidered" (PhD diss., University of Chicago, 2013).

22. As I have noted, Kantorowicz himself experienced firsthand the revival of this "archaic sphere" of doxological performativity. In the tumultuous mass politics of the early years of the Weimar Republic he belonged to the militant—and violent—far-right wing of the political spectrum; as a Jew, he would be forced to flee a homeland whose maniacally anti-Semitic regime had put into operation a vast doxological machine to sustain the bonds of the *Volksgemeinschaft*, to synchronize the frequencies at which its members "vibrated." He himself thus brought a finely tuned ear to the revival of interest in the *laudes* among theologians and musicologists in the 1920s as well as for their appropriation in fascist liturgies of power. In my book, *Stranded Objects: Mourning, Memory, and Film in Postwar Germany* (Ithaca, NY: Cornell University Press, 1990), I explore in detail Hans Jürgen Syberberg's often brilliant cinematic investigation into fascist doxology (and the place of cinema in it). The major critiques of Syberberg over the years could be summarized in the claim that his films succumbed to the spell they were spelling out, that they were insufficiently *para-doxological*. I will turn to this concept below.

23. In his Tanner Lectures on Human Values, Jonathan Lear argued that Aristotle's perverse achievement in his *Ethics* was, in effect, to establish just such a dimension of inoperativity in human life and to do so under the sign of happiness as the ostensible telos of human life. See his *Happiness, Death, and the Remainder of Life* (Cambridge, MA: Harvard University Press, 2000). "All the rest of animal nature," Lear writes, "is basically able to fulfill its nature unproblematically. There will be occasional mutants and occasions when the environment doesn't cooperate, but for the most part each species is able to flourish in its distinctive way. It is only humans who have a characteristic problem of failing to thrive. For humans, happiness *is* human flourishing, yet happiness by and large eludes them. Thus by injecting 'happiness' as the organizing goal of human teleology Aristotle manages to disrupt the teleological structure itself" (56).

24. The following section is deeply indebted to Moishe Postone's brilliant study, *Time, Labor, and Social Domination: A Reinterpretation of Marx's Critical Theory* (Cambridge: Cambridge University Press, 1993) and to numerous works by Slavoj Žižek.

25. Adam Smith, *The Wealth of Nations* (New York: Modern Library, 2000), 32 (emphasis added).

26. Smith characterizes the purchase of a commodity as a form of command that passes through the network of commodity producers; market economies are thus at some level decentralized "command economies": "After the division of labor has once thoroughly taken place, it is but a very small part of these [necessaries, conveniences, and amusements of human life] with which a man's own labor can supply him. The far greater part of them he must derive from the labor of other people, and he must be rich or poor according to the quantity of that labor *which he can command* or which he can afford to purchase. The value of any commodity, therefore, to the person who possesses it, and who means not to use or consume it himself, but to exchange it for other commodities, is equal to the quantity of labor which it *enables him to purchase or command*" (*Wealth of Nations*, 33; emphasis added).

27. Marx, *Capital*, 128 (translation modified); Marx, *Kapital*, 52. Subsequent references are made in the text.

28. This is similar to what readers have at times thought with respect to Freud's understanding of libido, of the sexual "labor power" that is, as Freud repeatedly emphasized, *perversely indifferent to its object*, only loosely "soldered" to it in the pursuit of its aim: more pleasure, pleasure in excess of any possible "use-value." Recent efforts to demonstrate the ways in which sex is beneficial to health should be seen, then, as attempts to "repurpose" sexuality, to demonstrate that it in no way swerves from teleological function, that it is in no way *wasteful*—that it is a materialism without *clinamen*.

29. Postone, *Time, Labor, and Social Domination*, 171.

30. Ibid., 170.

31. Recall Foucault's formulation about the king as the *physical-juridical* quilting point of social mediation in the ancien régime. What makes a nation, he writes, is the fact that its members "all have a certain individual relationship—both juridical and physical—with the real, living, and bodily person of the king. It is the body of the king, in his physical-juridical relationship with each of his subjects, that creates the body of the nation." Foucault, *Society Must Be Defended*, 217.

32. As I have indicated in the preface, it would appear as if in contemporary "cognitive capitalism" *data mining* has become the dominant extractive industry, data the value directly extracted/abstracted from "cognitively" laboring bodies.

33. Aside from Freud's writings on anal eroticism, of particular interest is Sandor Ferenczi's "The Ontogenesis of the Interest in Money," in *The Psychoanalysis of Money*, edited by Ernest Borneman, 81–90 (New York: Urizon, 1976). There Ferenczi suggests that feces undergo, under pedagogic pressure, a metamorphosis (by way of degrees of "dehydration") into mud, sand, pebbles, marbles, and, finally, gold.

34. Jean-Joseph Goux, *Symbolic Economies: After Marx and Freud*, translated by Jennifer Curtiss Gage (Ithaca, NY: Cornell University Press, 1990), 28. Georges Bataille's *The Accursed Share* is in its entirety a meditation on the laws of the "general economy" according to which living systems, whether organisms or societies, rid themselves of surplus energy that can serve no practical

purpose, are of no use. If this "excess cannot be completely absorbed in its [a system's] growth, it must necessarily be lost without profit; it must be spent, willingly or not, *gloriously or catastrophically.*" Bataille, *The Accursed Share: An Essay on General Economy, vol. 1: Consumption*, translated by Robert Hurley (New York: Zone Books, 1991), 21.

35. Johann Wolfgang von Goethe, *Faust: A Tragedy*, translated by Walter Arndt (New York: Norton, 2001), 76 (lines 2796–804). German text cited from *Johann Wolfgang Goethe: Faust-Dichtungen*, edited by Ulrich Gaier (Stuttgart: Reclam, 2010). In winter 2014, I sat in on a seminar on *Faust* conducted by my colleague, David Wellbery. My views on the play have been strongly informed by the seminar discussions. This casket containing gold will, of course, turn out to have the mortal consequences that Freud linked to the base metal, lead, in his reading of the three caskets in *The Merchant of Venice*.

36. This would be a productive site for exploring alternative readings in the spirit of Gil Anidjar's *Blood: A Critique of Christianity* (New York: Columbia University Press, 2014).

37. Smith, *Wealth of Nations*, 15. For a wonderfully lucid discussion of the Mephistophelian dimension of classical political economy, of its commitment to an "oikodicy," see Joseph Vogl, *Das Gespenst des Kapitals* (Zurich: Diaphanes, 2010).

38. Marx, *Capital*, 255; *Kapital*, 168–69. For Marx, only in modern capitalism do Aristotle's anxious insights about chrematistics find their truth.

39. Agamben develops the concept of "instrumental cause" in the sequel to *The Kingdom and the Glory, Opus Dei: An Archaeology of Duty*, translated by Adam Kotsko (Stanford, CA: Stanford University Press, 2013). Agamben's key point of reference is Aquinas, for whom the priest functions as "instrumental cause of an act whose primary agent is Christ himself" (22).

40. Hannah Arendt, *The Human Condition* (Chicago: University of Chicago Press 1998), 89; emphasis added. Subsequent references are made in the text.

41. Against this background one might say that for the Greeks, glory is linked to *immortality* sustained by literary and civic remembrance while in the Christian tradition it is linked to *eternity* sustained by faith embodied in cultic action. Arendt's concern with the fate of glory—and so of what is distinctive about the forms of action that constitute politics proper—is echoed in Alain Badiou's understanding of the "evental" opening of a "truth procedure" in the domain of the political. In *The Communist Hypothesis* (London: Verso, 2010), he writes: "The non-factual element in a truth is a function of its orientation, and this will be termed subjective. We will also say that the material 'body' of a truth, in so far as it is subjectively oriented, is an exceptional body. Making unabashed use of a religious metaphor, I will say that the body-of-truth, as concerns what cannot be reduced to facts within it, can be called *a glorious body*. With respect to this body, which is that of a new collective Subject in politics, of an organization composed of individual multiples, we will say that it shares in the creation of a political truth" (244–45; emphasis added).

42. As readers of *The Communist Manifesto* well know, large portions of that text read as quasi-hymnic, quasi-ironic praise—glorification—of the accomplishments achieved under the regime of the self-valorization of Value, above all, the destruction of much of what had heretofore been the object of doxological praise in European civilization.

43. Walter Benjamin's writings on nineteenth-century Paris including, above all, his unfinished *Arcades Project*, represent one of the landmark bodies of work in the field that Agamben, no doubt deeply influenced by Benjamin, called the "archaeology of glory." Agamben's reflections on the doxological dimension of modern democratic societies are largely prefigured there. Writing, for example, about what he sees as the deep affinity between world exhibitions and Grandeville's work, Benjamin writes, "World exhibitions glorify [*verklären*] the exchange value of the commodity. They create a framework in which its use value recedes into the background. They open a phantasmagoria in which a person enters in order to be distracted. The entertainment industry [*Vergnügungsindustrie*] makes this easier by elevating the person to the level of the commodity. He surrenders to its manipulation while enjoying his alienation from himself and others.—*The inthronement of the commodity, with its luster of distraction*, is the secret theme of Grandeville's art. This is consistent with the split between utopian and cynical elements in his work. Its ingenuity in representing inanimate objects corresponds to what Marx calls the 'theological niceties' of the commodity." Walter Benjamin, *Paris, the Capital of the Nineteenth Century*, translated by Howard Eiland, in *Walter Benjamin: Selected Writings, Volume 3: 1935–1938*, edited by Howard Eiland and Michael Jennings (Cambridge, MA: Harvard University Press, 2002), 37.

44. See *The Correspondence of Walter Benjamin and Gershom Scholem: 1932–1940*, edited by Gershom Scholem, translated by Gary Smith and André Lefèvre (Cambridge, MA: Harvard University Press, 1992). The letters, along with other relevant texts, are collected in *Benjamin über Kafka: Texte, Briefzeugnisse, Aufzeichnungen*, edited by Hermann Schweppenhäuser (Frankfurt a. M.: Suhrkamp, 1981). If my preoccupation with this debate has the quality of a repetition compulsion—I refer to it in several books—it is, I think, because the stakes of the debate concern the dimension of human experience that Freud located beyond the pleasure principle and that seems to involve the demand for repetition.

45. As I have suggested earlier, we might hear this formulation as standing in relation to the figure of the king who reigns but no longer governs.

46. Walter Benjamin, "Franz Kafka: On the Tenth Anniversary of his Death," translated by Harry Zohn, in *Walter Benjamin: Selected Writings. Volume 2: 1927–1934,* edited by Michael Jennings, Howard Eiland, and Gary Smith (Cambridge, MA: Harvard University Press, 1999), 815.

47. The village in question is, of course, the setting of Kafka's novel, *The Castle*. I would argue that in Robert Walser's novel, *Jakob von Gunten*, the Institute Benjamenta belongs to the same universe as this village and that Jakob counts

among those creatures in whom, precisely on the basis of his uncannily "vibrant" being, the absurdity of the hope mentioned by Benjamin is mirrored. And indeed, at the end of the novel Jakob becomes a kind of Sancho Panzo to Herr Benjamenta's Quixote.

48. Walter Benjamin, "Capitalism as Religion," translated by Rodney Livingstone, in *Walter Benjamin: Selected Writings, Volume 1: 1913–1926*, edited by Marcus Bullock and Michael Jennings (Cambridge, MA: Harvard University Press, 1996), 288. Subsequent references are made in the text. The German text is found in Walter Benjamin, *Gesammelte Schriften. Band VI: Fragmente vermischten Inhalts*, edited by Rolf Tiedemann and Hermann Sheppenhäuser (Frankfurt a. M.: Suhrkamp, 1986), 100–103.

49. See once more Vogl, *Das Gespenst des Kapitals*, for his compelling reading of the various forms of "oikodicy" that inform political economic doctrine. One could add to this Luc Boltanski and Eve Chiapello's *The New Spirit of Capitalism*, translated by Gregory Elliot (London: Verso, 2007). There the authors analyze, among other things, the quasi-theological literature on *management* that informs this new spirit.

50. What is rendered here as "utter fealty" is, in the original, [*die*] *äußerste Anspannung des Verehrenden*. The word *Anspannung* conveys the sense of stress, tension states, and, perhaps, the condition of *undeadness* that Benjamin referred to as *erstarrte Unruhe* or petrified unrest.

From Moral Neutrality to Effective Altruism:
The Changing Scope and Significance of
Moral Philosophy

PETER SINGER

THE TANNER LECTURES IN HUMAN VALUES

Delivered at

Linacre College, University of Oxford
June 9, 2015

PETER SINGER is often described as the world's most influential living philosopher. In 2005 *Time* magazine named him one of the one hundred most influential people in the world, and in 2014 he was third on the Gottlieb Duttweiler Institute's ranking of Global Thought Leaders. He is known especially for his work on the ethics of our treatment of animals, for his controversial critique of the sanctity of life ethics in bioethics, and for his writing on the obligations of the affluent to aid those living in extreme poverty. He first became well-known internationally after the publication of *Animal Liberation* in 1975. In 2011 *Time* included *Animal Liberation* on its "All-TIME" list of the one hundred best nonfiction books published in English since the magazine began, in 1923. Singer has written, coauthored, edited, or coedited more than forty books, including *Practical Ethics, The Expanding Circle, How Are We to Live?, Rethinking Life and Death, The Ethics of What We Eat* (with Jim Mason), *The Life You Can Save, The Point of View of the Universe* (with Katarzyna de Lazari-Radek), and, most recently, *The Most Good You Can Do.* His works have appeared in more than twenty-five languages.

Peter Singer was born in Melbourne, Australia, in 1946, and educated at the University of Melbourne and the University of Oxford. After teaching in England, the United States, and Australia, he has, since 1999, been Ira W. DeCamp Professor of Bioethics in the University Center for Human Values at Princeton University. Since 2005 he has combined that position with the position of Laureate Professor at the University of Melbourne, in the School of Historical and Philosophical Studies. He is married, with three daughters and four grandchildren. His recreations include hiking and surfing. In 2012 he was made a Companion of the Order of Australia, the nation's highest civic honor.

My topic is the startling change in moral philosophy that has taken place since I came to Oxford as a graduate student in 1969. The story is one in which Oxford philosophy has played a particularly important role, so it seems an appropriate topic for a Tanner Lecture given in Oxford.

In 1972, when I was a Radcliffe Lecturer at University College, Oxford, I published a short article titled "Moral Experts," in which I challenged the view that, as C. D. Broad put it: "It is no part of the professional business of moral philosophers to tell people what they ought or ought not to do."[1] Why, for a time, did most of the leading moral philosophers think it a mistake to look to their discipline for guidance? Why do we see the subject so differently today?

AGAINST PRACTICAL ETHICS

In the article I quoted from C. D. Broad and also from A. J. Ayer, both of whom held what was then the dominant conception of the proper role of the moral philosopher. In this lecture I will add a third, Bertrand Russell. I begin with Ayer, because he is the clearest example of the view I had in mind.

A. J. Ayer

In 1949 A. J. Ayer published an essay called "On the Analysis of Moral judgments."[2] It was later reprinted in his widely read book *Philosophical Essays*. Ayer was, at the time, Grote Professor in Philosophy at University College, London. Earlier he had published *Language, Truth and Logic*, his manifesto for logical positivism, in 1936, when he was only twenty-six, and a lecturer in philosophy at Oxford, and he was to return to Oxford as Wykeham Professor of Logic in 1959.

In "On the Analysis of Moral Judgments," Ayer restates in a somewhat more sophisticated form the view of what it is to make a moral judgment that he first presented in *Language, Truth and Logic*—namely, that such judgments do not state propositions, but express our attitudes, and so cannot be true or false. In explaining the implications of this theory, he makes some firm statements about the scope of moral philosophy:

> I am not saying that morals are trivial or unimportant, or that people ought not to bother with them. For this would itself be a judgement

of value, which I have not made and do not wish to make. And even if I did wish to make it it would have no logical connection with my theory. For the theory is entirely on the level of analysis; it is an attempt to show what people are doing when they make moral judgements; it is not a set of suggestions as to what moral judgements they are to make. And this is true of all moral philosophy, as I understand it. All moral theories, intuitionist, naturalistic, objectivist, emotive, and the rest, in so far as they are philosophical theories, are neutral as regards actual conduct. To speak technically, they belong to the field of meta-ethics, not ethics proper. That is why it is silly, as well as presumptuous, for any one type of philosopher to pose as the champion of virtue. And it is also one reason why many people find moral philosophy an unsatisfying subject. For they mistakenly look to the moral philosopher for guidance.

It is indeed to be expected that a moral philosopher, even in my sense of the term, will have his moral standards and that he will sometimes make moral judgements; but these moral judgements cannot be a logical consequence of his philosophy. To analyse moral judgements is not itself to moralize.[3]

In saying this, Ayer is dismissing a tradition of moral philosophy that goes back to Socrates who, at least as he is portrayed in Plato's dialogues, challenged Athenians to examine their lives. Presumably, by unsettling accepted views, Socrates would have been influencing his interlocutors' ideas about how they ought to live. Other moral philosophers who offered guidance about how to live and what to do included Aristotle, the Epicureans and Stoics, Christian scholastics like Thomas Aquinas, and later Western philosophers such as Hume and Kant, the utilitarians Bentham, Mill, and Sidgwick, and the intuitionist W. D. Ross. All of them thought that moral philosophy has practical implications. Ayer's rejection of this conception of the subject is, however, consistent with the radical view of philosophy that he had put forward in *Language, Truth and Logic*, which maintained that statements for which there is no possible form of verification are meaningless. This included statements about the existence of God, and moral judgments. Ayer was therefore quite deliberately turning his back on the history of philosophy, and setting out a new, and much more limited, program for what philosophers, including moral philosophers, should do.

C. D. Broad

Whatever we think of Ayer's position—and it will not surprise you to learn that I do not think much of it—it at least has the merit of being straightforward and consistent with his overall views. The other philosopher I quoted in "Moral Experts" is C. D. Broad, and his case is more puzzling.

This is the quote I originally used from Broad:

> It is no part of the professional business of moral philosophers to tell people what they ought or ought not to do. . . . Moral philosophers, as such, have no special information not available to the general public, about what is right and what is wrong; nor have they any call to undertake those hortatory functions which are so adequately performed by clergymen, politicians, leader-writers.[4]

When I quoted this, in 1972, I took it at face value, including the reference to "hortatory functions which are so adequately performed by clergymen, politicians, leader-writers." Now that I know more about Broad, it seems to me that he must have meant this ironically. He was a homosexual who in 1958 joined others in signing a letter to *The Times* supporting the repeal of the law that made homosexual acts illegal. Clergymen, at the time, were not generally supportive of such reforms. Although the article from which I quoted was written eighteen years earlier, it seems unlikely that Broad would have then thought that clergymen, along with politicians, were performing their hortatory functions "so adequately."

A second puzzling aspect about the quote is that it is from an essay titled "Conscience and Conscientious Action," which was first published in wartime, in 1940. The opening sentence, which immediately precedes the passage I quoted, indicates its topic: "At the present time tribunals, appointed under an Act of Parliament, are engaged all over England in dealing with claims to exemption from military service based on the ground of 'conscientious objection' to taking part directly or indirectly in warlike activities." So this looks very much like a contribution to practical ethics! Broad's argument is that "for anyone to decide rationally as to whether another person's action is conscientious or not" is an "almost impossible" task, and that therefore the tribunals set up to consider claims to exemption based on conscientious objection "have been given a task which is, from the nature of the case, incapable of being satisfactorily performed." Nor does Broad hesitate to draw the conclusion that this is, "a strong ground against allowing exemption from military service on grounds of conscience and against setting up Tribunals at all," although he does acknowledge that there could be other reasons that point in the opposite direction. Perhaps he has in mind public policy considerations such as reducing the opposition to compulsory military service, or the cost of imprisoning people who refuse to serve. But in any case, Broad clearly comes very close to doing what he says it is not the professional business of philosophers to do—namely, telling people (including those in government) what they ought or ought not to do.

A clue to resolving the seeming contradiction between the passage I quoted in my *Analysis* article (in which Broad says it is no part of the professional business of philosophers to tell people what to do), and the fact that the article in which it appears does tell people what to do, lies in the following sentences, which immediately follow the passage I quoted. Broad writes:

> But it is the function of a moral philosopher to reflect on the moral concepts and beliefs which he or others have; to try to analyse them and draw distinctions and clear up confusions in connection with them; and to see how they are interrelated and whether they can be arranged in a coherent system. Now there can be no doubt that the popular notions of 'conscience' and 'conscientious action' are extremely vague and confused. So I think that, by devoting this paper to an attempt to elucidate them, I may succeed in being topical without being impertinent.

What Broad here describes is in fact the basis for a great deal of what goes on in practical ethics. The reference to clearing up confusions in our moral concepts and beliefs resembles at least part of what I claimed, in "Moral Experts," was the advantage that moral philosophers would have over people in assessing what we ought to do. As I put it then, the moral philosopher's

> specific experience in moral philosophy gives him [or her] an understanding of moral concepts and of the logic of moral argument. The possibility of serious confusion arising if one engages in moral argument without a clear understanding of the concepts employed has been sufficiently emphasised in recent moral philosophy and does not

need to be demonstrated here. Clarity is not an end in itself, but it is an aid to sound argument, and the need for clarity is something which moral philosophers have recognised.[5]

Beyond that, however, Broad says something more far-reaching when he recognizes that it is the function of a moral philosopher to see how "moral concepts and beliefs ... are interrelated and whether they can be arranged in a coherent system." Broad could hardly deny that this is properly the function of a moral philosopher, because it is at least part of what Henry Sidgwick sets out to do in *The Methods of Ethics*, a book that Broad had earlier described as "the best treatise on moral theory that has ever been written."[6] This activity is not normatively neutral. In Sidgwick's hands, in Book 3 of *The Methods*, it leads to the rejection of the form of intuitionism he refers to as "common sense morality" and the suggestion that it needs to be supplemented and underpinned by utilitarianism.

A good deal of my own work in practical ethics could be seen as arguing that our moral concepts and beliefs are *not* coherent, and therefore should be changed. To give some examples:

1. The traditional ethical doctrine of the sanctity of human life, as held by, for instance, the Roman Catholic Church, insists that all human life is of equal worth, irrespective of its quality. Yet it also permits the withdrawal of life support, such as a respirator, from patients who have irreversibly lost consciousness. Although various justifications are given for this permission, such as that the provision of life support in these circumstances is an "extraordinary" rather than an "ordinary" means of treatment, or that it imposes a "disproportionate" burden on the patient, these justifications themselves can be shown, when scrutinized, to rest on a quality of life judgment of the kind that the doctrine of the sanctity of life rejects.[7]

2. Most of us believe that it would be seriously wrong to fail to rescue a small child in danger of drowning in a shallow pond, even when rescuing the child would mean that one has to replace a very expensive pair of shoes. Yet most of us do not condemn a failure to aid children in developing countries, even though we can save their lives for a comparable cost.[8] These beliefs at least appear to be at odds. In several works, I explore some ways of making them coherent, but argue that they do not succeed.[9]

3. We reject the view that, in our dealings with other human beings, we may give extra weight to the interests of those who are members of our own race

or sex, merely because they are of our race or sex. Yet we accept that we should give extra weight to the interests of those who are members of our own species. Although we sometimes disguise the nakedness of such speciesism by referring to characteristics, such as rationality, or self-awareness, or autonomy, that are typically manifested by members of our species and not, or not to the same degree, by members of other species, the fact that we continue to regard even members of our species who do not, and never will, have these characteristics as having a higher moral status than any nonhuman animal suggests that this is not the real basis of our views. There is, therefore, a lack of coherence in our opposition to racism and sexism, and our acceptance of speciesism.[10]

If one argues that an opposing position has this kind of incoherence, one is offering a person who holds the position a choice. In each of these examples, it would be possible for someone to avoid the conclusion for which I am arguing by dropping one of the premises: by saying, in the first example, "it is wrong to withdraw a respirator when one knows that will result in death, even if the patient has no prospect of recovering or again having an acceptable quality of life," and in the second example, "it is not wrong to leave the child to drown in the shallow pond," and in the third example, unpalatable as it may be, by saying that racism and sexism are not wrong.

Thus a more careful reading of Broad than I gave in "Moral Experts" suggests that his conception of the function of a moral philosopher allows considerable scope for practical ethics, and that he himself was engaged in practical ethics in the article from which I quoted. It therefore looks very much as if my younger self seriously misrepresented Broad; but in fact there is other evidence that, though quite unknown to me in 1972, supports the view that he thought moral philosophers have very little to contribute to practical issues. The first comes from *Five Types of Ethical Theory*, written a decade before the article from which I quoted, Broad wrote: "We can no more learn to act rightly by appealing to the ethical theory of right action than we can play golf well by appealing to the mathematical theory of the flight of the golf ball. The interest of ethics is thus almost wholly theoretical."[11] The second piece of evidence arose after Eugene Freeman invited Broad to contribute to a festschrift for Paul Arthur Schilpp, the theme of which was "Philosophy and the Public Good." The volume was to have a particular focus on the issue of nuclear weapons. Broad replied: "I find myself with nothing of the slightest interest or importance to contribute" and expressed the view that this was not merely a result of his own inability, but that it was unlikely that philosophy has anything to contribute on the nuclear threat.[12]

It appears therefore that although Broad recognized that moral philosophers have the tools to contribute to some practical ethical questions, he believed that the occasions on which these contributions are likely to be useful are going to be extremely limited. There was, one might feel, considerable, and I would argue, excessive, modesty about venturing far beyond the academic world and one's area of expertise. He seems to have felt that this would be, to use his word, "impertinent."

In contrast to Broad, the next philosopher I will discuss was not at all modest about writing for a broad public, nor at all constrained about going beyond his professional expertise.

Bertrand Russell

Bertrand Russell was the best-known British philosopher of the twentieth century, and at the same time the author of a large number of books and essays on practical ethical issues, from social justice to sexual morality, and from happiness to nuclear disarmament. How then can he be included among philosophers who think that practical ethics is not philosophy? The answer is that when Russell was writing on what we might now think of as practical ethics, he did not regard what he was doing as philosophy.

Russell's work in ethics is the subject of Charles Pigden's fine contribution to *The Cambridge Companion to Bertrand Russell*, and in what follows I draw on this work.[13] As Pigden points out, Russell himself contributed to a narrow view of what philosophy is, writing: "The only matter concerned with ethics that I can regard as properly belonging to philosophy is the argument that ethical propositions should be expressed in the optative mood, not the indicative."[14] The issue that Russell is referring to is one in what we now call metaethics, and refers to whether we should understand statements like "X is good" as making a statement about X that can be true or false, or as an expression of a wish or hope that makes it another way of saying something like "Would that everyone desire X!" So Russell's view is similar to that of A. J. Ayer and the emotivist account of ethics later defended by C. L. Stevenson. From 1913 onward, Russell held that normative ethical judgments are not the kind of utterance that can be true or false, and since he thought of philosophy as an inquiry into truth, this, Pigden suggests, explains why he thought his writings on issues in normative and applied ethics were not part of philosophy.

This view appears to have affected not only the way in which Russell regarded his own writings on ethical issues but also the way in which he went about that writing. Consider this passage: "Persuasion in ethical matters is necessarily different from persuasion in scientific matters. According to me, the person who judges that A is good is wishing other persons to feel certain desires. He will therefore . . . try to rouse those desires in other people. . . . This is the purpose of preaching and it was my purpose in the books in which I have expressed ethical opinions."[15]

Elsewhere, in defending himself against a lack of precision in his writing, Russell refers to his *Principles of Social Reconstruction* and "to some extent my other popular books" as "not intended as a contribution to learning" but rather having "an entirely practical purpose."[16]

Russell is therefore distinguishing "preaching" from philosophy, and putting practical ethics—indeed, all normative ethics—in the former category. There is one qualification to be made here: work that takes an end as given, and then shows that a particular practice does or does not conduce to that end, is scientific, and it is possible to formulate rational arguments about how best to achieve the given end. For example, if we take, as Bentham did, the maximization of utility as the sole end, we may write a scientific work inquiring whether capital punishment does or does not conduce to this end. But this work would then not be normative either, and would only guide those who accept that utility is the end. This is, therefore, not an exception to Russell's rule that normative ethics is more akin to preaching than to philosophy—or at least, Russell did not think that it was.

We can, I believe, see the effects of this in some of Russell's own writings, especially about nuclear disarmament. It is the plain duty of everyone, he says, to make known two key facts: that nuclear war is "not improbable" and that it would cause the death of all, or almost all, human beings. Given this, a philosopher or other person of "any academic capacity" must, after studying the probable effects of nuclear war, "devote himself, by whatever means are open to him, to persuading other people to agree with him as to these effects and to joining him in whatever protest shows the most chance of success."[17]

What view of normative ethics or applied ethics is Russell displaying here? Note that again the philosopher is not distinguished from others, and the persuasion should be by whatever means are open to him. Here

Russell really is assimilating practical ethics to preaching and reserving the term "philosophy" for something that is clearly not preaching.

Broad and Russell *could* have said that when they were doing practical ethics, what they were doing was part of their professional work as philosophers. It is interesting that they nevertheless chose not to do so. As I have said, some kind of discomfort about venturing into the public eye seems to have been a factor for Broad, and for Russell, given his attitude to religion, perhaps avoiding any suspicion that philosophy is involved in "preaching" could have been a significant factor in denying that practical ethics is part of philosophy. But practical ethics is not the same as preaching, and it is not just a matter of arousing desires, or emotions, in readers. Practical ethics is about producing and assessing arguments for ethical views. It is subject to academic standards. When we grade student essays, we do not grade them on the basis of our agreement or disagreement with the conclusions the student reaches, but on the quite distinct criterion of the quality of the argument presented. Academics seek to publish in peer-reviewed journals, or in books published by respected academic presses that also use reviewers, or if they publish in more popular places, they seek to win the regard of their colleagues, who can tell an emotional appeal from a well-reasoned one. So it is not all that difficult to separate practical ethics from preaching, and it is surprising that Russell himself makes such a crude assimilation. He should have been aware of the work of his many philosophical predecessors who did practical ethics, and should have recognized that, whether he agreed with it or not, it was not the same as preaching. Indeed, Charles Pigden argues that Russell, in at least some of his work—for example, his Hobbesian argument for world government—makes philosophical arguments and therefore is doing philosophy. Pigden writes of Russell: "When he wrote on these topics he often wrote as a moral philosopher and not—as he sometimes pretended—an unphilosophical moralist."[18]

WHAT CHANGED AND WHY?

The rise of student activism in the 1960s—focused initially, in the United States, on the civil rights movement in the South, but subsequently dramatically increased by opposition to the war in Vietnam, and then also by the emerging environmental and feminist movements—led to a demand that university courses should be relevant to the major issues of the day. For some disciplines this was easy. Historians of Southeast Asia had a prominent role to play in teach-ins about the Vietnam war, as did experts on international relations. But what about the rights and wrongs of going to war? Or of disobeying the law requiring young men to register for the draft? Philosophy professors recalled the long tradition of just war theory, and the arguments of social contract theorists like Hobbes, Locke, and Rousseau for a qualified obligation to obey the law. Encouraged by their students—and by departmental chairs seeking larger enrollments to justify maintaining or expanding their academic staff—teachers of philosophy became more willing to venture out beyond the limits of philosophy prescribed by Ayer, Broad, and Russell.

As an undergraduate and master of arts student at the University of Melbourne, I had been involved in the antiwar and anticonscription movement before I came to Oxford as a graduate student in 1969. In 1971, I attended a conference held in London that aimed toward founding an organization called Radical Philosophy. The idea was to change academic philosophy—which most of those attending saw as essentially conservative, elitist, and dominated by Oxford—into something more relevant to people outside academic life, and more in tune with the values of those who saw a need for social change. I shared these aims, and initially supported the organization. To my disappointment, however, the organization came to be dominated by those who thought that what is truly radical is Marxist philosophy, and not the analytical Marxist tradition developed by philosophers like Gerald Cohen, but the interpretations propounded by French writers like Louis Althusser.[19] Whatever one thinks of Marx, to discuss Marxism in the style of Althusser is to ensure that one's work is completely incomprehensible to everyone except the few who enjoy struggling with obscure, jargon-ridden texts. What would really be radical, I thought, would be to use the tools of analytical philosophy in a way that would enhance discussions of important issues outside academia.

In seeking to do philosophical work about practical ethical issues, I was, notwithstanding the conservative reputation of Oxford philosophy, pushing on an open door. This was in part a generational change—younger philosophers like Derek Parfit and Jonathan Glover were already working on what we now consider to be practical ethics. Glover was doing preliminary work for *Causing Death and Saving Lives*, though this seminal book was to be published only in 1977, and Parfit was raising questions about whether it would be better to have a small population of extremely happy people, or a much larger population of people who were, on average, less happy, but could nevertheless be seen as having, because of their numbers, a greater total amount of happiness—a surprisingly difficult issue to resolve that, despite its abstract nature, has important practical implications.[20]

It was not, however, only members of the new generation of Oxford moral philosophers who were interested in practical ethics. R. M. Hare had long thought that the point of doing moral philosophy is to help us reach better decisions on practical issues. In his second book, *Freedom and Reason*, published in 1963, Hare gave examples of moral reasoning that showed that he believed that his analysis of the logic of our use of words like "ought" had practical implications.[21] His 1966 lecture "Peace" was another early foray into practical ethics, although it was little-known until it was reprinted in one of the first anthologies in practical ethics, James Rachels's *Moral Problems*.[22] Later Hare wrote on abortion and other issues in bioethics, and in one article he explored what is wrong with slavery—a topic that was not remote for him because, as he used to say, he had actually been a slave.[23]

Another important source of encouragement of practical ethics came from the founding of *Philosophy and Public Affairs*, which rapidly set the standard for the discipline, publishing, in its first two volumes influential articles such as Judith Jarvis Thomson's "In Defense of Abortion," my own "Famine, Affluence and Morality," and Michael Tooley's "Abortion and Infanticide."[24] Each of these articles used reason and argument to make new points in a way that was distinct from previous discussions of these issues.

THE SIGNIFICANCE OF PRACTICAL ETHICS

To illustrate the significance of this new development in philosophy, I will use two fields that I know well because I have contributed to their development.

The Ethics of Our Treatment of Animals

One way of gauging the extent to which the ethics of how we treat animals has become more prominent in philosophy is to look at Charles Magel's comprehensive bibliography of writings on the moral status of animals. Magel found only 94 works on that subject in the first 1,970 years of the Christian era, but 240 works in the next 18 years, up to the date when he completed his work.[25] The tally must now be in the thousands.

Leading works on animals and ethics have been translated into, and discussed in, most of the world's major languages, including Japanese, Chinese, and Korean. For those who think, as Hegel did, that the Owl of Minerva takes wing at dusk and philosophy follows trends rather than instigating them, it is worth noting that, at least in this instance, the philosophical arguments came first and the animal movement followed. As James Jasper and Dorothy Nelkin observed in *The Animal Rights Crusade: The Growth of a Moral Protest*: "Philosophers served as midwives of the animal rights movement in the late 1970s."[26] Several leaders of the animal movement have attributed their initial awareness of the issue to reading my own book, *Animal Liberation*. These include Henry Spira, who was the first animal campaigner to succeed in stopping a series of experiments on animals, and was also responsible for causing major corporations like Revlon and Avon to cease testing their products on animals, and Ingrid Newkirk, the founder of People for the Ethical Treatment of Animals, the largest radical animal rights organization in the world.[27] Forty years after the publication of *Animal Liberation*, people are still coming up to me and saying that they became vegetarians or vegans after reading the book (in some cases, they tell me that they have been lifelong vegetarians or vegans because their parents read the book). It is, of course, more difficult to say how much the book has contributed to changing attitudes to animals, or to the significant, though regrettably far from sufficient, improvements in animal welfare that have occurred in many different jurisdictions since it was published. These include European Union regulations that have eliminated the most extreme forms of confinement for veal calves, pigs, and hens in factory farms and so have improved the living conditions of hundreds of millions of farm animals, and similar reforms in California.

We can find, I believe, some confirmation of the importance of clarity and rigor in argument in the fact that it is practical ethics in what we can still, for want of a better term, refer to as the analytic tradition that has influenced people in favor of radical changes in their attitudes to animals, and not the continental philosophical tradition, which in this area, at least, has failed to live up to its own standards of social critique. There is, as far as I am aware, no evidence that any of the impetus for changing our practices regarding animals came from writers in the philosophical traditions of twentieth-century continental Europe, that is, from thinkers such as Heidegger, Foucault, Levinas, Derrida, Badiou, or Deleuze, nor from those strongly influenced by these writers.

Obligations of the Affluent to the Poor

"Famine, Affluence and Morality," which I published in 1972, did not have the immediate practical influence of *Animal Liberation*. It was published in an academic journal, not in a book by a trade publisher, and so it reached a larger audience only when it began to be reprinted in anthologies used in teaching ethics courses. Even then, though, it was often taught as if it raised an intellectual, rather than a moral, challenge. Joshua Greene, a professor of psychology at Harvard and the author of *Moral Tribes*, introduced a talk I gave at that university in 2015 by saying that when he was an undergraduate at Harvard, he had taken an ethics course in which students were told to read "Famine, Affluence and Morality," but the professor teaching the course said, in effect, "Well clearly this can't be right, but it's interesting to figure out where he goes wrong."[28] Until recently that was the prevailing response to my views about the obligations of the affluent to the poor; but in the past decade, things have changed. There is an emerging new movement, known as effective altruism, which is taking seriously the idea that we ought to be doing the most good we can, and that one plausible candidate for doing the most good is to give a lot more to help people in extreme poverty. This movement emphasizes the importance of using evidence and reason to determine the most effective ways to improve the world. Although some of this can be seen as science, rather than ethics—assessing the outcomes of specific antipoverty programs is a scientific enterprise—the idea of "improving the world" or "doing the most good you can" implies that we know what is an improvement, and what is not, and are able to compare different possible improvements. The effective altruism movement has therefore spawned a good deal of philosophical discussion, much of it taking place online.[29]

Oxford University has been at the center of the growth of effective altruism. When I wrote "Famine, Affluence and Morality," I was a Radcliffe Lecturer there. More than thirty years later, Toby Ord was a graduate student in philosophy at Oxford when he decided to calculate how much good he could do if he were to become an academic and, for the rest of his career, live on something like his graduate studentship, donating whatever else he earned to a charity. He did the sums and calculated that the money he would be able to donate would, over his lifetime, be sufficient to prevent eighty thousand people in developing countries from becoming blind. He was astonished that one person could, without a particularly high income, do so much good. He thought that if other people knew this, they might be prepared to donate a portion of their income to effective charities, so with assistance from Will MacAskill, another Oxford graduate student in philosophy, he founded Giving What We Can in 2009. MacAskill also set up another organization, 80,000 hours, which provides advice to those who are thinking about choosing an ethical career. The term "effective altruism" was coined when a group of effective altruists, many of them from Oxford, decided that the movement needed a name, and chose it from a list of possibilities. The Centre for Effective Altruism is also now based in Oxford. Many other past and present Oxford philosophers have links to effective altruism.[30]

Effective altruism is a movement based on a set of values that tend to be consequentialist, but not strictly so. Effective altruists take a universalist and timeless perspective. They are concerned about improving the lives of people and other sentient beings, wherever they are, and whenever they exist. They discount the future only for uncertainty, not merely because future goods are yet to come. Many effective altruists think about principles like justice, fairness, and equality in a consequentialist way— that is, they regard them as having great instrumental value, because a society that is just, fair, and not too unequal is likely to have higher welfare than one that does not instantiate these principles; but they do not see such principles as having intrinsic or overriding value.

Effective altruists are concerned with outcomes, not with moral merit. They do not spend much time worrying about whether someone is acting in a purely altruistic way, rather than because he or she is interested in having a good reputation, or living a better life. In fact, effective altruists promote their way of life as one that is more rewarding—because more fulfilling and meaningful—than one that is less altruistic. That may seem paradoxical, but if the result is more help for those in need, that is what really matters.

Effective altruists are spread across a wide spectrum with regard to what they do for others. Some of them provide remarkable proof of the extent to which ethical argument can alter people's lives. Ian Ross, for example, has been a management consultant and is now involved in a video game startup. In 2014 he earned $400,000, and kept only $20,000 for himself, donating 95 percent of his income. Some effective altruists deliberately choose a career that will enable them to give more. Matt Wage, a Princeton philosophy major who had thought of going on to an academic career, turned down Oxford University's offer of a place in its graduate program, and instead went to Wall Street, where for the past three years, he has been earning enough to donate a six-figure sum to effective charities. He believes that this enables him to do more good than he would have been likely to do as an academic.[31]

In January 2013, I learned of a particularly dramatic example of how philosophy can lead people to do something they would not otherwise have done. I received an e-mail that began as follows:

> In *The Life You Can Save*, you remark that as far as you know no student of yours has ever actually donated a kidney. Last Tuesday, I bit the utilitarian bullet: I anonymously donated my right kidney to whoever could use it the most. By doing so, I started a "kidney chain" that allowed a total of four people to receive kidneys. The idea of donating a kidney popped into my head in an Ethics class.

The writer was Chris Croy, a student at St. Louis Community College, in Meramec, Missouri. He went on to tell me that although he had never taken a class with me, my writings on humans' moral obligations to others had played a role in his decision to donate his kidney. After reading my article "Famine, Affluence and Morality," Croy continued, the class had considered a counterargument by John Arthur that contained the following passage:

> One obvious means by which you could aid others is with your body. Many of your extra organs (eye, kidney) could be given to another with the result that there is more good than if you kept both. You wouldn't see as well or live as long, perhaps, but that is not of comparable significance to the benefit others would receive. Yet surely the fact that it is your eye and you need it is not insignificant. Perhaps there could be cases where one is obligated to sacrifice one's health or sight, but what seems clear is that this is not true in every case where (slightly) more good would come of your doing so.

Another student in the class said that we need both of our kidneys to live, but Chris knew that that was wrong and replied that donating a kidney has little to no effect on one's health and thus is actually an insignificant sacrifice. Then he spent the rest of the class thinking about what he had said. He read everything he could find about kidney donation. When his friend Chelsea told him that she was thinking of donating a kidney, the idea suddenly did not seem so crazy. He decided to do it, and after building up his courage called the hospital. Chelsea did the same, but a scan showed that she had polycystic kidney disease, so her offer to donate was rejected. Chris went ahead on his own. More than a year after the donation, Chris was doing fine. One morning he got a call from an unfamiliar number, and a voice said, "Hello, it's your kidney calling." The kidney was now working for a forty-three-year-old schoolteacher at a school that mostly serves poor children. Chris felt good about that.[32]

Effective altruism raises many interesting philosophical questions, and challenges some views that philosophers have defended. Bernard Williams argued, against Henry Sidgwick and utilitarians more broadly, that humans are not the kind of beings who can take a universal point of view: "There is simply no conceivable exercise that consists in stepping completely outside myself and from that point of view evaluating *in toto* the dispositions, projects and affections that constitute the substance of my own life."[33] Some effective altruists come very close to being living refutations of that claim. Williams also argued, in his famous example of George and the chemical weapons factory, that there is something wrong with taking a job that goes against your values, even if by doing so you will bring about better consequences than any alternative open to you. This is, Williams seems to have thought, to give up the projects that are central to all our lives, and making yourself a hostage to circumstances. I am not going to compare working on Wall Street with building chemical weapons, but the many people who have successfully chosen a career with higher financial returns in order to give more seems to refute this aspect of Williams's thought too. Doing the most good you can is itself a project that one can, and arguably should, adopt and take to be overriding of other projects.[34]

PRACTICAL ETHICS AND THE VALUE OF PHILOSOPHY

In 2013 a report from Harvard University set alarm bells ringing because it reported that, for the United States as a whole from 1966 to 2010, the proportion of students completing bachelor's degrees in the humanities fell from 14 percent to 7 percent. Even elite universities like Harvard itself have experienced a similar decline. Moreover, the decline seems to have gotten steeper in recent years. There is talk of a crisis in the humanities.[35]

Nicholas Kristof, in one of his *New York Times* columns, raised the question "What use could the humanities be in a digital age?" Skeptics about the value of the humanities, he wrote, "may see philosophy as the most irrelevant and self-indulgent of the humanities." He then responded to these skeptics by referring to three philosophers who have shaped the way he understands the world: Isaiah Berlin, John Rawls, and myself. "These three philosophers," Kristof wrote, "influence the way I think about politics, immigration, inequality; they even affect what I eat," and he concluded that "To adapt to a changing world, we need new software for our cellphones; we also need new ideas."[36] It hardly needs to be said that all three of the philosophers Kristof names wrote on substantive normative issues in ethics or political philosophy. Kristof is saying, in other words, that philosophy has been redeemed from irrelevance and self-indulgence by precisely the modes of thought that go beyond philosophy, as Ayer, Broad, and Russell sought to define it.

It is, of course, possible to defend the value of areas of philosophy that Kristof does not mention. Yet it is curious that philosophers, who should be the first to question the assumptions on which their discipline rests, rarely mount such defenses of what they are doing. Effective altruism therefore poses a challenging question to everyone thinking of pursuing a career in philosophy: will you, by making that career choice, be doing the most good you can? The prospects of giving this question an affirmative answer seem brighter if you are planning to work on normative questions, and in that way may help others to do more good (although even then, for some people there may be better options, as Matt Wage decided there were for him). If, however, you are not intending to work in an area of philosophy that will make a difference, either directly or indirectly, to how people live, the question as to whether you should choose a philosophical career becomes more acute. Why not choose a different career that will do more good? To answer that question—or a broader question about the value of pursuing other areas of the humanities or the arts—is, however, a much larger topic than I can address here.

NOTES

1. Peter Singer, "Moral Experts," *Analysis* 32 (1972): 115–17. The quote is from C. D. Broad, "Conscience and Conscientious Action," *Philosophy* 15 (1940): 115–30, here 115. Reprinted in C. D. Broad, *Ethics and the History of Philosophy* (New York: Humanities Press, 1952).
2. A. J. Ayer, "On the Analysis of Moral Judgments," *Horizon* 20 (1949): 171–84, reprinted in A. J. Ayer, *Philosophical Essays* (London: Macmillan, 1954), 231–49.
3. Ayer *Philosophical Essays*, 244–46.
4. Broad, "Conscience and Conscientious Action," 115.
5. Singer, "Moral Experts," 117.

6. C. D. Broad, *Five Types of Ethical Theory* (London: Kegan Paul, Trench and Trubner, 1930), 143.

7. See Helga Kuhse and Peter Singer, *Should the Baby Live?* (Oxford: Oxford University Press, 1985); Peter Singer, *Rethinking Life and Death* (Oxford: Oxford University Press, 1995).

8. When I first made this claim, the available information on the cost of saving a life by donating to an aid organization indicated that it was comparable with the cost of an expensive pair of shoes. Subsequently, much more thorough investigation of the cost of saving a life by donating to an effective aid organization put the figure at around $3,000. Although it is possible to find shoes priced at $3,000, few of us would pay that much for a pair of shoes. On the other hand, Peter Unger's example of Bob and the Bugatti suggests that most people believe it would be wrong to fail to save a life even if the cost to oneself were *much* more than $3,000. See Unger, *Living High and Letting Die* (New York: Oxford University Press, 1996), 136–39.

9. See, for example, Peter Singer, "Famine, Affluence and Morality," *Philosophy and Public Affairs* 1 (1972): 229–43; *The Life You Can Save* (New York: Random House, 2009).

10. See especially Peter Singer, *Animal Liberation*, rev. ed. (New York: Harper, 2009).

11. Broad, *Five Types of Ethical Theory*, 285. I owe this quote to Dale Jamieson, "Constructing Practical Ethics," in *The Oxford Handbook of the History of Ethics*, edited by Roger Crisp (Oxford: Oxford University Press, 2012), 845.

12. C. D. Broad to Eugene Freeman, March 13, 1964, quoted in Eugene Freeman, ed., *The Abdication of Philosophy* (La Salle, IL: Open Court, 1976), 2–3

13. Charles Pigden, "Bertrand Russell: Moral Philosopher or Unphilosophical Moralist?" in *The Cambridge Companion to Bertrand Russell*, edited by Nicholas Griffin (Cambridge: Cambridge University Press, 2003), 475–506; for a fuller account of Russell's work in moral philosophy, see Pigden's "Russell's Moral Philosophy," in *The Stanford Encyclopedia of Philosophy, edited by* Edward N. Zalta (Winter 2014 ed.), http://plato.stanford.edu/archives/win2014/entries/russell-moral.

14. Bertrand Russell, "Reply to Criticisms," in *The Collected Papers of Bertrand Russell*, vol. 11, edited by John Slater and Peter Köllner (London: Routledge, 1997) 47. I owe this quote to Pigden, "Bertrand Russell," 478.

15. Russell, "Reply to Criticisms," 11:47, quoted in Pigden, "Bertrand Russell," 480.

16. Russell, "Reply to Criticisms," 11:55–6, quoted by Pigden, "Bertrand Russell," 481.

17. Bertrand Russell, "The Duty of a Philosopher in This Age," in Freeman, *Abdication of Philosophy*, 17–18. Freeman indicates (on p. 22) that this paper was written in 1964, when Russell was ninety-two, though published only after his death.

18. Pigden, "Bertrand Russell," 493.

19. This trend can be seen by a perusal of the early issues of the organization's journal, *Radical Philosophy*, available at www.radicalphilosophy.com.

20. Jonathan Glover, *Causing Death and Saving Lives* (Harmondsworth, Middlesex: Penguin, 1977). A full presentation of Parfit's work did not appear until his *Reasons and Persons* (Oxford: Clarendon Press, 1984).

21. R. M. Hare, *Freedom and Reason* (Oxford: Oxford University Press, 1963).

22. R. M. Hare, "Peace," a lecture given at the Australian National University, Canberra, 1966 and privately printed. Reprinted in James Rachels, ed., *Moral Problems* (New York: Harper and Row, 1970), 323–41, and in R. M. Hare, *Applications of Moral Philosophy* (London: Macmillan, 1972), 71–89.

23. R. M. Hare, "What's Wrong with Slavery?" *Philosophy and Public Affairs* 8 (1979): 103–21. Hare had been a slave during World War II, when he was, as a prisoner of the Japanese, forced to work on building the notorious Burma Railway.

24. Judith Jarvis Thomson, "A Defense of Abortion," *Philosophy and Public Affairs* 1 (1971): 47–66; Peter Singer, "Famine, Affluence and Morality," *Philosophy and Public Affairs* 1 (1972): 229–43; Michael Tooley, "Abortion and Infanticide," *Philosophy and Public Affairs* 2 (1972): 37–65.

25. Charles Magel, *Keyguide to Information Sources in Animal Rights* (Jefferson, NC: McFarland, 1989).

26. James Jasper and Dorothy Nelkin, *The Animal Rights Crusade: The Growth of a Moral Protest* (New York: Free Press, 1992), 90.

27. On Spira, see Peter Singer, *Ethics into Action: Henry Spira and the Animal Rights Movement* (Lanham, MD: Rowman and Littlefield, 1998). For Newkirk, see Ingrid Newkirk, "What is Animal Liberation? Philosopher Peter Singer's Groundbreaking Work Turns 40," http://www.peta.org/about-peta/learn-about-peta/ingrid-newkirk/animal-liberation/.

28. Joshua Greene, introducing my lecture, "The Most Good You Can Do: How Effective Altruism Is Changing Ideas About Living Ethically," Harvard University, April 12, 2015. Greene's remarks can be heard at https://www.youtube.com/watch?v=MAXTmLsIx7g, around eighteen minutes after the beginning of the video.

29. See Peter Singer, *The Most Good You Can Do* (New Haven, CT: Yale University Press, 2015); and Will MacAskill, *Doing Good Better* (New York: Gotham, 2015). Web sites include www.effectivealtruism.org; www.thelifeyoucansave.org; www.givingwhatwecan.org; and www.80000hours.org; and www.givewell.org.

30. An incomplete list includes, in alphabetical order, Nick Beckstead, Nick Bostrom, Iason Gabriel, Michelle Hutchinson, Jeff McMahan, Andreas Mogensen, Derek Parfit, Theron Pummer, Janet Radcliffe Richards, and myself.

31. E-mails from Ian Ross to me, 2013–14, and e-mails and conversations between Matt Wage and me, 2013–15.

32. E-mails from Chris Croy to me, 2013–14.

33. Bernard Williams, "The Point of View of the Universe: Sidgwick and the Ambitions of Ethics," *Cambridge Review*, May 7, 1982, 191; reprinted in Bernard Williams, *The Sense of the Past: Essays in the History of Philosophy*, edited by Myles Burnyeat (Princeton, NJ: Princeton University Press, 2006).

34. Passages in this section are based on my book *The Most Good You Can Do*.

35. *The Teaching of the Arts and Humanities at Harvard College: Mapping the Future*, a report of a Working Group chaired by James Simpson and Sean Kelly, Harvard University, 2013, http://harvardmagazine.com/sites/default/files /Mapping%20the%20Future%20of%20the%20Humanities.pdf. See also "Addressing a Decline in Humanities Enrollment," *Harvard Magazine*, June 6, 2013, http://harvardmagazine.com/2013/06/reinvigorating-the-humanities; and Anthony Grafton and James Grossman, "The Humanities in Dubious Battle," *Chronicle of Higher Education*, July 1, 2013, http://chronicle.com/article/The -Humanities-in-Dubious/140047/.

36. Nicholas Kristof, "Don't Dismiss the Humanities," *New York Times*, August 13, 2014.

THE TANNER LECTURERS

1976–1977

OXFORD   Bernard Williams, Cambridge University

MICHIGAN   Joel Feinberg, University of Arizona
"Voluntary Euthanasia and the Inalienable Right to Life"

STANFORD   Joel Feinberg, University of Arizona
"Voluntary Euthanasia and the Inalienable Right to Life"

1977–1978

OXFORD   John Rawls, Harvard University

MICHIGAN   Sir Karl Popper, University of London
"Three Worlds"

STANFORD   Thomas Nagel, Princeton University

1978–1979

OXFORD   Thomas Nagel, Princeton University
"The Limits of Objectivity"

CAMBRIDGE   C. C. O'Brien, London

MICHIGAN   Edward O. Wilson, Harvard University
"Comparative Social Theory"

STANFORD   Amartya Sen, Oxford University
"Equality of What?"

UTAH   Lord Ashby, Cambridge University
"The Search for an Environmental Ethic"

UTAH STATE   R. M. Hare, Oxford University
"Moral Conflicts"

1979–1980

OXFORD   Jonathan Bennett, University of British Columbia
"Morality and Consequences"

CAMBRIDGE   Raymond Aron, Collège de France
"Arms Control and Peace Research"

HARVARD   George Stigler, University of Chicago
"Economics or Ethics?"

MICHIGAN   Robert Coles, Harvard University
"Children as Moral Observers"

STANFORD   Michel Foucault, Collège de France
             "Omnes et Singulatim: Towards a Criticism of 'Political Reason'"

UTAH   Wallace Stegner, Los Altos Hills, California
             *"The Twilight of Self-Reliance: Frontier Values and Contemporary
             America"*

1980–1981

OXFORD   Saul Bellow, University of Chicago
             "A Writer from Chicago"

CAMBRIDGE   John Passmore, Australian National University
             "The Representative Arts as a Source of Truth"

HARVARD   Brian M. Barry, University of Chicago
             *"Do Countries Have Moral Obligations? The Case of World
             Poverty"*

MICHIGAN   John Rawls, Harvard University
             "The Basic Liberties and Their Priority"

STANFORD   Charles Fried, Harvard University
             "Is Liberty Possible?"

UTAH   Joan Robinson, Cambridge University
             "The Arms Race"

HEBREW   Solomon H. Snyder, Johns Hopkins University
UNIV.   *"Drugs and the Brain and Society"*

1981–1982

OXFORD   Freeman Dyson, Princeton University
             "Bombs and Poetry"

CAMBRIDGE   Kingman Brewster, President Emeritus, Yale University
             "The Voluntary Society"

HARVARD   Murray Gell-Mann, California Institute of Technology
             "The Head and the Heart in Policy Studies"

MICHIGAN   Thomas C. Schelling, Harvard University
             "Ethics, Law, and the Exercise of Self-Command"

STANFORD   Alan A. Stone, Harvard University
             "Psychiatry and Morality"

UTAH   R. C. Lewontin, Harvard University
             "Biological Determinism"

AUSTRALIAN   Leszek Kolakowski, Oxford University
NATL. UNIV. *"The Death of Utopia Reconsidered"*

1982–1983

OXFORD   Kenneth J. Arrow, Stanford University
             "The Welfare-Relevant Boundaries of the Individual"

CAMBRIDGE H. C. Robbins Landon, University College, Cardiff
"Haydn and Eighteenth-Century Patronage in Austria and Hungary"

HARVARD Bernard Williams, Cambridge University
"Morality and Social Justice"

STANFORD David Gauthier, University of Pittsburgh
"The Incompleat Egoist"

UTAH Carlos Fuentes, Princeton University
"A Writer from Mexico"

JAWAHARLAL Ilya Prigogine, Université Libre de Bruxelles
NEHRU UNIV. *"Only an Illusion"*

1983–1984

OXFORD Donald D. Brown, Johns Hopkins University
"The Impact of Modern Genetics"

CAMBRIDGE Stephen J. Gould, Harvard University
"Evolutionary Hopes and Realities"

MICHIGAN Herbert A. Simon, Carnegie-Mellon University
"Scientific Literacy as a Goal in a High-Technology Society"

STANFORD Leonard B. Meyer, University of Pennsylvania
"Music and Ideology in the Nineteenth Century"

UTAH Helmut Schmidt, former Chancellor, West Germany
"The Future of the Atlantic Alliance"

HELSINKI Georg Henrik von Wright, Helsinki
"Of Human Freedom"

1984–1985

OXFORD Barrington Moore, Jr., Harvard University
"Authority and Inequality under Capitalism and Socialism"

CAMBRIDGE Amartya Sen, Oxford University
"The Standard of Living"

HARVARD Quentin Skinner, Cambridge University
"The Paradoxes of Political Liberty"

Kenneth J. Arrow, Stanford University
"The Unknown Other"

MICHIGAN Nadine Gordimer, South Africa
"The Essential Gesture: Writers and Responsibility"

STANFORD Michael Slote, University of Maryland
"Moderation, Rationality, and Virtue"

1985–1986

OXFORD Thomas M. Scanlon, Jr., Harvard Univesity
"The Significance of Choice"

CAMBRIDGE   Aldo Van Eyck, The Netherlands
"Architecture and Human Values"

HARVARD   Michael Walzer, Institute for Advanced Study
"Interpretation and Social Criticism"

MICHIGAN   Clifford Geertz, Institute for Advanced Study
"The Uses of Diversity"

STANFORD   Stanley Cavell, Harvard University
"The Uncanniness of the Ordinary"

UTAH   Arnold S. Relman, Editor, *New England Journal of Medicine*
"Medicine as a Profession and a Business"

1986–1987

OXFORD   Jon Elster, Oslo University and the University of Chicago
"Taming Chance: Randomization in Individual and Social Decisions"

CAMBRIDGE   Roger Bulger, University of Texas Health Sciences Center, Houston
"On Hippocrates, Thomas Jefferson, and Max Weber: The Bureaucratic, Technologic Imperatives and the Future of the Healing Tradition in a Voluntary Society"

HARVARD   Jürgen Habermas, University of Frankfurt
"Law and Morality"

MICHIGAN   Daniel C. Dennett, Tufts University
"The Moral First Aid Manual"

STANFORD   Gisela Striker, Columbia University
"Greek Ethics and Moral Theory"

UTAH   Laurence H. Tribe, Harvard University
"On Reading the Constitution"

1987–1988

OXFORD   F. Van Zyl Slabbert, University of the Witwatersrand, South Africa
"The Dynamics of Reform and Revolt in Current South Africa"

CAMBRIDGE   Louis Blom-Cooper, Q.C., London
"The Penalty of Imprisonment"

HARVARD   Robert A. Dahl, Yale University
"The Pseudodemocratization of the American Presidency"

MICHIGAN   Albert O. Hirschman, Institute for Advanced Study
"Two Hundred Years of Reactionary Rhetoric: The Case of the Perverse Effect"

STANFORD   Ronald Dworkin, New York University and University College, Oxford
"Foundations of Liberal Equality"

UTAH Joseph Brodsky, Russian poet, Mount Holyoke College
"A Place as Good as Any"

CALIFORNIA Wm. Theodore de Bary, Columbia University
"The Trouble with Confucianism"

BUENOS Barry Stroud, University of California, Berkeley
AIRES *"The Study of Human Nature and the Subjectivity of Value"*

MADRID Javier Muguerza, Universidad Nacional de Educación a Distancia,
Madrid
"The Alternative of Dissent"

WARSAW Anthony Quinton, British Library, London
"The Varieties of Value"

1988–1989

OXFORD Michael Walzer, Institute for Advanced Study
"Nation and Universe"

CAMBRIDGE Albert Hourani, Emeritus Fellow, St. Antony's College, and
Magdalen College, Oxford
"Islam in European Thought"

MICHIGAN Toni Morrison, State University of New York at Albany
*"Unspeakable Things Unspoken: The Afro-American Presence in
American Literature"*

STANFORD Stephen J. Gould, Harvard University
"Unpredictability in the History of Life"
*"The Quest for Human Nature: Fortuitous Side, Consequences, and
Contingent History"*

UTAH Judith Shklar, Harvard University
"Amerian Citizenship: The Quest for Inclusion"

CALIFORNIA S. N. Eisenstadt, The Hebrew University of Jerusalem
*"Cultural Tradition, Historical Experience, and Social Change: The
Limits of Convergence"*

YALE J. G. A. Pocock, Johns Hopkins University
"Edward Gibbon in History: Aspects of the Text in The History of
the Decline and Fall of the Roman Empire*"*

CHINESE Fei Xiaotong, Peking University
UNIVERSITY *"Plurality and Unity in the Configuration of the Chinese People"*
OF HONG
KONG

1989–1990

OXFORD Bernard Lewis, Princeton University
"Europe and Islam"

CAMBRIDGE Umberto Eco, University of Bologna
"Interpretation and Overinterpretation: World, History, Texts"

HARVARD
Ernest Gellner, Kings College, Cambridge
"The Civil and the Sacred"

MICHIGAN
Carol Gilligan, Harvard University
"Joining the Resistance: Psychology, Politics, Girls, and Women"

UTAH
Octavio Paz, Mexico City
"Poetry and Modernity"

YALE
Edward N. Luttwak, Center for Strategic and International
Studies
"Strategy: A New Era?"

PRINCETON
Irving Howe, writer and critic
"The Self and the State"

1990–1991

OXFORD
David Montgomery, Yale University
*"Citizenship and Justice in the Lives and Thoughts of Nineteenth-
Century American Workers"*

CAMBRIDGE
Gro Harlem Brundtland, Prime Minister of Norway
*"Environmental Challenges of the 1990s: Our Responsibility toward
Future Generations"*

HARVARD
William Gass, Washington University
"Eye and Idea"

MICHIGAN
Richard Rorty, University of Virginia
"Feminism and Pragmatism"

STANFORD
G. A. Cohen, All Souls College, Oxford
"Incentives, Inequality, and Community"

János Kornai, University of Budapest and Harvard University
"Market Socialism Revisited"

UTAH
Marcel Ophuls, international film maker
"Resistance and Collaboration in Peacetime"

YALE
Robertson Davies, novelist
"Reading and Writing"

PRINCETON
Annette C. Baier, Pittsburgh University
"Trust"

LENINGRAD
János Kornai, University of Budapest and Harvard University
"Transition from Marxism to a Free Economy"

1991–1992

OXFORD
R. Z. Sagdeev, University of Maryland
"Science and Revolutions"

UC
LOS ANGELES
Václav Havel, former President, Republic of Czechoslovakia
(Untitled lecture)

UC BERKELEY
Helmut Kohl, Chancellor of Germany
(Untitled lecture)

CAMBRIDGE   David Baltimore, former President, Rockefeller University
"On Doing Science in the Modern World"

MICHIGAN   Christopher Hill, Oxford
"The Bible in Seventeenth-Century English Politics"

STANFORD   Charles Taylor, McGill University
"Modernity and the Rise of the Public Sphere"

UTAH   Jared Diamond, University of California, Los Angeles
"The Broadest Pattern of Human History"

PRINCETON   Robert Nozick, Harvard University
"Decisions of Principle, Principles of Decision"

1992–1993

MICHIGAN   Amos Oz, Israel
"The Israeli-Palestinian Conflict: Tragedy, Comedy, and Cognitive Block—A Storyteller's Point of View"

CAMBRIDGE   Christine M. Korsgaard, Harvard University
"The Sources of Normativity"

UTAH   Evelyn Fox Keller, Massachusetts Institute of Technology
"Rethinking the Meaning of Genetic Determinism"

YALE   Fritz Stern, Columbia University
"Mendacity Enforced: Europe, 1914–1989"
"Freedom and Its Discontents: Postunification Germany"

PRINCETON   Stanley Hoffmann, Harvard University
"The Nation, Nationalism, and After: The Case of France"

STANFORD   Colin Renfrew, Cambridge University
"The Archaeology of Identity"

1993–1994

MICHIGAN   William Julius Wilson, University of Chicago
"The New Urban Poverty and the Problem of Race"

OXFORD   Lord Slynn of Hadley, London
"Law and Culture—A European Setting"

HARVARD   Lawrence Stone, Princeton University
"Family Values in a Historical Perspective"

CAMBRIDGE   Peter Brown, Princeton University
"Aspects of the Christianisation of the Roman World"

UTAH   A. E. Dick Howard, University of Virginia
"Toward the Open Society in Central and Eastern Europe"

Jeffrey Sachs, Harvard University
"Shock Therapy in Poland: Perspectives of Five Years"

UTAH   Adam Zagajewski, Paris
"A Bus Full of Prophets: Adventures of the Eastern-European Intelligentsia"

PRINCETON   Alasdair MacIntyre, Duke University
              *"Truthfulness, Lies, and Moral Philosophers: What Can We Learn
                  from Mill and Kant?"*

CALIFORNIA   Oscar Arias, Costa Rica
              "Poverty: The New International Enemy"

STANFORD   Thomas Hill, University of North Carolina at Chapel Hill
              "Basic Respect and Cultural Diversity"
              "Must Respect Be Earned?"

UC SAN   K. Anthony Appiah, Harvard University
DIEGO   *"Race, Culture, Identity: Misunderstood Connections"*

1994–1995

YALE   Richard Posner, United States Court of Appeals
              *"Euthanasia and Health Care: Two Essays on the Policy Dilemmas
                  of Aging and Old Age"*

MICHIGAN   Daniel Kahneman, University of California, Berkeley
              "Cognitive Psychology of Consequences and Moral Intuition"

HARVARD   Cass R. Sunstein, University of Chicago
              "Political Conflict and Legal Agreement"

CAMBRIDGE   Roger Penrose, Oxford Mathematics Institute
              "Space-time and Cosmology"

PRINCETON   Antonin Scalia, United States Supreme Court
              *"Common-Law Courts in a Civil-Law System: The Role of the
                  United States Federal Courts in Interpreting the Constitution
                  and Laws"*

UC SANTA   Nancy Wexler, Columbia University
CRUZ   *"Genetic Prediction and Precaution Confront Human Social
                  Values"*

OXFORD   Janet Suzman, South Africa
              "Who Needs Parables?"

STANFORD   Amy Gutmann, Princeton University
              "Responding to Racial Injustice"

UTAH   Edward Said, Columbia University
              "On Lost Causes"

1995–1996

PRINCETON   Harold Bloom, Yale University
              I. *"Shakespeare and the Value of Personality"*
              II. *"Shakespeare and the Value of Love"*

OXFORD   Simon Schama, Columbia University
              *"Rembrandt and Rubens: Humanism, History, and the Peculiarity
                  of Painting"*

CAMBRIDGE   Gunther Schuller, Newton Center, Massachusetts
I. "Jazz: A Historical Perspective"
II. "Duke Ellington"
III. "Charles Mingus"

UC RIVERSIDE   Mairead Corrigan Maguire, Belfast, Northern Ireland
"Peacemaking from the Grassroots in a World of Ethnic Conflict"

HARVARD   Onora O'Neill, Newham College, Cambridge
"Kant on Reason and Religion"

STANFORD   Nancy Fraser, New School for Social Research
"Social Justice in the Age of Identity Politics: Redistribution, Recognition, and Participation"

UTAH   Cornell West, Harvard University
"A Genealogy of the Public Intellectual"

YALE   Peter Brown, Princeton University
"The End of the Ancient Other World: Death and Afterlife between Late Antiquity and the Early Middle Ages"

1996–1997

TORONTO   Peter Gay, Emeritus, Yale University
"The Living Enlightenment"

MICHIGAN   Thomas M. Scanlon, Harvard University
"The Status of Well-Being"

HARVARD   Stuart Hampshire, Emeritus, Stanford University
"Justice Is Conflict: The Soul and the City"

CAMBRIDGE   Dorothy L. Cheney, University of Pennsylvania
"Why Animals Don't Have Language"

PRINCETON   Robert M. Solow, Massachusetts Institute of Technology
"Welfare and Work"

CALIFORNIA   Marian Wright Edelman, Children's Defense Fund
"Standing for Children"

YALE   Liam Hudson, Balas Copartnership
"The Life of the Mind"

STANFORD   Barbara Herman, University of California, Los Angeles
"Moral Literacy"

OXFORD   Francis Fukuyama, George Mason University
"Social Capital"

UTAH   Elaine Pagels, Princeton University
"The Origin of Satan in Christian Traditions"

1997–1998

UTAH   Jonathan D. Spence, Yale University
"Ideas of Power: China's Empire in the Eighteenth Century and Today"

PRINCETON   J. M. Coetzee, University of Cape Town
                "The Lives of Animals"

MICHIGAN   Antonio R. Damasio, University of Iowa
                "Exploring the Minded Brain"

CHARLES   Timothy Garton Ash, Oxford University
UNIVERSITY   *"The Direction of European History"*

HARVARD   M. F. Burnyeat, Oxford University
                "Culture and Society in Plato's Republic"

CAMBRIDGE   Stephen Toulmin, University of Southern California
                "The Idol of Stability"

UC IRVINE   David Kessler, Yale University
                "Tobacco Wars: Risks and Rewards of a Major Challenge"

YALE   Elaine Scarry, Harvard University
                "On Beauty and Being Just"

STANFORD   Arthur Kleinman, Harvard University
                *"Experience and Its Moral Modes: Culture, Human Conditions,
                and Disorder"*

1998–1999

MICHIGAN   Walter Burkert, University of Zurich
                *"Revealing Nature Amidst Multiple Cultures: A Discourse with
                Ancient Greeks"*

UTAH   Geoffrey Hartman, Yale University
                "Text and Spirit"

YALE   Steven Pinker, Massachusetts Institute of Technology
                "The Blank Slate, the Noble Savage, and the Ghost in the Machine"

STANFORD   Randall Kennedy, Harvard University
                "Who Can Say 'Nigger'? . . . and Other Related Questions"

UC DAVIS   Richard White, Stanford University
                "The Problem with Purity"

OXFORD   Sidney Verba, Harvard University
                *"Representative-Democracy and Democratic Citizens: Philosophical
                and Empirical Understandings"*

PRINCETON   Judith Jarvis Thomson, Massachusetts Institute of Technology
                "Goodness and Advice"

HARVARD   Lani Guinier, Harvard University
                "Rethinking Powers"

1999–2000

YALE   Marina Warner, London
                "Spirit Visions"

MICHIGAN   Helen Vendler, Harvard University
                "Poetry and the Mediation of Value: Whitman on Lincoln"

HARVARD   Wolf Lepenies, Free University, Berlin
            "The End of 'German Culture'"

CAMBRIDGE   Jonathan Lear, University of Chicago
            "Happiness"

OXFORD   Geoffrey Hill, Boston University
            "Rhetorics of Value"

PRINCETON   Michael Ignatieff, London
            "Human Rights as Politics"
            "Human Rights as Idolatry"

UTAH   Charles Rosen, New York
            *"Tradition without Convention: The Impossible Nineteenth-
            Century Project"*

STANFORD   Jared Diamond, UCLA Medical School
            "Ecological Collapses of Pre-industrial Societies"

2000–2001

MICHIGAN   Partha Dasgupta, Cambridge University
            "Valuing Objects and Evaluating Policies in Imperfect Economies"

HARVARD   Simon Schama, Columbia University
            "Random Access Memory"

UC SANTA   William C. Richardson, The Kellogg Foundation
BARBARA   *"Reconceiving Health Care to Improve Quality"*

OXFORD   Sir Sydney Kentridge Q.C., London
            "Human Rights: A Sense of Proportion"

UTAH   Sarah Blaffer Hrdy, University of California at Davis
            "The Past and Present of the Human Family"

UC BERKELEY Joseph Raz, Columbia University
            "The Practice of Value"

PRINCETON   Robert Pinsky, poet, Boston University
            "American Culture and the Voice of Poetry"

YALE   Alexander Nehamas, Princeton University
            "A Promise of Happiness: The Place of Beauty in a World of Art"

CAMBRIDGE   Kwame Anthony Appiah, Harvard University
            "Individuality and Identity"

STANFORD   Dorothy Allison, novelist
            "Mean Stories and Stubborn Girls"
            "What It Means to Be Free"

2001–2002

MICHIGAN   Michael Fried, Johns Hopkins University
            "Roger Fry's Formalism"

UC BERKELEY Sir Frank Kermode, Cambridge, England
            "Pleasure, Change, and the Canon"

HARVARD   Kathleen Sullivan, Stanford University
               "War, Peace, and Civil Liberties"

YALE   Salman Rushdie, New York
               "Step Across this Line"

CAMBRIDGE   Seamus Heaney, Harvard University
               "Homiletic Elegy: Beowulf and Wilfrid Owens"
               "On Pastoral: Starting from Virgil"
               "On Pastoral: Eclogues in extremis"

UTAH   Benjamin Barber, University of Maryland
               "Democratic Alternatives to the Mullahs and the Malls:
                   Citizenship in an Age of Global Anarchy"

STANFORD   Paul Krugman, Princeton University
               "Intractable Slumps"
               "Currency Crises"

PRINCETON   T. J. Clark, University of California, Berkeley
               "Painting at Ground Level"

OXFORD   Laurence H. Tribe, Harvard University
               "The Constitution in Crisis: From Bush v. Gore to the War on
                   Terrorism"

                            2002–2003

MICHIGAN   Claude Steele, Stanford University
               "The Specter of Group Image: The Unseen Effects on Human
                   Performance and the Quality of Life in a Diverse Society"

UC BERKELEY   Derek Parfit, Oxford University
               "What We Could Rationally Will"

HARVARD   Lorraine Daston, Max Planck Institute, Berlin
               "The Morality of Natural Orders: The Power of Medea"
               "Nature's Customs versus Nature's Laws"

AUSTRALIAN   Martha C. Nussbaum, University of Chicago
NAT.   *"Beyond the Social Contract: Toward Global Justice"*
UNIV. AND
CAMBRIDGE

PRINCETON   Jonathan Glover, King's College London
               "Towards Humanism in Psychology"

STANFORD   Mary Robinson, New York
               "Human Rights and Ethical Globalization"
               "The Challenge of Human Rights Protection in Africa"

YALE   Garry L. Wills, Northwestern University
               "Henry Adams: The Historian as Novelist"

OXFORD   David M. Kennedy, Stanford University
               "The Dilemma of Difference in Democratic Society"

2003–2004

UTAH
Sebastião Salgado, Paris
"Art, Globalism and Cultural Instability"

PRINCETON
Frans de Waal, Emory University
"Morality and the Social Instincts: Continuity with the Other Primates"

HARVARD
Richard Dawkins, University of Oxford
"The Science of Religion"
"The Religion of Science"

MICHIGAN
Christine M. Korsgaard, Harvard University
"Fellow Creatures: Kantian Ethics and Our Duties to Animals"

CAMBRIDGE
Neil MacGregor, The British Museum
"The Meanings of Things"

UC BERKELEY
Seyla Benhabib, Yale University
"Reclaiming Universalism: Negotiating Republican Self-Determination and Cosmopolitan Norms"

YALE
Oliver Sacks, Albert Einstein College of Medicine, New York
"Journey Into Wonder: Reflections on a Chemical Boyhood"
"Awakenings Revisited"

STANFORD
Harry Frankfurt, Princeton University
"Taking Ourselves Seriously"
"Getting It Right"

OXFORD
Joseph Stiglitz, Columbia University
"Ethical Dimensions of Globalization"

2004–2005

HARVARD
Stephen Breyer, United States Supreme Court
"Active Liberty: Interpreting Our Democratic Constitution"

CAMBRIDGE
Carl Bildt, Sweden
"Peace after War: Our Experience"

UTAH
Paul Farmer, Harvard University
"Never Again? Reflections on Human Values and Human Rights"

UC BERKELEY
Axel Honneth, Johann Wolfgang Goethe-Universität Frankfurt/Main
"Reification: A Recognition-Theoretical View"

STANFORD
Avishai Margalit, Hebrew University
"Indecent Compromise"
"Decent Peace"

OXFORD
Lord Winston, Imperial College, London
"Manipulating Reproduction"
"Stem Cells: Hope or Hype?"

2005–2006

YALE
Ruth Reichl, *Gourmet* magazine
"Why Food Matters"

HARVARD
James Q. Wilson, Pepperdine University
"Politics and Polarization"
"Religion and Polarization"

MICHIGAN
Marshall Sahlins, University of Chicago
"Hierarchy, Equality, and the Sublimation of Anarchy:
*   The Western Illusion of Human Nature"*

STANFORD
David Brion Davis, Yale University
"Exiles, Exodus, and the Promised Lands"

UC BERKELEY
Allan Gibbard, University of Michigan
"Thinking How to Live with Each Other"

UTAH
Margaret H. Marshall, Supreme Judicial Court of Massachusetts
"Tension and Intention: The American Constitutions and the
*   Shaping of Democracies Abroad"*

OXFORD
Carol Bellamy, former executive director of UNICEF
"From Taliban to the Tsunami: True Stories from the Front Lines
*   of Making a World Fit for Children"*
"Stealing Childhood: Poverty, War, and Disease"

PRINCETON
Emma Rothschild, Cambridge University
"The Inner Life of Empires"

2006–2007

YALE
Anthony Grafton, Princeton University
"Rat's Alley? The Humanities in the American University"
"Clio's Catastrophe? History and the Humanities"

CAMBRIDGE
Kurt Biedenkopf, Germany, former President of Saxony
"Germany Reunited: A Lesson in Political Transformation"
"Germany's Role in the Enlarged European Union"

UTAH
Bill Viola, video artist, Long Beach
"Presence and Absence: Vision and the Invisible"

PRINCETON
Michael Doyle, Columbia University
"Anticipatory Self-Defense: The Law, Ethics, and Politics of
*   Preventive War"*

HARVARD
Mary-Claire King, University of Washington
"Genomics, Race, and Medicine"

MICHIGAN
Samantha Power, Harvard University
"Human Rights: The Risk of Politics"

STANFORD
Glenn Loury, Brown University
"Ghettos, Prison, and Racial Backlash"
"Social Identity and the Ethics of Punishment"

UC BERKELEY   Joshua Cohen, Stanford University
              "On Public Reason"
              "Democracy's Public Reason"

2007–2008

YALE   Santiago Calatrava, architect, Zurich, Paris, and Valencia
              "Wings and a Prayer"
              "A Collection of Pearls"

CAMBRIDGE   Judy Illes, University of British Columbia
              "Medicine, Neuroscience, Ethics, and Society"

MICHIGAN   Brian Skyrms, University of California, Irvine
              "Evolution and the Social Contract"

PRINCETON   Susan Wolf, University of North Carolina
              "Meaning in Life and Why It Matters"

OXFORD   Simon Deakin, University of Cambridge
              "The Diversity of Contemporary Corporate Governance"

TSINGHUA   David Miller, University of Oxford
UNIVERSITY   *"Global Justice and Climate Change: How Should Responsibility
                  Be Distributed?"*

UC BERKELEY   Annabel Patterson, Yale University
              "Pandora's Boxes: How We Store Our Values"

HARVARD   Tony Kushner, playwright, New York
              "Fiction That's True: Historical Fiction and Anxiety"

UTAH   Howard Gardner, Harvard University
              "What Is Good Work?"
              "Achieving Good Work in Turbulent Times"

2008–2009

YALE   Steven Chu, Stanford University
              "The Epistemology of Physics and Scientific Revolution"
              "Golden Eras of Scientific Institutions"

CAMBRIDGE   Lisa Jardine, University of London
              "The Process of Communication Is the Process of Community"
              "Communication Is a Whole Social Process"

STANFORD   Michael Tomasello, Max Planck Institute for Evolutionary
                  Anthropology
              "Ontogenetic Origins of Human Altruism"
              "Phylogenetic Origins of Human Collaboration"
              Roberto Unger, Harvard University
              "The Future of Religion"
              "The Religion of the Future"

HARVARD   Sari Nusseibeh, Political Activist, Jerusalem
              "Of Hedgehogs, Foxes, and Swans"
              "Of Folly, Faith, and Miracles"

PRINCETON   Marc Hauser, Harvard University
                "Humaniqueness and the Illusion of Cultural Variation"
                "To Do, or Not to Do"

MICHIGAN   Uwe Reinhardt, Princeton University
                "American Values in Health Care: A Case of Cognitive Dissonance"

UTAH   Richard Davidson, University of Wisconsin
                "Order and Disorder in the Emotional Brain"

OXFORD   Brasenose College 500th Anniversary Lectures, Christopher
                    Timpson, Convener
                "Meeting the Challenges of the Twenty-first Century"

UC BERKELEY   Jeremy Waldron, New York University
                "Dignity and Rank"
                "Law, Dignity, and Self-Control"

                            2009–2010

YALE   John Adams, composer, New York
                "Doctor Atomic and His Gadget"

HARVARD   Jonathan Lear, University of Chicago
                "Becoming Human Does Not come That Easily"
                "Ironic Soul"

CAMBRIDGE   Sir Christopher Frayling, Royal College of Art
                "An Instinctive Sympathy?"
                "To Do the Right Deed for the Wrong Reason"

UTAH   Isabel Allende, social activist, Chile
                "In the Hearts of Women"

OXFORD   Ahmed Rashid, reporter, Pakistan
                "Afghanistan"
                "Pakistan"

UC BERKELEY   Abdullahi An-Na'im, Emory University
                "Human Values, Self-determination and Global Citizenship"
                "Taming Utopia: Pragmatic Means for Transformative Vision"

PRINCETON   Bruce Ackerman, Yale University
                "An Extremist Presidency"
                "A Politicized Military"

STANFORD   Mark Danner, University of California, Berkeley
                *"Imposing the State of Exception: Constitutional Dictatorship,
                    Torture, and Us"*
                *"Naturalizing the State of Exception: Terror, Fear, and the War
                    Without End"*

MICHIGAN   Susan Neiman, director, Einstein Forum
                "Victims and Heroes"

2010–2011

CAMBRIDGE Susan J. Smith, Mistress of Girton College, University of
Cambridge
"Moral Maze: Dealings in Debt"
"Ethical Investment? Attending to Assets"

HARVARD James Scott, Yale University
"The Late-Neolithic Multispecies Resettlement Camp"
"The Long Golden Age of Barbarians, a.k.a. Nonstate Peoples"

MICHIGAN Martin Seligman, University of Pennsylvania
"Flourish: Positive Psychology and Positive Interventions"

STANFORD Elinor Ostrom, Indiana University
"Frameworks"
"Analyzing One-Hundred-Year-Old Irrigation Puzzles"

PRINCETON Robert Putnam, Harvard University
"Americans Are Religiously Devout and Divided, yet Tolerant. Why?"
*"Religious Americans Are Better Neighbors and Citizens, though
Less Tolerant. Why?"*

UC BERKELEY Leon Botstein, president, Bard College
"Music Literacy in the 19th Century"
"The Recorded Age"

UTAH Spike Lee, film director and political activist, Brooklyn
*"America Through My Lens: The Evolving Nature of Race and
Class in the Films of Spike Lee"*

YALE Rebecca Newberger Goldstein, writer, Boston
"Morality and Literature"
"Metaphysics and Literature"

2011–2012

CAMBRIDGE Ernst Fehr, University of Zurich
"The Lure of Authority Motivation and Incentive Effects of Power"

HARVARD Esther Duflo, Massachusetts Institute of Technology
"Paternalism versus Freedom?"
"Hope as Capability"

MICHIGAN John Broome, Corpus Christi College
"The Public and Private Morality of Climate Change"

PRINCETON Stephen Greenblatt, Harvard University
"Shakespeare and the End of Life History"

STANFORD John Cooper, Princeton University
"Ancient Philosophies as Ways of Life I: Socrates"
"Ancient Philosophies as Ways of Life II: Plotinus"

UC BERKELEY Samuel Scheffler, New York University
"The Afterlife"

UTAH   Abraham Verghese, Stanford University
                "Two Souls Intertwined"

YALE   Lisa Jardine, University of London
                "The Sorcerer's Apprentice: C. P. Snow and J. Bronowski"
                "Science and Government: C. P. Snow and the Corridors of Power"

2012–2013

CAMBRIDGE   Joseph Koerner, Harvard University
                "The Viennese Interior: Architecture and Inwardness"

HARVARD   Robert Post, Yale Law School
                "A Short History of Representation and Discursive Democracy"
                "Campaign Finance Reform and the First Amendment"

MICHIGAN   Craig Calhoun, London School of Economics
                *"The Problematic Public: Revisiting Dewey, Arendt, and
                   Habermas"*

OXFORD   Michael Ignatieff, Harvard University
                "Representation and Responsibility: Ethics and Public Office"

PRINCETON   Ian Morris, Stanford University
                *"Each Age Gets the Thought It Needs: Why Hierarchy and Violence
                   are Sometimes Good"*
                *"The Evolution of Values: Biology, Culture, and the Shape of
                   Things to Come"*

STANFORD   William G. Bowen, Andrew W. Mellon Foundation
                "Costs and Productivity in Higher Education"
                *"Prospects for an Online Fix: Can We Harness Technology in the
                   Service of Our Aspirations?"*

UC BERKELEY   F. M. Kamm, Harvard University
                "Who Turned the Trolley?"
                "How Was the Trolley Turned?"

PARIS   Claude Lanzmann, filmmaker, Paris
                "Resurrection"

UTAH   Michael Sandel, Harvard University
                *"The Moral Economy of Speculation: Gambling, Finance, and the
                   Common Good"*

2013–2014

CAMBRIDGE   Phillippe Sands, University College London
                "The Tale"
                "The Troubles"

HARVARD   Rowan Williams, Archbishop of Canterbury
                "The Other as Myself: Empathy and Power"
                "Myself as Stranger: Empathy and Loss"

MICHIGAN Walter Mischel, Columbia University
"Overcoming the Weakness of the Will"

OXFORD Shami Chakrabarti, Liberty organization (formerly National
Council for Civil Liberties)
"Human Rights as Human Values"

STANFORD Nicolas Lemann, Columbia University School of Journalism
"The Turn Against Institutions"
"What Transactions Can't Do"

UC BERKELEY Eric Santner, University of Chicago
"On the Subject-Matter of Political Theology"
"Paradoxologies"

UTAH Andrew Solomon
"Love, Acceptance, Celebration: How Parents Make Their Children"
Neil deGrasse Tyson, Hayden Planetarium
"Science as a Way of Knowing"

YALE Paul Gilroy, King's College London
"Suffering and Infrahumanity"
"Humanities and a New Humanism"
Bruno Latour, Sciences Po Paris
"How Better to Register the Agency of Things"

2014–2015

CAMBRIDGE Peter Galison, Harvard University
"Science, Secrecy, and the Private Self"

HARVARD Carlo Ginzburg, UCLA
*"Casuistry, For and Against: Pascal's Provinciales and their
Aftermath"*

MICHIGAN Justice Ruth Bader Ginsburg, U.S. Supreme Court
*"A Conversation with Ruth Bader Ginsburg, Associate Justice of the
United States Supreme Court"*

OXFORD Peter Singer
*"From Moral Neutrality to Effective Altruism: The Changing Scope
and Significance of Moral Philosophy"*

PRINCETON Elizabeth Anderson, University of Michigan
"When the Market Was 'Left'"
"Private Government"

STANFORD Danielle Allen, Princeton University
"Two Concepts of Education"
"Participatory Readiness"

UC BERKELEY Philip Pettit, Princeton University
"From Language to Commitment"
"From Commitment to Morality"

UTAH Margaret Atwood, Author
"Human Values in an Age of Change"

YALE   Dipesh Chakrabarty, University of Chicago
                  "Climate Change as Epochal Consciousness"
                  "Decentering the Human? Or, What Remains of Gaia"